Michael Randle

Rebel Verdict

Michael Randle

Rebel Verdict

IRENE PUBLISHING

Michael Randle

Rebel Verdict

Published by Irene Publishing
Sparsnäs 1010, 667891 Ed, Sverige
First edition 2022
ISBN 978-91-88061-56-0 (Paperback)

Executive Editor: Gavin Randle

Layout: J. Johansen
Cover: Freya Randle-Helgesson
Drawing on cover: Priscilla Coleman/MB Media
Cartoon before page 1: Chris Vine

www.irenepublishing.com
irene.publishing@gmail.com

ISBN 978-91-88061-56-0
9 789188 061560 >

Dedication and Acknowledgements

Dedicated to Anne Randle and to our sons, Sean and Gavin, who were unwitting accomplices in the escape itself, but continued to support us when they learnt of our - and their! - involvement; and to my co-defendant at our Old Bailey trial in June 1991, the late Pat Pottle, and his widow, Sue.

Special thanks are due to our legal team - our solicitors Ben Birnberg, John Wadham, and Caroline Bowman; our counsel, Tom MacKinnon QC, Ed Fitzgerald QC, Anthony Scrivener QC, and Geoffrey Robertson QC who advised us and, in the pre-trial hearings, represented us on a pro bono basis. Thanks also to Jørgen Johansen of Irene Publishing and the team involved in the production of this book, including Freya Randle-Helgesson, who was responsible for the overall design of the cover, and to the numerous other friends and colleagues, many of them in the peace movement, who supported us through a difficult and testing time. Thanks, finally, to the courageous members of the jury who faced criticism, and at times abuse, from some sections of the press when they followed their consciences and pronounced the 'rebel verdict' of Not Guilty.

It takes real courage to go against the whole political and military establishment, mainstream media, and most ordinary citizens. Michael Randle and his friends risked everything in helping George Blake to escape from prison. They challenged the law and lived many years in fear, but were proven right in a court! Like some other activists - Plowshares and climate justice protesters - they managed to convince a British jury that the law and the judge were wrong. I hope this book and its powerful story will inspire more people to follow in their footsteps; to resist injustice and stand up for the value of all human life.

- Stellan Vinthagen

Endowed Chair in the Study of Nonviolent Direct Action and Civil Resistance, Professor of Sociology at University of Massachusetts, Amherst

Michael Randle helped us to smuggle literature into occupied Czechoslovakia in the early 1970s. He risked imprisonment by driving the first van across the Iron Curtain. Only about 20 years later did I discover that he had built the same secret compartments in an earlier van with which he smuggled George Blake out of the UK to East Germany. I agreed to be his character witness in the court because I admired his courage, integrity and strength of convictions. I was happy to support him even though at that time I had to defend myself against accusations that I have worked for the Communist Secret Service and any, even indirect association with a Soviet spy made my position more difficult. However, I understood Michael's fight for peace and human rights. His credo - plague on both houses. Neither US nor Soviet missiles. Neither gulags nor Guantanamo. No repression of any kind. As an MP I helped to incorporate into the Czech law the still topical provision that "Citizens have the right to resist anvone who endeavours to abrogate the democratic order of human rights and basic liberties established by the Charter of Funda- mental Rights and Freedoms, if the rightful actions of constitutional organs and the effective usage of proper legal measures are made impossible"

- Jan Kavan

Former Foreign Minister and Deputy Prime Minister of the Czech Republicformer President of the UN General Assembly

Contents

...and in 1991.... the most perverted verdict from an English jury....
VINE.
GUINNESS BOOK OF RECORDS

Chapter 1:

'We have lost one of our chaps over the wall'

It got dark early that evening, Saturday 22nd October 1966. Low clouds had threatened rain most of the day and by four thirty it had started to drizzle. Seán Bourke phoned me from the public phone box in the hall-way of his flat at 28 Highlever Road, West London.

'Well, my friend,' he said, 'I'm just setting off.'

'How are you?'

I've known better days, but I'm all right. I'll manage.'

According to his own account[1], Seán then returned to his flat, put on a macintosh and trilby hat, and carefully placed a rope ladder into a large carrier bag. On the bed was a set of clothes for the visitor who, if things went well, would be joining him within the next few hours. There was a London A to Z guide on the table, a map of the underground, and a plain brown envelope containing Anne's and my telephone number, disguised in the simplest of codes. (Each digit of the number had been advanced by one; a simple code to remember, but a childishly simple one to break had it fallen into the wrong hands.) We would provide the fall-back refuge if things did not go quite so well and the visitor needed to leave Highlever Road in a hurry.

The visitor in question was Wormwood Scrubs prisoner number 455, George Blake, the double-agent sentenced to 42-years imprisonment in May 1961 for passing secrets to the Russians. Seán had got to know him while himself serving a seven-year sentence in Wormwood Scrubs for sending an explosive device in the post to a policeman against whom he had a grievance (fortunately, the explosive device either failed to go off, left the officer unharmed. If the officer had been killed, Seán could have faced the death penalty - which was not abolished for murder until 1965). I had become friendly with both of them when I spent a year in Wormwood Scrubs in 1962-63 for my part in organising an anti-nuclear demonstration at Wethersfield USAF base in December 1961 on behalf of the Committee of 100.

---

1 See Seán Bourke, *The Springing of George Blake*, Cassell & Co, 1970, Chapter 2, 'The Escape'

The remaining members of the 'Escape Committee' on the outside, were my wife Anne and Pat Pottle. Pat was also convicted and sentenced for the Wethersfield demonstration and had been on the same mailbag workshop as Blake during the four months he spent in Wormwood Scrubs in 1962. They had briefly discussed an escape plan at that time though Pat was transferred to an open prison before it could be developed. None of us were communists or had the least sympathy for the espionage activities of East or West. It was the cruelty and hypocrisy of the 42-year sentence that prompted us to help Blake.

Seán set out on foot in the direction of East Acton, taking the route along Du Cane Road. As he approached Wormwood Scrubs prison on his right he glanced up Artillery Road, the lane that runs between the high east wall of the prison and Hammersmith Hospital. It was dark and deserted. At the main entrance to the prison he recognised some officers from his own time inside. But he was on the far side of the road from them, and they did not appear to notice him. By now it was raining more heavily, adding to the gloom of the day.

In Old Oak Common Lane, the right turning at the end of Du Cane Road, he bought a pot of pink chrysanthemums in a florists and continued down the road to the spot where, earlier that afternoon, he had parked a two-tone green Humber Hawk car. It was old, dented in several places, but 'a runner'. He had bought it for £60 in mid-August from Barbara Sanson, the manageress of a butcher's shop and the wife of William Sanson serving time in the Scrubs for robbery. Seán put the carrier bag in the boot, and the pot of chrysanthemums on the passenger seat beside him. In the back was an overcoat containing a spare set of keys for his flat, and a hat. His guest would put these on as soon as he picked him up. His appointment was for six o'clock.

To kill time, he drove round the area, along East Acton Lane, stopping near the King's Arms. He listened to the car radio, and sucked sweets, trying to calm his nerves. At a quarter to six he began driving slowly back again along East Acton Lane. It was raining heavily now, drumming on the roof of the car.

When he turned left into Old Oak Road he found there was a traffic jam all the way to the junction with Westway. It was six o'clock by the time he edged his way to it in mounting frustration. Blake would be switching on his two-way radio by now, waiting for their call sign. Eventually the policeman on point duty beckoned him on. Seán wound down his window.

'Thank you officer,' he said as he drove past.

The policeman was too absorbed in his work to respond. Had he done so he might have noticed that the Humber displayed no licence plate. And if he'd been in a position to ask Seán for his driving licence, he could not have produced it; he'd had a few lessons at the locally based Leo School of Motoring during the previous few weeks, but had never passed a test. However, the policeman could not stop to question an individual motorist during rush hour traffic even if his suspicions had been aroused; nor were foot policemen in those days routinely supplied with two-way radios. So Seán drove ahead into Old Oak Common Lane and then turned right into Du Cane Road and back past the front entrance of the prison. At ten past six he turned into the still deserted Artillery Road.

At the end of the lane, there were bollards to the left blocking off traffic from the Common beyond it. To the right was a hinged and padlocked barrier; here the lane continued on to a wooden sports pavilion. Seán did a three point turn, drove back down Artillery Road, and stopped at the point where two turrets, rising high above the outer wall, marked the south end of D wing. Holding the pot of chrysanthemums in front of his face, he took out a two-way radio from his pocket.

> **'This is Fox Michael calling Baker Charlie, Fox Michael calling Baker Charlie. Are you receiving me? Over.'**

The voice that responded contrasted strongly with Seán's own soft Limerick accent. It was refined and educated but retained traces of the guttural vowels of the speaker's native Dutch tongue.

> **'This is Baker Charlie calling Fox Michael, Baker Charlie calling Fox. Come in please. Over.'**
>
> **'Stone Walls do not a prison make, nor iron bars a cage. Over.'**
>
> **'Minds innocent and quiet would take this for a hermitage. Over.'**
>
> **'Richard Lovelace must have been a fool. Over.'**
>
> **'Or maybe just a dreamer.'**

Blake and Bourke had read Lovelace, the 17th century English poet, on the English literature diploma class in the prison, run by the extra-mural department of London University. I had been on the same course during my time inside and it was principally on the unsupervised study sessions every Monday morning that were part and parcel of it that I had got to know George. There was a literary connection too with their code names, invented by Seán. Fox Charlie (FC) was a reference to the legendary Irish giant, Finn McCumhail, Baker Charlie (BC) to his right-hand man, Baldy Canaan.

> **'Sorry for the delay,' Seán said. 'I got caught in a traffic jam. Everything's ready now. You can get your friend to see to the window.'**

Three minutes later, the voice sounded again.

> **'This is Baker Charlie calling Fox Michael. The window has been seen to. I am ready to make my exit now. Over.'**

Seán was about to respond when he was blinded by the headlights of a van turning into Artillery Road. He dropped the transmitter onto his lap and pretended to sniff the flowers as the van drove past him. At the far end the driver got out and unlocked the barrier. A security guard, Seán concluded. He called up 'Baker Charlie' and told him what had happened and that they would have to wait till the van returned and left the area.

But when the van returned it did not continue on to Du Cane Road but parked a few yards ahead of Seán. The driver, wearing a donkey-jacket and turned-down wellington boots, got out and stared suspiciously at Seán, who again began sniffing his chrysanthemums to give the impression that he was waiting to visit someone in Hammersmith Hospital. The man continued to stare straight at him. Then he opened the back of the car to let out a large Alsatian dog and began walking resolutely towards the Humber with the dog straining on a short leash.

There was nothing for it. Without even being able to call through to 'Baker Charlie' to tell him what was happening, Seán started the car engine, drove past the man, and turned left into Du Cane Road. This retreat itself would confirm the man's suspicions. Even now, Seán thought, as he drove past Hammersmith Hospital and away from the prison, he might be phoning the police from the nearest call box. It would be foolhardy to go ahead with the plan. But what must George inside be thinking? And how would he explain things to Pat, Anne and myself? Would we even believe him?

The plot to spring Blake from prison had been hatching for over a year, just before Seán had left D-wing to go on the Hostel Scheme. (Men on the hostel worked during the day outside the prison, and had weekends free, but had to spend their nights in a separate 'hostel' within the prison walls. Seán's work was at the CAV factory in Acton, a subsidiary of Lucas.) They kept in touch at first via smuggled notes, taken into the wing by a trusty prisoner with access to the hostel. In April, however, while Seán was still on the hostel, he managed to get a two-way radio – a 'walkie-talkie' – to Blake. He also recorded all their exchanges on a portable tape recorder. Seán was released from prison on 4th July 1966, and, over the next few months smuggled in other items of equipment in preparation for the escape including wire cutters, and a stop-watch with which Blake timed the intervals between the appearance of the wall patrol near where he planned to scale the wall.

Saturday was the evening for the weekly cinema show in the Recreation Hut adjoining D Wing. It was chosen because there would be far fewer prisoners on the wing and only a skeleton staff. Films usually finished at 7pm, so there was some leeway regarding the escape time set for 6pm. On the evening in question, 22nd October 1966, 107 men remained in the wing under the supervision of two prison officers – 33 year-old William Fletcher, and 26 year-old Colin Townsend. The latter, by his own account, was 'a disciplinarian' and 'considered a bit of a bastard' by the men.[2] However, the atmosphere that evening was relaxed. Fletcher spent much of the time watching the television situated at the North end of the wing, while Townsend occupied the desk in the centre, or patrolled the landings. He may or may not have spent part of the time playing table tennis.

Exit from the wing was to take place from the large gothic window at the south end. There are gothic windows at each end of the wing, stretching from the first floor landing – 'the twos' – to the top of the building. However, the north window was ruled out as a point of exit because it was too close to the newly installed look-out post at the corner formed by the north and east walls of the prison. The windows are divided by cast iron bars into oblong panes measuring approximately 9 inches x 6 inches. The previous night an accomplice inside the prison, Phil Morris, smashed one of the sections, using tape to deaden the sound of the breaking glass, and to secure the broken bar in position. When the bar was removed it would leave a space measuring 18 inches x 12 inches, just large enough for a man of Blake's small build to squeeze through. It was unlikely that the missing panes would be noticed since many others in all the wings had been missing for some time.

The following week a steel grid was due to be attached to the outside of the window as had already been done with A and B wings – the Young Offenders wings – and C wing, the wing for short term prisoners. Common sense might have suggested to the prison authorities that they should start with the long-term wing, especially as some prisoners had attempted – unsuccessfully – to escape through the window some weeks earlier. But the prison authorities are nothing if not methodical. The windows had to be strengthened in alphabetical order.

After most of the men from the wing had gone off to the cinema, Blake looked in to Kenneth de Courcy's cell to say goodbye to him. De Courcy, a former Secret Intelligence Service agent serving time for fraud, had found out about the escape plan as a result of a potentially fatal mishap. The trusty who smuggled notes and equipment to Blake, also carried clandestine messages to de Courcy, and on one occasion got the two messages muddled up; thus Blake got the message intended for de Courcy, and de Courcy the message intended for him. Fortunately de Courcy had taken a liking to Blake and decided not

2 Statement by Townsend to the police, 1st November 1966.

to inform the authorities. As a parting present, Blake gave him his copy of the Koran in Arabic which he had been reading as part of his Arabic studies.

Blake then wandered down to where the television was situated at the north end of the wing, and watched the all-in wrestling for a while before remarking to the officer Fletcher that it was a fake and he was going to his cell – No. D.1-8 on the ground floor – to read. The time, Fletcher later recalled, was about 5.30pm. Blake made himself a mug of tea in the canteen on the ground floor, drinking it slowly in his cell as he braced himself for the task ahead. Then he took a shower and returned to his cell for the last time. Townsend, he noticed, was no longer at the centre desk and had gone into the 'pantry' cell behind it to play chess. Blake changed into gym-shoes, stuffed the walkie-talkie under his prison sweater, and walked up the iron stairway to Phil's cell on the top floor, the 'fours'. There the two men waited anxiously for the signal from 'Fox Michael'.

At 6.15 Seán's voice came over the walkie-talkie. Phil should go ahead now and see to the window. Blake walked out with him as far as the landing outside the cell and peered over the railing. He could see Fletcher still standing near the television; Townsend had not yet returned to the centre desk. Even if he was there his line of vision to the escape point would be blocked by blankets slung over the landing railings in front of it. This would not arouse suspicion as it was common practice for inmates to clean out their cells at the weekends and to hang their bedding over the railings while they did so.

Phil returned to the cell so quickly that Blake wondered if there had been a hitch. But no. One kick had sufficed to remove the already broken bar. Blake called Seán on the walkie talkie and told him he was ready to make his exit.

But there was no response. Several minutes passed. Then Seán's voice came back on the air. He told them about the security van and that they would have to wait until he gave them the all clear. Silence again.

Ten minutes went by, then twenty. Every so often Blake tried to call up Seán, but got no response. Had he been picked up? Had he lost his nerve at the last minute? It seemed unlike him, but you could never tell how people would react when put to the test. At twenty to seven the gate in the centre of the wing opened and the men began to file back in from the cinema; the film had finished early. Within a few minutes there would be men clambering all over the wing, and obstructing the stairway down to the threes. Blake made one last desperate attempt to make contact.

> **'Baker Charlie calling Fox Michael, Baker Charlie calling Fox Michael. Come in please, Fox Michael. If I do not leave now, it will be too late.'**

***

Seán had a choice when he drove away from the prison. He could turn left at the junction with Wood Lane and return to safety – and defeat – at Highlever Road. Or he could turn right, and return via Westway and Old Oak Road to the far end of Du Cane Road, and the prison to make another attempt. He hesitated. But the thought of defeat, and the humiliation of having to explain to George and the rest of us why he had called the attempt off was too bitter. He pulled over into the right hand lane.

It was 6.30 as he turned into Westway. Traffic had eased now, and within a few minutes he was turning again into Du Cane Road. As he did so a man who had just stepped off the pavement to cross the road recognised him, and called out to him.

'Seán!'

He braked and stopped, and wound down the window. The man was Alan Morton, a prisoner on the hostel scheme. According to his own account in a statement made under caution to the police on 26 October, Seán said something like "Clear Off". But another ex-prisoner who knew both men told the police on 28 October that Morton had been smuggling parcels into the wing for Seán, and that Morton himself had told him that Seán stopped the car that night to tell him he would be delivering £300 to him the following day.[3]

Whichever version is correct, Seán quickly resumed his journey down Du Cane Road. Outside the Governor's house, he pulled up and walked along to Artillery Road. The van had gone, but there was another car parked in the same spot. Was it, he wondered, a police 'Q' car? Realising there was no time to be lost if the operation was to go ahead, he returned to the car, drove into Artillery Road and did another three point turn before returning to the appointed spot opposite the end of D-wing.

The parked car was facing him, just a few yards away, and he could see a young couple in the front fondling and kissing each other. He got out of his car, and, in the pouring rain, stared straight at them. For a minute or two they seemed not to notice him, then they straightened up. The man started the engine, did a three-point turn and drove off. Seán glanced at his watch and noted that it was now 6.40.

He called Blake and the reply, terse and clipped, came back at once, telling him that the men were on their way back from the cinema. 'I must come out now,' he said.

---

3 Statement by Stanley Nicholls to Detective Inspector H. Nichols on 28 October 1966.

'OK, Baker Charlie. Go Ahead. Over.'

A few minutes later, Blake was back on the air. He was in the yard at the end of the wing, just fifteen yards from the perimeter wall. 'Throw the ladder now,' he said.

But it was getting close to visiting time at Hammersmith Hospital, and now another car with dazzling headlights pulled into Artillery Road. The headlights remained switched on and the couple showed no inclination to move. Seán got out of his car again, holding the chrysanthemums, and walked towards the car. As he passed it the headlights were switched off and the couple got out. Seán walked slowly to the end of the road, allowing the couple to overtake him, and then hurried back to his own car.

As he opened the door he could hear Blake's voice on the two-way radio, desperately pleading for him to throw the rope. But yet another car was approaching, and Seán could only slam the door shut and wait until this car too was parked and its occupants had moved off.

It was now five to seven. The prison officers on the wing would be opening the cell doors ready for the final count of prisoners for the night. Blake came again on the air. 'You must throw the ladder now, Fox Michael. I expect to be taken at any moment. There is no more time.'

Seán pressed the call button on his set.

'Fox Michael to Baker Charlie. The ladder is coming over.'

Leaving the pot of chrysanthemums at the foot of the wall, Seán climbed on top of the car and threw over the ladder, keeping firm hold of the rope at his end and flicking the ladder a few feet down the wall to be clear of the car. He jumped down from the roof and held the trailing rope taught, standing as close to the wall as possible to increase the drag of the rope against the top of the wall. For an age, nothing happened. Seán banged his head against the wall and kicked it in frustration. There had been no cars now for several minutes, but this could not last. At last he felt the pull on the rope and the vibration of footsteps climbing the wall. Two hands appeared on the coping stone, followed by Blake's anxious, pale face.

Blake lowered himself down by his hands to be that much closer to the ground, while Seán positioned himself underneath to catch him and break his fall. Then came the first serious mishap. Blake, fearing he might injure Seán if he landed on top of him, threw himself in mid-air to one side, and fell awkwardly, hitting his head on the gravel path.

As he lay there, bleeding and unconscious, yet another car swept into Artillery Row, and parked in front of the other one, just a few feet from the Humber. Its headlights remained switched on. Seán, in full view of its occupants, opened the rear door of his car on the driver's side. He then returned to Blake who had started to come to and was groaning where he lay. The open back door protected the two men from view, as Seán half-dragged, half-carried his dazed companion to safety.

Seán started the engine and drove off. At the end of Artillery Road, he turned left and raced along Du Cane Road. Then as he wiped clear the steamed-up windscreen, he saw, too late, that the traffic ahead had stopped at the pedestrian crossing opposite the hospital. He slammed on his brakes, but skidded into the car ahead. Their bumpers collided with a loud crash. When the traffic started moving again, the car ahead pulled into the side and signalled Seán to do the same. He ignored this and drove on, speeding towards the traffic lights which were still at red. 'Bugger the lights!' he exclaimed.

Blake in the back was struggling into the coat and hat, half blinded by the blood coursing down his forehead and into his eyes.

> **'Take it easy, Seán! Take it easy!' he said. 'It would be a pity to spoil everything now!'**

Fortunately the lights had turned to green by the time Seán reached them and he drove on to Highlever Road without further mishap.

Because of Blake's state and appearance, Seán decided he should accompany him into the room. Blake pulled the hat well down over his eyes to conceal his injuries, but fortunately there was no-one about. Having made sure his guest was safe, Seán drove off again to dump the car. He drove around distractedly for some while before leaving the car in a street which he imagined must be some distance away from the prison, and made his way back to the flat.

***

Meanwhile, back at the prison, officers Fletcher and Townsend, an officer named Stanley Crawley (who was in charge at the cinema) and one or two others were locking up the prisoners for the night, and checking the numbers. At approximately 7.15, according to his statement to the police, Fletcher noticed that Blake was missing from his cell and 'told officer Williams on the Boundary wall to watch out for any movement.' He tried to contact the Orderly Officer, Whittaker, but was unable to reach him at that time, and also telephoned the Gate-Keeper, Cooper.[4] He and his fellow officers checked various places where the prisoner might have been – the canteen, the pantry, de Courcy's cell. Not long afterwards Williams from the Boundary Wall watch came into the wing with the rope ladder and handed it over to prison officer

---

4 Statement by William Fletcher taken by Detective Superintendent William Marchant of Shepherds Bush Police Station, on 24 October 1966.

Rowe.[5] Evidently, however, Williams had not seen the rope coming over the wall or Blake scrambling up it some twenty or thirty minutes earlier. In fact the various mishaps that had delayed the planned escape time by nearly an hour had worked to Blake's advantage since it was much darker than it would have been if the operation had gone exactly according to plan.

The officers then began a systematic search of the wing. Eventually, Townsend on the Threes landing spotted the broken window and the missing bar.[6] (Fletcher found the broken bar early next morning in the yard below, bound at either end with black adhesive tape.)[7]

It was not until more than half-an-hour after Fletcher first noticed Blake's absence that the prison authorities alerted the police at Shepherds Bush Police Station, and then in an extraordinarily casual fashion. The Information Room register at the station shows that the call was received at 7.52pm and taken by PC Stanley Frankling. His statement about the call is worthy of a Monty Python script:

> On Saturday 22nd October, 1966, I was employed at Shepherds Bush Police Station on Communication duty.
>
> At a time I recorded as 7.43pm[8] I received a 'phone call' from a man who said he was the Deputy Governor of Wormwood Scrubs Prison. To the best of my recollection the conversation went as follows: 'This is the Deputy Governor of Wormwood Scrubs, I have just been informed by my Chief that we have lost one of the chaps over the wall. We think it's Blake'. I said 'Blake?' and he said, 'Yes the one doing 42 years.' I said 'Can you give a description?' and he said 'Not at the moment. He's probably in prison grey. He went over the east wall. Look I'm a bit tucked up at the moment, I'm in the middle of releasing a man. I'll ring you back when I get more information.'
>
> I am aware that a coded form of message 'Patterson calling' is in use for escape messages from the Prison. This had not been used. I therefore asked the reserve officer P.C. 622 'F' Child to ring the prison to verify the

5 From the statement by Prison Officer Stanley Crawley to Detective Sergeant Peter Cornish, `F' Division, Shepherds Bush Police Station, 27 October 1966

6 From the statement by Colin Clive Townsend made to Detective Superintendent William Marchant of `F' Division, Shepherds Bush Police Station, 24 October 1966.

7 Fletcher's statement to the police, 24 October 1966.

8 Later in the statement Frankling agrees that he probably made a mistake about the time and that the Information Room was correct in logging the call at 7.52pm.

> information. Whilst he was doing this I contacted all local units (T/T car, van, motor cycle and foot P.C.s) via the personal radio system and directed them to the prison.[9]

The phlegmatic reaction of the prison governor appears to be symptomatic of a general relaxed attitude to prison security. Some months before the escape, a prisoner Derek Madren rummaging inside a large cardboard carton he had found outside the wing discovered remnants of packaging marked '9-inch Transistor Transmitter'. He thought no more of it at the time, but then noticed that on several occasions when watching television that bleeps appeared on the screen every so often. He 'quickly figured out what it was – every time you press the "Send" button on a walkie-talkie a TV will show a pinging on the screen.' Subsequently the interference stopped and he concluded that either the transmitter was no longer operating or that it was being used further away from the television.[10]

On 19th August, Madren told the officer in the Laundry where he worked – George Allen – that a two way radio was operating from D wing. He wrote a note about the bleeps on the television and his conclusion that they were caused by a walkie-talkie. Allen in turn made a report to the prison Governor, and handed over Madren's note.

The Assistant Governor John Rham, dealing with the reports about a two way radio on the wing, had this to say to the police on 3rd November 1966:

> **About three months ago I heard a jocular remark from a member of the staff to the effect that Radio Wormwood Scrubs was operating again. I did not consider that this was meant seriously, but at the same time, was aware that I did have men who were capable of making a transmitter and of obtaining access to the necessary materials. I did not consider that they would manufacture a transmitter because there was too much to lose from their point of view if it was discovered. I did, however, see all the men concerned and warned them.**
>
> **I consider that all the information received since that date is as a result of that warning. There has been no direct evidence to my knowledge of a two way radio being used in 'D' Hall or 'D' Recreation Hut.**

However, it is true that one of the Governors of Wormwood Scrubs was worried about having Blake in a prison of only medium level security.

9 Statement of Stanley Frankling, Police Constable 436`F'/137388 on 2 November 1966.

10 Note by Madren to prison officer George Allen handed over to the police during their enquiries in the Blake escape.

On 14th January 1966, Governor Leslie Newcombe was asked by the Prison Department if he 'had any Security Risks who would be safer elsewhere.' Hesubmitted three names for transfer, one of them Blake's.[11] Fortunately for Blake, the Prison Department did not act on this suggestion.[12]

This was not the only occasion on which the success of the escape hung by a thread. One morning a prisoner doing life came to George's cell to warn him to be careful. He had been idly playing with the tuning dial on his radio the previous night and by chance had tuned into their conversation. He thought at first that it was part of a play, but soon recognized the voices. He stood to gain a great deal by telling the authorities since this could have advanced the date of his release. Instead he chose to warn George and to say nothing to the authorities.

If the reaction of the prison authorities to Blake's escape was – at first – surprisingly low key, there was no lack of enthusiasm on the part of the prisoners when it was reported on the BBC nine o'clock news it that evening. A fellow prisoner who had come to have a great respect for George, Gerald Lemarque, records the response:

> **A growing murmur of sound breaks into my thought … the men with radios are shouting the news to those without. The excitement in the voices I hear is unbelievable. There must have been nearer a hundred than fifty escapes in the years I have spent here, but I have never known a reaction like this. By concentrating, I can distinguish words and snatches of conversation.**
>
> **'Blake … Blake … over the wall … George … had it away. Good old George.' Cowboy yells of 'Yippee', only once or twice sheer savagery, directed against authority more than in support of Blake's escape. 'He's fucked 'em …' And then, far away and faintly from the south end of the prison, singing, 'For he's a jolly good fellow.'[13]**
>
> **(from Life by Zeno, Lemarque's pen name.)**

***

I did not learn the details of the escape until the following day. But Seán phoned me as soon as he got back to the flat after abandoning the car.

---

11 Statement by Leslie Newcombe, Governor Class 1, Wormwood Scrubs Prison made to Detective Superintendent William Marchant, `F' Division, Shepherds Bush Police Station, on 7 November, 1966.

12 See also the Mountbatten Report on the Escape about this point.

13 Zeno, Life, Macmillan, 1968, pp.163-4.

'I threw the bait', he said enigmatically, 'and our friend took it, hook, line and sinker.'

But there was a problem; 'our friend' had hurt his wrist. It was probably nothing more than a sprain, but there was a chance it was broken. He would contact me again the next day if necessary. This was the first small hint of the crisis that would engulf us over the next ten days and force Pat, Anne and myself to improvise desperately to prevent the whole enterprise coming to grief. Had we known just how close the authorities came during that period to uncovering us, our anxiety would have bordered on panic. And as if to forewarn us of the imminent danger in which we had placed ourselves, I received further phone calls that night from two journalists – one who worked for the Daily Telegraph, the other, I think, for the Daily Mail. As someone who had been in prison with Blake, they said, had I any idea who might be behind the escape? I said No to both of them and put the phone down. But I was shaken. If journalists were already asking that question, could Special Branch and the Security Service be far behind?

Chapter 2:

Manhunt

The front page headlines in the Sunday newspapers were like a blow to the guts for Anne and myself and no less for Pat who lived on his own in a flat in the Hampstead area. It was the lead story too on radio and television. All the media were stressing the scope and intensity of the police hunt. Air and sea ports were being watched; 'iron curtain' embassies had been placed under special scrutiny; an intensive investigation was to be carried out at the prison itself to trace current and previous associates of Blake. We had told ourselves beforehand that there would be this kind of reaction. Still when it came, it came as a shock.

Anne and myself had not finished reading the reports in the selection of newspapers we had gone out and bought when I saw the stocky figure of Seán coming down the garden path. We lived at the time with our two young children, Seán aged four, and Gavin two years nine months, in a small housing cooperative in Kentish Town, a pleasant backwater tucked away behind Leighton Road. I had just graduated in English from University College, London, and was doing some part-time teaching of English as a Foreign Language; Anne was doing part-time secretarial work.

We had not expected to see Seán, for the plan was that we would have no contact with either him or Blake except to provide money for the latter's planned exit on a forged passport. Yet we were delighted to see him and hugged and congratulated him in the hallway. He then sat down and relayed to us the adventures of the previous evening, his voice frequently choking with emotion and excitement.

But his visit had a more sombre purpose. It was to seek our advice on what to do about George who had indeed broken his wrist jumping down from the wall. He had been awake in agony all night, and could not cope for much longer. To our consternation, Seán proposed taking him to a hospital, arguing that he would not be recognized from the crude prison mugshots that had appeared in the press. We vehemently opposed the idea, yet we couldn't immediately think of any doctor who might help.

After talking it over for a while, Anne and I thought of some friends in South London who had a lot of contacts and might possibly be able to suggest someone. Seán agreed to delay taking George to a hospital until I had had a chance to sound them out; he would phone Anne from time to time to see if I was having any success. We did not think it advisable for us to phone him on the public phone in his hallway, and, to our later regret, did not even take the precaution of noting the phone number. We left the house together. His final words to me were that if I didn't find a doctor quickly he would have to take George to a hospital.

That was the longest day. My friends – 'Matthew' and 'Rachel' – did know of a doctor who might be willing to help, but couldn't immediately get hold of him. Several times during the morning and early afternoon I tried to phone Anne from a public telephone box to let her know that we now had a particular doctor in mind and to tell Seán to hang on. But the line was constantly engaged. I was conscious at every moment of Seán's parting words to me, and feared that George might be tempted to go along with the plan because the pain of his broken wrist had become unbearable. I felt quite certain that such an action would mean disaster and am more than ever convinced of it today. Apparently it is standard procedure for the police to alert hospitals after a break-out because of the possibility that the escaped prisoner would have been injured. All day, the radio and television news bulletins were full of the escape. I could already see the newspaper headlines announcing his recapture. Preventing such an eventuality became for me an absolute priority. I was determined at whatever cost not to let it happen.

Finally I did get through to Anne. No-one had been able to phone for most of the day because we were on a shared line and the other party had failed to replace the receiver properly. Frustratingly, Anne could hear the voices of children playing in the other house every time she picked up the phone. She used a neighbour's phone to let the telephone exchange know what had happened, but they said it was not their policy to tell subscribers the name and address of people with whom they shared a line, and their own efforts to alert the other subscriber by putting a buzz on the line proved fruitless.

At around 7 we saw the doctor at his house. As soon as I mentioned an escaped prisoner he said 'Ah, George Blake'. He made it clear at once that he had no sympathy for the Soviet regime, and could not forgive the Communists for what they had done in Spain during the Civil War. However, he understood that Blake had been active in the resistance in occupied Holland during the war, and he was conscious of the terrible effect resistance activities could have on people; to that extent he was sympathetic and was prepared to do what he could. However, it would be a makeshift job; the wrist ought to be x-rayed and dealt with under proper conditions at a hospital. Moreover, as a GP, he had not had to deal with fractured limbs since he was at medical school.

I took leave of my friends, thanking them warmly for their help, and left with the doctor in his car for Highlever Road. He had no plaster bandages in the house and was unable to get to the supplies in his surgery on a Sunday. So on the way we stopped off at the BBC Limegrove Studies to pick some up from a friend who worked in the Wardrobe department there. Little did the newsreaders reporting Blake's escape and the hunt to find him know how close to home the fugitive was or how vital a role the BBC itself was unwittingly playing in preventing his recapture.

It was about 8.30 when we arrived. Seán opened the door to us and led us down a long narrow corridor to his room at the end. George was there in trousers and vest looking pale and battered, with ugly lacerations across his forehead and down the left side of his face. One eye too was partially closed. His manner was subdued and he was clearly in pain.

To my surprise, Pat was there too. He had phoned Anne in the afternoon and, realising something was seriously amiss, went straight to Highlever Road. There he found Seán in a distraught state standing in the middle of the road in his shirt-sleeves in the pours of rain. 'I've got him in here!' he had shouted to Pat. And then: 'Where's Michael?'

The doctor was methodical and efficient, saying only what was absolutely necessary for the task in hand. He had come, he said, because he understood the injured person had an aversion to hospitals. After briefly examining George's distorted left wrist, he confirmed that it was broken. He then gave George a local injection which he warned would do no more than dull the pain and got him to lay his forearm on the kitchen table. Seán gripped George's upper arm and shoulders firmly as the doctor began manipulating the wrist, trying to put it back into place. George's face was contorted in pain. Beads of sweat stood out on his forehead.

Having satisfied himself that the wrist was as straight as he was going to be able to get it, the doctor wrapped it and George's forearm in the plaster-impregnated bandage. Finally he wet the bandage thoroughly from a bowl on the table, ignoring the headlines about the escape and the mugshots of George on the newspapers Seán had placed there to soak up the surplus water. Nor did he react in the slightest when George's face appeared on television at the start of a news bulletin. Finally he gave George an anti-tetanus jab in the backside while the rest of us looked fixedly out of the French windows into the blackness beyond. Then, warning us again that the arm needed to be dealt with properly at a hospital, he quietly took his leave.

The doctor is dead now so we would no longer be putting him at personal risk if we revealed his identity. But when I talked to him many years later about the episode he told me he had some qualms of conscience about having helped someone who had spied for such an odious regime. Out of respect for his views and his impressive integrity, we have to keep his name secret.

Not long after he left, Anne arrived, and the evening turned into something of a celebration. But it was a celebration clouded by fears and worries. One cause for concern was the getaway car. Seán told us he had parked in Harvist Road, and when we checked its whereabouts in an A-Z we found it was quite close to the prison at the back of Wormwood Scrubs Common. Pat and I insisted that it ought to be moved, and he said he knew of a tip in North Wales where I could dump it. Seán replied that he had thrown away the key after abandoning the car, and that brought the discussion to an abrupt halt.

We were worried about the car on several levels. Well before the escape, Pat and I had urged Seán to sell the Humber as it was registered in his name, and would lead the police straight to him if it was discovered. Seán agreed, and subsequently assured us that he had sold it and was using another which he had not yet registered. But he was always vague about this new car and Pat never saw it all the time Seán was lodging with him. Seán explained that he always parked it some distance away so that it would not be seen in the vicinity of Pat's flat, but Pat was not entirely convinced. During the week of the escape he mentioned his suspicions to me, but I dismissed them. I trusted Seán and didn't think he would lie to us on so crucial a matter. Pat had particular reason to worry because once, after Seán had promised to sell the Humber, he had taken a ride in it. He was not wearing gloves at the time so his fingerprints could be inside the car. When we were walking down Highlever Road on the night of the doctor's visit, Pat raised the matter again. He was now more than ever convinced that Seán had used the Humber, and he didn't believe his story that he had thrown away the car keys. I was now inclined to believe him and agreed to try to talk Seán round to giving me the key so I could drive the car away.

However, while we were all together that night an even more urgent problem occupied our thoughts and discussions. This was the first time that Pat, Anne and myself had seen what Seán had described as a 'self-contained flat'. In fact it was no more than a bedsit with a bathroom in the corridor which presumably was shared with the other tenants, at least on the ground floor.[1] More disturbing still, Seán informed us that every Wednesday morning,

1 But possibly Seán had exclusive use of it. In her statement to the police on

the landlady and an assistant cleaned out the bedsit. We simply could not take the risk of leaving George here, and were suddenly faced with the major task of finding him alternative accommodation in only two days. We had more or less ruled out our own places because of our association with George and, in my case, the fact that I had regularly sent him Christmas cards.

Actually Blake's situation at Highlever Road was more precarious than any of us realised. Giving evidence in the High Court in October 1990, the Irish journalist Kevin O'Connor recalled that a retired Special Branch Officer, Rollo Watts, told him in 1984 that Seán's landlady, Mrs Lotte Heveringham had become suspicious of him shortly before the escape took place. This was because he 'would sometimes go out clean-shaven and return with a beard and wearing spectacles'. She went to her local, Shepherds Bush police station which was to become the hub of the enquiry into the escape, and told them of her suspicions. But the desk sergeant refused to take this 'little old lady' seriously. 'Keep on taking the tablets' he said, and 'You will be seeing Martians next!'[2]

Over the next couple of days Pat, Anne and myself racked our brains about whom we could dare ask and who might possibly be in a position to help. Finally I again approached Matthew and Rachel; at least they already knew of our involvement in the escape and we were not adding to the risk by approaching them. They reluctantly agreed to put up George but only George for just a few days while we found him somewhere more permanent. Their situation was far from ideal. Another couple had a self-contained flat in the house but frequently dropped by for coffee and a chat. There was no possibility of having both Seán and George, so it would be necessary to split them.

On Tuesday evening, 25th October, Anne and I moved George to his new hiding place, using a car borrowed from a friend, 'Bernard'. (We had no car ourselves). We stayed with them for a while helping them to cut up his prison clothes into small pieces ready for incineration. Matthew and Rachel were, understandably, extremely nervous and anxious and wanted to minimise the risks. During his stay with them, George was locked all day in a spare bedroom with a bucket to pee in. Rachel brought him his meals, and let him

---

16 January 1967, the landlady, Mrs Lotte Heveringham, describes the let as comprising a 'double room, bathroom, and kitchen, at a weekly rental of £4.15.0d'. So possibly Seán had exclusive use of the bathroom.

2 Kevin O'Connor under cross-examination by Mr Julian Bevan at the High Court on 2 October 1990. The quotes appear in the court transcript p.5, and refer to contemporaneous notes by O'Connor of his conversation with Rollo Watts in 1984.

out to use the bathroom at night when the other lodgers in the house had gone to bed.

Seán was visibly taken aback when we told him that he and George would have to be separated, but put a brave face on it. There was as yet no reason to believe that the police were looking for him though it was certain he would be a prime suspect because he was a known associate of with Blake while in prison. Indeed, for this reason we had taken elaborate – and expensive – precautions to put them off the scent. At our suggestion, Seán had quit his previous bedsit at number 26 Perryn Road and his job with CAV in September, informing all and sundry that he had decided to return permanently to Ireland. On 23rd September he moved into Pat's flat, using it as a base from which to do his own flat-hunting. In October, with some of the money I had raised earlier, he flew to Limerick, and stayed there for a week before flying back under an assumed name.[3] He returned to Britain on Sunday, 16th October, and on the following day managed to rent 28 Highlever Road through the agency Rupert & Evans of Praed Street, London, W2.[4] The landlady, a German woman named Lotte Heveringham, lived in another building a few streets away. Seán moved in on 18 October, just four days before the escape.

Seán tells in his book how on the Tuesday evening, sometime after we had taken George to our friends, he made an anonymous phone call to the police and telling them that the getaway car used in the escape of George Blake was a Humber Hawk parked in Harvist Road, NW6. His account is confirmed by the police records which show that an anonymous phone call telling them about the car was received at 9.45pm on Tuesday 25th October.[5]

The reason Seán gives for what he did is that it would focus police attention on himself and deflect it from anyone else. This doesn't stand up. There was no reason at all for the police to assume that Seán had acted on his own. His action also meant that the elaborate precautions we had taken to lead the police to believe that Seán had returned to Ireland for good were a waste of time.

---

3 Our suggestion to him was that he should travel from Limerick to Dublin and fly back from there, partly to minimise the chances of his being recognized at Limerick airport. However, he decided to cut out that part of the operation and flew back from Limerick.

4 This last detail is contained in the statement to the police made by Mrs Heveringham on 16 January 1967.

5 See Appendix A, the report by Detective Inspector R. Bird on 7th March 1990 in preparation for the trial of Pottle and Randle, p.l.

In fact they had already been compromised. On 18th October, following his return from Ireland, Seán was spotted in Perryn Road near his previous lodgings by two other co-tenants, Mrs Rosemary Brown and Mrs Jennifer Lucy; the latter also saw his Humber Hawk car parked round the corner in Shae Road. This emerges from statements they made to the police on 26th October 1966.[6] The date, however, is significant, for it was the day after Seán had phoned the police and tipped them off about the car.

Prior to that Seán was certainly marked down as a suspect. A prison officer, Percival Porter, in a police interview on 24th October named Seán as a close associate of Blake. Bourke, he said, 'was perhaps the closest to Blake'. He described him as 'an anti-social, anti-authority rebel, self-educated and self-centred'. Later on in his statement he came close to the truth when he speculated: 'For about six months before his discharge, Bourke was living in the Prison Hostel and working out. Amongst those who still live in 'D' wing and had occasion to pass the hostel every day was Lemarque, who worked in the prison college. Messages could have been passed from Blake to Lemarque.' In fact it was not Gerald Lemarque (author of Life written under the pen name 'Zeno') who acted as go-between but another trusty who had access to both the hostel and 'D' wing. Lemarque was the 'Blue Band' Trusty for the Education Wing, an ex-army officer doing life for killing his wife's lover. Despite his conservative views on most topics, he had become very close to Blake as the extract quoted earlier from his book indicates. But Blake had not taken him into his confidence about his plans.

But while Seán was from the start an obvious suspect, it appears that the police took no serious steps to discover his whereabouts until after he phoned them and the car provided concrete evidence of his involvement. After that all the clues, and concrete evidence, pointed to his involvement. One of the prison Governors, Leslie Newcombe, interviewed on 7th November, told the police of the incident on 4th July in which Seán was allegedly seen at his hostel window with a camera by an officer on escort duty from Brixton prison. Alan Morton, the prisoner in the Hostel had – as noted in the previous chapter – informed the police in an interview on 26th October that he had seen Bourke at the west end of Du Cane Road driving a 'dark Humber car' between 6.45pm and 7pm on 22nd October, and that Seán had stopped and spoken to him. On 28th October, an ex-prisoner who had been released in September, Stanley

6 Statement by Mrs Rosemary Brown to Detective Sergeant Frank Harris, 'F' Division, Shepherds Bush Police Station, 26 October 1966, and statement by Mrs Jennifer Lucy (nee Fairington) taken down by Detective Constable R. Slatter of Shepherds Bush Police Station, 26 October 1966.

Nicholls, claimed that Morton had smuggled parcels into the prison for Bourke on two occasions. He also claimed that Morton smuggled a camera out of Wormwood Scrubs for Seán on 4th July, presumably the camera that Seán had been spotted using on that day. Morton, in a subsequent statement on 4 November, said he knew nothing about the camera and had never smuggled parcels into the Scrubs for Seán.[7] On 5th December, a chauffeur, Christopher Day, when shown a photograph of Seán by the police said he resembled the man he had seen carrying a flower pot on 22nd October in the vicinity of Du Cane Road. Later still, 19th December, Special Branch interviewed Blake's mother, Katherine Blake, who told them that Seán had approached her and her daughter prior to the escape asking for money in order to carry it out. But despite the accumulating evidence of Seán's involvement the police did not release the name of the 'Irishman' they wished to interview in connection with the escape until January 1967.

The police became curious about the Humber car parked in Harvist Road before Seán's phone call, though until then they had no inkling that it was the one involved in the prison breakout. On Monday 24th October, at 1pm, Police Constable Michael Sims, attached to Harlesden Police Station, noticed a 'two tone green Humber Hawk saloon motor car, index number 117 GMX, parked stationary and unattended about 50 yards west of Kingswood Avenue, close to and parallel with the north kerb of Harvist Road, facing east.'[8] This was about 100 yards from the rear entrance to the police station. His attention was drawn to it because cars rarely parked on the north side of the street. He then noticed that it displayed no road fund licence, placed a note under the windscreen wiper, and reported the fact to the station on his return. Early the following morning when he returned on duty at 5.35am he noticed the vehicle was still there and checked it with the Central Vehicle index to make sure it was not a lost or stolen vehicle. ' The reply direct was "No trace." '

In the early hours of Wednesday morning, at 1.30am, just a few hours after Seán had phoned the police, another Police Constable, David Fryer, was instructed to bring the car into the compound of Harlesden police station and told that 'it was to be preserved for fingerprints'.[9]

7 Statement by Alan Morton, made under caution, on 4 November 1966 to Detective Inspector W. Bridges in the presence of Detective Superintendent Marchant at Shepherds Bush Police Station.

8 Statement by Michael Sims, Police Constable 398 'Q'. Undated, but evidently made in early November 1966.

9 Statement of David Fryer, Police Constable 415, made to Det Sergeant R.

Unaware of any of this, I met Seán at Goodge Street Underground Station on Thursday and broke the news gently to him that we were aware that he had never sold the Humber, and that it was imperative it should be moved. Not only was it registered in his name, but it was possible that Pat's fingerprints would be found. He assured me the latter was out of the question since he had thoroughly wiped down the interior. When I persisted, and asked for the keys, there was a flicker of panic in his eyes. He had flung them away he said. Then he changed the story at once and said that he had dropped them down a drain. This convinced me he still had them. He finally said that he had a spare key he could give me, but warned that I would be making a huge mistake if I attempted to move it. It was quite possible the police had the vehicle under observation and that I would be arrested the moment I approached it. I said I would prefer to take that risk, than leave the car where it was.

The next day, Friday 28th October, we met again and he handed over the key, once again giving me dire warnings of the dangers to which I was exposing myself. The one thing he could not bring himself to do was to tell us that he himself had already informed the police about it. Bernard, the friend with the car, drove me to Harvist Road. Seán had told me exactly where it was parked, but we drove the length of the road without seeing it. Could we have missed it? We drove slowly back down again, scanning every parked vehicle. There was no doubt now. The car had been removed.

Bernard dropped me off at a nearby underground station, and as I approached it I saw the scrawled headlines on the news-vendor's box 'Blake Escape Car Found'.

I phoned Seán at once, telling him that a certain car had been found. He took the news phlegmatically.

'It's just as I expected,' he said

I then rang Pat at his printing works. For him the news was much more of a blow. He made it clear that he wouldn't be around for a few days. Obviously if his fingerprints were discovered and he became a suspect, it was best if he broke off all contact with the rest of us for a while. Otherwise he might lead the police straight to the person they were looking for.

We had meanwhile arranged for both George and Seán to move to another house, this one in West London, not far from the MI6 building where George used to work. The owner and his wife – 'Will' and 'Mary' – were away at the time, but I phoned them telling them that we had a couple of friends who needed to be put up. Thinking we were referring to a couple of

---

Harding at Harlesden Police Station, 14 November 1966.

US deserters unwilling to fight in Vietnam, they agreed readily. His mother, he said, lived in the house, and would let us in and give us a spare key. I drove Seán there on the Friday night, and George the following morning.

The morning papers headlined the discovery of the car and reported that the police were looking for an Irishman who was the legal owner of the car and had recently been released from prison. The evening papers gave a fuller description of Seán, though again without mentioning his name. The Evening Standard said he was aged thirty-three and from Limerick; the Evening News added the information that he had served a seven-year sentence for causing bodily harm, and that police throughout Britain had circulated a description of him which said he was heavily built with only a slight Irish accent. The press and media reports also stated that two Scotland Yard detectives had travelled to Limerick to interview his mother and other people there. The *Daily Express* said the police no longer believed that Blake had been sprung by the agents of a foreign power, but by a 'small time Communist … helped by a group of sympathisers'.[10]

On Sunday, the friends, Will and Mary, returned to London, and I met Mary by arrangement in the West End, in the heart of the theatre area around St Martin's Lane. She was clearly worried.

> **'Who are these two men,' she asked me, 'and why are they hiding?'**
>
> **'Well, one of them is George Blake …'**
>
> **'George Blake!' Her voice rose to a scream. I desperately tried to calm her, certain that everyone in the street must be listening to us.**

Things were now unravelling in a serious way. The car had been found; Seán as well as George was being hunted by the police; soon they might also be looking for Pat. That evening, when I went round to Will's house he told me that it was not safe to put Seán and George up for more than a day or two. The problem was not his mother; she was extremely deaf, never watched television for that reason, and was unlikely to suspect anything. However he had a secretary who worked from the house all during the week who might well become curious and suspicious. I would have to find somewhere else for the two men to stay.

Monday's papers reported that the police had discovered an aerial in a bedsit at 26 Perryn Road, formerly the residence of the Irishman they wanted to interview. The report in the *Daily Telegraph* quoted another tenant, Rosemary Brown, as saying that two men called Pat and Terry had been regular visitors of the Irishman – we didn't see that report at the time. At least it was gratifying

10 *Daily Express*, 29 October 1966

to know that our precautions prior to the escape meant that there would be no leads from Perryn Road to the Highlever Road address.

With the options closing, Matthew, Rachel and I discussed a plan to hoist George up over the wall into the grounds of the Soviet Embassy. They themselves walked round the area and found a spot where they felt this could be done without much risk or difficulty. However, when I broached the idea with George the next day, he reacted with disbelief. He had not come out of prison to do a 'Cardinal Mindszenty' in the Russian Embassy. What I was suggesting was a counsel of despair. If we wanted to involve the Embassy I would have to approach them, tell them the situation and 'await instructions'. The words struck a chill inside me. I had no intention whatever of 'taking instructions' from the Soviet Embassy, and becoming in effect their agent.

That evening, with a Censure Motion on the Home Secretary Roy Jenkins due to be debated, Will came in to tell us there was a small matter he felt he should raise with us. It sounded as though he was going to raise some small domestic matter.

> **'My wife,' he said, 'is undergoing a course of analysis. This requires her to be absolutely frank with her analyst and not to conceal anything from him.'**

We looked at him in disbelief.

> **'Are you saying,' George asked, trying hard to keep his composure, 'that she has told him about us?'**
>
> **'Yes,' Will replied calmly, 'Everything. There is no point in it if she isn't completely frank. You must understand, of course, that what she says to him is in the strictest confidence.'**

Shocked silence.

> **'And what did the analyst say when she told him?' George asked.**
>
> **'He said it was part of her neurosis. Blake's name had been in the news so she had imagined he was hiding out in her house.'**

Another pause.

> **'In view of what you have just told us,' George said, his voice taut with the effort to maintain his self control, 'I think we should move back to our previous address.'**

Seán said nothing but dived under the bed, grabbed his case and began stuffing his clothes into it.

In the end we agreed that Seán should return immediately to Highlever Road. I would move George in a day or two as soon as I had found him somewhere else to stay. At that point, the only option seemed to be for Anne and myself to harbour him, despite the obvious risks and disadvantages. Our idea was to keep him hidden under the stairs during the daytime and construct a kind of 'priest hole' there so that even if the police called they would not necessarily find him.

But next day I met Pat who argued that it made much more sense for George to move in with him. The police had not come round to interview him following the discovery of the car, so presumably they had not found his fingerprints in it. George would be far more secure in his flat than in our house, where there were two children, a lodger, and neighbours and their children in the Housing Cooperative who frequently looked in. On the evening of Wednesday, 2nd November,[11] I once again borrowed Bernard's car, and drove George to Pat's flat. He remained there for the next six weeks or so until we got him out of the country.

Unbeknown to us, the police came as near to apprehending us that day as at any time in the period following the escape. In the morning the Security Service, MI5, phoned Special Branch naming both Pat and myself as possible suspects. Their report had been prompted by a report in the Daily Telegraph of 31st October, mentioned earlier, which quoted Rosemary Brown as saying that a 'Pat' and a 'Terry' were regular visitors of the Irishman the police wanted to interview. MI5 wondered if the two men might be Pat Pottle and Terry Chandler. [Pat and Terry were two of the six people jailed in 1962 for planning an occupation of the United States Air Force base in Wethersfield, Essex. The other four were Michael Randle, Ian Dixon, Trevor Hatton and Helen Allegranza.] They pointed out also that both men had been in Wormwood Scrubs at the same time as Blake. I was a possible suspect for the same reason and because I had sent greetings cards to Blake after my release.[12]

As a result of this tip-off, Detective Inspector Henry Nicholls, from Shepherds Bush Police Station went to 26 Perryn Road. His report reads as follows:

> At 5 p.m. today I visited 26 Perryn Road, W.3. where I saw, separately, Mrs Brown and Mr. and Mrs. Lucy.
>
> To each of them I showed a photograph of four men together, Dave Thomas, Terry Chandler, Patrick Pottle, and Douglas Breewood. Mrs.

11 In *The Blake Escape* we put the date of the move as Tuesday 1 November. But a more careful examination of the diary of events convinces us it must have been on the Wednesday. On Monday, Seán left the West London flat, it was the next day that I again made contact with Pat, and on the Wednesday that we moved him.

12 See Appendix A, the report by Inspector Bird listing the sources on which he based his report dated 7 March 1990, and specifying those for which the Crown was claiming Public Interest Immunity.

> Brown and Mr. and Mrs. Lucy were not able to identify any of the four men and were quite certain that they had never seen them visiting Seán Bourke at 26 Perryn Road.[13]

It emerged that the report in the *Daily Telegraph* had contained an error: it was not a 'Pat' and 'Terry' who had been frequent visitors of Seán but a 'Paul' and 'Terry'. The following day Nicholls paid Mrs Brown another visit during which she identified a former prisoner John Mantle from a photograph as the man she knew as 'Paul'.[14] Later, on 10th November, Nicholls interviewed John Mantle at Shepherds Bush police station and he confirmed that he was often known as Paul and that he had visited Seán at Perryn Road. On 3rd November, Mrs Brown and Mrs Lucy were also visited on the same day by a Detective Sergeant Frank Harris and both positively identified Alan Morton from a photograph as the man they knew as Terry.

But while it became quickly apparent that there was a mistake in the *Daily Telegraph*, it is surprising when the police were spreading their net so wide that they did not approach either of us to rule us out of their enquiries. After all it wasn't just the coincidence of the two names that had prompted MI5 to make their suggestion, but the fact that we both had been in prison with Blake, and that I had subsequently corresponded with him. Had they visited Pat that night, and arrived by chance at the very time we were moving Blake in, they would have caught Pat, Anne, myself and George Blake in a single swoop. Even if they had delayed by a day or two, Blake would have been in the flat when they arrived.

While we were quite unaware of the enquiries that had been going on behind the scenes, we were extremely well aware of Seán's predicament, rather more aware of it, we suspected, than Seán himself. The police were now on the look-out for him as much as for George, and he might be spotted and picked up at any time. We were afraid that if he got lonely and bored on his own he might seek out some of his ex-prisoner friends. We now know that he had done this – by phone at least – the very first day he was on his own in Highlever Road after we moved George to Matthew and Rachel's house. Andras Egey-Samu, an ex-prisoner and friend of Seán's, made a statement to the police on 31st October 1966 telling them that Seán had phoned him 'on Tuesday 25th

---

13 Statement by Detective Inspector H.J. Nicholls dated 2nd November, 1966. All four men mentioned had been active in the anti-nuclear organisation, the Committee of 100.

14 Further statement of Detective Inspector Nicholls, dated 3rd November 1966

or Wednesday 26th October.'[15] Seán had maintained contact with Egey-Samu and his family both when he was on the hostel scheme, as well as after his release; in fact Egey-Samu and a woman friend of his had gone with Seán to inspect the Humber car when he was contemplating buying it in mid August. He promised to inform the police if Seán phoned again.

Meanwhile I had met Seán again and persuaded him to join George at Pat's flat. He left a note for the landlady saying he had been called away on an assignment to another part of the country and would send the weekly rent by post. According to Seán's own account, he moved into Pat's flat on 7th November. But if we thought that had brought matters under control, we were mistaken. Seán, continued to leave the flat during the day when Pat was at work, blithely dismissing all fears and warnings, and contemptuous of the risks.

On 11th November, at about 2.30pm, he phoned Egey-Samu again. The latter immediately informed the police and made a statement the same day to Detective Inspector Rollo Watts at New Scotland Yard. It reads in part as follows:

> I am the managing director of the Hot Potato Ltd, and about 2.30pm today I received a telephone call at my restaurant, The Hot Potato, at the Elephant and Castle Shopping Centre, S.E. The call was from Seán Bourke. He told me that he had been out of the country for two or three weeks and had just returned and realised that police were looking for him. I told him that of course they were and asked him if he was going to give himself up. He replied, "Not to those fucking bastards – let them earn their fucking money." He asked me if police had been in touch with me and I told him that they had and that I was very worried. He told me not to worry as I hadn't had anything to do with it and they couldn't do anything about it. I pointed out that I was still a foreigner and he said that did make a difference and apologized for any trouble he had caused my family. I asked him where he was speaking from and he said, "Why would you give me up?" I said, "What do you think?", but he wouldn't tell me where he was. I told him that I would like to see him for old times sake but he was non-committal … Bourke did not actually mention Blake or the escape but took it for granted that I knew why he was wanted. He did not make any arrangements to see me or telephone

15 Statement by Andras Egey-Samu taken down by Detective Inspector D. Elvet Price and witnessed by Detective Constable J.M. Sillence at 1.30pm on 31 October 1966.

me again, but I will continue to co-operate with police and let you know immediately should he contact me.[16]

With George and Seán safely under the same roof in Pat's flat we were able to take stock of our situation. Our immediate problem was to raise more money. Prior to the escape Pat and I had tried two or three people in the anti-war movement, all of whom had turned us down flat. When I approached Dr Alex Comfort – whom I had worked closely with in the Direct Action Committee and Committee of 100 – he reacted as if I had struck him. He didn't want to know anything about it, he said, or to hear the subject ever raised again; what we were contemplating was madness and could bring the peace movement into disrepute. Pat and I realised that people who had never met George as we had done were quite likely to react in this way, and we felt at this stage that we could jeopardise the whole operation if we went on touting for support and spreading the circle of people who knew about it.

The solution fell into our lap unexpectedly. Shortly before the escape, a friend of ours 'Bridget' who was involved in the peace movement and was deeply committed to egalitarian principles, approached me to say she had inherited money which she wanted to put to a worthy cause. Had I any suggestions? I didn't immediately tell her of our plans to help free Blake, and afterwards waited until we had concrete plans for getting him out of the country before confiding in her our predicament.

Our original plan regarding Blake was both daring and original. We would turn him black – actually change the pigmentation of his skin – before providing him with a false passport. I had read a book by a white American writer, John Howard Griffin,[17] who had temporarily changed the colour of his skin through a combination of drugs and treatment under an ultra-violet lamp. Pat and I had found out from another doctor friend the name of the drug – meladinin – and Pat had forged a doctor's prescription for it. The day before the escape, Seán and I had obtained it, and an ultra-violet lamp, at chemist shops in Central London. Seán was to provide the false passport through underworld contacts.

16 Statement taken down by Detective Inspector Rollo Watts at the Hot Potato Restaurant, The Elephant and Castle shopping Centre, 11 November 1966, between 7.pm and 7.30pm. Presumably Egey-Samu telephoned the police after receiving Seán's call, and Scotland Yard sent Watts to the restaurant to interview him.

17 John Howard Griffin, *Black Like Me*, Panther, 1964.

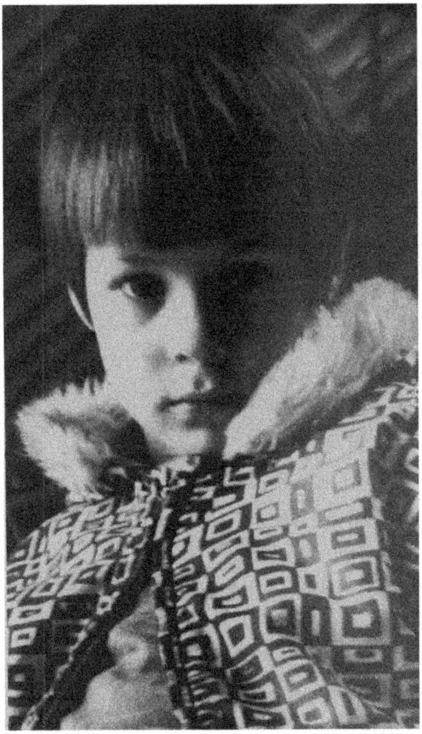

Left: Gavin (aged almost three), Christmas 1966, soon after our return from Germany.

Below: Sean (aged four-and a half) Christmas 1966

Above: Sean and Gavin playing in the snow in Goslar, two days after leaving George on the autobahn near the East Berlin checkpoint.

Below: The campervan in which Blake was taken to East Germany, hidden in secret compartment..

But George never took to the idea of turning black. There were risks attached to it, as an overdose of meladinin could damage the liver. Moreover, George was in no condition to undergo the treatment for a couple of weeks after the escape because of the injuries he had received. By then it was out of the question to have Seán touting round the underworld for a false passport. We had to find an alternative approach.

We eventually settled for building a secret compartment in a camper van where George would hide while I drove him to East Germany. (I was the only one of the group with a driving licence). Anne at once offered to accompany me with our two children, Seán and Gavin. This would make it look as though we were a family taking a winter holiday and greatly reduce the risks of being caught. The whole plan, however, depended upon our being able to raise the money.

It was at this point that I spoke again to Bridget. She was stunned by the revelation that the three of us were involved in Blake's escape, but agreed at once to help. Thus about three weeks after the escape, she handed me over a cheque for £1,000. With this we were able to buy a second-hand Commer van in good condition, and to start work on modifying it.

The work was done by Matthew who had the skills and equipment necessary for the task. Over a period of several weeks I drove the van to his garage where he worked into the early hours, while I acted as his assistant. He created the space under a fold-out bench/bed which ran the length of the driver's side at the back. Originally the bed when it was folded down was supported by two open cupboard doors which gave access to the storage space underneath. We replaced these with drawers which could be filled with clothes and other items to account for the space. Only if customs men became suspicious and attempted to push the drawers fully shut would there be a problem. The secret compartment where Blake would hide was right at the front end. Matthew did a thorough and professional job, matching up all the wood and the facings with those in the rest of the camper. No one, when the job was complete, would suspect it had been modified unless they had the original plans in front of them.

At about 8pm on Saturday, 17th December, Anne, myself and the two children left Pat's flat to board the midnight ferry from Dover. Once, just outside Canterbury, we had to stop to let George out to get some air. He was feeling nauseous but put this down to the smell from a rubber hot-water bottle we had given him to pee in if he felt the need. At Ostend, all was so quiet inside the van that we were seriously worried that he might have suffocated. However when we stopped the van a little way outside Ostend, we found him alive, well and busting for a pee. Anne created a kind of tent around the two boys in the front, while I released him.

After that he travelled openly with us except at the frontier crossings and for the final leg of the journey. There was no inspection of any kind at the Belgium/West German border, or on the Western side at Helmsted. The East German border guards did get us to open the back of the van, but made no move to disturb the two children asleep on the bed. We then drove on to the autobahn that used to link West Germany to Berlin, situated deep inside East Germany.

Anne and myself were shaken by the grimness of the border with its high fences surmounted by barbed wire, its tall watchtowers with their armed sentries and their searchlights trained on the fence and gates below. The East German autobahn too was dark and depressing, and the road pitted and in poor condition, in stark contrast to the brightly lit and well-maintained autobahns of West Germany. We drove non-stop for a further four hours or so, with George hidden the whole time. Stopping along this stretch of road was prohibited, and we had decided not to risk drawing attention to ourselves by ignoring the prohibition. For the same reason we kept George in hiding until we were quite close to Berlin; if we were stopped by a passing East German police patrol we would have to explain how we came to have an extra passenger with no passport or other documents. We might even have been detained for hours, or days while George's story was checked out, and this in turn would increase the risk of arousing the suspicions of Western guards or Security Service.

It was near midnight when, a few miles from from the East German checkpoint, just past the bridge over the Elbe, we released George from his hiding place. By then we were anxious and overtired and unable to share in his obvious elation. I had been driving virtually non-stop for 28 hours, keeping myself alert towards the end with pills supplied by the good doctor that had fixed George's wrist. I began to worry that George's arrival on foot would be observed from the West Berlin checkpoint, or that the Western Intelligence services would soon find out by one means or another how he had made good his escape. George tried to reassure us, and promised that he would never do or say anything that would put us at further risk. On this he has been as good as his word. He was, I think, genuinely touched by Anne's willingness to put so much at risk when she had two young children. His other preoccupation was whether or not he should retain the beard he had grown during his period in hiding, and he insisted on having our opinion on the matter. Finally, about a mile from the East German checkpoint, he left the van. At the side of the road we made our farewells, promising ourselves that one day we would meet again and have a proper celebration. We then drove on into West Berlin, stopping there one night at the Hotel am Zoo in the Kurfurstendamm before driving back to West Germany where we spent a couple of days in the picturesque town of Goslar, recommended to us by George.

We had to make other plans for Seán. He had neither the build nor the temperament to lie hidden in a coffin-like box for nine or ten hours at a stretch. He himself favoured taking the mailboat back to Ireland, but we thought this was too dangerous. If he wasn't spotted boarding the ferry, he would probably be extradited after his return to Ireland. He could fight extradition on the grounds that his offence was a political one, but we doubted if he could win his case when his offence was to free a notorious double-agent working for an atheistic communist power. We urged him, for all our sakes as well as his own, to follow George to Moscow and lie low there for six months or so until the pressure eased. Reluctantly he agreed. This has been the one episode that gave us qualms of conscience afterwards for we should have realised some of the problems and difficulties that would arise – and at some level at least we did.

In the end we solved the problem of getting him out of the country by the same kind of do-it-yourself improvisation that had been the hallmark of the whole enterprise. By trial and error I found a way of transferring the official embossment on a passport photograph onto a quick-setting plastic filler paste. By using the brass rubbing technique, the embossment could then be transferred onto any other photograph. We steamed off the original photo from Pat's passport, and replaced it with one of Seán, duly embossed and properly aligned with the rest of the embossment on the page. The result was not perfect, and might just be spotted by an alert official at the British end; but if it passed that test, it was unlikely to be queried anywhere else in Europe. Armed with this improvised forgery, we arranged for him to take the Golden Arrow Express train from Victoria to Paris, and to fly from there to Berlin. He would then cross into East Berlin at Checkpoint Charlie and meet up with George.

On Saturday 31st December, Pat, Anne and myself took him in the Commer to Victoria Station to catch the midnight train. It is a non-stop journey as the carriages were loaded directly onto the ferry at Dover and hooked up to a French engine at the other side. Thus the British customs and passport checks were carried out at Victoria, and we would know immediately if the passport had stood up to its first and most hazardous test. We had several drinks in the bar next to the departure platform, and then the three of us watched Seán going through the ticket barrier and into the building where the customs and passport control was carried out. When he emerged some minutes later and boarded the train we felt all our problems were finally behind us.

But we reckoned without Seán. He phoned me from Paris the next day to say that on no account must Pat or I go to the Highlever Road flat to clear the belongings he had left there. We had continued sending the rent every week to the landlady in case George and/or Seán needed to return there in an emergency. Before he left we'd had long discussions as to whether or not it would be advisable for us to clear it after Seán left. He was strongly against this. Now he was phoning to say that he actually knew for certain that the police had it under observation. It would be suicidal for us to return. Once again he assured me that there was absolutely nothing there that could incriminate us or point the police in our direction.

When Seán's book was published, he revealed that on 31st January, before leaving for Paris, he posted a photograph of himself to a national newspaper with his name and address on the back. This, he felt sure, would result in the immediate discovery of the flat by the police. The reason he gives for this extraordinary action was that he wanted to prevent Pat going there since he believed that he wanted to be caught, so that he could stand up in the dock and denounce the authorities for their treatment of Blake.

At the time, of course, we were quite unaware of all this, and now faced a dilemma. Should we risk going to Highlever Road despite Seán's dire warning? Or were we putting ourselves at even greater risk if we did not do so? Perhaps, after all, there were clues there to our involvement that Seán had overlooked. In the end I drove there with Pat. We parked the Commer round the corner in Oxford Gardens and let ourselves in. There was a light showing in the panel above the bathroom door as we crept past. Wearing gloves, we quickly and quietly emptied the surfaces and drawers, and left carrying Seán's typewriter, television, and his suitcase stuffed with photos, letters, the walkie-talkies and other oddments. A few doors away two women who had been chatting over the garden fence fell silent and eyed us curiously.

> **'They either have us down for sneak-thieves,' Pat said as we loaded the van, 'or we are from a rental firm come to repossess the telly.'**

Among the items we collected were photographs taken on a self-timer by Seán while still on the hostel scheme standing by the window with the walkie-talkie in his hand. In the background the towers of the prison wings were clearly visible. Far more serious, however, from our point of view, was the bundle of letters which Blake had written to Seán before he smuggled in the walkie talkie. These strongly urged him to get in touch with me. He didn't mention me by name, of course, referring to me as 'our friend' but he did emphasise that I had been sending him Christmas cards since my release, and for this reason he felt confident I would be sympathetic. This information would have narrowed suspects to a mere handful, perhaps to no more than two or three people. Given the phone call made by MI5 to Special Branch on 2nd November drawing attention to the fact that I had been sending greetings cards to Blake, it is inconceivable that the police would not have followed up this clue if it had fallen into their hands. They would have found the van with its secret compartment still in place, and no doubt discovered about the £1,000 paid into our account and our recent trip to Berlin. We would also have been vulnerable to pressure because of having two young children to worry about.

The next shock came on Friday, 13th January when the Evening Standard ran a front page story headlined in large black print: 'Blake Hunt Murder Threat'. A letter, the story ran, posted on New Year's Eve and bearing a Hampstead postmark had been sent to a Sergeant Michael Sheldon in Crawley, Sussex the same policeman to whom Seán had sent an explosive device back in 1961. Police wanted to interview the man in connection with the escape of George Blake; a warrant for his arrest had been issued by the Director of Public Prosecutions and Interpol had been alerted. The Standard did not publish Seán's name or print his photograph, but next day the Times did so.

None of us saw the item in the Times, but it was spotted by Mrs Lotte Heveringham who recognized Seán from the photograph and went at once to the police. The following Friday, 20th January, the Evening Standard headlines announced that the police had discovered the flat in Highlever Road which they believed had been the hideout for the escaped prisoner George Blake. It had been cleared, the story said, only ten days previously. The story was accompanied by a full-length photograph of Seán occupying most of the right hand front page of the paper. Next day the Guardian published photos side by side of George and Seán and a report by Adam Raphael stating that the police now believed that Blake was still in hiding in London.

Once again, because of the police files that came into our possession in 1990, we are now able to fill in some more details of how matters developed. Seán sent the threatening letter to Sheldon by registered post from Hampstead Post Office at around 2pm on Saturday, 31st December. The Post Office clerk who dealt with it was 26 year old Robert Cramp who also happened to be a Special Constable. On 5th January he made the following statement to the police:

> **I am employed as a Postal and Telegraph Officer at Hampstead Post Office, 63 High Street, Hampstead, N.W.3. I would mention that I am also a Special Constable stationed at Finchley (No.133 'S').**

> **On 31st December, 1966, at about 2pm, I was working on the counter. A man handed me a large envelope, brown and about 12 inches x 10 inches. It was not the normal Post Office envelope. He asked that the envelope be sent by registered mail. I filled out Receipt No. R.7884 and I wrote on this receipt 'Sheldon Police Station, Crawley'. I recall that the letter was addressed to a Detective. I marked the envelope with blue lines and stamped the envelope.**
> **I remember that the man was an Irishman. I would say he was aged about 35 years, 5 feet 10 inches tall, thick set. He was unshaven and generally scruffy. I have been shown a photograph (Seán BOURKE) and I would say that to the best of my recollection that this was the man.**
>
> **I cannot remember having seen this man in the area before.**[18]

Had the police publicised the death threat to Sheldon as soon as he received it, or even as soon as they interviewed Cramp, we might never have been able to clear Highlever Road. We are uncertain at this point about exactly when we did so. Our recollection is that we did so the day after Seán left for Paris and Berlin, that is on New Year's Day, 1967. But several statements made to the police in January 1967 concur in placing the date at around the 5th or 6th January. Thus Margaret Lawrence of 20 Highlever Road, one of the women Pat and I had seen talking to her neighbour when we went by with Seán's possessions, told the police on 17th January:

> **About a fortnight ago, I think it was 6th January 1967, between 3.p.m. and 4.pm, I saw two men come out of 28 Highlever Road, W.10, carrying something like a large trunk. I particularly remember this incident because the trunk was very heavy and the two men seemed to have difficulty in carrying it. The two men did not have a car and did not use a taxi, I thought this rather strange. They struggled up the road towards Oxford Gardens. They passed my house and continued up the road. I did not see the men once they had passed my house. One man I would say was aged about 30 years to 33 years, 5' 10", well built. He was wearing a short car coat coloured tan or brown with a white fur collar. He had a small beard which covered just his chin and the lower part of his face. I have been shown two photographs (Bourke's) and I would say that this was the man. [It was in fact Pat she was describing]. However, the full length photograph is the best likeness whilst the man is barely recognisable from the other photograph. The**

18 Statement of Robert Cramp to Detective Sergeant C.R. Jones, in the presence of another detective,D.S. Harris D.S. Harris at Hampstead Post Office on 5 January 1967 between 12-40 pm and 12.55 pm.

> **other man was aged about 30 years, slightly taller than the first man, slim build. He was wearing a dark suit. I have looked at a number of other photographs but I cannot pick out the other man.**[19]

Another statement, made on 16th January, came from 28 year old Robin Taylor who occupied room number 3 on the ground-floor at 28 Highlever Road. His statement reads in part:

> **Just before he [Bourke] left the premises (about 5 or 6th January) I heard the sound of movement from his room and the sound of voices, although subdued. I had the impression that there was another man there but did not see the other person. This was mid afternoon at about 3.30pm and I went out shortly after this and never saw them leave.**[20]

Possibly, then, it was him who was in the bathroom as we went to empty the bedsit.

Finally Eileen Griffin, who worked for Mrs Heveringham, the owner of 28 Highlever Road, said in a statement on 16th January:

> **I normally go to 28 Highlever Road on Mondays and sometimes on other days in the week. For the first few weeks, I saw the man in his room when I went to change his linen. On those occasions he was just walking about his room, not doing anything very much. He would not talk to me, and seemed anxious to avoid me.**
>
> **He was away for about seven weeks, and used to send his rent by post. During that time I am fairly certain he had not been in the house, for his bed had not been slept in. I remember seeing some false beards and moustaches in his room. On the first occasion I saw him he was clean shaven, but each time after that he had a very dark beard and moustache, and I should think it was false – although it looked real enough.**
>
> **I also remember seeing in his room an Insurance Card in the name of Bourke but cannot remember any other details.**
>
> **I did not see the man after he started writing the letters, but he must have come back between the 2nd and 7th January. On the 2nd I noticed that his belongings (a small suitcase, a television set and a typewriter) were still there, but they had gone on the 7th.**[21]

---

19 Statement by Margaret Rose Lawrence taken by Det Sergeant A.R. Jones in the presence of D.C. Gray between 7.45 and 8.5.-.m. on 17 January 1967.

20 Statement by Robin Patrick Taylor at Shepherds Bush Police Station to R. Haslett, Detective Sergeant 'B', at Shepherds Bush Police Station.

21 Statement of Miss Eileen Griffin, Aged 28, made at her home in Finstock Road

If we did not clear the flat until 5th or 6th of January, as these statements suggest, then indeed we escaped detection by a very narrow margin indeed.

The landlady, Mrs Lotte Heveringham, interviewed on the same day, explained how she had gone to the police after seeing Seán's photograph in the newspapers. She tells how on one occasion, on 15 November, she found two National Insurance Cards, one in the name of O'Riordan, the other in the name of Seán Bourke. Inside a book on the Great Train Robbery, she also found 'four or five false moustaches and beards, in different colours, ranging from blonde to dark in colour.' But there was an even more bizarre twist to her story:

> **About three weeks ago, some R.A.F. Policemen came to my address in Finstock Road, saying they were looking for a deserter. They showed me a photograph of a man they were looking for, but I did not recognize him. They said that the man they were looking for had left behind a note of my name and address. I took them to Highlever Road, and told them that I was rather suspicious about my tenant called Sigsworth. They came with me to his room and they took a note of some numbers which they found on a large piece of paper. We noticed that the Insurance Card of O'Riordan was missing, but the one for Bourke was still there.**[22]

Next day Detective Inspector Nichols spoke to Flight Sergeant Thompson of the R.A.F. police who confirmed that he and another R.A.F. policeman had called on Mrs Heveringham on 25th December 1966.

> **Mrs Heveringham took them to a house owned by her at 28 Highlever Road, W10, where in Flat 5, there was a tenant about whom she had suspicions. She took them into the flat and F/S Thompson there saw an Insurance Card in the name of Bourke, a small case containing a number of small Japanese Transistor radios, a number of newspapers and some correspondence with the Press Council.**[23]

Some of the information and suggestions received by the police were entertainingly irrelevant. James Hill, a Customs Clearance Officer, on his way home on a bus at 5.30pm on 24th October read a report in the *Daily Express* that Blake's wife had sent him a Bokhara rug. He must have phoned the police

---

on 16 January 1967 from 8 p.m. to 8.30 p.m. to Det. Insp H.J. Nicholls, in the presence of D.C. Day.

22 Part of the statement by Lotte Heveringham , aged 64, of 37 Finstock Road W.10 made to Detective Inspector H. J. Nicholls.

23 Statement by Detective Inspector Harry Nicholls made on 17 January after talking to F /S Thompson.

as soon as he arrived home, for later that evening he made a statement at his home to an officer from the Surrey Constabulary to say that he had worked as an auctioneer of antiques for many years and that in his opinion 'it is possible that a message can be woven into this type of rug and could be read by an expert.'[24]

Less fanciful, but probably more misleading, were the suspicions entertained by the journalist Adam Raphael. On 24th October he went to Shepherds Bush Police Station and made a statement to Detective Inspector R. A. Watts ('Rollo Watts'). The implication here was that the Soviet Embassy was somehow involved in the escape:

> **I am a member of Hurlingham Tennis Club, Ranelegh Gardens, Fulham and on last Saturday afternoon at about 3.15pm I overheard a fellow member named Walters complaining that his partner had let him down at the last moment. He said that his partner, a Russian, had telephoned to say that his Ambassador had called him away at short notice. To my knowledge there are only two Russian members of the Club – the Russian Ambassador and a secretary named Valentin Elistratov. Presumably the latter was the partner in question. It is possible that from the timing, this may have some connection with the escape of Blake. The facts could no doubt be verified from Mr. Basil Walters whose telephone number is Flaxman 8755, but I would prefer that my name is not given to him.**[25]

The police clearly took this lead seriously, for that same evening Detective Inspector Rollo Watts went to Basil Waters' home at 18 Old Church Street, and took a statement from him. He confirmed that he had arranged a match between Mervyn Brown, a Foreign Office official, Kenneth Low, a Director of Heron Arts Ltd, Kong Tan, the owner of the Shangri-La and other Chinese restaurants and Yari I. Loginov, 1st Secretary (Political) at the Russian Embassy.

> **I did not wish to play myself as I had slightly injured my leg, so Loginov had agreed to take my place. I have been told that about mid-day on Saturday, Loginov rang the 'Tennis Organiser' at the Club to say that he would be unable to play. However, he was referred to me and did, in fact, ring me at home at 12.55pm. He apologised profusely but said that a spate of work had arrived which would prevent him**

24 Statement by James Allen Hill, aged 53, at his home at 3 Wolverton Close, Horley, Surrey, to Police Constable 326 Dance at 7.45 pm on Monday 24th October 1966.

25 Statement taken by Detective Inspector RA.Watts on Monday 24th October, 1966, between 12.15 p.m. and 12.30 p.m. at Shepherds Bush Police Station. and signed by Raphael.

playing that afternoon as his Ambassador had asked him to remain and deal with it. It is highly unusual for anyone to cancel a game at Hurlingham at such short notice and Lovinov was quite aware of this. In the end I played myself despite my leg. When I realised the possible implications of Loginov's absence, in view of the escape of Blake, I telephoned Mervyn Brown at about 3pm. today and drew his attention to it.[26]

Whether or not the police attached any great importance to this incident, we do know that from the start they were working on two theories about the escape. As Detective Inspector R. Bird put it: 'The view taken at the time was that this escape had either been undertaken by a criminal element for financial gain or by agents of a country hostile to the United Kingdom. It was the latter which had greater credibility.'[27]

The strong suspicion on the part of the police and the authorities that foreign agents had organised the escape worked to our advantage; it meant that from the start they felt deep down that they had little chance of finding Blake. To quote from one of the officers involved in the hunt, Wilf Knight:

We ran around a bit like headless chickens, working out where we were going to go. We assumed that Blake had been sprung by an Eastern bloc country, because of the organisation, the mechanics of doing such a thing, and, therefore, they must be ready to take him out straight away. Two o'clock in the morning, the Czech State Orchestra checked-in to go out on their own state aircraft, and we turned them over – bassoons, cello cases, people man or woman. I mean we looked for him everywhere. There was one or two people we weren't happy with. We caused quite a furore diplomatically.[28]

Perhaps if the police had been working with a rather more open mind, and had been less weighed down with the feeling that they were on a hiding to nothing, they might have followed up the suggestion from the Security Service on 2nd November 1966 and checked out Pat and myself. Had they done so, the story would almost certainly have had a very different ending.

---

26 Part of the statement by Basil C.J. Waters, Executive of British Iron and Steel Federation, to Detective Inspector R. Watts, at his home at 18 Old Church Street, S.W.3, between 7.25 and 7.40 p.m.on 24th October 1966.

27 Report by Detective Inspector R. Bird of Special Branch dated 7th March 1990 after inspecting the police files from 1966 onwards about the escape. See Appendix 8

28 Wilf Knight speaking to Richard Lindley for the Thames Television drama documentary, The Blake Escape, first broadcast 26 April 1989.

Chapter 3:

The 'Outing' of the Secret

Seán soon got itchy feet in Russia. He had never had any illusions about the nature of the Soviet regime, and before long he had become disillusioned with Blake. This might not have happened, or not have happened so soon, but for a well-intentioned gesture on Blake's part. Seán had originally been housed by the KGB in a Moscow hotel where he had little company and easy access to vodka. Realising he was getting bored and lonely, Blake invited him to share his own, ample, KGB flat.

The friendship forged in the particular circumstances of prison did not long survive the strains of living in close daily contact. Soon they were getting on each other's nerves. Blake was punctilious, reserved, dedicated to a quiet orderly existence; Seán was untidy, impulsive, unpredictable – as we ourselves had discovered. Both men were like fish out of water in a strange country, without a clear role. Blake had at least a reasonable command of the language, and, according to Seán's account, spent many hours during his first few months in Moscow talking to KGB officials. Seán was given work for a time checking translations from Russian into English for Progress Publishing House in Moscow, but gave up the work after checking one book on Scientific Communism. His main project was to write up the story of the escape and its aftermath.

The two men became more and more estranged. Seán decided that the patient, understanding character he had known in Wormwood Scrubs was a fraud. The Blake he now saw at close quarters was 'sullen, intolerant, arrogant and pompous.' There were petulant scenes and quarrels – for instance, over how loud Seán had the radio, and over noise after 11 o'clock at night. Seán alleges that on one occasion, in a fit of pique, Blake hurled the sandwiches he had been preparing at the wall and refused to go on their planned outing together accompanied by their KGB minder, Stanislaus (Stan). Blake was also, Seán decided, the vainest man he had ever met. He loved to dress up and preen himself in front of a full-length mirror, and was excessively proud of two medals he had been awarded, the Order of Lenin, and the Order of the Red Banner, for his services to the Soviet State.

This is Seán's side of the story. We are inclined to accept that the particular incidents he relates did take place though his account of them may be rather jaundiced. Blake undoubtedly does have a vain streak. During the last stage of the journey to Berlin, after we had released him from his hiding place, his chief concern seemed to be whether or not he should keep the beard he had grown while in hiding. He insisted on having our view on this matter when we were worried sick about whether we would survive the next few days and weeks without being arrested and split up as a family as a consequence of what we had done. Still, few of us would fare well from the close daily scrutiny of a critical onlooker. Moreover, some of Seán's comments tell us as much about himself as they do about George. He is contemptuous, for instance, about Blake's fondness for children. 'On one occasion,' he remarks, 'Victor [another KGB official] brought his six-year-old son to the flat, and Blake fussed over him and fondled him with a maternal devotion that was embarrassing to watch.'[1]

Seán also leaves out of his account crucial facts that are unflattering to himself. He mentions the fact that he made an anonymous phone call to the police to tell them the whereabouts of the getaway car three days after the break-out, but not that he was prepared to put my liberty on the line, and the whole operation in jeopardy, by giving me the key of the car to drive it away a few days later simply because he could not bring himself to admit to us what he had done. He mentions that the KGB officials brought him copies of British papers in late January which reported that the police were hunting for him in connection with the escape, and had published his name and photograph, but not the fact that he had sent a death threat to a Sussex policeman, or that it was this which had led to his being publicly named for the first time.

The release of Seán's name by the police and the attendant publicity – for which he himself was directly responsible – led the KGB to harden its opposition to his early return to Ireland. It had, Stan told Seán, altered the whole picture. Now there could be no doubt that the British government would seek his extradition from Ireland if he returned there and thus put Pat, Anne and myself at risk. Seán vehemently disagreed. He had always assumed, he said, that his identity would quickly be known to the police and that the British would seek his extradition if he returned to Ireland.

Clearly he was right about that, at least once he had tipped the police off about the whereabouts of the getaway car. But there was no basis for his further argument that it also meant that his friends would 'have an even greater chance

1 *The Springing of George Blake*, p.250.

of escaping detection because the police hunt would be focused on him.'[2] This argument is based on a misapprehension and a fiction. The misapprehension is that the police would assume that Seán must have acted on his own. There was no reason at all why they should do so – and nor, of course, did they. The fiction was that neither Pat nor I had been in Wormwood Scrubs prison at the same time as him and George. In my own case, I had worked closely with Seán for about seven months in the Tailor's Shop, had been on the English Diploma Class with both him and George, and corresponded with him after my release. Thus it is highly improbable that George ever have uttered the words Seán attributes to him when Stan brought them the news from London:

> **The police will now concentrate on checking up on his known friends … including those he had known in prison, and so Michael and Pat are in the clear. As I see it, this discovery and [Seán's] established guilt … is a blessing. It is the best thing that could have happened from the point of view of our friends in London.**[3]

At all events, George sided with the KGB in opposing Seán's early return to Ireland. To Seán, this amounted to betrayal by the man he had taken so many risks to free. Some months later, he claims to have overheard George saying to Stan:

> **'You can go out there now and tell him that he must stay in this country for at least five years whether he likes it or not – and if you like I will tell him for you. Or, you can …'**

The sentence was left unfinished, but Seán had no doubt what was intended. Blake was suggesting that if he would not fall in with the KGB plans, they should kill him.

Blake's version of events is – naturally – quite different. In his autobiography published in 1990 he makes no reference to this alleged incident, but states that over the period in which they were in Moscow together their relationship 'soured', mainly because of the disagreement about when or whether Seán should return to Ireland. Blake says he felt the ideal solution would have been for Seán to settle down in Russia, though he soon realised this was not going to happen. He opposed Seán's early return, he says, because he was concerned for the safety of the three of us who had, after all, strongly urged Seán to come to Moscow in the first place precisely because we were worried that he would be extradited if he attempted to settle down in Ireland.

Seán dismisses this concern on George's part – which he had strongly expressed to him during their time together in Moscow – as so much humbug.

2 *The Springing of George Blake*, p.246.

3 *The Springing of George* Blake, p.246.

The real explanation, he says, is that Blake was a born traitor. As he put it later to his brother, Kevin: 'Blake does not betray for ideals; he betrays because he *needs* to betray. If Blake had been born a Russian he would have betrayed the K.G.B. to the British. That's how he's made.'[4]

This explanation doesn't bear examination. If Blake had an irresistible compulsion to betray, why did he not betray the three of us? Not only did he not do so, but he went out of his way to restrain Seán from acting with a blithe irresponsibility that would indeed give MI5 and Special Branch the information they required to identify us, and would, in the longer term, lead to our being publicly named and standing trial at the Old Bailey. Whoever or whatever else he betrayed, George Blake kept faith with us.

To return to Blake's account. Since Seán was determined to leave the Soviet Union, the KGB put forward an alternative plan. They would provide him with false papers and a passport which would enable him to settle in the country of his choice under a new identity. Seán would have none of it; he would settle for nothing short of returning to Ireland under his own name. He does not mention this proposition in his own book, but it seems entirely consistent with the manner in which the KGB are known to have behaved towards him that they would have put forward such a plan – and no less consistent with his own character and disposition that he would have flatly rejected it.

We are not in a position to say whether or not the conversation which Seán alleges he overheard ever took place. It seems unlikely that he would have invented the whole story, but no less unlikely that Blake would have used English to propose Seán's murder when he could perfectly well have said the same thing in Russian. (Seán notes, for example, how George addressed the servants assigned to them in Russian). Moreover, George had absolutely nothing to gain by proposing Seán's murder; if the latter's continued presence in the same flat had become intolerable he had only to say so and Seán would have been moved to another flat – as eventually he was. The most likely explanation is that Seán did indeed overhear a conversation but misconstrued it.

Seán now determined upon a desperate course of action and carried it through with the kind of verve he had shown in springing Blake from prison in the first place. Evading the Russian guards on duty outside the British Embassy in Moscow, he made his way inside, announced who he was and asked the astonished officials to supply him with a passport so he could return to Britain.

4 *The Springing of George Blake*, p. 341.

He describes the two officials he first encountered as 'snotty bastards'. The vice-consul whom he eventually saw was more sympathetic but he explained to Seán that as he was an Irish citizen there was nothing they could do immediately. The Irish government had no representation in Moscow, so the British Foreign Office would have to contact their counterparts in Dublin to see if he could be given an Irish passport; he should come back in a week and try again.

To Seán this sounded like a cruel joke. He was convinced that once he left the Embassy he would never be given a chance of returning for a second visit. Moreover, without the protection of either a British or Irish passport he would be at the mercy of the KGB who, he assumed, would never forgive him for what he had done. The Consul's words, therefore, amounted to a death sentence.

He was stopped by the Russian guards upon leaving the building but managed to convince them he was a tourist and that his passport was at his hotel. He then phoned George from a call box to tell him what he had done and took the metro to the stop at the end of the line on the Western outskirts of the city. That night he slept rough in a dense forest. However, by the evening of the following day, with only a single rouble left in his pocket, he decided that a quick death from a bullet in the head was preferable to a slow death from starvation and exposure in the forest. He therefore phoned Blake again and returned to the flat.

To his surprise he found the KGB man Stan sympathetic and conciliatory. If he was that determined to return to Ireland, Stan said, then of course he could do so; the Soviet authorities themselves would make all the necessary arrangements. But would he be prepared to wait a few more months until the fuss subsided? Seán, scarcely able to believe his good fortune, agreed. He moved out of Blake's flat, spent some time touring the Soviet Union, and formed a relationship with a young Russian woman, Larissa. Back in Moscow, he continued to work on a book about the escape and his subsequent adventures. In August 1968, his brother Kevin visited him and attempted to smuggle the manuscript out of the country; it was confiscated by KGB officials at the airport. On 22nd October 1968, two years to the day after Blake's escape from Wormwood Scrubs, Seán flew back to Ireland.

For the rest of us this was a tense period. There was huge press and media interest in Seán's story. He told television reporters who accompanied him on the plane from Amsterdam to Dublin that he and Blake had left Britain on forged passports. The next night, he told Granada Television's World in Action about the two-way radio used in planning the escape, and that he personally had driven Blake to East Germany concealed in a secret compartment of a camper van; he claimed that he then drove on into West Berlin before returning to London. Later, he said, he left Britain on a forged passport and eventually joined Blake in Moscow.

Next day Anne was shocked to get a phone call from Seán. (I was away in Bradford at the time.) He wanted the tapes he had left with us which recorded the conversations between him and Blake over the prison wall while they were planning the escape. Fearing his phone, or ours, might be bugged, she pretended he had got through to a wrong number and hung up.

The British authorities wasted no time in seeking his extradition. On 31st October 1968, Irish police arrested Seán on a Scotland Yard warrant. However the case did not come before the High Court until the following January, and meanwhile Seán was released on bail. No sooner was he out than he phoned us again. This time I spoke to him, and told him I did not think it was a good idea to post the tapes. A few days later a journalist from *RTE* (Radio Telefis Eireann) turned up on the doorstep saying he had come at Seán's request to collect the tapes. He gave us a solemn assurance that he would not reveal our identity to the police, and to his credit he never did so.

During the High Court hearings, more details of the escape emerged. Seán's lawyers revealed that three friends of his had raised £1,000 for the escape, and Seán himself, giving evidence on his own behalf, stated that it was one of them – not himself as he had earlier claimed – that had driven Blake to East Germany in a concealed compartment of a camper-van. The worrying thing from our point of view was that every time Seán retold the story, he edged that bit nearer to revealing the nature and extent of our involvement.

However, the High Court hearing had an unexpectedly positive outcome from our point of view. On 3rd February the judge, Mr Justice O'Keefe, ruled that although Seán's motives in helping Blake to escape were not in themselves politically motivated, Blake's original offence undoubted was so. Therefore Seán's action fell within the category of 'an offence committed in connection with a political offence' which is excluded from the provisions to the extradition treaty between Britain and Ireland. The following July, the Supreme Court rejected an appeal by the Irish Attorney General against the decision, and our troubles seemed finally to be at an end.

But once again we reckoned without Seán. In June 1970 he published his book, *The Springing of George Blake*. In it he describes in detail the role played by Pat, Anne and myself, gives us the pseudonyms 'Pat Porter', 'Anne Reynolds' and 'Michael Reynolds'. He also includes details about our age, family circumstances and background, political sympathies, and the area of London in which we lived. Thus he says of Anne and myself that we had two young children aged two and a half and four, that we lived about twenty minutes walk from Camden Town underground station, and that we were socialists but not communists.

The one detail he did not reveal – indeed went out of his way to conceal – was that Pat and I had been in prison with him and George. (A Special Branch report which eventually fell in to our hands commented – 'Even Bourke was unlikely to go that far.'[5]). But the clues to our identity were unmistakeable; as we said to one another at the time, a boy-scout could have worked out from them who we were. In fact a journalist friend of mine on *New Society*, saw a review copy and rang to warn me of what was in the offing. I agreed to review the book, and got as far as sending a piece to the journal. However, I decided that this was tempting providence too far, and called him again to ask him not to run it.

The history of Seán's manuscript is a saga on its own and also throws considerable light on Blake's motivation in the quarrels with Seán. We have already said that the KGB confiscated it from Seán's brother Kevin as he attempted to smuggle it out of Russia in August 1968. When Seán returned to Ireland he sent several letters to Stan in Moscow, care of the KGB, requesting its return. The letters went unanswered, but in the Spring of 1969, the exercise books arrived unexpectedly through the post to Seán's solicitor in Dublin. The final section dealing with Seán's stay in Moscow and his alleged betrayal by Blake had been removed. Other passages in the manuscript had been heavily blacked out.

Blake has since confirmed what we immediately suspected, namely that he himself had done the censoring. We have never seen the complete manuscript, but Seán in his book reproduces some of the censored pages. All the excised passages in them relate to names and descriptions that pointed to us as Seán's helpers, such as our first names, our descriptions, the age of Anne's and my children and so forth. In other words the clear purpose of the censorship was to protect us. Seán, however, not only reinstated the passages but drew attention to their significance by reproducing the censored pages and noting what had been excised.

Why, one may wonder, did the KGB return the manuscript, or rather the greater part of it, to Seán? In fact, however, there was little point in not doing so for what Seán had written once he was perfectly capable of writing a second time, now perhaps with an added grudge against the KGB for seizing

5 Report by Chief Inspector R.A.Watts of the Metropolitan Police Special Branch dated 23 March 1970, p.3.

the original manuscript and putting him to so much trouble. Nor, of course, could they prevent Seán from reinstating the passages that had been blacked out. This was not censorship at all in the normal sense of the word since the Soviet authorities could exercise no control whatever over the final shape and content of the book. Rather it was an urgent plea to Seán to think again about the implications for the rest of us of including the passages that had been blacked out. The KGB's decision to withhold the final portion of the manuscript was presumably motivated also by the hope that now that Seán had been allowed to return to Ireland, and all his fears about being assassinated laid to rest, he might see things differently. That didn't work either, and indeed the fact that Seán was able to re-write that section of the book underlines the fact that refusing altogether to send him the manuscript would have been pointless.

We now steeled ourselves for police interrogation and the likelihood of arrest and a lengthy term of imprisonment. But publication day came and went without incident. Gradually as the weeks passed we were able to breathe again. We concluded that the most likely explanation was that MI5, Special Branch and the authorities in general had decided that it would be too much of an embarrassment to arrest us at this stage when the principal actors had eluded their grasp. It was preferable from their point of view to let the public go on believing that the whole operation had been masterminded by the KGB, using Seán as their instrument, rather than have it revealed that it was all the work of a bunch of amateurs working on a shoe-string budget and desperately improvising to stay a step ahead of the police. The alternative explanation was that the police had not picked up on Seán's clues and still didn't know who we were. But that seemed highly improbable.

I managed to track down Seán's whereabouts in Dublin the following year and arranged to meet him at his flat in Sandymount in the southern outskirts of the city. He greeted me with a revolver in his hand, and then apologised for the dramatics saying that some unionist students from the north were threatening to abduct him. Over lunch in the city, we discussed several points about the book and about his stay in Moscow. But when I asked him why he had used pseudonyms so close to our original names he was clearly embarrassed.

> **'It goes to show,' he said after a long pause, 'that I am not the simple, straightforward Irishman that some people take me for.'**

It was no explanation, but I didn't press the point. The thing was done now, and, for whatever reason, none of us had been arrested. Seán also told me he had had several telephone conversations with one of the Special Branch officers involved in the case – probably Inspector Rollo Watts – who told him that they knew the identity of his helpers but had decided to take no action against us.

***

There the matter rested for a further seventeen years. I visited Seán twice more in Limerick in the early 1970s, once on my own, once with Anne and the children. I last heard from him in early 1977 when he wrote to say that he had decided to return to Britain and give himself up as there was nothing left for him in Ireland. I didn't reply, and simply hoped he would change his mind. In January 1992 the news came that he had died in the seaside town of Kilkee from a heart condition exacerbated by his heavy drinking and the general neglect of his health.

But Seán's book, written so many years previously, was to prove a time-bomb that would eventually explode the issue onto the front pages and present us with an acute dilemma about how to respond. In late September 1987, the writer and former MI5 officer, Montgomery Hyde, published a new book about Blake entitled *George Blake: Superspy*.[6] I was forewarned about it by the same journalist who had tipped me off about Seán's book in 1970. He was now working for *the Guardian* and I agreed to write a review for that paper.

Hyde's book is essentially a rehash of Seán's, indeed much of it is straightforward plagiarism. However, it included details about Pat and myself that Seán had been careful to leave out and thus positively identified all three of us beyond any possibility of doubt. The key passage in this respect reads:

> In addition there were two other prisoners [in Wormwood Scrubs] with an Irish background – Michael Reynolds and Pat Porter (these were not their real surnames). They both belonged to the Committee of 100, the nuclear disarmament group formed by Bertrand Russell, the philosopher and social reformer, who was the first president of the Campaign for Nuclear Disarmament. In 1960 he had split the CND to form the more militant Committee of 100 dedicated to civil disobedience in pursuit of its aims. Michael Reynolds and Pat Porter had helped to organise the civil disobedience demonstrations at Wethersfield RAF base in December 1961, for which they were imprisoned from 1961 to 1963.[7]

There were only five of us in Wormwood Scrubs for organising the Wethersfield demonstration, and none of the other three had the first name Pat or Michael. So Montgomery Hyde might just as well have gone the step further and given our, and Anne's, full names. It seemed certain, in any case, that if he didn't, it wouldn't be long before some other writer or journalist did.

6 Montgomery Hyde, *George Blake: Superspy*, Constable, 1987.

7 *George Blake: Superspy*, p. 63.

I showed Pat the review I had written and we agreed that it should appear under both our names. In it we virtually acknowledged our involvement in the Blake escape but without saying so in so many words since this might provoke a prosecution which the authorities would otherwise be reluctant to initiate. We also decided, however, to hold back publication of it until we had a chance to judge whether any notice was taken of the book. It was such a second-rate rehash of Seán's book that it might just be passed over unnoticed.

There was nothing in the press on the day of publication, 28th September 1987. The following day, however, there was a short news item by Richard Norton-Taylor in the Guardian headed 'Nuclear disarmers freed spy Blake, author says', and the story noted that two members of the Committee of 100 imprisoned in Wormwood Scrubs after the Wethersfield demonstration in 1961 were 'given thinly disguised aliases' in the book. The Guardian, it continued, had contacted former members of the Committee of 100 who were seeking legal advice. Pat and I had, in fact, had lunch with Richard during the week who had decided not to publish our names at this point.

But just over a week later, on 4th October, the lead story by Barrie Penrose in the Sunday Times was headed 'Soviet Spy was sprung by CND men'. (We knew it was coming since Penrose, a Committee of 100 turncoat, had been badgering us with phone calls all week and sending round photographers to sit in cars outside our homes in the hope of obtaining sneak pictures). The 'News In Focus' section inside carried a feature article by the same journalist headed 'The Blake Escape Committee' which included prominent photographs of Pat and myself taken in the late 1950s and early 1960s as well as more recent pictures. Penrose's feature article read in part:

> The descriptions of Reynolds and Porter by Bourke and Hyde match Randle and Pottle in almost every detail – religion, parentage, wives, mortgage, addresses, qualifications and political sympathies. Indeed Randle and Pottle expected MI5 to call when Bourke's book was published in 1970.

We decided to reply by way of an exclusive statement to Richard Norton-Taylor in the Guardian who had treated us with such fairness and courtesy. It appeared (in shortened form) on Friday, 9th October, together with a lengthy review of Montgomery-Hyde's book. Like the review, the statement stopped short of an outright admission of our involvement in Blake's escape while making it as clear as we could that we were indeed involved and thought we had been absolutely right to be so. To quote from the statement:

> We do not intend to confirm or deny the allegation made obliquely by Mr H. Montgomery Hyde in his new book, and explicitly by a Sunday

newspaper last weekend, that we assisted in the escape from Wormwood Scrubs, and subsequent flight to the Soviet bloc, of George Blake in 1966.

Mr Hyde relies almost entirely on a book published by Seán Bourke in 1970. If the events surrounding Blake's escape correspond with Bourke's account, no stigma in our judgement would be attached to any persons identified as his assistants …

We have no doubt that after Bourke's book was published the British Security Service were fully aware that we two matched the descriptions of Porter and Reynolds. If the police did not act then, and did not even question us, it was presumably because they realized that there was no real evidence of our involvement. We are confident they will take the same view today. Nevertheless should Scotland Yard wish to interview us, we will be happy to meet them at any time – preferably over a glass of Irish whiskey in memory of Seán Bourke!

Neither of us in the course of a long association has ever had any dealings with the espionage services of any state. We have, however, campaigned against the nuclear war preparations of both East and West as well as interventionist and repressive policies by both sides …

We do not condone Blake's role as a double agent, particularly if, as has been alleged, his activities led to the execution of western agents and double agents whom he named to the Soviet authorities. But Western Intelligence agencies also have blood on their hands … The time indeed is long overdue for a reassessment by both East and West of their extensive espionage activities which ruin lives, poison international relations and contribute to an unhealthy public obsession with spies and spying.

The 42-year sentence on Blake reflects no credit on British justice. It was clearly influenced by the Cold War. As Blake's QC, Mr Jeremy Hutchinson, said at the Appeal Court in 1961: 'This sentence is so inhuman that it is alien to all the principles on which a civilized country would treat its subjects.' His escape, as the then Prime Minister Wilson stated, posed no threat to British security. For our part we do not regret that he escaped instead of deteriorating slowly down the years in a succession of British jails.

If we were involved in Blake's escape we clearly could not say so publicly without pointlessly inviting prosecution. But we would have no apologies or regrets for an act of human solidarity that cut across political disagreements and across the lies, and murderous obsessions of superpower politics and the Cold War. If we were not involved we would not regard it as a slur on our character to be named as having been so.

> Thus on the basis of what has been said so far we will be issuing no writs and making no denials.

A few days later I agreed to meet an Irish journalist, Kevin O'Connor who worked freelance for RTE. He rang me from Bradford university after flying over from Dublin and I thought he might be the journalist to whom I had handed over Seán's tapes so many years ago. He wasn't, but the meeting nonetheless proved important. O'Connor had taken a special interest in the case ever since he was a young man living in London at the time of Blake's escape. He had got to know Bourke in Ireland and made a radio programme about him for RTE which had been broadcast in January 1983, round about the time of the anniversary of Seán's death. This included extracts from the tapes Seán had made of the discussions between him and Blake while they were planning the escape; the originals, he informed me, were now in the hands of Seán's solicitor in Dublin.

But more interesting still was the account he gave Anne and myself of an interview he had had in 1984 with a retired Special Branch Officer, Rollo Watts, who had been what he described as 'the legman' in the investigation into Blake's escape. Watts, he said, had told him that Seán used to phone him from Ireland after his return there in 1968 and engage him in long conversations. He also said that the police had known the identities of Seán's helpers soon after the escape but had decided not to take any action against them because they were decent people leading useful lives in the community. Watts was working for a security firm, Saladin Security, and we should certainly contact him if we were ever prosecuted.

Our invitation to the police to discuss the matter with us was taken up a few weeks later – though there were no toasts in whiskey to Seán! On Friday 30th October, Pat and I were interviewed separately in the presence of our solicitor and old campaigning friend, Ben Birnberg, at Holborn Police Station by a (female) Detective Inspector Crampton and a (male) Detective Sergeant Lynch. On Ben's advice we said nothing beyond identifying who we were. The interviews were polite, formal – and very short. The two police officers shook hands with us, expressed the hope that I would soon get over the nasty cold I had at the time, and saw us out of the building.

We could have left it at that, but it didn't feel right. Our statement and review had clearly indicated that we had been involved in the escape, and indicated what our motives were. But unless and until we told the full story, speculation was bound to continue, and there would inevitably be some people – sympathizers as well as opponents – who would wonder what the exact nature of our involvement was and whether we had at any level co-operated with the KGB or other intelligence agencies, or been their unwitting dupes. Thus an article in the Daily Mirror the day after the Sunday Times' revelation suggested that the KGB and MI5 had jointly organised the escape. Much more serious, however, was the allegation in the Sunday Times on 3rd November that the actress Vanessa Redgrave had put up the money for the escape. There was no truth in this, but we could not authoritatively deny it without at the same time acknowledging openly our own involvement. The statement we did make served in a sense to underline the impossibility of the situation in which we now found ourselves. It was cited by the Sunday Times and reads in full:

> As the two people named by Mr Barrie Penrose in the Sunday Times as having assisted in the escape of George Blake, we wish to state categorically that neither in 1966 nor at any other time, did we receive or use money or any other assistance from Ms Redgrave for the kind of activities Mr Penrose describes.[8]

Pat and myself got together to discuss what we should do. One proposition was that we should make a further statement straight away acknowledging our involvement in the escape and stating that we would be writing a book to clarify exactly what had happened. The problem with this idea was that we were likely to be arrested before we had a chance to write the book. Pat suggested that the book could tell the story but with an ambiguously worded title which would leave it open as to whether it was fact or fiction; this might be a way of saying what actually happened while reducing the chances of arrest and a long prison sentence. However, we decided after many hours of discussion and heart searching, that the time for ambiguity was past, and that if we said or wrote anything more, it should take the form of a frank acknowledgement of the facts and an explain of why we had acted as we did.

Neither Anne nor Pat's wife Sue were happy about the decision. However, they could see the logic of it and did not oppose it. Anne was not prepared though to expose herself to prosecution by being named as a co-author of the book. Aside from the fact that she dreaded the thought of a long prison sentence, she also risked losing her nursing qualification if she was convicted of a criminal offence. She had only qualified in 1986 having started the nursing course after our two sons had grown up and left home.

I started work on writing the book in February 1988 while Pat concentrated on research, including getting copies of newspaper reports from the time of the escape. By Easter it was clear that we had the makings of a book and responded to an offer we had had the previous November from the publishers Harrap. We agreed to deliver a completed typescript by the end of

8 As published in full in Bradford's *Telegraph & Argus*, 20 November 1987.

the year; publication would be in the spring of 1989. After some negotiation, Harrap agreed on an advance royalty of £15,000 each for Pat and myself, half to be paid when we signed the contract, the rest when we delivered the completed book. By this time I had come to an agreement with the School of Peace Studies at Bradford University to resign my post as a Research Fellow at the end of the year.

Blake himself, meanwhile had broken cover. On 25th April he appeared on Moscow Television and spoke for the first time publicly about his escape and his subsequent life in Moscow. He confirmed that he had been smuggled to East Germany in the hidden compartment of a van, but gave no information about the people who had assisted him. *The Daily Express*, reporting the story, said detectives now believed he was aided by 'two CND men'. Another report said he had been helped by 'communist sympathizers.' These reports and speculations strengthened our conviction that we were making the right decision in going public.

We had hoped for a period of calm while we worked on the book, but it was not to be. The first problem came when I had to be rushed to hospital in April for a blood transfusion after collapsing with a bleeding duodenal ulcer, caused, at least in part, by overwork. (I had other writing and research commitments in addition to the work on the book). The second problem proved even more disruptive. As a result of a phone call I made to Kevin O'Connor, and Seán's former solicitors in Dublin, Barrie Penrose (author of the original Sunday Times story) got wind of the fact that we were writing a book on the escape. He phoned Pat several times and was due to publish a story in his paper on 13th November. In order to pre-empt his report we agreed that Pat should give an interview to the Observer which would appear on the same date. In this he confirmed on behalf of both of us that we had helped in Blake's escape and were writing a book about it. (Ironically, Penrose's report was not published that weekend in the Sunday Times – and obviously by the following Sunday it had no news value.)

There was an immediate outraged reaction from the Chairman of the 1922 Committee, Marcus Fox, MP for Shipley, quickly followed by other conservative MPs. 'He needn't think he can get away with and make money out of telling his story.' he told Yorkshire Television. 'The police will have something to say about it. And Parliament will have something to say about it!' He then went on to attack the School of Peace Studies at Bradford University. *The Sun* was incensed. On Monday 14th November it ran an editorial entitled 'Nasty duo':

> Two CND supporters, Pat Pottle and Michael Randle, claimed to have helped the escape of the Soviet spy George Blake.
>
> Maybe they are simply big mouths seeking attention for themselves.
>
> But how can they possibly take pride in helping a traitor believed responsible for the deaths of many brave British agents?
>
> Blake served less than two years of a 42-year sentence.
>
> It would be poetic justice if this nasty pair could be locked away for the remaining 40 years.[9]

Actually Blake had served about four and a half years of his full term, but the *Sun* was marking Prince Charles' 40th birthday and carried a 'forty' theme throughout the paper. A little inconvenient fact was not going to be allowed to stand in their way when it came to our case. Scotland Yard, on the other hand, reacted coolly. A spokesman told the *Bradford Telegraph & Argus*: 'There is no investigation [of Pottle and Randle]. A check has been made with Special Branch and the official view is that there is no investigation.'[10] I learned from Michael Clarke of the *Yorkshire Post* the full text of a Scotland Yard statement on 16th November which read: 'The matter was thoroughly investigated on a previous occasion and there was insufficient evidence to support any further action. Unless fresh evidence is forthcoming that will remain the case.'

It was around this time that we decided to make a serious effort to contact Blake with a view to possibly including an interview with him in the book's final chapter. We had not been in touch with him since Anne and myself dropped him off in East Germany as this would have meant running an unnecessary risk. But now that the truth was out, there was nothing to be lost by doing so. By chance I found out from a colleague the name of the institute where he worked – the World Institute for Economics and International Affairs – IMEMO in the Russian acronym. My friend had been in Moscow on a delegation when the Soviet chaperon pointed out the building where Blake now worked. One afternoon I linked the telephone to a small tape-recorder and phoned the number. A man answered in Russian, and I said:

> **'My name is Michael Randle. I want to speak, please, to George Blake.'**

There was a long silence. Then the man spoke in English in a veritable caricature of a Russian accent.

> **'*Who* do you say you want to talk to?'**
>
> **'George Blake.'**
>
> **Another pause.**

---

9 *The Sun*, 15 November 1988

10 *Telegraph & Argus*, 15 November 1988.

'One moment please.'

Several minutes passed. I could imagine the intense discussion at the other end. Another man came to the phone – but it was not George. He too asked me who I wanted to talk to, and then responded that Mr Blake was not in at present. I should phone back the following day. Next day, when I did so, I was asked to leave my telephone number for Mr Blake to phone me back. But I heard no more. Possibly the IMEMO people suspected a trick and that I was a British journalist trying to ferret Blake out of hiding. Soon afterwards we decided that it might be a mistake to include an interview with Blake in our book since all the media attention would tend to centre on that rather than our own story and the reasons we gave for our actions.

Pressure did now begin to build up for us to be prosecuted. On 19th December, Graham Riddick, Conservative MP for Colne Valley, and member of the right-wing pressure group the Freedom Association, put down an early day motion, signed at that stage by 80 fellow conservative MPs, demanding the prosecution of the two peace campaigners who had admitted helping Blake escape. The motion described our actions as 'illegal and treacherous', and called for steps to make sure we did not profit from a book we were believed to be writing. Riddick speaking to the motion devoted more than half his time to a blistering and ignorant attack on the School of Peace Studies – for which he was roundly attacked by two Bradford MPs, Bob Cryer (MP for the Bradford South constituency where Anne and I lived) and Max Madden, MP for Bradford North.

By the beginning of January Riddicks's motion had gained 110 signatures from the ranks of conservative MPs. Norris McWhirter of the Freedom Association also wrote to the Director of Public Prosecutions threatening to take out a private prosecution if the he would not act. In response, the DPP, Alan Greene, announced on 3rd January 1989, that he was ordering a re-opening of the enquiry into the Blake escape.

There was instant pandemonium. That night our phone rang constantly until, at midnight, we took it off the hook. Next day, Wednesday 4th January, our homes were besieged by press and television reporters. We spoke briefly to all enquirers, confirming that we had indeed assisted in the escape of Blake and saying that the full story would be in our forthcoming book.

By now, however, our publishers were worried that there would never be a book. The first draft was still not quite complete, and there seemed every possibility following the spate of press and media coverage that we would be arrested before it could be so. They urged – and finally ordered – us to answer no more press enquiries and make no further incriminating statements. They also decided to bring forward the publication date from June to April, but without making any public announcement of this. In consequence, I spent several weeks working through most of the night, on some occasions snatching no more than an hour's sleep before resuming the work. To add to the pressure, a Detective Inspector Richard Bird of Scotland Yard's Special Branch phoned Harrap asking for an undertaking that they would send the book to them as soon as it was available. Reluctantly they agreed, knowing that the police would get a search warrant if they refused. However, since the police had requested the book rather than the typescript, Harrap delayed sending out a copy until the eve of publication. As an added precaution, Harrap also decided not to send out any advance review copies, but to launch the book with a press conference on the day of publication.

We were able to deliver the first draft of the book to Harrap by the end of January 1989, though following suggestions from their excellent editor, Susanne McDadd, I did some substantial work on it in the weeks which followed, much of it turning indirect into direct speech and sharpening up the narrative. The book starts with a description of the trial of Pat, myself and four others from the Committee of 100 in February 1962 which landed us in Wormwood Scrubs prison where we first met George. It tells the story of the planning and execution of the escape in the chapters which follow, and concludes with a long chapter dealing with our reasons for becoming involved, why we believed our actions were justified, and the stance we would adopt if we were arrested and tried. We called this chapter 'The Antigone Choice' after the heroine of Sophocles's play who defied King Creon of Thebes by performing a ceremonial burial ritual on the body of her dead brother Polynices. This chapter confronted the principal arguments which had been, or were likely to be, levelled at us for aiding Blake escape. It outlines Blake's own story, including the secrecy and manipulation surrounding his trial and appeal in May and June 1961, and called for the release of the transcripts of these, both of which had been held *in camera*. In a section headed 'Blood on his Hands?' we freely acknowledge that he may well have been responsible for the death of British agents, but point to the 'covert operations' by Western Intelligence agents which also involved assassinations and murders, and that Blake's particular role in his work for MI6 was to suborn the members of Soviet and East-European intelligence agencies. In the final section we sum up our case. It reads in part:

> The final and crucial criticism we have to respond to is that however cruel and unjust the 42-year sentence on Blake was, we had no right to take the law into our own hands. This raises a general issue of profound

importance in modern societies where new technology places enormous power in the hands of the centralized state.

We accept that laws, or at least some kind of codes and norms, are necessary in any society in order to ensure that the exercise of freedom by one individual does not deny the basic freedom and rights of others. In the end that is the only justification for placing restrictions on the individual's freedom of action …

Elected governments, like dictatorships, may pursue aggressive, even genocidal policies, or introduce laws which are manifestly unjust and deprive individuals or sections of the community of their basic rights. When the Eden government, in collusion with France and Israel, launched a military attack on Egypt in 1956 some people, including servicemen, engaged in acts of civil disobedience to obstruct it. In the United States in the 1950s and 1960s, Martin Luther King and his followers defied manifestly discriminatory laws, not because they were passed by unrepresentative bodies but because the laws themselves were inherently unjust …

In the case of the Blake escape, the laws which we contravened – against aiding a prisoner to escape, forging passports, smuggling someone out of the country – are not in themselves unjust or unreasonable. For that matter the laws against obstructing the highway, or railway tracks, or occupying aircraft runways are not unjust in themselves. It may nevertheless be right and necessary to disobey them on occasions to prevent a more serious crime or to put right a flagrant injustice. No-one could have complained of an unacceptable breach of the law, for instance, if thousands had sat down in front of the trains taking victims to the concentration camps in Nazi Germany, even though there is nothing inherently unreasonable in a law forbidding people to block railway tracks.

The crucial proviso in all such cases is that the breaches of the law should not cause injury to innocent people. Unlawful acts may sometimes be justified; criminal acts which harm innocent people cannot be so …

The rights and liberties of a section of the community were not directly at stake in the 42-year sentence on George Blake. He had broken the law and confessed to it. The crucial point, however, is that the 42-year sentence was indefensible … the policy of imposing what are virtual life sentences removes from a prisoner any real hope of resuming normal existence and has major implications for a country's whole penal policy – and even beyond that for the norms and values society accepts. As John Lilburne, the 17th-century Leveller, put it: 'what is done to anyone, may be done to everyone.'

> Clearly if there was generalised law-breaking, society would be threatened with chaos … The State, however, has powerful coercive sanctions at its disposal to induce conformity, besides those operating within the social structure itself. For if the rule of law is necessary for an orderly society, the willingness to disobey it where basic rights and values are violated is an essential constraint on State power …
>
> Although we are convinced we were justified in breaking the law by helping Blake to escape, we do not claim any special rights or privileges and are prepared if necessary to face trial and go to prison for what we did.
>
> Generally, if laws are defied for reasons of principle they should be defied openly so that the issues will be publicly debated and the authorities forced to confront them. However, sometimes it is necessary to act clandestinely – for instance in smuggling American army deserters and draft dodgers to Sweden during the Vietnam war …
>
> When all is said and done we had a choice. A man we had grown to like and respect was facing the terrible prospect of a lifetime behind bars; we better than most had some idea of what that meant. When he asked us to help him escape, we could either agree and accept the risks involved, or we could plead that concern for our own or our families' safety, or for the reputation of the peace movement, or some other consideration, made this impossible.
>
> George was no dangerous criminal whose confinement was necessary for the safety of the public – the only possible justification there can ever be for restricting a person's liberty. He had betrayed a trust by passing information to the Soviet Union. We have never supported that, but we knew he was employed by this country in a profession whose hallmark is treachery and double dealing, and that he had acted out of genuine conviction. The 42-year sentence was not an act of justice but of revenge - A man's a man for a' that. All the calculations of the possible political consequences of helping George are in the end a matter of opinion and guesswork. The one thing that was beyond question was that if the escape succeeded George personally would have the chance to start a new life instead of facing the terrifying prospect of twenty or more years in prison. Now that our involvement has been made public we will have to live with whatever consequences that may bring. But we could not have lived with ourselves if we had acted differently. We make no apologies for what we did. We have no regrets.

That was the core of our argument that we put in all our public statements, and that we were determined to take to the court in the event of a trial.

Some months earlier, in November 1988, we had had a lunch meeting with Roger Bolton and others at Thames Television in London and agreed to cooperate in the making a drama documentary about the escape and our part in it for the This Week programme. After the DPP re-opened the case, they too became seriously worried we would be arrested before they could make their programme, and wanted everything 'in the can' at the earliest opportunity. We therefore worked with them intensively over two days in January 1989. The first session, in the basement of the director's house in North London lasted the best part of eight hours during which the interviewer, Richard Lindley, questioned us upon every aspect of the escape, and challenged us to justify our actions. On day two we went with the television crews to the various places that had figured in the escape: the outside of Wormwood Scrubs itself, the hideout in Highlever Road, Torriano Cottages in Kentish Town where Anne and myself had lived at the time, and Pat's old flat – now alas altered beyond recognition – where Blake and Bourke had remained concealed for nearly two months while we make preparations to smuggle them out of the country. Filming on the common at the back of the prison, was a bizarre and disturbing experience. Looking at the high perimeter wall, and seeing again the four wings side by side with their gothic turrets, brought back memories of our time inside, and impressed upon us that as a result of our decision to go public we could expect to spend the next two, three or more years in one or another such grim, dreary place. Even so we could speak the opening lines of the documentary with total conviction:

> **Michael: We helped to get the spy George Blake out of Wormwood Scrubs Prison, and we smuggled him across to Eastern Europe.**
> **Pat: And we would do exactly the same thing again tomorrow.**

Publication day for The Blake Escape was Thursday, 27th April. On the eve of publication, Pat, Sue, Anne and myself, and several other people involved in its production met at the flat of Camilla Nicholls of Harrap for a celebration dinner party and to watch the Thames television drama documentary, also entitled The Blake Escape. We had not been able to see it in advance of the broadcast, but the team had done a good job and honoured their undertaking to ensure that we would have a fair hearing. At a crucial moment, however, when the filmed reconstruction had reached the point where Anne and myself and our two children were crossing the checkpoint into East Germany, the transmitter broke down and the screen went blank. The broadcast was resumed after a delay of some ten or fifteen minutes, but Thames Television was inundated with calls from people who were convinced that MI5 had pulled the plug on the programme. This we learned from Chris Cowley, the producer,

Richard Lindley, who had interviewed us for the programme, and others on the production team who came round to Camilla's flat later that evening.

The press conference next day had a conspiratorial air about it. Journalists were not informed of where it was to take place but were picked up by coach at a meeting point near St Pauls and driven to the Waldorf hotel for the conference. The conference itself passed off without incident, though the coverage of it was disappointing. Next day Pat and Sue, Anne and myself, accompanied by two people from Harrap, Camilla Nicholls and Diane Spivey, and a young journalist from the Guardian, travelled to Ireland. There Pat and myself appeared on the Pat Kenny television programme on the Saturday evening and did signings during the day at two leading bookshops, Easons (next door to the GPO in O'Connell Street) and Waterstones.

For Anne and myself, the trip to Dublin was a chance to meet up with friends and relatives. I had spent the war years as a child there living with my aunt (my mother's sister), and grandparents in Dublin, and Anne and I have been regular visitors to Ireland down the years. Our good friend Dr Maire Woods put on a celebration party on the Sunday evening and we were showered with good wishes, and offers to Anne to come and stay in Ireland if I was sent down for a long spell in prison. This seemed a real possibility since, soon after our arrival, we received a phone call from our solicitor Ben Birnberg in London to say that the police wanted to interview us on our return to Britain; he had made an appointment with them to meet us in his office the following Wednesday.

The Pat Kenny show went well. A straw vote in the studio audience half-way through showed overwhelming opposition to the idea of our being prosecuted and sent to prison. Also a viewer in Inchicore, the area of Dublin I had lived in as a youngster, phoned the programme to offer us asylum in a shed at the bottom of his garden!

One of our happiest memories of the trip is meeting the redoubtable Phyllis McGee, a friend of Maire's and a self-confessed and outspoken atheist and communist – though a communist who thought that the Soviet Union had, as she put it, 'disgraced the very name of communism'. While Pat and I were doing our signings in Waterstones she came and introduced herself, holding two copies of the book for us to sign, one for herself, one for the Limerick MP, Jim Kemmy, who had been a friend of Seán's. Already seriously ill with cancer, she retained a great sense of fun and a zest for life that was truly extraordinary. Currently she was busy badgering all her friends to provide accommodation for a 40 strong delegation from Nicaragua which was touring all the EC countries to muster support of the Sandinista government. She accepted the fact that she had only a limited time left to live with impressive equanimity. In fact she had appeared not long before on one of the television chat shows and spoken about her attitude to death and her atheist convictions. People had written to her from all parts of Ireland, she told us, saying how much they agreed with her. However, some of the clergy were furious.

> **'But sure what could they do?' she said gleefully. 'I had them by the short and curlies because they didn't dare attack a dying woman!'**

She was delighted about the escape of Blake, and that it was friends of Maire, and supporters of nuclear disarmament, who had helped to bring it about.

> **'I used to feel terribly sorry,' she told us with a sympathetic lilt in her voice, 'for poor Kim Philby. It must have been terribly hard for him living in Moscow after the kind of life he'd been used to. So do you know what I did? Every month I made up a parcel of those fancy cheeses wrapped in silver foil and sent them to him. I wonder now did he ever receive them?'**

Anne and myself stayed on in Dublin for a few more days after the Pat Kenny show to attend Maire's party and spend time with friends and relatives. (Pat and Sue, and the people from Harrap had to return home on the Sunday). We saw Phyllis several more times during this period, and she drove us to the airport on the Tuesday afternoon when we were leaving. All the time she entertained us with hilarious anecdotes and with words of encouragement that helped us to put our present difficulties and anxieties in perspective.

She parked her car immediately outside the entrance to the airport, ignoring the repeated warnings on the loudspeaker that on no account were cars to be parked there.

> **'Don't worry,' she said, as she gave us a final hug, 'even if you do spend a couple of years in prison, sure what does it matter? At least you've done something worthwhile in your life.'**

Coming from someone facing so cheerfully and courageously the prospect of impending death these words gave us a real lift. We carried them with us as we boarded the plane taking us back to England and police interrogation.

Chapter 4:

Arrest

We spent Tuesday night with my mother, by then living on her own in the family farmhouse in Sussex. (My father had recently been moved to a nearby nursing home when mother could no longer manage to take care of him.) During the evening we received a phone call from Ben. The police had been back in touch to say they now wanted to interview Anne as well as Pat and myself. This was a shock, especially for Anne herself who had deliberately avoided co-authoring the book and made no public statements about her involvement in the escape to avoid any possible risk of imprisonment and, more important, of losing her nursing qualification. (In principle at least, she would do so automatically if she was convicted of a criminal offence.)

> **'Is there any likelihood,' I asked Ben, 'that the police will actually arrest us tomorrow?'**
>
> **'I shouldn't think so,' he replied, reassuringly. 'All the indications are that it will be a routine interview at this point. But I will ring my opposite number in the morning to check with him.'**

Like Phyllis, Nell, my mother is a tonic to be with in a time of stress. Then aged 84, her movements were beginning to be impaired from a disease affecting the joints, but she had lost none of her mental alertness, her sense of fun, and her fondness for the Irish card game of 25s which we and other members of our large family play whenever we visit. She too has an extraordinary composure associated in her case with strong, but in no way narrow or sectarian, religious convictions. She had supported us completely since the Sunday Times story first appeared in October 1987.

Born in Dublin in 1905, mother had lived through, and can vividly recall, the 1916 rebellion, the guerrilla war and later the civil war in Ireland. Her father's cousin, Seán (Johnny) Treacy, had been with the Irish Volunteers defending the GPO during Easter week. And she herself, living at the time in Inchicore not far from Kilmanham Jail, remembers as an eleven year old girl hearing the shots from the prison yard when Pearse, Connolly and the other leaders were executed. Her older sister too, my Aunt Peg, married a young IRA volunteer who later fought on the republican side in the civil war and had been imprisoned in Kilmainham Jail. Thus her natural sympathies were with the prisoner and the underdog – though on the other hand she had a deep aversion to spies and spying. When she first learnt of our involvement in Blake's escape, she told us of the tremendous excitement there used to be during the Irish war of Independence whenever there was an IRA jailbreak, and particularly the occasion when 20 prisoners escaped from Mountjoy.[1] She recited a popular ditty of the time celebrating the event and sung to the tune of Molly Malone:

I'll sing you a ditty
Of Dublin's fair city
And a place called Mountjoy
Which all of you know.
It was there of all places
That the boys kicked their traces
And got out of prison
Alive, Alive O!

JJ Walsh and Pieras Béaslaí
The trick did quite easy,
Some poor German devil
A ladder did throw,
And twenty Sinn Feiners
Like acrobat trainers
Climbed the walls of Mountjoy
All Alive, Alive O!

I'll finish my tale now,
I think it is time now,
The people are laughing
Wherever I go.
It's causing elation
In this ancient nation
Of Sinn Feiners and rebels
Alive, Alive O!

Next morning, in brilliant sunshine, Anne and myself drove to the house of our friends Tess and Mario in Welwyn, Hertfordshire, taking the train from there to London and then making our way to Ben's office near London Bridge. Pat was there already as was Ben's colleague John Wadham – soon to become the legal advisor of Liberty – the National Council for Civil Liberties. The

---

1 This was in March 1919 See Piaras Béaslaí, `Twenty got away in the big daylight escape from Mountjoy jail' in *Sworn to be Free: The Complete Book of IRA Jailbreaks, 1918-1921*, Foreword by Florence O'Donoghue, Anvil Books, Tralee, 1971.

office is small, overflowing with books and papers, and has that dishevelled, makeshift air characteristic of left-wing campaigning organisations working on shoe-string budgets. Anne always says it reminds her of the Committee of 100 office.

> **'There's been a further development,' Ben announced as soon as we had sat down. 'The police now say they want to interview us at a police station instead of here.'**
>
> **'Why do you think that is?' Anne asked, immediately suspicious we were being led into a trap.**
>
> **'Probably nothing more than that they want to question you in a place where there are recording facilities. I rang my counterpart in the police department who assured me that there was no question of an arrest at this stage. Everything, they said, will be done in a gentlemanly manner, and they will let us know if and when an arrest is likely. Of course you can never be sure. If you like I can ring them now and postpone the appointment until another day.'**

We turned the question over. If we postponed the meeting, Anne and I would have to travel down again to London for the next appointment. Besides, we were keyed up for the interrogation and my own inclination was to get it over and done with so that we would have a better idea of where we stood. Anne remained uneasy, but agreed finally we should let the existing appointment stand. Soon afterwards the three of us, and the two lawyers, piled into two taxis in the hot sunshine and told the drivers to take us to the appointed police station in Gerald Road, more or less at the back of Buckingham Palace. Our appointment was for 1pm.

Gerald Road turned out to be a poky little police station. We arrived about ten minutes early, and the desk officer told us that those in charge of the case had not yet arrived. It was a small, oblong shaped, room with the counter at the far end, and seating for only a couple of people. We stood around, making nervous conversation in low voices.

Finally a middle aged woman dressed in a blouse and skirt followed by two other men, also in civvies.

> **'I am Detective Superintendent Eggington,' she said. She had frank brown eyes, and smiled as she spoke. She introduced us to the two other men: Detective Inspector Bird, a tall, well-built man, with a high forehead, regulation close-cropped haircut and upright stance, and a Detective Sergeant Lloyd, somewhat more rotund, with gingerish hair. Bird we already knew by repute since he had been in charge of the case since it was re-opened by the DPP in January. He it was who had phoned Camilla Nicholls at Harrap's and requested a copy of *The***

> ***Blake Escape*** **a few weeks before its publication.**
> **'Shall we go through?' Eggington said, and we followed her into a rather grim little room that had the smell of prison about it. To the left as we entered was a counter where a man being charged was emptying the contents of his pockets. Nearby, against a wall, were a couple of wooden forms to which she conducted us.**
> **'I want to speak first,' she said, 'to Mr Pottle and Mr Randle – not Mrs Randle at this stage.' She and Bird took us to a narrow passageway leading to some lock-up cells, directly opposite the door by which we had come in.**
> **'I am arresting you,' she said, 'on suspicion of assisting in the escape of a convicted prisoner, George Blake, on 22nd October, 1966. You do not have to say anything, but anything you do say may be taken down and used in evidence …'**
> **'Do you understand?' Bird asked.**

We both said we did.

So Anne had been right. For whatever ounce of psychological pressure it might bring to bear on us, Special Branch had decided to lull us into a false sense of security before making their arrests. I looked across at Anne. She was pale but calm, finding an inner strength at the moment of crisis. Presently we rejoined the solicitors while Bird explained that Anne was not under arrest but would be interviewed along with the two of us. We two would then be fingerprinted, photographed and taken to our respective homes for a police search. After that we would be released on bail.

Pat and I had to empty our pockets and hand over all our possessions to the officer behind the counter. We were then taken to separate lock-up cells at the end of the corridor. I was thankful I'd had the presence of mind to bring a book with me and that I had been allowed to keep it while waiting to be interviewed. It was Maurice O'Sullivan's *Twenty Years a Growing*, translated from the original Irish, about life on the Great Blasket Island off the Kerry coast in the early decades of this century. The outdoor life he describes in a farming and fishing community on a weather-beaten Atlantic island could hardly have been in greater contrast to the confines of the dingy, ill-lit police cell where I was reading it.

Pat was the first to be interviewed. His interview lasted about 15 minutes, after which I was unlocked and led up a flight of stairs to a small office. There Superintendent Eggington and Sergeant Lloyd sat side by side on the far side of a small table. Ben was sitting at one end of the table. Eggington repeated the formal police caution, and the interview began.

It was a brief and perfunctory affair, for, on Ben and John's advice, we refused to answer any questions. I felt uncomfortable about this – after all we had admitted everything in our book, so what was the point of refusing at this stage to answer police questions? Eggington herself later that day told Pat she was surprised we were unwilling to say anything. However, Ben and John argued that if the authorities were undecided as to whether or not to prosecute, admissions made under caution by us to the police might tip the balance in favour of their going ahead.

Eggington asked the questions, Lloyd laboriously wrote them down in longhand, as well as my stock reply – 'On the advice of my solicitor, I am not making any statement or answering any questions.' The first question was whether I had appeared in the ITV film entitled The Blake Escape; when I said that I was not answering any questions, Eggington responded that she nevertheless intended to put certain questions to me. Were the statements made by me in the film about my involvement in assisting George Blake to escape true? Was I one of the authors of this book? – pointing to 'Exhibit RJM/1'. a copy of *The Blake Escape*. Was my role in the escape including harbouring of George Blake as related in the book true? When I stonewalled yet again, she concluded the interview, saying these were all the questions she wanted to put to me at this stage. I then had to initial each (non) reply of mine, and sign at the bottom of each page. The pages were also countersigned by Eggington and Ben.

Pat had been asked an almost identical set of questions, but Anne, who was the last to be interviewed, faced a longer interrogation. When did she first become aware of the escape plan? When did she meet Seán Bourke? Did she help raise money for the escape? Did she supply the knitting needles for the escape ladder? When and where did she first meet George Blake? Was she ever present at 28 Highlever Road? Was she involved in finding a doctor for George Blake? Was she present during the journey with George Blake when her husband drove him to East Germany? And so on. Anne gave the answer we had all previously rehearsed. In her case, of course, it was crucial that she should remain silent if she was to avoid arrest.

After the interview I was photographed with equipment in permanent place in the charge room. Then came the fingerprinting, carried out by a young woman PC. 'Just try and relax,' she said as she used a small inking roller to cover thumb and fingers of one hand in a black sticky ink. She took the thumb and each finger in turn and pressed it firmly, with a small rotating movement, onto a paper marked out to show where each print should appear. Then she inked up my whole hand and pressed it on another paper to obtain a palm print. The procedure was repeated with the other hand.

After I had cleaned up, Bird told me we would be leaving right away for Bradford. First I was allowed to have a word with both Anne and John Wadham. John asked Bird for a lift in the police car to Bradford.

'Sorry, we're not insured to take passengers', Bird replied. Odd, since he was about to drive me some 200 miles up the motorway. John then went into a huddle with me and, speaking very quietly, warned me not to engage in any conversation about the case with the police on the journey. Probably everything would be straightforward, but it was best to avoid giving them any opportunity to put words in my mouth.

The point was well made. Pat was given a lift home at 10.15 that evening by Eggington and Lloyd after his house had been searched and he had been taken back to the police station to be bailed. Almost eight weeks later, on 26th June, Sergeant Lloyd made a statement with an account of an alleged discussion that took place on the journey. Part of it reads:

> Once in the car we discussed a number of topics which centred mainly around Russia and Pottle's excitement and enthusiasm for Gorbachev and his reforms. He said that life in Russia in the next ten years would be very exciting and he almost wished he could be there as the freedoms come and the restrictions soon become relaxed. At one stage our conversation turned to his arrest and the events of the day. Pottle said that he thought the police enquiry into his and Randle's roles in the Blake escape had been perfunctory and little interest had been taken until they had decided to write their book The Blake Escape and to make the TV documentary of the same name. He said that he was surprised that he had not been arrested earlier and that in fact he and his wife had gone on a ten day holiday to Ireland just before the book was published in order to avoid being arrested. He admitted that sales of the book would increase following their arrest and that he thought they would have been arrested before it was published and an injunction taken out by the authorities to ban the publication. Both Det. Supt. Eggington and I made no comments on these admissions by Pottle and Det. Supt. Eggington emphasised that we were not able to make any comment as to the police action both past and present in the whole matter of the Blake Escape.[2]

2 Witness Statement of William Geoffrey Lloyd, aged 40, of SO12 Special Branch, Metropolitan Police on 26 June 1989.

On 30th June, four days after Lloyd wrote his statement, Detective Superintendent Eileen Eggington wrote a longer statement about the arrests and interviews of 3rd May. In this she too referred to the alleged conversation in the car, much of it the same, word for word, as Lloyd's version, including the statement that Pat had said he had gone to Ireland with his wife ten days before the book was published. In fact, Pat had never been to Ireland in his life prior to the three-day visit to launch the book there after its publication. The two detectives, writing after a lapse of nearly two months, had become confused about what Pat had told them: he had left London to stay with friends in another part of England ten days before publication, and spent three days in Ireland after publication. The mistake was a trivial one, but the fact that both detectives had made the same mistake, and that the wording was for the most part identical, strongly suggests that they had colluded in making their statements. Moreover, had the trial taken a quite different turn, Pat's alleged statements expressing enthusiasm for the Gorbachev reforms in the Soviet Union, taken out of context, might have been used against him.

Pat's recollection of the journey is that very little was said on it. However, earlier, during the house search, there was a good deal of discussion of political and other issues, with Eggington expounding her own views as well as listening to what Pat had to say. It was in the context of that discussion that Pat had expressed support for the Gorbachev reforms.

We are not suggesting that Lloyd and Eggington set out deliberately to distort the record or manufacture evidence; they were recollecting discussions some time after they had taken place and got the facts wrong. The disturbing thing is that this material could have been presented as evidence in court had the prosecution so decided. (In the event they did not, probably because they realised we could have shot it down.) It was a classic case of 'verballing', even though there was no intention to deceive. Pat was not under caution at the time of the alleged conversation and the account was not based on contemporaneous notes. Such 'verballing' completely by-passes, and indeed makes a mockery of, the elaborate precautions taken to record suspects' statements under proper conditions in the police station.

To return to my own story, before Anne left we were allowed briefly to embrace.

> **'If you get home ahead of me,' I whispered to her as we held each other, 'could you look out a box of computer discs which I've hidden in one of the earthenware pots in the attic, and get them out of the house?'**

'I won't be able to get there in time' she whispered back. I still have to travel to Welwyn to pick up the car.'

It was not a matter of life or death, but the discs contained some earlier drafts of the book and I was afraid one or two passages – which I had subsequently changed – might provide clues as to the identity of the person who had done the work converting the camper van. The discs also contained letters I had written to various people about the case, including an angry one to a friend who disagreed with our decision to help Blake escape, and even more vehemently opposed our decision to go public about it. I had left most of the other material, including the typescript of the book, background material and other letters, in the care of a friend in Bradford,

In fact we didn't leave for about another half-hour – at 3.45pm according to the police records. I had decided by that time that I probably wasn't going to sleep in my own bed that night but would be spending it in a police cell, and I steeled myself mentally for that event. After the cell door was opened again, Bird held me firmly by the arm and led me to his awaiting car – a maroon Cavalier with automatic gear-change.

'I take it there is no need for handcuffs?' he said – and I was grateful for that. He drove, with another tall, well-built policeman in plain clothes, Detective Sergeant David Nesbitt. They sat together in the front while I was on my own in the back. We sped up the A1 as far as the M18, then cut across to join the M1 near Sheffield. At one point on the AI Bird slowed down suddenly and pulled into the inside lane. He had spotted a police car in his rear-view mirror! We listened to the 'PM' programme at five o'clock on the car radio which reported the arrest of Pat and myself and quoted Pat as saying that he expected we would be sent to prison. Bird laughed:

'He's very frank about it,' he said.

As we pulled into the police station at Bradford, just before 8pm, we spotted John Wadham a few yards ahead of us.

Once again I had to hand over, and sign for all my personal belongings. This time, however, the police insisted at first on taking my book as well. I wouldn't have time to read, they told me, as we would be going to my house as soon as the officers involved had had a cup of tea. But I pressed to be allowed to keep it, and grudgingly they agreed.

Almost two hours later I was unlocked after a supper consisting mainly of dried-up baked beans and rice, most of which I left. It was ten o'clock by the time we reached the terraced house in Lidget Green, a few minutes drive from the police station in the town centre. So Anne could in fact have made it to the house before us had we known there would be such a long delay.

'Hope we're not breathing curry all over you,' Bird said laughing. They had all been for a meal at the locally well-known Silver Jubilee eating house in Oak Lane. I didn't begrudge them their meal. But why did they have to pretend they were only going to have a quick cup of tea and that I wouldn't even have any time to read?

Five officers took part in the search – Bird, Nesbitt, a Detective Sergeant Dainis Ozols, a Detective Constable James Hill and a young woman Detective Constable, Sharon Coles. John Wadham was there to keep an eye on things. There was a minor verbal duel between him and Bird in the course of the evening about the police abusing their powers during interviews of suspects, and about whether the Metropolitan police adopted a tougher demeanour than their counterparts in the provinces. John, slightly built, lean-faced, wearing glasses confronted the tall, stolid policeman, two people from different worlds. Bird said he liked to think that 'verballing' and other abuses by the police did not occur. He also thought it was right for an arresting officer to maintain a certain formality in his dealings with a suspect. When all was said and done, the officer was depriving that person of their liberty, and it was bogus to pretend that relations could be friendly.

In keeping with this, perhaps, he firmly refused an offer from me to make him and the other officers a cup of tea. However, he said I could make one for the uniformed policeman on duty outside the back gate, keeping guard over a posse of cameramen and reporters. Bird, in fact took complete charge in the house. He would not allow me to stand near the kitchen window where I might be photographed by the cameramen outside, he got me to open the mail in his presence that had come while we were away, and he answered all telephone calls, including one from Anne to say she would not be coming up until the following morning. (Eggington had been much more relaxed with Pat, and he was able to give a couple of telephone interviews with the press before she thought better of it and said that as he was under arrest, he wouldn't be allowed to say any more to the press.)

The search was much more thorough and systematic, than I had expected. I had directed the attention of the police to the two filing cabinets in the back bedroom and thought they might be satisfied with searching that. Hill and Nesbitt, began their search there, but Ozols and Cole were sent up to the attic bedroom where I have my office – and piles of unsorted papers, some of them dating back to the 1950s. Bird directed operations from the kitchen.

I stayed with the detectives in the back bedroom for a while but I soon got bored and went down to watch television. That night the police uncovered letters to and from our publishers, a letter from Thames Television about the *This Weekend Special* programme, a piece of hardened plastic padding in a drawing pin container with the reverse impression of an official passport stamp, an old passport of mine that had been used to produce this impression – and, inevitably, the box of computer discs I had hidden in the earthenware pot. Bird said they would examine these on my computer at the conclusion of the search. The plastic padding with the official stamp imprinted on it was not of course the one we had used back in 1966 but one Pat and I produced a few months earlier to provide an illustration for the book. At 1am, Bird announced that they were suspending the search overnight, and that I would have to spend it in Bradford police station to make sure nothing was removed from the house.

The cell was spartan, but clean, with distempered, pinkish walls. A notice on one wall warned that anyone damaging the cell would be liable for prosecution. I smiled. The only furniture in it was a plain wooden bench affixed to the wall. High above it, and well out of reach, was a barred window divided up into small, semi-opaque panes. The bench was my bed for the night. I was given a mattress to place on it, and a few grey army blankets.

I didn't sleep at all. I kept thinking of the events of the day and became obsessed with the idea of preventing the police from finding some items in the house. One was the tape of my telephone conversations with IMEMO in Moscow asking to speak to George Blake. It would tell the police nothing significant except that I had made a very recent effort to contact Blake. Another item I didn't want them to find was a postcard Anne had sent her mother from Goslar, dated 22nd December 1966, just a few days after we had dropped Blake off on the autobahn. Could this, if discovered, provide evidence on which to arrest her as well?

Next day the search resumed at 10.15. Anne had arrived well before us to find an empty house; she had set out at dawn from Welwyn, also after a sleepless night. It was a relief and a joy to see her. John Wadham arrived soon afterwards; he had stayed overnight with a friend in Bradford.

It was a blisteringly hot day, and you could not help feeling sorry for the officers in that stuffy back bedroom sorting through years of accumulated papers, 99 per cent of them of no interest or relevance to them. They had to keep the bedrooms curtains drawn too to hide themselves from the attentions of the press and television reporters outside with their long-range lenses.

After a shower and some breakfast I began to feel human. Then an incident occurred which further lifted my morale. I was alone in the bedroom after my shower when I located the tape of my conversations with IMEMO in Moscow. I looked round the room for a hiding place, and finally settled for forcing it down the back of the blocked-up fireplace. It made a hideous scraping noise as I pushed it down, and I was sure this would attract the attention of the plain clothes detectives on the landing immediately outside the room. But they suspected nothing, and it was with relief I heard the tape drop down onto the grate behind. In a small way, at least, I had retaken the initiative.

However, the police had the last laugh over another piece of evidence I attempted to destroy. During the morning, several more officers arrived from London so that for part of the day there were eight or nine of them scattered over the house. In the early afternoon, Bird and the original crew went off for lunch and I was able to go up to the attic where the search had been completed. I started up the computer and systematically erased all the files on the discs containing drafts of the book, and letters and other material connected with it. My heart was pounding as I did so for I realised that if I was discovered this could lead to another charge and to the end of police bail.

While I was busy erasing the files, an officer came in unexpectedly.

> **'Doing some research, are you?' he said affably.**

When the search finally ended at around 7pm, Sergeant Nesbitt got me to start up the computer to examine the contents of the discs. I felt a glow of triumph as the screen showed that there were no files on them. He, nevertheless held on to the box of discs with labels dated 1988 and 1989 on them and took them downstairs to show Inspector Bird.

> **'All the files have been deleted,' he said. 'However, I am keeping these because, as you know sir, deleting only erases the titles, not the material itself which can be retrieved.'**

I certainly didn't know that and tried not to look non-plussed. Apparently I should have reformatted the disks to erase the material beyond any possibility of retrieval. The police laboratories were in fact able to restore all the material I had deleted, some of which the prosecution put in evidence. However, none of it assumed any importance in the trial itself or received even a mention.

Bird did unwind in the course of the day, allowing Anne to make tea for his team. (Probably he felt there would be no impropriety in this because Anne, unlike me, was not under arrest.) He offered to get one of his men to do some shopping for her if she did not want to run the gauntlet of the awaiting press, and gave me some advice on looking after a rather sorry-looking camellia a friend had given us. He also pointed to the crack in one corner of the kitchen ceiling and advised us to get it seen to before it collapsed. What he did not realise was that the crack had been caused, or at least made worse, by the fact that during the last couple of months when I was working on the book under constant threat of arrest, I used to hide the print-outs and computer discs every night under a floorboard in the room above – the back bedroom. (In addition I parked completed chapters with a friend in Bradford). At around midday, having first phoned through to London, he and Nesbitt drove me back to the police station to get police bail. The conditions were that I would report back to Gerald Road police station on 7th June.

But there was a more bizarre, and at the same time touching, incident. John Wadham was present in the attic when one of the officers found a minute quantity of hash in a twist of plastic in one of the small earthenware pots. He called over his colleague and got him to sniff it.

'What do you think?' he asked.

'Put it back,' the other replied. 'They're in enough trouble as it is!'

After a lapse of six years this story can, I hope, be told without risking anyone's reputation or career. And all right, if the police had been dealing with someone who was poor, and black and living in Brixton they might have taken a different attitude. The officers in charge of the search, too, had they known about it, might have responded differently. Still the fact remains that those two detectives could have added considerably to our problems and decided not to do so out of human decency. Their action deserves an honourable mention.

In addition to the computer tapes, the plastic padding with the impression of an official passport stamp, the police carried off several notebooks which I had used while working on The Blake Escape, a bundle of letters which Anne had written to me soon after we were married while I was serving an 18 month sentence in Wormwood Scrubs in 1962, a set of prison notebooks from the same period which I had managed to smuggle out from the prison, several sets of photographs and negatives, including one showing the interior of the van and the gap under the fold-out bed where Blake had hidden, and some shots taken in Goslar in 1966, and various other letters and notes, among them three letters I had received in prison from Bertrand Russell in 1962.

The letters also included recent correspondence with my dissident Czech friend, Jan Kavan who had been living in exile in London since 1969-70. The background here needs to be briefly summarised. In 1970, myself and another friend in Bradford had adapted a Volkswagen camper van – in much the same way that the Commer Van had been adapted earlier for the Blake escape – and I had driven this to Brno in Czechoslovakia in January 1971 loaded with books and magazines for the democratic opposition movement in the country. Subsequently that same van, and others adapted in a similar way, was used to make regular trips to Czechoslovakia taking in literature and equipment, such as duplicators, printing machinery and eventually computers. The operation had to be halted in 1981 when the border guards, in response to a tip-off, stopped the van and took it apart. The correspondence with Kavan that the police found in the house dated from early 1989 when he had sought my advice on adapting a Transit van so he could arrange for further, bulky material to be smuggled in. The police also found, in the glove compartment of the car, early sketches of a plan I had drawn from adapting the Transit van. The police must also have handled Anne's postcard from Goslar to her mother dated 22nd December 1966, but its significance obviously did not strike them.

Despite the fact that the police had acted throughout with propriety, Anne and myself felt drained and empty after they had gone. Our private space had been invaded, our personal letters perused, all our belongings sifted through and moved about. The attic was unrecognisably tidy but at the cost of having all the papers and oddments stacked in a heap in one corner. There was a huge imprint of a policeman's boot on the seat of the black, plastic-coated easy chair in the attic; one of the detectives, it appears, had climbed on it to open up the small trap-door leading up to the header tank for the central heating system in case anything was hidden there. There was a strange chemical smell in the attic and to a lesser extent throughout the house, which lasted for weeks. This came from some bottles of chemicals which Bird and Nesbitt had been using, though for what purpose I never discovered. Somehow, the place no longer seemed our own. An alien force had occupied it and left its smell and its traces everywhere.

Chapter 5:

Charged on Three Counts

Since Pat and myself had not yet been formally charged, we were free to talk to the press and media without either them or us infringing the sub judice rules. And there was much media interest. Pat was sympathetically interviewed by Brian Redhead on the Radio 4 Today programme the morning after our arrest, and both of us subsequently gave interviews on local and regional television and radio stations – Yorkshire Television, BBC TV Leeds, BBC Radio Leeds, Radio Piccadilly in Manchester, London Broadcasting Company and several others. The tapes and videos of these broadcasts were assiduously collected by the police and submitted as evidence in the trial since in all of them Pat and / or I openly acknowledged our involvement in Blake's escape.

But several major television opportunities fell through because the companies, or programme makers, succumbed to pressure and withdrew their invitations. Pat recorded a programme for the *BBC* programme *Kilroy*, and was assured it would be broadcast. However, when we tuned in to listen to it, the BBC had substituted another programme for it. Channel 4 booked us to appear on its live, open-ended discussion programme *After Dark* on 13th May on the topic of espionage. Lined up to debate with us were Norris McWhirter of the Freedom Association – whose threat to take out a private prosecution helped to push the DPP in taking action against us – the historian Lord Dacre (Hugh Trevor Roper), and the ex-MI6 officer, Sir Anthony Cavendish. A condition of the booking was that we would not in the meantime appear on any other television programme and on the basis of that we turned down an invitation to appear on Central Television on 12th May. But just two days before the *After Dark* programme was due to be broadcast, the producer, Claire Powell, phoned to say the arrangement was off. The IBA, she explained, had banned the appearance of either of us. She was extremely sorry, and said we would be receiving a grovelling letter of apology. It never came.

Central Weekend then booked us to appear on Friday 26th May, assuring us that they had taken legal advice and there would be no question of a last-minute cancellation. Yet they too cried off, this time on the day before the broadcast, after Pat had already travelled to Birmingham to take part in it. (Ironically, while there, he gave two half-hour interviews to local BBC and commercial radio stations.) It would be interesting to discover what behind-the-scenes pressure was put on the programmes to cancel.

Still more disappointing in a way was the decision of the *New Statesman & Society* not to run an article they had commissioned from me about these last minute television cancellations – an article I entitled 'Screened Out'. Not only did they not publish it but they kept up a pretence that they had not received it until I was able to tell them the exact time a friend of mine had faxed it to them – at 9.26 am on Monday 5th June – to meet the deadline they themselves had set. The editor then feebly agreed that they had got it but said that it was by now too late to run it.

However, not all the media were so pusillanimous. *Leeds Other Paper*, the excellent local alternative paper, ran a long interview with me conducted by Michael Hughes, and Thames Television re-broadcast their drama documentary *The Blake Escape*. Friends and colleagues in the peace and anti-nuclear movement could not have been more supportive; more on that in due course.

The most amusing radio broadcast I made was for the local radio in Skegness on 5th June. It was an outside broadcast which took place on the sands where I was surrounded by children, donkeys and a yapping dog that almost drowned out my voice. It was a surreal setting for a serious discussion about the escape of a 'masterspy'. To add to the incongruity, the interviewer suggested to me that we might have made up the whole story of our involvement in Blake's escape and that our arrest was a publicity stunt. It would be a good trick certainly if you had the DPP and Crown Prosecution Service in your pocket – and a guarantee from them that they would not actually press charges!

Pat and I duly surrendered bail at Gerald Road on 6th June – coincidentally just two days after the Tiananmen Square massacre – and were again interviewed by Superintendent Eggington. This time the interviews were more prolonged, and they concentrated on items found during the search. In my case they included questions about the computer discs, the impression of the official stamp, the out-of-date passport used to make the stamp, the agreement with Harrap, notes on, and draft chapters of, the book. The questions to Pat too revolved around whether or not he had partly written *The Blake Escape*. Our authorship of the book was, I suppose the one thing they had to establish beyond doubt for they had to shut and bolt the door against the possibility that we would get up in court and deny that we had anything to do with it, and perhaps claim that someone had set us up by using our names.

Back in the charge room after the interview, Pat asked Eggington what happened next. She replied that she would submit her report to the Director of Public Prosecutions who would decide whether or not to press charges.

> **'I'm sure you're going to say,' Pat said with a smile, 'that these two men have suffered enough and that the matter should be allowed to rest.'**

Eggington laughed.

> **'Suffered enough! – I think you are enjoying it. It's your wives I feel sorry for.'**

There was an element of truth in what she said. Having the whole thing out in the open after suppressing it for so long was like lancing a boil. There was a sense of elation too in defying the authorities to do their worst and making plans for the battle ahead should the prosecution proceed. Nevertheless there was another side to it – of butterflies in the tummy, raw nerves, strain, sleepless nights. It was more of a psychological blow than we had anticipated when Ben phoned a few days before we were due to surrender bail back at Gerald Road in July to tell us that the CPS had decided to press charges and that we should now report instead to Bow Street Magistrates' Court.

On 10th July we duly appeared before the Stipendiary Magistrate, Mr Ronald Bartle. Waiting for our case to come up, we and our family and friends were witnesses to a succession of summary cases involving prostitutes, vagrants, drunks – and two men whom a policeman had spotted engaged in mutual masturbation in a public park. Then it was our turn. Pat, was first to go into the dock. The formal indictment was read out:

> a) Michael Randle and Patrick Pottle on the 22nd October 1966 aided George Blake, a prisoner, to escape from Her Majesty's Prison, Wormwood Scrubs.
> Contrary to Section 39 of the Prison Act 1952.
> b) Michael Randle and Patrick Pottle on divers days between the 1st day of May and the 31st day of December 1966 conspired together and with Seán Bourke knowingly to harbour George Blake, who had escaped from Her Majesty's Prison, Wormwood Scrubs.
> Contrary to Section 1 of the Criminal Law Act 1977.
> c) Michael Randle and Patrick Pottle on divers days between the 1st day of May and the 31st day of December 1966 conspired together and with Seán Bourke knowingly to give assistance to George Blake who had escaped from Her Majesty's Prison, Wormwood Scrubs, with intent to prevent, hinder or interfere with his being taken into custody.
> Contrary to Section 1 of the Criminal Law Act 1977.

Pat pleaded Not Guilty, and I in turn did the same. Then Ben began to deliver a short statement to make our position clear:

> **'My clients have asked me to say that although they admit their involvement in the escape of George Blake, they will be contesting these charges. They intend to expose what they consider to be the cruel and inhuman sentence passed on George Blake and the danger to democracy posed by the Security Service in Britain …'**

Mr Bartle, interrupted him. These arguments, he said, could be dealt with in due course. Outside the court, Ben completed his statement for the benefit of the press in which he spoke of 'the spy mania of both of the power blocs.'

The court appearance was widely and sympathetically reported. *The Daily Telegraph*, *Independent*, and *Guardian* carried prominent reports and pictures and quoted Ben's statements, as well as comments of ours. 'Blake charge pair pledge to expose Security Service' was the Independent's headline, and the *Guardian*, too, in a sub-heading stated: 'Anti-nuclear activists aim to expose "cruel sentence".' *The Daily Mirror* carried a picture of the two of us drinking beer in the sunshine on a wooden table outside a pub and bore the caption: 'Men of Peace.'

The first of the three counts carried a maximum sentence of 5 years, the second and third, 2 years each. In principle then, if we were convicted and given consecutive maximum sentences, we could go down for 9 years. That was never a real possibility, but a four or even five year sentence undoubtedly was, and it was this prospect to which we now had to adjust ourselves.

On 7th August we made another brief appearance at Bow Street for the Committal hearing. Under the law as it then applied, defendants could insist on full committal proceedings if they wished to force the prosecution to present their evidence. That made sense, however, only if the defendants thought there was a reasonable prospect that the magistrate would rule there was no case to answer. Since this did not apply in our case, we opted for the more usual, formal, hearing. We were committed to appear at the Old Bailey at a date to be fixed.

From the outset, Pat and myself had agreed that when we were arrested – for in our own minds it was a matter of 'when' rather than 'if' once the book was published – we would take the offensive. We would not hide behind legal technicalities, even supposing there were some available, and either one or both of us would conduct our own defence.

A week after the committal, we received the full prosecution 'bundle', comprising over 1,000 pages – much of it repetitive. There were for instance many pages of the same draft typescript of The Blake Escape, some found in Pat's house, some in mine. We were puzzled at first by the duplication, but realised it was evidence that both of us had been involved in writing the book. This conclusion was confirmed when Mr M Biddy, of the Special Casework Division of the Crown Prosecution Service, wrote to our solicitors on 12th September inviting them on our behalf to make the following admissions under Section 10 of the Criminal Justice Act 1967:

> 1. The Defendants are the authors of the books, The Blake Escape, copies of which are RJM/1 and SMD/2.
> 2. In particular, passages in the said book headed either 'Narrated by Pat Pottle' or 'Narrated by Michael Randle' were written by the said Pat Pottle and Michael Randle (subject to minor editions by the publishers).
> 3. Where in the said book facts are stated by either Defendant in the parts of the book described in para 2 above, or in parts of the book without specific attribution, to be within the personal knowledge of either or both Defendants, those facts are true to the best of his / their knowledge and belief.

On the advice of the solicitors we admitted nothing. The reason for this was that if we did so, the prosecution might decide that it would be unnecessary to produce witnesses whom we wanted to cross-examine to bring out some of the wider issues in the case.

Fortunately Pat and I were in complete accord about the approach we should adopt at the trial. In a memo to our solicitors dated 25th August, based on the discussions between us, I set down what we saw as the nature of our defence and our strategy for presenting it. Essentially it was a moral and political defence, not a legal one, and was encapsulated in the last chapter of our book: in no way did we approve or condone what Blake had done, but we believed we were right to have assisted in his escape because the 42 year sentence he had received was inhuman and hypocritical. However, we recognized the problem we could face in the court, namely that 'the judge could succeed in totally blocking the presentation of this moral / political defence unless we [could] find some legal hook to attach it to.'[1]

One possible line of approach on the legal side, we thought, was to argue that the 42 year sentence on Blake 'amounted to cruel, inhuman and degrading treatment' and therefore breached the European Convention on Human Rights; but this was something we needed to explore further with the barristers. It would be important, too, and would add dramatically to the

---

1 Michael Randle, 'First Notes on Defence in Blake Escape Case', 25 August 1989

interest in the case, if we could produce a sworn statement from George Blake. A subsidiary argument, and one with which we could seriously embarrass the prosecution if we could uncover concrete evidence to support it, was that the police had known about our involvement not long after the escape as the retired Detective Inspector Rollo Watts had told Kevin O'Connor in 1984. O'Connor had given us the name of the security firm – Saladin Security – which Watts was working for at that time so there was some chance we would be able to trace him.

There were a number of other witnesses we considered calling at that stage in support of our broader political and moral case. One was the former prime minister Harold Wilson, who could repeat what he said in the House of Commons at the time of the escape, namely that it had in no way endangered national security. Another possibility was Lord Hutchinson, QC, who defended Blake at his trial and appeal. In January 1989, while we were working on the book, we met him and asked him 'if there could possibly be any truth in the rumour that Blake's 42-year sentence corresponded to evidence produced at the trial about the number of British agents betrayed to imprisonment or death.' He replied that this story was 'absolute rubbish'. Other prospective witnesses were John Stockwell, a former CIA agent who had detailed many of the covert operations conducted by the CIA; former CIA agent Miles Copeland who was quite open in his book *The Real Spy World*, and in a recent broadcast on *BBC Radio 4*, about the fact that the CIA sometimes murdered people; and Jan Kavan, the Czech dissident exile who could speak about the work I had done with him smuggling material into Czechoslovakia.

Ben and John had always been aware of our intention to plead Not Guilty and for one or both of us to conduct our own defence. But whilst in sympathy with our approach, they urged us to apply for legal aid to engage the best barristers we could get hold of so that we would have the benefit of their experience in the period leading up to the trial. We accepted their advice and were initially granted legal aid for one leading counsel and one junior to represent both of us.

The first barrister to be engaged was Tom Mackinnon, a Canadian by birth, married to a charming and attractive young woman from Moscow named Katya. They had met and fallen in love while in adjacent beds in the mixed ward of a hospital in Leningrad (where he was on holiday) and now had a baby daughter. He had got to know Ben slightly when the latter was doing some conveyancing work for him and asked if he could be on the defence team. He was also about to go on a trip to Moscow with his wife and baby daughter and volunteered to contact Blake on our behalf.

Tom, Pat and Ben met for a preliminary 'case conference' at Ben's office on 20th August and discussed chiefly the best way of trying to reach Blake and what he should ask him to do. Pat was able to give him the address and phone number of IMEMO where Blake worked; he also gave him a letter for Blake and photographs of the Chinese wall hangings that Pat had had in his flat in Hampstead when Blake was in hiding there. Tom, it was decided, would go to the Soviet Consulate in London before departing for Moscow to inform them of his intention to contact Blake and, if possible enlist their support. To this end, Ben gave him letters of introduction explaining about the forthcoming trial and indicating that he had been engaged for the defence team. Tom would also sound him out about making a statement that could – if the judge agreed – be read out in court, and about Pat and myself visiting him some time before the trial started.

Armed with the letters and photos, and a copy of *The Blake Escape*, Tom and his family went to the Soviet Consulate the next morning. The first junior official they saw looked at Ben's letter and asked Tom to translate it into Russian. After some delay they were ushered in to see the First Secretary of the Consulate, a Mr Igor Kuzmin. He read and kept the letter from Ben and listened in silence to what Tom had to say. He also put the copy of *The Blake Escape* on one side – presumably to examine later. But he did not comment, or commit himself in any way.

That afternoon Pat went with Tom to see Geoffrey Robertson, QC, who had agreed to act for us. He is an experienced and highly regarded QC who had been involved in a number of celebrated cases including the successful appeal of the Guildford Four. Recently he had been appearing on a series of drama documentaries on television related to the courts. Pat found him refreshingly informal. He dispensed with the protocol of having a solicitor present and discussed the case in his chambers with Pat and Tom over a bottle of wine – something that would have been unthinkable back in the 1960s when Pat and I last had experience of these matters. He came up, too, with one particularly imaginative idea about how to present the case. Assuming Tom managed to see Blake and secure his cooperation, we should arrange for a video link to be set up between the court and Moscow so that George could give his evidence live on television in the courtroom. Technically it was entirely feasible and would add enormously to the drama of the occasion.

Next day, Tom and his family set off for Moscow and lost no time in the attempt to track down Blake. Soon after 9am on Wednesday 23rd August, the morning after their arrival, Katya phoned the Institute of World Economy and International Relations (IMEMO) from her brother's flat. The man she spoke to confirmed that Blake did indeed work there. However, he did not start work till 10 o'clock; he also believed that Blake was on holiday, and asked Katya to phone back after 10am. She did so, this time speaking to a man who gave his name as Boris Igorevich Sorochinski who confirmed that Blake was away on holiday and would probably not be back until 1st September. Katya said she had a book, a letter and some photographs from Blake's friend Pat Pottle. Sorochinski said he knew about Pat Pottle and would pass the message on to Blake as soon as he returned from holiday and took down the telephone number of Katya's brother. That evening Tom took the metro to Profsoyuznaya station and located the IMEMO building at number 23 Profsoyuznaya Street, a huge Stalinist-type building, 20 floors high.

Suspecting that he and Katya were being given the brush-off and that Blake was not in fact on holiday, Tom returned there at 9.20 on the Friday morning and scrutinised those going in to see if anyone resembled the picture of George Blake that had appeared on television the previous year. No-one did, and after an hour he left.

In fact there had been no brush off. On the Monday morning, Blake phoned Katya's brother, and on the following Thursday he came by appointment to his flat. Tom's diary entry for the meeting begins:

> 31 August, 1989, 10.55am – 1.15pm. George Blake arrives at our flat. He is approx. 5 feet 7 inches tall, of medium or slight build and speaks English with a Dutch accent. He looks just like the photo of his 1988 Soviet television interview and the other photos of him in *The Blake Escape*. He has the same beard and moustache, same largish nose and wrinkled forehead. It is evident from speaking to him that he is George Blake. He is very polite to my wife's relatives, and I am told he speaks fluent Russian but with an accent.
>
> I gave to him the letter from Pat Pottle with 3 photos. He recognizes the Chinese painting / tapestry in one of the photos which he said was on the wall of Pat Pottle's flat at Willow Buildings where he hid after his escape. I also gave him a copy of *The Blake Escape* signed by the authors, a photocopy of the edition of the *T.V. Times* telling of the *Thames Television* documentary film, and a photo of Chapman Pincher's article in the *Daily Express* of June 20, 1961 ('40 Agents Betrayed'). George Blake stated that he in fact already had 2 copies of *The Blake Escape* book and he was also in possession of a video of the *Thames Television* documentary film, the latter having been sent to him by his sister. He remembered having read the Chapman Pincher (he thinks) when he was in prison in 1961. I also gave him a letter of introduction from B. M. Birnberg, solicitor for Pat Pottle and M. Randle, together with the entire committal documents.

Section 23 of the Criminal Justice Act 1988 was explained to George Blake, together with section 25, ie. that it may be possible for him to provide a statement in Moscow which could be read at Pat Pottle and Michael Randle's trial in London, dealing with what involvement they had had with his escape from Wormwood Scrubs prison. I explained that there were 4 options:
(i) he could choose not to provide anything;
(ii) he could make a written statement in Moscow in the presence of a Soviet lawyer and myself;
(iii) he might make an oral statement on video;
(iv) a hearing relayed to the court by satellite might take place in Moscow with a prosecution and defence barrister asking questions of George Blake.
George Blake said that 'his friends' would have to agree to any co-operation on his part. If he were to agree to be asked questions by barristers on satellite transmission, he did not want this to be shown on television, ie. public television (so as not to embarrass family in England?) I mentioned that one factor perhaps against the 4th option is that George Blake may be asked whether Anne Randle assisted or was present on the journey to the G.D.R. I explained that the trial judge may somehow refuse to admit a Section 23 statement under his discretion under section 25, so that we might be left with the 4th as the only option.[2]

Blake stayed for just over two hours while he and Tom talked about the forthcoming trial. He said he had been told in advance that Tom would be coming, presumably as a result of the latter's visit to the Soviet Consulate in London and that it had been agreed he could see him; and he had genuinely been on holiday that week, on a boat trip on the Volga. Personally he was willing to give evidence on our behalf if we thought this would help, though everything was subject to the agreement of 'his friends'. With Tom's help he then drafted a statement which, amongst other things confirmed that Pat and myself had received no payment or any assistance from the Soviet authorities, that we appeared to be acting out of humanitarian concern and that we had asked him to intervene on his arrival in Moscow on behalf of two imprisoned Soviet dissidents, Sinyavsky and Daniel. He kept the draft statement and said he would discuss with his 'friends' whether they would have any objection to his making a formal written statement to be read at the trial. Finally he was enthusiastic about the idea of Pat and myself coming over to see him, and

2 From Tom Mackinnon's diary of his trip to Moscow in August/September 1989

> offered to pay the airfare if we decided to do so. (We were never prepared to contemplate this as it could have compromised our situation in the run-up to the trial).
>
> George came to the flat on two further occasions on Saturday 2nd and Monday 4th September – the latter being the day Tom was leaving. However, Blake's 'friends' remained unsure whether he should sign a witness statement since they feared that anything he said would make matters worse for us. In the end a compromise was agreed. George would write a draft statement on the proper legal forms (Section 23 Statement), countersigned by Tom as the witness; this would stay in Moscow until the Soviet authorities came to a final decision. To prove that the statement, was authentic, Katya took a photo of Blake and Tom together, with Blake holding up the statement, and Tom displaying Blake's old driving licence which his mother had brought him on one of her visits to Moscow. Tom also made a copy of the draft statement in his own handwriting to take back to us to study.

Soon after his return from Moscow, Tom appeared on our behalf in court to fix a date for the Old Bailey trial.[3] It was set, appropriately enough, to start on 23rd April – St George's Day. The court also agreed to extend the legal aid provision to cover a leading and junior barrister for both Pat and myself. This was good news, though, as the lawyers were quick to point out, it meant the court recognized the seriousness of the charges against us.

The first full legal 'conference' took place on 31st October at Geoffrey Robertson's chambers, No. 1 Dr Johnson's Buildings, just off the Strand, attended by the two barristers, Geoffrey and Tom, our solicitors, Ben Birnberg and John Wadham, and Pat and myself. Geoffrey was keen to explore the abuse of process issue at a pre-trial hearing; if we could establish that the police had indeed known of our involvement since at least 1970 and had taken no action against us, we would have, on the face of it, a strong case. He was dismissive, however, of the principal defence we had suggested, namely that the 42 year sentence on Blake was inhuman and therefore a breach of European law. If the abuse of process application failed, our best bet, he thought, was to plead guilty and make our moral and political points in mitigation.

Tom agreed to start researching possible technical defences. The solicitors, meanwhile, would contact Kevin O'Connor, and try to track down Rollo Watts – the detective who had told him the police knew the identity of Bourke's helpers soon after the escape. They would ask the prosecution for police documents relating to Blake's escape, especially any produced after

3 Before Mr Justice Nolan on 15 September 1989

Seán's book was published in June 1970, which might indicate that the police knew at that time of our involvement. John, in addition, agreed to write to the State Department in Washington, the CIA in Virginia and the FBI requesting copies of exchanges between British and US Intelligence concerning the Blake escape under the terms of the Freedom of Information Act. (In the event, we received nothing from these US sources). John, finally, would apply for copies of the transcripts of Blake's trial and Appeal Court hearing in 1961. These transcripts, if we could obtain them, should give the lie to the rumour that Blake's 42 year sentence was related to evidence about the number of agents who had been imprisoned or executed as a result of his activities. However, the lawyers warned us that these transcripts didn't have a direct bearing on the case, and the chances of obtaining them were slight.

Tom's letter to Geoffrey on the technical defences written two days later (2nd November) was not optimistic. In *Bell v D.P.P. of Jamaica* (1985),[4] he pointed out, convictions for serious offences were set aside on the ground that the criminal proceedings were not brought within a reasonable time. On the other hand in *R. v. Derby Crown Court, ex parte Brooks* (1985)[5] the Divisional Court ruled that a delay of 5 or 6 years did not amount to an abuse of process in that it had not prejudiced the applicant in the preparation of his defence as he had always admitted his guilt. Tom's advice continued:

> It is my initial view that it is extremely difficult to rely on the doctrine of 'abuse of process'. I say this as we cannot show that the long delay in proceeding against our clients resulted in prejudice in that defence witnesses have died, disappeared or suffered a loss of memory. Indeed the prosecution would likely say that there was little if any delay at all, as there was no evidence against Patrick Pottle and Michael Randle until they published their book and made the Thames television documentary …
>
> Perhaps one of the most discouraging aspects of the 'abuse of process' issue is the fact that the judge in the absence of the jury would decide the point as a preliminary issue. Thus, we cannot use it in the hope that against all odds the jury would render a perverse verdict. This is a point you raised at Tuesday's conference.

He was not much more optimistic about a defence based on the contention that Blake's 42 year prison sentence amounted to 'inhuman treatment or punishment' and therefore violated Article 3 of the 'Convention for the Protection of Human Rights and Fundamental Principles', Council of

4 Bell v DPP of Jamaica (1985) 2 All E.R. 585, P.C.

5 R.v.Derby Derby Crown Court, Ex parte Brooks (1985) 80 Cr. App. R 164.

Europe 1950:

> We would have to argue that if George Blake had taken his case to the European Commission alleging a breach of Article 3, the European Commission and the European Court would have ruled in his favour. Therefore, his sentence was an illegal one and our clients were justified in what they did to assist his escape and apprehension.
>
> Obviously the prosecution would say that this submission has no merit as it depends on so many contingencies. Moreover Blake's sentence was upheld by the Lord Chief Justice in the Court of Appeal. Further, Patrick Pottle and Michael Randle helped Blake after only 5 years of the sentence. In any event there was no case taken to the European Commission.

Still, we had put forward, in his view, powerful reasons for claiming that Blake's sentence was utterly inhuman 'and would have in essence destroyed him as a functioning human being' and therefore the issue was worth pursuing. Unlike the abuse of process submission, the submission that Blake's 42 year sentence was an inhuman punishment and therefore illegal ought to be left to the jury. 'The presiding judge will obviously think this submission is wrong, but he should not be able to stop the jury making the ultimate decision.'

We had a second meeting with Geoffrey Robertson, Tom Mackinnon and John Wadham on 4th December, in which Geoffrey reviewed the options. He still thought our best chance lay in a pre-trial application to have the case discontinued on the grounds that it represented an abuse of the judicial process. To this end, we needed to press hard for the discovery of the police documents after Blake's escape, and again after the publication of Seán Bourke's book. If this failed and we were tried, he could see only two possible defences. The first was to put the prosecution to proof – to say, in effect, where is your evidence? (As far as Pat and I were concerned, that wasn't on since we had already confessed in the most public fashion possible to our role in the escape and were not prepared to renege on this). The second was to suggest that MI5 or MI6 might have been involved in the escape, as several commentators had speculated. If we were the dupes of the Security or Intelligence Services, our actions would not have been criminal.

We both reacted vigorously against this approach. We had written our book, we said, to put the record straight and to scotch the speculation and rumour surrounding the escape and our role in it. If we put up a defence like that, it would defeat our whole purpose.

But Geoffrey had clearly been mulling over the idea for some time, and now warmed to his theme:

> It wouldn't be you saying you had been dupes of MI5, but me suggesting to the jury that you might unwittingly have been so – or that, even if you were not their dupes, your actions suited their purpose, and they turned a blind eye to what you were doing and helped to protect you. The half-hearted attempts to extradite Bourke in 1968-69 would support that theory. And by running it, we could create a climate of criticism of the security forces. It would also fit in with your argument that the intelligence and Security Service were out of control.

This was getting worse. We pointed out this would be playing a game that would fool no-one since it would be clear that Geoffrey could not be making this suggestion without our agreement. John intervened at this point. He understood our reservations. But after all we could not be certain that MI5 or MI6 was not involved in some way. Kim Philby in fact, in an interview with the writer Philip Knightley which appeared in his book *Kim Philby: KGB Masterspy*, had hinted at the possible involvement of the British Secret Intelligence Service [SIS, often referred to as MI6].[6] If Geoffrey was able to find evidence – perhaps from Blake himself or from Phillip Knightley – that MI5 or MI6 were involved, would we reconsider our attitude? We repeated that we were sure they were not involved – but had no objection to Geoffrey or the others trying to find evidence. Geoffrey agreed to talk to Knightley, stressing again that we had no other defence to put to a jury. The defence that the sentence of 42 years imprisonment was a breach of the European Convention on Human Rights, he thought would not wash.

The lawyers, too, for the most part, were nervous about the prospect of Pat and myself going to see Blake in Moscow. John thought it could give an impression that we were closer to him than was actually the case. However, if we were determined to go, one at least of the solicitors should accompany us.

'Perhaps,' Ben interjected, 'I could get funding from legal aid to cover the cost of the travel to Moscow!' The remark may have been tongue in cheek, but

6 Phillip Knightley, *Kim Philby: KGB Masterspy*, Andre Deutsh, 1988, pp.242-43: 'I tried to get Philby to tell me how Blake brought off his amazing escape from Wormwood Scrubs prison in West London, and made his way to Moscow. He said: "I know how Blake got away but I can't say anything about it because it involves KGB operational matters." I said: "Not even who sprang him? Can't you end the rumours? Was it the IRA? The Committee of One Hundred [a militant section of the Campaign for Nuclear Disarmament]? Seán Bourke [an Irish adventurer who had been in jail with Blake and who claimed credit for Blake's escape]? Philby interjected: "You've left out SIS. Maybe British Intelligence sprang him"'.

everyone was delighted at the idea, and Ben agreed to make the application.

By this stage, the eminent QC Anthony Scrivener had agreed to take on the case on my behalf. Someone – I can't remember who – suggested Ed Fitzgerald to act as his junior. (Ed had been involved in a number of political type cases with Geoffrey, and people thought he would be sympathetic and a good choice.) By chance we saw him as we left the building at the end of the meeting, and he said at once that he was willing to act as Scrivener's junior, provided of course that Scrivener himself was happy at the idea. Our barrister team – once Scrivener had agreed to take on Ed – was now complete: Geoffrey Robertson and Tom Mackinnon were officially acting for Pat; Anthony Scrivener and Ed Fitzgerald for me. In practice, as there was no clash of interest between Pat and myself, they all represented and spoke for both of us.

We could not have hoped for a more committed and intelligent team. Over the next twelve months we had a series of the most lively and entertaining meetings in which no-one pulled any punches in expressing their point of view, yet during which there was much banter and laughter.

The fact that Pat and I were bound in the end to go down for a long prison sentence, and knew it, gave a bitter-sweet sharpness to the meetings, and a nervous edge to the laughter. Several times the barristers said they had never before dealt with such cheerful clients, especially clients who were clearly destined to be convicted. In reality the fact that we knew we had no hope of winning the legal battle freed us from inhibiting caution and allowed us to concentrate on how we could use the trial to put across our arguments to the best effect and cause the maximum embarrassment to the authorities. I suspect, too, that our unorthodox approach had an unnerving effect on prosecuting counsel at the trial itself because they never knew what we might do next and were prepared to flout the polite conventions of court procedure when there was an advantage in doing so.

The plans to see Blake and have him give evidence on video, or through a direct satellite tv link-up, was indicative of our approach to the forthcoming trial. In one sense we would be putting new evidence in the hands of the prosecution since his statement would provide independent confirmation of our involvement in his escape. Indeed it was this very point that initially worried him, and even more so his 'friends'. However, from our point of view a statement by him would be helpful in several ways: he could confirm, as he did in the draft statement Tom and he had drawn up, that we had had no contact with the KGB or the Soviet authorities and received no money for what we did; he might be able to say something about his activities for British as well as Soviet Intelligence; and he could help scotch the notion that the 42 year prison sentence was related to evidence given at his secret trial that he had been responsible for the betrayal to imprisonment or death of that number of British agents. Finally, his statement to the court, in whatever form it was given would be a theatrical coup which would ensure extensive media coverage of the trial, thus providing us with a further opportunity to put our message across.

We were meanwhile preparing two other projects aimed at enhancing the political impact of the trial rather than affecting the legal outcome. The first was the publication of a paperback version of *The Blake Escape*, updated to include a short account of our arrest and our plans for the conduct of the forthcoming trial. This was due to be published on the 19th April 1990, four days before the start of the trial, and to be launched with a £30,000 publicity drive, including posters on the London Underground, in bus shelters, and on public hoardings across the country. It would be published by Star Books, the paperback imprint of W. H. Allen, which in turn was now part of Richard Branston's Virgin Publishing empire.

The choice of publisher had been rather thrust upon Pat and myself. Originally Harrap had arranged for it to be published by Abacus. But on 31st May 1989, Virgin had acquired the general lists of Harrap and insisted that they wanted the paperback to be published by Star Books. Initially neither Pat nor I were happy about the prospect as Star Books did not have a reputation for serious publishing. But on 6th July we went to the W. H. Allen office and met its director, Tim Halestone, and other members of the editorial and marketing staff, and were impressed by Halestone's enthusiasm and his ambitious plans for promoting the new edition. It was Hobson' s choice for us, in one sense, since under the terms of the contract we had signed with Harrap, Virgin had the ultimate say in who published the paperback. But certainly the W. H. Allen staff were keen to convince us that they would make a good job of it, and on 13th July I wrote to them on behalf of Pat and myself expressing our agreement for W. H. Allen to be the paperback publisher.

In December I sent W. H. Allen our postscript which briefly covered the legal developments since the trial. It maintained the same defiant note we had struck in the hardback edition and gave advance notice of how we intended to approach the trial:

> We are sticking to our decision to plead 'not guilty'. This does not mean that we will in any way be denying the fact that we helped George Blake escape from prison and from the country, or retracting our testimony in this book. We will be inviting the jury to take the view that, given all the circumstances, our actions were justified.
>
> Even if we have to go to prison we will have the satisfaction of knowing

> that we helped to prevent the senseless waste of another man's life. And if the Cold War does now come to a close, if the bloc system in Europe continues to wither away, and if at last there is some real progress towards nuclear and conventional disarmament, we will be satisfied that we have played a part in the struggle that has led to those changes.

The other initiative launched in the late autumn of 1989, was a public appeal by War Resisters International and the European Nuclear Disarmament campaign to have the charges against us dropped. Clearly, there wasn't the slightest chance of this happening, but the appeal provided another chance for us to state our position publicly, attack the Intelligence services of East and West and show that our actions had considerable public support. By May 1990, when it appeared as an advert in the New Statesman & Society it had gained over 250 signatures from peace and human rights campaigners from Australia, Austria, Belgium, Czechoslovakia, Denmark, Finland, France, F. R. Germany, the GDR, Hungary, India, Ireland, Israel, Italy, the Netherlands, Norway, Poland, South Africa, Spain Sweden, Switzerland, the USA and Yugoslavia.

There were two Nobel Prizewinners among the signatories – Mairead Corrigan of the Peace People from Northern Ireland, and Esquival from Argentina. Among the British and Irish signatories were John Arden and Margaretta D' Arcy, John Berger, Frank Blackaby (Director of the Stockholm International Peace Research Institute), Bob Cryer MP (my local MP in Bradford South), Bishop Tony Dumper, Lol Coxhill, the jazz saxophonist, Adam Curle, former Professor of Peace Studies at Bradford, Julie Christie and Dorothy and Edward Thompson. Many of the signatories from East and Central Europe came from former activists in the democratic opposition movements in the various countries.

This is to jump ahead of the narrative. In the meantime, on Friday 9th January 1990, we had another case conference, this time at Anthony Scrivener's chambers at 8 New Square, just across from the High Court in the Strand. The whole legal team of barristers and lawyers, plus Pat and myself, were assembled together for the first time.

Tony Scrivener is a tall, dynamic man, witty and sure of touch, with an impressive capacity to think on his feet. He sat in his shirtsleeves at the head of a table cluttered with books and documents.

> 'I love your book,' was his opening line – 'in fact I must get you to sign my copy before you leave. My wife's Hungarian, and she was particularly interested in your protest against the Soviet invasion of Hungary in 1956. You've both done an excellent job in getting the public on your side by

> the way you have reacted since your arrest. But you should seriously reconsider your plans to plead Not Guilty and conduct your own defence. You will be convicted and go to prison for a much longer period than if you had pleaded guilty in the first instance. You will also have lost some of the moral high ground because you'll have been found guilty by a jury of your peers. You could be looking at a prison sentence of three or four years, plus a hefty fine. Frankly I don't want to be the one who has to see your wives when you've been sent down for a long period.'

Like Geoffrey at the previous meeting, he went through the possible options. The abuse of process was certainly worth pursuing and might go as far as the House of Lords on Appeal. There was an outside chance of this succeeding, but no more than that. (In connection with the abuse application, John undertook to phone Kevin O'Connor in Dublin to see if he would be willing to make a statement and even to appear at the pre-trial hearing at the Old Bailey). Assuming, however, that the trial went ahead, our only real option was to plead guilty. We had no defence in law unless we were willing to say we had been set up by MI5 or MI6, and clearly we were not prepared to do that. The judge would not allow us to put forward in our defence the kind of political arguments we wanted to make since they were not relevant in law. On the other hand, if we pleaded guilty we could make all those points and more in mitigation. Moreover, the prosecution might be prepared to drop one or more of the charges if we let them know of our intention to plead guilty.

> **'I know the prosecuting counsel, Julian Bevan,' Tony Scrivener continued. 'He's a reasonable sort of chap. If you like I'll have a word with him.'**

Pat and I remained unconvinced. In my case this was based in part on a bad experience back in 1967 when I faced charges for occupying the Greek Embassy along with about forty other people after the Greek colonels' coup in April of that year. I had gone into the Old Bailey determined to plead Not Guilty and defend myself. However the defence and prosecution counsel got in a huddle, and our lawyers informed us the deal offered by the Prosecution was that they would drop the charge of assault on one of the accused, Terry Chandler, only if everyone else pleaded guilty. Out of consideration for Terry's situation, and especially because he faced the likelihood of a longer sentence due to his many previous convictions, I then agreed to plead guilty. But it stuck in my craw. I did have the opportunity on that occasion to make a short statement stating why I thought our actions were justified, but several other people who wanted to make a statement did not have the opportunity of doing so. (I also got sent down for 12 months, while Terry got 15 months, as long probably as if he had been charged and found guilty of assault).

But Tony was persistent.

> **'Don't make a final decision now,' he urged. 'Think over what I have said. Meanwhile, if you have no objections, I will sound out Julian Bevan about whether they would drop any charges if you pleaded guilty.'**

We agreed that nothing would be lost by his doing that, provided it was clearly understood that our intention was to plead not guilty.

Tony was also worried about the plans to publish a paperback version of the book just a few days before the opening of the trial.

> **'It will get right up the judge's nose,' he said. 'He might even regard publication as a contempt of court.'**

John supported him on this. He was particularly concerned that the postscript in its present form would give the prosecution too much information about the strategy we intended to adopt at the trial.

I caught a late train back to Bradford that night and had to change at Doncaster. I had found Tony's arguments persuasive, yet instinctively reacted against the course of action he was suggesting. Finally I put my finger on one of things that was bothering me. Once we pleaded guilty, the drama would go out of the trial. No-one, including the press, was likely to be interested in what we had to say, since nothing depended on it. It was a bit like watching the video of a football match when you already knew the result. I phoned Pat from the station and said that to him. He needed no persuading, and I think had been less swayed than myself by Tony's arguments.

I phoned Ben's office a few days later to let him know our decision and at his request wrote a letter (dated 30th January 1990) confirming that I would be defending myself. Pat wrote a letter on the same lines, and also a longer memo which took up some of the issues we had discussed. It reads in part:

> The argument that we in some way lose face or credibility because a jury has heard our case and decided against us, has some meaning only if we have been allowed to put our full arguments.
>
> As we fully expect our main points are going to be ruled irrelevant and inadmissible, the jury will never be in a proper position to decide the merits of our arguments.
>
> There has never been any doubt in our minds that once we had taken the decision to write the book the end result would be prison. Obviously on occasions, you grasp at straws, but deep down we have always known where we would end up.
>
> The strength of our case is that we stand up in court and say: 'Yes, of course, we did these things, we were right, and when you have listened to

> our arguments we invite you the jury to agree with us.'
>
> The real weakness in our case would be if after our book and public pronouncements we in any way look as if we are retreating. We would come over as fudging and compromising, and lose what I think we have gained, a certain amount of public sympathy.
>
> Obviously we could plead guilty and try to put our arguments in mitigation. However, whatever way I look at mitigation it is undeniably arse-licking, with no guarantees that the judge will hear our arguments anyway. It's not the Judge we want to win over but the jury.

On the question of visiting Blake he wrote:

> I feel very strongly about the possibility of Blake giving evidence – written or video. If we have to get the judge's approval before it can be admitted, the content cannot be too controversial. But what he can do is confirm our story.
>
> The dramatic effect of Blake giving evidence would guarantee maximum publicity for our case. Not for us as individuals, but for our arguments.
>
> Once we accept that we are going down, what becomes important are the political arguments, not the legal ones, and how we can make them to the best effect.
>
> What we should discuss is how we can improve Blake's statement [i.e. the statement he made to Tom Mackinnon] and I believe that Michael and I should go to see him as soon as possible. We cannot and should not attempt to distance ourselves from Blake. After all we did break him out and in all our comments since, we have maintained we were right.
>
> Geoffrey's initial reaction to Tom going to see George was, I think, absolutely right. He said: 'I see this case as all about the Cold War.'
>
> If we are now saying we need to distance ourselves from Blake we are becoming victims of the very thing we are attacking. We see Blake as no better but no worse than someone doing the same job for MI6.
>
> If, as a result of Blake's evidence or our trip to see him, the prosecution attempts to make propaganda out of it, then surely they are themselves opening up the case.
>
> If Michael and I do go to see Blake, we should do so quite openly – not in a blaze of publicity, but, also, not by a surreptitious route which could well be used against us.[7]

Shortly after the conference, Ben phoned with the heartening news that the Legal Aid Board had agreed to grant legal aid for the travel costs of one

7 Pat Pottle, memo entitled 'Our Defence' – undated but written soon after the case conference of9 January 1990.

lawyer to Moscow to interview George and get a statement from him. Both Ben and John decided to come with us, but now had only to share the cost of one return flight.

We began at once to make travel arrangements, and, as we had agreed, did so quite openly, though without any public fanfare. We all booked on regular Thompson's tours. Pat, Sue, John and Ben all managed to get on the same tour which gave them a week in Moscow; Anne and myself booked on a separate tour which gave us three days in Moscow and three in Leningrad. Their flight was around midday from Heathrow; ours, several hours later from Gatwick.

Since the screening of the Thames programme The Blake Escape the previous year, Pat and Sue had kept in contact with some of those involved – especially with the director Clive Edwards and with Richard Lindley who had interviewed us and been the link person reading the script in the programme. When they learnt of our intended visit they asked us to use our good offices to try to persuade Blake to give them an interview. They lent us a professional-quality video camera owned by Thames, to record our reunion with Blake, and gave Pat and Sue a lesson in how to use it. We could also use the equipment to record his witness statement which we would attempt to have shown during the trial.

John meanwhile had managed to contact Kevin O'Connor who faxed him a letter dated 16th January 1990 confirming that he had met Watts at the offices of Saladin Securities and that the latter had said the police knew who we were a short time after the escape but that a decision had been taken 'from above' not to prosecute us because we were 'perfectly law-abiding citizens in every other respect.' O'Connor also told John on the phone that in principle he would be willing to give evidence in court.

We had a further case conference on 8th February, the day before our trip to Moscow. The barristers again spent much of it urging us either to plead Guilty, or to run one of the defences they had suggested: that Blake had been sprung with the connivance, if not the actual help, of MI5 or MI6; or that we would challenge the prosecution to prove that what we had written in our book was true. However, one new idea was put forward at the meeting – I think by Tony Scrivener; this was a defence of 'necessity of conscience'. We probably wouldn't get very far with it, he thought, but at least it provided some kind of legal peg on which to hang our essentially moral and political argument. Pat and I seized upon this idea. Tom said he would look into its possibilities, and I undertook, with the help of the lawyers, to do some research of my own.

Anne and myself spent that Thursday night with my mother in Sussex. If she was anxious about our trip she did not show it – 'At least,' she commented as we left next morning, 'you can both say you've had an interesting life.' My sister Anne drove us to Haywards Heath station to catch a train just after midday for Gatwick. Her parting present was a rabbit's sheepskin hat with ear flaps which she had bought for five shillings years ago at a village jumble sale. Armed with this, and with the best wishes of the family, we set off in some excitement for Moscow – our first ever trip there, and our first meeting with George since we had left him on the autobahn near Berlin nearly a quarter of a century earlier.

Chapter 6:

Reunion with Blake

'That's him!' Sue said, pointing to a small, bearded figure in a long overcoat and black, wide-brimmed hat walking up the steep curving ramp to the Cosmos hotel where we were staying. Strange that she, who had never set eyes on him, was the first to recognize him. Perhaps Pat, Anne and myself still retained a mental image of the younger man we had known.

It was just before 5pm on the Sunday evening, 11th February 1990. We had spent the morning on a conducted Thompson's coach tour of Moscow, and much of the afternoon preparing questions with the solicitors to put to Blake. We had to meet him outside the hotel because, as a Soviet citizen, he could only enter it as the guest of a foreigner. (It was a law introduced to discourage speculators, George later explained to us, but was deeply resented by the ordinary citizens of Moscow.) As he came nearer his face broke into a smile. He embraced Anne, Pat, and myself in turn. 'I just can't believe this,' he kept repeating; 'I just can't believe this is happening!'

Pat introduced Sue, and we went into the hotel together where John and Ben were waiting in the lobby. They had insisted that they should be with us when we first met George so that they could hear his account at first hand and forestall the possibility of the prosecution claiming later that Pat and I had got together with him and concocted a story.

After the introductions, John said: 'I suggest we go to our room to talk.'

> **'No, no,' George said hastily. 'I don't think we should do that. It may be perfectly all right, but you never know in these places. Could we talk here in the lobby? – or perhaps there's a quiet corner somewhere?'**

We looked at him in surprise. Was he suggesting that our rooms were bugged? And anyway why should he worry since it would presumably be the KGB doing the bugging?

There were armchairs in the main lobby, but it is a vast noisy place, like a station concourse with people going back and forward the whole time, not at all suitable for a private discussion. ('The Hotel Cosmos,' our Soviet guide Tanya had informed us when Anne and myself arrived the previous evening, 'has 3,500 rooms. In front of it you will see a monument to the conquerors of space.' This was a sculpture perhaps 50 or 60 foot high representing a rocket which trailed a gilded mosaic behind it to the ground.) We suggested the Heineken Bar, just off the main lobby, which was all but deserted. George apologised that he couldn't buy any drinks: it was a hard-currency bar and he had none with him. We were learning some of the realities of life for the Soviet citizen under reform communism.

I bought a round and we settled down to the discussion.

> **'When you made your confession,' John asked, 'were you given any kind of inducement, such as a promise that you would get a lighter sentence?'**
>
> **'Not at all,' George said. (His voice was much more recognizable than his face; there was still the unmistakeable Dutch accent which had not changed at all during his years in Russia). 'In fact,' he continued, 'when it was suggested to me that I might express regret for what I had done, I said no. It would have been hypocritical for me to have done so since obviously if I had not been arrested I would have gone on passing information to the Russians.'**
>
> **'There have been some reports,' Ben said, 'that British Intelligence might have had a hand in your escape.'**
>
> **'That, I can assure you is totally untrue. It's complete nonsense. And after all why should they?'**

No-one spoke for several seconds. Then John said with a laugh: 'Well, there goes Counsel's favourite defence!'

George was able to corroborate the other elements in our story – as indeed he had already done in the statement he made to Tom Mackinnon. Crucially, he confirmed that we had never had any contact with the KGB or Soviet officials, and never received any remuneration for our part in the escape.

The discussion lasted longer than we had expected and by seven o'clock George showed signs of anxiety; his wife, he said, was expecting Pat, Sue, Anne and myself and he didn't want to keep her waiting too long. We ended the conference, arranging for another one the following morning when Ben and John would take a formal statement. The four of us then left the hotel with George.

We walked to the end of the drive where we discovered that a driver in uniform had been waiting in a black Volga Saloon car ready to take us to our destination. (The Volga at that time was a step up in the prestige hierarchy from the ubiquitous Ladas, though some way below the long, sleek black Zils used by state and party leaders. The Zils even had a lane set aside for them on the motorway from Moscow airport to the city centre.) Four of us managed with some difficulty to squeeze into the back, with Sue sitting on Pat's knee, and George sitting in the front next to the driver.

After ten or fifteen minutes, we turned down a narrow street and stopped outside a low rise bloc of flats with a small tree-lined green in front of it. George pressed a series of numbered buttons on the wall just inside the entrance and the door opened to let us into the downstairs lobby. There was a flight of stone stairs immediately in front of us; the walls were covered for two thirds of their height in white glazed tiles, reminding me of a police station – or a prison. The lobby was clean, but had a dilapidated air, as if it were an area it was no-one's responsibility in particular to take care of.

'I'm afraid the entrance isn't very imposing,' George said apologetically.

At the top of the flight of steps was a small wooden lift into which we could all just manage to squeeze. The lift, George told us, had been added some years after he moved into the flat, the lift-shaft being simply clamped onto the outside of the building. When we got out of the lift we had to go down one flight of steps to the entrance to George's flat.

The door was opened by an attractive woman of perhaps fifty, flushed and slightly nervous. A retriever with a lovely reddish-brown coat scurried round her feet protectively, barking loudly and wagging its tail. Beside her stood a tall, good-looking young man in his late teens.

George introduced his wife Ida and their son Mischa. She embraced us all warmly, kissing us on both cheeks.

'This is a fantastic occasion,' she said. 'Why didn't it happen years ago?'

Mischa shook hands with us. He was nineteen, in his second year of studying physics at Moscow university, and spoke good English. He seemed perfectly at ease with us from the start. ('Mischa,' George said later, 'is the Russian form of Michael. What else could I call him?')

The retriever continued to scurry and bark. George said he was friendly, but when I put my hand down to stroke him, he snapped and backed away suspiciously.

'Well he's a bit nervous,' he said. He'll soon get used to you'.

The first thing that surprised us as we began to take stock of our surroundings was the ornamental plate hanging high on the wall opposite the front door – a plate celebrating the wedding of (Prince) Charles and Diana!

'One of my sons brought it for me from England some years ago,' George said. This didn't explain why it occupied such a place of honour in the Blake household, unless it was intended as an ironic gesture. (But I don't think so). Underneath it, at eye level, was a framed copy of a religious homily, the Desiderata that begins 'Go quietly …' The original was reputedly discovered in a monastery in the late 16th century. On the other walls in the square entrance hall hung reproductions of classical paintings – city views by Canaletto, interiors by the Dutch masters.

George led us past the dining room to a sitting room / study. One complete wall, to the left as you entered, was lined with books. The other walls were hung with Russian religious icons.

> **'They came from Ida's family,' George said. 'They are reproductions, of course, not originals.' He pointed to the rows of books. 'Most of these,' he said, came from Donald Maclean. 'He left them to me when he died.'**

Maclean was his hero. On a table in one corner were two framed photographs, one of his mother, the other of Maclean. It was Maclean, he told us, who had found him his present job with IMEMO some two years after he arrived in Moscow.

George's desk, bare except for a stylish green phone and some writing materials, was situated under a window on the wall opposite the bookshelves. There was also a settee and easy chairs ranged round a coffee table where we made ourselves comfortable. George poured champagne and proposed a toast.

> **'I owe my life, to you,' he said. 'Without you, I would never have met Ida, and Mischa here would literally not exist. It is marvellous that we can all be together at last, and the only cloud on the horizon is that Pat and Michael face trial and could go to prison. I can assure you that I have never forgotten what you did for me, and have always hoped that one day it would be possible for us to get together. So I give you a toast – To our reunion!'**

We raised our glasses.

> **'And now I want to propose a second toast to someone who will always be a heroine in my eyes – Anne. I don't think our trip across Europe could have succeeded without her, or that we would even have attempted it.'**

I was especially pleased about this. Media attention had focused almost exclusively on Pat and myself – inevitably so since Anne had not publicly acknowledged her role in the escape. Anne accepted this, but could not avoid feeling at times that she was being written out of the history of the event.

> **'Why didn't we get together before this?' Ida asked again.**
>
> **'Only because it would have put Anne, Pat and Michael at risk. 'Now that everything is out in the open, that problem no longer exists.'**

We told George that while working on our book we had visited Jeremy Hutchinson, QC – Lord Hutchinson of Lullington – Blake's counsel at his trial and appeal in 1961 – who had expressed disappointment at not having heard from him after his escape. His prison visitor in Wormwood Scrubs, Roger Falk

– now Sir Roger – had also spoken to our solicitors and said that he would like to hear from him. George promised to write letters to both of them which we could take back with us to Britain.

We had brought George and his family some small presents from England and handed these over. Pat and Sue had brought tea and soap – which Tom Mackinnon had told us were in short supply in Moscow; Anne and myself had brought stoneware goblets.

'These are coals of fire on my head!' he said as he unwrapped them.

Among the books on his shelves were two copies of The Blake Escape, and, next to it, Montgomery Hyde's book, *George Blake: Superspy*, whose publication had led directly to our being named. There was also a copy of Seán Bourke's book *The Springing of George Blake* which had, so to speak, laid the fuse, and given Hyde his essential clues to our identity.

George said he had greatly enjoyed reading our book – but still did not seem to have entirely grasped why we had written it. We explained again the sequence of events.

'You weren't upset at any of things we said in the book?' Pat asked, thinking no doubt of the criticisms of Blake's espionage activities and occasionally of his behaviour during the period we were harbouring him.

'No, no. Not at all.'

I spotted Lemarque's book *Life*, written under the pen-name of Zeno. Lemarque had been the blue-band Trusty on the Education wing while I was in Wormwood Scrubs prison in 1962, and a leading light in the English Literature Diploma class that George, Seán and myself attended. In our book, we had quoted several passages from *Life* that dealt with Blake's escape and the reaction to it inside the prison.

'You know what happened to him, I suppose?' George asked.

'No.'

'It was tragic. He found he couldn't cope with the outside world when he was released. Several people tried to help him, but finally he committed suicide.'

This was a shock. If anyone had appeared to come to terms with prison life and make the most of it, it was Lemarque. Only George himself appeared his equal in this respect.

Soon after we had settled down around the coffee table, Pat asked George if he would be willing to give an interview for the Thames TV Weekend programme which had made the drama-documentary about the escape. George had seen this and liked it, and we were able to say that we had been impressed by the integrity of the team who produced it.

> **'Well, obviously I would like to be able to help,' he said. 'However, I have to tell you in confidence that I am working on my autobiography which will be published in Britain in the autumn – well after your trial of course. I have signed an exclusive contract with the agent in London not to give any interviews until after publication. In any case he has been negotiating with Thames Television about a possible interview for the last two months. If he has no objection, then I am perfectly willing to cooperate.'**

We were dumbfounded. The Thames TV people had told us nothing of any negotiations when they lent Pat and Sue a video recorder and asked us to use our good offices to obtain an interview. Yet George was bound to tell us as soon as we put our request to him.

> **'I've arranged to ring Clive Edwards tonight in London,' Pat said. 'I'll ask him what the bloody hell is going on.'**

George now came back at us with a counter-request. The Soviet News Agency, Novosti, which was now also a Television Company, was making a programme for the Soviet media about George. They had already interviewed him and were keen to have some footage reconstructing our first meeting with Blake in over twenty years. He assured us that we were under no pressure or obligation. If we decided against doing it, that would be an end of the matter, but he had said he would put the proposition to us. We agreed without hesitation. After all, we had nothing to hide. The filming was provisionally set for the following Tuesday.

We moved into the dining room next door where Ida had prepared a dinner of assorted cold dishes: salads, caviar, fish, liver paste etc; it had to be a cold dinner as she didn't know what time we might be arriving. George produced a bread and butter pudding. Puddings remain a speciality of his. Pat had remarked on this in our book.

> **'Every year,' George said proudly, I invite our friends round to a traditional English Christmas Dinner including turkey, roast potatoes and greens in the main course, and Christmas Pudding for dessert. I make the Christmas Pudding myself, except for one year when one of my sons brought us over one from Sainsburys. But I have to say that it was not as good as the ones I make myself!'**

Once we were seated he got Anne and me to explain what had happened to us after we dropped him off near the East German checkpoint in December 1966. He then, in turn, told us what happened to him. The guards at the East German checkpoint were curious and suspicious when he arrived in the middle of the night on foot without a passport or any form of identity. He asked to see the commandant of the Soviet command post – which is situated

Above: George Blake in Moscow hotel (with our solicitor John Wadham) signing witness for use at the trial.

Below: L to R : Anne, Michael, George, and Pat in Blake's apartment in Moscow, February 1990.

Michael in conversation with Blake, Moscow, 1990.

in between the East German and West German checkpoint – but for an hour or so the East German officer pumped him for information and tried to find out who he was. Eventually a young Soviet officer arrived.

> **'I am George Blake,' George told him. 'I was serving a forty-two year sentence in Britain for giving information to the Russians, but I escaped last October. My friends have just dropped me off about a mile down the autobahn.'**

The young officer looked blank. It was clear the name Blake meant nothing to him. However, George was given something to eat and a bed for the night in a room within the checkpoint. Next morning the guards brought him breakfast in bed! While he was still eating it the door opened and three men looked in.

'It's him! It's him!' one of them cried excitedly – and George recognized Vassili, a KGB officer who had been a contact of his during espionage activities in London. George was astounded. Could it be that Vassili had been flown overnight from Moscow to identify him? The explanation proved simpler. Vassili was attending a conference in East Berlin when he got word that someone had turned up at the East-German checkpoint claiming to be Blake and he was asked to check if it really was him.

George was taken to a house in East Berlin and remained there for several days while his 'friends' kitted him out with a new set of clothes. They kept making journeys to West Berlin to buy the clothes, and he wondered why they didn't wait until he arrived in Moscow to do this. (Once he was in Moscow, the reason was quite obvious; it was much easier to get what was needed in West Berlin.) Finally they flew him to Moscow and put him in a 'temporary' flat.

> **'But as you know,' he said, 'nothing is more permanent than a temporary arrangement. This is the flat they took me to; I have remained here ever since!'**
>
> **'So it was here that Seán stayed when he was living with you?' I asked.**
>
> **'That's right,' he said.**

We talked about Seán. George confirmed that it was he personally – as we had assumed – who had deleted passages in the manuscript of Seán's book that could lead the police in Britain to identify us – all to no avail, as it happened, since Seán promptly re–instated them.

> **'But why on earth did he give all those details?' George asked.**

I told him that when I had visited Seán in Ireland I had put that question to Seán and that after reflection he had said:

> **'Well you see I am not the simple uncomplicated Irishman that some people imagine.'**

> **'Ah!' George said, 'that was always his problem. He had this tremendous inferiority complex that affected his whole outlook.'**

George wondered why the police had never interviewed us after Seán's book appeared in 1970. He had felt sure we would be arrested. We said if the British authorities had succeeded in their efforts to have Seán extradited from Ireland they would almost certainly have come after us. But with the two principal characters – George and Seán – out of their reach, it would have been enormously embarrassing to the security authorities to have put us on trial – especially after all the emphasis there had been on the escape being a KGB operation. Of course they might also have felt that they didn't have sufficient evidence to bring us to trial, but this did not explain why we were not even interviewed.

George was able to throw an interesting light on the attitude and morale of the police trying to track him down immediately after the escape. They had been to see his mother within 24 hours and one of the officers had remarked to her that they 'were on a hopeless quest.'[1] They took it for granted that the operation was professional and well financed and that George had probably fled the country within hours of getting over the wall. This had undoubtedly given us a crucial psychological advantage.

He talked about Seán's stay in Moscow and his allegations that he, George, had tried to have him killed. When Seán first arrived he had been put up in a hotel room on his own where he felt lonely and isolated; he knew no-one and could not speak a word of Russian. Before long he was drinking heavily. George then suggested that he should move into the flat with him, and Seán was happy to accept the invitation.

Soon, however, there were tensions. It was a difficult period for both of them living in a strange country and having to learn to adjust to a totally different life. There were also major differences in their upbringing and temperament.

> **'I, being Dutch, have always been very tidy – excessively so perhaps. He, being Irish, was exceedingly untidy.'**
>
> **'Hold on!' Anne interrupted him, laughing. 'We're not going to have any slanders against the Irish!'**

Then Seán had began to insist that he should return to Ireland. George had pleaded with him that if he did this, and was extradited by the British

1 The earliest statement by Mrs Adele Blake in our files is of an interview that took place in December 1966. However, the pagination of the police files shows that there are gaps, and it would be surprising indeed if Mrs Blake had not been one of the first people to be interviewed.

authorities, it would put all of us in danger. Seán was totally dismissive of this; no–one, he said, would ever get any information out of him.

'He then got into his head the notion that the KGB wanted to kill him, and that I was plotting to have him killed. This was the last thing that I or anyone else wanted. Seán invents things in his books, and dramatises everything for effect. But in fact there was never any wish or suggestion that he should be killed.'

George was able to confirm some of the other elements of Seán's story. He did meet an attractive young Russian woman from Moscow university, Laura, and they all hoped he might settle down. But it didn't happen. Instead Seán, as he says in his book, approached the British Embassy, and afterwards disappeared overnight into a wooded park on the outskirts of Moscow.

> **'As a matter of fact,' George said, 'the Russian police suspected where he had gone to hide and combed the woods hunting for him. But they didn't find him, and next day he phoned here to say he was returning.'**

At that stage it was clear to all concerned that if Seán was determined to go, there was no way they could stop him. However, he agreed after some discussions to postpone his departure for a little longer. He moved back into a hotel in Moscow, though he and George met once a week for a meal and a drink. George added that he regretted that Seán could not be with us for this reunion. Was he being disingenuous. Who can say?

The conversation moved on to other topics. George again waxed lyrical in his appreciation of Donald Maclean. He told us that Maclean had become disillusioned with the Soviet Union and gave half his monthly salary to support the families of dissidents who had been imprisoned. Some years previously he had written a paper arguing for what amounted to Perestroika and Glasnost, the policies then being pursued by Gorbachev. George himself expressed strong support for the Gorbachev reforms; socialism could not be imposed by force from above as Stalin had attempted, but must be introduced democratically. (It was exactly what we had said to him all those years earlier when he was holed up in Pat's flat.) But he was deeply worried by certain developments, particularly by the resurgence of anti–semitism in the Soviet Union. If the reforms did not succeed, he said, there could be civil war.

He did not have the same respect for Kim Philby. The latter, according to George, was fascinated by the whole business of espionage and revelled in it. George said that for him personally, as for Donald Maclean, it was an unpleasant fact of life, a necessary evil. I was surprised at his evident coolness towards Philby because the first pictures of George to be published in Britain after the escape showed him on holiday with Philby and his family. In fact it was those very pictures, George explained, that marked the beginning of their estrangement. They were taken by Kim's son – on a visit to his father – on the understanding that they were for private use only and would not be published. Yet soon after Philby's son returned to Britain from Moscow they appeared in a British national newspaper. It wasn't Kim Philby's fault, George said, but still it rankled.

George claimed too that Philby was nettled that he, George, had received the Order of Lenin in January 1967, within a month after his escape to the East. Philby, was not given this award until many years later, even though he had occupied a much higher position in British Intelligence.

A more recent event increased the divide between them. Interviewed by the writer Philip Knightley in 1988, Philby had suggested that the SIS (MI5) might possibly have been involved in his (George's) escape from Wormwood Scrubs in 1966.[2]

> **'He had no right to say that,' George said vehemently. 'It was very wrong of him to do so.' He had not shown such passionate conviction all evening.**

He nevertheless defended Philby against the charge of being a womaniser. True he was married a number of times, but he was only interested in one woman at a time, and it was not until a marriage or partnership had broken down that he would look at another woman. He had in fact met his Russian wife through Ida. She was a woman, very much younger than Kim, with whom he had fallen in love 'at first sight' when they were introduced.

George said something about his own difficulties in the first two years after his arrival in Moscow. During this period he had worked as an editor at home which meant he was on his own most of the time and met very few people. He'd hoped at first that his wife Gillian and their three children would come over from England and join him. She had been in the process of divorcing him when he escaped as she had found someone else she was fond of

---

2 Phillip Knightley, *Philby: KGB Masterspy*, Andre Deutsch, 1988, pp.242-243. The passage reads: I tried to get Philby to tell me how Blake brought off his amazing escape from Wormwood Scrubs prison in West London, and made his way to Moscow. He said: `I know how Blake got away but I can't say anything about it because it involves KGB operational matters.' I said: `Not even who sprang him? Can't you end the rumours? Was it the IRA? The Committee of 100 [a militant section of the campaign for Nuclear Disarmament]? Seán Bourke [an Irish adventurer who had been in jail with Blake and who claimed credit for Blake's escape]? Philby interjected: `You've left out SIS. Maybe British Intelligence sprang him.'

who wanted to marry her. George had felt it would have been unfair to have stood in their way given that he might remain in prison for another twenty or more years, and agreed to the divorce. He was in fact planning his escape at that stage but felt he could not take her into his confidence.

On reflection he decided it was as well she had not joined him in Moscow. She was very English and would not have adapted to living in Moscow. Even when they had been in Berlin in the 1950s she bought none of the children's clothes locally but waited until they were visiting Britain. George had never met her second husband but it seemed he was a kind and considerate man and had been a good father to the three boys. They now came to visit him from time to time. The oldest was a missionary, the second eldest a fireman in London. (I forget what he said about the youngest son – the one who was born in fact in 1961 in the period between George's conviction in early May and his Appeal Hearing on 19th June.) He had met Ida on a riverboat excursion down the Volga when they were both on holiday. She was a translator, working in French and Russian, and at first they conversed mainly in French before George had become fluent in Russian.

I asked George what section of IMEMO (The Institute of World Economics and International Affairs) he worked at and said I had heard Alexei Arbartov from the Institute speaking at a meeting in New York in 1983.

> **'He's my immediate boss!' George said. 'I work in the Security and Disarmament section of the institute and edit the English language edition of its yearbook Security and Disarmament.'**

He explained that this was a recent endeavour by the institute to put Soviet security studies on a serious footing – an attempt to match the famous SIPRI yearbooks on armaments and disarmament.

It was not a suitable occasion on which to quiz George again about the allegations that he was responsible for the death of British agents. He, himself, however, brought up the case of the East German defector Bialek which we had mentioned in our book on the basis of Montgomery Hyde's account. Bialek – according to Hyde – had become a Western agent while an Inspector General in the East German People's Police and Head of the GDR's State Security Service (SSD).[3] After fleeing to the West in 1953 he allegedly moved into the same block of flats as Blake in West Berlin. In February 1956 he was kidnapped by the East German secret police, taken back to the GDR and, after prolonged 'interrogation', was executed. Hyde claims that it was George who tipped off the East Germans about Bialek's whereabouts, even directly assisting

3 Montgomery Hyde, *George Blake: Superspy*, pp. 47-48

in his kidnapping by informing his contacts when Bialek left the flat without his usual bodyguards.

George said he had never heard of Bialek until he read about him in Hyde's book. He claimed that Bialek could not possibly have occupied the same block of flats as himself since these were reserved exclusively for members of the British mission in West Berlin. He found the whole story hard to credit. It seemed to him inconceivable that a defector as important as Bialek purportedly was would have been installed in so vulnerable a location as West Berlin. Normal practice would have been for anyone like him to have been moved as far behind the lines as possible – in West Germany, or even Britain.

I then raised the Popov case, which we had also referred to in our book. Popov, according to accounts by Montgomery Hyde and Nigel West, was a Russian officer in the GRU (Soviet Military Intelligence) who passed secrets to the West, was betrayed by Blake and executed by being thrown alive into a furnace in front of GRU colleagues.[4] George said he had never heard of Popov but again thought the gruesome story improbable. Even if it had happened, how would anyone in the West know about it?

George said he had still to write three chapters of his autobiography and would draft something on the Bialek and Popov cases and show us what he had written. (He had a text ready by the time of our next meeting on Tuesday, and it duly appeared in his book published in the autumn of 1990.)[5]

> **'But you know,' he added, 'one of my interrogators back in 1961 warned me I would become the scapegoat for all the errors and cock–ups of the British security service, and would be accused of every kind of atrocity.'**

At one point in the evening, he became very serious. Leaning forward and lowering his voice he said: 'There is one thing I want to raise with you. My friends over here have asked me to tell you that if you wished to remain in the Soviet Union you are welcome to do so. The authorities are fully prepared to grant you political asylum.'

We thanked him, but said we couldn't think of accepting the offer; it would put a wholly different light on our actions and appear to confirm the allegations of those who said we had acted on behalf of the KGB.

> **'Well, yes, I can see that,' he said. Then he smiled: 'At any rate if you do go to prison, you will be very popular inside with the other prisoners.'**
>
> **'But perhaps not quite so popular with the screws!' I ventured.**

4 Montgomery Hyde, *George Blake: Superspy*, pp.48-49.

5 George Blake, *No Other Choice*, Jonathan Cape, London, 1990, pp.208-211.

He spoke about how close the plans for his own escape in 1966 had come to disaster – when the business tycoon Kenneth de Courcey had inadvertently received a note from Seán intended for George, and when another prisoner, Fletcher, had overheard on his radio the exchanges between George and Seán on their walkie talkies.

> **'I am a fatalist,' he said at one point, confirming the conclusion we had already reached about him back in the 1960s, 'and believe that if something is going to happen circumstances will conspire to make it happen.'**

De Courcey, despite his right-wing views, decided not to inform the authorities. This was partly because he had got to know and like George when they worked next to each other in the canvas shop, but mainly because he was a member of an obscure religious sect, the British Israelites, who believed mankind was divided into those who were 'saved' and those who were not, and had come to the conclusion that George was one of the saved.[6] Fletcher had also decided to stay silent, even though, as a lifer, he stood to get early parole if he informed the authorities of what was being planned.

The animated discussion had been going on steadily for perhaps an hour or hour and a half when we became aware of a low hum coming from the end of the table where Ida was sitting.

> **'Too much talking!' she said 'Too much talking.'**

Then the hum got louder, and finally Ida launched into an emotional Russian folk song – followed immediately by another. It was the highlight of the evening – though followed inevitably by still more talk.

We left at about 11.30pm and were dropped back at the hotel in the chauffeur-driven Volga.

On Monday we met George at ten o'clock outside the hotel. On this occasion he had no hesitation about doing the interview in Ben and John's hotel room. This suggested to us that the reason he had declined to go there the previous night had nothing to do with thinking it might be bugged. Pat's guess was that he wanted to take the measure of the lawyers before going to their room. Perhaps his 'friends' had warned him to be careful.

Preparing and writing the statement took all morning. The wording was similar to the one in the statement he had written the previous September for Tom Mackinnon but elaborated some of the points, emphasising in particular that there had been no allegation at his trial in 1961 that he had been responsible for the death of British agents.

---

6 See George Blake, *No Other Choice*, pp.225-227.

In the afternoon, Ben – who had previously been to Moscow – acted as our guide. We saw some of the palatial metro stations, and visited the New Virgin Convent on the outskirts of the city, its gilded turrets sparkling in the winter sunshine. (It was an unusually warm winter that year in Russia. George said he had known nothing like it in the 23 years he had lived there.) Later we took a bus to the city centre and strolled down the Arbat which was thronged with street pedlars selling everything from icons to soft porn, from painted eggshells to Babushka dolls bearing the likeness of all the Soviet leaders starting with Lenin and finishing with Gorbachev. Several times we were accosted by beggars, often children directed by a parent or other adult.

That evening, Anne and I had dinner with the *Guardian's* Moscow correspondent, Jonathan Steele whom I had becomes friends with when he worked on the Alternative Defence Commission in Britain. Another friend from Dublin, Bill McSweeney, was there, and a well-known independent thinker Tair Tairov who, by coincidence, had worked at IMEMO for a time and knew Blake by sight. Tairov, from the Caucasus, was sharply critical of Gorbachev's policy in the region, confidently anticipated that the Baltic Republics would be independent by the time the European Nuclear Disarmament movement met in Tallinn in Estonia in the autumn, and prophesied the eclipse of Gorbachev by Yeltsin.

It was colder and greyer when we got up at eight o'clock the following morning. A light dusting of snow covered the approaches to the hotel, and all the spaces to which people and traffic had no access were white.

At breakfast Pat and Sue told us they had spoken the previous evening to Richard Lindley and Clive Edwards in London. Pat had confronted them with the fact that George's literary agent had been negotiating with Thames for the past couple of months. Clive said he had known nothing about this; Richard acknowledged that he did know, but had only been informed shortly before we left for Moscow. The unexpected news was that both of them were flying out to Moscow and would be there that evening.

We did some further sight-seeing that morning, taking in the famous Gum store on the perimeter of Red Square. Pat stayed behind to change the lens on the Thames TV video camera. At two o'clock Pat, Sue and myself met George outside the hotel and set off to do the filming with Novosti. We'd all had some hesitation about this, not least John and Ben. Sue pointed out that once Novosti had filmed us we would have no control over how the material was used. Nevertheless, Pat and I decided to go ahead, though we would insist on a straight interview rather than re-enacting the first meeting with George in 23 years. When we explained our position to George he said that as far as he knew, Novosti did not intend to interview us at all but simply to take some footage of the three of us together.

We got off a stop earlier than necessary in order to walk past the KGB Headquarters in Dzerjinsky Square. Dzerjinsky's statue still stood there with its back to the solid grey building which housed the notorious Lubyanka prison in the basement. Above one of the ground floor windows was a stone bas-relief of Andropov, former Soviet leader and one time head of the KGB. In the old days, George said, people were so terrified of the power of the KGB, that they would not even walk on the pavement in front of the building.

We walked from Dzerjinsky Square down to the river where the camera crew was awaiting us. Further up the river on our side, you could see the walls of the Kremlin. But right beside us was a huge featureless hotel, and on the opposite bank a power station belching smoke out of fat low chimneys.

> **'At one time,' George said, 'from a point just up the river from here you would have had a beautiful view of the Kremlin, St Basils and the older part of the city. Then they plonked down the power station and this monstrous great thing (indicating the hotel) and spoiled it all.'**
>
> **'It seems like a gesture of contempt,' I said.**
>
> **'That's exactly what it was!'**

We were introduced to the camera crew and the rest of the team – I think there were three women and two or three men. George spoke to them for a few minutes in Russian and then indicated to us to get into one of the awaiting cars; George, Sue and I got into the back, Pat sat beside the driver in the front.

> **'Now they are going to take us to the Kremlin,' George said, 'where they will shoot us.'**
>
> **'Now you tell us!' – I said.**

In fact the first lot of filming was not in Red Square but in a tree–lined street nearby, leading down to the river. Pat, George and myself were filmed walking up the street towards the cameras, engaged in conversation. As George had anticipated, we were not wired up for sound and the sequence was for the visual image only.

While the filming was going on, I asked George if he could confirm the reports in the Cookeridge and Montgomery Hyde books that while he was a prisoner in North Korea he had escaped from a camp and been sentenced to death by a Korean patrol.

> **'It wasn't quite like that,' he said. 'Yes I did escape, and that wasn't at all difficult as there was no perimeter fence to scale. Philip Deane, the Observer correspondent, originally planned to come with me after we heard that US forces under McArthur were not far away. However, at the last minute, Deane changed his mind and I set off on my own.**

> **'I was captured by sheer chance by a North Korean patrol whose commandant spoke a little Russian. I managed to persuade him that I was a British diplomat who had been interned, not a spy or part of an American patrol, and that probably saved my life. The patrol held me overnight before returning me to the camp next morning. Later in the day I was ordered to stand on a small wooden box in the centre of a circle formed by the prison guards and other inmates while there was a public discussion of what punishment to impose. Lord, the Salvation Army chaplain, acted as interpreter while the camp commandant denounced my offence. Eventually they decided to let me off with a severe warning though telling me that if I ever again attempted to escape I would be executed. And there is no doubt they would have carried out that threat.'**

Shortly after this incident, George told us, all the prisoners were taken on a forced-march further north across bleak and hostile terrain. Many prisoners died on the march, and indeed any that fell by the wayside were shot. This might seem very cruel, he said; however, had they been left they would have died miserably from cold and starvation.

The Novosti crew, meanwhile, carried on filming. Pat and I became absorbed in George's tale and became less self-conscious in front of the cameras. After three takes, the Novosti crew were satisfied. However, because it was cold and snowing, they decided to go straight to George's flat where Ida would be expecting us. So, after all, we were spared the ordeal of being shot in Red Square! Sue went off in a separate car to collect the others at the hotel.

Back at his flat, we found the Novosti crew already setting up cameras and lights. George had a few words with them in Russian and then turned to us in some embarrassment and said that, contrary to what he had understood, they were hoping to do an interview with us. Pat and I said we were concerned that the interview would be edited and we would not have a record of everything that had been said. The Novosti people said they understood our concern, and promised to let us have two copies of the complete video tape on VHS the next day on the understanding that it would not be made available to anyone else.

The interview – from our point of view anyway – went well. A young woman, squatting on her haunches to keep out of the line of vision of the camera put the questions in Russian, with one of the men squatting beside her acting as interpreter. Behind him, standing next to the camera, was another, dark-haired woman whose function seemed to be to nod encouragement to us as we responded.

The first question was whether people in Britain might believe that we were working for Soviet Intelligence in helping George to escape. I said that if we had refused to respond to the allegations, first publicly made in 1987, then people probably would have come to this conclusion. Our main reason for writing the book when we did was to put the record straight and end speculation of this kind. The point arose again later when the interviewer asked us to explain why we had decided to write the book when we knew it was likely to result in our prosecution and imprisonment. We were then able to indicate the precise sequence of events and the dilemma we faced once we had been publicly named by the Sunday Times in October 1987. In subsequent questions, Pat succeeded in drawing attention to the fact that we were opposed to the espionage system of both sides and had demonstrated against the nuclear policies and military interventions of East and West.

> **'If you were sent to prison,' the young woman asked through the interpreter at the conclusion of the interview, 'is there anything you would like George to do?'**
>
> **Pat laughed.'We would like him to drive up to the prison,' he said, 'and throw a rope ladder over the wall – and then smuggle us out of the country hidden in a camper van!'**

They all laughed. But the young woman pressed the point.

> **'But seriously, is there anything you would like him to do?'**
>
> **'No,' Pat said. 'he has given us a sworn statement for use at our trial – there's nothing much else he can do.'**

George now intervened for the first time.

> **'If they are sent to prison,' he said, 'I am prepared to go back to England and give myself up if this would secure their release. However, I don't suppose either side would agree to that.'**
>
> **'And nor would we!' Pat said emphatically, drawing the interview to a close.**

At about four thirty the others arrived. George changed into a smart navy blazer with brass buttons to record his statement not only for the court but for *Thames Television* and *Novosti*.. After some negotiations with the Novosti people, it was arranged that both they and Pat would video the statement simultaneously, using the lighting arrangements they had already set up. They undertook not to use their copy prior to the trial, and to give us a copy of their video the following day. (At one point they were proposing that they alone should do the videoing and provide us with the copy – but John and Ben thought it important from a legal point of view that we should have our own original video rather than a copy of a video made by a professional Soviet company).

In a smart navy-blue blazer, and with a silk scarf knotted under his chin, he was now unmistakeably the same man featured in the press photographs in 1953 as he stepped down from the plane bringing him back from captivity in Korea. Indeed he still seemed remarkably young and sprightly for his age (sixty-seven), and told us he still kept up the regular yoga exercises for which he had made a name for himself among the prisoners and prison officers alike in Wormwood Scrubs. He read out his sworn statement, flanked by John on one side and Ben on the other. It was all rather stilted – but it gave us what we wanted to take back to Britain.

When all the Novosti people had gone we settled down to an evening of celebration and discussion. George opened more champagne – which he and Ida kept on a balcony off the bedroom along with other provisions that need to be kept cool. It was Shrove Tuesday in the Russian Orthodox calendar, so the meal consisted of a large quantity of freshly-made pancakes which we ate with caviar, jam, or George's own home-made marmalade.

We talked a good deal during the evening about the political situation in the Soviet Union since Gorbachev had assumed the leadership of the Party, the rise of anti-semitism and the state of East-West relations. Once or twice Ida seemed uncomfortable.

'My poor country! My poor country!' she said.

Up to that point she had never been outside the Soviet Union, though she planned to visit George's mother in Holland later that year. George confessed to us when she was not in the room that he was somewhat concerned that she would be lured by the attractions of the West and want to stay there. However, when she and Anne went out on a short excursion together during the evening she told Anne that his fears were groundless: 'Russia is my home,' she said. 'I don't want to live anywhere else.'

The purpose of the excursion was to take Anne to a nearby shop so that she could choose a present for herself. She came back with a pair of ceramic earrings and a Babushka doll.

The regular chauffeur-driven Volga returned for us at about half past ten. In the hallway as we collected our hats and coats, George picked up an old tweed flat–cap, its inner lining stained and frayed.

'This was Donald Maclean's cap,' he said.

We all trooped down the stone staircase to go. But then there was a difficulty. There were too many of us to fit in the car at one time; either the car would have to make a second journey or two people would have to travel by Metro. Ben and John immediately volunteered to take the Metro. George gently but firmly resisted this, and in the end Anne and I walked with George and Ida to the metro station. On the way George confided to Anne that his 'friends' had been anxious that the lawyers should go by taxi rather than by the metro so that they wouldn't know exactly whereabouts in Moscow he and his family lived.

When the others had gone, Anne suggested to George and Ida that instead of setting out at once for the Metro we return to the flat for a final drink as we would be leaving the next day for Leningrad. They said it was an excellent suggestion, but we decided to first take a short walk round the square in front of the flat. Ida had their dog with her, and almost at once it became embroiled in a fight with another dog which was being taken by its owner on a late-night walk. Ida grabbed her dog by the behind and dragged it away snarling and snapping, while the owner of the other dog did likewise with his pet.

It was snowing gently, but was not cold, and we strolled through the trees to the far end of square where there was a small children's playground. I asked George about the meaning of some graffiti painted onto the playground wall. I can't remember exactly what it said, only that it was a play on the Russian word Luba which means 'love' and is also a very popular first name for girls in Russia – along with the words for Hope and Charity. We took several photographs of each other to record the occasion.

When we got back to the hotel, Anne suggested we phone through to Pat and Sue's room to see if they were having a party with Clive Edwards and Richard Lindley of Thames Television. It was about half-past midnight, and I thought we shouldn't risk disturbing them, especially as Pat had been complaining of a bad headache during the day. As a compromise we decided to go up to the room and listen to see if there were signs of merriment from within – in which case we would make our presence known. Sure enough when we got there we could hear the sounds of voices and laughter, and when Sue let us in we found Clive there sitting on one of the beds, and Richard in one of the easy chairs.

After the greetings, Pat said: 'I'm glad you've both come. Richard and Clive have some news.'

> **'Novosti,' Clive said, 'is trying to do a deal with a British television company for a film about Blake. Your interview will be part of the deal. Tom Bower from the BBC is here in Moscow right now trying to arrange it all. And the person working with him is your old friend Barrie Penrose!'**

He sounded angry and fed up; Thames television had been pipped at the post by the BBC, and the meeting between us and Blake which they had been trying to organise had gone to the other side. But I was feeling tired too and pissed off that Thames Television had kept us in the dark about the fact that they had been negotiating with Blake's agent, Andrew Nurnberg, for several months. Had they warned us that Novosti were trying to come to an arrangement with the BBC, and that Barrie Penrose was involved, we would obviously have refused to do the filming.

> **'I don't mind very much who shows the interview of Pat, George and myself,' I said tetchily.**
>
> **'Well of course,' Richard said, smiling with bitter irony, 'I can see that from your point of view you've done very well. The meeting has been filmed and it doesn't make much difference to you who now gets hold of the material.' Clive snapped the pencil he was twisting between his fingers and threw it down in anger and frustration on the bed. Sue intervened.**
>
> **'You can't really mean that, Michael. After all if Penrose and Bower had approached us directly, you'd obviously have refused.'**

That was certainly true. Richard and Clive were also worried that George's interview with Novosti might have been conducted in English, and that Penrose and Bower would buy that up as well as the film of the interview with us. Thames, he said, would not be able to match such dramatic footage and their own project would probably fall by the way.

> **'Why can't Thames buy the Novosti material?' Pat asked.**
>
> **'Because we are in enough bother as it is making another programme about George Blake. We can't afford to add to it by buying material from an official Soviet news agency.'**

Pat and I finally agreed to ask George when he came to the hotel at 11am the following morning if he would be prepared to be filmed with the two of us on the understanding that the tape would only be released to Thames if and when his agent gave his consent. The schedule would be very tight indeed, because Anne and I had to be ready to leave the hotel by 12 noon to set off for Leningrad.

George arrived next morning, prompt as ever, and Pat and I took him up to Anne's and my room on the 9th floor. We explained the situation to him, but he was still unwilling to give an interview without the consent of his agent, Nurnberg. However, he was able to confirm that the interview he had given to Novosti had been conducted in Russian, and assured us that there was absolutely no question of any of the film being released before our trial in April. Nor, he said, would Novosti be in a position to sell the video to a foreign company without official permission. Things had opened up a great deal in the Soviet Union, but Novosti still did not have the same freedom of action as would a television company in the West.

Pat left us at about half eleven so that Anne and myself could have a bit of time on our own with George before we left. We mainly talked about personal things, including the forthcoming trial and the possibility of us making a return visit to Russia when everything had finally been cleared up. However, I took the opportunity to clarify one further point – whether or not the first count against him in his trial in 1961, namely that he had passed secrets to the Russians in 1951 while still a prisoner of the North Koreans, had been trumped up. Montgomery Hyde, amongst others, had surmised that he had been persuaded to plead guilty to this charge even though it was untrue, in the hope of receiving a lighter sentence. He said he could see why I was puzzled about this. But in fact it was while he was in Korea that he first approached a Soviet military advisor working with the North Koreans and indicated his willingness to pass on information on their behalf.

We gave him as a parting present for Mischa two pairs of jeans which a friend in England had given us. He was clearly delighted.

'They're a bit old and torn,' I said.

'Even better!' he said. 'It adds to their value.'

I learned from Pat on our return to England that there was a sequel to the Novosti / Thames / Bower contest. Novosti failed to deliver the copies of the video tapes of the interview with Pat and myself, putting forward one lame excuse after another to explain why the tapes could not be delivered. Probably they were afraid that if they handed over the tape it might fall into the hands of a British TV company and pre-empt their negotiations for the sale of the film as a whole. There could be no such consideration in respect of the film of George reading his own statement for the court, but they could hardly deliver one tape to us without the other. As the days passed and there was still no tape from Novosti, George became more and more agitated and angry. Finally he said that if Novosti still had not come up with the tape by the Friday he would after all allow us to film Pat and himself in conversation.

So there was after all an interview with George to give to Thames – though by that time Richard and Clive had returned to London and knew nothing of this unexpected turn of events. The interview was conducted in Pat and Sue's hotel room, with Sue operating the camera. George was anxious and on edge. He told them he was fearful that the room was bugged, that the KGB would realise they were making a video and that they would confiscate the tape as Pat and Sue left the country. The discussion had therefore to be conducted as if there was no video camera present. Despite the constraints this imposed, the interview went well. On their return to London, Pat and Sue phoned Clive and he and Richard came round personally to the house to collect the tape to make sure it did not fall into the wrong hands in the Thames TV building.

There was another unexpected sequel to our visit. George had duly written letters, as he had promised, to Lord Hutchinson and Sir Roger Falk which Ben Birnberg sent to them on his return. Falk, the vice-president of the Sadlers Wells Theatre and former deputy chairman of the gaming board, informed the press that he had received the letter and released its contents to the *Sunday Correspondent.* On 4th March their columnist Neil Mackwood featured it in a sympathetic piece headed 'The masterspy comes in from the cold'. 'In a characterful hand,' Mackwood wrote, 'Blake reveals himself as a charming and thoughtful person.' He quotes Falk as saying: 'He [Blake] was a popular man in the Scrubs. He used to give up time to teach other prisoners foreign languages and used to play bridge with the governor and his wife. I honestly feel that his sentence was grotesque. It was ghastly. With good behaviour he would only have got out in 1989. He was a deeply interesting man but I wasn't overcome with pity or by deep affection. He struck me as a humane man and I have pondered that he began to cast a shadow then about things which are happening now in the East.'

The Sunday Express, by contrast, sought to sensationalise the story of our visit. 'Blake spy pair's secret trip to him in Moscow' their headline read in a report by Michael Dove. 'Their mystery trip,' he claimed, 'was revealed in the Sunday Express. [In fact, the Guardian had carried a report the previous day.] Their cover was blown by one letter addressed to Sir Roger Falk, the industrialist knighted by Harold Wilson, in his London flat.'

There was of course no mystery about the trip, and nor was there any cover to blow. We travelled under our own names with a regular courier, and the prosecution must have known about it since one of the lawyers that accompanied us received legal aid to cover the travel costs. True we did not call a press conference to announce our departure. But our trip was no more secret than that of all the other passengers on the two flights that took us to Moscow.

Chapter 7:

Paperchase

'You've got no chance,' Prosecuting Counsel Julian Bevan told John Wadham when he first indicated to him that we wanted to see all Special Branch and MI5 documents related to the investigation into the Blake escape at various periods. The question of what documents in the possession of the Crown we would be allowed, or not allowed, to see had been a bone of contention from early on in the case and it led to the first skirmish in the Crown Court (Old Bailey) two weeks after we had returned from the Soviet Union.

On 16th February, the day of our return from Russia, the two junior counsel, Ed Fitzgerald and Tom MacKinnon, wrote an 'Advice' for the Crown Prosecution Service listing three separate sets of material that it was essential for use to see 'in the interests of justice.'

Firstly, we required access to the complete investigation by the police and Security Service into the escape of Blake from Wormwood Scrubs in 1966:
a) in the aftermath of the escape;
b) during the period 1968 – 1970, including files concerning the attempt to extradite Seán Bourke and the investigations following the publication of Seán Bourke's book, *The Springing of George Blake* in 1970; and
c) all files in respect of investigations following the Sunday Times story by Barrie Penrose in 1987, including the police interview with Penrose.

Secondly, we required a copy transcript of the entire sentencing proceedings of Blake on 3rd May 1961, and of the proceedings in the Court of Criminal Appeal on 19th June 1961. In particular we required access to the *in camera* proceedings in both instances since 'without going into our proposed defence, at the very least it is essential to know what degree of culpability was attributed to Blake in court if our clients are to be convicted of the charges they face.' In short, we wanted confirmation of the point that Hutchinson, Blake's QC, had told us, namely that there was no mention at the trial of Blake being responsible for the death of 42 British agents. John had previously written to the Lord Chancellor's office about the transcript and received a reply to the effect that they had looked in the Central Criminal Court file and that 'no transcript appears among the papers.'[1] We were convinced however that the

1 As noted in a letter from John Wadham to Michael Randle dated 25 January

transcript of such an important trial would have been kept, and that it had perhaps been moved to the Security Service files.

Thirdly, we required access 'to the files of the DPP and any other prosecuting authority dealing with the events leading up to the eventual decision to charge and prosecute Mr Pottle and Mr Randle.'

> The most important point in the reply of Mr Michael J. Bibby, Acting Head of Special Casework for the Crown Prosecution Service, dated simply 'February 1990,' was that they were not prepared to give us access to their files or to produce any police reports taken throughout the history of the enquiries. There was no objection, he said, to our having access to and copies of statements taken as a result of the escape of George Blake except where disclosure could be refused under the terms of the Attorney General's Guidelines. He enclosed copies of material related to the attempt to extradite Bourke from Ireland in 1968 – 69, including the draft affidavit of the Director of Public Prosecutions at the time and copy warrants against Bourke in relation to the prison escape, and to his threat to kill a Sussex policeman in January 1969. As far as the period following the Sunday Times article in 1987 is concerned, he said that 'your clients were interviewed by the police shortly after the appearance of the newspaper article and such information as was in the possession of the police was put to them.' The interview with Penrose could be disclosed.

On the other points Ed and Tom had raised, he stated that if we required material from the *in camera* proceedings in the trial and appeal of Blake, we would have to apply to the trial judge. Mr Bibby undertook to send us transcripts of the proceeding that had taken place in the open court both at the Old Bailey and the Court of Criminal Appeal. The letter concluded:

> The decision to prosecute [Pottle and Randle] was taken on consideration of the evidence which had emerged in the television programme closely followed in time by the publication of the book. *We are not prepared to give you access to our files nor are we prepared to produce any Police Reports taken throughout the history of these enquiries.*
>
> What we are prepared to provide is a statement from a police officer setting out the salient points in the enquiries from the date of the escape insofar as they may affect your clients, and this will be provided as soon as possible.
>
> Any other information asked for and not specifically replied to must be a matter of an application to the Court. [Emphasis added]

1990.

Mr Justice Auld heard our application for the disclosure of all the material mentioned in the Advice from Ed and Tom at the Central Criminal Court – the Old Bailey – on 2nd March 1990. All four defence barristers were present – Geoffrey Robertson and Tom Mackinnon formally representing Pat, and Tony Scrivener and Ed Fitzgerald representing me; Julian Bevan, and his junior Mr Calvert-Smith, were there for the prosecution.

Pat attended the hearing and met the two Crown Counsel for the first time. Calvert-Smith kept his distance, but Bevan was casual, even friendly. While they were waiting outside the courtroom he approached Pat, introduced himself, and, in Pat's words 'bummed a cigarette' off him.

> **'I think you know how I feel about the prosecution,' he said in a confidential aside as he took a pull on the cigarette, 'but well ... it has been decided otherwise.'**

According to the notes made at the time by Tom Mackinnon, Bevan also stated in informal conversation with the barristers that he considered we should have access to all the statements taken at the investigation into George Blake's escape. Tony Scrivener sounded him out about what the prosecution's attitude would be if we pleaded guilty to one of the lesser charges to which Bevan replied that the prosecution would probably be willing to drop the serious charge of assisting in the actual escape, and one of the conspiracy charges.[2] Tom Mackinnon's notes also mention a remark by Calvert-Smith, again in conversation outside the court, that Pat Pottle's photo had been shown to Seán Bourke's landlady. That, in fact, was the most intriguing piece of information to come out of the day's proceedings.

In the Court, Mr Justice Auld instructed the prosecution to disclose to the defence within seven days all such documents as they felt ought to be disclosed, and ordered Detective Inspector Bird to produce a 'Section 9' statement for the defence about the police enquiries into Blake's escape since it occurred in 1966.[3] The Prosecution also undertook to consider acknowledging that at the *in camera* proceedings at George Blake's trial and appeal no mention was made of any deaths having resulted from Blake's actions.[4]

---

2 Bevan himself at the Old Bailey trial in 1991 insisted that the `deal' would have been that if we pleaded guilty to both the lesser charges he would recommend dropping the most serious charge.

3 A statement made in accordance with the provisions of Section 9 of the Criminal Justice Act 1967 and therefore admissible as evidence in a court of law.

4 These points are all included in the Tom Mackinnon's `backing sheet' - that

About a week later the lawyers received copies of Special Branch documents relating to the Blake escape and dating from late October 1966 to February 1967 – the ones in fact that Mr Bibby had indicated in his letter of February that they were willing to disclose. They comprised statements by Special Branch officers, prison governors and other prison staff, current and past inmates of Wormwood Scrubs, Blake's mother and sister, and others who had known Blake and / or Bourke, or who on their own initiative volunteered information they thought might be helpful to the police in pursuing the investigation. A number of these statements have been cited in earlier chapters.

The documents were divided, on no very obvious principle, into 'Statements Material' and 'Statements Non-Material.' There were 53 of the former covering a total of 124 pages, and 33 of the latter covering 51 pages. It was quickly evident, however, that we had been given only a selection of the documents since the pages were numbered consecutively and there were substantial gaps at various points. Originally there had been at least 265 pages of Material Statements, and 340 pages of Non-Material statements.[5]

The solicitors sent Pat a set of the statements for him to copy and send to me. He read them all at a sitting, underlining passages and inserting crosses and exclamation marks in the margins as he went along. He then phoned me in a state of exhilaration – and shock. For the first time we could see just how close we had come to being detected in those hectic days and weeks immediately after the escape. I have the notes I took down at the time of this conversation and see from these that Pat spoke first of the photograph of himself, Terry Chandler, Dave Thomas and Douglas Brewood which Detective Inspector Henry Nicholls showed to Mrs Rosemary Brown at Seán's previous bedsit in Perryn Road. (All four had been active in the Committee of 100, and Terry was sentenced with us in February 1962 to 18 months imprisonment for the Wethersfield demonstration.)

> **'She couldn't identify any of us,' Pat said. 'But the question is, what made the police show her that photograph in the first place?'**

He went on to read passages from other documents – including those that showed how a policeman had spotted the Humber getaway car two days after the escape parked only yards away from the back entrance to a police station and noted that there was no vehicle licence displayed on it; how Seán

---

is the notes he was obliged to make at the time in relation to fees and expenses claimed for work on the case.

5 These are the final page numbers on the respective sets of documents the police sent to our solicitors.

had been seen in Perryn Road, three days before the escape by two former fellow lodgers at No 26 – Mrs Rosemary Brown and Miss Jenifer Lucy; how, blind drunk, he had phoned a former fellow prisoner in Croydon a few days after the escape to ask if the police were looking for him; how RAF police had searched the hideaway bedsit at 26 Highlever Road on Christmas Day 1966 looking for a deserter; how Seán had sent a threatening letter by registered post from Hampstead Post Office to detective Sheldon in Crawley on the day we were getting him out of the country; and how Pat and I had been spotted by a woman resident in Highlever Road carrying away Seán's belongings from Seán's flat early in January 1967, her suspicions aroused by the fact that we didn't seem to have a car to put them in. Several of the statements, Pat noted, had been taken by a Detective Sergeant Rollo Watts – the same Rollo Watts that Kevin O'Connor had told us he interviewed in 1984.

These statements brought back such vivid recollections, and such a sharp reminder of the risks we had all run, that my legs began to shake involuntarily. Finally, however, amid explosions of mirth, Pat read the statement from Detective Constable Stanley Frankling of Shepherds Bush police station recording his telephone conversation with the Deputy Governor of Wormwood Scrubs on the evening of 22nd October 1966 who told him 'we have lost one of our chaps over the wall' but didn't have time to give a detailed description because he was 'a bit tucked up at the moment.'

But interesting – and occasionally hilarious – as these documents were, they did not give us the evidence we were looking for that the police had known of our involvement in the Blake Escape for some twenty years. Nor was this surprising, since none of the documents dated from the period after Seán published his book in 1970. It was otherwise with the report from Inspector Bird summarising the course of investigations from Blake's escape in October 1966 to our arrest in April 1989. Bird's report, dated 7th March 1990, indicated that we had been regarded as possible suspects soon after the escape and, more importantly, confirmed that the police had identified Pat, Anne and myself in 1970 from the descriptions in Seán's book. Here is his statement in full, as we received it:

> 1. I have been engaged on enquiries concerning the alleged involvement of Michael Randle and Patrick Pottle in the escape from HM Prison Wormwood Scrubs on 22nd October 1966 of the convicted spy George Blake. I have familiarised myself with the police enquiries carried out following the escape and as a result can say: –
>
> George BLAKE was sentenced at the Central Criminal court on 3.5.61 to a total of forty two years imprisonment for offences against the Official

Secrets Acts. He was imprisoned in Her Majesty's Prison Wormwood Scrubs, London, from where he escaped on the night of Saturday 22nd October, 1966. He is still unlawfully at large and is a resident of Moscow. The escape was effected by BLAKE leaving his prison wing via a window and then scaling the outer prison wall by means of a rope ladder thrown into the prison from beyond the perimeter.

At 9.45pm on the 25th October 1966 an anonymous call was received by Special Branch to the effect that the car used in the escape was parked in Harvist Road, NW6.[6] Enquiries revealed that this was a two tone green Humber Hawk, registration 117 GMX which had been seen there at 1pm on 24th October by a patrolling police officer.

Forensic examination of the vehicle and its contents confirmed that the pot of chrysanthemums found at the spot where BLAKE had climbed over the prison wall had been in the car and, therefore, the car was the one used in the escape. It was established that the vehicle had not been abandoned in Harvist Road prior to the escape and that it had been purchased by Seán BOURKE in August 1966 from the wife of a man serving a term of imprisonment at Wormwood Scrubs.

BOURKE, it was discovered, had rented a room at 26 Perryn Road, W3 from July 1966 until 30th September 1966 when he told a witness, Rosemary BROWN, that he was going to Ireland. She was shown a photograph of four men by Detective Inspector Henry John Nicholls, one of whom was of Patrick POTTLE. BROWN was unable to identify anyone from the photograph but was certain that none had visited BOURKE at Perryn Road. When shown other photographs the following day she had no hesitation in identifying a man named John MANTLE as a person she knew as 'Paul' and 'Terry' as Alan MORTON. Both these men were on the hostel scheme at Wormwood Scrubs.

The landlord of 26 Perryn Road, Beno William HABER, was shown photographs and was only able to identify Seán BOURKE.

Mrs Jennifer Maud Carol LUCY, who lived in the adjoining flat at 26 Perryn Road, W3, was shown photographs and identified from them a man known to her as 'Terry' who had visited BOURKE. MANTLE and MORTON were interviewed by police but whilst admitting that they had visited BOURKE at Perryn Road, denied any connection with the escape.

6 This confirmed for the first time Seán's claim in his book that he made an anonymous call to the police just after Anne and myself moved Blake out of 26 Highlever Road on the Tuesday evening after the escape, 25th October, telling them the whereabouts of the getaway Humber car.

Early in the investigation police became aware that POTTLE and RANDLE had been imprisoned at Wormwood Scrubs at the same time as BLAKE and that RANDLE had sent him Christmas cards. These two, along with many others, had been considered as possible suspects but, in view of the early identification of 'Paul' and 'Terry' and the involvement of BOURKE, enquiries into RANDLE and POTTLE were not pursued.

Despite tracing the presence of BLAKE to 28, Highlever Road, W10 and establishing that Seán Alphonsus BOURKE (deceased) had been involved in the escape, no-one was arrested for the offence neither was there any evidence to suggest that this had been other than a lone effort by BOURKE. Whilst numerous stories and theories abounded as to who and how the escape had been carried out, detailed investigations, which were commented on by the Lord Mountbatten Enquiry, did not disclose any evidence linking RANDLE and POTTLE to the affair. The view taken at the time was that this escape had either been undertaken by a criminal element for financial gain or by agents of a country hostile to the United Kingdom. It was the latter which had greater credibility.

In 1968 BOURKE returned to the Republic of Ireland from Russia and en route gave an interview to Granada Television. Very shortly afterwards he gave interviews to journalists and presented an account which differed in small details to that related to Granada Television, thus casting further doubt on his credibility.

Application was made in the High Court in Dublin for the extradition of BOURKE on two warrants; one granted at Bow Street Magistrates Court on 25th October, 1968.

In this book BOURKE described two men and a woman, Michael and Anne REYNOLDS and Pat PORTER, whom he claimed had assisted in planning and effecting the escape. BOURKE had, since his return from Russia on 22nd October 1968, boasted of his part in the escape of BLAKE and arranging his journey to the USSR. BOURKE had always considered himself to have a flair for writing and whilst in Wormwood Scrubs had been editor of the prison magazine 'New Horizon.' The style and phraseology used in his book was in accord with articles known to have been written by BOURKE and the details provided by him in it agreed closely with the facts revealed by the police investigations.

BOURKE described his early life in Ireland and his subsequent time in Wormwood Scrubs where he met BLAKE. He claimed that upon release when he was on the hostel scheme, he contacted BLAKE by two way radio. Also, with the assistance of another prisoner, he passed messages and material to BLAKE. In the book this prisoner is called 'Peter MARTIN' whose correct identity is believed to be Philip MORRIS who was suspected by police at the time but against whom there was no evidence. Assuming that this identification was correct BOURKE retained the initials of his associates but changed their names. It was therefore surmised by police that Michael and Anne REYNOLDS were most probably Michael and Celia Anne RANDLE and that Pat PORTER was Patrick POTTLE.

Michael RANDLE and POTTLE had been imprisoned in Wormwood Scrubs in 1962 and 1963 and it was then that RANDLE had come to know both BLAKE and BOURKE. After his release RANDLE had on occasions sent greetings cards to BLAKE. The details supplied by BOURKE in the book about the age, family lifestyle of REYNOLDS and PORTER were compatible with those of RANDLE and POTTLE.

Despite reaching this conclusion, there was no evidence to substantiate this and it was based solely on the allegations made in the book written by Seán BOURKE who was not available to be questioned. In view of the lack of evidence and the extreme improbability that they would admit their involvement no action was taken against RANDLE and POTTLE.

There the affair rested until renewed interest was kindled by the publication in 1987 of a book by Montgomery HYDE entitled "George Blake Superspy." He made the claim that PORTER had been members of the peace movement and the Committee of 100, a fact not publicised previously. Armed with this information Barrie PENROSE, a journalist with the Sunday Times, published an article in the paper on 4.10.87 in which he named RANDLE and POTTLE.

On 30th October, 1987, the two men were interviewed under caution at Holborn Police Station using tape recording facilities by WDI Helen Crampton of SO12. On advice of their solicitor Mr BIRNBERG, who was present, apart from providing their personal details both refused to answer any questions. PENROSE was interviewed later but was unable to provide evidence of the involvement or RANDLE and POTTLE in the BLAKE escape. He did not make a written statement at the time although the interview was tape recorded. He has now signed a statement saying that he did not have evidence to satisfy a criminal court.

In November 1988 articles appeared in the 'Sunday Times' and the 'Observer' newspapers in which it was reported that RANDLE and POTTLE had 'confessed' to journalists that they had assisted BLAKE to escape and were proud of what they did.[7] Consequently a number of

---

7 Bird got his facts slightly wrong here. It was Barrie Penrose's claim that he was about to publish a piece in the *Sunday Times* stating that Pat and I were writing

Members of Parliament signed a motion urging that they should not be permitted to gain from their alleged crime by publishing a book about the escape. Police once more considered the allegation and determined that upon publication of the book, the matter would be reviewed."

[Signed]
R Bird
Detective Inspector

We met on Friday 16th March 1990 with the full legal team – all four barristers and the two solicitors – at Tony Scrivener's chambers to plan our next moves. Bird's report showed that he must have had access to police files that we had not seen. Thus there was nothing in the documents we had received to indicate that Pat and I had figured in the police investigations in 1966, that the police were aware that Pat and I were in prison with Blake or that I was known to have sent him greetings cards after my release from prison in 1963. And nor, of course, had we any police documents that postdated the publication of Seán's book. Our next step therefore was clear; we must write to the DPP asking for these further documents on which Bird had based his statement, and if necessary go back to the Crown court to apply for their disclosure.

By now we knew who the judge would be – Mr Justice MacPherson of Cluny. The lawyers told us he was a tough ex-military man who held the position of honorary colonel in the SAS.[8] He was what lawyers call 'robust'.

'You won't get much change out of him,' Tony said cheerfully. 'But if we play our cards right he might lose his temper and make a ruling that will give us grounds for an appeal later on.'

John Wadham wrote to the DPP after the weekend. A letter to Pat and myself dated 21st March, began:

Just to bring you up to date on the current position. I have now written to the CPS requesting the documents suggested at the conference and I am attempting to book time in court on Friday 30th March for the hearing. I have noticed in the previous correspondence of the CPS that they have already refused to provide the information we want but in any

---

a book that prompted us to go public at that point. But in the event, Penrose's story was not published and nor was there any mention of our `confession' in the *Sunday Times*. Only *The Observer* carried the story that day in a piece written by David Leigh. Next day the *Guardian* carried the story in a piece by Richard Norton-Taylor.

8 The Special Air Services, a crack military unit within the British Army.

> event I have given them 7 days. I expect they will refuse and therefore that is why I have fixed the court hearing. This date is not confirmed as yet and may not be confirmed until quite close to the time.

The date of 30th March was subsequently confirmed and the hearing to force disclosure took place before Mr Justice Rougier at the Old Bailey with Geoffrey Robertson and Tom Mackinnon appearing on our behalf. Again I didn't come down specially from Bradford for the hearing. But Pat phoned me later that day to tell me what had happened. Here is the account he gave me in his own words:

When we get to the court, there is no sign of either Bevan or Calvert-Smith for the prosecution. Rougier, the judge, is furious, and adjourns the case for 15 minutes while court officials chase frantically round the building trying to find him. It turns out he is involved in a murder case in another court in the building.

When Rougier returns there is still no Bevan. He's now even more angry and says he will hear the case without him. Geoffrey reads Bird's statement and lists the documents we want.

Just then in rushes Bevan, looking like a guilty kid coming up before the headmaster. He is dishevelled and red with embarrassment, falling over himself in his apologies to the judge. Rougier stops the hearing and orders Bevan to come with him into the room at the back. Five minutes later Bevan comes back into the court rubbing his bum.

'Six of the best!' he announces.

'Well, at least then,' I said, 'You both had a good time!'

When the case resumes, Bevan says that he has not seen all the documents, and that it is rare for the prosecution to do so in cases where national security is involved. But he assures Rougier the Crown will cooperate, though they may possibly wish to claim Public Interest Immunity on some documents. Rougier orders Bird to list the documents on which his report dated 7 March was based and to indicate any on which the Crown were claiming Public Interest Immunity.

A few days later Bird's second statement arrived. As will be seen, the Crown claimed Public Interest Immunity for every document referred to – apart from the one for which it would have been impossible anyway to have done so, namely the report in the *Daily Telegraph* of 2nd November 1966. On next page is the text of Bird's second statement in full:

Date	Document	Paragraph in Det. Insp. Bird's Statement	Privilege Claimed	Grounds of Privilege
26/10/66	Report by Det. Insp. Murray of Special Branch	First sentence of paragraph 2 on page 1 commencing "At 9.45 p.m. on the 25th October 1966"	Yes	Public Interest Immunity
2/11/66	Telephone message from Security Service to Special Branch	First sentence of paragraph 1 on page 3 commencing "Early in the investigation"	Yes N.B. Telephone message prompted by article in Daily Telegraph of 31.10.66 for which privilege is not claimed	Public Interest Immunity
		Paragraph 2 of page 3	NB This Paragraph is prepared on police assumption on an analysis of the known facts. The main Police Report on the Blake escape by Det. Supt. Marchant dated 4/3/67 has been consulted	Public Interest Immunity
23/3/70	Report of Det. Ch. Insp. Walts	Third and fourth sentence of paragraph 1 on page four commencing "Burke has always concidered himself"	Yes	Public Interest Immunity
2/11/66	Telephone message previously referred to from Security Services	Second sentence of paragraph 1 on page 5 commencing "After his release"	Yes	Public Interest Immunity
23/3/70	Report previously referred to of Det. Ch. Insp. Wats	First sentence of paragraph 2 on page 5 commencing "Despite reaching this conclusion"	Yes	Public Interest Immunity
14/4/89	Report by Det. Insp. Bird	Last sentence in final paragraph on page 6	Yes	Public Interest Immunity

The first startling discovery from this document was that it was as the result of a tip-off from 'the Security Service' – MI5 – that Pat and myself had 'been considered as possible suspects' within less than a week after Blake's escape. Hardly less surprising – though entirely reassuring – was the fact that once Special Branch realised that the MI5 suggestion had been prompted by a mistake in the *Daily Telegraph*, and once Seán's fellow lodger at 26 Perryn Road, Mrs Rosemary Brown, failed to recognize Pat Pottle or Terry Chandler from the photographs the police showed her, they didn't pursue the matter further. Had they done so they would have caught us red-handed – or, to put it another way, with a 'red' on our hands.

However, for us the main interest of the new document lay in the fact that it revealed the existence of a report written by Rollo Watts, now Detective Chief Inspector, on 23rd March 1970. Watts, as Kevin O'Connor had predicted in October 1987, was turning out to be a key player for in this report he had identified Pat Pottle as the 'Pat Porter' of Seán's book, and Anne and myself as the 'Michael and Anne Reynolds' in the book. Watts was now the witness we simply had to track down, assuming he was still alive, and his report of 1970 the crucial document we had to insist on seeing. Not surprisingly, the prosecution were equally determined to block the disclosure of the Watts' report.

Our first efforts to find Watts himself were unsuccessful. Saladin told John Wadham when he phoned them that Watts no longer worked for them. Nor, they said, could they give him Watts' home address as this would contravene company policy. The best John could do was to write to Watts care of Saladin and ask them to forward the letter.

There was rather discouraging news too about Hutchinson whom we were keen to have at the trial itself if the abuse of process application failed. In a phone conversation with Ben on 20th February he said he was reluctant to appear. However, he wanted to help and would phone Ben to arrange a time to come to the office.

Kevin O'Connor, however, confirmed his willingness to come to court. He said he still had the notes he had made in 1984 of his meeting with Watts and could bring these with him. On 2nd March he faxed Ben's office a section 9 statement he had written the previous day. It reads:

> I am a journalist and radio producer with RTE the state broadcasting service in the Irish Republic. In January 1984 I wrote and produced a documentary for Radio entitled 'A Death in January' which was on the life of Seán Bourke.
>
> After the programme was broadcast, I was contacted by a number of

> people who said they had further information to offer. One of these mentioned that Michael Holiday then a reporter on the Mail on Sunday had seen Seán Bourke before he died. I subsequently met Holiday. He introduced me to the Crime Correspondent of the Mail. He arranged for me to meet Roly Watts.
>
> Sometime in 1984 I went to the offices of Saladin Security in Sloane Street and met Mr Watts. We had a meeting for about 20 minutes in Watts Office.
>
> Watts wore a business suit 3 piece pin stripe. He told me that months after Seán Bourke returned to Ireland from Moscow, Bourke would telephone him from Ireland and they would have a conversation along the lines that Bourke's old Humber was still in the Metropolitan Police Pound and when could he arrange to claim it.
>
> Watts said that he was an ex Scotland Yard Officer, a Sergeant who was involved in the investigation which surrounded the escape of George Blake. He said that the authorities had known within a very short time that there were two other people besides Seán Bourke involved in the escape. They knew that two of the people were part of the 'intellectual mafia' at the prison. Watts said that there were conversations about the prosecution of these two people and his superiors had told him that they should leave well enough alone.
>
> Watts said that the police had quickly established Bourke as the prime suspect days before the description of Bourke was released to the media.
>
> I have a note of the conversation and Watts said 'Of course we knew who they were in a short time but a decision was taken not to prosecute them. The reason (which came from above) was they were perfectly law abiding citizens in every other respect. One was a teacher married to a teacher they had young children why break up the family and put them away at the cost of the tax payer when there were lots of other real villains about that it was our job to catch.'
>
> At that stage from information available from elsewhere I knew that Randle lived in Bradford. I tried to get Watts to say where the two men were now and he said something to the effect of 'Up the Midlands somewhere'.
>
> It was clear to me he knew more than he was prepared to say if only to protect the full identity and location of Randle.

In a subsequent statement, O'Connor confirmed that he had visited Pat and myself in 1987 shortly after Barrie Penrose's article which named us appeared in the Sunday Times. Clearly if we could ever get Watts into the witness box he would have some explaining to do.

Easter was now fast approaching – Easter Sunday fell that year (1990)on 15th April. The date for the commencement of the trial had been put back a couple of days to Wednesday 25th April 1990 because of some kind of annual ceremony for barristers on the 23rd at which they parade in their wigs and gowns in and around the Central Criminal Court. On 11th April the lawyers met on their own at Tony Scrivener's chambers to review their tactics.

That same evening Inspector Bird and another officer arrived at Pat and Sue's house in Dashwood Road, Muswell Hill. Pat greeted them with his usual generosity and bonhomie: 'Hello, Mr Bird. Come in and have a cup of tea.'

Bird looked embarrassed.

'No thank you,' he said stiffly. And then: 'This is for you' – handing Pat a large brown envelope, 'I think you've been expecting it. This one,' he added 'is for Mrs Pottle.' He waited until Sue came to the door so he could hand the second envelope to her personally, then he and his fellow officer went back down the path and drove off.

Pat and Sue went back inside to study the documents. One was a court order signed that very day by Mr Justice Kennedy at an ex parte hearing in the Queen's Bench Division of the High Court. It imposed a 'charging order' on the houses of Pat and Sue, and Anne and myself under the provisions of Section 78 of the Criminal Justice Act 1988 which deals with the confiscation of the 'proceeds of crime.' With it was an affidavit sworn two days earlier on 9th April by Inspector Bird which had been presented to the court in support of the application. This stated that Pat Pottle had benefitted from his crime to the tune of £15,000, and Michael Randle to the tune of £16,100. (More on this difference in a moment.)

Pat phoned John Wadham straight away who explained that the effect of the order was that the four of us were legally prohibited from selling our houses until after the trial. If we were found guilty the court could order them to be confiscated and sold and the proceeds seized up to the value of our alleged criminal gains.

'But we didn't even know about this hearing? Can they really do this without us even being there?'

> **'I'm afraid they can,' John said. 'An *ex parte* hearing is one in which only one side is present.'**

The claim that I had made £1,100 more than Pat from the crime was comical in its small-mindedness. Back in 1966, as I had stated in our book, I had been given £1,000 to buy the camper-van in which we smuggled Blake out of the country, and to meet the travel and living expenses of Blake and Bourke. It was used for this purpose and indeed in 1967, some time after Anne and

I had returned from our trip, we sold the van and gave the proceeds back to 'Bridget', the woman who had given us the money in the first place. (This last fact is not mentioned in *The Blake Escape* though the prosecution could easily have found it out by asking us.) The claim for the additional £100 was still more absurd. I had raised £200 in June or July of 1966, all of which I handed over to Seán. However while telling this part of the story in the book I made a cross-reference to Seán's book, mainly to show how closely our accounts tallied. This passage reads:

> Seán was released on Monday 4 July and moved into a flat in Perryn Road not far from the prison. According to his account I handed over an initial £100 to him on 24 July which he used to buy a second-hand car costing £65, and other tools and equipment.[9]

From this Bird – and presumably also prosecuting counsil – jumped to the conclusion that I must have pocketed the other £100 myself and sought to claim it back retrospectively from the Crown under the provisions of an Act passed 22 years later!

But if this was simply laughable, another statement in Bird's report infuriated us. On page 4 he states: 'Furthermore, within the book, both Randle and Pottle state clearly their financial motives in writing the book and thereby benefiting from the crimes.'

We knew very well that we had made no such statement. The reasons for our decision in late 1987 to write the book are in fact set out in detail on pages 240 – 241 of *The Blake Escape*. The relevant passage reads:

> The rumours concerning Vanessa Redgrave's involvement, and the suggestion that the KGB might have masterminded the escape, underlined the inadequacy in the long-term of our *Guardian* statement.[10] As a holding statement it was about as good as we were capable of producing. But it did not enable us to deal with the speculation that must inevitably arise. Thus, within a few weeks of the original allegations, Pat and I had a long discussion about whether we should not issue a second statement acknowledging our role, and saying that we would be writing a book which would set the record straight.
>
> We made no hasty decision. We knew that if we went public we were likely to be prosecuted and perhaps imprisoned, and we had to think carefully about what that would mean for our future and that of our

9 *The Blake Escape*, p. 60

10 In this statement, published in *The Guardian* 9 October 1987, we neither confirmed nor denied our involvement in the escape but made it clear we were happy it had occurred and would see it as no disgrace to be associated with it.

> families. Neither Anne nor Pat's wife Sue were happy about what we were proposing, though they acknowledged the strength of the arguments in its favour. But the more we thought about it, the more it seemed to us that we really had no option but to reveal in full what we had done and why we had done it. We had not sought the publicity in the first place, and down the years had done our utmost to prevent our role being made public. But once the Sunday Times had named us, the genie was out of the bottle for good.[11]

Pat and I both checked what we had written and could only conclude that this part of Bird's sworn affidavit was pure invention, a straightforward lie. I knew Bird would be delivering copies of the charging order on our house within a day or two and brooded over what I would say to him when he showed up.

He had not arrived by the following evening and Anne and I went out to see the film *Born on the 4th July* at the new American style Showcase Cinema situated just off the M62 between Bradford and Leeds. We returned late, soon after 11.30pm, and as we were driving down the rough, unadopted road at the back of the house we noticed a car parked by our back gate. Anne, who was driving, cursed mildly at the inconvenience, and then, suddenly tense and alert, said: 'I know that car. It's Bird!'

It was the same B-registered Cavalier car in which he had driven me up to Bradford a year earlier, but I would not have spotted this so quickly. Now my heart was pounding and I could feel the anger rising. 'I must keep calm,' I told myself. 'I will tell Bird what I think, but calmly.' I mentally rehearsed what I would say to him.

As we drew near, the Cavalier pulled ahead and parked on the opposite side of the lane a few yards further down.

> **'Don't lose your temper with him,' Anne said as we pulled up.**

As I got out of the car, I saw Bird get out of the driving seat of the Cavalier and lean in to get something out.' Then he called twice – 'Michael! Michael!'

Michael indeed! A fine moment to decide we were on first name terms. Anne and I waited at the back of our car by the gate while Bird approached carrying two envelopes. As he reached me I said:

> **'I want to say one thing to you. Up to now I had some respect for you …'**

He stiffened and his eyes glazed over:

> **'This is for you,' he said, trying to hand me the envelope. I put my hands behind my back so he tucked it under the back windscreen**

11 *The Blake Escape*, p.240

wiper of the car. He handed a second envelope to Anne. My voice was now rising in anger as he continued to ignore me and to turn his head away.

'You lied to the court yesterday. You know the passage I am talking about – where you claim that we said in our book that we had a financial motive in writing it.'

Still ignoring me, he began walking back to his car. I walked beside him, continuing to harangue him.

'You know there is not a single passage in the book where we say anything of the kind.'

We had now reached Bird's car. He turned round and spoke past me to Anne:

'Mrs Randle, speak to your husband!'

I walked the few yards back to our gate, but as Bird got back into his car I shouted at him at the top of my voice:

'You lied to the High Court!'[12]

It wasn't at all how I had intended to handle it. But my plan to deliver a quiet, telling rebuke went out the window in face of Bird's hard-faced response. After he left I went straight upstairs to my attic office and wrote down an account of what had occurred.

Next day I phoned John Wadham, feeling I'd mishandled the situation.

'Don't worry about it,' he said. 'You were right to be angry, and it's right the police should feel your anger when they behave like that.'

A little over a week later the solicitors received a letter from Mr Michael Bibby of the Crown Prosecution Service dated 18th April enclosing a copy of a Notice to the Court under Section 72 of the Criminal Justice Act 1988. This is a notice which must be served by the prosecutor in advance of a case if the court is to consider confiscating the proceeds of crime in any given case in the event of the accused be found guilty. With it was a further supporting statement by Inspector Bird giving relevant information – again as required by the Act. Bird's statement – a financial profile of Pat and myself – was dated 9th April 1990, that is the same date as the other statement by him submitted to Mr Justice Kennedy at the hearing on 11th April. In the Financial Profile Bird again alleges, in identical words, that 'both Randle and Pottle state clearly their financial motives in writing the book' but then goes on to cite the passage on page 83 on which he is relying. As he puts it:

> They admit (line 28 et seq) "We could, however, offset the disaster" (if convicted) "to some degree by writing up this story; this would help to

12 From my own notes written immediately after Bird's departure and timed at 11.45pm.

> defray the legal costs and provide some minimal support for Anne and the children if I (Randle) was in prison." It was agreed that Seán (Bourke) "would leave the taped discussions between him and George" (Blake) "with me the day before the break so that these could be used to support any written account, whether in the form of a book or newspaper articles."

The full extent of the prosecution team's dishonesty was now apparent – for we can take it that Bird did not act alone and that his action was approved by the others most closely involved in the case. The passage he cites referred to a discussion not in 1987 when Pat and I made the decision to write *The Blake Escape* but to a book we might have written in 1966 or early 1967 if Pat and I been arrested and given a long prison sentence at a time when Anne's and my sons, Seán and Gavin, were still toddlers, both under school age, and when Anne would have had the responsibility on her own of looking after them.

Twenty-one years later the circumstances were completely different. Seán and Gavin were grown up and had left home, the tapes had long since been returned to Seán Bourke, and we were writing a book not after we had been arrested and imprisoned for helping free George Blake but to put the record straight following Montgomery Hyde's and the *Sunday Times* revelations. Indeed by writing the book in 1988-89 we were providing the Crown with the very evidence they needed to bring a prosecution. Any profit we made from it would have to be balanced against the losses we would incur from the long term of imprisonment that seemed certain to follow publication, and from the fact, in my case, that I would have to resign my post at Bradford University. I had been advised, too, by the Professor of Peace Studies, James O'Connell, that if the book led to my prosecution and imprisonment I would cut myself off from the possibility of ever being employed again at any university either in Britain or any other country. Anne had also resigned her full-time job as a staff nurse at the Bradford Royal Infirmary and went instead onto the temporary nursing register. This meant she would be employed on an occasional basis as and when the hospital needed her. She had taken this step so that she could be present at the trial and the preliminary court appearances. A knock-on effect was that when she did eventually get another permanent post she lost out on the grading. We have no complaint about any of this, since it was our decision to write the book and face prosecution; we simply want to lay to rest the notion that we did so in order to make money.

Had Bird cited the passage he was relying upon in making his allegation in the statement submitted to Mr Justice Kennedy, the judge might have been astute enough to have realised that it was referring to a book that might have been written in 1966 or 1967 not to the book that actually was written more than twenty years later under entirely different circumstances, and might have questioned Bird, or the prosecuting counsel, about this. But though the statement submitted to Kennedy was drawn up on the same day as the Financial Profile, this key revealing passage was omitted from it.

Here, to complete the picture, is the fuller context of the passage on page 83 of *The Blake Escape*:

> Although our own confidence was now high [a few days before the escape in October1966] we couldn't help thinking about the consequences for us and our families if we were caught. Even if everything went smoothly on the night itself, and we managed to get George safely out of the country, the Security Service might discover our involvement in the weeks and months that followed. Pat recalled how a team of plain-clothes detectives had been used to follow Lonsdale[13] and find out who he was meeting. One day a team of detectives would follow him a certain distance and then break off contact; the next day an entirely new team would watch out for him at the point at which their colleagues the previous day had stopped. This procedure continued until his destination was discovered, and virtually ensured that he would not suspect he was being followed. If the Security Service were to investigate the escape with that kind of thoroughness, we had to face up to the fact that their investigations might lead to us.
>
> We went through our reasons for being involved and how we would put them across in the event of an arrest and trial. We decided that if it came to it we would not deny our involvement, or shelter behind a legalistic defence, but would concentrate on the moral and political issues involved.
>
> We also discussed the kind of sentence we could expect if convicted. Seán's researches had indicated that a five-year sentence was the maximum for assisting an escaped convict. However, we knew that if we were convicted of conspiracy, there was no statutory limit to the sentence that could be imposed and the length was likely to be influenced by the prevailing atmosphere and the temperament of the trial judge. We could, however, offset the disaster to some degree by writing up the story; this would help to defray the legal costs and provide some minimal support for Anne and the children if I was in prison. It was agreed that Seán would leave the taped discussions between him and George with me

13 The Soviet spy Gordon Lonsdale, alias Konon Molody, the leading figure in the 'Portland Spy Ring' sentenced to 25 years imprisonment in 1961 but exchanged three years later for the British businessman Greville Wynne.

> before the day of the break so that these could be used to support any written account, whether in the form of a book or newspaper articles.[14]

This whole shabby manoeuvre by the prosecution was probably unnecessary. They might well have got the charging order on the houses without making the dishonest claim that we had 'clearly stated our financial motives in writing the book.' They could have argued that whatever our motives the fact was that we were paid money for writing the book, and that the book could not have been written but for our freely acknowledged involvement in the criminal offence of helping Blake to escape, harbouring him and smuggling him out of the country. Perhaps they felt that this argument was not sufficiently strong in itself. The section of the Criminal Justice Act 1988 was largely aimed at drug traffickers and the like who profited directly from their crimes and in some cases invested the proceeds in the property market. It was open to argument as to whether it was ever intended to cover money obtained from the perfectly legitimate act of writing a book, albeit one that described illegal acts in which the authors had been involved.

We had good grounds on which to apply for the charging order to be set aside. First, as just noted, it was clearly stretching a point to say that money legally obtained from the sales of a book amounted to 'proceeds of crime' within the meaning of the Act. Second, on a narrower legal point, Pat and I had received half the advance royalties prior to the Act becoming law. This meant that the amount we received after that point fell short of the amount specified in the Act as the minimum to which charging and confiscation orders could apply.

However, Easter was now upon us, so we couldn't think of an appeal against the Order until after the holiday. Moreover the barristers took the view that when the holiday was over it would be too near the trial date to be worth trying to get the order rescinded. Any judge, they thought, would be likely to take the view that matters should be left as they were until the trial result was known. No doubt this was why the prosecution had sprung the matter upon us so close to the trial date. Bird, however, was quite wrong if he really believed that we or our lawyers had expected this move on their part. Our lawyers had indeed warned us that we faced the possibility of a heavy fine in addition to imprisonment, and that we were prepared for. In fact, in anticipation of this eventuality I had signed over to Anne the house we had previously jointly owned.

There had been developments, meanwhile, on the publishing front. Sometime in February or March the Virgin Group decided to halt publication

14 *The Blake Escape*, p.83.

on virtually all the W. H. Allen list, including the paperback version of The Blake Escape. Thus the grand plan for publication coupled with a £30,000 publicity drive to coincide with the start of the trial came to nothing. Moreover, if the paperback was still to appear on time, the new publishers would have to be found fast, and to move fast.

There were no shortage of offers, and we settled finally on Sphere books, part of the MacDonald Group. They produced it with impressive speed, publishing on the 19th April. But the publicity was modest and the event had no great impact. It might have been otherwise if the Crown had reacted as Tony Scrivener had anticipated they would and kicked up a fuss about it. Perhaps they knew better than to do this. The book sold moderately well, but its publication never came across as the act of defiance we intended it – amongst other things – to be.

***

As the trial date approached so the intensity of Pat's and my preparations increased. Pat typed pages of notes on questions to ask two of their key witnesses – Superintendent Eggington and Inspector Bird. I prepared a 'scenario' of the trial, clarifying points of procedure with the lawyers as I wrote it.

I also spent hours in local libraries checking the defence of necessity which the barristers had pointed us in the direction of at an early stage as a possible – if exceedingly fragile – basis on which to base our argument that it is sometimes justified to break the letter of the law in order to prevent a greater crime. Some leading authorities doubted if the defence existed at all in English law; others, notably the distinguished law professor Granville Williams were equally confident that it did.

Chris Vincenzi, a close family friend in Bradford, and lawlecturer at what was then the Huddersfield Polytechnic drew my attention to a ruling in a case before the Court of Appeal in 1989. This was the case of R. v Martin in which Mr Justice Simon Brown quashed the conviction of a man found guilty of driving while disqualified on the grounds that the judge had not permitted him to put forward a defence of necessity.[15] 'English law,' he ruled 'does in extreme circumstance recognize a defence of necessity.' This decision has turned out to be a landmark in clarifying the law in this area and is now cited in all the standard works on English criminal law. Relying on this judgement, and on the proposition that the 42 year sentence on Blake amounted to 'cruel and unusual punishment' as prohibited under the Bill of Rights of 1688, I developed an argument to which the judge – and we hoped also the jury if

15 (1989) 88. C.A. 12, 345.

they were allowed to stay and listen to it – would at least have to give serious consideration.

There was a sense of exhilaration as the day of confrontation drew close. But the tension too was considerable. The barristers told us that the abuse of process application would almost certainly fail; the best we could hope for from it were points for an appeal at a later point. And – with the possible exception of Tom – the lawyers were in no doubt at all that once the trial proper started we stood no chance whatever of an acquittal.

At a cold rational level, we shared this view, and in a sense acquittal was not even our principal aim. We wanted to use the trial to advance a moral and political argument. I can remember that we said to one another that if we could convince one member of the jury to agree with us and force a majority verdict this would represent a stunning moral victory. However, to achieve even that we needed as it were to suspend disbelief and argue our case as if a Not Guilty verdict was the only one that a sensible and compassionate jury could arrive at. The tension that we felt as the trial approached stemmed only partially from the prospect of imprisonment, loss of our homes and so forth: we had, after all, known of such possible consequences from the moment we signed the contract with the publishers of The Blake Escape and had braced ourselves for them. The more immediate worry was whether we could acquit ourselves well in the court and make good use of the opportunities it gave us to present our case.

The support of friends and colleagues at this time, particularly friends in the peace movement, was crucial. We received many cards and letters wishing us well and this gave our morale a much needed boost.

Friends in and around Bradford were especially supportive, sometimes introducing a lighter touch into the proceedings to keep Anne and my spirits up. Two friends John Arden and Margaretta d'Arcy sent us cards regularly from their home in Galway, and there were messages of support too from friends and relatives in Dublin and Wicklow. Another very good friend, Mary Wilkinson from the Peace Pledge Union, sent us cards at every critical moment. As she said in one of them, no matter how thoroughly you have braced yourself for arrest and court appearances the events themselves impose a heavy strain. She had lost her partner / companion, Myrtle Solomon – another dear and courageous friend of ours in the peace movement – who had died of cancer in 1985, and Mary herself was also suffering from the same disease. She faced this infinitely more serious trial with great courage, never giving her illness more than a passing mention in her cards. To our great regret she died before the case finally came to trial at the Old Bailey.

On Sunday 22nd April, Anne and I drove to London, complete with the nearly 2,000 pages of (repetitive) prosecution evidence, my extensive notes on the defence of necessity, on questions to put to prosecution witnesses, and on a final speech to the jury. I brought with me also a portable computer and a printer so that I could continue working during the trial itself. We stayed in North London with our good friends Tony and Jean Smythe whom we had known since our early campaigning days at the beginning of the 1960s. Tony and I had also been on the Council and Executive of War Resisters International for many years, and he was one of the people who encouraged Pat and myself to write our book setting the record straight once we had been publicly named in the Sunday Times. Tony and Jean installed us in the room of one of their daughters who was away at the time, gave us the free run of the house, and made us warmly welcome.

On Tuesday morning we had a final conference with the lawyers at Tony Scrivener's chambers in New Square. New Square is a quiet retreat to the back of the North side of the Strand where Georgian buildings overlook a pleasant green, away from the noise of the traffic. It seemed particularly serene and unthreatening in the warm Spring sunshine, the epitome of elegance and good order. But suddenly, as I walked by the side of the green approaching Tony's office, I heard a rustling noise in the hedgerow that surrounds the green and looking more closely saw that what had appeared to be heaps of old cardboard and newspaper were makeshift shelters for some of the thousands of homeless people living rough in London.

The discussion that morning was focused not so much on how Geoffrey and Tony would present their case at the pre-trial hearing on abuse as on the tactics Pat and I should adopt once we were on our own at the trial itself – probably starting on the following Monday. Geoffrey suggested we request the judge to ask the prosecution if the jury had been vetted, explaining that the prosecution has to get the permission of the Attorney General to do so. If the jury had been vetted, this would be a good appeal point to take to the European Court. We spent some time reviewing the main points I should put forward when it came to making a legal submission on the defence of necessity. We also debated whether to object formally to having MacPherson as the judge because of his association with the SAS and the Security Service. One of the lawyers pointed out that he would have been a serving member of the SAS at the time Pat and myself were organising the Wethersfield demonstration and when we were sentenced to 18 months imprisonment under the Official Secrets Act for doing so. (Much later on, Justice Macpherson, to his credit, was to play an important role in exposing institutional racism in the police force in his official report in 1999 into the killing of the black teenager, Stephen Lawrence on 22nd April 1993.)

John Wadham had one piece of disappointing news. Lord Hutchinson had now confirmed that he regretted he could not appear as a witness for us. Furthermore, he had said that although no *evidence* had been produced at the *in camera* trial of George Blake that he had been responsible for the death of agents, the prosecution had made the *allegation* that about 40 agents had lost their liberty or vanished without trace because of what Blake had done.

This was a blow indeed. When Pat and I had seen Lord Hutchinson in January 1989 and asked him if there could possibly be any truth in the rumour that Blake's 42-year sentence corresponded to evidence produced at the trial about the number of British agents he had betrayed to imprisonment or death, he told us that this story was 'absolute rubbish' and said we could quote him on that.[16] His statement to John was not quite incompatible with this, since making an allegation is not the same as adducing evidence, but it did put matters in a very different light. We agreed that at an early stage during the trial, Pat and I should again apply for the transcripts of the *in camera* proceedings to be disclosed to us so that this matter could be settled once and for all.

As far as the abuse of process application was concerned, John had had both bad and good news. The bad news was that they had not managed to track down Rollo Watts; the good news was that Kevin O'Connor was flying over from Dublin for the hearing. It only remained to ensure that we could also call Inspector Bird. To this end John obtained later that day a witness summons obliging Bird to 'attend before the Central Criminal Court, Old Bailey … there to give evidence and produce the following documents or things:

> 'All those documents not so far disclosed to the defence relating to the investigation, prosecution and disposal of the escape of George Blake and in particular all those documents referred to and considered in the statement of the above witness made on 7th March 1990. And in addition all documents relating to decision to proceed, not to proceed, prosecute or not prosecute from 1961 to today's date.'

We were now ready to join battle.

16 See page 255 of *The Blake Escape*.

Chapter 8:

The Home Secretary Intervenes

Wednesday 25th April was again bright and sunny, heralding a glorious hot summer. We got up early, tensed for the day ahead and walked to the nearest British Rail station at Haringey to take the train and tube to St Pauls. At a newspaper shop opposite the station I bought a Guardian and found that the lead story on the Home News page was a piece about the trial by Richard Norton-Taylor headed 'Crown in the dock as spy case opens.' There was a large picture of Pat at the top left of the page with a caption underneath which read: 'Pat Pottle at his home, which is already the subject of a confiscation order, should he be found guilty;' there were also inset photos of George Blake and myself. It was an entirely sympathetic piece, quoting from what Geoffrey Robertson had said at the hearing before Mr Justice Auld in March that the police had known about our involvement 20 years ago and 'had details which even Inspector Clouseau could not avoid connecting with these defendants.' The report also noted our intention to plead not guilty and quoted Ben Birnberg as saying that we would do so 'to expose … the cruel and inhuman sentence passed on George Blake, and the danger to democracy posed by the Security Service in Britain.' There was a good piece too by Nick Cohen in the Independent which mentioned the international petition calling for the charges to be dropped, noting that former Czech dissidents were among the signatories to it and recalling that I had organised protests in Warsaw Pact countries against the Russian invasion of Czechoslovakia in 1968 and helped smuggle literature into the country.

Outside the court we met up with Pat and Sue. The last time Pat and I had been there together had been in February 1962 when we faced charges under Section 1 of the Official Secrets Act for organising the Committee of 100 Wethersfield demonstration. In those days you walked up the broad stone steps to the imposing main entrance. But more than 20 years of the Irish troubles, and bombing campaigns on the British mainland, had altered all that. Now everyone involved in court proceedings, from witnesses and defendants, to prosecuting and defence council used a small side entrance lower down the building, and had to announce their business to security staff seated behind toughened glass panels.

This is followed by airport style security. A revolving door allows through only one person at a time, who then places his or her bags on a conveyor belt for X-Ray examination, and has to walk through a screening arch which tests for metallic objects. Visitors, however, including the relatives of the accused, have to use a separate, shabby side entrance at the north end of the building and climb up flights of stone steps to the gallery over the courtroom. Surprisingly, they are not subjected to screening. There was already a queue at the visitors' entrance by the time Anne and Sue found it and they were lucky to get a place inside at all. Again this was quite different from 1962 when relatives had been able to sit in the well of the court.

I felt a surge of confidence as Pat and I walked into the imposing, oak-panelled courtroom. The formal lay-out, the wigs and gowns, the archaic procedures, seemed faintly ridiculous rather than intimidating. No doubt it helped that I had been here before, once in this very No 1 courtroom, once in one of the other courtrooms in the building. In due course Pat and I would be sent down and that was not a happy prospect. But we had always known that. Meanwhile the trial itself gave us a platform to put our case, and an opportunity to test our wits against the professionals.

For the time being, however, it was the professionals' turn. Pat and myself sat in the well of the court on the right hand side (as you face the judge), a few rows behind our legal team. The two Crown Counsel were also in front of us, slightly to our right, with the visitor's gallery, jutting out into the courtroom immediately behind us. Julian Bevan was much as Pat had described him – slim build, affable, anxious almost to the point of self-deprecation that we should not see him as a demon figure bent on exacting retribution. Calvert-Smith was of similar physical build but entirely different in style and personality. He was reserved and distant, and there was a nasal twang to his speech which increased the impression of aloofness – perhaps unfairly.

Much of the argument was highly technical, involving the lengthy citation of cases. But the main issues were straightforward enough. Had there been excessive delay on the part of the authorities in bringing the prosecution? Had our defence been prejudiced by the delay? Should the Watts' report and other documents for which the Crown were claiming Public Interest Immunity be disclosed? And should the defence be permitted to call two live witnesses, Inspector Bird who had examined all the documents appertaining to the case, and Kevin O'Connor who had talked to Watts in 1984?

The order of play, so to speak, was as follows. First Geoffrey Robertson and Julian Bevan made brief opening statements outlining their positions, and then in turn made their full presentations. Anthony Scrivener began his presentation at the end of day one, continuing into the next day, Thursday. After further argument and exchanges involving the judge and all three counsel, Robertson and Bevan made their concluding speeches. Macpherson gave his ruling on the application on the Friday afternoon.

Geoffrey Robertson in his brief opening statement said was that the police had known of our involvement since 1970 and had taken no action. The charges were not so serious that they should be pursued whatever the lapse of time; this was evident from the fact that the main charge of aiding a prisoner to escape carried a maximum sentence of five years. The judge should set aside the Public Interest Immunity (PII) claim of the Attorney General because the documents in question, particularly the Watts' report, might show who decided and on what grounds, not to pursue an investigation once our involvement was known in 1970. There was a particularly strong case for doing so in a criminal case where the normal balancing act to decide between conflicting interests should not apply.

Bevan in his opening concentrated on persuading the judge to set aside the witness summons on Inspector Bird. If he went into the witness box and was subjected to cross-examination by counsel he, Bevan, would simply have to repeat that the documents in question fell into a class to which Public Interest Immunity applied. In any case Bird could only offer hearsay evidence and we did not need to go behind the PII claim.

Macpherson commented that PII claims could be challenged in court. However he ruled that the witness summons on Inspector Bird had not been made out in the proper form and that he was therefore setting it aside. For the time being, he was not prepared to order the disclosure of further documents, and asked Geoffrey to continue his presentation on the Abuse of Process application.

Geoffrey now put an argument which Pat and myself found acutely embarrassing. Indeed when he had suggested it at one of the legal conferences we made clear that we did not want it to be put. He argued that the fact that no action was taken against us in 1970 when Seán Bourke had all but named us in his book had aroused a false expectation on our part that the issue was no longer alive and that no action would be taken against us when we published our book. This was an ingenious attempt to show that, despite our open and repeated acknowledgement of our involvement in the Blake escape, our case had been prejudiced by the elapse of 20 years between the time the police definitely knew of our involvement and the instituting of proceedings against us. We could see why Geoffrey wanted to put this argument, but it was not less embarrassing for that. It demonstrated indeed the problem of being represented at any stage of a political case. Quite understandably, the barrister's priority is to present a legal argument that might secure his or her client's acquittal – or in this instance ensure that no trial would take place. Our priority was to put our case to the court and the public. Neither Pat nor I wanted to go to prison, but we would prefer that to muddying the moral and political argument with suggestions that had no foundation in fact. We had written our book in the first place primarily to put the record straight, and it would defeat that purpose if we now advanced spurious arguments to evade prosecution. We both resolved to raise this matter again with Geoffrey at the earliest opportunity.

Geoffrey moved on to discuss the implications of previous cases in which prosecutions had been halted because of undue delays in bringing them.

Bevan in his presentation said had been no delay whatever in this case for there had been no evidence to substantiate charges until Randle and Pottle published their book. In 1970, after Seán Bourke's book was published they became suspects, but no more than suspects; there was no actual evidence on which to charge them. He continued:

> **Neither of them were visited by the police in 1970, and nor were their houses searched. Why not? My Lord, the answer is simple: it would have been a fruitless exercise. We are dealing then and today with two highly politically active individuals who had spent time in prison in 1962. Had they been questioned they would have refused to make any statement. This is in fact what happened when they were interviewed by the police seventeen years later, in October 1987, following the publication of an article in the Sunday Times by Barrie Penrose which named them. Barrie Penrose, too, was unable to provide any evidence against Pottle and Randle.**

Lunch break – and we all adjourned to the pub across the road for a beer and a cheese or ham roll. The pub was heaving, but we were able to sit on a bench outside in the sunshine. We were joined by a number of journalists, including Richard Norton-Taylor from the Guardian who had become a personal friend, and John Mullin from the Scotsman. Also with us was the British Isles' correspondent for the leftist German daily paper, *Die Tageseitung* (Taz), Ralf Sotschek. Ralf is big and round, instinctively as well as intellectually sympathetic to our case, who is married to an Irishwoman, Aine, and lives in Dublin. He learned his English in Belfast and Dublin and speaks it with a wonderfully hybrid accent, mainly Irish, with Irish expressions and turns of phrase, but with an occasional German inflection coming through. We were to meet Aine later that year and struck up a friendship with both her and Ralf which has continued ever since.

After lunch, Bevan completed his presentation. 'When Pottle and Randle published their book in 1989,' he said, 'and took part in a TV documentary about the escape, the police had real evidence for the first time to support a charge. The defendants were arrested within days, and since then there had been no delay in bringing a prosecution.

> **'Could they now have a fair trial? Of course they could! They are charged with a serious offence ...'**
> **Macpherson: 'Helping a prisoner to escape is, of course, a very serious offence ...'**
> **Bevan: 'They assisted a convicted spy to escape, and it is in the public interest there should be a prosecution.'**

He agreed that very prolonged delay could be regarded as oppressive. But this was where the delay occurred between having evidence and doing something about it, or between a defendant being charged and brought to trial. The police had no evidence prior to 1989. In the Cherry case, which Mr Robertson had cited, the judge had stated that the defence had to show that the delay caused general prejudice and unfairness. Here the defence was not prejudiced. Mr Robertson had argued that the delay led the defendants to expect that there would be no prosecution. However, on page 243 of their book, the two men had written:

> If we are arrested and the case goes to trial we intend to plead Not Guilty. This does not mean we will at any point deny that we helped Blake to escape – the Not Guilty pleas would be a pure technicality to allow us to present our case and call witnesses as to the kinds of activities British and Western Intelligence agencies have engaged in during the period after the Second World War.

And on page 284 they had stated:

> Although we are convinced we were justified in breaking the law by helping Blake to escape, we do not claim any special rights or privileges and are prepared if necessary to face trial and go to prison for what we did.

The TV documentary also provided the police with evidence. The transcript of the documentary formed exhibit 32 of the prosecution evidence. On page 1086 both men confirmed their role in the escape, and on page 1110 Randle had stated:

> Well I think it is now up to the authorities to decide, after twenty-two years, whether they want to prosecute us, and we are quite prepared to face prosecution. We do not, in breaking the law, claim any different position from anybody else, and having broken the law, we are quite prepared to face trial and to face imprisonment if it comes to that.

Here, of course, Bevan was quite right. We had always assumed we would be prosecuted if we published our book, and had been warned by our solicitors that the rules of evidence were such that our self-confessions could be used as the basis of a prosecution.

At this point Macpherson ruled that there was no need for the Crown to call Inspector Bird. Any cross-examination of him 'would reach a dead end.'

Geoffrey's reply concentrated on the things the police could have done in 1970 after they had identified us from Bourke's book. 'They knew the time and date of the ferry sailing from Dover which Randle had taken when smuggling Blake out of the country, and could have checked the passenger lists. They could have carried out fingerprint and other forensic tests at Pat Pottle's flat, and could have shown photographs of Blake and Bourke to neighbours. The vehicle licensing office would have shown when Mr Randle bought and sold the camper-van, and the vehicle itself could have been checked for forensic evidence. They had done none of these things, and the inference was that someone decided not to look for evidence. The defendants' book had been written in the reasonable belief that a decision had been taken not to prosecute.

'The Watts' report may indicate who decided not to prosecute or pursue the investigation. We do not need to use our imaginations here, because this report exists. There is a paper trail which could reveal who made the decision and at what level.'

> **Macpherson: 'I will be making no further order of discovery. I can put everyone out of pain on that point.'**

The first afternoon ended with Anthony Scrivener making a start on his presentation. He concentrated on the reasons for calling Inspector Bird. He had made statements on which there was no evidence before the court and his statement was not evidence unless he appeared in the Box.

> **Macpherson: 'What would you ask Bird?'**
> **Scrivener: 'I would ask him – On what evidence did you base your judgements?'**

There were three possibilities, he suggested. The first was that the police had no evidence in 1970; we would want to probe that. The second was that there was no diligent enquiry based on evidence in the hands of the police in 1970. If that was the case, then to proceed now would be an abuse of process. The third was that there was a policy decision in 1970 not to prosecute – in which case, again, a trial now would be an abuse. The prosecution had referred to evidence and judgements but had called no-one for us to cross-examine. In the last paragraph of his statement of 7th March, Inspector Bird had referred to the fact that a number of MPs had signed a motion urging that Pottle and Randle should not be permitted to gain from their alleged crime. This suggested that the prosecution was the result of political pressure. He would want to question Bird about this part of his statement.

He continued to press for the disclosure of documents. There were times when disclosure would be against the public interest, but other times when withholding documents would be so. The court had to decide which interest predominated. In the Australian case of Sankey v. Whitlam and others (1978), where the documents in question were Cabinet papers, it was held that there was no absolute or permanent right to immunity against disclosure even for these. In the present case, the prosecution were not submitting that disclosure of a particular document was prejudicial but that the documents belonged to a class to which PII applied.

At 4.30 the court adjourned. Next day's broadsheet papers gave the case good coverage. 'Evidence on Blake escape "20 years old" ' was the headline above Richard Norton-Taylor's report in the Guardian. The Times report by John Young was headed 'Prosecutions over Blake's escape "would be unfair!" ', and there was an inset photograph of Pat and me looking very pleased with ourselves – but taken, I should add, some time earlier. There was a full report also in the Scotsman by John Mullin who noted that 'both defence barristers made a lengthy critique of Mr Bevan's arguments, pouring scorn on the contention that police in 1970 never had the evidence to mount a case.'

Thursday's proceedings were dominated by the Crown's production of a certificate signed by the Home Secretary, Mr Waddington, on 24th April claiming Public Interest Immunity for all the documents our barristers were requesting to be disclosed. 'They are internal police reports,' the certificate said, 'in pursuance of criminal investigations. As such they belong to a class of documents which should be protected from production ...' He advanced four reasons why documents in this class should not be disclosed.

> First, it was necessary for the police pursuing investigations to be able to comment freely; they might also contain allegations against suspects who were not subsequently charged or lines of enquiry which had not yet been pursued;
>
> Second, they might contain information received in confidence, and if it were to be thought that such documents might at some future date pass into the field of public scrutiny, such information would not be forthcoming; informants, too, might be put in danger;
>
> Third, individuals who had featured in police reports might be 'held up to public suspicion and contempt';
>
> Fourth, it was undesirable that the inner working of the criminal

investigation process should be revealed since this information might prove to be of use to criminals.[1]

Macpherson's first reaction to the production of the Home Secretary's certificate was to say that it settled the issue. But Scrivener at once challenged this; it was for the court, he insisted, to decide where the balance of interest lay. We were not asking for the disclosure of reports from the police to the DPP but simply reports passing between police officers. He denounced the sweeping terms of the certificate:

In my thirty years in the courts, he said,
I have never seen a certificate in this form which gives blanket protection for all internal police documents. If it were allowed, the administration of justice would be greatly affected. The defence would be unable to see any internal report recording what a witness had told the police. Nor could they do so in cases where there were allegations that the police had beaten someone up.
The Guildford Four would still be in prison because in their case it was internal documents which revealed that dishonesty had taken place.
Just when we were getting to a period of openness, this would be a step back to the Middle Ages.

Scrivener also pressed for us to be allowed to call Bird and O'Connor. If Bird was not called, his statement could not be challenged. Moreover, Bevan had asserted things that were not contained in Bird's statement – for instance that no enquiries could be made in 1970. In the *Cherry* case, a police officer was called upon to give evidence in court.

But Macpherson was not persuaded and rejected the application to call Bird. Undeterred, Scrivener continued, demanding to know why, if the police had no evidence in 1970, they took no steps to obtain it.

Scrivener: 'Bill Sykes would have got away with murder if the police in Oliver Twist had taken that attitude.'
Macpherson: (dryly) 'Bill Sykes didn't have the benefit of the advice of Mr Benedict Birnberg!'

Macpherson took a step back from completely ruling out calling Bird and O'Connor, saying he would consider the issue of the documents first and then come back to the matter of calling witnesses.

Geoffrey Robertson took over and asked again for the four documents mentioned in Bird's list. He concentrated, however, on the Watts' report. This was written on 23rd March 1970 although Bourke's book was not published until June. Thus the police could have moved during those three months,

1 For the full text of Waddington's Certificate, see Appendix 1

interviewed Randle and Pottle, carried out searches and so forth. The Watts' report should be disclosed because it was 'on the cards' that it would throw light on why no action was taken. Bevan had informed the defence that the Watts' report had been sent to the Director of Public Prosecutions and the Home Office at the time.

Bevan interrupted him.

> **'The Watts' report,' he said, 'was sent to the DPP and the Home Office – but the advice of the DPP and the Home Office was not sought. No decision by the DPP or anyone else at that time.' Despite this qualification, Bevan's public admission that the Watts's report had gone to the DPP was highly significant. Why would it have been sent to him if not for him to consider initiating a prosecution? Robertson had the bit between his teeth.**
>
> **'Now that we know the Watts' report was sent to the DPP and the Home Secretary, it is clear that the matter was handled by the police at senior level in communication with these two ministers. The strong inference is that the authorities made a decision not to proceed. If it is the case that a policy decision was made by the DPP, then clearly the abuse of process application would be irrefutable.**

Robertson went on to consider Waddington's certificate in detail. Paragraph 2 of the document made it clear that the claim was based on the class of documents not on their content. This weakened the arguments he was putting forward in the rest of the document. Paragraph 3 would bar the disclosure of even the most routine of police reports. However, various judgements supported the view that in criminal cases especially the fullest possible evidence should be available to the defence. Time also affected the argument put forward in paragraph 4, namely that police reports might contain information which had been received in confidence, and the argument in paragraph 6 about revealing police methods since the documents in question were over 20 years old. As for the risk, mentioned in paragraph 6, of exposing individuals who had come under suspicion, or against whom allegations had been made, this could be dealt with very simply by blocking out the names.

> **Macpherson: Where does it take us if the police did decide to take no action in 1970.**
>
> **Robertson: If Rollo Watts concluded in 1970 that Randle and Pottle were involved, a decision must have been made not to pursue the matter.**
>
> **Macpherson: So what? What's to stop the authorities from proceeding in 1989?**
>
> **Robertson: There is of course no statute of limitation. It is simply a question of fairness.**

Macpherson: Even if a policy decision was made, I still have to decide if it is fair for the case to go ahead now.
Robertson: Your Lordship would have to decide if it would be right for the trial to go ahead twenty-three years after the event, and twenty years after a decision had been made that it would not be in the public interest to proceed. The alleged offence is a serious one, but not so heinous that a prosecution ought to proceed no matter what time had elapsed.
Macpherson: I have to decide.
Robertson: Clearly it would have been right to prosecute in 1970. But if a decision was made in 1970 not to proceed, how could it be right to do so in 1990?

Over lunch we talked with the lawyers.

'By rights Macpherson really ought to let O'Connor take the witness stand,' Tony Scrivener said, adding with a chuckle: 'But I think I can wind him up sufficiently so that he'll refuse. That will give us an appeal point later on.'

When we returned to the court Geoffrey completed his presentation followed by Scrivener who continued to press for the disclosure of documents. Macpherson interrupted him: The only disclosure I would consider making is the Watts' report.[Addressing Bevan]. Could I see it?'

Bevan: Your Lordship will understand that I am wearing two hats here. As the representative of the Crown, I have to support the claim for Public Interest Immunity for the Watts' report. However, as the prosecutor in this case, I also have a duty to disclose everything relevant to the defence. The PII certificate can be waived only if it is thought likely to help the defence; that principle would have to be fulfilled. I have assured you that I have carried out my duty to the defence. The defence therefore are saying 'we cannot accept your word'. A judge has the power to assure himself that the Crown has fulfilled its duty to show the defence relevant documents. However, I don't want to set a precedent here.
Judge: How long is Watts?
Bevan: Six or seven pages.

Macpherson said he would dismiss the application for its disclosure and didn't need to see it. However, as a double check he would look at it though he did not intend to order its disclosure.

From the back of the court, Bird came forward with a large brown envelope which was handed to the judge. He had already opened the envelope and was about to pull out the document when – to Pat's and my surprise – Scrivener objected:

Scrivener: If your lordship thinks we have a case, he should examine the documents. Otherwise not.

Judge: If you don't want me to look at it, I won't.

Geoffrey: There is no suggestion by the defence that the Crown has not fulfilled its duty.

Macpherson put down the envelope.

Macpherson: I am making no further order for the discovery of documents.

The grounds for the objection by our Counsel to the judge personally checking the Watts' report has always puzzled me. It can hardly have been to save the feelings of Prosecuting Counsel; he had given us an assurance before the application ever began that there was nothing to assist us in the Watts' report yet this had not prevented our side from pressing for its disclosure. In a sense by demanding the disclosure we were casting doubt if not on Bevan's integrity then at least on his judgement. Presumably the real reason for the objection by our two counsel was that Macpherson had clearly made up his mind in advance that he would not order the disclosure of the report and we stood a better chance of getting hold of it if the matter came up before another judge at a later stage.

Scrivener said he would move on to the argument about Kevin O'Connor taking the stand.

Macpherson: I can tell you now that I am not going to grant this.

Scrivener, in real or simulated rage, slammed his papers down on the bench in front of him.

'If your lordship is not even prepared to listen to my argument, there is no point in my continuing.'

He sat down. The display had visibly affected the judge.

Macpherson: Please, Mr Scrivener, continue. Obviously I will consider what you have to say on the matter.

Scrivener stood up again. Watts he said had been involved from the start in the enquiries into the Blake Escape. In 1966, as an Inspector in Special Branch he had conducted a number of interviews in connection with the escape. In 1970, by then a Chief Inspector, he had identified Pottle and Randle from clues in Seán Bourke's book. He had told Kevin O'Connor that a decision was taken not to prosecute, and this information was passed on to Randle by O'Connor in 1987.

'Macpherson: I will not allow Mr O'Connor to take the stand, but I will accept his Section 9 statement.

Ben half-turned to Pat and myself, and we all gave one another the thumbs up; Scrivener had won his appeal point. Macpherson saw us and scowled.

After Scrivener finished, Geoffrey and Bevan summed up their argument. Macpherson then announced that he would give his decision on the application the next day, Friday, at 2pm. It would take approximately 20 minutes.

Since it was quite evident that Macpherson would find against us, the solicitors began at once to make arrangements to seek an *ex parte* judicial review in the Divisional Court – the Queen's Bench Division of the High Court. The principal difficulty was that it was not clear that the Divisional Court had jurisdiction to deal with such an application from a Crown Court. However, by the time we returned to court on Friday afternoon the lawyers had arranged for a hearing before a single judge, Mr Justice Hodgson, to adjudicate on the jurisdiction issue. If he found in our favour the case would then go to a full hearing before two judges at a later date.

Macpherson, as anticipated, turned down our application on abuse of process. The crucial passages are those dealing with his reasons for not allowing Bird and O'Connor to be called to give evidence, and his reasons for rejecting the applications: On the first point, he had this to say:

> **My reason for not allowing evidence to be called [in relation to Bird's statement] extended later to an application made by Mr Robertson, on behalf of both the accused, to hear orally the evidence of Mr. Kevin O'Connor, a journalist, who had a conversation with Mr Watts in 1984. It seemed to me absolutely clear that it would be wrong to conduct this application as if it were a full trial. Such procedure would simply be inapt. For example, Mr Bird would, in connection with 1970, be able to say nothing other than that which he had learned from the documents and reports. Mr. O'Connor would be able to say no more than that he had been told that which is set out in his statement. Cross-examination properly conducted would truly lead nowhere and factual issues, as such, are not truly involved at this stage. I agreed, however, with Mr. Bevan's acceptance, that I would look at the O'Connor statements simply as part of the information contained in varied and indeed voluminous documents which have been put before me. Regina v Pottle and Randle (Revised) Ruling on Application to Stay Proceedings, p.3.**

Macpherson's judgement concludes:

> **I have come firmly to the conclusion that these applications fail, and for the following reasons.**
>
> **1. In 1966 there was no evidence against these two men.**
>
> **2. In 1970 there was, as a fact, still no evidence against them which would stand up in a court of law. Whatever I or others may feel now about the steps which might have been taken in 1970, the fact is that**

nothing further was done and there was no case to put before the court. I do not believe that this inactivity is so reprehensible that it should be held to outweigh all the other considerations.

Indeed, neither I nor anybody else can know fully what the situation was in 1970. Four years had passed. And I am simply faced with the important but, in my judgment, not overwhelming fact that nothing was done, and that a decision was made at the time to do no more. I do not accept that the use of the expression "policy decision" advances the defence case. If that means a decision to abandon any idea of prosecution or a high level decision that nothing would ever be done about the case, then there is no evidence of any such decision having been made at all. I prefer simply to accept that at that time the matter could not and would not be prosecuted. The defendants were never informed that the cloud had lifted. No positive step of any kind was taken to lead them to a conclusion that all was forgotten and over. Indeed, insofar as it is relevant, their own book suggests nothing of the kind. And, as Mr. Bevan stressed, they certainly knew in 1987, before they wrote the book, that the case was not dead.

3. I believe that it would be quite wrong to suggest that the offences said to have been committed, if proved, are anything other than serious offences. They are very serious in themselves. They were not offences which allowed a man to be freed from a short sentence arising from a slight crime. They involved, if proved, the freeing of a notorious traitor.

4. The anxiety and the personal position of these two men is of course palpable. And I take those factors into account, of course, as one of the heads of relevant circumstances and considerations which the cases and common sense and humanity indicate must be taken into account.

5. The relevant material for this prosecution is now that which is set out in the defendant's own book and television admissions, should those matters be true. That material was not available until April, 1989.

6. The charges made are simple. There is no complexity in the case as charged or the evidence to be led by the Crown.

7. Nobody has suggested that there are any missing witnesses or any particular problems for the defence in presenting its case. Guilt or innocence is of course not under discussion at all today. And, indeed, since there will now be a trial on Monday, I say nothing at all about any view which I may hold about the likely outcome of the case. That is wholly irrelevant and that will be a matter for the jury.

8. The passage of these 23 years, particularly the years since 1970, is, of course, apparent. It is the background of the whole case. But it has

> to be looked at in the light, particularly, of the nature and seriousness of this particular case.
>
> 9. I do not accept that any improper pressures or motives have actuated the prosecuting authorities. Of course, there has been comment, probably both ways, from the public and in Parliament. But I detect no improper pressure of any kind. The procedure for freezing the book's proceeds is not a matter for me at this stage. An order to that effect has in any event been made by another judge. That will not in any way influence the course of this case.
>
> Against that background, I have had to form my own value judgement. I stress, finally, then, that justice and fairness are not one sided. Those who sympathise with these two men who now have to face trial should bear that well in mind. I believe that the nature and seriousness of the alleged offences and all the relevant circumstances establish beyond any doubt that it is fair, right and just that this case should proceed. I say again that its outcome will be decided next week by a jury. That is for the future. I detect at this stage no such unfairness, nor such prejudice to these two men as to allow me to impose a stay. The Crown have satisfied me beyond any doubt that the case should proceed and these applications are accordingly dismissed.

Having delivered his judgement, Macpherson confirmed that the trial proper would commence on Monday morning. Scrivener informed him that Pat and I would not be represented at the trial as we had elected to defend ourselves. Macpherson turned to us in what appeared to be genuine consternation.

> 'I am very sorry indeed to hear this,' he told us. 'You have in Mr Robertson and Mr Scrivener two of the country's leading barristers.'

Scrivener then told him about the High Court hearing on the following Tuesday, and suggested the commencement of the trial should be postponed until the Wednesday at least.

> Macpherson: 'Well now, that depends, doesn't it, on how confident I am of my judgement.'

Mr Bevan intervened with a 'helpful' suggestion. His opening statement would not be lengthy and he expected to have completed it by lunchtime. The prosecution then proposed to give the members of the juries copies of the defendants' book to read and to suggest that they should be given several days to do so. 'It would be quite unfair,' he added for the prosecution to pick out particular passages in the book without giving the jury the opportunity to read it in its entirety.' If his lordship was agreeable to this proposal, the case could open as planned on Monday, and the defendants would still be free to attend the Divisional Court the next day.

It all sounded so reasonable and helpful, and it seemed for a moment that Counsel would go along with it. But Pat and I were astonished, for this was virtually to assume that the High Court application would fail. I jumped up and tugged John Wadham's elbow.

Supposing we win?' I said.

There was a hasty discussion among the lawyers and then this point was put to the judge. He turned and addressed us directly:

> **Since you are going to be defending yourselves, what is your feeling on the matter. Do you want the opening of the trial postponed until Wednesday?'**
>
> **I think this would be best,' Pat said.**
>
> **'Very well then,' Macpherson said. 'I will see you back here at ten o'clock on Wednesday.'**

Chapter 9:

Leave to Appeal

On Monday, 30th April Pat and I met John and Ben at the latter's office to discuss tactics. The Divisional Court (High Court) hearing on the preliminary issue of jurisdiction the following day would be heard by a Mr Justice Hodgson. He was unlikely, however, to grant us leave since to do so would create a legal precedent. We therefore needed to be fully prepared for the beginning of the trial on Wednesday.

We mainly discussed whether or not to challenge the suitability of the judge to hear the case in view of the fact that he had been serving in the SAS when Pat and I were imprisoned in 1962 over the Wethersfield demonstration and was still an honorary colonel in that regiment. The chief argument against doing so was that it would mean delaying still further the commencement of the trial. Ben and John both planned to be in court as 'McKenzie Friends'[1] – which is to say they could advise us on legal issues and points of procedure during the trial, though they could not conduct any cross-examination, or address the court on our behalf.

They had one interesting piece of information about the judicial review: the court had instructed a senior Treasury solicitor, John Laws, to act as *amicus curiae* – a 'friend of the court' to advise it on issues of law. This suggested some uncertainty on the part of the Crown about the outcome of the hearing.

Tony Scrivener next day didn't seem in much doubt about it when I saw him in the High Court, just before the commencement of the hearing. While we were standing in the corridor outside the courtroom he took me on one side and said in a low voice:

> **'You do understand the strategy here, don't you? We will lose this one – but it will give us points for an appeal after the tria1.'**

The main lobby of the building is a lofty cathedral-like hall with high gothic windows, and, underneath them, low archways along either side. The archways lead via winding stone steps to the narrow corridors which give access

1 A McKenzie friend is someone, not necessarily legally qualified, who is present in court to assist a defendant conducting his or her own defence. The name somes from the civil case of *McKenzie v McKenzie 1970.*

to the courtrooms. To my surprise while we were waiting in the corridor I spotted both Julian Bevan and Calvert-Smith.

'How come they're here?' I asked John Wadham. 'We weren't able to be present when they had an *ex-parte* hearing.

John shrugged.

'There's nothing to stop them coming,' he said, 'Presumably they won't be addressing the court.'

You couldn't avoid bumping into your adversaries in the narrow space and soon afterwards I saw Julian Bevan approaching accompanied by a stocky, red-faced man, rather like a cut-down version of our old adversary Manningham-Buller, later Lord Dilhorne, who prosecuted Pat, myself and others in 1962 – and also George Blake the previous year.

Bevan stopped when he reached us while his companion walked on.

'That's Mr Laws,' he explained. 'He is neutral – a friend of the court who advises it on legal issues.'

I thanked him for this information. Nevertheless when we entered the courtroom I noticed that Mr Laws sat on the bench immediately in front of Bevan and Calvert Smith on the right hand side, while our barristers were on the opposite side. The room is arranged much more informally than a criminal courtroom as it deals mainly with civil cases. The judges sit at the front on a raised platform; the lawyers, litigants, police officers, and members of the public sit on the tiered wooden benches facing them. The walls are lined from floor to ceiling with law books. To the left, near the front are the press benches, facing sideways. Pat and Sue, and Anne and myself sat on the bench immediately behind Bevan and Calvert-Smith so we were able to examine their behaviour closely.

Robertson opened for us. The reason he went first had nothing to do with strategy or seniority. It was simply that as soon as he had presented his case he was rushing off to get married in Finsbury Town Hall to the Australian writer and wit Kathy Letts! He hoped to be back in court to hear Hodgson's decision before flying off on honeymoon.

We had to convince the judge on two points. First, that the High Court had jurisdiction to carry out a judicial review once a case had reached the Crown Court – or at least that there was an arguable case for jurisdiction. Second, that there was a case for saying that Macpherson had acted incorrectly in refusing to disclose the Watts' report and to allow Bird and O'Connor to give evidence.

Argument throughout the day focused mainly on the first point, for if the High Court didn't have jurisdiction, there was no point in arguing about the merits of the abuse of process application. Normally, applications for judicial review relating to abuse of process in criminal cases come from the magistrates' court, and here there is no ambiguity about the High Courts' jurisdiction. However, there had never been an instance in which the High Court had judicially reviewed a prosecution once it had reached the Crown Court.

The argument over jurisdiction, backed up by numerous references to previous cases, hinged on an apparently narrow point of law. Section 29(3) of the Supreme Court Act, 1981, extended the High Court's jurisdiction 'to make prerogative orders in relation to Crown Court decisions,' but specifically excluded from this jurisdiction 'matters relating to trial on indictment.' But was the hearing before Macpherson at the Old Bailey a matter relating to trial on indictment? No, said our counsel, it was a pre-trial issue; the arraignment of the accused had not taken place or the jury sworn in. The judge was being asked to decide whether the trial on indictment should take place at all. Yes, said Laws and Bevan. When an issue of abuse of process was raised at Magistrates' Court level, the magistrates were being asked to quash the indictment. When it arose at the Crown Court, the judge was being asked not to quash the indictment but to stay the proceedings, and this was 'manifestly … a matter relating to trial on indictment.'

Hodgson himself evidently found the issue puzzling. He even questioned the jurisdiction that Macpherson was exercising in hearing the application.

> **Hodgson: The jurisdiction that Macpherson was exercising was the inherent jurisdiction which is discretionary?**
> **Robertson: Yes it is. It was an inherent jurisdiction described by Lord Devlin in some detail in the Connelly case.**
> **Hodgson: Quite a lot of Law Lords say that it does not exist, but there we are.**
> **Robertson: Viscount Dilhorne took that view a little later, but he seems to have been outnumbered. Indeed, the Divisional Court last year, in the case of the Wapping policemen, described abuse of process as something of a growth area in the law … The Wapping police case was stopped after an eighteen month delay between the time at which the police became aware of the evidence against the police officers and the time at which the men were charged … It is quite clear that his Lordship was exercising an inherent jurisdiction based on the court's power to ensure fairness and to ensure that no citizen was put on trial which is unfair through lapse of time and that the public spectacle of man undergoing an oppressive trial is not seen …**

Robertson advanced several reasons why Macpherson's decision did not affect the conduct of a trial and was therefore subject to review by the High

Court. Firstly, while the jurisdiction to arraign and to try was a statutory one, the jurisdiction to stay proceedings on the grounds of abuse of process was an inherent one possessed by all courts. Secondly, this inherent jurisdiction to prevent unfairness to a defendant did not affect the conduct of a trial in any way; it affected whether the trial process should be embarked upon at all. Thirdly, it would be a serious anomaly if the High Court did not have the power to review an order on abuse of process made by the trial judge given that it did have such power where that same point was taken at the committal proceedings. This anomaly would also mean that the prosecution would have no redress if the abuse issue was heard in the Crown Court immediately before the trial. Defendants might in fact delay applications until after the committal proceedings so as to avoid the possibility of judicial review. Fourthly, while the applicants might be able to go to the Appeal Court following a trial, if the High Court declined jurisdiction, the mischief of an oppressive trial would already have occurred.

The substantive issue of abuse of process did not figure much in Robertson's presentation – and subsequently was not taken up at all by Laws who confined himself to considering the jurisdiction issue. However as Robertson was drawing toward the close of his address, Hodgson asked him on what grounds Macpherson's ruling would be attacked if he were to hold that the jurisdiction point was arguable at least. Robertson replied that there were four points. Macpherson had been wrong in law to rule that no evidence could be called; he was wrong to uphold the Home Secretary's PII claim over police reports which were over twenty years old; he should have inferred from the evidence that a policy decision had been taken at that time not to prosecute and therefore ruled that a trial now would be oppressive; and finally he should have ruled that a prosecution for crimes that were not of a heinous nature should not be pursued twenty-four years after the event.

> **Hodgson: What is the position so far as the jurisdiction point is concerned? Do I have to decide that?**
> **Robertson: Your Lordship has to decide jurisdiction. As far as the substantive issue [ie. the issue of abuse of process] is concerned, your Lordship merely has to be satisfied that there is an arguable case. I take the view that we should satisfy your Lordship on jurisdiction. Mr Scrivener takes the view that we have to satisfy you that there is an arguable case on jurisdiction. That is a matter that he has looked at.**

This was the first indication Pat and I had that Geoffrey and Tony were in disagreement on the issue. The latter now put his position. It would not be right, he argued, 'to encourage … a full argument on jurisdiction to take place on an application for leave…[2] The final decision on jurisdiction would be made at the full hearing before two judges if Hodgson decided there was an arguable case for them to consider.

> **My submission is that your Lordship's approach is the same as any other lead case. It is an arguable case on jurisdiction. It is not appropriate for a new procedure whereby points which go to jurisdiction, which are not infrequent, should be dealt with at a full hearing on the application for leave. It so happens that we have made sure that the prosecution were informed of the hearing today so that they should attend. Your Lordship has the added assistance, or will have of Mr Laws.**
>
> **'In my submission, all the points which arise in judicial review cases have to pass the threshold of the arguable case point. It would not be right to encourage … a full argument on jurisdiction to take place on an application for leave in each case.'**

At one point the neutral Mr Laws turned round and said to Bevan and Calvert-Smith in a voice so loud that I missed Tony's next few words: 'If he is right about that point …' and he went on to expound some legal argument.

Scrivener returned to one of Geoffrey's points which had clearly impressed the judge.

> **Scrivener: If the only route is by an appeal after conviction, there are two consequences. The first is that the prosecution do not have a right of reviewing the matter at all.**
>
> **Hodgson: That had occurred to me. I do not know what view the prosecution take about this matter. I can see that there might be a case before an assistant recorder in the Crown Court where he might be persuaded to stop a trial which is quite wrong.**
>
> **Scrivener: Yes. It becomes even more absurd if one considers this. Your Lordship rightly put to my learned friend [Robertson] 'Was this taken at committal?' It could have been. In the Wapping case … it was taken at committal. It was the prosecution who took the matter to the Divisional Court. This point could have been here at the committal stage, but it was not …**
>
> **There is then the final point on oppression. If the purpose of the procedure is to operate to prevent oppression in that the procedure should be stopped, then it would be a very strange remedy if before an appeal can be heard or a review can be heard, the whole procedure [ie. the prosecution] must be gone through. The words 'conduct of the trial' mean, in my submission, anything that happens during the**

2 Transcript, p.20 at G

> **trial once it has started ... If that be right and proper, then this court has jurisdiction, and it is right and proper that it should have and that both sides can come to this court on the question of jurisdiction and it is the appropriate place for the matter to be tried ...**
> **The final point is an important one ... A number of cases recently were quite serious cases. The court declined jurisdiction because of oppression. It has not been argued before. It is a novel point and, on novelty alone, your Lordship ought to grant leave.**

The 'neutral' Mr Laws rose. He emphasised the difference in the positions adopted by our two QCs on the question of jurisdiction: Mr Robertson had accepted that his Lordship had to decide the issue whereas Mr Scrivener had argued that he had only to be convinced that there was an arguable case for it. The latter approach, Laws argued, was 'wholly incorrect.' If on the correct interpretation of the statute there was no jurisdiction, there could be no basis on which leave could be given. This was 'a pure isolated crystalline question of construction.' Section 29 conferred jurisdiction but limited it.

> **Laws: Moving on to the words 'other than its jurisdiction in matters relating to trial on indictment' and looking at the facts of this case, it is my principal submission that a decision whether or not to stay an indictment is manifestly, and if necessary I will say unarguably, a matter relating to trial on indictment.**

Laws went on to argue the point summarised earlier. At Magistrates' court level the court, in an abuse of process application, was being asked not to commit; at Crown Court level, it was being asked to 'stay proceedings.' In law this was different. It meant that the matter remained on the file 'not to be proceeded with without the leave of the court;' in effect the judged adjourned the proceedings *sine die* [literally 'without a date', or indefinitely]. And since the question at issue at Crown Court level was whether or not to order a stay of the indictment, it followed that the hearing itself must be 'a matter relating to trial on indictment.'

Hodgson, however, was not sure whether the Crown Court hearing an application for abuse of process was being asked to stay the proceedings or quash the indictment. Moreover, if a decision by Lord Goddard in the case of Downes was still binding on a Crown Court judge, then 'my brother Macpherson J. could not have done what he was being asked to do anyway. In another case, that of Connelly, it was not clear what the judge was being asked to do.'

> **Laws: The present practice is clearly not to quash the indictment but to stay the proceedings ...**
> **Hodgson: What worries me is that I do not know how I decide a**

> **jurisdiction point until I know what it is that the Crown Court judge was doing.**

A further point made by Laws was that if, as both sides agreed, the issue of abuse of process could be taken to the Appeal Court (Criminal Division) at the end of the trial, the strong implication was that it must be an issue related to trial on indictment. 'If it were otherwise,' he said, 'the implication would be that the Court of Appeal (Criminal Division) may concern matters which do not relate to trial on indictment.'

He turned to Geoffrey and Tony's point that if a Crown Court decision was not reviewable except by going to the Appeal Court at the end of the trial, the prosecution would be left without a remedy if a wrong decision was made.

> **Hodgson: You can imagine an assistant recorder being faced with Mr Robertson and Mr Scrivener.**
>
> **Laws: Yes, but I am sure that assistant recorders are made of stern stuff. The answer is to be found in Lord Bridge's speech in Smalley where he recognizes the absence of any prosecution remedy …**
>
> **If it is the prosecutor who is aggrieved by such a decision, it is in no way surprising that he has no remedy, since prosecutors have never enjoyed rights of appeal or review when unsuccessful in trials on indictment.**

Laws' final argument was that if Hodgson granted leave, it would open the floodgates to many other cases.

> **Laws: It is also asserted that this matter is important not least because the abuse of process applications have become something of a growth industry in recent times. If that is so, then this case – never mind the merits – would mean that any and every defendant whose application for a stay on abuse grounds is refused can come to this court for leave … It is my submission as *amicus* to the court that the correct resolution of this leave application is that it should be refused for want of jurisdiction.**

The neutral Mr Laws sat down, turned round at once to Julian Bevan and Calvert-Smith, and said: 'Was that all right?'

Bevan and Calvert-Smith nodded approvingly. Bevan then stood up and told the judge that he had 'nothing to add.' What surprised Pat and myself about this was not Bevan's reply but the fact that his view had been solicited at all. In an *ex-parte* hearing brought by the defence, surely he as prosecutor had no standing in the court and therefore no right to add anything?

Geoffrey, responding, said that the Crown Court, when it found in favour of an applicant claiming abuse of process, ordered 'a permanent stay.' There was really no question of the case being resurrected after that. This was what was indicated by the *Grobb* case. He cited several other authorities, concluding on the question of whether the granting of leave to appeal would lead to a host of other applications.

> **Robertson: Finally my learned friend came to the flood gates argument, the skies will fall argument …**
> **Hodgson: That never impresses me.**
> **Robertson: Then I will say no more about it.**

Tony Scrivener began his response shortly before the lunch break, pressing the argument that the judge did not have to make a final ruling on the jurisdiction issue but simply satisfy himself that there was an arguable case for it.

> **Scrivener: There are two very good reasons why that cannot be right. The first is that the court here would always be determining this issue on a one-judge basis. The court would not be able to say 'This is a matter of such importance that it may be a two or three judge court.' The second matter, of even greater significance, is that it would deprive any applicant, who is arguing a point of jurisdiction, the right to take his case to the House of Lords, the highest court in the land. On a refusal of application for leave, you cannot get to the house of Lords. What would happen is that there would therefore be created a special class of case, namely cases which deal with jurisdiction. In that class of case, the final court will be the Court of Appeal in the case of a civil matter, and in the case of a criminal matter it will be the Divisional Court. That is where it would end.**

Hodgson seemed inclined to agree.

> **Hodgson: I am quite worried about the question as to whether I think the jurisdiction point is arguable and whether I should give leave. When I glanced at the papers and without thinking through it very carefully, I thought that if it was arguable I ought to give leave.**

When we met up with the legal team at the lunch break, Geoffrey and Tony were on a high. Hodgson seemed likely after all, to grant us leave to appeal.

> **'Laws made a big mistake,' Tony explained, gleefully, 'when he put forward the "floodgates" argument. I know Hodgson. He never has any time for that argument.'**

Resuming after lunch – while Geoffrey hurried off to get married – Scrivener accepted Laws' argument that we would eventually have the right to appeal to the Appeal Court (Criminal Division) – but if the prosecution was oppressive, as we contended, it would be odd to say that there could be no remedy until after trial and conviction. Section 29 made the courts of record amenable to the jurisdiction of the Divisional Court for the first time. He then pressed home the advantage over the floodgates issue:

> **Scrivener: 'I am not going to address your Lordship on a floodgates argument. I have seen the way your Lordship has dealt with other cases on that basis before.'**

Laws, by contrast, prudently avoided raising that issue again when he made his final address to the court. He concentrated instead on persuading the judge that he must give a definite ruling on the question of jurisdiction.

> **Laws: My friend says with great energy that once your Lordship says that there is an arguable point here, then, on the ordinary principles applicable to leave applications, leave should go. This misapprehends the position. The fact that my friend and I are able to advance separate and opposing arguments does not demonstrate that the matter is arguable once your Lordship has concluded the question. If I persuade your Lordship that there is no jurisdiction, then, in the eye of the law and subject to any higher court, it is not arguable …**

But Hodgson was not persuaded. After a short adjournment, he announced his decision that the case should go before two judges to decide the issue. The key passage in his full judgement reads:

> If I were going to make a decision in this case, as at present advised, I am undecided as to how I should decide it and, if Mr Laws is right, I would, as at present advised, take time to consider not only the arguments that have been put before me but also, which I think may be important, the actual nature of the jurisdiction which my brother Macpherson J. was exercising. But I have decided that it would not be right for me on an application for leave made *ex parte*, although, as I have acknowledged, with the great assistance of Mr Laws, to come to a decision on a point which I consider arguable and indeed difficult.
>
> In those circumstances it does seem to me that the right thing I should do is to grant leave to move for judicial review to these applicants. I also think that there ought obviously to be as much expedition as possible. [3]

We were jubilant at this unexpected success – the lawyers especially.

In my case, however, – and Pat's too – the jubilation was tempered by a certain sense of anti-climax after we had keyed ourselves up for the courtroom battle and the prison sentence that would follow it. Now there would be several more weeks – perhaps months – of delay. Nor did the lawyers hold forth any prospect of an ultimate victory in the High Court, or of any outcome but conviction and imprisonment once the case reached the Old Bailey. When I spoke to Tony in the corridor outside the courtroom he again pressed me to

3 Court Transcript as approved by the judge, p.5.

reconsider my plea and said he would be more than willing to represent me at the trial if I did so.

The ambiguity of Pat's and my feelings was expressed in comments we made to the reporters who surrounded us as soon as we left the courtroom. 'We want the trial,' I said, 'to be over as quickly as possible, but on the other hand the trial judge made a number of mistakes last week, so it is right they should be reviewed.' Pat's comment was characteristically forthright: 'We were all geared up for the start of the case tomorrow morning. Mr Justice Macpherson last week had the bat and the ball and seemed to be making up the rules as he went along, but now the umpire has pulled him up.'[4]

On Tuesday, the broadsheet newspapers emphasised the unprecedented nature of Hodgson's decision.[5] Richard Norton-Taylor in the Guardian noted that 'Mr Hodgson's decision means that for the first time the High Court has given leave for a challenge at this stage of criminal proceedings on what lawyers described as an abuse of process issue. It is understood that lawyers in other trials with arguments over delays and alterations in the charges have been closely watching this case.' Andrew Moncur in the same paper added a titbit in the Diary section on Geoffrey Robertson's performance:

> A remarkably cool show by barrister Geoffrey Robertson at the High Court in London yesterday. He was there as counsel for Pat Pottle, half of the Wormwood Scrubs Two, charged with helping to spring from jail the double agent George Blake. A significant legal argument had to be thrashed out. The hearing plodded on. Not a sign of haste or anxiety from Mr Robertson. But at 2.30pm he finally had to depart – just five minutes before it all ended in his favour. And where was he off to? Finsbury Town Hall. Why? To get married to Kathy Letts. [6]

Now, however, there was a new problem. Immediately after the High Court hearing, and without consulting our solicitors or barristers, the Prosecution had arranged for the hearing before two judges to take place a fortnight later on 16th May. As it turned out neither Geoffrey nor Tony were available on that date. Pat and I met John Wadham at the offices of Liberty – whose Legal Adviser he had recently become – on Thursday 5th May. John thought the most likely outcome at the resumed High Court hearing was that the judges would find against us on the issue of jurisdiction. In fact our case

4 *Scotsman*, 2 May 1990.p.2. Report by John Mullen.

5 See the reports in *The Times*, *Guardian*, *Independent*, *Daily Telegraph* and *Scotsman.*

6 Guardian, 2 May 1990.

had been 'listed for mention' at the Old Bailey on the following day – that is to say provisionally booked to take place. However, if we lost on the jurisdiction issue at the High Court we could seek leave to appeal to the Lords and John thought we probably could obtain a Certificate to say the issue was one of public importance, the first step in getting to the Lords. The lawyers were also applying for a postponement of the hearing. If it was delayed, or if it went ahead and we were granted leave to appeal to the Lords, the chances were that Macpherson would be off the case by the time it got back to the Old Bailey. In fact the Listings Officer there had told our solicitors that there might not be time to have the trial before October.

The prospect of such a considerable delay was far from welcome to us. But John had more cheering news. Tom Mackinnon had managed to track down an address for Rollo Watts in West London – or at any rate an address where he had been living up to two or three years ago. He had tracked him down through past records at Companies House where he was listed as a director of Saladin Security. So at last there was a realistic prospect of serving him with a witness summons and forcing him to come to court. John warned us however that unless Waddington's claim for Public Interest Immunity on the Watts' Report of March 1970 was set aside we would not be able to ask Watts any question about its contents.

We then discussed serving a witness summons on Waddington himself. John said Pat or myself could get the necessary form from the 2nd floor at the Old Bailey and either send it to the Home Office or serve it on him personally at his home address which we could get from Who's Who.

The meeting concluded with a further discussion of the strategy and tactics to pursue at the trial. John advised against renewing the request for the transcript of Blake's trial at an early stage in the proceedings. If Bevan referred to the heinousness of Blake's offence, or suggested that he had been responsible for the death of agents, we should interrupt him and ask for the transcripts then. But he warned that we could not be sure they would help us if we succeeded in getting them, and that the prosecution were insisting that some mention was made during the *in camera* trial of the death of British agents. On more general matters he advised us to speak slowly, especially in cross-examining prosecution witnesses, not to be rushed or harried by the judge or to be afraid to stop and consult one another.

> **'If you can introduce an element of humour,' he said. 'that's always a good tactic. Try to get the jury laughing with you. And if the judge makes a ruling you think is unreasonable, try adopting an "Inspector**

Clouseau" approach: "I don't understand your point here, my Lord – and I don't think the jury understand it either."

These sound practical tips, however, were not to be put to use for some time. On Monday 14th May, Lord Justice Watkins and Mr Justice Potts sitting in the High Court were persuaded by Ed Fitzgerald and Tom Mackinnon to postpone the hearing due to begin two days later. Somewhat to Pat's and my dismay, it was then postponed until 11th July. As a result the Old Bailey trial was also postponed and 'listed for mention' on 2nd October. When I phoned Anne from the High Court, she sighed.

'How much longer is this whole business going to drag on for?'

The plus side was that Macpherson would definitely be off the case.

We heard along the grapevine he was furious about losing it and this was an additional satisfaction. On 16th May we were back at the Old Bailey for a new date for the trial to be fixed, with Tom Mackinnon acting for the two of us, and Calvert Smith acting for the prosecution. Macpherson's annoyance was palpable.

Macpherson: I have had papers served on me, which is unusual. Rumours have reached me, without anyone having the courtesy directly to inform me, what went on at the Divisional Court, and I am told now that the case is fixed for the Divisional Court for the 11th of July. Is that right? Calvert-Smith: My Lord, that is right. That occurred as a result of an application on behalf of the accused on Monday of this week to adjourn here which had been fixed for today, in fact.

Macpherson: Yes.

Calvert-Smith: And it was granted. I apologise to your Lordship if the Crown have been dilatory.

Macpherson: No, I am not complaining about the Crown. Anyway, there it is, it has been adjourned … Mr Mackinnon, do you simply want the date today of the trial, preliminarily fixed for the 5th June?

Mackinnon: Yes, I would like to apply to vacate that in the light of the Divisional Court …

Macpherson: Yes, it will have to be vacated.

Mackinnon: … and, indeed, I have a copy of the order of Mr Justice Hodgson.

Macpherson: Yes, well, eventually I saw that.

Tom argued against trying to fix a new date for the trial until after the July hearing at the Divisional Court. But Macpherson would have none of it.

Macpherson: This matter has to be further delayed because the two accused men want counsel of their choice [ie. at the Divisional Court].

> They are entitled to make that application, they have made it, and they have succeeded. The Divisional Court Hearing, therefore, will not be until the 11th of July, but delay has been cried so often in this case that I am not going to take the risk of the trial being further delayed should they be unsuccessful in the Divisional Court. As a preliminary and commonsense move I therefore fix the trial – purely as an administrative arrangement, of course, because the Divisional Court Hearing may affect the matter – for Tuesday, the 2nd of October, 1990.
> Mackinnon: My Lord, may I address your Lordship on that date? Neither leading counsel are available on that day.
> Macpherson: I have been told in the clearest possible terms that leading counsel are not going to take part in the case. I was told that by leading counsel a fortnight ago in this court. The case is fixed for Tuesday, the 2nd of October, 1990. Thank you very much.[7]

The delay also meant that Anne and I were able to fit in a holiday, and in June we spent a happy week in Minorca at a holiday home owned by the family of our son Seán's partner. It was situated in the quiet fishing village of Es Grau, right on the edge of a bay. We went swimming two or three times a day, took afternoon siestas, and ate out most evenings in the many excellent cafes and restaurants. Yet it did have a little bit the feel of the last good meal before execution.

7 Court Tranacript, 16 May 1990, pp.3-4

Chapter 10:

Special Branch Report Disclosed

The weekend before the start of the hearing in the Divisional Court in July, Anne and I travelled down to London and again set up home and office with our good friends Tony and Jeanne Smythe in North London.

On the evening just prior to the trial, we also met for the first time our German fan club – or at least one half of it – in the form of Gerda Kistner. Gerda had been phoning us from her home near Hanover from time to time since she first spotted an item in the Guardian about us, the previous autumn. In fact it was she who first alerted *Taz* to the case and was perhaps instrumental in having them assign Ralf Sotschek to cover it. Her story, when we could decipher it from the disjointed telephone calls in broken English, was a fascinating one. In 1946 she and her identical twin sister, Doris Meyn, had met and struck up a friendship with George Blake when he was an officer in naval intelligence interrogating former Nazis. They were young nurses at the time and travelled with him in his jeep across the country. Later, he took over some pictures for Gerda to relatives of hers in England. Whatever may have been the relationship between them and George, they clearly had a strong emotional attachment to him and held him in high esteem. In recent years they had both been actively involved in protests against nuclear weapons and nuclear power plants. On discovering the date of the High Court hearing, Gerda phoned us up excitedly to say she had booked a cheap boat and train passage via Hamburg to London.

She turned out to be a petite, elderly, white-haired lady of 70. Her English, never good at the best of times, almost deserted her altogether at first in the excitement of meeting the people who had rescued 'our George'. She brought with her presents for all of us from her and her sister, including a gold bracelet for Anne which had been a family heirloom, and a pot of artificial pink chrysanthemums. (The flowers were, of course, a reference to the pot of pink chrysanthemums which Seán Bourke had carried with him in the getaway car outside Wormwood Scrubs prison to give the impression that he was visiting a patient in Hammersmith Hospital and which he finally ditched at the foot of the prison wall at the exact spot where George jumped down to freedom.) She also brought along a copy of the German magazine *s* for 30th April 1990 which carried a long report about the Blake escape and our involvement in it and included a photograph of Pat and myself leaving Bow Street Magistrates Court in July of the previous year.

Next morning, Wednesday 11th July the battle in the High Court resumed before Lord Justice ('Tusker') Watkins and Mr Justice Hutchison. Watkins is a tough-minded judge with a reputation for forthrightness. During the war he had won the VC for flushing out single-handed a German machine-gun nest; with this military background, he was unlikely to be sympathetic to our case. It might be different, our lawyers said, had we been prepared to apologise for what we had done and to say it had been the result of youthful indiscretion – rather than standing by our actions and stating would do the same again in similar circumstances. He sat enthroned in the centre of the judges' seats, square jawed, bewigged, wearing black horn-rimmed classes. His mouth, turned down at the corners, gave him at once a grim and determined aspect. And indeed while he treated the two QCs with circumspection, he tried to bully the two junior counsel on the occasions when they appeared before him on their own. Sitting to his left, and slightly behind him as if to acknowledge his junior position, was Hutchison. He was taller and leaner than Tusker, with a pale, oblong face. Watkins dominated proceedings, but Hutchison intervened from time to time with questions and comments.

'Hutchison is one of our best, younger, liberal judges,' Tony Scrivener told us at a meeting in his chambers before the hearing. 'Oh, They're the worst!' I said – only half in jest. My experience was that tough minded conservatives were sometimes better at standing up to Establishment pressures than their more liberal counterparts. Watkins, I found out later, had on one occasion given an important judgement against the authorities on an immigration issue. He had also been the presiding judge in the case of the Wapping policemen – the 'Cherry case' – to which our counsel had referred several time in the hearing before Hodgson. Watkins had ruled in that case that it would be an abuse of the judicial process to prosecute four policemen for alleged offences because of a delay of eighteen months between the time the authorities first had evidence against them and their being arrested and charged. Our counsel went out of their way during the hearing to mention the case, talking facetiously about 'a second bite at the Cherry'.

Both prosecution council were in court – despite the fact that this was supposedly an *ex-parte* hearing. So too was a representative of the Crown Prosecution Service, Mr Bibby, and an *amicus curiae*. The ambiguous status of the 'neutral' friend of the court was well illustrated by a letter to the Court from the Treasury Solicitors Office, signed by R. N. Ricks, Principal Assistant

Treasury Solicitor, and dated 10th May 1990. (Copies of the letter were sent to our solicitors and to the CPS). It reads in part:

> As you are aware Mr John Laws argued the jurisdiction issue before Hodgson J. on the application for leave as *amicus curiae*. I take it that the Divisional Court would wish Mr Laws to address them on the jurisdiction issue but I should be grateful if you would confirm this … The Crown would wish Mr Laws to be able to address the Court on the public interest immunity issue as well if it arises. In my opinion he can do this consistently with remaining *amicus curiae* since the public interest immunity issue is one which arises independently of any particular partisan issue and indeed is one which the Court should have regard to of its own motion if necessary. If there is any difficulty in this, then the alternative would be for Mr Laws to argue the jurisdiction issue and, if it arises, the public immunity issue on *behalf of the Crown* and for him not to appear as *amicus curiae*. It is proposed that Mr Julian Bevan will be briefed on the issues arising out of MacPherson J's. decision not to stay the criminal proceedings. (Emphasis added).

So if Mr Laws was disqualified from appearing as a neutral friend of the court he would put the same argument as a non-neutral representative of the Crown. And of one thing we could all be certain – the hat he was wearing wouldn't make a ha'porth of difference to what he said. The letter also clarified Julian Bevan's standing in the High Court. He was not appearing for the prosecution as such but for the Treasury Solicitors; the latter just happened to brief the same individual who would be conducting the prosecution if the trial went ahead.

In the event, Laws was engaged in the House of Lords on 11th July and his place was taken by Mr Philip Havers. Pat and I had had a previous brush with a member of the Havers family. Philip Havers' grandfather, Lord Justice Havers, had sent us and four others down for 18 months in the Wethersfield trial in February 1962 – ironically the event that led to us getting to know Blake in the first place.

The opening day and a half was taken up with the jurisdiction issue and followed much the same pattern as the preliminary hearing before Hodgson with both sides citing case law in support of their argument. Geoffrey opened again, followed by Anthony and then Havers. For those of us sitting at the back of the court it was difficult to hear what counsel were saying, and when we could hear it was sometimes impossible to follow arguments which required a knowledge of the particular case being cited. The press corps sitting on benches at the front left-hand side of the court at right angles to the rest of us got bored at times and wandered out into the corridor for a smoke. Smalley,

Grobb, Raymond and Brownlow were frequently mentioned – Grobb so often that eventually the very word became a signal for the press people to get up and leave en masse.

What Gerda made of it all, we can only surmise. But she was thrilled to be there, and both thrilled and shocked to find herself sitting next to the two chief Special Branch officers involved in the case – Superintendent Eggington and Inspector Bird.

> **'Such a thing,' she told us in a scandalised voice, 'would never be allowed in Germany.'**

Just before lunch on the Thursday, Watkins announced that the court was deferring a decision on jurisdiction, but would in the meantime hear argument on the substantive issue of abuse of process and MacPherson's ruling on the matter in the Crown Court. Everyone was surprised at the decision; the Crown's team, in addition, were dismayed. It didn't make sense for the court to consider the abuse case before first deciding that it had jurisdiction to do so, but the implication was that Watkins and Hutchison had decided in their own minds to find for our side on this issue.

Again many by now familiar arguments were put forward on both sides. Geoffrey, who opened, said that there were two possible reasons for police failure to act in 1970 following the publication of Bourke's book. One was that the police decided to turn a blind eye to the offences; the second was that there was a policy decision from on high not to prosecute. The Crown had initially accepted that the Watts report which named Pottle and Randle had been sent 'for information' to the DPP and the Home Secretary, amongst others, though subsequently Mr Bibby of the CPS had thrown doubt on whether it had gone to the DPP. If a decision had been taken at the level of the Home Secretary or the DPP not to prosecute, it would be wrong – as Mr Bevan himself acknowledged – to pursue it 20 years later.

Watkins stopped him to ask Bevan if this was the case.

> **'If the Home Secretary or the DPP had evidence in 1970 of the involvement of Pottle and Randle in the escape of George Blake,' Bevan replied, 'but decided to take no action, the Crown would drop the case at once. However, there is nothing to suggest that this was the case.'**

Despite the rider, it was a significant concession and one we could use to advantage later on.

Geoffrey went on to say that if there had not been a high level decision and the failure to act had been due to police slackness, the abuse argument was less strong – though still strong enough for the prosecution to be halted. Once again he outlined the history of the case, suggesting we had been prejudiced by the delay because we had some reason as a result of talking to the Irish journalist Kevin O'Connor to believe that a decision had been taken not to prosecute us and because we had been put under pressure to tell our story when innocent parties had been named as playing a part in the episode. (A reference to the suggestion in the Sunday Times that Vanessa Redgrave had put up the money for the escape).

Hutchison commented that Geoffrey's 'best point' (a favourite phrase amongst lawyers) was that the offence we had been accused of did not fall into the most serious category because it carried a maximum sentence of five years. But Watkins was not impressed. 'People who cock a snook at the law, ' he commented, 'ought not to be allowed to get away with it.'

Scrivener concentrated his fire on Macpherson's decisions and the way he conducted the pre-trial hearing. He had been wrong to debar us from calling either Bird or O'Connor and wrong not to order the disclosure of the Watts report. He had ruled that Bird could only speak directly of events in and after 1989 – yet in his judgement he had relied on things Bird had said in his statement about earlier events and decisions. Thus Bevan had contended that the police had no evidence until Randle and Pottle published their book though this contention was based entirely on Bird's statement. Mr Bibby had changed tack on the issue of who the Watts' report had been sent to – something which showed how important cross-examination could be.

> **'How far would you have got in cross-examination?' Hutchison asked. 'We would have been able to test matters relied upon by the Judge on page 10 of his judgement.' (This is where Macpherson deals with the state of police knowledge in 1970 after the publication of Seán Bourke's book.)**

Hutchison suggested that extensive cross-examination prior to a trial was undesirable. Could it only take place at a pre-trial hearing? Why shouldn't a trial be stopped in mid-course if evidence was brought to show that it amounted to an abuse of the judicial process? Scrivener agreed that it could be, but argued that the judge was wrong in law in making a judgment of the facts on the basis of uncontested statements.

Turning to the issue of the documents, he conceded that in civil cases the general rule was that courts would not release documents, even relevant documents, if that was considered injurious to the national interest. But there was a stronger argument for disclosure in criminal cases:

> 'To deny the disclosure of documents on the grounds that it could not help the defence would leave defendants with a sense of grievance. Justice

> would not be seen to be done. Perhaps the courts have not yet grasped the importance of disclosure in criminal cases. It is not right for the defence to have to rely on the prosecution to survey documents on its behalf.'

Hutchison commented that the burden of proof here rested on the defence. In the present case, we had to convince the court that the Watts' report could be relevant to the plea of abuse of process. It must be on the cards, at least, that it would help us. Scrivener responded that had we been allowed to call Kevin O'Connor his evidence might have thrown light on this question. According to his sworn statement, Watts had told him in 1984 that the police knew of Randle and Pottle's involvement soon after the escape but that a decision was taken high up not to prosecute because they were decent people doing a useful job in the community.

Had we attempted, Watkins asked, to call Watts? Robertson fielded this question, saying that we had not done so because Macpherson had ruled out hearing live witnesses. (Actually we hadn't traced his whereabouts at that point, but I think Geoffrey was reluctant to say so since Watkins might have said that that was our funeral and we should have tried harder to do so.) Watts, Robertson said, had been subsequently contacted and had indicated his willingness to appear, though after talking to Inspector Bird he now said he would not do so voluntarily.

Bevan responded, speaking not in his capacity as prosecutor but as counsel briefed by the Treasury Solicitors to take up the issues raised by Macpherson's ruling.

The most significant element in his presentation was a retraction of his earlier statement at the Old Bailey that the Watts report had been sent to the DPP in 1970. He had thought this was the case he said, but had subsequently learned that it was not so.

Was this the truth? If the Watts report had never been sent to the DPP, it was an extraordinary blunder to have stated in court that it had been so. On the other hand none of the various Special Branch and MI5 documents that were eventually to come into our hands indicate that the DPP did receive it.

For the most part Bevan repeated the arguments he had deployed in the Old Bailey. The police had decided against taking action in 1970 after Seán Bourke's book was published because they had no concrete evidence and nor did it seem worthwhile to interview experienced campaigners like Randle and Pottle who would refuse to answer questions. The fact that the authorities attempted to secure the extradition of Bourke from Ireland in 1968-69 showed they were serious about bringing those responsible to book and had they succeeded in that, Pottle and Randle might well have been investigated at that point. Pottle and Randle had been interviewed by Special Branch in November 1987 after they had been named by the Sunday Times, and this showed clearly that the case was not dead and buried. Yet they went ahead and published their book.

> **Watkins: They trailed their coats.**
>
> **Bevan: They almost welcomed arrest – and certainly they courted it.**

He again cited passages from the book to show that we expected to be arrested and charged once it was published and intended to use the trial to expose the activities of western intelligence agencies. Yet now they claimed there had been an abuse of process. As for the seriousness of the offence, they had not only helped a convicted spy to escape, they had smuggled him out of the country.

> **Watkins: Their confession is scandalous. Why should they now complain? As Churchill said: This is an ill conceived world, but it is not as ill conceived as that.**

Finally, Bevan moved on to the subject of Public Interest Immunity. The Prosecution had a duty to disclose documents that could assist the defence and every single statement made during interrogations from 1966 to 1989 bar two had been disclosed to the defence. (He did not, of course, mention that we had to go to the Crown Court to get the Crown to let us have these documents). One of those not disclosed was by a relative of George Blake, and there was one other. Police reports were another matter; they were by their nature covered by Public Interest Immunity. However, Inspector Bird's statement had culled all the relevant matter from the police reports. He, Bevan, had been able to assure Macpherson that Bird had done his duty and that his statement covered everything. When Macpherson had nevertheless asked to see the Watts report, he had agreed. It was the defence at that point who had objected to Macpherson seeing it unless he was first satisfied that it was 'on the cards' that it might assist.

Tony Scrivener stood up to object, and Watkins interposed:

> **'Macpherson was more cautious than I would have been' – and he went on to chuckle over another judge who would pretend to be discussing whether or not to read a document while surreptitiously glancing down at it to see what it said. It was a clear warning. If he made up his mind to read the Watts' report, nothing either the prosecution or defence would say was going to stop him.**

The case continued until Monday of the following week when it had to continue without the benefit of the two QCs. Calvert-Smith took up the argument where Bevan had left off. There had been no application at the Crown Court, he pointed out, to call Rollo Watts, and different considerations would have applied in his case than in that of Bird or O'Connor. There was a burden of proof on the applicants to show that a prosecution would constitute abuse. But what was the prejudice they were claiming? True they had suffered anxiety in the period between 1970 and 1989 and this had been taken into account, but this Sword of Damocles had been placed there by the defendants themselves. There were no missing witnesses or other difficulties for the defence arising out of the delay. Nor had the Crown's behaviour in any way led them to expect there would be no prosecution when they published their book.

Calvert-Smith was followed by Havers, speaking now not as *amicus curiae* but as the Crown's representative on the question of Public Interest Immunity. He repeated the point that police reports belonged to a class of documents that should be given public interest immunity. The court had to perform a balancing act here, weighing the importance of not revealing police reports against the claims of the defendants. But this was a judicial review, not an appeal on the merits of the case. He then cited various cases and authorities to support his claim that the Watts report should not be disclosed.

> **'Mr Bevan,' he concluded, 'has given an assurance that the Watts report would not assist the defence. What then do the appellants expect to get out of it? – Nothing. There is no reason not to rely on Mr. Bevan's assurance.'**
>
> **Watkins: The judge has the discretion whether or not to hear witnesses.**
>
> **Havers: Yes, my Lord. Surely in seeking to call Inspector Bird as a witness the defence were engaging in a fishing expedition?**
>
> **Watkins: What could they expect to gain from calling him? Counsel has assured them that there is nothing in the report that could help them.**
>
> **Havers: My Lord, I agree. The defence already have all the evidence to deploy the argument that the police failed to act in 1970. What possible prejudice to their case can arise from a refusal to disclose documents? In my view, my Lord, none.**

Ed Fitzgerald, and then Tom, responded. Inevitably they too went over a lot of ground that had been covered before, but Ed made some telling points about the reason for wanting to see the Watts report and putting Bird in the witness box. There were unanswered questions about Watts' statement, he said. Who was the report to? What was the response to it? How far did it square with O'Connor's report of his conversation with Watts in 1984? Bevan had doubtless done his duty in disclosing documents, but there were things he could not explain. Whom did he ask about the events of 1966 and 1970? What answers did he get?

> **Watkins interrupted him: 'Sounds like an application,' he said, ' to cross-examine Mr Bevan!'**

We were not doubting Bevan's word, Ed continued. But was he shown everything? This was not an appropriate way of dealing with the issue. As to our failure to sub-poena Watts to appear, the effect of Macpherson's ruling regarding Bird and O'Connor, was to bring the gates down. He was saying in effect that no oral evidence would be allowed. Thus we knew very well he would have debarred Watts if we had attempted to call him.

Watkins asked Ed why the defence had objected to Macpherson reading the Watts report himself. The only basis, Ed replied, on which he could properly have done so was if he ruled it was on the cards that it would point to an abuse of process – and in that case he should have ordered its disclosure to the defence. Macpherson was not prepared to do this. Yet in fact it must be on the cards that the report would help, for instance by showing at what level a decision was taken not to prosecute Pottle and Randle. Hutchison commented that the fact that PII had been claimed not because of the content of the document but because of the class to which it belonged undermined Ed's argument here.

Watkins and Hutchison gave Ed short shrift when he tried to introduce again the argument that the offence was not of a particularly grave kind as the maximum sentence of five years indicated.

> **Watkins: Many members of the public are likely to be struck rather by the enormity of the crime. It is neither interesting nor compelling that it carried a maximum sentence of five years.**
>
> **Ed: It may be a serious offence of its kind but the order of gravity is indicated by the five year maximum penalty.**

Tom, in his presentation, concentrated on the history of the case and the failure of the police to follow up obvious leads, particularly after they had obtained the text of Seán Bourke's book. They could have checked Randle's and Pottle's fingerprints against those found at the hideout in Highlever Road but failed to do so. They had not interviewed us or searched our houses which still contained vital evidence of our involvement including letters from George to Seán discussing the escape before they had established a two-way radio link-up, the passports Anne and I had used for the journey to Berlin and back, photos of George and Seán I had taken in Pat's flat when we were planning to get false passports for both of them, and the plans for the conversion of the camper van.[1] They had not questioned Pat's neighbours to see if they had noticed anything during the time Blake and Bourke were staying with him, and they had not bothered to trace the whereabouts of the camper-van and examine it for Blake's fingerprints.

Hutchison seemed to accept some of these points. The police, he commented, were not normally deterred from interviewing suspects by the expectation that they would not respond. He also accepted that the police would have found a 'treasure trove' if they had searched our houses in early 1970.

Tom said that the policy decision not to prosecute would not necessarily have been taken at top level. Blunt in 1964 had been offered immunity in exchange for a confession without the Home Secretary being informed.

> **'Blunt was a spy,' Watkins observed.'Ministers of the Crown don't usually want to know about such matters. What are you driving at – that MI6 and MI5 were involved?'**

Tom said he thought it would be extraordinary if MI5 had not been involved in the decision not to prosecute, as they had been in the Blunt case. His Lordship was in a difficult position because of the secrecy surrounding the case. But if the prosecution were seeking to maintain secrecy, they should have to pay the price for this.

> **Watkins: Do you want Mr Bevan to go to prison.**
> **Mackinnon: We are not suggesting that.**
> **Watkins: Do you mind if we look at the documents?**
> **Mackinnon: We have no objection provided you decide the documents are relevant.**

Watkins adjourned the case and said he would give his decision later. We had no doubt from the way things had gone what that decision would be.

On Thursday of that week I flew to Berlin to attend the Council meeting of the War Resisters International, staying for the first few days with Ralf Sotschek and his wife, Aine. Ralf is a native of Berlin and was able to show me round the city and to take me into the bleak part of it that used to be East Berlin. What was striking was the relative dilapidation of the area. Many buildings were still pock-marked with bullets fired into them in the closing days of the war in 1945. But there was a sadness too in the fact that East German products were now totally undervalued and the shops were being flooded with West German goods at inflated prices. Ralf told me that farmers were even unable to sell potatoes and other produce, and were setting up roadside stalls in a desperate attempt to dispose of their produce.

---

1 See pp. 214-215 of *The Blake Escape.*

While in the city, I took the opportunity to visit the Hotel Am Zoo in the Kurfurstendamm where Anne and I and our two children had stayed all those years ago in December 1966, the night we dropped George Blake on the East German autobahn. It had a new modern entrance clamped on to the front of the old building and, inside, the foyer was unrecognisable. I went in and asked the proprietor if he had any guest records dating back to the 1960s but unfortunately he had not.

On the evening of my arrival, Thursday 19th July, I had an unexpected phone call from Pat. There had been a dramatic development in the High Court. Watkins had summoned both sides to court that day and, brushing aside all objections from Tom and Ed, had announced he was going to read the Watts' report. Having done so, he returned and ordered that it should be released forthwith to the defence *because he could not say for sure that it would be of no assistance to them.*

In a later chapter I am severely critical of Watkins. But in deciding to view the Watts report despite the Home Secretary's Public Interest Immunity claim, despite the repeated assurances from Bevan that there was nothing in it that could possibly be of assistance to the defence, despite even the opposition of our own counsel unless he first ruled that it was 'on the cards' that it might be relevant, he showed a determination and an independence of mind that is entirely admirable. It is even more to his credit that having read Watts he immediately recognized its possible significance and ordered its disclosure. By implication at least, this was also a severe rebuke to both Bevan and Havers who had given such bland assurances that the Watts report had no relevance to our application.

Something of the flavour of the occasion comes across in the official transcript:

> **Watkins: Mr MacKinnon, Mr Fitzgerald and Mr Bevan, we propose to read the documents.**
> **Fitzgerald: I do not know whether this is the appropriate stage but I wonder whether you would hear me on two points.**
> **Watkins: We have heard all about it. We do not intend to hear any more. We are going to read the documents. When they have been read, you can have something to say.**
> **Fitzgerald: I will address you then.**

Watkins also extracted an important statement from Bevan.

> **Watkins: We are going to retire to read the documents. There is one further point on which we want your help. Let us suppose for the moment that we came to the conclusion that it is a proper inference to be drawn from the whole of the circumstances that there**

was a policy decision sometime not very far after the event not to prosecute. Following that finding, is it permissible – reasonable – for a prosecuting authority to change its mind?

Bevan: Although I have taken no instructions with regard to the matter, it was my view on behalf of the Crown that had a policy decision been made that it was not in the public interest or whatever not to prosecute these two individuals in 1970 … I would be hard pressed to persuade any court that it would not be an abuse suddenly in 1989 to change that decision and to prosecute. That has always been my stance.

The answer to your Lordship's question is that, if a policy decision had been made in 1970 not to prosecute these two individuals for whatever reason, I would have advised the Director of Public Prosecutions not to have instituted these proceedings … If I had been instructed that a policy decision had been made in 1970 not to prosecute these two individuals, I would not have advised the Director to institute proceedings in April 1989, 19 years after that decision had been made.

Pat made no attempt to hide the excitement he felt at the turn of events.

'Mike,' he said, 'just listen to this opening sentence of the Watt's report:

> With their letter dated 30th January 1970, reference PF.607,084/K3/NLM, MI5 enclosed a photostat copy of the manuscript for a book written by Seán Bourke which, it is understood, will be published by Cassell & Co Ltd, 35 Red Lion Square, WC1 in May this year. They ask for comment regarding the material contained therein.

'So it was MI5 who asked for the report! How could Bevan have possibly maintained that it couldn't help us in any way?'

In fact Bevan himself confirmed that he realised just how helpful the Watts report could be to us. After Watkins had ordered the release of the Watts report, Bevan and Pat were standing in the corridor together outside the court.

'You could well get away with it, now' he said gloomily to Pat.

Pat, Anne and myself – as we already knew – were all clearly identified in the report which contained appendices detailing the points of similarity between the 'Pat Porter', 'Anne Reynolds' and 'Michael Reynolds' of Seán's book and the three of us. Pat read me the final paragraph of the report:

> It should be stressed that, at this stage, there is no actual evidence to substantiate any of these possible identifications and no enquiries have been made by police of the persons concerned. It must be said, however, that if Bourke's story is true, these persons, with their ideological beliefs, their militant backgrounds, and their wide circle of associates, fit very well into the pattern of the escape as we know it. Even the final details of the escape, where 'Michael Reynolds' and his wife allegedly drove

> through Dover with Blake hidden in the secondhand Dormobile they had purchased, would have been quite feasible for Randall and his wife, both of whom had current passports and had travelled abroad extensively."

Watkins had ordered both sides back to court the following Wednesday, 25th July where he was prepared to hear oral evidence. He had said he wanted Watts to be present in court at the start of proceedings at 10.30 to give his evidence. Other Special Branch officers involved in 1970 would also be there, as would Kevin O'Connor.

> **'It's a drag, I know,' Pat said. 'But you're going to have to cut short your stay in Berlin.'**

I agreed to return on the Tuesday, even though it meant missing part of the WRI Council meeting. I stayed out late on Monday night with Ralf and Aine, and set my alarm for 5am the following morning to catch an early flight to London. Despite the early start, the taxi ran into some fearful traffic jams and I was on the edge of my seat most of the journey wondering if I would be able to catch the plane. I was exhausted and had a splitting headache by the time we reached London, and could not keep awake as the tube train trundled from stop to stop on its way from Heathrow to Kings Cross. There Pat met me with news of a further unexpected turn of events which I will come to in the next chapter.

Chapter 11:

The Note for File

The new development was the release by the prosecution of a set of seven documents from Special Branch files dating from January to May 1970. On Friday, 20th July, the day after Watkins had ordered the disclosure of the Watts report, Havers and Bevan, had gone back to the court – without informing us or our lawyers – and successfully applied for Watkins and Hutchison to order the release of these documents.[1] The other important news was that Watts, former Commander Arthur Cunningham, the acting head of Special Branch in 1970, and one other Special Branch officer, ex-Commander 'Jock' Wilson, would all be giving evidence; so too would Kevin O'Connor who had flown over from Dublin to do so.

In the case of Watts, the Crown's hand had been forced. On the Thursday, 19th July, when Watkins had made his decision, either John Wadham or Ben phoned Watts to tell him what had happened and that he was expected in court on 25th. Watts said he was willing to come, but that he would like to have a *sub poena* to attend.[2] Accordingly, the next day, Tom made an *ex parte* application for a *sub poena* to be issued to Watts for him to appear, bringing

1 The defence received the new documents on Friday, 20 July, but the Crown may have sought and obtained the permission of the court to release them the previous day, that is on the same day that the Watts' report was disclosed. The official transcript of the High Court hearing on 25th July reports Havers as referring to `the seven documents that your Lordships ordered disclosure of on Tuesday' (Page 2 at F.). (There were in fact nine documents but contained on seven pages). But the reference to Tuesday is a mistake, either on Havers' part or on the part of the shorthand writers; Tuesday 17 July was prior to the disclosure of Watts and Havers himself told the court that the Crown had applied for the extra documents to be released only after Watkins had ordered the Watts' report to be disclosed. (Transcript 25 July, p. 2 at A). The following, Tuesday 24 July, was the day before the resumed hearing, by which time the documents had been in our hands for several days. Perhaps Tuesday should have read Thursday.

2 From the contemporaneous note of the telephone conversation made by John or Ben of the telephone conversation and now in the files at Birnberg's office.

with him his report dated 23rd March 1970 'and all other documents relevant to the suspected culpability of Michael Joseph Randle and Patrick Brian Pottle concerning the escape of the said George Blake.' Only at this point did the Crown agree to produce him voluntarily as their witness.

The new documents comprised correspondence between Special Branch and 'Box 500' – the code name for the Security Service, MI5 – internal Special Branch minutes and a copy of a letter from Cunningham to Sir Philip Allen at the Home Office. They are all stamped 'Secret' (in one case 'Secret and Personal'), and even more clearly than the Watts' report itself fall into the class of document covered by Public Interest Immunity. But whereas the Watts' report was helpful to us, the new documents, on the face of it at least, were helpful to the Crown in that they appeared in places to support the contention that it was lack of evidence that led the police to take no action against us in 1970. So instead of going to the Home Secretary and getting him to sign a Public Interest Immunity certificate, as they had done with the Watts' report and other documents they wanted to keep from us, Bevan and Havers went to Watkins and Hutchison to get them to order their release.

It is certain that D.I. Bird had seen all these documents because the Watts report, numbered 19D in the series, comes from this set of documents – as Havers himself was to acknowledge in court. Yet Bird made no mention of them in the list Rougier had ordered him to make of the documents he had referred to in drawing up his report of 7th March. This was dishonest – and indeed a contempt of the court's ruling. Had he taken the witness stand in the High Court we could have publicly confronted him over this, but unfortunately he never did.

The probable explanation for his – and the Crown counsels' – decision not to mention the documents until this late stage is that to have done so would have alerted us to the involvement of MI5 in 1970 in the events surrounding the writing of the Watts' report and strengthened our hand in arguing that both Special Branch and MI5 files should be disclosed. Once the Watts' report had been released to us, the situation changed. We could see from the first sentence that MI5 had sent a typescript of Seán Bourke's book to Special Branch and that it was at their request that Watts had written his report. Now they had nothing to lose from releasing the other documents in the file and – on the face of it at least – much to gain.

Pat had studied the documents carefully and typed up notes to bring to a meeting with the lawyers that afternoon. They start with the covering letter dated 30th January 1970 which MI5 sent to Special Branch with the typescript of Seán Bourke's book. Paragraph 2 was the most significant as far as we were concerned. It reads:

> I have been asked to stress that this typescript was received on a confidential basis and *we would ask you not to take any action on matters revealed in the typescript or make any enquiries which would reveal that it is in our possession.* (Italics added)

In short, MI5 had obtained the typescript in advance of publication from one of their contacts who was presumably working inside the publishers Cassel & Co, and were anxious that no action should be taken which could expose him or her.

The documents also show that MI5 sent copies of Bourke's typescript to both the Home Office and Foreign Office, and that Special Branch sent the Watts' report on its completion on 23rd March 1970 not only to MI5 but to Sir Philip Allen, Permanent Secretary to the Home Office, and to an officer in the Criminal Investigation Department, D.I. Chapman. Mr Peter Brodie, the Acting Commissioner for Crime, in overall charge of CID and Special Branch, also saw the report and endorsed Cunningham's comments upon it.[3] The documents show too that the Information Research Department at the Foreign Office, which we understand was part of, or closely linked to, the Secret Intelligence Service (SIS/MI6), was sent the Watts report minus the identifications.

From the Crown's point of view, the most useful document was Cunningham's minute of 25th March 1970 which states that 'The possible identifications [i.e. of Randle and Pottle in the Watts' report] are interesting, but there is no evidence to substantiate any charge' – a conclusion endorsed by Brodie. Somewhat more ambiguous in its implications is Watts' final comment in his minute of 9th May 1970 which reads: 'Apart from the warrants for Bourke's arrest, which remain outstanding, the matter would seem to rest there.'

Pat commented on Watt's concluding comment in his notes for the lawyers as follows:

> How can he (Watts) possibly come to that conclusion? – there is nothing in the MI5 reply that says that. Surely Mr Watts who has spent some deal of time working on his report – which has been greatly praised by MI5

3 See Appendix 3 the note numbered 21 signed by Cunningham which has a tick in the top left corner and the handwritten initials P.B. (looking more like M.B.) against the typed initials ACC. In court Watts confirmed that this meant that the Assistant Commission Crime (ACC), Mr Peter Brodie, had seen Cunningham's note and the Watts report, numbered 19D.

for its identification of Randle and Pottle – must say to himself or ask his superiors "Well what do I do now – shall I start gathering evidence – shall I start making enquiries?" That would seem a natural response by anyone, especially a policeman who has been given a task, does it well, clearly identifies Bourke's helpers. Surely he would want to see the job through and get the evidence that is lacking. But no he merely says '… the matter would seem to rest here.'

WHY???

The first letter received from M15 clearly states:

"I have been asked to stress that this typescript was received on a confidential basis and we would ask you not to take any action on matters revealed in the typescript or make any enquiries which would reveal that it is in our possession"

That instruction is never countermanded at any stage. We must assume that Special Branch were still acting upon it up until 1987. Although commonsense would say that once Bourke's book is published the confidential sources are no longer in danger of exposure. Why did Special Branch make no further enquiries – this is not explained at all.

The documents do our case no damage, in fact I feel that they help us.

What the prosecution will make great play of is 3 senior Special Branch officers all getting into the box and denying any knowledge of a policy decision …

I do not see these 3 officers as damaging to us – unless they can give a feasible reason for no action being taken. It has to be made clear that MI5 are the decision makers – that they call the tune and that we are being given evidence by the 3 monkeys and not the organ grinder.

The clear directive from MI5 to Special Branch contained in their letter of 30th January states that they should do nothing. This is the only clear statement, the only clear instruction and the only clear decision contained in the documents and it has never been rescinded.

The lawyers, when we met that afternoon in Ed Fitzgerald's chambers, did not share Pat's confidence. Our two senior Counsel, Anthony Scrivener and Geoffrey Robertson, were still away so the conference was attended by Ed, Tom, Ben and John plus ourselves. Ed felt Cunningham's assertion in his memo of 25th March 1970 that there was 'no evidence to substantiate any charge' would carry a lot of weight, no matter what he or Tom said. Cunningham himself would be there in person and no doubt he and the other Special Branch officers would insist that the lack of evidence was the only reason for not proceeding against us in 1970.

Ben raised what turned out to be a key question; who would have been responsible for deciding whether or not to prosecute? Would the Home Office have any say in the matter? John's view was that formally the decision would have been made by the police and the Director of Public Prosecutions, and that if a case had gone to the DPP it would be wrong in law for the Home Office to intervene.

'But in practice', Ben insisted, 'would the DPP go ahead if MI5, Special Branch and the Home Office were opposed to this?'

My notes do not indicate whether anyone responded to that, although probably we were all convinced that Ben was right in what he was implying. The DPP, after all, is obliged in law to take the issue of 'public interest' into account in deciding whether or not to prosecute, and in a case with such political overtones and implications he would surely consult, at least informally, and take into account, the views of these other government institutions. In a sense it would be a dereliction of duty if he did not do so.

Ben also thought we should approach Lord Allen – formerly Sir Philip Allen – to find out if he had informed the then Home Secretary, James Callaghan, after receiving the Watts' report. Lord Gifford – who looked into the room as we began our discussion – said Allen was a 'reasonably enlightened' person and it seemed worth doing.

As it turned out, the most important decision taken that afternoon was that Ed should phone Havers and ask for the disclosure of MI5, CID and Home Office files related to the Blake escape, and advise him we would be requesting their disclosure during the hearing. Ed subsequently told us that when he said this to Havers he 'went mad'.

After the meeting Pat and I had a drink at a nearby pub and mulled over the situation. The meeting had rather deflated our optimism of the morning.

On July 19th I went to Berlin for a War Resisters' International Council meeting, returning to England on July 24 to be in time for the hearing following day in at the High Court. Anne travelled down from Bradford to meet up with me, and we arranged to stay for the duration of the hearing with good friends in Welwyn, within easy reach of London. I had had a very early start to the day and, what with that and all the stress and anxiety, by the evening I was feeling desperately tired and had developed a persistent headache.

It proved to be the harbinger of something more serious. Next morning when I got up to shave I started feeling giddy and vomiting blood and, soon afterwards, collapsed. The duodenal ulcer was bleeding again, and this time the attack was much more severe than the one I had experienced in 1988. I was taken by ambulance to the Queen Elizabeth Hospital in Welwyn Garden City to await surgery and, following a blood transfusion, I began to feel somewhat better. Obviously, however, I wasn't in a fit state to go to the High Court, so Anne agreed to go there with Pat and report back to me on proceedings. I had the operation that evening and though I subsequently made a good recovery, it was apparently touch and go at one point whether I would pull through.

During the day, however, the ulcer haemorrhaged again and I needed urgent surgery – but I wanted to see Anne and Pat first to hear what had happened in Court at teatime to say that there had been yet another dramatic development, and that the whole prosecution appeared on the verge of collapse.

Pat and Sue wanted to come up so that he could personally tell me all about it, and Anne had come on ahead to check if I was well enough to see them. I was – and even had I been on my last breath I don't think I could have said no to the visit, so overcome was I with curiosity about what had occurred.

When Pat arrived some while later – on his own because Sue was unwell – he could scarcely contain his excitement. An MI5 document had come to light at the end of the day's hearing which appeared to belie the testimony Watts and Cunningham had given earlier in the witness box and to support our claim that there had indeed been a policy decision not to prosecute us in 1970. To put the development in context, it is necessary to go chronologically through the events of the day. In doing so I have referred both to the accounts of Pat, Anne and others who attended and to the official court transcript.

The day began with an attempt by Ed to have the hearing postponed because of my absence. Watkins said he was sorry I was unwell but that my presence wasn't necessary and the hearing would go ahead. Then came the first unexpected development. Without warning, the Crown produced a memo from MI5 files, dated 25th February 1970. Marked 'Note for File', it was a minute by an MI5 officer – name blanked out – of a meeting between her[4] and Watts at Special Branch 'to discuss Seán Bourke's book "The Springing of George Blake" (See Appendix 4 for a copy of the Note) Several passages were blanked out, including one speculating on the identity of the doctor who had attended to Blake's broken wrist and the writer at Cromwell Road who had harboured him for a few days in 1966. However, Pat and I are both named. Paragraphs 3 to 6 read:

> 3. Chief Insp. Watts asked if we were interested and I said we were very interested although of course any action was a matter for the Police. What particularly interested us was any evidence, or evidence to the contrary, of Russian involvement in the escape.

---

4 It subsequently emerged that the officer was a woman, referred to only as `Miss A'.

> 4. Chief Insp. Watts said that Michael Randle had been in Wormwood Scrubs at the same time as Blake and knew him there. He thought it was possible that Blake himself might have assessed Randle as an idealist who would have sympathy with an attempt to help him escape from his 42-year incarceration and asked Seán Bourke to approach him.
> 5. Chief Insp. Watts gave me his hand-written notes comparing the descriptions of Reynolds-Randle and Porter-Pottle and they are attached.
> 6. He said that even if the identities are confirmed it is very unlikely that any of those identified could be prosecuted unless they themselves admitted their involvement. *However a course of action would be decided after his preliminary investigations were completed.* (Italics added)

This meeting took place on the same day, 25th March 1970, that the acting head of Special Branch, Arthur Cunningham, had noted 'The possible identifications are interesting, but there is no evidence to substantiate any charge.' The last paragraph of the Note for File confirmed Pat's conclusion that although there was no evidence at that stage, the matter was still open and, officially at least, a prosecution not ruled out after 'preliminary investigations were completed.'

Ed at once asked Watkins for the complete MI5 and Home Office files relating to the Blake escape to be opened. Every document so far, he said, apart from this latest note had come 'in dribs and drabs' from the Special Branch file. Havers objected:

> **Havers: May I deal first with the suggestions that these documents have been appearing in dribs and drabs. That, in my submission, is wholly unjustified and baseless. The police report (i.e. the Watts' report) was the only document that was in, as it were, "issue" until the end of last week when your Lordships ordered disclosure of it. As I indicated, a few moments ago, *in the light of that order* the Crown then, in my submission properly and rightly considered the police file from which, as it were, the report came and, again in my submission rightly, concluded that your Lordships should see, or would probably wish to see, the documents on that file surrounding the report.** (Italics added).
> **This further document [i.e.the MI5 Note for File that had just been produced] has been shown to your Lordships *only because the defence indicated late yesterday afternoon that they might well seek discovery or disclosure of both the Home Office file and the Security Service File.* With respect, when viewed against that background, it is wholly**

> **unjustified to suggest that the documents are coming out in dribs and drabs.**[5] (Italics added)

The only question at issue, Havers continued, was whether there was a decision or not to prosecute 'these two men' in 1970. That decision would not have been made either by the Security Service or the Home Office but by the police and ultimately the DPP. Therefore there could be no grounds for allowing the defence to 'trawl their way through' these files. He continued:

> **'Although I say it with some diffidence, in view of the refusal of the applicants to accept the assurance that Mr Bevan gave in relation to the other matter, can I assure your Lordships that there is nothing in that file which is either relevant or in any way touches upon the issue with which your Lordships are concerned.'**

His 'diffidence', however, had almost certainly less to do with the fact that the applicants had refused to accept the assurance of Mr Bevan than with the fact that when Watkins had read the Watts report he had concluded that he could not say for certain that it would not help us.

Havers continued that he had also seen 'whatever documents either are or may be relevant in the [MI5] file' and could say that the one produced was the only one that 'either is or could be relevant'. The application for further disclosure, he submitted, 'entered into the realms of a true fishing expedition'. He did not need, he said, 'to draw [their] Lordships attention to authorities for the proposition to show that this is not to be permitted.[6]

Ed in response pointed out that in one document there was an item saying 'await comments from Box 500'. (See Appendix 3, the page headed 18) Presumably, therefore, there must have been a response at some point and this might throw light on why nothing further was done in 1970. There must also be another police file since the Assistant Commissioner Crime, Commander Brodie, had been kept informed and seen the Watts report, and because the report had been sent to an officer in CID, D.I. Chapman. Moreover, the question of whether or not there was a policy decision not to prosecute in 1970 was not the only one at issue. 'As your Lordships have pointed out there is a quite separate issue if there is a gross negligence, or if there is a completely unexplained refusal to take matters further. That of itself could be a reason for your Lordships to take the view that there was inordinate and inexcusable delay.'[7]

---

5 Court transcript for Wednesday 25 July 1990, pp.1-2.

6 Transcript 25 July 1990, p.3

7 Transcript, p.4, at D.

Tom stood up to support the application. He got a curt reaction from Watkins, a foretaste of the harassment he was to receive later in the day:

> **Watkins: This is not your application, is it?**
> **Mackinnon: No, but I wanted to make it clear that I am supporting the application and I would like to be allowed to add a few words in furtherance of that support.**
> **Watkins: What is it you want?**

Tom insisted that the new documents showed that many other government departments were involved: Special Branch, the Home Office, the Foreign Office and the CID.

> **Mackinnon: 'These files in fact … are of great importance. When the advance manuscript and Mr Watts's report are sent to these various organisations certainly I would concur with Mr MacKinnon that your Lordships should be able at the very least, now that we know this for the first time, to inspect those files and make the decisions that your Lordships have been making … I would also briefly conclude by mentioning that, in my submission, the documents in fact have been elicited and obtained in dribs and drabs.'**
> **Watkins: That comes rich from you. You did not want the learned judge below to see them. When he wanted to look at them in the court below you said not.**
> **Mackinnon: We in fact listed the matter before Rougier J. and had further arguments before various tribunals before we finally get to Mr Bird's report. In any event I am obliged, my Lord.**
> **Watkins: Very well. That application is refused Mr MacKinnon.**[8]

Watts then took the stand. No doubt both sides were aware that the outcome of our application could depend on his performance, and in particular how he dealt with the O'Connor testimony. It has to be said that he made a good witness for the Crown – at this stage. His written statement, dated 24th July 1990, which Bevan took him through in the examination in chief reads:

> I am a former Metropolitan Police Officer and served from 1947 until 1978, spending from 1949 until my retirement in Special Branch. When in October 1966 George Blake escaped from Wormwood Scrubs I was a Detective Inspector and was a member of the Special Branch liaison team attached to the investigation of the escape which was being conducted from Shepherds Bush Police Station by Divisional C.I.D. About six months after the escape I returned to my Special Branch duties. I recall that the names of Randle and Pottle had been mentioned because they had been in Wormwood Scrubs prison at the same time as Blake but that

8 Transcript 25 July 1990, p.5.

> there was nothing to connect them with the escape. Because of my initial involvement in the Blake escape enquiry I assumed the role of the Special Branch officer to whom subsequent queries could be referred.
>
> In 1970 I was a Detective Chief Inspector and was requested by my senior officer to respond to a letter from the Security Service who had sent the Branch a copy of a manuscript of a book written by Seán Bourke about the escape of Blake. The book was due to be published later in the year. I submitted my report dated 23rd March 1970 to my senior officer. In reading the manuscript I made the conjecture that the persons named by Bourke as assisting him in the escape of Blake, that is Reynolds and Porter, could have been Michael Randle and Patrick Pottle. When submitting the report to my Chief Superintendent I made the recommendation that a copy be sent to D.I. Chapman who was then the officer maintaining an interest in the case. I should point out that my recall of the fact that Randle and Pottle's names had been mentioned early in the enquiry was made in 1970 when I was asked to prepare my report.
>
> I retired from the Force as Commander in 1978 and shortly afterwards became a director of a commercial security company specialising in executive protection. I remained with this company until July 1987. I have been told that a journalist called Kevin O'Connor claims to have had an interview with me during this period and that I told him that a policy decision had been taken not to prosecute Randle and Pottle. Whilst a director I was interviewed by numerous press and TV reporters regarding the expertise of the company. Although I cannot remember O'Connor it is possible he is one of the journalists I gave an interview to regarding the work of my company. As a matter of course I would not have mentioned the names of Randle and Pottle to him. As far as I was concerned there was insufficient evidence against them to justify prosecuting them. To my knowledge no such policy decision has ever been taken not to prosecute them and therefore it would be out of the question for me to have made such a statement.

In the examination in chief he insisted that he knew of no discussion as to whether or not we should be prosecuted. Moreover, as a Special Branch officer 'he was not directly involved with the investigation of crime' which was a job for the CID. Thus when he had said in his minute of 9th May 1970, 'the matter would seem to rest here' he was referring to the role of Special Branch which had completed its task with the writing and distribution of his report.

Bevan questioned him about points in O'Connor's statement.

> **Bevan: My Lords, I am going to put to him, if I may, part of the statement … of Mr O'Connor … I would like you to listen to this Mr**

Watts. It is alleged that in, I think it is 1984, you met Mr O'Connor at the offices of Saladin Security in Sloane Street. During the course of the meeting you said this, and I am going to read the three paragraphs [i.e. from O'Connor's statement] if I may that contained the matters:

'Watts said that he was an ex Scotland Yard officer, a sergeant, who was involved in the investigation which surrounded the escape of George Blake. He said that the authorities had known within a very short time that there were two other people besides Seán Bourke involved in the escape. They knew that two of the people were part of the 'intellectual mafia' at the prison. Watts said that there were conversations about the prosecution of these two people and his superiors had told him that they should leave well enough alone.

'Watts said that the police had quickly established Bourke as the prime subject days before the description of Bourke was released to the media.'

It goes on to say in the statement:

'I have a note of the conversation and Watts said "of course we knew who they were in a short time but a decision was taken not to prosecute them. The reason (which came from above) was they were perfectly law abiding citizens in every other respect. One was a teacher married to a teacher. They had young children. Why break up the family and put them away at the cost of the tax payer when there were lot of other real villains about that it was our job to catch."

From that do you recall a meeting with this journalist, Mr O'Connor, that touched upon Mr Randle and Mr Pottle?

Watts: No, I do not.

Q. Did you ever say to the journalist, Mr O'Connor, that a decision had been made not to prosecute these two men?

A. No, I cannot remember at all meeting this person, although I did meet quite a number of journalists in connection with my work. I cannot possibly have made a statement like that because I had no knowledge of such a decision. No.

Q: If you had said it, and I underline the word if, Mr Watts, would it have been true?

A: No I think there are a number of points you have mentioned in there and one that sticks in my mind is that we knew almost immediately – what did he say? – "who those two people were."

Q: He said … 'the authorities had known within a very short time that there were two other people besides Seán Bourke involved in the escape. They knew that two of the people were part of the "intellectual mafia".

A: Totally untrue.

Q: Secondly, I read it before and this is you speaking: 'of course we knew who they were in a short time but a decision was taken not to prosecute them.'
A: a) We did not know who they were and b) the first inclination of who they might have been is of course from the book. [9]

Bevan then referred to the new documents, and in particular to Watts comment in the last of them: 'the matter would seem to rest there'.

Q: Did you write that?
A: Yes.
Q: What lay behind those words, Mr Watts?
A: My work in this respect is as a Special Branch officer and not as a criminal investigation officer. From the Special Branch point of view, MI5 had written the letter which was mainly concerned with the question of whether what Seán Bourke said in his book was likely to be the true story. The concern, clearly, at that stage still was whether there had been involvement with the Russian Embassy or one of the iron curtain embassies. The letter had answered that. I had drawn some speculative identifications.
Q: In the report?
A: In the report, yes. These had been passed to the persons investigating the crime. What I am saying here is that from our point of view in Special Branch the matter would appear to rest here, there appears to be no further enquiries to be made.

Bevan's final question was:

Q: Do you know, Mr Watts, of any discussions whatever with regard to pursuing enquiries about this matter that stem from the book?
A: No, as I say, my personal involvement was to answer that particular letter that had been given to me. If I could say at that point for what it was worth, I was then the second in command of the squad dealing with countering Irish terrorism which was coming very much to a head at that time in 1970 and therefore I was very much involved in other work. From my point of view this was something which had been given to me, I completed it, handed it in and that was the end of it.[10]

Cross-examined by Ed Fitzgerald, Watts again insisted that it had been up to the Divisional CID, to whom his report had been sent, 'to take decisions as to whether further enquiries were to be made and whether there was any evidence of any kind to justify prosecution.' Later he explained the role of Special Branch in the enquiry in more detail:

---

9 Transcript of 25 July 1990, pp.9-10

10 Transcript 25 July 1990, p.12.

Watts: Could I just possibly explain to the court if I may. As Special Branch officers we were sent down to assist the Divisional CID enquiries mainly from a political point of view at that time. It was not known who had assisted Bourke or who had assisted in the escape at all. Quite clearly there was a strong thought at the time that it could have been either the Soviet Embassy or one of the Iron Curtain embassies. Since that was mainly our field of work that was our main reason for going down. We went into great depths interviewing the Czech Philharmonic Orchestra who left the country the following day I believe. I would suggest, although I cannot remember specifically … people like Philip Morris [a trusty 'red band' prisoner in Wormwood Scrubs at the time who was suspected of smuggling in material to help in the escape] would have been interviewed … by the Divisional CID officers.[11]

This gave Ed one telling point. Philip Morris, a prisoner in Wormwood Scrubs in 1966 who was suspected of having assisted in the escape, had been interviewed in 1966 even though at that point there was no evidence against him. Yet when Randle and Pottle were identified as suspects early in 1970 the CID took no action.

Fitzgerald: … Are you surprised to hear that [Randle and Pottle] were not interviewed in 1970?

Watts: It is a difficult one for me to answer quite honestly, because you are now asking me to say what an experienced Divisional detective actually would do.

Q: I am asking you for your reaction as a police officer with years of experience to the fact that these two defendants were not interviewed in 1970.

A: I would certainly have thought that if they felt any progress could have been made in the case that they could have done so …

Q: It is surprising, is it not, that they were not interviewed?

Watts: Unless they had some knowledge there was no point in doing it. It is a difficult one for me to answer.

Watkins: These questions are matters of comment. We are not a jury.[12]

Watts acknowledged that Seán Bourke had phoned him from Ireland – 'He phoned me and invited me out to give a joint press conference in the Gresham Hotel in Dublin.'

Fitzgerald: Were you still an officer in Special Branch at that time?

Watts: I was still with Special Branch, yes.

---

11 Transcript of 25 July 1970, p.14.

12 Transcript 25 July 1990, p.15.

Q: Was this something that was publicly made known at the time?

A: I certainly reported it to my senior officers.

Q: Did it appear in the newspapers or anything?

A: Good heavens, no.[13]

Here Ed was leading up to O'Connor's testimony, since he had said in his sworn statement that Watts had told him Seán used to phone him from Ireland. Establishing that Seán's phone calls to Watts had not been publicised would therefore help to confirm the authenticity of O'Connor's testimony.

Ed now moved on to the new documents and in particular to the covering letter from MI5 to Special Branch dated 30th January 1971 in which they asked the latter not to take any action that would reveal Seán's Bourke's typescript was in their possession.

Fitzgerald: ... Were you being asked by MI5 to do nothing in the way of making further enquiries or interviewing the defendants themselves?

Watts: We were being asked not to disclose, in so many words, that we had received the typescript.

Q: Yes, but did you go further than that? If you had investigated in any way, at that stage at any rate, it would have revealed that this typescript was floating around and therefore you were being asked not to investigate the matter of Mr Randle and Mr Pottle's involvement.

Bevan: My Lords I am sure the court are not mistaken and I appreciate that the court are not a jury. My Lords, that is not quite what the paragraph is saying. It is saying 'do not make any investigation which will reveal the fact that we have the transcript' which is a little different.

Fitzgerald: I entirely accept that that is what it says ... The only way the revelation which MI5 asked not to be made could be avoided would be that no further action be taken on the matters until the publication of the book. I am asking the witness whether that is a reasonable interpretation of what is being said.

Watts: I think what it is saying is, if you should decide to make any further enquiries, please do not do it is such a way that it discloses that you have had a transcript of the manuscript.[14]

The cross-examination continued into the afternoon when Ed raised the matter of O'Connor's interview with him:

Fitzgerald: You have confirmed that it is right to say that in 1984 you were working in Saladin Securities. Do you deny that a conversation took place between yourself and Mr O'Connor in 1984?

---

13 Transcript 25 July 1990 p.17.

14 Transcript 25 July 1990, pp.18-19.

Watts: I do not deny it. I cannot confirm it either because I have no memory of it at all.

O'Connor was then brought into court to see if his appearance might jog Watts' memory:

Watts: I cannot recall him.
Fitzgerald: Thank you very much. As I understand it you are saying, looking at Mr O'Connor who had just come in, does not jog your memory
Watts: It does not in the slightest, no.
Q: Now you do not say that the Blake case was something you would never have discussed?
A: What I can say is that for the 29 years in Special Branch there was not a single occasion when I spoke to a member of the press. That is something which is absolutely taboo and is totally out of bounds. After having retired I was approached many, many times to appear on television and radio and I declined on every occasion. I was asked on many occasions to write memoirs, which I declined. I cannot recall ever having spoken to anybody on police matters and that would include this statement.
Fitzgerald: You cannot recall it, but you are not denying that you ever discussed it?
A: I cannot possibly over a period of time say absolutely categorically when somebody was talking to me that I did not mention something, but certainly cannot agree with this.
Q: Would you accept that it is difficult now because you simply cannot recall it. What Mr O'Connor is saying is that you certainly did not name Mr Randle and Mr Pottle and that is something that would be in accordance with your approach – that it would be wrong to name them specifically. What he does say is that you identified one of them in the course of your remarks as a man who, at the time that the question of prosecution was being considered, was married with young children and you would accept that that fits in with Michael Randle?
A: Yes, it would.
Q: Would you accept that it is right that by 1970 you had become aware that there were other people involved in the escape and who they were?
A: Yes; through the report.
Q: Would you accept that it was a perfectly reasonable description for you to have adopted – that they were part of the 'intellectual mafia' of the prison?

A: Yes.[15]

Watts acknowledged that he had worked for Saladin Security and that some of the statements attributed to him conformed to the facts as he knew them. But he categorically denied that he would ever have said that a decision was taken 'from above' not to prosecute the other people involved.

> **Fitzgerald: I am putting it to you that the decision about the prosecution came from above. I am putting to you that there had been consultation between yourself and your superiors about the Randle and Pottle case in question.**
>
> **A: I could not possibly have made the statement that the decision was taken from above not to prosecute them and that the reason which came from above was that they were law abiding citizens. Absolutely not.**
>
> **Q: Are you denying that conversation?**
>
> **A: Absolutely. I could not possibly have said that.**
>
> **Q: I have put it to you in full that the reason that you gave was that 'they were perfectly law-abiding citizens in every other respect. One was a teacher married to a teacher. They had young children. Why break up the family and put them away at the cost of the tax payer, when where were lots of other real villains about.'**
>
> **A: It is not the way I talk.**
>
> **Q: Can I just ask you this. You are saying it is not the way you talk. Is it the way you thought about this case?**
>
> **A: No, not at all.**[16]

Finally Ed asked him if he could think of any reason, other than there was some policy decision, why there was no further investigation and no interview with Randle and Pottle after the book was published and the question of protecting MI5 sources no longer applied.

> **Watts: I can only give a personal view. It is possible that the detective in charge of the case looked at it and felt that, with the length of time that had elapsed, any question of fingerprint evidence – anything like this – would not be obtainable whether they were interviewed or not and decided that there was no future in it. That is a personal opinion and is all I can give.**

Tom Mackinnon in his cross-examination could get little further. He did, however, press him on the role of Special Branch:

> **Mackinnon: Can I put to you that in this particular case, the case of Mr Randle and Mr Pottle writing the book which is the subject matter**

15 Transcript 25 July 1990, p.29.

16 Transcript 25 July 1990, pp.30-31.

> **of these proceedings, every single officer involved in this case, the interviewing officers, the arresting officers and the charging officers are all Special Branch officers. This is what I am putting to you: in this sort of case with a political connection it is not quite as clear-cut as perhaps, after all these years, you gave us the impression this morning.**
> **Watts: Perhaps I might explain that things have changed very considerably since the time of 1970 in Special Branch. At that time Special Branch officers did not conduct prosecutions or investigations other than those connected with Official Secrets Act offences. Since then it has changed very considerably. Special Branch officers now go out and gain expertise with the CID or uniform branch. It is now, I understand, quite common practice for Special Branch to take up and deal with prosecutions.**

Tom then referred to the prosecution of Pat, myself and others in 1962 – when already Watts was serving with Special Branch:

> **Mackinnon: At that stage they were arrested, interviewed and brought to court. Every officer in that case was a Special Branch officer was he not?**
> **Watts: Am I not correct in saying that it was an offence against the Official Secrets Act?**
> **Bevan: The offence was brought under a section of the Official Secrets Act. I think the Attorney General prosecuted.**[17]

They were both correct about that particular case. But Tom was on to a good point. It was not only in the Official Secrets Act case of 1961-2 that Special Branch were directly involved in interviewing and prosecuting anti-nuclear protesters; they had been involved in fact in almost all the cases since the Direct Action Committee against nuclear war first embarked on civil disobedience back in December 1958. Indeed so familiar had I become down the years with the Special Branch officer assigned to the task of monitoring our actions, Detective Inspector Stratton, that when he arrested me outside a pub in Fleet Street in December 1961 he tapped me on the shoulder and said – 'You know me, Mike'. Unfortunately Tom was not aware of all this when cross-examining Watts and the moment passed.

Tom also did a valuable job, amid increasing heckling from Watkins, in sorting out who in the new document were the various people referred to by initials indicating their rank

> **Watkins: What is the purpose of all these questions? What are they going to tell us? It is we who are deciding first, the relevance (of which**

17 Transcript 25 July 1990, pp.32-33.

> I do not hesitate to remind you again) and secondly, what do we make of these letters. Please tell me what on earth these questions are directed to?
>
> Mackinnon: My Lord, our submission has been that you can infer from all the circumstances of the case that a policy decision was made by someone not to prosecute Mr Randle and Mr Pottle. We have been given … these documents and it is very, very difficult to tell to whom they are sent as names are not printed out and this witness can give us those answers.
>
> Watkins: Just ask him who is X? We do not need a lot of rigmarole of reminding him what is in the documents. He can see it. Just ask him, who is X?
>
> Mackinnon: I did just ask him who these three persons were. We could never know from looking at them who they were.
>
> Watkins: Of course you would not. Why do you not ask him: who is AC?
>
> Mackinnon: I thought I just did that.[18]

Towards the end of the cross-examination, Tom got one useful admission out of Watts, namely that the appendix to his report of 1970 would give any investigating officer important clues to follow – though he insisted that this was not its purpose.

> Mackinnon: You yourself have listed headings: the hide-outs; the final plans; Bourke's departure for Moscow; Blake's departure from the country and you have also given page numbers. Try to think back 20 years ago, this must be a list of particular interest to the police and on your account you are handing over your report to CID or whatever.
>
> Watts: Yes.
>
> Q: Is it to help them obtain evidence against the two people you have identified?
>
> A: I cannot see it that way. I cannot remember what was in my mind 20 years ago. I would still see it, knowing my style, as an abbreviation for anybody referring my report against the book.
>
> Q: In effect you've presented to the police what they never ever get in another case. You put it on a plate, all the clues, the page numbers, the references to the date of the departure and the hide-outs. There is everything for them to go to if they wanted to obtain evidence in appendix A, is there not.
>
> A: Yes
>
> Q: Can you, Mr Watts, remember in you long years of service any other case where a criminal wrote a book telling everything – the

18 Transcript 25 July 1990, p.37.

dates and the hide outs – and the police had that in their possession in which to obtain evidence?
A: Not in my personal recollection.
Q: In your report at Appendix B you have also told of the actual address where Mr Randle was staying in Camden Town: 25 Torriano Cottages, NW5.
A: Yes.
Q: So the police, when they refer to that passage, would actually know the address he was staying at.
A: If they could read they would.[19]

In his re-examination, Bevan put only one question to Watts.

Bevan: Mr Watts, tell me this. Would you have expected to have become aware, after your final memorandum, of a decision not to prosecute these two me whatever the state of the evidence? Do you understand the question?
Watts: Yes, I think I do. I think my answer to that must be that I do not think anybody would have addressed such a thing to me personally, but certainly I was not aware.[20]

Watts' position seemed unassailable. He had no recollection of any discussion of whether or not to bring a prosecution. He had no recollection of ever meeting O'Connor, but he could say categorically that he would never have made some of the statements O'Connor attributed to him. However, while that got him personally off the hook, the court had to explain the fact that Watts had indeed been working for Saladin Security where O'Connor said he interviewed him only six years previously, and decide whether his account of their conversation was credible.

Ex-Commander Cunningham, the acting head of Special Branch in 1970, was no more forthcoming than Watts. His sworn statement, taken on 24th July 1990, reads:

> I served as a police officer in the Metropolitan Police from 1934 until my retirement in 1971. I joined Special Branch as a Detective Constable in December 1936 and retired as a Commander in charge of Special Branch Operations on 27th August 1971. When George Blake the Soviet Spy escaped from Wormwood Scrubs in October 1966 I was a Detective Superintendent in charge of the Irish Squad and was sent to liaise with the Garda Siochana in Dublin in an effort to locate Seán Bourke. I also visited Bourke's mother in Limerick. My enquiries proved

19 Transcript 25 July 1990, pp.42-42.

20 The official transcript reads at this point (p.42 at G) `...I do not think anybody who have address such a thing to me...' but the who is clearly a typist's error.

to be fruitless. I was not involved further in the investigation into the Blake escape. On 23rd March 1970 a report by Detective Chief Inspector Rollo Watts, which gave an analysis of Seán Bourke's manuscript, was referred to me for information. D.C.I. Watts concluded that two possible identifications named by Bourke could have been Michael Randle and Patrick Pottle. However, there was no evidence to substantiate this. I discussed the content of the report with Chief Superintendent Rodger. At that time I was Commander Operations, but Acting Deputy Assistant Commissioner in charge of Special Branch. We concluded that there was not evidence to substantiate any charge and that there was no merit in pursuing enquiries. I referred the report up to the Assistance Commissioner of Crime, who was in charge of the CID and Special Branch, and advised him that there was no evidence at that time to substantiate any charge. He initialled my minute. I do not recall having any discussion with him about this. I subsequently sent a copy of D.C.I. Watts' report with a covering letter to both the Security Service and Home Office. I have been asked whether there was any policy decision taken not to prosecute Randle and Pottle at that time. There was no such decision.

In the Examination in Chief from Bevan, he elaborated his account of his discussions in 1970 with Chief Superintendent Roger – inadvertently undermining Watts' categorical assertion that Special Branch would not have been directly involved in pursuing the investigation with a view to prosecution:

Bevan: As a result of your discussion with Mr Rodger, what was your conclusion of the whole matter with regard to this report?
Cunningham: I came to the conclusion that there was no evidence which we could put before the court in any way to prosecute these two individuals.
Q: Secondly, did you discuss the possibility of pursuing any lines of enquiry that flowed from the manuscript of the Bourke book?
A: Yes, we did discuss that.
Q: Tell your Lordships about that discussion and the conclusion you came to.
A: We came to the conclusion that we had no positive evidence whatsoever to pursue investigations. We feared that if someone was sent down to see them they would more or less laugh at us because there was no evidence that we could produce and interrogate them on.[21]

Cunningham also stated that the initialling by the Assistant Commissioner Crime, Mr Brodie, of his minute of 25th March 1970 meant that he concurred

21 Transcript 25 July 1990 p.44.

with the judgement that there was no evidence at that stage, and confirmed that Brodie would be responsible for initiating any prosecution or any action which should be taken.

> **Bevan: You were a very senior police officer. Did you know at that time in 1970, of any decision whatever, from whatever source, not to prosecute these two men – Mr Randle and Mr Pottle – whatever the state of the evidence?**
> **Cunningham: No, sir. There was nothing like that at all sir, nothing whatsoever.**
> **Q: Secondly, I ask you this. Had such a decision been made by someone somewhere else not to prosecute these two men, whatever the state of the evidence, would you have expected in position to have learnt of such a decision?**
> **A: I should have done sir, certainly yes, but I did not. There was no such order or agreement on the basis of that. It was only my decision here which went to the Assistant Commissioner Crime and he initialled it. There was nothing else. Letters were sent to the Home Office and to the Security Service enclosing copies of this report. There was nothing said at all which would indicate that they wanted us to take certain actions.**
> **Q: Mr Brodie, of course, as you have said, was not merely head of the Special Branch but he was also head of the investigative part of the police at that time.**
> **A: That is correct. Yes, head of the CID for London.**[22]

Cunningham's assertion that not only was there no decision not to prosecute us regardless of the evidence, but that if there had been he would certainly have known about it, was particularly damaging to our case if his testimony was accepted. However, Tom in his cross examination managed to pry him away slightly from that position:

> **Mackinnon: … Mr Cunningham, you were a member of Special Branch in 1964 when Anthony Blunt was offered immunity?**
> **Cunningham: In 1964, yes I remember that.**
> **Q: I think you know, it is a matter of record, that even the government minister did not know of that offer of immunity until some years later.**
> **A: I was not involved in that case. I cannot comment upon it.**
> **Q: You say you were not involved in the case in any event.**
> **A: I was not involved in that case at all.**
> **Bevan: So far as immunity is concerned, the only person who can give immunity is the Attorney General, not the Home Office, not the**

22 Transcript 25 July 1990, pp.46-47.

Special Branch, not even D.I. Chapman, but the Attorney General.
Mackinnon: Mr Cunningham, what I am putting to you is that there have been cases involving swapping of prisoners with foreign countries after a very short period of incarceration, these sorts of decisions in cases involving spies.
A: I have read about such cases but I have never been involved one myself.
Q: I am suggesting to you that in that very limited class of case, policy decisions and the like can be made and they may be communicated only to the very top officers, such as perhaps Mr Brodie or perhaps the very top officer in the Special Branch – your superior officer.
A: I did not know of any in the present case.
Q: You have heard of such things happening, have you not?
A: I have heard, yes.[23]

Cunningham also acknowledged, under cross examination by Ed, that the option of obtaining a warrant to search Pat's and my premises was considered but rejected – 'on the basis that we believed that there would be no evidence at all found.'[24] He also accepted that 'to the best of his knowledge' no steps were taken to find any further evidence.

The next witness, ex-Commander Wilson could throw no light whatsoever on the affair. He had been in Special Branch in 1970, but had no connections with the case and had never even seen the Watts' report until the day before his appearance in court. There seems to have been no reason for the Crown calling him as a witness and it only remained for Watkins to wish him well in his retirement and to say how nice it was to see him again.

It was now after 4pm and Watkins accepted Bevan's proposal that they adjourn proceedings for the day, though O'Connor had not yet had the opportunity to give his evidence. Ed renewed his application for files to be disclosed:

Fitzgerald: ... I would limit [the application] to the CID files being brought to court and inspected by your Lordships. If indeed only Special Branch officers are being called, as indeed is the case, and they all say 'It is nothing to do with us and any steps to be taken to pursue this matter are to be done by the CID,' then it could well be that some decision has been made or there is very relevant information in the CID file on this matter. That appears to be exactly what Mr Cunningham said. Mr Watts stressed all he was really to do was to

23 Transcript, p. 5.

24 Transcript, 25 July 1990, p. 49.

> **prepare the report and Special Branch does not get concerned in these matters …**
> **Bevan: The instructions that I have received are that the CID file as it is termed by my learned friend contains nothing about Randle and Pottle at all. What it concerns is the Blake escape, but not Randle and Pottle. Those are my instructions. I can but ask those behind me to bring all the papers that touch upon this matter and for myself and Mr Havers to look through it and to see if that is really the position.**
> **Watkins: Very well, perhaps you will do that, Mr Bevan. It is to be hoped that we start at ten o'clock in the morning.**

The hearing appeared to be over for the day, when two men came into the courtroom and handed a note to Havers who in turn took it to the judge. Earlier Pat had noticed them sitting at the front of the court and leaving it at some point in the afternoon. It appears from what followed that they were members of the Security Service, MI5. The official court transcript does not mention the incident itself, only its aftermath. But the document which Watkins then showed to the Counsel for both sides so traumatised Mr Bevan that the exact time etched itself on his memory and he subsequently referred to it as the '4.13' document. Like the note that had been produced that morning, it was a minute from an MI5 file of 1970, this one made on the 29th April recording a conversation between the same female MI5 officer and Chief Inspector Watts. It read:

Note for File

> 1. While I was speaking to Chief Inspector Watts of S.B. yesterday he mentioned their report [blanked out words] and asked if we had any comments to make on it.
>
> 2. Chief Inspector Watts added that the S.B. decision at present was to take no steps to interview or attempt to prosecute the Randles, Pottle or Goodwin.[25] It was considered that to do so might be persecution – a big fish had got away so they were taking it out on the little fish. It was considered, however, that it had been necessary to investigate their suspicions and place them on record.
>
> 3. First of all I had I already had it in mind that S.B. would want to know how much of their report had been passed on to the I.R.D. and I said that in order not to prejudice their enquiries we had omitted all

25 Goodwin was another person identified, much more tentatively, by Watts in his report. He thought he might possibly be the writer living in the area of Cromwell road that Seán mentions as having harboured Blake and Bourke for a few days. Here Watts was mistaken. Pat and myself didn't know Goodwin and he was not involved in any way.

parts which disclosed the possible identifications they had made.

4. Secondly, I said that before commenting on their report we were awaiting the results of our own enquiries. I said I would see that S.B. would receive our comments as soon as possible.

[The signature and endorsements have been blanked out. See the photo of the Note in Appendix 4, second document]

Watkins at once ordered that Watts, who had by now left the building, should be recalled the next day to take the stand again and be confronted with this new evidence. He was not to be shown the document in advance, and the press were warned not to report what had occurred for the time being. To quote the court transcript:

Watkins: Gentlemen of the press, you should be very circumspect about reporting what has happened in the last five or ten minutes because as you appreciate a witness is coming and he should know nothing about what has been happening here. I do not want to make any particular order, but you understand what I mean about how circumspect you should be in circumstances of this kind.

In the corridor outside the courtroom the defence and Crown advocates and their entourages were huddled in separate groups. There was no mistaking the dismay of the Crown lobby. Pat overheard Chief Inspector Eggington enquiring urgently of Bevan.

'This means we've lost, doesn't it?'

He did not hear Bevan's reply. Perhaps, indeed Bevan was too furious to answer, for as the *amicus curiae* Havers walked away, Bevan hissed after him – 'Little shit!'

The significance of the document is clear. It proved beyond doubt that considerations other than the strength of the evidence did figure in the deliberations about whether further steps should be taken, that these were discussed between Watts and an MI5 officer, and that the Special Branch, contrary to what both Watts and Cunningham had asserted, could have played a direct role in obtaining evidence and in conducting a prosecution. ('*The S.B. decision* at present was to take no steps to interview or attempt to prosecute the Randles, Pottle or Goodwin'). The document, in fact, blew a mighty hole in the stonewall defence that the Special Branch had constructed to prevent us from prying further into what had occurred and threatened it with total destruction.

But when the court resumed next morning, Bevan announced that Watts had been taken ill with renal spasms and was in hospital. He was therefore applying for an adjournment. Watts, he said, was not a well man, had had a stroke three years ago and suffered from angina. It was impossible in these circumstances for our Counsel to oppose the adjournment, and the hearing was postponed until the beginning of the new term on or around 2nd October. Meanwhile the injunction that Watts should not be shown the Note for File was lifted, though he was not to discuss the issue with the retired MI5 officer concerned. The restrictions on press reporting were also lifted.

The impossibility of pressing home our advantage was a disappointment – tempered in my case by the satisfaction of knowing that with luck I would now be able to attend the resumed hearing in October. In some ways, too, it would have been an anti-climax for us to have won the case in the High Court procedure rather than being able to defend ourselves and put our case to the jury at the Old Bailey.

The only other significant development that day was that a renewed application by Ed for MI5 files to be disclosed to us was flatly rejected by Watkins. Bevan and Havers also told the court that they had read the CID files and there was no mention of Randle or Pottle in them. This point was confirmed by Watkins after he had adjourned the session for about an hour to read them. In fact the omission of any mention of us in the file was perhaps more surprising than anything that it might have said about us, since the CID had received the Watts report in 1970 in which we had been clearly identified as suspects. This point was not lost on our own counsel who obtained from Bevan a formal admission that there was nothing in the file 'to indicate that the CID carried out any investigations of Randle or Pottle at any time in 1970 as a result of the Watts report.' 'Obviously,' he continued, 'we may be, at the end of the day, inviting inferences from that.'

Most of the papers next day prominently reported the emergence of the MI5 document and the illness of Watts. 'MI5 document stalls case against Pottle and Randle' was the Guardian headline above a report by Richard Norton-Taylor in which he said that 'The prosecution case against two peace campaigners charged with helping the double agent George Blake to escape from prison in 1966 broke up in disarray yesterday after an intervention by MI5.' In the Scotsman, which throughout gave the case extensive coverage, John Mullin's story was headed 'Key witness in Blake escape case taken ill' and the report stated that Watts had 'collapsed after being told he had to face fresh questioning at the High Court in London yesterday.' The Independent made the story, by Nick Cohen, its front page lead. 'MI5 files throw spy case into disarray' was the banner headline. One paragraph in the report read:

> In a series of extraordinary events at the review of whether the Government's attempts to prosecute Pat Pottle and Michael Randle are an abuse of the judicial process, the High Court asked journalists to suppress details of the discovery [of the MI5 document on Wednesday afternoon]. They did not want Mr Watts to be 'forewarned of its contents'. But Mr Watts was taken to hospital on Wednesday night after being told to reappear. He is expected to be released on Monday.

How is one to explain the sudden appearance of the second MI5 document on the Wednesday afternoon? We ourselves speculated that it might be result of feuding between MI5 and Special Branch whose relationship is known to have been marked at certain periods by friction and rivalry. Havers' explanation to the court was quite different. The document had been uncovered, he said, in the course of Wednesday as the result of 'an abundance of caution' on the part of MI5 officers who had discovered it in a file which did not appear to be relevant. Here, in fairness to him, is his full statement to the court on the matter:

> The position is, as I think your Lordships already know, that on Tuesday evening both Mr Bevan and I were notified by counsel for the applicants that they were proposing yesterday morning, as indeed they did, to apply to your Lordships for disclosure of both the Home Office file and the security service file. The intention was obviously passed on by me to the appropriate channels and the matter was investigated, in so far as it could be on Tuesday; in fact it was not until Wednesday morning that sensible investigations could be made. As a result of that, on Wednesday morning what appeared to be the relevant files from both sources were produced. As a result of that exercise, the document – that I think is now page 8 of the small bundle, the one that was produced yesterday morning – was produced. In fact thereafter, in other words after the production of that document yesterday morning and the resumption of this hearing, other files which were not on the face of them relevant to the issues in this case were also examined out of an abundance of caution. As a result of that exercise that further document came to light. As soon as it did, naturally the appropriate steps were taken, and the matter was brought to your Lordships' attention yesterday afternoon.[26]

Despite the absence of Watts, Ed Fitzgerald urged that O'Connor, who had flown over specially from Ireland to attend, should be allowed to give his evidence. But Bevan objected. He could not, he maintained, conduct a satisfactory cross-examination of O'Connor until after Watts had taken the

26 Transcript 26 July 1990, p.5.

stand for a second time and responded to the new evidence. So for the second time, O'Connor went away empty handed. And he was understandably reluctant to commit himself to making a third trip to the attend the resumed hearing in October. There was thus a risk that as a result of the debacle our key witness would not be able to give his evidence in person in the Divisional Court.

Chapter 12:

Blake's Boast

Before we went back to the Divisional Court in October, George Blake himself made a dramatic re-entry into the public arena. We knew from our visit to him that he was working on an autobiography but he was able to assure us it would not be published until well after our trial, set at that time for the latter part of April. We had also done our filming with Novosti on the understanding that any programme would not be shown before the trial. However, the successive postponement of that event threw out our calculations.

Some time in late July or early August we learned that the BBC planned to broadcast the following month a major television documentary on Blake in their *Inside Story* series to coincide approximately with the publication of his autobiography by Jonathan Cape. The documentary, produced by Tom Bower, was the joint BBC-Novosti production in connection with which he and Barrie Penrose had been in Moscow the previous February. It would almost certainly include some of the footage Novosti had shot of Pat and myself with Blake in February. This was no disaster as far as Pat and myself were concerned because we had said nothing to Novosti that we had not said in our book, in the Thames Weekend programme, and a dozen times in interviews to the press and media. But the lawyers were concerned. They feared that our appearance with Blake himself in Moscow represented an additional twist of the knife and could affect how a judge and jury might view our actions, and the severity of the sentence if we were found guilty. On 6th August Ben wrote to the BBC asking to be put in touch with the producer of the programme and those responsible for its transmission. (I was still in hospital at the time and learned only later about the exchanges with the BBC on the programme).

The real shock came some ten days later. On 19th August the *Sunday Express* ran a lead front page story about Blake under the banner headline – 'How I betrayed 600 British Spies.' Written by our old adversary Barrie Penrose, it claimed to be an 'exclusive' account of how Blake had admitted to betraying 600 British agents. The reader should bear in mind at this point that it was the sister daily paper of the *Sunday Express* – the *Daily Express* – which in 1961 first claimed that Blake had been responsible for the death or disappearance of over 40 British agents and that his 42 year prison sentence represented one year for every agent betrayed. Since then Express newspapers had taken a proprietorial interest in Blake and in bolstering his image as the master-spy who eclipsed all others in the depth of his treachery and the damage he had caused to Western intelligence. The story was accompanied by a colour photograph of George, Ida and Misha and their dog outside his dacha, and began:

> Traitor George Blake has emerged from hiding in Moscow after 24 years to reveal that he betrayed 600 British agents.
>
> The MI6 double agent was speaking publicly for the first time since he escaped from Wormwood Scrubs in 1966 and slipped through an international dragnet to flee to the Soviet Union.
>
> Despite his denials, some of the agents he betrayed would almost certainly have been executed.
>
> His disclosures will lead to a dramatic reassessment by Whitehall intelligence chiefs – for the depth of his treachery suggests the damage he did to Britain and the West during the Cold War has been massively underestimated.
>
> Blake's confession means he ranks as the biggest traitor who ever worked for British Intelligence, causing more damage than did Kim Philby, Guy Burgess, Donald Maclean or Anthony Blunt.
>
> He was previously thought to have identified 42 British spies to the KGB and he was sentenced to 42 years imprisonment – one for every life betrayed.
>
> His new claim will cause shock and consternation within MI6.

The consternation within MI6 – if it existed at all within an organisation that had had ample time and opportunity to assess the damage wrought by Blake – was certainly nothing compared to the consternation it caused Pat and myself, our families and our lawyers. What the hell, we asked ourselves, was George playing at? Had he actually given an exclusive interview to Barrie Penrose of all people, after having assured during our visit in February that he would never do so? Did he have no idea of the impact this could have on our trial, assuming, as we must, that it would eventually go ahead? Here we were pouring scorn on the story of 42 years for 42 betrayed agents, only to have George intervene to say that, by the way, it was probably 600! It was surely a boast, though a boast of a particularly perverse kind. It was hardly likely he had kept a tally of agents betrayed to put in his memoirs. In an odd way Blake and the Sunday Express shared an interest in boosting his importance by exaggerating the damage he had done.

The view that Blake was bragging was apparently shared by former MI6 officers. Richard Norton-Taylor has good contacts in these circles and sounded them out for their reaction to the story. His report appeared in the Guardian on August 20th, the day after the Sunday Express story. Headed: 'Blake's claim he betrayed 600 doubted', it said that former intelligence officers treated the figure of 600 as 'a wild overestimate'. One source suggested that 'Mr Blake was simply showing off.'

Pat phoned George in Moscow to ask him what was going on. George was contrite, apologised profusely and said the last thing he had wanted was to make things more difficult for us. He could promise us he had never met or been interviewed by Penrose and could only suppose that one of the Russians who had been present when Tom Bower interviewed him had passed on the information to Penrose. From this, Blake supposed, the latter had constructed his 'exclusive' report. (In fact it seems more likely that Tom Bower himself passed on titbits of information to Penrose.)

> **'I'm really sorry if all this has made things worse for you and Michael', Blake repeated.**
>
> **'Well, never mind that now,' Pat said, 'the damage has been done. But it would help if you would give an interview to a responsible journalist to put things into perspective. Would you be prepared to talk to Richard Norton-Taylor of the Guardian who had been closely following our case?'**
>
> **'Of course! I'll do whatever you and Michael think will help.'**

So it was that Pat and Richard Norton-Taylor travelled to Moscow to see George.

By now the media build up to the publication of Blake's autobiography, orchestrated by his agent Andrew Nurnberg, was gathering momentum. Simon Garfield wittily described the goings-on behind the scenes in a piece in the Independent on Sunday on 9th September headed 'George Blake: a story of intrigue, secrets and agents … and that's just the media.'

> 'We should brace ourselves for an autobiography, newspaper interviews, an 80-minute BBC film about Blake, and a nice line in backbiting about who would unveil 'exclusives' first.
>
> It is a story of agents, predominantly of the literary sort, and of how a journalist, a specialist spy writer, a television film-maker, a publisher and two Sunday newspapers came to break bread with a traitor who had done much to destroy the work of British intelligence since the war.'

Garfield said that there was intense rivalry and bad blood between the makers of the BBC film on the one hand and Tom Maschler of Jonathan Cape, publishers of Blake's autobiography, on the other. Andrew Nurnberg, the literary agent, straddled both camps, negotiating the timing of the publication and the broadcast to ensure the maximum exposure for his client. The official publication date of the book was to be 17th September with the broadcast following two days later. Nurnberg had also struck a deal with the *Sunday Times* whereby they would help to promote the book by serialising a lengthy interview between Blake and Phillip Knightley, the well-known writer on espionage matters, who had also written an introduction to Blake's book.

But the film-makers preempted the *Sunday Times* with Penrose's story in the Sunday Express claiming Blake had admitted naming 600 British agents. (In fact in both his book and interview the figure Blake gives is 400; Penrose throws in another couple of hundred victims for good measure.) Penrose had formerly worked for the Sunday Times where he had published his story about our involvement in the Blake escape in 1987 so maybe he had a score to settle with his former employers. As it turned out, the *Sunday Times* were so furious about the Penrose article, and about the fact that copies of the book had been distributed ahead of an agreed embargo date – thereby allowing other papers to publish information from the book – that they refused to pay Jonathan Cape the sum they had agreed.

Penrose was a key figure on the film-makers side – this much we already knew from what the Thames Television people had told us during our trip to Moscow in February. Indeed, according to Garfield, Penrose had initiated the project some eighteen months earlier when he obtained permission through a Soviet diplomat in London to do a television interview with Blake in exchange for financing a group of Soviet film-makers from Novosti to work in London for a month. He teamed up with Tom Bower and together they negotiated a deal with the BBC and Novosti to produce the documentary. To cover its back, the BBC insisted that they would have the final word on editing the film, and that Blake himself would receive no money from it. In February, after the BBC and Novosti had reached an agreement, Penrose and Bower flew to Moscow. Filming began the following month. However, the interview with Blake was conducted not by Penrose but by Bower. Perhaps this was because Pat and myself had warned Blake off Penrose, though we don't know that. But at any rate Penrose continued to liaise with Bower and was able to obtain the information on which his 'exclusive' non-interview with Blake was based. His article in the *Sunday Express* included an inset plug for Bower's BBC programme – though significantly not for the book – whilst in the documentary Penrose is credited as a 'consultant'.

If Garfield's date's are correct, the BBC had already clinched a deal with Novosti by the time we went to Moscow in February armed with a video camera from Thames Television. Roger Bolton, the head of Thames' current affairs and documentaries, was quoted in an article in the Observer on 2nd

September by its Media Editor, Richard Brooks, as saying that he was offered the interview the previous year but rejected it 'because the co-production deal limited editorial independence.' The article chiefly focuses on the severe censure of the BBC for making the film 'by one of the corporation's most distinguished journalists,' Charles Wheeler – a man whom, incidentally, all of us also held in high esteem. 'Blake sees the interview,' Wheeler is reported as saying, 'as a chance to rehabilitate himself as does the KGB. The man is a professional liar'.

The report goes on to say that once the Russians had gone to Bower, Thames expressed interest again but lost out to the BBC. Presumably then when Thames asked us in February for our cooperation in getting an interview with Blake they were making a last ditch attempt to outwit the BBC. They did not see fit to inform us that they had been negotiating with Nurnberg or that Novosti had approached them the previous year and by then were committed to co-producing a film with the BBC, or at the very least were on the verge of clinching the deal. Blake, too, unless he was kept altogether in the dark about the negotiations, must have known more than he was prepared to tell us when he asked us to do some filming with Novosti – and the Novosti people themselves gave us no hint that they were involved in a co-production with the BBC.

The serialisation of Knightley's interview with Blake began in the Sunday Times on 9th September. On the same day the Sunday Express featured another 'World Exclusive' by Barrie Penrose on Blake headed 'Why I Betrayed my Country'. More blatantly than the earlier piece, it was presented so as to give the impression that Penrose himself had interviewed Blake. 'The Sunday Express,' it claimed,' in a front page report drawing attention to the feature, 'has obtained the first exclusive interview with Blake.' The introduction to the feature itself concludes: 'Over a period of several weeks the spy who had no shame spoke candidly of his treachery and why he betrayed Britain. Barrie Penrose tells the story.' No one could imagine from this that the interview in question had been given to someone else – namely Tom Bower for the BBC-Novosti film – and that Penrose was simply weaving in some of its contents in his re-telling of the Blake story. Penrose's 'World Exclusive' also repeated the assertion that Blake admitted he 'had betrayed 600 agents to the deadly KGB.'

By contrast, Knightley's piece was, in general sympathetic in tone as this passage from his introduction shows:

> In three days of interviews in Moscow … Blake told me the amazing story of his life.
>
> I was under no illusion as to why he did so. He wants to promote his

> autobiography No Other Choice which will be published in the West later this month. There are things in this book and many others Blake told me during our talks that I find hard to believe, as will many readers, but without access to the archives of SIS and the KGB, it is impossible to be certain.
>
> However, in general, I think Blake answered my questions frankly and truthfully, and those statements that I could check bear out this impression. But we must not forget that Blake receives a KGB pension, that he had to seek KGB approval for our interviews, and that the KGB, like all intelligence agencies, is interested in establishing its version of our recent history.

Later in the article – which overlaps considerably with the introduction to Blake's book – Knightley writes:

> Unless Blake was playing some deep KGB game, we have to cast aside all our preconceptions about him and think again. I know this will infuriate the many people who detest George Blake; but I decided I was dealing with a very sincere man who is in the process of coming to terms with the fact that the side he chose 40 years ago has lost the ideological battle.

The first article in the series, however, put a new spin on the 42 years for 42 betrayed agents myth. The judge at Blake's trial, readers were told, had said that '*he had given the KGB the name of every British agent behind the Iron Curtain*, and most damaging of all in the public view, he had been responsible for the deaths of 42 of them – hence his sentence, "a year for each life betrayed." In fact the judge had said nothing at all about Blake betraying British agents or being responsible for deaths – and the original Chapman Pincher version of the story was that Blake had betrayed over 40 British agents *some of whom* had disappeared or been executed. Moreover the claim that he had betrayed 'every British agent working behind the Iron Curtain' was an absurdity – an insult as much to the British Intelligence Service as to Blake himself. Not even his – or the SIS's – worst enemies had ever suggested he was in a position to do that. My letter setting the record straight was published in the *Sunday Times* two weeks later. Knightley himself subsequently acknowledged in the paper that he was mistaken on this point.

Much more damaging, because it came as it were from the mole's mouth, was Blake's statement that the number of agents he betrayed was 'more likely 400 than 40.' Nor did he make any apology for his actions, commenting that those he named 'were working against communism.' Knightley is sceptical about Blake's claim that the KGB promised him that none of the agents he identified would be executed but only imprisoned. Even if the KGB told him that, it was an extraordinary feat of self-deception for Blake to have persuaded himself that they would feel the slightest obligation to honour this commitment.

Our lawyers meanwhile had been attempting to get the BBC to postpone the showing of Bower's film and to secure the backing of CPS itself for this 'since we consider there is an equal interest on the part of the prosecution and defence to restrain the showing of prejudicial material before the trial.'[1]Neither responded positively. The BBC's solicitor – appropriately called Mr Law – noted that 'your clients have made no secret of their involvement with that escape, quite the reverse, as is immediately apparent from their readily available book The Blake Escape – How we freed George Blake and why – detailing their part in it.' In view of this there seemed 'no likelihood that the programme will give rise to any substantial risk of serious prejudice to the criminal proceedings against them.'[2] They stuck firmly to this position in subsequent exchanges. Michael Bibby of the Crown Prosecution Service passed copies of the correspondence between our lawyers and those of the BBC to the Legal Secretariat of the Law Officers, together with 'two recent articles in the Sunday Express.'[3] The latter responded, in a letter dated 10th September, saying in effect that it was up to us if we wanted to seek an injunction.

> The Solicitor General is of the view that in the circumstances, the material placed before the Crown Prosecution Service does not provide a sufficient basis for an application for injunctive relief or other action on the part of the Law Officers but that it is open to your clients to bring this matter before the court if they are so advised.[4]

By this stage Tom Mackinnon had been able to see a video of the film. It contained very little of the discussion between Blake, Pat and myself in his Moscow flat – in fact just a short passage of me speaking to camera. However, we did appear briefly walking beside him in the street. In Tom's view, the most damaging part of the film was Charles Wheeler's vehement attack on Blake as 'a cold calculating liar.' However, we decided it wasn't worthwhile pursuing the matter further. My own feeling, in retrospect, is that if by any chance we

---

1 Letter from Ben Birnberg to Michael Bibby of the Crown Prosecution Service dated 22 August 1990.

2 Letter from Mr RM.Law, BBC Solicitor's Department, 16 August 1990.

3 Letter from Michael Bibby to B.M. Birnberg dated 29 August 1990.

4 Letter signed by S.J.Wooler of the Legal Secretariat to the Law Officers at the Attorney General's Chambers, addressed to B.M. Birnberg & Co, dated 10th September 1990.

had succeeded in having the screening postponed this would have prejudiced us more than anything the film contained since the press and the public might have concluded that there was some dark secret we were attempting to hide.

In early September, Pat and Richard Norton-Taylor travelled by train to Moscow to interview George. They brought back with them a signed copy of George's biography for Anne and myself – and a bar of soap from the Hotel Am Zoo in the Kurfurstendamm in Berlin where they had stayed for a night on their journey back.

Richard's account of his meeting and interview with Blake was published in the Guardian on 19th September, the morning of the day on which the BBC showed the Bower film. Richard noted that Blake could be 'pedantic and disingenuous in his answers' but that he had 'an emotional, perhaps sentimental, side to him'. On the crucial issue of the 400 betrayed agents, Blake had this to say:

> **I deliberately used the figure of 400 by way of shock treatment to try and get rid of the completely fabricated story [i.e. that the 42 year sentence represented one year for every agent betrayed]. The number of agents whose identities I passed on indeed exceeded 40. Exactly how many I simply don't know. I never added them up …**

The last point rings true. But it is hard to credit that he decided to claim he had betrayed around 400 victims to 'get rid of the fabricated story' of 42 years imprisonment for 42 betrayed agents. The whole rationale behind that government-inspired rumour was to convince the public that the unprecedented sentence was justified. You could hardly expect to convince them otherwise by saying that actually the number was nearer 400. The article continues:

> 'To drive home the point – and not for the first time praising his former employer, MI6 – he later added that no competent intelligence service would allow a single agent to have access to as many as 400 names. Pressed to give a figure Blake replied: 'I don't know; I really don't know and I don't know who knows.' He added: 'These people were not innocents, they were agents working willingly and knowingly against their own governments'. Just like him.

Blake said again, as he does in his book and in the Bower and Knightley interviews, that he made a special arrangement with the KGB to ensure that none of the people he named would be executed. However, he conceded one point that he had not done elsewhere, namely that it was impossible to have a 'definitive answer' about whether any agents were in fact killed.

There were no great surprises in the Bower interview on BBC television that evening given what had already been published. Nor indeed were there any very startling revelations in the autobiography. A passage on the opening page, rich in unintended irony, explains why:

> ... As my life unfolded day by day before my eyes, it did not seem to me all that extraordinary and worth writing about. To do so might seem presumptuous. What is more, I have always been of the opinion that secret intelligence operations should remain secret and that those who are called upon to take part in them should remain silent, except perhaps within the small circle of those who are in the know, who are 'indoctrinated' as the term has it.'[5]

Pass information to the agents of the other side – ok. But reveal it to the general public, the hoi polloi who are not 'indoctrinated' – never! This reticence on Blake's part did not, however, deter the authorities from taking action in the courts to prevent him or his family receiving royalties from the book. He had been paid a £35,000 advance by Jonathan Cape, so that they could do nothing about that. He had arranged for the balance to be paid into a Trust Fund for the benefit of his children. The Treasury Solicitors sought and obtained a court order freezing these royalties on the grounds that the book was produced in breach of confidentiality. Our solicitor, Ben Birnberg, represented Blake in the court hearings on the issue.

According to a report in the *Sunday Express*, the then Prime Minister, Mrs Thatcher, personally intervened to prevent Blake receiving the royalties. The paper quotes from a letter she wrote in reply to the espionage writer, James Rusbridger, who had written to demand why the government had not taken action on the matter. She is quoted as saying that the government considered it 'wrong for Blake to make money from publishing the story of his treachery as a Crown servant'.[6] (Apparently there was no such objection to Jonathan Cape making money from publishing the book, or the Sunday Times from publishing extensive interviews with him which cover almost all the material that could be considered confidential or sensitive in the book.) But Blake had the last laugh on this issue. In April 1996 the case again came before Mr Justice Scott in the High Court when the Crown sought to confiscate the £90,000 that had amassed in royalties since 1990. Blake was unrepresented as he had been refused legal aid, but a barrister was appointed to represent his interest. The Court rejected the Crown's claim and the royalties were freed. The public significance of the case lies in the fact that the Crown acknowledged that Blake's book revealed nothing that was not already in the public realm but claimed

5 George Blake, No Other Choice, Jonathan Cape 1990, p.l.

6 'No 10 acts to block cash for Blake', Barrie Penrose, *Sunday Expres* 23 September 1990.

he had a lifelong duty of confidentiality as a former Crown servant. Had this claim been upheld it would have prevented any former civil servant, and perhaps ex-government minister, from writing his or her memoirs, or speaking about their work, without official permission and thus placed extensive new powers of censorship in the hands of the government.

There are interesting insights in the book – and the interviews – into the way intelligence services become entangled in their own webs of betrayal and deceit. Blake is reviled for his treachery in acting as a double-agent, a role neither Pat nor I have ever defended. But ironically his principal task whilst working for six years in Berlin for SIS/MI6 in the 1950s was to try to induce Soviet intelligence officers to betray their country and the service they worked for by becoming double-agents on behalf of the West. This was done not by appealing to any ideals they might have concerning human rights and democracy, or any antipathy they might feel for an authoritarian system, but by an appeal to material self-interest and greed. Blake, at least, acted out of conviction – as did a handful of other 'traitors' on both sides.

To illustrate the point. Blake tells how the SIS recruited a German called Trautmann with extensive criminal and black market contacts to open up a 'shop', situated unobtrusively inside a luxury block of flats near the Russian sector boundary selling luxury goods such as silk stockings, watches and cameras. Black market touts, unaware even that they were acting on behalf of British Intelligence, would attempt to lure Soviet personnel into the shop where they could be flattered and softened up by British agents. As it turned out, the operation was a fiasco. The only 'Soviet agent' ever recruited, a young woman called Nina, turned out to be in the employ of the rival US intelligence agency, the CIA. Shortly afterwards this scheme collapsed altogether when Trautmann and his mistress, defected with the funds and stock to East Germany. It then emerged that he had been working for the East Germans for some time.

The one major catch that Blake delivered to his SIS masters was a senior KGB officer he calls 'Boris'. It will come as no surprise that he was a plant, a double agent, feeding British Intelligence with what the Russians wanted them to know. This, of course, would have included some genuine information to convince them they had recruited a genuine top-grade agent.

The full story behind this episode is convoluted but worth retelling because it shows how Intelligence Agencies fall into traps of their own devising. Blake, on behalf of the SIS was running a German agent, Horst Eitner – nicknamed 'Mickey' because of his physical resemblance to Mickey Mouse. He worked in a Jewish tailor's shop in a poor working class suburb of West Berlin, and again the intention was to attract Soviet intelligence personnel in search of bargains into the shop and induce them to work for the West. In fact, unknown to the SIS, 'Mrs Mickey' was already working for the Russians. As a young woman after the war she had been recruited by the CIA, uncovered by the Russians and imprisoned for 25 years. Then, after serving five years, she was granted an amnesty on the understanding she would now work for the Russians. Subsequently Blake was tipped off by his KGB handler that Soviet Military Intelligence, GRU, had also recruited Mickey, though the later remained unaware of Blake's role as a double agent. The KGB then arranged with Blake for Boris to be 'recruited' to British Intelligence by way of Mickey's shop, a move which would allay suspicion that he was a plant, and at the same time give a boost to Blake's own reputation within SIS. For the next two years, until moved to a different post, Boris played this double-game without arousing the least suspicion on the part of the British.

However, there was an ironic sequel to the Mickey / Boris sting. After Blake left Berlin in the summer of 1959, Mickey got a new MI6 case officer, an agent by the name of Johnny Spears. The Russians, curious to find out the discussions that were taking place between them, got Mickey to agree to have hidden microphones installed in his flat. Not long afterwards, 'Mrs Mickey' (as Blake calls her) in a fit of jealous rage denounced him – and herself – to the West German police. At first they refused to take her seriously. Then she took them to the flat and showed them various items including the hidden microphones, presumably also telling them when they had been installed. She and Mickey were arrested.

Later a senior officer in British counter-intelligence, Harry Shergold, examining the case wondered why the microphones had been installed only after Blake had left Berlin. Reluctantly he concluded that the most plausible explanation was that they did not need them during Blake's time because he was working for the KGB. This then tied up with information which came from the former deputy head of Polish Intelligence, Michael Goleniewski, who defected to the West in 1960 and warned that the Russians had two important spies in Britain, one in the Navy, one in the British Intelligence Service. Gordon Lonsdale, of the Portland Spy Ring, was the one in the Navy; Blake was the one in British Intelligence.

Even so, when Shergold and the others interrogated Blake in London on Easter Tuesday, 1961, they had no solid evidence on which to charge him and had to hope that, under pressure, he would confess. He did so on the third day of interrogation when his interrogators suggested to him that he had been tortured by his Korean captors in 1951 and forced to admit that he was working with British Intelligence. He writes:

> Suddenly I felt an upsurge of indignation and I wanted my interrogators and everyone else to know that I had acted out of conviction, out of belief in Communism, and not under duress or for financial gain. This feeling was so strong that without thinking I burst out, 'No, nobody tortured me! Nobody blackmailed me! I myself approached the Soviets and offered my services to them of my own accord …
>
> My reaction in the end was no different from that of my friends Michael Randle and Pat Pottle when it became known, in 1989, that they were the people who had helped me to escape and had been named in the press. They wrote a book The Blake Escape in which they admitted their role in the escape. What was important to them was that everyone should know exactly why they had done it. They chose to face the danger of prosecution and a prison sentence rather than have the wrong motives ascribed to them.[7]

Blake calls his autobiography *No Other Choice*, reflecting his fatalistic philosophy. Everything that happens, he maintains, is predestined to happen, every choice we make, the one we were bound to make. Free will is an illusion. His religious upbringing in Holland had inculcated in him a belief in predestination, and it was reinforced by the communist doctrine of historical necessity. But fatalism, he insists 'is not sitting back and accepting what has occurred; it is also the impulses which force you to act in a particular way.' Thus if it was his fate to be sentenced to 42 years imprisonment, it was also his fate to act and organise his escape.[8]

But if predestination does not preclude an active human response to circumstances and events, it does, in Blake's reading of it, totally absolve the individual of all moral responsibility. 'If all depends on the will of God, he writes, it follows that he has made every individual exactly as he is with all his virtues and all his faults, some with more virtues, and others with less, in accordance with His own inscrutable purposes.' He goes on to quote from an epistle of St Paul to the Romans: 'Nay but, O Man, who art thou that repliest against God? Shall the thing formed say to him that formed it, why has thou made me thus? Hath not the potter power over the clay, of the same lump to make one vessel unto honour, and another unto dishonour?'[9] Blake concludes that it is justified for someone to say, 'You cannot punish me for my sins because my sins were put inside me and are not my fault.'

7 *No Other Choice*, p. 199.

8 *No Other Choice*, p.109.

9 Cited in *No Other Choice*, p.108.

This is a cop-out – one might say an Almighty cop-out. Discussion of guilt or innocence, or indeed individual responsibility of any kind, loses any meaning if one takes that position. Everyone does what they have to do, and thinks what they cannot help but think. Morally speaking, Adolf Hitler and Mahatma Gandhi are on the same level, one programmed to act and behave in one way, the other in a different way – all part of God's inscrutable plan.

Not surprisingly, Blake doesn't push the logic of his argument that far. He admires some individuals – like Donald Maclean – for their selflessness and dedication, and censures others. He relies on what are in essence moral arguments to justify or explain his own actions. He finally became convinced, he tells us, that he was working for the wrong side as a member of British Intelligence during his period as pro-Consul in South Korea through witnessing the corruption and tyranny of the Syngman Rhee regime and the ruthless bombing of Korean villages by the Americans. His motive in switching sides, he says, and becoming a double agent was to help thwart the attempt of Western intelligence agencies to undermine the socialist experiment which he still regards as a noble one. Even his confession to Harry Shergold and his other interrogators in London occurred because, according to his own account, he was stung by the suggestion that he had acted under duress and wanted them and everyone to know that he had offered his services to the Russians 'of his own accord'. (How you 'act of your own accord' when freewill is an illusion is a moot philosophical point). At his trial, he even refused to let his QC Jeremy Hutchinson, apologise on his behalf for what he had done because he felt it would be hypocritical to do so given that, if he had not been caught, he would still have been working for the KGB.

The central contradiction in his book is that he now acknowledges that the communist system, as imposed with coercion and terror from above in the Soviet Union, failed, yet he will not acknowledge that he was therefore utterly and profoundly wrong in spying for it, and still speaks of Western Intelligence undermining 'socialist' countries – as though they were socialist in some real and admirable sense of the word. He gives particular defences for his actions, but when he runs out of these there is always the ultimate cop-out: I was made that way, I had no other choice. This comes across most trenchantly in the final part of Tom Bower's interview with him in the Inside Story programme:

Bower: Any regrets about your life?
Blake: No, none whatsoever.
Bower: No recriminations?
Blake: No, no, no.
Bower: Most people have regrets though.

> **Blake: Well, but I haven't.**
> **Bower: Why are you so self-righteous?**
> **Blake: I'm not self-righteous. Everything that happened in my life was meant to happen. There was no other possibility. I want to remind you of the words of St Paul who said that the potter uses the clay to form vessels, some to honour and some to dishonour. And it is not for the clay to ask the potter why he does it. That is my outlook on life. I have been formed in this way and it is not for me to ask why. And I would say that I have been an unusual vessel in that I have been fashioned both to shame and to honour.**

Blake's extraordinary boast, and his feeble defence of it, occasioned no final rift in our relationship with him. But it did leave a sour aftertaste. His book, too, and BBC television interview, while ultimately they did no harm to our case emphasised the gap between his outlook and ours. None of this, however, altered our view that the sentence he received was inhuman and that we had been right to help him all those years ago.

Chapter 13:

Curtain call for Miss A

Presumably former Chief Inspector Watts' illness back in July was genuine since he had a doctor's certificate to say so and was admitted to hospital. The strain of giving evidence and the shock of hearing that he was to be recalled might indeed have caused many a younger and fitter man to have renal spasms – or 'the shits' as Pat put it. If, as we were all convinced, he remembered only too well his conversation with Kevin O'Connor this would have added to the tension.

At all events the delay in the hearing was a boon to the Crown side, giving them time to recover their balance and come up with some kind of plausible response to the MI5 'Fish' note. In late August they took new statements from Watts, Cunningham and two former MI5 officers – 'Miss A', the author of the two Notes for File, and 'Mr B', her senior officer at that time.

Watts relied on his continued loss of memory, Cunningham on a miraculous recovery of his. Watts' new Section 9 statement, dated 31st August 1990, reads:

> Further to my statement dated 24th July 1990, I have today been shown a copy of a Security Service file note dated 29.4.70, exhibit No. A/I. This refers to a conversation between myself and, I am told, a member of the Security Service. From the note it is not clear whether the conversation was by telephone or person to person. Understandably, after 20 years, I have no recollection of this conversation. I can only repeat that at no time was I aware of any evidence existing which would justify a prosecution against Randle and Pottle. I can accept that I may have told the person concerned that no further action would be taken in the matter at that time, for that was the recommendation made by our A/DAC, which was agreed by the AC. I have no recollection whatsoever of the A/DAC's recommendation being based upon the notion that to make further enquiries might be seen as 'persecution'. Sight of this document does not in any way alter the statement I have previously made or the evidence I have given in the High Court.
>
> (Signed) Rollo A Watts.
>
> (Signature witnessed by) E Eggington D/Supt.

Cunningham's statement, taken ten days earlier on 21st September reads:

> Further to my statement dated 24th July I now recall that towards the end of April 1970 I was telephoned by the Security Service case officer concerning Michael Randle and Patrick Pottle. This call related to a telephone conversation the Security Service had had with Mr. R. Watts, who was at that time a Detective Chief Inspector. I was told, in effect, that Mr Watts had informed the Security Service in a telephone conversation that Special Branch was not going to take action against Randle and Pottle as they were minor figures in the George Blake escape from Wormwood Scrubs Prison in 1966 and that the Branch was going to concentrate on arresting Seán Bourke, the prime suspect. I was asked my views. I replied that what Mr Watts was alleged to have said was not correct. There was no evidence to substantiate any proceedings against Randle or Pottle and in view of the lapse of time since the escape, October 1966, the prospects of obtaining such evidence were not good. I referred the caller to my letter to the Security Service, dated March 1979, which enclosed a copy of DCI Watts report which said inter alia there is no evidence to substantiate any proceeding against Randle and Pottle. As I did not agree with what Mr Watts had allegedly said I went to seek him out to obtain an explanation. However he was not in his room and I did not pursue the matter further. I have been shown a photocopy marked 'AII' of a Security Service memo dated 29th April 1970. I do not agree with what is set out in paragraph 2. I certainly have never held the view that to consider prosecuting Randle and Pottle might have been persecution.
>
> (Signed) A. Cunningham.

This statement from a man who had insisted under oath in July that there had never been any discussion of a policy decision not to prosecute us is unconvincing. A defendant in a criminal trial blessed with such a sudden and convenient recovery of memory would not be taken seriously by any court. It needs, moreover, to be read in conjunction with the statement on 30th August 1990 by the author of the MI5 Note known to us only as 'Miss A'.

> 'I worked for the Security Service from 1950 until 1982. In 1970 I had dealing with the Special Branch of the Metropolitan Police in connection with a book being written by Seán Bourke about the escape of George Blake from prison in 1966. I had spoken a number of times to Detective Chief Inspector Watts who was preparing a report on the manuscript of Bourke's book which we had passed to Special Branch for comment and their information. Some time after receiving the report from Chief Inspector Watts I had a conversation with him and prepared a note of this the following day. I have seen this note and produce a photocopy of

> it with certain names and references deleted. (A/I). This note was made on 29th April 1970 and was normal procedure. I was aware that Special Branch had no evidence against Randle and Pottle and that at that stage no steps were to be taken by Special Branch to interview or prosecute them. My note in paragraph 2 contains the words 'It was considered that to do so might be persecution – a big fish had got away so they were taking it out on the little fish.' This phrase was noted by me, not as an explanation as to why there was to be no interview but as an afterthought since there was no evidence to support a prosecution. The reason why the possible identifications made in the Watts report had been omitted before being passed to the I.R.D. of the Foreign Office was to avoid prejudice to police investigations.'
>
> (Signed) Miss A.[1]

If, as Miss A maintained, the decision not to prosecute for the time being was based on lack of evidence, and the phrase about a big and little fish was simply a matter of consolation, why would a senior officer in MI5 have rung Cunningham and asked him what Watts was doing giving the impression that the decision was based on a fear that to prosecute would be a form of persecution? It is certainly not believable that he would have done so without first checking with Miss A exactly what Watts had said and how she interpreted it.

The police also took a statement from another former MI5 officer, Mr B – the Head of the Section where Miss A was employed.

> From 1956 until 1972 I was a member of the Security Service. In April 1970, I was 'Head of Section' where Miss A was employed. I had delegated to her the task of following up any leads in respect of the escape of George Blake. I did, however, regard the identifications and prosecution of those who assisted him as a matter for the police. I have been shown a piece of paper headed 'Note for File' dated 29 April 1970 (All). I do not recall having seen it before and as it is headed 'Note for File' it would not have necessarily been brought to my attention.

In the event Mr B was too ill to attend the renewed hearing. Clearly, however, if he did not remember the Note for File of 29th April 1970, he certainly would not have recalled making a telephone call to Commander Cunningham in connection with it.

The biggest problem for the Crown was O'Connor's testimony. He had agreed to make yet another trip to London to appear at the hearing. How was Bevan to explain the fact that what Rollo Watts told him in 1984 coincided

1 Statement by 'Miss A'.

so closely with what Miss A had recorded him as saying to her some fourteen years earlier? This surely was an issue that the court itself could not duck.

At a conference with all senior and junior Counsel and solicitors on 24th September, Ben informed us that he had corresponded with, and spoken directly to, Lord Allen. He had no clear recollection of the Watts report, so, with the agreement of Michael Bibby of the Crown Prosecution Service, he was sent a copy of it and of the subsequent Special Branch and MI5 documents that had later been disclosed by the Crown. Allen was helpful, in so far as he could be, and told Ben that the Watts report would almost certainly have ended up on the desk of the then Home Secretary, Lord Callaghan. Geoffrey said he would be happy to meet Allen, and if necessary we should sub-poena him to appear. We also talked about seeing Callaghan, and possibly serving him too to appear. But whether through inertia, or because the lawyers ultimately decided it would not be worthwhile, the matter was not pursued further. When we met again on 1st October, the day before the resumed hearing, Ed argued that in the light of the evidence that had emerged it was now up to Bevan to prove beyond reasonable doubt that there had been no policy decision not to prosecute in 1970.

Watts was the first to take the stand at the resumed hearing. It was the first time I had seen him in the flesh. He is shortish, red-faced, still with a good head of (grey) hair and long sideboards. He held himself erect, military fashion, and refused the offer from Judge Watkins of a seat.

He stuck to the line that he remembered nothing. 'I have no recollection of ever having had the matter discussed with me as to what action would be taken,' he told Bevan during the examination in chief, 'or what was going to be done about it.'

> **Bevan: May we turn to the word 'persecution' contained in the note? … Do you recollect now any decision being made on the basis of persecution?**
> **Watts: Absolutely not.**
> **Q. Let me put it a different way. Was any decision made to your knowledge, with regard to the prosecution or non-prosecution of these individuals, based upon persecution?**
> **A. No, not to my knowledge.**
> **Q. Do you have any recollection whatever of a conversation about 'the big fish having got away so they were taking it out on the little fish'? Can you help us with regard to that note at all?**
> **A. I can only say, from the file note that I have in front of me, that it would appear to be an informal conversation that I had held with someone from the security service and that I was expressing some**

personal views of some sort. I have no memory of it but that is the only explanation that I have for this.
Q. Do you have any personal views – personal views to yourself – with regard to persecution of the big fish and little fish?
A. I think it quite possible that I could have said something on balance, it is the big one but I cannot remember myself using the phrase a 'big fish' – perhaps I did. A personal opinion is that Blake himself had got away and, in comparison anyone else was a comparatively minor figure.
Q. What about Bourke himself? Did you consider Bourke the big fish in any context since extradition proceedings had failed against him?
A. No.
Q. What was your own personal view, Mr Watts, with regard to the prosecution or non-prosecution of Messrs Randle and Pottle whom you had identified in your report? What was your personal view?
A. It is very difficult for me to remember what my personal views were over 20 years ago. I cannot believe that they would be different from my present views. Those are that, at the end of the day, it is not a question of police decisions on this, it is a question of the court's decision. The court in this particular case had found Blake's offences so serious that they sentenced him to 42 years' imprisonment. Bourke – and as it turns out these other people as well, anyone who is responsible for flouting that decision of the court and enabling someone to escape justice – should be brought to justice. I cannot think I have ever held any views other than that.
Q. Are you saying to this court, in effect, that you did not hold the view that it would be persecution to attempt to prosecute Messrs. Randle and Pottle or, indeed, Goodwin.
A. Most certainly not because, as a police officer, if we were not to prosecute people because they claimed they were persecuted we would have very few cases before the court.[2]

In his cross-examination, Geoffrey returned to the fish:

Robertson: I suppose, as you said, the big fish – the great white shark – in the form of Blake and the rather plump Irish salmon had got away, Mr Bourke, and you are left with a couple of little CND sardines.
Watts: I can only say that … I think the wording of this note does not really represent what I said at the time. I have no recollection of saying it, so I can only conjecture, my Lord. I could understand that I would say words to the effect of, 'if we have no evidence against these people it is a pity but the big one has got away'. Blake himself got away and,

---

2 Transcript, 2 October 1990, pp.1-2

in comparison, they are nothing. This is dialogue and in black and white it tends to give a totally different meaning.[3]

Geoffrey did get Watts to acknowledge that MI5 and Special Branch worked in close cooperation, citing the conclusion of Lord Denning's enquiry into the Profumo affair:

Robertson: 'You were working in harmony and your actions were subject to their comment, correction, and indeed direction, is that right?'

Watts: Yes.

When, later on, Robertson suggested that MI5 might have a say in deciding whether or not a prosecution went ahead, Watkins intervened:

'It is neither the function nor the practice of MI5 to request the police to prosecute nor do MI5 have it in their power to direct the police to prosecute.'

Robertson: I certainly accept that as the constitutional and, indeed, the legal position because at the time we are speaking – which is not the time now because there is an Act that has been introduced – the MI5 had no constitutional existence, no legal existence and no legal power to do anything whatsoever other than, I suppose, that power possessed by the ordinary citizen who has certain powers of arrest. The operation which was carefully scrutinized by Lord Denning and led to publication which looked at this relationship between Special Branch and MI5 indicated, certainly, that there was a very close and harmonious working relationship. On several occasions, indeed, I think, that MI5 decided or advised – put it that way – the Special Branch to do this or to do that or advised the Special Branch to direct CID officers to do this or to do that. While the legal position is that MI5 had no power to do so, in practice an MI5 view that it was in the national interest that a certain course should be taken either by CID or Special Branch would carry enormous weight.

Watkins: I hear what you say, Mr Robertson. It is very interesting.[4]

Robertson questioned Watts closely on the similarities in the Note for File of 1970 and O'Connor's testimony about their conversation in 1984:

Robertson: The two comments that [O'Connor] recalls that interest us are that you said that there were conversations about the prosecution of these two people and your superiors told you to leave well enough alone. Then five lines from the bottom [of O'Connor's statement] it says why 'put them away at the cost of the taxpayer, when there

3 Transcript, 2 October 1990, p.14.

4 Transcript 2 October 1990, p.19.

> **were lots of other real villains that it was our job to catch.' That is not dissimilar language to the language in the file note, is it, that you have been shown? It is about the little and the big fish getting away and taking it out on the little fish – catching the little fish while you had some big Irish villains and a lot of other villains in 1970 to be getting on with. You were a Branch that was badly pressed and understaffed were you not?'**
> **Watts: May I say something about this conversation? This is a person who I cannot remember having seen before in my life. He claims that I gave him an interview to talk about the Blake escape – which is breaking the habit of a lifetime.**

Was it? O'Connor had explained in his statement, and there is no reason why he should have been untruthful, that the way he got to hear about Watts was from the crime correspondent of the Daily Mail whom he was introduced to by another journalist on the paper, Mr Holiday. It was the crime correspondent who told him that Watts was the 'leg-man' on the follow-up investigation into the Blake escape, a fact which he presumably learned from Watts himself.

Watts then focused on those points in O'Connor's statement that he knew did not correspond with the facts:

> **Watts: He says that I said that the authorities had known within a very short time that there were two other people besides Bourke involved. Well, we did not. They knew that two of the people were part of the intellectual mafia at the prison – since we did not know about the two people we could not have known those. I am very intrigued that in this file note [he is in fact referring to the O'Connor statement] at the end it says that I said 'One was a teacher married to a teacher. They had young children. Why break up the family.' I cannot remember either of them ever being married to a teacher. It may be so but I would not have remembered in those days – in nineteen eighty something-or-other. I cannot accept that.**

Again, the fact that the police did not know of the identity of Pat and myself until 1970, doesn't destroy the credibility of O'Connor's statement. After all, Watts himself might have been tempted to exaggerate the sagacity of the police and the alacrity with which they solved the mystery of the other people involved. Even if it was O'Connor who got it wrong here, and misunderstood what Watts was claiming about how soon the police knew, this doesn't affect the significance of the fact that O'Connor's testimony of what Watts told him in 1984 is too similar to that contained in the MI5 record of 1970 to be a coincidence.

Watts was clearly being evasive too over the issue of the 'intellectual mafia', attempting to dismiss the point by linking it to the issue of how soon after the escape the police identified us. He is saying in effect – How could I have described them as part of the prison's 'intellectual mafia', when we did not know until 1970 who they were? But the date the police knew of our identity is irrelevant here. The question is, once they did know, was it credible that Watts would have described us as part of the intellectual mafia of the prison? Here he is convicted out of his own mouth. As noted in Chapter 11, at the July hearing, Ed Fitzgerald asked him:

> **Fitzgerald: Would you accept that it is right that by 1970 you had become aware that there were other people involved in the escape and who they were?**
> **Watts: Yes, through the report.**
> **Fitzgerald: Would you say that it was a perfectly reasonable description for you to have adopted – that they were part of the 'intellectual mafia' of the prison?**
> **Watts: Yes.**[5]

After Robertson concluded his cross-examination the court broke for lunch. When it resumed, Scrivener took up the questioning, concentrating on the follow-up investigations the police could have carried out after Watts had made his identifications of Pat and myself.

> **Scrivener: Having read the references to these two men in the book, did there not appear to you to be obvious lines of possible enquiry?**
> **Watts: I cannot recall lines of enquiry which we could have taken. There was one aspect of course which was to go around and confront them with it. Whether that would have been good judgment or not is not for me to say.**
> **Q: You have been involved in investigations for a long time – for 23 years?**
> **A: Yes.**
> **Q: There were references to the use of a motor vehicle, were there not?**
> **A: Yes.**
> **Q: There were obvious inquiries that could be made with respect to that, were there not?**
> **A: From whom? I am sorry.**
> **Q: I am asking you to rely on your experience of 23 years as a police officer. Here is a very serious crime which has been committed. Every effort has been made to find who assisted Blake to escape. Here is the evidence that they had available; is the police force or your Branch impotent to deal with that?**

5 Transcript, 25 July 1990, p.30.

A: My opinion would be that presumably enquiries could have been made of neighbours who perhaps could have said there was a Dormobile at some time but I do not know.
Q: It would be elementary, would it not, to go round to the neighbourhood and to see in fact if either of them had ever owned this type of vehicle?
A: Yes.
Q: It is obvious is it not? You do not need to be in the police force for 23 years to think about that as a possibility, would that be right? A: Quite, but whether that would lead anywhere.
Q: You could say nothing was going to lead anywhere and never bother to carry out any investigation at all. That [i.e. making enquiries of neighbours] would help to establish whether or not there was an independent evidence that they had the vehicle, would it not?
A: Had a vehicle, yes.
Q: It would not be beyond the resources of the police force to check garages to see if the vehicle had ever been serviced, would it?
A: Yes that is a possibility.
Q: To your knowledge were any of those steps ever taken?
A: No, not to my knowledge.
Q: The book revealed that the two gentlemen concerned had travelled abroad, did it not?[6]
A: Yes
Q: To East Germany?
A: I cannot recall.
Q: To an iron curtain country?
A: Was it?
Q: Assuming that to be so, would it have been useful to look at the passports of the two individuals concerned?
A: Possibly, yes.
Q: Obviously, it would do, would it not?
A: Whether it would have produced evidence for a prosecution – it is not for me to decide.
Q: We are not gifted with the foresight of God. We do not know what the enquiries will reveal, do we?
A: Right.
Q: That is not the approach that is normally taken. They [the police] do not say it is hopeless and not bother; they get on with it, do they not? That was an obvious thing to do, was it not?

6 This was a minor slip-up by Scrivener; only Anne and myself and our two children had travelled with Blake to East Germany.

A: You are putting me in a very awkward position I am afraid with this question. You are asking me should I have taken decisions which I was not in a position to take. If you are asking me as a police officer solely 'Was that one line of enquiry that could have been followed up?' the answer has to be, of course, yes.
Q: I am asking you as an officer who had 23 years' experience at that date – that is why I asked you originally. On that basis that would have been an obvious enquiry to make, would it not?
A: It would have been one to have been made, yes?[7]

Scrivener went on to question him about the possibility of comparing Pat's and my fingerprints with those, other than Blake's and Bourke's, at the hideout in Highlever Road, emphasising that the police had thought it worthwhile to make the comparison some twenty years later in 1990, after we had been arrested and charged.[8] Scrivener also established an important point about the role of Special Branch in any follow-up investigation.

Scrivener: I turn now to the 'Note for File' … Can we look at point 2, 'Chief Inspector Watts added that the S.B. decision at present was to take no steps to interview or attempt to prosecute the Randles, Pottle or Goodwin.' I pause there for a moment. The word I want you to concentrate on is the word 'decision'.
Watts: Yes.
Q: Would Special Branch have made a decision as to the future progress of this investigation?
A: I would interpret that as meaning that, at that stage, whilst the report had gone over to the security service it had been decided in Special Branch to take no further steps to interview or anything until we received a reaction from them.
Q: I am grateful for that. It does follow that the answer to the question I put to you is, 'Yet Special Branch would have made a decision about it' does it not?
A: Yes
Q: Would you have expected to have known about the decision?
A: Yes, I would think so.
Q: It goes on to say 'was to take no steps to interview or to attempt

7 Transcript, Evidence of Watts, 2 October 1990, pp.25-27.

8 The comparison, as Bevan made clear, would have been with fingerprints taken at the time and kept on record in the police laboratory. As noted elsewhere, the police found in 1990 that Pat's and my fingerprints did not match any of those at Highlever Road

> to prosecute.' Would those have been two options available to Special Branch? Take one at a time – 'interview.'
> A: To interview is one aspect; it had been decided not to interview them at that stage.
> Q: It would have been open to Special Branch to interview if they had wanted to, would it not?
> A: Or to divisional CID, yes.
> Q: I am talking about Special Branch at the moment. 'Or attempt to prosecute' – that would have been within the power of Special Branch to put up, no doubt, some lawyers to see whether they could prosecute or not.
> A: It could have been. I am trying to get clear in my own mind the actual stage of the relationship between Special Branch and Divisional CID. The escape of George Blake was a Divisional CID enquiry, not a Special Branch enquiry. Any attempt to prosecute, I would have thought, would have been a decision taken by the criminal investigation department and not by Special Branch. I cannot remember the detail.
> Q: I am sorry to interrupt but the possibility would be that if both branches were involved in it both would have a say in it. It would be possible for the Special Branch to make a decision on these matters – to interview or to prosecute, would it not?
> A: Yes.

Compare these answers with Watts' categorical assertion back in July that 'at that time [1970] Special Branch officers did not conduct prosecutions or investigations other than those connected with Official Secrets Act offences'.

Kevin O'Connor now took the witness box. Both sides – and the judges too – knew that his testimony, and how well he stood up to cross examination could be crucial to the outcome of our application.

> 'We have heard a lot about 'Mr O'Connor', Lord Justice Watkins remarked just before he took the stand.

O'Connor is clean shaven, slimly built, medium height. He was an excellent, one could say an ideal witness, answering questions promptly and clearly and wasting no words. Robertson took him through his evidence, establishing that he was 'some 50 years old', had worked for many years in London and Dublin as a writer and journalist, and was currently employed by RTE – the national television service in Ireland. He was able to speak in convincing detail of his meeting with Watts:

> O'Connor: ... I later came to London and met Mr Holiday who introduced me to the crime correspondent of the Daily Mail and I

had a conversation with him. He said Rolly had been the leg man on the follow up investigation into the escape. He gave me a telephone number for Rolly Watts. I rang Watts and he was very affable. He agreed to see me. I met him at Saladin Security in Sloane Street. He was wearing a pin-striped suit and sat behind a desk in the room … He was extremely helpful. He referred very fondly to Seán. He said: 'Poor old Seán. He died sadly.'
Robertson: Did you make any notes?
O'Connor: Not during the interview but I made them shortly afterwards. I went across to a restaurant and I made some notes.
Q: Do you have them?
A: I have them here. They are a mixture of shorthand with gobbledegook …[9]
Q: Can you tell us what your notes indicate?
A: Saladin is spelt out and Sloane Street. Then I have in shorthand 'real life effing and blinding villains.' That is a reference to a phrase that Watts used. He said that the people who had sprung George Blake were not your 'real live effing and blinding villains.' 'Of course we knew all along' means that the authorities were involved in the conspiracy to release Blake from on high and that they decided not to prosecute.[10] The 'respectable' refers to the fact that the people who were involved in the conspiracy were in police eyes respectable people.
Q: Do go on.
A: 'Shepherds Bush police station' and 'little old lady' refers to the follow-up investigation when they were doing a lot of interviews. They found that a little old lady had been suspicious of Bourke and had gone into the police station to say she had a suspicious lodger and they said to her 'Yes, Ma' am, keep on taking the pills.'
Q: He was telling you an anecdote of how a little old lady was told to go away.
A: This was before the escape. She became suspicious of Bourke before. That was one anecdote. He would not tell me where they were. He said 'up North somewhere.'
Q: They meaning?
A: The British-based conspirators of the escape.
Q: Know SB's Associates in WAS'?

---

9 See Appendix 5 for a copy of O'Connor's contemporaneous notes of his meeting with Watts.

10 Clearly O'Connor was mistaken in drawing this conclusion. There may well have been a decision 'from on high' not to prosecute, there was no such decision to free Blake.

A: They knew who his associates were in Wormwood Scrubs. He indicated to me that they had known within a short time, through researching, who Bourke's intimate circle consisted of in Wormwood Scrubs. He said they were respectable people: 'One was a teacher married to a teacher.' It was not quite correct; it was a teacher married to a nurse. He said 'One was a teacher married to a teacher' as he thought, and: 'Why put them in gaol when there were real live villains about.' Why go after these people and put them away. It was a waste of taxpayers money.
Q: Is that a recollection or is there a note of shorthand there?
A: 'Respectable' I have given you. The 'WAS' is for Wormwood Scrubs and associates. I do know that he said that they would not have pursued them because of the type of people they were.
Q: Do you have a direct note to that effect?
A: No, only to the associates in WAS.
Q: But your recollection is of him saying, 'Why put them away at the cost of the taxpayer rather than the real villains that it was our job to catch?'
A: To that effect.
Q: Did you subsequently tell anyone about this conversation you had with Mr Watts?
A: Not at the time, no.
Q: Did you come to tell Mr Randle about it?
A: Later when I went to see him because I had information from the source I am not prepared to divulge that he was involved …
Q: Did you then tell him [Randle] that you had spoken to Watts and he had indicated that a decision had been made at the time not to proceed.
A: Yes.

Scrivener had nothing to add in the way of questions, so Bevan began his cross-examination. It was a floundering performance because Bevan was at a loss to decide how to challenge the authenticity of O'Connor's testimony. He began with a line of questioning apparently aimed at suggesting that Watts, as a retired Special Branch officer would not have said the kind of things O'Connor attributed to him. Normally it is the witness who can be nonplussed by a skilled advocate asking a series of tendentious questions. In this instance, it was Bevan who was thrown by the directness and confidence of the witness.

Bevan: Mr O'Connor, do you have a date of this meeting?
O'Connor: No.
Q: What is the time gap between speaking to him [i.e. on the phone] and meeting him?

A: A day.
Q: Did you tell him why you wanted to see him?
A: I did.
Q: Did you tell him you were a journalist?
A: I did.
Q: Did you tell him you wanted to talk about the Blake escape?
A: I did.
Q: Did you tell him what you would do with the information you received from him?
A: No.
Q: Did he ask you, 'If I give you information about the Blake escape what use are you going to make of it as a journalist?'
A: No.
Q: Did he ask you any questions about whether or not you as a journalist would reveal the fact that he, Mr Watts, as a Special Branch officer was giving you the information about the escape?
A: No.
Q: So this was Watts giving you information about the Blake escape without knowing what you were going to do with it?
A: He was a retired Special Branch officer.
Q: I accept that. You are quite right. As a retired Special Branch officer he did not question and did not know what you were going to do with the information he was giving you; is that right?
A: Yes.
Q: During the course of your conversation with him he was telling you, was he not, sensitive and private information?
A: He was.
Q: Did it surprise you as a journalist that he, as a Special Branch officer, did not know what you were going to do with it?
A: Not in the circumstances.
Q: This man was a complete stranger to you, was he not?
A: He was.
Q: And you, of course, to him?
A: That is correct.[11]

So far Bevan had got nowhere. He now got O'Connor to go again through his notes of the conversation with Watts:

Q: I obviously cannot translate your shorthand note. Would you translate the words you have in your note for the convenience of this court?
A: 'BOG' is about stuff with the file. 'Holiday – Mail' is the name of a

11 Court transcript, 2 October 1990, the Evidence ofO'Connor,pp.3-4.

journalist. It refers to a journalist at the Mail in Fleet Street, my Lord. 'Sloane Street' is where the offices are and 'real life effing and blinding villains.' 'Holy Jihad' is the Holy Jihad.
Q: Would you explain Holy Jihad.
Watkins (intervening): I am a frequent visitor to Ireland and I have met a lot of Irish people who say that.
O'Connor: I believe you are thinking of 'Holy Jaysus', my Lord.[12]

The whole court resounded with laughter. Watkins was not amused. It is clear from his eventual written judgement that the incident rankled with him. Q'Connor then continued:

O'Connor: Mr Watts worked with a security firm in the Middle East and said that the people you really ought to be looking at these days were the Holy Jihad. He was referring to his work in the Middle East.
Bevan: It is a terrorist group?
O'Connor: Yes.

The one problem with Q'Connor's evidence was that it attributed to Watts the claim that the police knew of our identities 'soon after' the escape. As noted earlier, it was essentially a trivial point since Watts himself might have wanted to exaggerate the efficiency of the police in tracking down Bourke's accomplices, and even if it was O'Connor who had misunderstood Watts on this point, it didn't detract from the significance of his testimony. But it was all Bevan had, and he made the most of it.

Q: Would you just take your time. Before we deal with any passage in your statement, did you get the plain impression in everything that Watts said that the police, if I may use that, Special Branch and everybody else in the police knew within a very short time who was involved?
A: Yes.
Q: They knew that these respectable people were involved as well?
A: Yes, sir.
Q: You got that impression?
A: I did.
Q: Did you also get the impression that the police knew very soon after the Blake escape that the two people involved with Blake were part and parcel of the intellectual mafia?
A: Can you rephrase that?
Q: Did you get the impression from Watts that the police knew very soon after the Blake escape that the two people involved with Blake were part and parcel of the intellectual mafia?

12 Transcript, 2 October, O'Connor's Evidence, pp.4-5

A: I did.
Q: Did you get the impression from Watts that a decision was taken very soon after the Blake escape not to pursue the two respectable people?
A: Exactly.
Q: Was there any suggestion whatever by Watts that they did not in fact know the identity of the two respectable people until after the publication of the Bourke book?
A: No, sir. On the contrary he gave me the impression that the police had known the extent of the conspiracy and this was a decision at a level above him.
Q: Because, of course, you knew Seán Bourke and a great deal about him?
A: I did.
Q: And you may have implied to Watts that you knew about him?
A: I did.
Q: At no stage did Watts say to you, 'If it was not for the Bourke book we had much less.' Watts was telling you that they knew of the involvement of the two respectable people well before Bourke published his book?
A: I cannot be clear on that.
Q: Did Watts ever say to you it was Seán Bourke that let the cat out of the bag?
A: No, sir.[13]

In answer to further questions, O'Connor said he did not find it 'at all odd' to hear that a decision had been made from on high not to prosecute us:

O'Connor: I did not find it all that odd because with due respect to you the state settles the political establishment and the police function in response. I was aware that the kind of work that Watts did was subject to political control. The Special Branch works a bit removed but closely to the Home Office. Had he been prepared to tell me exactly I would have been even more intrigued because at the time there was a certain speculation in the public print that perhaps the escape of Blake had been a clever triple-cross engineered privately between the intelligence services. I have no evidence that that is true but it had been raised among people investigating the case at a journalistic level. Were that to have been the case it could well be that a decision was taken not to prosecute the suspects in England because of some wider transactions at national level.

13 Transcript, 2 October 1990, O'Connor's Evidence, pp.6-7.

Bevan: Did you ask him questions that might resolve that?
A: I nibbled around the edges of that.
Q: Why did you ask him?
A: I was curious to know.
Q: Let us approach this from a different angle. Was it simply because they were respectable people and it did not matter what they did or was it a much more sinister and political decision somewhere higher up; did you want to know that?
A: I did want to know.
Q: Did you not ask Watts?
A: He was unable to give satisfactory answers.
Q: What were his answers?
A: The answers were that the decision not to prosecute came from on high and when I tried to get him to define what on high meant he closed up on me. He would not go into that area.
Q: Did Watts give you the impression that the police in fact had evidence upon which they could have prosecuted these two respectable people had they wished?
A: Not evidence that he might present to a court.
Q: Did you ask him what they had?
A: No I did not.[14]
The final series of questions from Bevan seemed designed to cast doubt on whether O'Connor had ever met Watts.
Bevan: You entered the door as a journalist. He gave you all this information and you walked out. How could he get hold of you?
O'Connor: If he had wanted to contact me he would have gone back to Holiday. Holiday had my number so he would have got back to me via the route that I got to him.
Q: That is a roundabout route to get hold of you, you a journalist?
A: Yes.
Q: What time of day was the meeting?
A: I am not sure. It was in the day. I know I got out at Sloane Street.
Q: You were in an office were you?
A: Yes. He was up the top of the building. The meeting took place. I did not invent it.
Bevan: I was not suggesting that you did invent it.[15]

O'Connor's direct challenge had punctured Bevan's approach. If Bevan was not trying to suggest that the meeting had never taken place, of what

14 Court Transcript, 2 October 1990, O'Connor's evidence.

15 Court Transcript, 2 October, O'Connor's evidence, p.9.

possible interest or relevance could it be to check again that it had occurred in an office, or the time of day it had taken place?

The former Chief Superintendent M.D. Rodger, who had countersigned the Watts report in 1970 and whose name appears on some of the documents subsequently disclosed to us, was next to take the stand. He had little to say and remained in the witness box for only a brief period. Examined by Bevan he expressed his view that there would have been no point in re-opening investigations in 1970 into an escape which had occurred in 1966. He was also unaware, he said, of any decision in 1970 in relation to Pottle and Randle. One point of interest Geoffrey Robertson managed to establish in a brief cross-examination was that Watts would certainly have been consulted about any decision whether to prosecute us or to conduct further enquiries concerning us. Rodger also agreed with the suggestion put to him by Geoffrey Robertson that the Blake escape had been followed by 'one of the largest manhunts in British history.'

Next morning it was the turn of the anonymous author of the Notes for File, the former MI5 officer, 'Miss A'. As far as we are aware, this was the first time ever that an MI5, or former MI5, officer had given evidence in open court, and the judges were at pains to ensure that her identity should remain a secret. So the court was cleared while court officials rigged up a curtain in front of the witness box and the judges satisfied themselves that this shielded her effectively from the gaze of the court. (They neglected to check if she could be seen by the journalists sitting at the very front of the court at right angles to the rest of the audience. In fact she could be as several journalists told us later. However, if any of them managed to identify her, the news did not trickle down to us.) When the judges were satisfied, we all trooped back into the court.

The scene was bizarre. 'Miss A, can you hear me?' said Bevan addressing the curtain. 'Yes, thank you' said the curtain, in a clipped, educated voice. Thus was a new chapter inscribed in the history of the British courts.

Bevan, having established that Miss A was indeed the author of the two Notes for File, focused on the second of them, dated 29th April 1970 – the 'Fish' note. He drew her attention to the second paragraph:

> **Bevan: 'Chief Inspector Watts added that the [Special Branch] decision at present was to take no steps to interview or attempt to prosecute the Randles, Pottle or Goodwin'?**
>
> **Miss A: Yes, right.**
>
> **Q: Pausing there for a moment, did he inform you of that or not, namely the decision.**

A: I am sorry, I do not understand. I am awfully sorry.
Bevan re-read the passage.
Miss A: Yes. This was in the context that, as far as I remember, he had not been able to find any ammunition with which to prosecute them.
Bevan: Any?
Miss A: Any evidence or information on which to base a prosecution. In that context that is what he said.
Q: I will continue with that paragraph, if I may. You see the words, 'It was considered that to do so might be persecution – a big fish had got away so they were taking it out on the little fish.' Pause there for a moment.
A: Yes.
Q: That is what is written?
A: Right.
Q: What is the basis of those words that appear?
A: It may have been my understanding of what he was saying or it may have been almost word for word. I cannot be sure which it was, but it was certainly my understanding and I understood it really as a word of consolation that so far he had not been able to find any evidence and nor had I. To take a case without proper firm evidence would have looked like persecution. That was the way I understood it.
Q: From what Mr Watts told you during the course of this conversation, did you understand that the persecution factor in any sense influenced any decision that was being made?
A: No, certainly not. That was not my understanding of it, definitely not. I understood that simply as an aside, a comment, if you like, but certainly not a basis for their decision. That was not the way I understood it at all.
Q: May I probe to this extent, Miss A. What did you understand to be the basis of any decision that was being made at that time, namely 28th April 1970? I take the day before because the note is written the day after. What was the basis of any decision as Mr Watts informed you?
A: I understood that the decision was a temporary one because if you look in paragraph 4 of that note, you will see that I was not going to do anything that would compromise or – sorry paragraph 3 that is it – that would prejudice their further enquiries it. So I understood that was the decision taken at the moment and the basis I understood of the decision to be the lack of evidence or the lack of the confession, lack of any collateral at all.[16]

16 Court Transcript, pp.2-3, Evidence of Miss A and Mr Cunningham, 3 Oct

Whatever may have been Miss A's understanding at the time, there is no mention in the Note itself of lack of evidence. The only reasonable construction to be put on the words it contains is that the decision not to interview or prosecute was taken because 'to do so might be persecution.' The 'afterthought' or 'consolation' was there, not the alleged thought itself.

Robertson began the cross-examination. He was at pains in the early part of this to establish the kind of relationship that existed between MI5 and Special Branch.

> **'We had a good liaison,' Miss A told the court, 'and if my seniors had had any view [ie. on further steps to be taken in relation to the two of us] I have no doubt that would have been taken into account' and she concurred with Robertson's suggestion that the two bodies 'worked together closely and harmoniously.'**
>
> **Robertson: Special Branch would not have taken any action which would be deplored or which they would be advised strongly against by MI5?**
>
> **Miss A: I am sure that is true.**
>
> **Q: Equally, if MI5 had encouraged Special Branch to take a certain action as being in the national interest, you would expect Special Branch to take it?**
>
> **A: Yes.**
>
> **Q: It would have been inconceivable at that period that Special Branch would have taken an action that MI5 had indicated they should not be taking.**
>
> **A: I agree.**[17]

Next Robertson got Miss A to confirm that the covering letter to Special Branch dated 30th January 1970 sent with the typescript of Seán Bourke's book was almost certainly written and signed by her.

> **Robertson: Paragraph 2 of that letter indicates that no action was to be taken which would – may I put it this way – put at risk the identity of your source?**
>
> **A: Right.**
>
> **Q: So you would not expect to hear that police officers of Special Branch or CID had gone off and taken any investigative action over the next few months before the book was published which might indicate that the police had an advance copy of the manuscript?**
>
> **A: That is true.**

1990, pp.2-3.

17 Court Transcript, 3 October 1990, Evidence of Miss A.

Q: If any such action was contemplated you would expect to hear of it and to advise on it?
A: I would hope so.
Q: You would expect that no action of an investigative nature based on the manuscript would be taken without your agreement given the sensitivity of the source?
A: Yes
Q: If a CID officer had rushed off to see Mr Randle immediately and shown him the manuscript and said, 'This is clearly you,' that would have been most unfortunate?
A: It would indeed.
Q: At that stage?
A: Certainly.
Q: You would have expected MI5 to know and to be kept immediately informed of, and to discuss, indeed, contemplated police action?
A: Yes because my words were, if they are mine, which I assume they are, are fairly strong. – 'have been asked to stress.' That was fairly strong language.[18]

With an eye on the testimony of ex-Commander Cunningham of Special Branch who would be next to take the witness stand, Robertson established that Miss A's Note for File would have been seen by her senior officer.

Robertson: Were you regarded as the case officer in relation to this matter?
A: Yes, but under supervision.
Q: I do not want to ask you about identities, but you were supervised by a senior officer?
A: That is right.
Q: Who was himself supervised by a very senior officer?
A: Yes, 'supervised' in his case was perhaps not the right word. In my case it was. In his case he had a senior but I would not say he was supervised. That would be, at his level, not quite correct, but he was answerable to a senior officer.
Q: You would assume that your file note was seen by those two individuals and certainly by your senior officer.
A: I would not assume. I know they were.
Q: Did either of those persons or any other person ever say a word to you about the accuracy of this file note?
A: No.
Q: It was never called into question?
A: No.

---

18 Court Transcript, 3 October 1970, Evidence of Miss A, pp.9-10.

Q: If at the time, and I am speaking of April 1970, this file note had been discovered by your superiors to be inaccurate as a result of an additional communication from Special Branch, would you expect to have been told of that matter?
A: Yes I would expect that.[19]

Miss A's answers here comprehensively undermined Cunningham's new testimony that he had been phoned by an officer in MI5 about what Watts was allegedly saying and had put them right on the issue.

Miss A was rather more successful in parrying Robertson's questions over her assertion that the decision not to interview or prosecute had been due not to the fear of seeming to persecute but to the lack of evidence:

Robertson: Then you go on to record it as being said that it was considered that to do so might be persecution; a big fish had got away, so they were taking it out on the little fish?
A: Yes.
Q: There is nothing there about it being persecution if they prosecuted without evidence, is there?
A: No, but if you look down to paragraph 3 you will see that we understood that the inquiries were still going on and at the end of that I would have expected further decisions in the light of any information coming.
Q: I accept that.
A: I certainly did not understand any decisions being made on the basis of a question of persecution, but what would have been considered persecution by anybody would have been going into action without any evidence.
Q: You see, if they prosecuted without any evidence the case would be thrown out by the magistrate, or at least by the judge, and they would have egg on their face would they not?
A: Yes, but also any person being accused would also rightly be upset if they were accused and no evidence was presented. It is surely a question of what is right, not just what suits one party. It is obviously what it is right to do.
Q: But, Miss A, you simply cannot prosecute without any evidence and if you look at this note, '... a big fish had got away so they were taking it out on the little fish,' you take it out on the little fish by catching them and in this case putting them behind bars. 'Taking it out' implies that it would be seen as persecution if these people were jailed perhaps for a long time where Blake and Bourke had got away?
A: No, that was not my understanding. My understanding was that it

19 Court Transcript, 3 October 1990, Evidence of Miss A, pp.12-13.

would seem like persecution if we insisted or they insisted on taking a case to court on their assumption of identities without any evidence. Clearly they had made very good identifications on their reading, but they still had not got any evidence, and to take a case to court on poor evidence would have seemed like persecution.
Q: Miss A, you cannot, in this country, take a case to court without evidence. It would be, I suggest to you, thrown out at the magistrates' court and, far from seeming to be persecution, it would make the Security Service laughed at, particularly by reasonably …
Watkins: All that is comment which we might be interested in later. What about questions, Mr Robertson?
Robertson: What I suggest to you is, and it may be that 20 years later you cannot recall exactly what you had in mind, that it is written on the basis that to put these individuals in prison would smack of persecution when the big fish had got away?
A: But surely there is no question of their getting put in prison if there was not evidence. A case can surely be taken to court on poor evidence, but we would hope that the case would be thrown out of court. But you can still take a case to court on poor evidence.[20]

Anthony Scrivener, in his, rather briefer, cross-examination pressed Miss A further on the point:

Scrivener: Would you be so kind as to look at the last sentence in paragraph 2 … To make sense of it, if you look at the previous sentence so that you can see it in context, the previous sentence goes like this: 'It was considered that to do so might be persecution – a big fish had got away so they were taking it out on the little fish'. This is the sentence: 'It was considered, however, that it had been necessary to investigate their suspicions and place them on record.' Can you see that?'
A: Yes, I do see that. That is correct. Then you need to read on to paragraph 3 where I said that I would not be passing on anything to IRD that might prejudice their enquiries. So the enquiries were presumably still going on. It was not a final decision.
Q: I was not to ask you to consider this for a moment. There is a difference between carrying out an investigation and attempting to prosecute, is there not?
A: Yes.
Scrivener: They are quite different, are they not?
Watkins: One leads to the other?
Miss A: Right.

---

20 Court Transcript, 3 October 1970, Evidence of Miss A , pp,15-16.

> Scrivener: One leads to the other; that is the point. Now I want to ask you some questions about what you understood and recorded here about investigation. That sentence I have just read to you records that it had been necessary to investigate the suspicions and place them on record only. Is that right?
> A: I do not like the word 'only'. 'It had been necessary to investigate their suspicions and place them on record' – full stop. Correct. That is correct but not 'only'. That was not only what they were going to do.[21]

Earlier, Scrivener had established that File Notes would be drafted carefully so that they would require no oral explanation, and probed Miss A about the procedure that would be followed if a File Note was found to be inaccurate on a matter of substance:

> Scrivener: So far as your 20 years' experience is concerned, it would have been part of your training to make sure that file notes were properly kept?
> Miss A: Yes.
> Q: The importance of a file note is so that a superior or another officer can read it and be informed. Would that be correct?
> A: Yes.
> Q: And he can be informed by reading it without any oral qualification.
> A: That would be the aim of a note certainly. Whether it always fulfilled that I would not like to say, but that would be the aim of a note – to provide a full record for the file.
> Q: Because you cannot always expect the maker of the note to be around, can you?
> A: No.
> Q: Can I ask you to look at document no. 7 again. Just have it in front of you … What would be the practice if you found that a file notes was inaccurate?
> A: A lot would – may I answer that?
> Q: I am hoping you will.
> A: It would depend on the circumstances, but never would a file note be destroyed or just taken out because it was found to be inaccurate for any reason. What would happen would be that another note would go on the file outlining the reasons why this earlier note had been inaccurate and a note should be made on this original incorrect note, either a line through it and 'See such and such because this has been found to have been superseded.' I cannot say that I have ever met that. I do not remember that having happened at any time, but sometimes a

21 Court Transcript, 3 October 1990, Evidence of Miss A, p.22.

> **note would have been superseded by events. Fresh information would come in, and then, if necessary, a handwritten note would be made on the note for file that this had been superseded by another note. I would not say that was always so because you would expect to read through the file anyhow and find the later notes, but it would make it easier for working on if one did that.**[22]

Bevan's re-examination was brief. He asked her where the ultimate responsibility lay regarding a decision to prosecute Randle and Pottle. She could not help on this point since she 'was not involved in policy-making or decision making.' Asked whether any pressure was put on the police, including Special Branch, by MI5 not to prosecute the two individuals concerned, she replied 'Not to my knowledge.' Surprisingly, however, Bevan too drew attention to the fact that there was no cross reference in the Note for File of 29th April 1970 which might suggest that it ought to be read in conjunction with a later correction, and said that he simply asked that 'in relation to the evidence of Mr Cunningham which your Lordships anticipate.'

Ex-Commander Cunningham now took the stand. He is a tall man with a shock of white hair who held himself erect, and was dressed in a suit, with a white shirt and a college, or company tie. Like Watts he refused the offer from Watkins of a chair.

Bevan took him through his evidence, which added little to his statement of 24th September and the evidence he had given to the court in July. He repeated his story that towards the end of April 1970 he had received a telephone call from 'the case officer'[23] in the Security Service dealing with Randle and Pottle and corrected the impression being given by Watts that a decision had been taken not to pursue them 'because they were minor figures in the case.'

Bevan's questions also drew attention again to the passage in the Watts' report which indicated that at the time it was written there was no evidence against the Randles and Pottle, and to Cunningham's own note to the Assistant Commissioner of Crime dated 25th March 1970 – 'You may wish to see 19D [the Watts report] for information. The possible identifications are interesting, but there is no evidence to substantiate any charge.' This note had been ticked and initialled by the Acting Commissioner for Crime, Mr Peter Brodie.

22 Court Transcript, 3 October 1990, Evidence of Miss A, p.20.

23 The 'case officer' in charge of the enquiries at MI5 was in fact Miss A. But Cunningham says he was phoned by a man, and in cross—examinsation by Robertson agreed that it was her senior officer who had phoned him.

Cunningham said this indicated that Brodie had seen the note and concurred with its conclusions. There was also a handwritten comment on the note 'Seen by F-S 15' and Cunningham reminded the court that this showed that Mr Ferguson-Smith, then Head of Special Branch, had read it.

Bevan then turned to the question of what action he had taken in relation to Watts after he received the call from the Security Service:

> **Bevan: … Having had that telephone call with the gentleman from the Security Service about the Watts conversation with the Security Service about Messrs Randle and Pottle, did you take it up with Mr Watts at all that he might have misled or not put the matter quite correctly to the Security Service?**
>
> **Cunningham: I would have put it to him, but I went to his office and he was not there. He was away and I could not find him. Eventually I found he was on leave. Other things happened and then I did not pursue it further. I did not discuss the case with Mr Watts.**
>
> **Q: You went to look for him, as I understand from your evidence?**
>
> **A: I was going to demand an explanation but he was not there.**
>
> **Q: You wanted an explanation, just to make it quite plain, for what?**
>
> **A: Why had he said that Special Branch intended to take no action against Randle and Pottle because they were minor figures in this case and that we were going to put all our energies into pursuing Seán Bourke, who was the prime suspect.**
>
> **Q: Did you yourself regard Messrs Randle and Pottle as minor figures or not?**
>
> **A: No. I was indifferent to what they were. We did not have any evidence and the information I had did not make me feel that we could obtain useful evidence. These were shrewd political activists, well versed in legal procedures, and I felt that it would be of no avail to interview them.**
>
> **Q: Was any decision whatever in relation to Randle and Pottle based upon persecution?**
>
> **A: No. There was no question of persecution or not persecuting them. The fact was there was no evidence.**

Cunningham was now cross-examined by Robertson. In the light of the judge's comment in their eventual judgement that Watts and Cunningham 'were witnesses of candour,' it seems worthwhile to quote in full the first few pages of the transcript of Robertson's cross examination. Readers can then decide for themselves whether they agree with the judge's view, or agree with our view which is that he was the least credible of all the witnesses who gave evidence at the High Court hearing or the subsequent trial:

Robertson: Mr Cunningham, I have to suggest to you that the evidence you have given to the court today about the telephone call from the Security Service is simply incorrect; your memory has played tricks with you?
Cunningham: No.
Q: You see you tell us very clearly that that was a call in April 1970?
A: It was about April 1970.
Q: March / April 1970 from a senior officer in the Security Service, MI5?
A: From the case officer.
Q: We know that the case officer who has come to this court this morning was a woman. You described the telephone call as being from a man?
A: That is correct.
Q: So it was presumably that woman's senior officer?
A: The man who wrote the 'Dear Arthur' letter?[24]
Q: Yes.
Q: A man whose name – I do not ask for it – you know?
A: Yes.
Q: A man who, today, you know has no recollection of making that call?
A: I did not know that but I know that he was ill.
Q: Too ill to come to court but he has made a statement in which he has no recollection of making that call?
A: Right. I recall that.
Q: It was a serious call, was it not?
A: Yes.
Q: Indicating that Special Branch had given incorrect information to MI5?
A: That is so.
Q: A matter of very considerable concern given the national interest of a very close and very active communication between Special Branch and MI5?
A: Yes.
Q: A matter of requiring not only correction of records and file notes but immediate speaking to Mr Watts?
A: Yes.
Q: Because the fault may have been at the MI5 side in their recording of what he said?

24 See document No7 in Appendix 3, a letter from 'Box 500' to Cunningham, dated 7 May 1970.

A: Yes. Mr Watts was not there. I went to seek him out to demand an explanation. He was not there.
Q: You would have done that immediately, would you not?
A: Yes.
Q: You tell us he was on leave?
A: He was away from his desk and I was told he was on leave.
Q: But he was not on leave at this period, was he, Mr Cunningham? We have seen the notes from him. If you look at the last note, it is on 9th May. He is there on 9th May. We know he was present on 28th April. This telephone call, if it took place at all, would have had to have been between 28th April and 30th April if it is said to be in April. It could not have been March?
A: I said it was the end of April. It may have been in May. I cannot be certain of that.
Q: Mr Watts is still there because he is writing file notes on 9th May.
A: It may have been before that time. I cannot recall the exact date that this phone call was made.
Q: I am putting it to you that it could not have been made because I suggest that, even if Mr Watts was away from his office, it was a serious enough matter to have spoken to him about?
A: I tried to speak to him.
Q: It was essential, was it not, to get his side of the story?
A: I do not agree with that entirely. I went to get an explanation from him and he was not there. I was told that he was away on leave, but he may have only been away for a day or so. I cannot say the exact date that this telephone conversation took place.
Q: It was an assertion by MI5 that they had been informed by a middle ranking Special Branch officer – by your officer – of something that you said was inaccurate. Is that right?
A: Yes.
Q It was essential to see Watts (a) to find out whether in fact he said what he was alleged to have said?
A: Yes.
Q: And (b), if he had, to have corrected his impression and even reprimanded him?
A: Yes, but this was what he was alleged to have said in a telephone conversation in a friendly fashion and I do not think that the whole of that conversation was recorded.
Q: It was still vital to see the man, was it not?
A: I tried to see him but he was not there.
Q: You did not leave him a note to see you when he got back?

A: No.
Q: How often in your experience at Special Branch had MI5 telephoned you and you discovered that one of your officers had given them incorrect information?
A: I cannot recall any apart from this one.
Q: It stood out in your mind. It stood out, if it occurred, far enough for you to have mentioned it to the court on the last occasion when you gave evidence?
A: I do not think I did.
Q: No, you did not. You did not mention it.
A: It was not raised at the time.[25]

Robertson had him on the ropes at this point. It was sheer evasion for Cunningham to have said that the point was not raised at the earlier hearing; it could not have been, because he was the only person who knew about the alleged telephone call. He had, however, comprehensively and emphatically denied that there was any discussion of a policy decision not to prosecute Pottle and the Randles. Robertson pressed him:

Q: You were questioned at length about the relationship between MI5 and Special Branch, were you not?
A Yes.
Q: During this period, and you never mentioned it?
A: I did not mention it because it was not raised.
Q: You did not mention it in your statement …
A: Not in my original statement, no.
Q: … when you were being asked to recall all you could remember about the decisions that were taken in relation to Randle and Pottle at the time?
A: I cannot recall being asked about this. I do not recall giving evidence about it.
Q: When you made the first statement in this matter it was dated 24th July?
A: That is correct.
Q: 1990?
A: Yes.
Q: Are you saying that you recalled your conversation with the Security Service official in July, at the time you made that statement?
A: No.
Q: Are you saying you recalled it at the time you gave evidence?
A: No.
Q: The position is that, when you were asked on 24th July to assist

25 Court Transcript, 3 October 1990, Evidence of Cunningham, pp.31-33.

this court with all that you could remember about decisions made in relation to these two men, you did not recall it then?
A: No.
Q: When you were asked questions on the last occasion, no question was asked which jogged your memory about this quite vital matter of you putting MI5 straight as to the basis for the decision of not proceeding against Randle and Pottle?
A: This matter was not raised in the court at that time. It was afterwards I was shown a memorandum from a file – a copy of a memorandum – and this showed Mr Watts had this conversation. That triggered my memory and that brought back to my mind the fact that the senior officer from MI5 had telephoned me.
Q: A telephone call that, again, I have to suggest, if it happened, you would have noted and ensured that Mr Watts had been put right about?
A: I did speak to his senior officer about it and I told him that I did not think it was correct.
Q: Who was that senior officer?
A: Mr Rodger.

This was the first time Cunningham had claimed to have spoken to Rodger about the incident. There is no mention of it in his second statement of 24th September or in his evidence in chief when questioned by Bevan. He knew, too, that Rodger had made a statement to the effect that he had no recollection whatever of the affair.

Q: Do you know Mr Rodger has no recollection of that at all?
A: Yes, I was told that. He had no recollection of the events at all.
Q: Neither you nor Mr Rodger made any note about the matter?
A: Not to my knowledge. I certainly did not.
Q: Or relayed by any means any information to Mr Watts putting him right about what he claimed you thought had happened?
A: No, I did not discuss it with Mr Watts.
Q: Namely that a decision had been made on the basis of persecution.
A: There was no question of persecution – no persecution. The facts were there was no evidence.[26]

Later Robertson pressed him on the matter of evidence:

Q: … It is plain from Mr Watts' report that Mr Randle was in prison with Bourke. MI5 had Christmas Cards he had sent to Bourke.[27] **He**

26 Court Transcript, 3 October 1990, Evidence of Mr Cunningham, pp.33-34.

27 In fact to Blake. This is either a mistake on Robertson's part or on the part of the official notetaker

> **had been known to express views that Blake's sentence was far too long. That is all in the Watts report?**
> **A: I accept that but I did not know that personally. I may have read it in Mr Watts' report and it was some time earlier.**
> **Q: But if you read it in Mr Watts' report it must have occurred to you that you had the makings of a case against Randle because you had evidence of motive: a belief that the sentence was wrong; sympathy for Blake; association with him; documentary evidence of that by way of Christmas cards and the like. You must have appreciated that you had some evidence – not enough for a prima facie case but some evidence?**
> **A: There was not enough to substantiate a prosecution.**
> **Q: The question was not whether there was enough to substantiate a prosecution but whether there was a reasonable prospect, or any prospect, of getting enough to substantiate a prosecution. That was the question, was it not?**
> **A: I assessed the situation at the time, and in my view there was not much chance at all of getting sufficient evidence to put before a court. In addition to that, there were three and a half years in which the investigation had gone cold. The investigation at that time was under the charge of Chief Superintendent Marchant [of CID]. He retired and it was taken over by Mr Chapman. I sent Mr Chapman a copy of Mr Watts' report. He could have taken action himself had he thought this a possibility.**
> **Q: Mr Cunningham, stopping you there, there is no evidence that Mr Watts' report was ever received by the CID because it is not in the CID files. Do you understand that?**
> **A: There is a note on my minute which says that it was sent to him.**
> **Robertson: I understand this to be the position from my learned friend [Mr Bevan] that, apart from a file reference in 1973 which does not concern Randle and Pottle, the CID files relating to the Blake escape are completely blank in 1970 and thereafter until 1987.**

Bevan rose to confirm that there was nothing in 'the district registry file or the general file sometimes mistakenly called the CID file' to indicate that the Watts report had ever been received, and no mention at all of Randle and Pottle.

> **Robertson: I am obliged for that, and that is the basis for my suggestion that there was no active CID investigation at all in 1970 by D.I. Chapman or anyone else.**[28]

Robertson also put it to Cunningham that their opportunity to act came

28 Court Transcript, 3 October 1990. Evidence of Mr Cunningham, pp.36-37.

in the period between Randle and Pottle being identified in the Watts report and the publication of the book:

> **Robertson: It is obvious, if you think about it, that as soon as that book is published they will realise that you are on to them and they will hold meetings. They will telephone each other. They will destroy the evidence they have. They will warn the doctor and the financier and the other co-conspirators to do the same?**
> **Cunningham: That is probably true.**
> **Q: As of 25th March 1970 you had a golden opportunity to detect what evidence there was, because it was as sure as eggs are eggs that after that book was published that evidence would be [there] no longer?**
> **A: I do not agree that it was sure as eggs are eggs when that book was published they were positively identified.**
> **Q: I have to suggest to you that on 25th March 1970 you must have realised that as far as prosecuting the co-conspirators of Bourke was concerned, not just two of them but up to six of them, it was now or never; in other words, three months later when the book was published they would take steps to destroy any evidence.**
> **A: No.**[29]

Robertson could get no further with this line of questioning and eventually Lord Justice Watkins warned him to avoid further repetition of questions already put.

Scrivener, in his cross-examination concentrated again on the things that the CID or Special Branch could have done to obtain evidence such as checking up on my passport to see if I had in fact been to Berlin in December 1966, to check with neighbours if I had ever owned a Dormobile and to check with local garages to see if I had had it serviced.

Bevan's re-examination produced nothing new. It enabled Cunningham to emphasise that the Special Branch officer given the task of sending the Watts report to D.I. Chapman in CID and ticked and initialled the relevant minute to indicate that this had been done. He also concurred with the suggestion put to him by Bevan that once Chapman had received the report 'he had a free hand' to investigate the matter further if he so wished.

The obvious question here is why then was there no record of CID having received the Watts' report or any mention at all in its files of the suspected role of Pat, Anne and myself? One explanation is that there was an extraordinary degree of inefficiency, all the more surprising given that the Blake escape itself had been followed, as Watts acknowledged, by one of the biggest manhunts in

29 Court Transcript, 3 October 1990, Evidence of Mr Cunningham, pp.42-43.

British police history. The other is that the report was delivered to Chapman at CID with a verbal indication that for the time being at least the view of MI5 and Special Branch was that no action should be taken in the way of investigating or prosecuting the three of us.

After Cunningham had given his evidence, both sides agreed that it was unnecessary to call Mr B [of MI5] who, we were told, was unwell and confined to a wheel-chair. He had said in his sworn statement that he remembered nothing of the events under discussion and it was clear there would be no point in having him come to the court.

Bevan began his final submission. There was no information he argued, that a policy decision had been taken not to prosecute regardless of the evidence. At its highest, the evidence could be read as indicating that a decision was taken not to prosecute, or attempt to prosecute, for two reasons. First that to pursue the matter could be perceived as persecution since Blake and Bourke had got away, and, second, that a decision was made not to investigate further on the grounds that the chances of success were negligible. Whether there was a dereliction of duty on the part of the police in 1970 was a matter for the court. But even if the court decided that the evidence showed that a decision was made in 1970 not to prosecute or investigate because prosecution would amount to persecution, the proceedings in 1989 after the two men had written their book would not amount to an abuse of process. If they had written it in 1970 they would have been prosecuted then, and the fact that they were interviewed by the police in 1987 after being named in a Sunday newspaper was a clear indication to them that the matter was not dead and buried.

Regarding O'Connor, he said he was not suggesting the meeting with Watts in 1984 had never taken place. But he found it odd that Watts had opened his mouth to a stranger whom he knew to be a journalist. O'Connor was claiming that Watts told him that the police knew the identity of Blake's helpers within a very short time of the escape, and this was certainly not the case. Nor was there anything about persecution in O'Connor's notes.

Randle and Pottle had played a vital part in the escape. Their Counsel had suggested that they were 'sardines' in the affair, but nothing could be further from the truth. They had helped plan the escape, provided finance, cars, a doctor to treat Blake's injury, a safe house in London. And finally they had spirited him out of the country.

Had the passage of time prejudiced a fair trial? No, he said, for the two men had acknowledged the principal facts in their book. There was no doubting the seriousness of their offence, and it was 'right and proper' and in the public interest that they should now stand trial.

The hearing continued into a third day when Scrivener and Robertson in turn made their final submissions. These mainly covered points they had dealt with earlier. Scrivener said that in the early period after the escape the Security Service, CID and Special Branch were all involved in the investigations. Miss A's note, and her evidence showed that the extent of the Security Service' interest was in establishing whether or not there was any Russian involvement in the escape. CID played a subsidiary role to Special Branch as was evident from the fact that their file contained virtually nothing beyond 1970 and that they did not even have a copy of the Watts report on their files. By 1970 it was Special Branch who was running the show and making the decisions. And they had evidently made a decision not to pursue the matter further. They did not take up an offer from MI5 to pursue enquiries abroad, or take the elementary steps that would be followed in a common burglary. Miss A had agreed – after a considerable pause – that Notes for File were intended to convey information without further explanation. And the only way her note of 29th April 1970 could be read was that Special Branch had decided not to prosecute, or interview, Randle and Pottle because to do so might be seen as persecution when the big fish had got away.

Scrivener also raised one procedural point which evidently nettled Watkins. There had been procedural errors at the Crown Court and for this reason no valid decision had been made there. The role of this Divisional Court was not to decide the substantive issue, but to rule on whether the Crown court had acted correctly, and if necessary send it back there.

Robertson reminded the court of previous judgements to the effect that delay of itself, if sufficiently prolonged, would make a prosecution an abuse of process. The Note for File of 29th April 1970 at the very least raised a reasonable doubt about whether a policy decision was made at that time.

Miss A, he said, had been an impressive witness. But we should put greater reliance on what she had actually written within 24 hours of speaking to Watts in 1970 than on her recollection of the event 20 years later. We also had the confirmation of O'Connor's testimony. He had no reason whatever to lie, and his notes showed that Watts had told him things that only he knew about. And aside from the fact that Watts claimed the police decision was made on humanitarian grounds, what he told O'Connor was remarkably close to what Miss A had recorded Watts as saying in 1970. Given all this, it was now up to the Crown to establish that there had not been a policy decision not to prosecute.

When he finished, Watkins announced that he and Hutchison were reserving their judgement and would give their decision at a later date. Consequently, some six weeks later, on 15th November, we found ourselves back at the court to hear their judgement.

Chapter 14:

Perverse Judgement

It was clear to us before Watkins uttered a word on 16th November that he would reject our application. But on what grounds would he and his fellow 'liberal' judge reject it? How would they deal with O'Connor's testimony, and with the conflict in the evidence of Watts, Cunningham, and Miss A? These were the real points of interest.

To recap the situation. Miss A's evidence told the court, in effect, that her Note for File of 29th April 1970 didn't mean what it appeared to mean. The crucial passage in the note read: 'Chief Inspector Watts added that the S.B. decision at present was to take no steps to interview or attempt to prosecute the Randles, Pottle or Goodwin. It was considered that to do so might be persecution – a big fish had got away so they were taking it out on the little fish.' Miss A now asserted that in fact the sole reason for Special Branch's decision was lack of evidence. The reference to 'persecution' simply meant that to interview or attempt to prosecute without evidence might be persecution. The reference to the big fish and little fish was no more than a consolatory afterthought. The passage in question had to be read in conjunction with the following paragraph which indicated that Special Branch enquiries were continuing.

Ex-Commander Cunningham fell into the same trap as the rest of us who read the note – he thought it meant what it said. On 25th July, before he was shown the Note, he stated under oath at the High Court that there had been no discussion whatever of a policy decision not to prosecute Randle and Pottle. However, when he was shown Miss A's Note it jogged his memory. Now he remembered that in late April 1970 he had received a telephone call from Miss A's senior officer in MI5 to tell him that Mr Watts was saying that Special Branch had decided not to interview or prosecute us because to do so might be persecution. He told the MI5 officer Watts was mistaken, and went straight away to Watts' office to put him right. But Watts was out of his office and didn't subsequently speak to him about it – this despite the fact that this was the only occasion in his career he had experienced anything like this happening. Late on in cross-examination he claimed that he had spoken to Watts immediate superior, Mr Rodger, about the incident.

If Miss A was correct in asserting that the Note didn't mean what it appeared to say, Cunningham could hardly have received a telephone call from her superior officer, Mr B, asking what Watts meant by the things he was reported as saying. It is inconceivable Mr B would have done so without first speaking to Miss A who could then have cleared up the misunderstanding. But Miss A stated categorically that her senior officer had not got back to her about the note, and that, furthermore, he would certainly have done so if its accuracy was being challenged by a senior officer in Special Branch. Moreover, if her Note had been found to be incorrect something would probably have been added to it to indicate this, perhaps in the form of a cross reference to a later note clarifying the position.

Watts claimed he had no recollection of his conversation with Miss A in 1970. He denied any memory of having given an interview to the Irish journalist Kevin O'Connor in 1984. According to O'Connor's notes made at the time, Watts told him that the police knew of the identity of Blake's helpers 'soon after the escape' but that a decision had been taken from on high not to prosecute them because they were law-abiding citizens doing a useful job in the community, not 'real life effing and blinding villains,' and that to pursue them would be a waste of the taxpayers' money. This explanation was not identical to that independently recorded by Miss A some 14 years earlier, but it was remarkably close to it – too close to be put down to coincidence. True the police had not in fact known of our involvement 'soon after' the escape but only after they received the manuscript of Seán Bourke's book in 1970. But this discrepancy could have been due to Watts wanting to make the police appear more efficient than they actually were. It is really a detail and took nothing away from the significance and credibility of O'Connor's testimony.

Another element in O'Connor's testimony lent it further weight – as Robertson had underlined in his examination. He reported Watts as telling him that Seán's landlady at Highlever Road had become suspicious of Seán because he would appear one day clean shaven and the next with a full black beard and had reported her suspicions to the police. This fact too was independently confirmed by the testimony of the landlady, Mrs Lotte Heveringham, which we received in April 1990. O'Connor could not have got this information from Seán, and did not get it from us since his first statement recording it was written in January 1990, some two months before we obtained the copy of the police interview with Mrs Heveringham. He could only have got it, in fact from Watts.

Since Watts claimed to remember nothing of his conversations with Miss A in 1970, or his meeting with O'Connor in 1984, his position was in a sense unassailable. Nevertheless from this unassailable position he did his best to undermine O'Connor's credibility by stating that he couldn't possibly have said the things attributed to him, and that it wasn't the way he thought or spoke. He claimed too that it would have been 'breaking the habit of a lifetime' if he had agreed to talk to a journalist about anything that had gone on in Special Branch. Yet it was another journalist, the crime correspondent from the Daily Mail, who had given O'Connor the lead to Watts and told him he was the 'legman' on the Blake escape case.

The judges had a clear choice to make regarding Miss A's note. Either it didn't mean what it said, in which case Mr Cunningham's memory 'was playing him tricks' – as Geoffrey Robertson charitably put it in cross-examination – when he claimed to have had a telephone call in late April 1970 from Miss A's senior officer. Or it meant exactly what it said and there really were factors other than the state of the evidence that influenced the decision of Special Branch to take no steps against us in 1970, at least for the time being. Moreover, assuming the Note did mean what it said, the alleged telephone conversation between Cunningham and Mr B still could not have taken place if Miss A was right in saying she would have been informed about it and that her Note for File would probably have been corrected or cross-referenced. In short, Cunningham and Miss A's testimonies conflicted. They couldn't both be right.

How did the judges resolve the dilemma? Quite simply they ignored it. Miss A was 'a most impressive witness'. Watts and Cunningham were 'witnesses of candour' and 'obviously frank … in all respects both as to the reason why the applicants were not prosecuted in 1970 and why neither of them, nor so far as they knew, anyone else had carried out an enquiry.' We had clearly underestimated the intelligence and ingenuity of the two judges. The implication of their judgement was that Miss A's Note both meant what it said and didn't mean what it said at the same time. They believed the candid Mr Cunningham about the telephone call from Mr B in late April 1970, and equally accepted Miss A's evidence that if it had taken place she would have been told about it by her senior officer and a comment would have been added to her Note for File.

The judges dealt with Miss A's evidence in a single paragraph:

> Miss A was a most impressive witness. When giving evidence she was screened from everyone's view save ours. She was a long serving member of M.I.5. who retired some time ago. She had, we thought, a most telling recollection of her dealings in 1970 with Watts and Cunningham and of the reason why in various of the disclosed documents statements material to the existence of a policy, or otherwise, not to prosecute appear and

> what the true significance of them is. She said she was not aware of any such policy. Her understanding was that there would be no prosecution at that time because there was no evidence but that that was a temporary decision. Moreover, M.I.5. did not have any evidence against the appellants.

Thus no specific mention of her crucial Note for File of 29th April 1970, no attempt to deal with the apparent contradiction between the words it contained and her interpretation of them. The Note was just another disclosed document whose true significance she had convincingly explained.
The shabbiest treatment was reserved for Kevin O'Connor.

Mr O'Connor was, we thought, more entertaining than truly enlightening. He said that he had interviewed Watts, then retired and working for a security firm, in 1984. Watts had no recollection of O'Connor with whom he was confronted in court. We are satisfied, however, that O'Connor went to Watts' office and spoke to him of the Blake affair. He was not the only journalist who had endeavoured to do that. O'Connor maintained that Watts told him there had been a policy not to prosecute. He said that Watts told him that this policy was formed in 1966 soon after Blake's escape.

This assertion by O'Connor is something of an embarrassment to the applicants. We are entirely satisfied that there is no evidence whatsoever to suggest that in 1966 – or at any time which, to quote O'Connor's evidence, could be described as 'very soon after Blake's escape' – the police knew or had any ground for believing who had helped Blake to escape, let alone that it was the applicants. There was no suggestion by Watts, O'Connor said, that their identities were not known until after Bourke's book – the decision was taken at an early stage. These statements which he attributes to Watts cannot sensibly be accepted as accurate, and we conclude that O'Connor's evidence as to the conversation is unreliable, and certainly does not establish that any policy decision had been made not to prosecute those responsible for the escape.'[1]

The sleight of hand here is in the treatment of the fact that the police did not know of our involvement 'soon after the escape.' It is quite true they did not. But the judges jump from that to the conclusion that it was O'Connor who got his facts wrong and that therefore his evidence is unreliable. The alternative explanation is that Watts used a vague phrase such as 'soon after the escape' either because he didn't want to go into greater detail about how they had come to learn of our involvement or because he wanted to impress O'Connor regarding the efficiency of the police. For the same reasons, Watts might have been reluctant to say that the police had no clue as to our identities until handed them on a plate in Bourke's book. Incidentally, O'Connor

1 From the official Judgement pp.39-41 in the unrevised version.

nowhere states that Watts told him the police knew 'in 1966' – but only that it was 'soon after' the escape – a minor point but not irrelevant if one is trying to assess the likelihood of Watts having said what O'Connor attributes to him. If Watts wanted to be vague but to give a general impression of police efficiency he would be more likely to use a phrase like 'soon after' the escape than to state a specific year.

Far more significant than the discrepancy over the year in which the police knew of our involvement is the remarkable closeness of the views O'Connor attributes to Watts in 1984 to those noted by Miss A in 1970. The judges avoid confronting this, as noted above, by not mentioning the latter specifically. Had they done so, it would have been far more difficult for them to have brushed aside O'Connor's evidence in the way they did. These are two highly intelligent men well versed in the subtleties of debate. Their treatment of this issue amounted to a perverse evasion of their responsibility.

A small but telling detail here is the judge's comment that Mr O'Connor was 'more entertaining than truly enlightening'. O'Connor made only one quip – and that at the expense of Watkins who was clearly put out by the incident. Watkins, readers will recall, said he was a frequent visitor to Ireland and that 'Holy Jihad' was a common expression there – to which O'Connor responded 'I believe you're thinking of "Holy Jaysus", my Lord.' For the rest of the time O'Connor was entirely direct and straightforward and certainly did not play the clown in the way the judge's comment suggests. In our own judgement, he was, in fact, by far the most direct and impressive witness to appear at the hearings. Again readers can judge the quality of his testimony and his responses to cross-examination from the passages quoted in the previous chapter or from the full transcript of the hearing.

We are of course, interested parties here, and our judgement is likely to be swayed by this fact. For this reason Pat and I have decided to deposit a copy of all the transcripts of the High Court proceedings in our possession – which includes the evidence given in July and October of Watts and Cunningham, and that of O'Connor and Miss A in October – in the Commonweal Library attached to Bradford University so that future researchers can read the proceedings if they so wish and draw their own conclusions. We will also be depositing at Commonweal the complete transcripts of the Old Bailey trial.

The judges could have rejected our application without recourse to these shabby tactics and evasions. They could have confronted honestly the conflicts in the evidence of Cunningham and Miss A, noted the significance of her Note for File and the degree of overlap between it and what Watts allegedly told O'Connor, but still adjudged that this did not amount to proof positive that a policy decision had been taken not to prosecute us, much less that a decision had been taken at a high level. Only by ignoring all these factors, however, could they arrive at the conclusion they did – namely that there was 'no evidence of the existence of a policy formed by the police at any time not to prosecute the applicants.' It is not their decision to reject our application that we quarrel with: it is the dishonesty of the methods they adopted to reach it.

Bevan in his closing speech presented them with the argument they could have adopted and still in good conscience turned down our application. The evidence, he argued, indicated 'at its highest' a reluctance on the part of the police to prosecute us in 1970 because this might be seen as persecution. This, coupled with a lack of evidence, and a sense that it would be a waste of time to interview us, would account for the fact that no action was taken against us in 1970. Perhaps the police were remiss in doing nothing, but this in itself was not sufficient to debar a prosecution once we had written our book. If it had been written in 1970, he had no doubt we would have been prosecuted then.

On this last point at least, I think he was right. The authorities were willing to let sleeping dogs lie, not only in 1970 but in 1987 when we were named by the Sunday Times. But if the dogs started to bark of their own accord that would change the situation. The unspoken bargain was – 'You keep your mouths shut and we won't prosecute.' We were prepared to buy that, but not once we had been publicly named and our continued silence was leading people to jump to wild conclusions about our possible collaboration with the KGB and fuel all the worst suspicions about the integrity of the wider peace movement.

With the other elements of the judgement we have no serious quarrel, even where, at times, we ourselves take a different view. It was reasonable for the judges to have rejected Robertson's argument that the pressure for us to go public once we had been named would make it unfair to prosecute us so long after the event. They were on strong grounds when they argued that the offence itself was a serious one and that, in view of the detailed account we had given of our actions in our book, we could hardly claim to have been prejudiced in presenting our case by the passage of time. As they put it:

> It would have been improper for us to have asked what defence the applicants have in the light of the contents of their book. However, it is in no sense inappropriate to observe that in the light of the contents of the book the plea of fading memory could simply not be advanced. Memories of events are seemingly all too clear …
>
> It is maintained that it is irrelevant that courts may suspect that the applicants have no good defence. We disagree. There is a significant

> difference in our judgment, between a case where guilt is squarely an issue and one in which it is suspected that it is not, or may not be. The value to be attached to that in the judgment of the court depends entirely upon the circumstances. It cannot, in our view, be left entirely out of account in this case but we regard it as being far from the most influential of the factors which should govern the decision. The judge appears have paid little or no attention to it.

The judges, too, backed Macpherson in rejecting the proposition that the prosecuting authorities had been unduly influenced by outside pressure from Parliament and the public in bringing the prosecution. Clearly that pressure existed, as indeed Inspector Bird's statement of 7th March 1990 acknowledged. But the fact that over 100 Conservative MPs had demanded our prosecution, and that the DPP was faced with the threat from Norris McWhirter of the Freedom Association to bring a private prosecution does not in itself prove that the authorities acted improperly in bringing charges once our book was written.

The judgement expressed some disagreement with Macpherson's decisions in the Crown Court. But the judges chose their words carefully, insisting that they should not be read as criticism:

> We have been concerned here with the decision making process. It has been asserted that the judge was wrong to disallow the calling of certain witnesses and to refuse to order disclosure of documents. In both respects we took a different course believing that to be right and, encouraged by counsel for the applicants, ordered discovery of documents to the widest possible extent and allowed, with like encouragement, witnesses to be called to deal with matters very much in issue. In implicitly finding the judge had been wrong not to do all that we should make it clear that we do not criticize him. He did not receive the wisest assistance from counsel for the applicants who, for instance, refused to agree to his seeing the Watts report so that he could be in a better position to tell whether he should disregard the Home Secretary's certificate and order discovery. Moreover, the request to him to hear oral evidence was on a very limited footing. Procedurally in error, as is alleged, he may possibly have been but that we have no doubt created no injustice for the applicants.
>
> The evidence we heard and the documents we have seen do not, as is apparent from what we have said, flaw the judge's separate conclusions to which the evidence and documents were relevant. They were that there was no evidence of the policy alleged by the applicants to have been made and "such a decision (not to enquire in 1970), whether it stemmed from inactivity or from a mixture of inactivity and other feelings which

> individual police officers may have felt in respect of these two men, cannot possibly end the matter. Nobody for a moment suggests that some kind of estoppel or bar exists as a result of that failure, for good or bad reasons, to take the matter further in 1970.

The judges also rejected Scrivener's 'eleventh hour submissions' that the High Court had acted improperly in hearing the case and in making findings of fact and that the right course of action would have been to refer the matter back to Macpherson in the Crown Court.

The judgement concludes:

> This is, of course, an extraordinary and unique case. The delay is obviously very long indeed but not so long as to disable the vast majority of the people of this country, we think, from recalling the consternation caused by the escape of Blake and its serious implications. Some people may sympathise with the predicament of the applicants. Whether that sympathy is misplaced is not for us to say. We have regarded, as we have most carefully the evidence, the arguments of counsel addressed to us on behalf of the applicants and the value judgment of the judge. In our judgment he came to a conclusion which cannot be criticised in principle. Nor can it be assailed on the basis that he disregarded matters which if taken into account might have affected his decision.
>
> These applications are refused.

***

By now the date for the Old Bailey trial had been fixed for 15th January 1991. We had two months, therefore, to make our final preparations. But we would be able to spend Christmas with our families and there was at least an end in sight to all the waiting.

Well, so we thought. But the lawyers now pressed us to consider seeking leave to appeal to the House of Lords which would certainly involve yet another postponement. The Crown side were hoping we would do so because they were unhappy about the court's ruling on jurisdiction. They couldn't initiate an appeal as the judgement on the main issue of abuse of process had been in their favour, but they could do so on the back of an appeal from us. In short, if we sought leave to appeal on the abuse of process they could tuck in an application on jurisdiction.

Somewhat reluctantly Pat and I consented to the lawyers going ahead with an application. The first stage in the process required Watkins to agree that there was an issue of public importance involved for the Law Lords to consider. The earliest date for the hearing which suited all parties turned out to be 24th May. Ten days before the hearing the Crown withdrew its own application on the jurisdiction issue, partly because there were other cases in the pipeline which they could use to test the issue[2], partly, no doubt, because our application on its own would have less chance to succeed.

It didn't. Watkins, already familiar to the point of boredom with all the arguments, gave it short shrift. He described a written submission from Ed Fitzgerald as 'intriguing but not very enlightening,' and listened with evident scepticism to what Geoffrey Robertson had to say on the matter. He then dismissed the application without further ado and expressed the hope that the trial would proceed as expeditiously as possible. The new date, which had already been provisionally booked, was for Monday 17th June.

In the end the postponement from January to June worked to our advantage. First, it meant that our trial did not overlap the Gulf War, an event which would certainly have eclipsed it completely in the press and media.

Second, the delay gave us the opportunity to appeal Mr Justice Kennedy's decision on 11th April 1990 to impose a Charging Order on our houses under the provisions of the Criminal Justice Act 1988. (The effect of this order, as noted in an earlier chapter, was that if we were found guilty our houses could be confiscated and sold and the advance royalties of £15,000 each we had received for our book seized – plus in my case a further £1,100 which the prosecution claimed I had gained during the escape itself). The appeal was heard before Mr Justice Webster in the High Court on 7th March 1991.

This too was unsuccessful. The judge concluded that although the payments did not fall into the category of property obtained 'as a result of the offences' as specified in the Act, they did constitute property obtained 'in connection with' them. It was, he said, 'the commission of the offences by the Applicants, if they are found guilty of them, that will have enabled them to write the book.' Doubtless our skill as authors also played a part, but this would lead him to conclude that 'the payments were obtained partly in connection with the commission of the offences and partly in connection with their skill as authors.'[3]

2 The ruling on jurisdiction was reversed in the Regina v Manchester Crown court and others, Ex parte Director of Public Prosecutions, House of Lords, 6 May 1993. Ironically, the Counsel for the defendants who successfully persuaded the Court that the Randle case was wrongly decided was Anthony Scrivener.

3 For a discussion of the issues involved, see Arie Freiberg, `Confiscating the Literary Proceeds of Crime', Criminal Law Review, Vol ? No ?, 1992, pp.96-106. Our case is one of those the author considers.

Thirdly, the delay also enabled me to finish a book I was working on the role of civil resistance in bringing about the collapse of East European communist regimes in 1989. The book, entitled People Power: the Building of a New European Home was published by Hawthorn Press (Stroud) in June 1991, coincidentally during the very week that Pat and myself stood trial at the Old Bailey. The second part of the book comprises interviews with various people who had taken an active part in the nonviolent revolutions, among them an old friend and colleague Jan Kavan. More on him later.

Finally the postponement of the trial from January to June provided us with the opportunity to hone our preparations. We held three all-day Saturday conferences at Pat Pottle's house – one in December and two in June – with Ben, John, Tom and, on the first occasion, Ed Fitzgerald in attendance so that we could go step by step through the case. We rehearsed questions we intended to put to witnesses, and legal points we would raise, and got the lawyers to interrupt us whenever they thought the judge or prosecuting Counsel were likely to do so. This partial role-play of the forthcoming trial was to prove of inestimable value. It meant we were in a position to anticipate the objections and could judge which points we needed to get in swiftly before the objections were raised.

The weekend before the start of the trial Anne and I spent the weekend in Sussex with my mother, Nell, and other family members. At 85 she still enjoyed relative good health, and was as alert as ever – still more than able to hold her own at the Irish card game of 25s which we always play when we visit her. But as we took our leave, she held me tightly and kissed me.

'Well, goodbye Michael,' she said simply.

She was sure I would be spending the next several years in prison and did not expect to be still alive when I was released. In her own mind she was saying goodbye to me for the last time.

Chapter 15:

'No Politics in my Court'

There was an officer waiting for Pat and myself as we entered the dock at No 1 Court at the Old Bailey. Despite the rigorous check we had already undergone to enter the building he took us half-way down the stairs leading to the cells under the court, checked our bags, and gave us a body check. There were the unmistakeable prison smells down there: I caught a glimpse of heavy iron doors. A prisoner was shouting out something and an officer was telling him to shut up. We walked back up the narrow stairwell, its walls lined with cracked white tiles, into the decorous oak-panelled architecture of the courtroom. It was 10.45am.

'All persons having anything to do with my Lords the Queen's Justices, let them draw nigh and give their attendance' a court official called out. Everyone stood up. Mr Justice Alliott strode in from an entrance behind the judges' seats. A well-built man, probably in his early fifties, he was dressed in red with white ermine borders on cuffs and collar, and carried silk gloves in one hand which he slapped down on the bench in front of him. He sat down, not in the most central seat, but on one to the left of it as we faced him.

Pat and I remained on our feet and said straight away that we wanted to argue that the trial would constitute an abuse of process. Our intention in doing so was to put down a marker in case anything came up at the trial which would allow us to argue that the abuse issue should be re-examined. Alliott responded that the Divisional Court had already ruled that there had been no abuse of process and he was bound by that. Having earlier been coached by the lawyers, I then cited the case of R v Grobb & Hart (January 1990), in which Judge Denison QC at the Central Criminal Court in Southwark agreed to stop the prosecution on the grounds that undue delay amounted to an abuse of the legal process, despite the fact that earlier Mr Justice McNeil had refused a similar submission in a pre-trial review.

> **Alliott: That was Judge Dennison on a retrial. I regard that case as distinguishable. Let them be arraigned.**
>
> **Randle: We want to raise it again at a later time.**
>
> **Alliott: You have raised it.**

The clerk of the court, Miss Russell, a woman of small stature but with a decisive, no-nonsense manner, read out the charges: aiding a prisoner, George

Blake, to escape; conspiring to harbour him; and conspiring to prevent his rearrest. We each in turn gave a firm Not Guilty reply to the charges.

Julian Bevan rose to introduce himself and his junior, David Calvert-Smith. The Crown case he said rested essentially on the book by the two accused published in April 1989. It would be necessary for the jury to read the whole book, so the Crown proposed, with the agreement of the defendants, to ask each prospective jury member if this posed a difficulty for them. Bevan then identified Ben and John as the two solicitors who would be advising us, and Caroline Bowman, a young trainee barrister who had agreed to take notes of the proceedings for our benefit.

Alliot leaned forward in his chair.

> Mr Justice Alliott: I think it would perhaps be sensible if I were to indicate to everyone my approach to this case. I have had the advantage of reading the book … and I have also had the advantage of reading various utterances made by one or other of the defendants in the approach to this trial. As I understand it, it is the intention not to contest the facts, but – to paraphrase the words of Mr Randle and Mr Pottle – to put the Government on notice for their espionage policies way back in the 1960's. I am bound to say I do not think that is appropriate. I am bound to say, I shall rule against that happening. I am sure Mr Randle and Mr Pottle will see why. If there are massive mitigations after a plea of guilty, I shall sieve through them. The only issues I am to have debated in the trial is whether or not it is proved by the Crown that the defendants did the acts constituting the three counts in the indictment. Now if having said that either of the defendants or Mr Birnberg or Mr Wadham think it appropriate for me to rise so that the defendants can digest that, I am happy to do so.

Pat interrupted.

> This was unrealistic he said. MI5 and MI6 had been involved in the case, and it was on their initiative that the case had been brought against us.

Alliott continued:

> All I am concerned with is the forensic process. In the light of what I have read, you have no defence. I am speaking in the absence of the jury. If the matter is tested, it will be for them to decide the issue. You can invite the Crown to prove its case. What I will not allow is cross-examination going other than to the issue of whether you did what the Crown said you did. I have very much in mind page 12 of the book (The Blake Escape), the brilliant exploitations by those unrepresented of judicial leeway.

The passage in question, dealing with our trial at the Old Bailey during the Committee of 100 period in 1962, noted how Pat had got round the Judge's ruling that he would not allow a political defence. The particular sentence reads: 'Pat brilliantly exploited the leeway the judge felt obliged to grant him as an amateur among professionals to put forward arguments and to question witnesses in a way not open to Hutchinson.'

The judge looked directly at us, emphasising his words:

> **You will not have any in this case. But I do not intend by anything I say to deprive you of some small pre-political platform you wish to have. In my view, the appropriate place for that is mitigation. Would anyone like me to rise so they can digest my attitude to that?**
> **Randle: I think so, yes.**[1]

The hearing was adjourned for half-an-hour while we consulted with the lawyers. We had not the slightest intention of changing our plea, but it was an opportunity to assess the import of Alliot's statement.

'It's clear,' Ben said, 'what Alliot's line is going to be. He's determined to shut you up completely.' The others agreed. John repeated the view he had expressed to us several times before – that we had been too frank in the book and in our public statements about the approach we intended to take at the trial. This had forewarned the judge and the prosecution who would now be on their guard to prevent us running the kind of arguments we wanted to. No-one even suggested at this stage that we should change our plea. We'd had that argument already, and everyone knew we weren't going to make a different decision at this stage.

As we made our way back into the court, Julian Bevan, caught up with us.

'I take it you are not changing your plea?' he asked quietly as we entered the court. We confirmed this, and he nodded understandingly, as much as to say, 'We always knew you wouldn't.'

Pat and I took our places back in the dock. The court was silent. The Clerk, Miss Russell, picked up the phone from the desk in front of her and cupped her hand secretively around the mouthpiece while she talked into it.

When his lordship came in again two minutes later, he did not trouble to enquire of Pat or me whether or not we had changed our minds but proceeded to talk about the conduct of the trial. Evidently Bevan had given the nod to the Clerk who in turn had telephoned the judge.

Alliot turned to practical matters. He ruled that the jury should be given two days to read the book and that they should do so in the controlled

1 Court Transcript, Vol 1, pp.6-8

environment of the juryroom rather than being allowed to take it home as Pat and I had suggested. Bevan then indicated, in response to a question from Alliott, that he expected the prosecution case to last for about a day and a half – though this would depend in part on the time taken by us in cross-examination. Alliott again took the opportunity to emphasise the limited scope we would be given.

> **Alliott: I am going to be tough on cross-examination, as you have gathered, gentlemen. I am going to restrict you to the genuine live forensic issue, which in my mind does not exist, and that is out of your own mouths that I take that attitude. Now again, within the confines of the case, as I propose strictly to maintain it, how long do you think your evidence will be?**

Pat replied that at the most it would take three days. In our strategy discussions with the lawyers they had emphasised how important it would be to indicate to the judge from the outset that we did not intend to waste the time of the court in a filibuster operation and would be as brief as possible. This way we had a better chance of quickly smuggling in some of the wider political and humanitarian arguments.

We had several other questions to raise, however, and now moved onto those.

> **Randle: My Lord, there were one or two other preliminary problems. One was, we have seen from this adjournment the inconvenience of us being up here and our lawyers being down in the well of the court.**
> **Alliott: You should have counsel; that would solve all the problems.**
> **Randle: We would not like to put the State to further expense in this case, and we feel we can put our own defence. In these circumstances – you can see there are two boxes of evidence, and we have one table up here – I wonder, just for the convenience of the court in this case, if it would be possible for us to sit in the well of the court rather than up here in the dock?**
> **Alliott: No. So long as the dock remains part of forensic furniture, there must be no special dispensation, nor in my view, should there be for you two gentlemen.**
> **Pottle: There certainly has been in the past, my Lord.**
> **Alliott: Not in my court.**
> **Pottle: This would be breaking new ground – would it be possible for Mr Birnberg and Mr Wadham to share the dock with us?**
> **Alliott: What I suggest they do is take up the position at the end of this table here so there is more ready access to you, but you must remain where you are, gentlemen.**

Pottle: Fine. We are not objecting to that. If your Lordship would give us a bit of leeway throughout the trial …

Alliott: Leeway is a word that rings alarm bells.

Pottle: (smiling): I'm sure it does.

Our reason for asking to be allowed to conduct our defence from the well of the court was not simply the convenience of being next to our two solicitors. It was also based on the fact that to be in the dock at all carries a suggestion of guilt, however much the judge may insist that a defendant is to be presumed innocent until proved guilty. We also knew that in at least one other case, that of the civil servant Clive Ponting who was tried under the Official Secrets Act for passing confidential information to an MP about the way the government was deceiving Parliament, the defendant had been permitted to sit with his solicitors and counsel. However, it was no great disappointment to us that the judge turned down our request, and we discovered in fact that it worked to our advantage. We had a natural platform from which to address the court and the jury which was denied to Bevan and Calvert-Smith.

I next raised the question of bail. This, Alliot said, would be continued, but not during the lunch period 'because of the risk of accidental contact with the jury.' Again in our rehearsals we had anticipated this response. We wanted, if at all possible, to be free during the lunch break so we could discuss between ourselves, and with our solicitors, how things were developing. Besides we had had experience of being locked up during the lunch breaks in the course of our trial in 1962, and knew how depressing it could be – even when friends outside sent in a reasonable meal. So when the judge gave his decision, we had our next move prepared.

Randle: We could give an assurance on that point that we would lunch entirely with our solicitors during that time … and they will back us on that. There will be issues that we need to discuss.

Alliott (addressing our solicitors): I have never imposed that, but it has been volunteered on your behalf, Mr Birnberg and Mr Wadham. Are you prepared to give that undertaking?

Ben and John agreed, and on that basis Alliott granted us bail at lunchtime.

Pat took up our two final preliminary points. First could our wives and immediate family be permitted into the court itself rather than having to queue up each morning for the public gallery and viewing proceedings from there. Alliot said that in his experience as a student was that one got rather better view of proceedings from the gallery than from the well of the court, but acceded to the request. Pat's next point was cheekier:

> **Pottle: There is just one further point I would like to raise. We fully accept Mr Bevan's suggestion that the jury should be asked whether they can read or not … and we ourselves would like to put a question to the jury which I think is perhaps even more relevant than whether they can read.**
> **Alliott: Any question to the jury will be through me. Put to me what you would like me to ask.**
> **Pottle: What I would like to ask through you, my Lord, is: 'Are you now or have you been a member of MI5, MI6, the CIA or the KGB?' That seems to me to be just as relevant as to whether a juror can read, and it would seem to me to be an automatic disqualification for the juror were they a member. They don't have to say, my Lord, which organisation they are a member of or whether they are a member of more than one of those. But it would seem to me to be a natural question to ask.**

A smile flickered across the judge's face – and of the faces of several others in the courtroom.

> **Alliott: I will not ask that question, Mr Pottle.**
> **Pottle: I accept your decision, of course, but under protest.**

I jumped up.

> **Randle: Is your Lordship saying that the jury would not be prejudiced if they were members of MI5 when MI5 are really very much involved in this case?**
> **Alliott: Conscious of the issue that the jury has to decide, I am not going to ask that question in the context of this case.**
> **Randle: We, of course, have to accept your ruling, but we do not agree.**
> **Bevan: May I make it plain to this Court that there has been absolutely no vetting of this jury, whatever. I know in some cases there is vetting of jurors. There has been no vetting of this jury whatever, and I say that to your Lordship so that Mr Randle and Mr Pottle know.**
> **Alliott: Of course I accept that because I know I would have been told, and so would Mr Randle and Mr Pottle have been told, that there was vetting.**
> **Bevan: I just say it so it is made plain; that is the position.**

The jury panel were now ushered in to the court, standing rather self-consciously in a group at the back to our left, just behind the jury benches. The judge addressed them. This trial could continue into early July; if any of them had holidays arranged, or had other urgent commitments within that period, he would be willing to excuse them. They would also be asked to read a book of 285 pages. Again if this presented a difficulty for any of them, they should say so and would not be asked to serve on this case.

The clerk then read out the names. Two of those called said they had holidays arranged and stood down. The others, as they were empanelled, took their places one by one on the jury bench. In the end we had what appeared a reasonably (if not ideally) balanced jury; four women, one of them a young Asian, and eight men. Three of the jury were black or Asian; one, judging from his name and appearance, was Greek, or Greek-Cypriot. They mainly had the appearance of being in their Sunday best that first day, though subsequently several of them dressed more informally – perhaps inspired by our – especially Pat's – example. The women were smartly, yet soberly, dressed. The men mainly wore suits – though the first to be empanelled, a tallish, slim, man with a bristle moustache, wore a greenish leather jacket. On subsequent days he usually had a rolled-up copy of the Sun newspaper in his hand or protruding from his pocket. It was past noon before they were all empanelled and the trial proper could begin.

Miss Russell first addressed the jury, setting out the three charges against us. 'To this indictment,' she said 'they have each pleaded not guilty, and it is your charge, having heard the evidence, to decide whether they or either of them be guilty or not.'

Bevan rose to present the prosecution case. It took up the rest of the morning session and continued for a further hour in the afternoon. He began by distributing to the jury four photocopied pages of The Blake Escape. These included our sketch of the layout of Wormwood Scrubs, and Pat's account of how he had approached George Blake in 1962 and said he would be willing to help him escape from prison.

He then took the jury through the events chronologically, starting with Blake's conviction under the Official Secrets Act on 3rd May 1961 and the sentence of 42 years imposed upon him in this same courtroom. He explained how we had met him in prison the following year, and how, with Seán Bourke we had become involved in assisting in his escape and flight from the country.

The Crown's case rested, he said, on the evidence of the book we had written and on a television documentary that the court would see in due course. There was, he said. 'no need to doubt their word.' Their account had all the hallmarks of truth – it was 'no fantasy dreamed up by the two men.' It was the account of two men who believed they were justified on moral grounds in freeing a spy serving a sentence of 42 years. They liked him and regarded his sentence as inhumane.

Quite early on I saw an opportunity to interrupt him. In 1962, he told the court, Pat and I had been on the same Wing, C Wing, as George Blake, and on the same landing. We knew he had got this from the statement of a prosecution witness, Peter Clark, who had been a prison officer in the Scrubs in 1962, but we also knew Clark had got it wrong. George Blake had been moved from C wing to D wing in October 1961 – as the Mountbatten report showed – and we had not arrived there until the following February. I stood up:

Randle: I think I can help you there.

Taken off guard, Bevan sat down.

Randle: We were never in the same wing as George Blake. He was in D Wing by the time we got to Wormwood Scrubs.

Bevan stood up again. The prosecution, he said, would present evidence to show that we had been in C Wing with George Blake. He looked flustered. When I saw him outside in the corridor at the end of the day's hearing I teased him gently about the incident. 'You shit!' he said, not entirely, I think in jest, and strode off. Later during the trial when I tried to pull off the same ploy again, he remained on his feet and said that this was a court of law, not parliament, and that he was not obliged to give way.

Bevan emphasised that the police had had no evidence on which to prosecute until Pat and I had written our book and co-operated with Thames Television in making their documentary on the Blake escape. The Bourke book in 1970 'provided clues' but we chose to remain silent in public until 1989. In 1987 Barrie Penrose had named them in the Sunday Times. Their response had been neither to confirm nor deny the allegation. They were questioned by the police at that point but chose to remain silent. Then in 1989 they wrote their book because 'they wanted to explain what they did and why they did it.' Within days they were arrested and questioned and their homes searched.

Bevan concluded by reading a passage starting on page 243 of the book:

> If we are arrested and the case goes to trial we intend to plead Not Guilty. This does not mean we will at any point deny that we helped Blake to escape – the Not guilty would be a pure technicality to allow us to present our case and call witnesses as to the kinds of activities British and Western Intelligence agencies have engaged in during the period after the Second World War.'

But, he concluded, giving assistance to a convicted prisoner to escape from prison and to flee the country was illegal. 'The defendants knew this at the time. They knew it when they wrote their book. My submission is that they know it now.'

Bevan sat down and took a long swig of water from a glass on the bench in front of him. I felt reassured by this. Clearly he was nervous too.

It was a very fair presentation – and we made a point of telling him this as soon as the court adjourned. The only thing we were unhappy about was that he had described Seán Bourke as an Irishman imprisoned for sending a bomb to a policeman but had not made it clear that this had nothing to do with the IRA and that his offence was related to a purely private grudge. But even here, there is no reason to think Bevan intended to give a false impression.

At five past three the court adjourned. The jury were told to report back the following morning at 10am when they would be given copies of the book to take to the jury room to read. They would report back to the court just before the lunch break at 1pm, at 2pm and finally at 4pm.

Counsel and solicitors were excused from attending until 2pm on Thursday when the period allocated for the jury to read the book would come to an end, and the court would start hearing evidence. A Mr Wells would be keeping a watching brief for the Crown. However Pat and I must remain in the precincts of the building each day, and be in the court itself whenever the jury were present.

This was a disappointment. We had hoped for a further couple of clear days to work together. We could do some work in the court canteen, but it would be without the benefit of typewriter or computer. I decided to raise the matter with the judge. 'I am not quite clear,' I said, 'what the purpose is of our being here.'

> **Alliott: Well, because it is your trial. We have all been so pleasant with one another, but do not let us overlook the fact, you are on trial on a number of very serious offences.**

It was a note of warning to us, and it was quickly followed by another. Addressing Bevan the judge said:

> **Alliott: You clearly, from the way in which you ended your opening, put the criminality as having three dimensions and cumulative.**
> **Bevan: That is right. That is how the three counts are phrased.**
> **Alliott: That is how I inferred it. So far as the substantive count is concerned, correct me if I am wrong, the maximum for that, where the jury convicts, is five years, and the conspiracy …**
> **Bevan: Two. My Lord, may I say this one could of course have decided to put three substantive counts in relation to the whole, which would only multiply two times three, making six, and added the final count for a further two. But in order to be a realistic and simplistic, the Crown have decided in relation to harbouring, the charge of conspiracy, to have one count rather than three substantive counts, and I tried to say that to the jury.**
> **Alliott: Well you specifically mentioned the three safe houses all being covered by Count 3.**
> **Bevan: They are. The harbouring offences, the three, your Lordship**

will remember – actually it is four. It is harbouring – naturally it could be four. Rather than have four separate counts in relation to the harbouring, it seemed simpler to charge the conspiracy count in relation to them all. So there is no sinister reason for the conspiracy, other than what I have just said. It just embraces all of those substantive counts in one.

The judge appeared to be doing his sums, and then announced, looking directly at us, that the possible maximum sentence we could receive was nine years.[2]

***

All the reports in the papers next day highlighted the judge's ruling that he would not allow us to make a political defence. The *Guardian* in addition carried a feature by Sue complaining of the treatment meted out to the relatives of defendants. It was of course written before Alliott had granted permission for our wives and relatives to be present in the courtroom, and as it appeared in the Features section, could not be withdrawn at short notice.

Anne and myself stayed in North London, with Richard and Anna Norton-Taylor during the trial, by now close friends. Next morning I travelled down to the Old Bailey on my own as we knew nothing much would be happening there. Inside the No 1 Court soon after ten, the judge leaned over confidentially to the jury and again carefully explained the procedure. They were not to feel rushed and had until lunch time on Thursday to finish the book. Every day at one o'clock, and again at 4 o'clock, he would find out from them how far they had got. If some of them were fast readers and completed the reading before Thursday, they would be excused from attending until the Crown began to call its witnesses on Thursday afternoon. (In the event the clerk, Miss Russell at her own suggestion ascertained privately from each member of the jury how far they had got with the book to save them the embarrassment of having to state this in open court).

Pat and I were conscious of a possible problem over the lunchtime bail. This had been granted on the understanding that we would spend it with our solicitors. Now that the solicitors had been excused from attending while the jury was reading the book, would the judge order us to be locked up over the lunch break?

'If he proposes that,' I said to Pat, 'I'll say we'll give our word to avoid any contact with the jury and point out that if our word wasn't to be

2 This concluding comment of the judge is not recorded in the official transcript though it was certainly made.

trusted there wouldn't be a prosecution at all in this case since it rests entirely on our own statements.'

It was a good line but not one likely to sway the judge if he had a mind to end the lunchtime bail during this part of the trial. Fortunately the problem didn't arise. Although it must have occurred to Alliott that our solicitors were no longer present to play gooseberry to us over the lunch-break, he didn't raise the matter. We certainly had no intention of doing so.

In fact the whole business of refusing bail at lunch-times is a farce. On several occasions, at the beginning or end of the day, we came across male members of the jury when we went to the toilet. There would be a constrained silence, a conscious avoidance of eye contact, a sigh of relief as the jury member left the toilet. In the evenings too several of them made their way, like us, to St Paul's Tube station. On one occasion the Greek or Cypriot member of the jury went through the automatic ticket barrier immediately in front of us.

One small incident outside the court itself gave us heart. Pat and myself had adjourned to the canteen to start work – a long narrow room with a self-service counter on the left as you enter, and windows on the right. It was nearly deserted at that time except for two young women with, I think, three children. The kids, bored, ran up and down the length of the room, played games, squabbled occasionally.

At a certain point the women recognized us, smiled and waved.

'Best of luck!' they called over to us.

That small gesture lifted our spirits wonderfully and strengthened our conviction that we had taken the right course of action in coming out into the open about our involvement in Blake's escape.

Next morning – Wednesday – I arrived at the court to find Pat on the opposite side of the road in earnest conversation with a stocky red-faced man in his late fifties or early sixties carrying a pile of books. This turned out to be Paddy Meehan, author of a book entitled Framed by MI5 which he intended to hand out to the members of our jury. Meehan, a habitual criminal from Glasgow who had been in prison many times, had been wrongly convicted of murder in the 1960s and subsequently pardoned, largely as a result of the efforts of Ludovic Kennedy. He claims in his book to have been approached by MI5 to spring Blake, and subsequently framed by them on the murder charge to silence him about their attempt to recruit him.

Meehan had sent me the book about a year earlier and I had read enough of it to decide that its central thesis was nonsense. First, Blake had not even been arrested when the supposed MI5 officer had approached Meehan with what he later interpreted as a request for his help to free him. Second, he had had nothing whatever to do with the escape and was himself in prison in another part of the country when it occurred. We did our best to discourage him from carrying out his plan. It would do no good, we said, and could get him into a lot of trouble. Nevertheless, as ten o'clock approached he crossed the road to start handing out his books at random to people entering the court.

We were working in the canteen when, at about 11am, we were summoned back to the court.

> **'It will be that Paddy Meehan!' Pat said as we went down the stairs to the floor below.**

Sure enough as the judge strode into the court in his customary manner he was holding a copy of Meehan's book in his hand. Mr Wells, the lawyer keeping a watching brief for the prosecution, told the judge that Patrick Meehan had been asking people if they were jurors on our case and handing out copies of his book, *Framed by MI5*.

The judge asked us if we knew anything about it. Pat said he had been approached by a man this morning whom he had never seen before who had given him a copy of his book and said he intended to hand it out to jurors. 'I said I thought he was absolutely mad.' I said I had seen the book before and read part of it. It contained some extraordinary statements and I didn't believe it. Alliott said he had only skimmed through Chapter 23, that Meehan's account was entirely inconsistent with ours because he was a great believer in the conspiracy theory. He would ask the jury at lunch time if any of them had received the book and 'just give them a little homily about not accepting anything as they approach or leave the building. If Mr Meehan appeared again outside the court the red bands should discourage him from remaining in the vicinity, and if he persisted he should be brought before the court.

We returned to the canteen – but fifteen minutes later were again summoned to the court. This time we saw Meehan himself, as we entered, standing at the back of the court guarded by an official.

When the judge came in he ordered Meehan to be brought forward so that he was standing in the well of the court, immediately below the dock.

> **Alliott: What was reported to me was that you had been endeavouring to distribute a book that you had written that touched upon the escape of George Blake from Wormwood Scrubs in Chapter 23.**
> **Meehan: That's correct.**
> **Alliott: You were endeavouring to get copies of the book into the hands of the jury trying the two gentlemen in the dock behind you.**
> **Meehan: Quite frankly, I handed out copies, and I wasn't paying too much attention who I handed them to. But when the officer told me**

to move on, I deliberately refused because I felt that I should come in here and explain why. It's a long story.
Alliott: Let me explain to you, very shortly, why you must not persist in distributing the copy of your book.
Meehan: It's available from the shops, my Lord.
Alliott: It is for this reason, the jury have to try the two men that are now in their charge upon the evidence and only upon the evidence. Any attempt to influence the jury by putting before them anything that is not evidence, I could treat as a contempt of court and get very stroppy about it. Do you understand?
Meehan: What I am trying to get across is that the two men on trial, admittedly they did what they said they did. But what I here am getting across is that they were tools – unwittingly, tools of MI5. That is what I am getting across.
Alliott: That is just what you must not get across to the members of the jury. Now, may I have an undertaking from you that you will remove yourself and such copies of the book that you have left in your possession from the precincts of the court forthwith?
Meehan: Well, I have only one or two copies left, and they have been taken before I came to court, so I have only a few copies left any way.
Alliott: May I have your undertaking that you and those copies will leave?
Meehan: Yes. I was in any case planning to leave for a caravan holiday tomorrow.
Alliott: I know you spoke to Mr Pottle earlier because he told me.
Meehan: I did speak to him.
Alliott: Then upon your undertaking, which is a solemn undertaking, you must leave the area forthwith with those copies and must not come back to this building during the continuance of this trial. Do you understand?
Meehan: Yes, sir.
Alliott: On that basis, I take no further action. You may go.

When the court reconvened before the lunch break, the jury were able to confirm that none of them had received a copy of the book. That was one hurdle over. If any of them had received the book the jury might have had to be dismissed and the proceedings restarted from scratch. And we had had enough of delays and false starts.

We were joined for our pub lunch by Tom Mackinnon and told him what had happened over Meehan's book. He looked troubled.

'Did Alliot make it clear to the jury that you had nothing to do with the incident?'

'No. He said nothing about that.'

'I think you should ask him to do so. Remember they'll have read in your book about the incident in 1962 when the Committee of 100 distributed leaflets outside the court at the beginning of your trial. They may just assume that you were involved this time. It could be quite prejudicial to your case.'

We raised the matter with the judge that afternoon after the jury had filed out of court to resume their task and he agreed at once to tell the jury that we were in no way involved. He recalled them to do so, apologising for not having made this clear earlier.

In the mid-afternoon we were again summoned to the courtroom. This time it was over Sue's article in the *Guardian* the previous day. (Clearly he was not himself a *Guardian* reader, but he said his attention had been drawn to the article.) He took it that it had been written before the start of the trial, but he did not want the jury to think we had been hard done by in this trial. He therefore proposed to ask the jury if any of them had read the previous day's *Guardian*.

Shortly before 4.30, the court reconvened for the final brief session of the day.

Alliott: Now there is one other matter I must inquire about. Did any of you read yesterday's Guardian newspaper?

They all shook their heads.

Alliott: Not one of you. Then I need say no more.

This saved a possible complication, but it was depressing that there was not a *Guardian* reader amongst them. It didn't bode well for us either, that two of them were in the habit of coming to court in the mornings carrying rolled up copies of the Sun.

However, it was on that day that I made my first human contact of any kind with two of the jury members. These were with two of the women – one slim and dark with sleek black hair framing her face, the other broader with shoulder-length hair permed into crinkles. Involuntarily perhaps each caught my eye as they came into the court, nodded, and smiled fleetingly. I wondered if they were enjoying the book and beginning to feel they knew us a little.

The various small exchanges with the judge had also subtly altered our relationship with him. When he had first strode into the courtroom and laid down the law about not allowing any politics in his courtroom, he must have thought he was dealing with two hard-line ideologues. Instead we had been polite and reasonable – though no less determined for all that to present our case as forcefully and persuasively as we knew how.

That evening we all had a celebration meal at the Red Dragon Chinese restaurant in Muswell Hill. The reason for holding it then – somewhat prematurely one might think – was that our two German friends, Gerda and her twin sister Doris, had come over for the trial but had to leave the following day. Our younger son, Gavin and his partner Anna were able to join us; so too were other close friends who were supporting us during the trial. It was a particularly happy occasion and for a few hours at least we managed to put the trial and its probable consequences for us out of our minds.

Chapter 16:

Round One to the Defendants

On Thursday afternoon, 20th June, at 2pm the trial resumed with the showing of the Thames Television film. A statement was read out from a secretary at Thames, Sarah Allen, confirming that the video supplied to the court was a true copy. Richard Lindley then took the stand to confirm that he was a journalist who had been involved in making the film. There was a small tv monitor in the witness box as well three other larger ones, for the jury and the rest of the court. The judge gave the order for the viewing to commence.

But sod's law prevailed. When Detective Sergeant Lloyd, who was in charge of the equipment, switched it on, the two larger monitors failed to work. There was sound but no vision. Beads of sweat stood out on Lloyd's forehead. He fiddled with the controls and tried again. Still no picture. The prosecution counsel looked sheepish.

> Calvert-Smith: I am putting forward the mitigation, it was tested and it did work.
> Alliot: I can think of nothing more embarrassing than being a technician whose efforts are viewed by all of us, so I think I am going to rise, ask you to go to your room, and if necessary, clear the court so the technician can do his work.
> Calvert-Smith: My Lord, this was installed by a technician who is contracted. When I checked it this morning, it was working perfectly well.
> Alliott: So you have to whistle someone up from outside?
> Calvert-Smith: May we find out how long it is going to take? I shall make enquiries now. My Lord, there will be other witnesses … If it came to it, I could change tack and go to other evidence.
> Alliott: Well, I would like to adhere to the timetable we had agreed, if we possibly can. Members of the jury, we get the book out of the way, we get the television out of the way, and then we can get on to live witnesses; that is what we planned. Let us clear the court for ten minutes and see what the situation is. If it was working recently, could it be that something has just come adrift?
> Lloyd: Yes. It might well be that there's a switch that I'm unaware of. I'm unqualified in these matters, apart from switching it on and off …
> Alliott: I will rise at least until half past, members of the jury. I think

it is better if you go to your room. I hope it is not too claustrophobic. Mr Pottle and Mr Randle, you may remain in the precincts of the building.

As we trooped out of the court Pat remarked – 'I wonder if they simply forgot to switch on the monitors.'

We had scarcely left the courtroom before it was discovered that this was indeed the problem. Ten minutes later the hearing resumed. Before the video show started, however, I pointed out that the people in the gallery would be unable to see any of the monitors properly. Justice should be seen to be done. Alliot said he assumed that the people in the public gallery could see the monitor near him, but he got the court official up there to take up different positions and had the angle of the monitor adjusted until the official confirmed that it could be seen by everyone in the public gallery.

The film-show began. But it was not the end of poor Mr Lloyd's troubles for at a certain point in the film the image on the screen broke up and the sound was distorted beyond recognition. Lloyd switched off and ran the video tape backwards a few minutes. Still no luck. When at the same point in the film, the image and sound broke up again. This time the judge told him to keep the video running, and after five or ten minutes the equipment righted itself.

From our point of view something was lost by this fault. It occurred at the point George Blake was describing his feelings as a young man witnessing the German bombing of Rotterdam in 1940, and the devastation of Korea by US bombers during the Korean war. Still the script of the video was in the hands of the jury, and we had to hope that they would read what he said.

There was one other surreal moment. At the point where the commercial break would have occurred in the original transmission, a clock appeared on screen, and the court watched solemnly as the seconds slowly ticked away. Finally the judge interrupted to propose that this section be fast-forwarded.

Before the examination of Richard Lindley began, Pat raised another procedural question with the judge.

Pottle: Michael and I are very conscious of the fact that we don't want to take up the court's time, and we don't want to be repetitive about what we do all the time. We have made a certain division of labour … Can we in fact take it in turns to cross-examine the witnesses called by the prosecution?

Alliott: There are a number of things I would like you to adhere to. First of all there is a formality about court proceedings and I would prefer you to refer to your co-defendant as Mr Randle when you are speaking publicly. Next, you must each cross-examine on your own

behalf. You cannot cross-examine on behalf of each other. But if between the two of you, one cross-examines first and the other second, then subject to anything Mr Bevan has to say, I am entirely easy.

Calvert-Smith, speaking on behalf of the prosecution had no objection. Pat and myself simply ignored the request to refer to each other formally and Alliott did not insist on his ruling.

Julian Bevan's examination of Richard Lindley was brief. He got Richard to confirm that he had met Pat and myself early in 1989, and that as far as he knew no money or other inducement was offered to us to appear in the film (though he himself had not seen the contract). He confirmed that actors had played our parts in the reconstruction scenes.

'I thought they cast Mr Pottle splendidly,' Alliott said good-naturedly. 'Mr Randle not quite so well.'

I stood up to cross-examine Richard. Pat and I had met him socially a number of times since the film was made and were on good terms with him. I had also sent him information I had uncovered about someone he interviewed in the film, Mr Richard Helms, the director of the CIA at the time of the Blake escape. I began by congratulating him on a very interesting film, and commiserating with him that yet again the showing had been dogged by breakdowns. (The original Thames TV transmission had broken down at a crucial moment in the story when Anne and I were depicted crossing the checkpoint into East Germany.)

Randle: I have only a few questions. First of all, when you first met us in February 1989, and when we agreed to make the programme – a programme which could expose us to the risk of arrest and imprisonment – did you form an impression as to why we were willing to do this?
Lindley: I did.
Q: Can you tell us what the impression was that you formed of that?
A: I think as I said in the film in my commentary, I believed you had found yourselves in a position where you either had to lie about what you had done because others were pointing fingers at you or you had to own up, and you decided to do that.
Q: Was it your impression that we told you the truth on that programme?
A: It was.
Q: As you told Mr Calvert-Smith, we never discussed any question of money or any financial award?
A: Certainly not.

Q: I turn now to some of the points within the film. You interviewed, in the film, a man called Mr Richard Helms?

A: Yes.

Q: Was he a former director of the United States Central Intelligence Agency, the CIA?

A: He was.

Q: And prior to becoming the director of the CIA, he had held various high posts within that agency?

A: He had.

Q: And the CIA is the agency responsible for foreign intelligence operations of the United States Government; that's correct, isn't it?

A: It is.

Q: He testifies in your programme to the damage George Blake had done to British and American espionage operations, this comes in the transcript on page 1096. Just let me look at it. He says at one point:

He was very damaging. Indeed this is the kind of damaging individual who when you are trying to run an intelligence operation with all its problems, with all the networks that you are trying to arrange, with the security that you need, with the covers, with the pseudonyms, with the peculiar communications that one requires, and so forth, to have somebody suddenly walk into that and sort of rip the whole thing out is very – well, it's daunting. That's all there is to it. And it's the kind of thing that you would have just about rather anything happen than that.

Q: He says that in that interview?

A: He did.

Q: He also testified to the consternation within the Central Intelligence Agency after the escape of George Blake. Again, I look at the bundle on 1105, that's Exhibit No. 32, 1105. This is when he was asked about the rift between the intelligence services of Britain and America brought about the Blake escape, and when you as commentator said that took a long time to repair, he replied:

'The reaction was – how in the world did the British authorities allow him to get away? And when it was discovered that it was really a rather simple jail break, we began to wonder whether they were really interested in doing anything about these issues.'

Do you recall that on the programme?

A: I do.

Q: I have a question to ask about Mr Helms. Is this the same Mr Richard Helms that was convicted by a Federal District Court on 4th November 1977 on two charges of criminal information and sentenced to a two-year suspended criminal sentence and a $2,000 fine?

Alliott: Do not answer that, Mr Lindley. What on earth relevance does that have?

Randle: My Lord I have read out the statements that a very prestigious person, the director of the CIA at that time, has made, statements which were extremely prejudicial to our case, and this question goes to the credibility of that witness. The fact is that he was convicted for not giving full information to a Senate Subcommittee of the United States Congress.

The full facts of the Helms' prosecution supported even more strongly our argument about the nefarious activities of espionage services on both sides. For what Helms had lied about was the subversive activities of the CIA in Chile in 1970. Asked by the Senate Sub-Committee if the organisation had attempted to subvert the democratic process there when Allende was elected he had replied that it had not. When the evidence subsequently emerged that this was untrue, Helms was indicted. Only a plea-bargain deal, and his willingness to plead guilty, saved him from serving a prison sentence. However, I knew I would have to put the question in the shortest possible time if I was not to be interrupted in mid-flow by the judge.

Alliott: Mr Randle, if the suggestion is that your offence, if the jury find it proved, was less heinous because the damage that Blake did was less than the film suggests, that is a matter for mitigation after conviction, if the jury were to convict, not for the jury's consideration of the issue before them.

Randle: But surely this is a point where we have been prejudiced by the statements of this man. It must be in justice that we are allowed to bring out the kind of person that he was and the activities that he had been up to. I'm genuinely puzzled by this.

Alliott: Members of the jury, I think it is probably better if we ask you to leave while we discuss this point.

Pottle: My Lord, could I bring up another point?

Alliott: Certainly, in the jury's absence.

Pottle: My Lord, it is relation to the very fact that you have asked them to leave.

Alliott: Would you prefer them to stay?

Randle: We would prefer everything in front of the jury.

Alliott: Certainly. Let me spell it out loud and clear. The issue that the jury have to decide, having read the book and seen the film, if I can put it that way, of you confessing that you were helping Blake to escape – if it is true, their task is done. Thereafter, it may be that there will be mitigation for you to place before me, but that is a matter for me and not for the jury.

Pottle: My Lord, can I just raise an issue on that?
Alliott: Yes.
Pottle: It seems, my Lord that you did make a ruling on Monday, prior to the jury being present, as to what was to be admissible in this case and what was not to be. You, as we have just seen – and in fact the jury have just seen – a television programme. Within that programme, there are former members of CIA, British Intelligence and English MP's making what I consider to be highly prejudicial remarks which have now been heard by the jury.
Alliott: Prejudicial to what issue?
Pottle: Prejudicial, whatever the issue, my Lord. They have heard remarks prejudicial to what George Blake did as a spy, and what should possibly happen to us.
Now, I'm not saying that those particular remarks go to guilt or innocence, but the fact that the jury have now heard highly prejudicial remarks, it seems to me, my Lord, means that you must allow us the chance either to challenge them or to rebut them or to try to explain them. But to actually say the prosecution can produce a piece of evidence which contains highly prejudicial remarks – which contains the very thing that your Lordship ruled against on Monday – it seems to me, my Lord, what's good for the goose is good for the gander.
Alliott: I had no idea of the content of the programme until I saw it a few moments ago. You raised no objection to the jury seeing it. Had you done so, we could have edited it so that only that which you said could have gone into evidence.
Pottle: Yes, my Lord. It's surely not incumbent upon us, who are defending ourselves and do not know procedure, not only to prepare our own case but to meet the case of the prosecution as well …
Alliott: Mr Pottle, you, of your own volition, dispensed with the services of counsel. You have an immensely experienced solicitor in the field of civil rights advising you, present in court, together with an assistant.
Pottle: … I'm sorry to press you on this, but I can't really understand the ruling. You have in this court allowed the prosecution to introduce the very evidence that you yourself ruled out on Monday … all we ask is the same kind of freedom to be able to rebut them.
Alliott: The only evidence contained in that television transmission that is admissible, so far as the jury is concerned, is that which you said, so far as the case against you is concerned; and that which Mr Randle said, so far as the case against him is concerned. All the rest is merely the background of the programme. Had you wished to object

to it, had Mr Birnberg suggested that it was objectionable, had Mr Wadham, his assistant, suggested that it was objectionable, we could have eliminated it and the jury would have seen only that which you two said.

Pottle: My Lord, the film has been in the possession of the prosecution for, in fact, now two years. I was quite happy with the situation over the last two years assuming that when it did come to trial … we would be able to ask the very questions we are now trying to ask the witness.

Alliott: Before the jury was sworn, I gave you three quarters of an hour, even then, to consider the matter with your legal advisors, so you knew exactly what my attitude was going to be.

Pottle: Of course, my Lord. And what has happened is that you made a ruling on Monday, and I would have thought the prosecution, on hearing that ruling, themselves – or your Lordship because I believe we do have this in transcript as well as actually seeing the film – would have realised that that programme contained highly prejudicial remarks.

Alliott: I am turning to page 12, Mr Pottle!

Pottle: The only things I am complaining about are what I feel are the absolute inconsistencies. There is now operating in this court one law for the evidence applied to the prosecution, and a different set of rules applied to the defence.

Calvert-Smith: My Lord, may I intervene briefly? I hope to assist. There was a time, of course, when these defendants were represented in the full sense of the word, and the case was about to be tried some months ago.

Alliott: That was before Mr Justice Macpherson.

Calvert-Smith: My Lord, indeed. An offer was made at that time for censorship.

Alliott: I prefer editing to censorship, but I understand.

Calvert-Smith: Editing – but it was declined

Alliott: Well, there it is.

Bevan: My Lord, may I assist on behalf of the Crown? I indeed asked Mr Calvert-Smith to say that in open court with regard to the censorship, because I understand that Mr Calvert-Smith took part in a conversation when that occurred when the abuse of process proceedings were taking place … The Crown cannot rely on damage, whatever it was, that George Blake inflicted. The Crown rely upon the evidence as to whether or not these two defendants helped in the escape, and thereafter, gave the assistance.

Alliott: That was what I was trying to explain to the defendants.

Bevan: My Lord, the damage great, small, middle, of George Blake, is not part of the Crown's case. Indeed, I did not touch upon it in the opening … in fairness to all.
Randle: Both of us have expressed privately to Mr Bevan that he made a very fair opening to the case, and we're not contesting that. But there is another issue that I want to raise here, and that is that we feel we do have a defence in law – the defence of necessity. Crucial to this defence is the question of proportionality, the various degrees of damage that are done by one course of action as against another. In that context, the question of the damage done by George – Mr Blake – being released as opposed to him remaining for the last 22 years, or whatever, in prison, is relevant not simply to mitigation, but to the question of our guilt or innocence, given the defence that we shall, in due course, be developing to your Lordship.
Alliott: But it is a non-defence, that is the trouble. This is back to your leeway point. This is why, I suspect, you felt obliged to dispense with leading counsel. It is a defence that they could not run and you are hoping to do it by appearing for yourself. I say this at your invitation in front of the jury. I would just as soon have the discussion without them here because that is the normal way if there is an issue of law, and this is, in fact, pseudo law.
Randle: I don't really want, at this point … to address your Lordship on the necessity defence. But I can just briefly note the ruling of Lord Justice Brown in the Martin case where he says definitively, the defence of necessity does exist in English law in exceptional circumstances. That is the point that we want to develop. We will argue that the question of proportionality does enter into this, and therefore, these issues are not simply issues of mitigation, but go to the question of guilt or innocence, and should not be ruled upon.
Bevan: May I say this, the defence of necessity, this the first time, of course, the Crown have been alerted to the point that is being taken. I hope Mr Randle and Mr Pottle will accept that. The Crown have not known that before. What concerns myself on behalf of the Crown is this: when the two defendants were given the opportunity of objecting, if I may say so, to the whole film – in other words, we can edit the film if you want it edited. That discussion took place, and I hope the defendants will accept that. The response from the defence, if I might put it in the plural was, Oh, no, we want the whole tape to be played. If that is the position, what concerns me is that having heard the whole tape played and then to use that as a platform, if I may say so, for putting forward matters which, in the Crown's submission – but

> I hear further argument from both of them – are really not relevant to the central issue of this case as to whether they assisted this man to escape...

Pat made the point that we had not heard his Lordship's ruling on the defence he would allow when we said we did not want the film to be edited – although in any case we certainly would not want it to be.

> Alliott: The significant thing is this, Mr Pottle, every lawyer knows that the only admissible part of that film is that which you and Mr Randle said. There was apparently a decision from your then advisors who said let the whole thing go in. Now on that basis, the Crown has shown it. Had there been any objection, the Crown I am sure would have edited anything out. Had it been submitted for me to decide, I would have ordered it to be edited out.
>
> Pottle: We certainly weren't objecting about that. We wanted it. We want everything to go before the jury. We want nothing excluded.
>
> Alliott: The one person who is inevitably going to be inconvenienced, I am afraid, is Mr Lindley, because it seems to me that this issue is going to raise itself in various guises during the course of the trial. We better sort it out once and for all on the issue of whether there is, in your case, the defence of necessity. Once we do it in this context, my ruling will stand in any other context.
>
> Pottle: We would like to point out, if we could, my Lord, we certainly at this stage would accept that Mr Lindley's evidence is now finished. We would have no further questions for him.
>
> Alliott: I am pleased, in a sense, to hear that because Mr Lindley can go, but you will remember that there is an unanswered question posed, that I have said that I will not let Mr Lindley answer until I have made my ruling.
>
> Pottle: Well, that's the trouble. Then to follow the strict procedure, we should have that issue settled and then finish it.
>
> Bevan: It does not need Mr Lindley to give evidence, having heard your Lordship, once your Lordship has ruled, if an admission is required to be put in evidence, I on behalf of the Crown, will of course make it.
>
> Alliott: Then can we release Mr Lindley? Thank you, sir, you are free to go.
>
> Well now, the next thing I am going to do is to say that the jury can go because I really would be happier to decide this issue of whether you have a defence of necessity in their absence. There need be no, as it were, secrecy. We can subsequently tell the jury what has transpired, but I think it would be kinder to them to let them go, and that is what

I am going to say. Members of the jury, 10.00 tomorrow morning. If you would be good enough.

Again we had anticipated this move and had our counter-arguments ready. From our point of view it was crucial for the jury to hear the substance of our argument on necessity, the only legal element in a defence based essentially on moral and humanitarian grounds. We did not want them simply to learn from the judge that he had heard our argument and had ruled out the defence we wanted to put.

Randle: We would still prefer the jury to be present, my Lord, if that's possible, because we don't want any issues to be tucked away to one side, so that they are not fully aware of what the argument …
Alliott: I think I am going to adhere to what is overwhelmingly customary procedure of dealing with this matter in the jury's absence, but I shall not, as I say, keep anything secret from them. In most cases, if I possibly can, I am a great exponent of Glasnost.
Randle: I would like to refer you to the case of Anderson who is quoted in that very fat book whose title has slipped my mind.

In the tension of the moment, I simply couldn't remember the name of the book. 'It's Archbold,' Pat interposed.

Randle: Yes, Archbold. It is the case of Anderson in 1930 where the judge there says quite categorically that the jury is entitled to be present unless the defence agree, or actually propose, that the jury should be absent. I can get the reference for that.

The judge and both prosecuting counsel looked at a loss. Bevan pulled a succession of wry faces. His junior, Calvert Smith, leaned over from the bench behind and engaged him in earnest whispered conversation. Alliot said:

1930! That was before I was born![1] All I can say is that the practice in the last 35 years, when I have been either at the Bar or upon the Bench, it is overwhelmingly usual for the jury to withdraw. Have you anything to say, Mr Bevan?
Calvert-Smith: My experience, certainly goes to your Lordship's experience. What I am concerned about is what the authorities say if the defence specifically say to a judge: We want the jury present during every legal argument. I am not quite sure on the authorities what the position is.

---

1 The official transcript has the following: Mr Justice Alliott: `I do recall the case. Needless to say I was not born then.' But this is clearly an error. The whole discussion at this points shows clearly that neither Alliott nor the prosecuting Counsel were aware of the case and were non-plussed when we cited it.

A court official approached the judge with a copy of 'the big black book.'

Alliott: Mr Watson looks like he is homing in on it.

Bevan: I have never known of such a case, but I learn a great deal in this one.

Randle: It appears in Archbold, Volume 1 of paragraph 4-303, page 477 in the judgment of Lord Chief Justice Hewitt:

> It is difficult to imagine any circumstances in which except at the request of or with the consent of the defence the jury can possibly be asked to leave the box in order that statements may be made during their absence.

Alliott: Give me the reference again?

Randle: That's paragraph 4, page 477.

Alliott read the passage, shook his head and handed the book to the court official to pass down to Bevan. Bevan read it in turn and handed the book to his junior, Calvert-Smith.

Alliott: It looks Mr Bevan as if that is indeed, what the Lord Chief Justice said in 1930. It is a ruling more honoured in the breach than the observance, in my experience.

Bevan: Your Lordship is right.

Alliott: Very well. Let the jury stay.

Randle: Thank you, my Lord.

It was a wonderful moment, all the more so because we had in fact outwitted our opponents. What the judge and prosecuting council did not realise – but were certain to discover before very long – was that the Anderson judgement had been superseded in a more recent case, that of *Hendy* in 1989 – in which the Lord Chief Justice, Lord Lane, ruled that 'whatever may have been the case in 1929' the judge had now complete discretion whether or not to allow a jury to remain while submissions were being made to him – though no doubt he would take into account any view expressed by the defence. The 9th supplement to Archbold (at paragraph 4, p.132) reports the ruling.

Alliott: Now let us hear about necessity in the context of this case.

Bevan: My Lord, may I just say this? Having specifically asked for the jury to be present during all legal argument, I hope we will never hear that they have been prejudiced by anything being said in the presence of the jury.

Pottle: Certainly not. We want the jury to hear everything, consider it, throw it out, or whatever they do.

Alliott: All right. Necessity.

I now had a problem; I had come without my notes on the necessity issue.

Randle: My Lord, would it be convenient to adjourn this until tomorrow, because I didn't expect this issue of necessity to have argue it out at this point? It came up in the context of a question which I was not anticipating. As it's near the time now, perhaps we could leave it until tomorrow.

'I can see what you are up to, Mr Randle,' Alliot said with a smile. 'You are trying to curry favour with the jury by seeing to it that they go home early. But all right, the court is adjourned until tomorrow morning at 10 o'clock.

As soon as the court adjourned, we retired to the canteen to review the situation with our lawyers. Tom was worried. The prosecution had been caught off-guard. But they would be burning the midnight oil to check out the precedents and it would be extraordinary if they did not discover the Hendy case. If the judge thought we had pulled a fast one he was likely to be extremely annoyed and insist that the jury should be sent away. It was quite possible he would ask me directly if I had been aware of this later case, thus putting me on the spot. The issue of what to do was still unresolved when we split up and went our separate ways home.

That night I worked late on the Necessity argument. But at the back of my mind all the time was the nagging uncertainty about how to handle the Anderson / Hendy issue. By morning I had come to the conclusion that the best thing was for us to take the initiative and inform the prosecuting counsel and judge that we had discovered a more recent case which indicated that the discretion now lay entirely with the judge. I was doubtful, however, if Pat would see it that way.

I was mistaken. Pat came to meet us next morning so that we could all to travel together to the court, and immediately came up with the same plan. The lawyers too, when we told them what we had in mind thought it was probably the best thing we could do at that stage. Tom, however, while not against the move, thought it probable that Alliott would send the jury out while he heard our argument.

Pat and I approached Bevan before the session opened and told him about the Hendy case. As we expected, he, or his researchers, had already dug it out. Indeed he had already passed on the relevant documentation to Alliot.

We were at some risk of losing the initiative after all. So as soon as the session began, Pat was on his feet.

Pottle: My Lord, I am sorry to interrupt so early. We referred you yesterday to the Anderson case of 1930 … Last night I was informed by our legal advisers that, in fact, there is another case of equal authority from 1988. We have not duplicated that case. I gave it this

> **morning, first thing, to Mr Bevan.**
> **Alliott: Is it the case of *Hendy*?**
> **Pottle: The case of *Hendy*.**
> **Alliott: Yes. A copy has found its way to me and it accords with my experience, as I mentioned yesterday, over 35 years. But you maintain the position that you want the jury to be present.**

Pat confirmed that we did, emphasising that the *Anderson* and *Hendy* cases were of equal authority, and that even in the latter case the judgement made it clear that the judge had discretion in the matter. The judge turned to Bevan, who argued that 'Anderson as an authority … is no longer live'. He agreed, however, that his Lordship had the final word and would have to exercise his discretion.

> **Alliott: What I propose to do, Mr Bevan, is this, to exercise my discretion in the light of the discretion that Mr Pottle and Mr Randle exercise. If the argument is conducted on a legal basis, then I am content that the jury stay. If they stray into addressing the jury through me, as it were, then I shall ask the jury to withdraw. Members of the jury as you will hear from me, the law is for me, I have to decide it. You have to take my direction upon the law as definitive and binding. If I get it wrong the Court of Appeal, Criminal Division, can put me right. Do you understand? The facts, of course, are for you. So for the time being the jury will stay. Now who is going to address me on this defence of necessity?**
> **Randle: I will kick off, my Lord.**
> **Alliott: Right.**

Chapter 17:

The Defence of Necessity

First task: to convince the judge that this was a serious application.

> **Randle: I want first of all to try and reassure the court and your Lordship regarding the nature of the argument that we are proposing to put in the light of your ruling at the beginning of the trial and all that has subsequently been said.**
>
> **It is actually a limited argument we want to put and it concerns chiefly the unprecedented sentence that George Blake received and the effect that this was bound to have on his mental and physical health. We want to argue that this amounted to a cruel and unusual punishment, contrary to the 1688 Bill of Rights, one of the great documents of liberty in the history of this country.**
>
> **We accept that it is not going to be possible for us to parade the examples of the intelligence services, east and west, much as we would like to have done. We are satisfied that the jury has read the book, everyone in this court has read the book, in which we put forward our arguments on those issues. They have also seen the film in which again we have argued at some length over our motives and why we think we are justified.**
>
> **So we hope those points will be taken into account. We fully accept that we are not going to be able to run a defence which goes through cases and so on or with questions along those lines. The other point I would emphasise is that we have no interest whatever in mounting a filibuster here. We want to get home as much as the members of the jury and your Lordship, perhaps a bit more. We do not want to bore the hind legs off the jury with a lot of legal argument. We want to stick to things that we think are essential. We do not want to waste the jury's time. But we do think we have a defence and we would like the jury to hear that defence and then to make up their own minds as to whether or not in all the circumstances we are guilty of the charge.**

The importance of re-assuring the judge had been emphasised by our lawyers. Alliott would be determined to prevent the case dragging on interminably. If we put the argument well and made clear that we intended to be brief, there was just a chance he would allow us to put our defence and leave it to the jury to decide whether or not to accept it.

Now this point about leaving it to the jury, I want to say a couple of things on that. The law, as I understand it, is that the judge must leave the issue of guilt or innocence to the jury, that if we have a lawful defence – that's what I will come on to – then that must be left to the jury to make their decision as to whether or not it stands up.

Alliott: From my overnight research, that is a very big if, because you have to persuade me that the facts of your case fall within the very, very limited range of the defence of necessity and I would invite you to embark on endeavouring to persuade me.

Well, at least Alliott's overnight research had shifted his thinking to some small degree. He was no longer referring to the defence of necessity as 'pseudo-law', but instead emphasising its very limited scope.

I continued for a while longer to press the point about the obligation of the judge to allow the jury to decide on the matter of guilt or innocence and not to direct them. I cited two cases in support of this, the reports on which we had photocopied. As I mentioned them, John Wadham handed them up to the judge with a polite bow. Alliott intervened again:

Alliott: You are hammering on an open door. I would never dream of directing a jury to convict. What I will direct the jury on, however, is the issue they have to decide and at the moment it is a simple issue of fact: did you or did you not commit the three acts that form the three counts of the indictment. You say there is the defence of necessity that I should leave to the jury and again I invite you to address me on that issue of law.

Randle: We see the defence of necessity as at least a partial recognition that there are extreme circumstances where it may be right, technically, to breach the law.

Alliott looked over to Bevan and Calvert-Smith and said in what was clearly intended as an aside to those who knew their law:

Alliott: It did not avail the three sailors who ate the cabin boy, did it?

But I had done my homework. I paused, then said:

Randle: I am coming to the case of Dudley and Stevens in a moment, my Lord.

It was a moment to savour. The judge clearly had not expected me to pick up on the reference. The Dudley and Stevens case, dating from 1884 – even longer before Alliott was born than the Anderson case of 1930 – is a classic one for the argument about the defence of necessity.

Randle: Professor Glanville Williams defines the necessity defence as follows:

'Necessity in legal context involves the judgment that the evil of obeying the letter of the law is socially greater in the particular circumstances than the evil of breaking it. In other words, the law has to be broken to achieve a greater amount of good.'

Of course that defence could not apply and should not apply to crimes which deny the fundamental rights of other human beings: murder, rape, torture and so on; and I think every authority talking about the necessity defence makes that distinction. Murder and crimes of that kind are in a different category and that was the argument that came up in relation to Dudley and Stevens.

What we argue is that the 42 year sentence on Mr Blake amounted to a cruel and unusual punishment, something which is actually forbidden in English law by the 1688 Bill of Rights. We broke the letter of the law which forbids helping a prisoner to escape to achieve the greater good of saving the life and sanity of an individual human being. We also, if I may say so, helped to save the British state, the judicial system even, from one of its cruellest excesses. We believe that the test of proportionality that we have just talked about, is satisfied in our case. George Blake faced virtually a lifetime in prison. The most serious offence with which we are charged carries a maximum sentence of five years imprisonment.

There are those who say that a 42 year sentence, or a swifter form of execution, is all that a spy deserves.[1] But these things have to be seen in context. That's why we wanted to raise the issues of what other secret services, do, both east and west … That's why we wanted to raise those issues but I will not do so now because I do not want to stray beyond the limit that you have set.

I then went on to the landmark judgement of Lord Justice Simon Brown in the Court of Appeal (Criminal Division) which authoritatively established that a defence of necessity does exist in English law.[2] Martin was tried at Snaresbrook Crown Court on a charge of driving while disqualified. The judge prevented him from advancing a defence of necessity, but at the Appeal Court, Simon Brown LJ, ruled that he should have been allowed to do so – despite the implausibility of his argument. Martin claimed that his stepson had overslept and that he felt bound to drive him to work, despite being disqualified, out of a fear that his wife would commit suicide if her son was late for work and yet again found himself without a job. Commenting on the substance of his defence, Brown, LJ, said:

---

1 The official transcript here reads: `...is all that a swine deserves' - a clear, but amusing, error.

2 Court of Criminal Appeal, 88, RA 12, 345.

'It is difficult to believe that any jury would, in fact, have swallowed the improbable story which the defendant desires to advance. There was, it emerged from evidence that was given in mitigation, at the house at the time a brother of the boy who was late for work who was licensed to drive and available to do so. The suggestion was that he would not take his brother because, a lot of aggravation in the house would have ensued. It is a further striking fact that when apprehended by the police the appellant was wholly silent as to why on this occasion he felt constrained to drive.'

Brown had gone on to set out the circumstances in which the defence of necessity was available:

> 'There are two questions to be answered: was the accused, or may he have been, impelled to act as he did because as a result of what he reasonably believed to be the situation he had good cause to fear that otherwise death or serious injury would result? If so, may a sober person of reasonable firmness sharing the characteristics of the accused, have responded to the situation by acting as the accused acted? If the answer to both those questions is yes, the necessity verdict applied and the jury is entitled to acquit.'

The difficulty for us was that we could not argue that George Blake faced death or serious injury, and it was therefore necessary to argue that Brown's criteria needed to be extended to cover serious psychological injury. On this issue I relied on research and notes by our counsel, Ed Fitzgerald, and would like to express again my appreciation of the help he gave us on this issue.

Randle: My Lord, the only modification of this basic test which is needed to meet the circumstances of our case is that serious injury should be understood to include both physical and mental injury. The test should, in our view, rightly be reformulated slightly as follows. '… has good cause to fear that otherwise death or serious injury or grave mental harm would result.'

As far as the legal implication of our case is concerned, it is worth noting here, and emphasising, that Alliott when he ruled on our application accepted that the scope of the necessity defence should be extended to include a reasonable fear that grave mental harm would ensue if the letter of the law was not broken. Even though his ruling to this effect in the course of the trial does not constitute a legally binding precedent, it strongly supports the extension of the necessity criteria.

Randle: The authority for this modification or this qualification or test is as follows. It is in *R v Bourne* in 1939, 1 Kings Bench, 687 and I will just find that. Mr Justice McNaughton laid down that it could

be a justification for abortion if what would otherwise be criminal act was done in order to prevent the likelihood that a continuation of the pregnancy would make the mother a mental wreck.

The circumstances of this case are that there was no legal abortion at that time but this young woman had been raped and the doctor decided that for her own mental and physical well being the abortion was necessary. Therefore despite the prohibition which in law at that time admitted of no exceptions he decided to carry out the abortion. This case came before the courts. He was finally acquitted of the charge because they found that in those circumstances, the duress of circumstances, the necessity argument, did apply and that he was entitled to do this despite the prohibitions in law he was nevertheless entitled, in those exceptional circumstances, to take that view. I think few people today, whether legal people or not, would want to quarrel with the decision in that case.

In that way the recognition that the prevention of intolerable mental harm, such as would make life not worth living, forms the defence of necessity, no less than the prevention of death or serious and critical injury.

My next case is *Rex v. Steane* (1947) 1KB. 997. Then Lord Goddard, who was the Lord Chief Justice, recognised that the defence of duress need not only be a threat of violence or bodily harm but could involve the threat of imprisonment. The circumstances of this case were of a man who was forced by the threat of imprisonment to broadcast on behalf of Nazi Germany during the war years.

His defence was not that he was threatened with immediate death but that he was threatened with imprisonment. In that case it was found that this was duress of circumstances and that this was not merely a point of mitigating circumstances, importantly, but that this was a complete defence for what had happened and so he was entitled to be acquitted, and indeed he was. Since necessity is, in fact, nothing less than duress of circumstances, the test proposed by Lord Goddard is no less applicable to the present case where the necessity defence is being considered. This shows that the category of recognised threats which may afford a defence is not fixed but may have to be extended in individual cases.

It may be that only the most extreme threats justify the most extreme breaches of the law. We take your Lordship's point that we are charged with serious offences. Nevertheless, these have to be seen in proportion that the maximum sentence is a 5 year sentence. Against that we have to set the threat to psychological survival, perhaps even the physical survival, of another human being. In any case psychological threat and threat to life can easily overlap.

Now there have been many cases that have been reported recently of suicide in prison. Anyone who has spent any length of time in prison, indeed anyone who is just a second below the well of this court in the cells underneath will understand how one can become suicidal faced even with a relatively short sentence. But certainly somebody faced with a 42 year sentence, it is perfectly possible that person would be suicidal, would attempt to commit suicide and even if they did not the chances of surviving in any kind of sane mental state are very slim. The status of the threat to George Blake may be relevant here. But it was very great and we submit by the standards of civilised society as well as by the law of this country, it was cruel and inhuman; those are the words of the Bill of Rights.

The prosecution have indicated to us, and your Lordship has already mentioned obliquely, the case of Dudley and Stevens. I do have some notes on that. This is a case that has been most frequently cited against the view that necessity is a valid plea in English law. It is a well known case where three shipwrecked men and a cabin boy were adrift in an open boat for a total of 22 days. After 18 days, two of them, Dudley and Stevens, proposed to the third man that they should kill and eat the cabin boy. He refused but two days later Stevens killed the boy and the three men then fed on the boy's body. Four days later the men were rescued. Dudley and Stevens were charged with murder and at their trial the jury found, by a special verdict – this is where they are asked to decide the facts of the case, I think, rather than to give a general guilty or not guilty verdict – that the two men would probably have died within four days had they not fed on the boy's body, that the boy would probably have died before them, and that at the time of the killing there was no appreciable chance of saving life except by killing one of the others in order to eat him.

Despite this, Dudley and Stevens were both found guilty of murder at the Royal Courts of Justice and sentenced to death. However, you will be relieved to hear that their sentence was commuted to six months imprisonment. Again I think here the authorities saw these circumstances as mitigating circumstances rather than as a complete defence in law.

Now the circumstances of that case could hardly be more different from those of the present case as regards the nature of the compulsion under which these men acted and the act which that they carried out. But more important in terms of the legal argument, opinion is sharply divided about the implications of Dudley and Stevens. Lord Simon took the view that the reason for the decision was the rejection of any defence of necessity. He took it that because they were found guilty that the necessity defence was being thrown out at that point. But Professor Glanville Williams, whose definition of necessity I quoted at the beginning, comments that most of the judgment is unconvincing and he argues, 'the court might conceivably have allowed the defence if it had been persuaded that the act was really necessary at the time when it was done.' He then continues, 'Even if the case decides that justification of necessity can never apply to taking life, it does not follow that necessity cannot be a defence for lesser departures from the ordinary law.'

That was Professor Glanville Williams on page 606 of his book on criminal law. I do have a copy of this if it is needed. I do not know whether to say any more on the subject except to say that I think the circumstances of our case are very, very different from that and it has not decided the necessity issue. In any case, it is a long time ago and a case in 1989 which is much more appropriate to our case should be the one that should be applied.

If you will bear with me just one moment. (Pause) One of the difficulties with our case is the question of immediacy. The definition put forward by Brown, LJ, however, does not require that the threat be of *immediate* death or serious injury. What is crucial is the reasonable belief that if the act is not done then death or serious injury would result. Extending that, it should also say, in our view, 'or serious mental deterioration of the possible victim.'

The crucial question is not whether the result will follow immediately but whether it is reasonably believed that if action is not taken at the relevant time the opportunity to prevent death, serious injury, or intolerable psychological harm will be lost. Again the authorities on the defence of duress are relevant here, in particular the judgment of the Lord Chief Justice Lord Parker, in *R v Hudson*, 1971, 2 QB 202 at 207A. I have the quote here. 'When however there is no opportunity for delaying tactics and the person threatened must make up his mind whether he is to commit the criminal act or not, the existence at the moment of threat sufficient to destroy his will, ought to provide him with a defence, even though the threatened injury may not follow instantly, but after an interval.'

The fact that the damage would not follow immediately is not a bar, in other words, to the necessity defence. The important thing is if we act at this time could we prevent that injury, even though the injury might

be taking place over a number of weeks, months or years later.
If a defendant reasonably believes that unless he or she acted at once the opportunity to save an individual from serious psychological injury or grave and intolerable psychological harm, they would entitled to put the necessity defence and it should be the jury who then make up their minds on the circumstances of the case and say whether does or does not apply in this particular case.
There are a number of other cases. I will quote a couple of those. Lord Justice Brown cited the case of *R v Conway*. You do not have that one … The circumstances of that case … were that there were two people in a car. There was a man in the back of the car and two policemen approached them, but they were in plain clothes and they looked in and ordered them to stop. The driver then drove off at reckless speed, went down a one way street and mounted the pavement and all sorts of other things that one is not normally meant to do in a car. The defence was that the driver honestly believed and could reasonably say that he believed, that the life of the person in the back of the car was being threatened. This person had been threatened quite recently and then when these plain clothes policeman came up the driver did not realise they were policemen and so drove off at high speed and recklessly.
The point I want to make is that even in circumstances where there is some danger to other people, nevertheless the defence of necessity was accepted in that particular case.
There is another case my Lord, which is quoted in Glanville Williams. I am afraid we do not have it separately but I can pass up something to your Lordship. It is the case of Johnson v Phillips. It is an interesting case because it puts a different twist on things. Phillips had driven down a one way street and parked just behind an ambulance. The policeman approached and said, 'Look, there's been an accident, there is another ambulance going to be coming down the street. Could you please reverse down the one way street to make way for the other ambulance to come.'
He refused and was prosecuted for – I do not know exactly what for - but anyway he was just disobeying a policeman, he was disobeying legitimate instructions. He was actually prosecuted and found guilty. This went to the Court of Appeal which found against the defendant Phillips.
Professor Glanville Williams comments on this case as follows:
'If Johnson had executed the manoeuvre on his own initiative and some stupid person had prosecuted him, Johnson would very probably have been convicted though given an absolute discharge, since convictions

are routine in traffic cases. But, the case having been decided, the conclusion was seen to be compulsory that Johnson would have had a good defence had he complied with the order and reversed in the wrong direction along the street. It would seem to follow also that in a sufficient emergency he might have done this without a policeman to tell him to do the obvious.'

Then he comments,'We are surely not members of a nanny state in which we cannot even help an ambulance without being told to do so by a policeman. The case may perhaps convince the courts that even a traffic regulation, absolute in its terms, may properly and lawfully be disregarded if this involves virtually no risk and the social gain is sufficiently large.'

There is also another case which perhaps will be cited; this is the case of *Buckoke v Greater London Council.* I can find where it was. It is in the *All England Law Reports* 254 – 258. I do not have a copy of it here, but I have the quote. This is Lord Denning who said – 1971, so it was some while ago.

'A driver on a fire engine with ladders approaches traffic lights. He sees 200 yards down the road a blazing house with a man at an upstairs window in extreme peril. The road is clear in all directions. At that moment the lights turn red. Is the driver to wait for 60 seconds or more for that light to turn green? If the driver waits for that time the man's life may be lost.'

Lord Denning, in those imagined circumstances, concurred with the view of both counsel in the case that the driver would commit an offence if he crossed the red light. However – and this is the important point – he added, ' nevertheless, such a man should not be prosecuted. He should be congratulated.'

But we have to ask ourselves what would happen if he was prosecuted. Surely Lord Denning himself would not pretend that a man whom he thought ought to be congratulated for his actions should not even be entitled to have a jury determine whether or not he should be convicted of a criminal offence. That would surely be totally illogical. If one took that view one would really be entering into the realm of the absurd.

The absurdity is underlined if one considers Lord Denning's whole situation in making that comment. Saying that a man should not be prosecuted is one thing. In English law the Crown does have – I forget the term – a right not to prosecute, given all the circumstances of the case; it does have that discretion.

To say that a man should not be prosecuted is one thing, that's entirely

within the law. If, however, Lord Denning is right in maintaining that the man would have committed an offence, then stating that he ought to be congratulated is prima facie evidence of incitement.
I am sure none of us here, and your Lordship, would not, want, the former Master of the Rolls, at his advanced age, to be faced with prosecution, perhaps initiated privately in an organisation like the Freedom Association!
But the strongest of the inadvertent espousals for necessity pleas comes from a different character of case altogether and I want to signal that I am now moving to different ground. This was the statement by Master of the Rolls, Lord Donaldson, in the Spycatcher case where he told the Court of Appeal on 22nd January, 1988,
'It is silly of us to sit here and say that the Security Service is obliged to follow the letter of the law. It isn't real.'
I do not have a photocopy, but it is cited by Mr Richard Norton Taylor in his book published by the Civil Liberties Trust, In Defence of the Realm, 1990, at page 8. We can make a photocopy of that. But as noted earlier, the fact is that at the same time Lord Donaldson was making his statement the Security Service had no special right or powers and its members were as much subject to the law as any other citizen.
Let me just explain about the situation, although your Lordship will be aware of it.
Alliott: I sometimes wonder from the direction you face, whether you are addressing me, Mr Randle.
Randle: My Lord, every time I look up at you have your head buried in your papers.
Alliott: I am trying to take a note.
Randle: I will endeavour to direct my remarks to you, and apologise if I have been remiss in that respect.[3]
The situation of the Security Service, MI5, has changed with the 1989 Security Service Act. They now do have a status within the constitution and within the law. It does not apply still to MI6 for which there are no such regulations. But at that time the members was Security Service were in exactly the same position as any other citizen.

3 The official transcript reports this exchange in a truncated form as follows:'*Mr Justice Alliott*: I sometimes wonder from the direction you face whether you are addressing me, Mr Randle. I am trying to take a note. *Defendant Randle*: I will endeavour to do so if I have been remiss in that respect.' I have relied on the fuller note by the student barrister Caroline Brown and on my own very sharp recollection of the incident.

English law has a long tradition of rejecting the notion that reasons of State could make lawful acts which would otherwise be unlawful and here the crucial case is that of *Entick v Carrington*. It is an old case, 1765, where Lord Camden said in a judgment to the Court of Common Pleas:

'With respect to the argument of state necessity or a distinction which has been aimed at distinguishing between state offences and others, the common law does not understand that kind of reasoning, nor do our books take notice of any such distinction.'

What is he saying there is that the state must be subject, the officers of the state are subject to the law, the same as everybody else. Indeed, Lord Donaldson himself, in the same Peter Wright case, stated in the Appeal Court on 10th February:

'It would be a sad day for democracy under the rule of law if the service were ever to be considered above or exempt from the law of the land, and it is not.'

Lord Denning too, states in his report on the Profumo affair:

'The members of the Security Service are, in the eyes of the law, ordinary citizens with no powers greater than anyone else. They have no special powers of arrest such as they can't enter premises without the consent of the householder, even though they may suspect that a spy is there.'

That the comes from Lord Denning's report, CMND 2152, published in September 1963.

Both their Lordships were making their statements before the passing of the 1989 Security Service Act which has changed the situation of MI5 but not the intelligence services, MI6. In any case this was before that Act; it doesn't affect the argument here.

So the situation we have is this. Lord Donaldson, Master of the Rolls states in the Appeal Court that it would be silly to pretend that the Security Service, MI5 is obliged to obey the letter of the law – in particular circumstances, of course. By this we can take it that he does not mean that in the normal course of events members of the Service can break the law, but that in certain exceptional circumstances it is understood that they can and will do so.

Yet in the same case he insists that the Secret Service is not above the law of the land. What he is saying about the Secret Service in this case applies to every other citizen. His predecessor, Lord Denning, spelt out the position even more clearly. The members of the Security Service are, in the eyes of the law, ordinary citizens with no powers greater than anyone else.

The conclusion I would suggest is that the circumstances which would excuse a member of the Security Service from obeying the letter of the law must logically apply to every ordinary citizen. Both are subject to the law and if they break the law they render themselves liable to prosecution. But exceptional circumstances would entitle them to break the letter of the law, perhaps in some situations place them under a moral obligation to do so. In those circumstances they could advance a plea of necessity whose merits the jury, and the jury alone, should decide.

How does Lord Donaldson propose to get around this difficulty? ie on the one hand he states that it would be – I quote – 'silly to say that the Security service is obliged to follow the letter of the law' and on the other hand he asserts that 'it would be a sad day for democracy under the rule of law if the service were ever to be considered above or exempt from the law of the land'?

I quote from the judge's comments in the Spycatcher hearing.

'The missing link is possibly this. Of course there has to be some control. Probably the best devised is to say the Security Service is bound by a strict rule of the law but you always bear in mind a prerogative power not to pursue criminal proceedings and the statutory powers in the Director of Public Prosecutions to stop criminal prosecutions.

'That procedure,' he continued, 'would be perfectly properly used in appropriate cases.' It was essential in the public interest, and this is an argument, for MI5 officers to break a law in some ways and for such breaches not to be prosecuted.

Let us note in passing that Lord Donaldson too set a limit stating, and I quote, 'murder is as an entirely different matter.' So again we can forget about Dudley and Stevens.

Here, in one particular at least, he was drawing a distinction which is crucial to our defence, the distinction between breaches of the law which might in exceptional circumstances be sanctioned and acts which are criminal in a much more fundamental sense, in that they deny the basic human rights of other human beings, murder, torture rape, these things which can never be justified under any circumstances.

Let us look again, however, at Lord Donaldson's proposed solutions to law breaking by MI5. It must surely be obvious to everyone that this is no solution at all. Indeed what he is proposing – that is that the authorities should use their prerogative to give a special status to people who in the eyes of the law are no different from any other citizen – would be a grave threat to civil liberties and the rule of law.

If the prerogative not to prosecute, and the powers of the DPP to stop prosecutions, were used in a systematic way to favour the members of a Security Service, as Lord Donaldson is suggesting, and to give MI5 or the Intelligence Services greater latitude in the matter of breaking the law than that enjoyed by other citizens, then the rule of law and the notion of equality before the law, which is at the heart of our ideas, would be radically undermined.

In a formal sense the Security Service would be subject to the law. In practice, in a crucial respect, it would no longer be so, and I think that is the least desirable solution.

Alliott: I am not going to stop you, Mr Randle, but you have strayed a long way from the theme that you set yourself, namely, persuading me that the defence of necessity was open in law for you and Mr Pottle.

Randle: Yes, well I thought I had not because I was trying to say that by looking at the situation which arises in the case of MI5, who are ordinary citizens like us and where the highest judges in the land have said everyone knows that they have a certain discretion, that by looking at that we can understand that that discretion and that rule of necessity must apply to the ordinary citizen. I will not pursue it further if your Lordship stops me.

Alliott: No, I said I am not stopping you but I was really bringing you back to the theme upon which you are addressing me.

Randle: Yes, well I think I was explaining how the theme relates to that particular case.

Alliott: I follow the point. What is sauce for the goose is sauce for the gander.

Randle: That's my point, yes. Lord Donaldson's solution would be more acceptable if he were suggesting simply that the prerogative power not to prosecute should be considered even-handedly in all cases. That means something different. Where the prosecuting authorities thought that a plea of necessity could apply they might say, 'Well, look, we won't bring a prosecution.' If that was applied even-handedly and not to give the Security Service some special status, then of course we would be approaching a better kind of solution. But that is not sufficient and the Law Commissioners, when they looked at this problem recognised that it wasn't sufficient that there could still be cases where a prosecution would be oppressive and unreasonable and that the defence of necessity should apply in those cases.

So it is not sufficient to say, well, maybe the prosecuting authorities will take account of the circumstances and not bring a prosecution in the first place. That is not a sufficient guarantee because if they make an error of judgment and do so prosecute then the defence of necessity should be open to the defence.

My Lord, I would conclude by briefly saying that I think the circumstances of our case do fit the definition and the tests as proposed by Simon Brown, J and the definition of necessity as defined by Professor Glanville Williams.

In this case a man was sentenced to a 42 year sentence. He was faced the with mental deterioration and who knows what else could have come from that. The circumstances of the case which I will not elaborate at this point, do not justify a sentence of that length.

It is arguable and we have argued it in our book, that by imposing consecutive sentences the judge was going against the intentions of parliament by extending the maximum sentence of 14 years and spreading it out to 42 years … that in any case it was oppressive, that it goes against the spirit and the letter of the 1688 Bill of Rights. We submit that the defence of necessity applies to all stages of the count against us. It applies to the help we gave Seán Bourke, who of course was mainly responsible for getting Mr Blake over the wall. It applies to the point at which Blake was already out of prison and there was a choice whether he should go back to prison and be kept under even stricter supervision and under even more restrictive conditions. And it applies, finally, to getting him out of the country so that he could lead some kind of normal, decent life.

We want to be able to put to the jury that this was the right thing to do in those circumstances and that the necessity defence is applicable in our case. Thank you.

Alliott: Thank you, Mr Randle. Now Mr Pottle do you adopt what Mr Randle has said?

Pottle: All that I completely adopt, and as I said, we have a division of labour. I think Mr Randle has done an excellent job of setting out this case. I have got no photostat pieces of paper to hand to anybody.

Alliott: Before you go on, specific pieces of paper. It is apparent, Mr Randle, that you were speaking from notes. I have endeavoured to take a note. Would you be minded to let me have a copy of your notes which would obviously be fuller than that which I have taken?

Randle: Yes. I was swapping around from about three different sets of notes but I could make up a set.

Alliott: It is entirely at your choice.

Randle: Yes, I will do that but I can't do it straight away.

I made a single text from the notes over the weekend and handed them to the judge on the Monday morning, with a copy for the shorthand writer who had also asked for this.

> Alliott: Thank you. Yes, Mr Pottle.
>
> Pottle: I will be very brief. I have not got any photostat copies for the jury and Mr Bevan because I am going to base my simple little talk on common sense and I do not think there are many authorities in these law books that deal with that particular matter.
>
> Common sense says to me what are we arguing about here? Your Lordship is asking us should we be able just to say to the ladies and gentlemen of the jury, this is what happened, that is why we did it.
>
> Alliott: Just a minute Mr Pottle. You are addressing me in the presence of the jury. You are not addressing the jury.
>
> Pottle: Having said that, if you or the jury think its a load of cods wallop, then you can say so. You can say I think what they have just said is a load of rubbish, on your bike! Have nothing to do with it! All we are asking is what seems to me to be common sense – just to say, look this is what we did. If you think it's a load of rubbish throw it out but at least give us the chance of being able to say it.
>
> Alliott: Thank you, Mr Pottle. Mr Bevan, as I define the issue that I have to decide I can put it in this way. On the apparently admitted facts of this case should I leave the defence of necessity to this jury? Would you agree that is the issue I have to decide.
>
> Bevan: My Lord, yes. My Lord, as to the jury returning a verdict I think your Lordship has already indicated that you would not, in any case, direct a jury.
>
> Alliott: Never have, never will.
>
> Bevan: What Mr Randle has said about that I endorse. In so far as the defence that is being put forward, as I understand the foundation of Mr Randle's case, and indeed Mr Pottle's, it is the principle as enunciated in Martin.
>
> My Lord it would be my submission, and indeed is my submission, that a person lawfully convicted and sentenced, as indeed the Crown submission is that Blake was, cannot provide grounds for the defence of necessity in relation to a person charged with assisting that individual convicted and sentenced, to escape, and thereafter to harbour him and, as in this case, to spirit him out of the country.
>
> My Lord, if the defendants are right in the submissions they have made and the facts of this case, it would allow an individual to take the law into his own hands, to act as judge and jury and to form his own conclusions and if his conclusion is the sentence that was passed upon

that man was cruel and inhuman, 'I am entitled by necessity to do everything in my power to help him escape.'
The consequences of that, your Lordship will appreciate, would be an anarchy because the individual who acts as such would be acting as judge and jury. The defence of necessity would centre upon that individual's view of the sentence that had been passed by a court and that would be his starting point in his defence that, 'I acted lawfully as a necessity.'
My Lord, one only has to spell it out, in my submission, for it to be apparent that this defence of necessity, cannot apply in this case where George Blake was, upon the evidence to be presented to the jury, lawfully convicted, indeed he pleaded guilty, and lawfully sentenced by the court.
What is perhaps curious in this particular case, of which these two defendants no doubt are well aware, is that a very great deal of the Blake case in fact was held *in camera*, and these two defendants as they sit here now, and indeed when they were in Wormwood Scrubs Prison and indeed when they wrote the book, and I venture to suggest at this present moment, do not in fact know the details of what Blake did.
Alliott: Now I think you are straying into the same area as Mr Pottle and Mr Randle were getting into.
Bevan: I am saying it simply for this reason.
Pottle: We could easily clear up the point if Mr Bevan wants to raise it, my Lord, by simply opening the case of George Blake.
Bevan: That is not what ...
Randle: We have already applied for the transcript of Mr Blake's trial and we would formally now like to make that application because the matter cannot be finally cleared up until one has that.
Bevan: I think with respect to Mr Randle, and I do not mean to be impertinent, he is missing the point I am making. The point I am making is that in this particular case, they, if their defence be of necessity, can in fact be applied to these charges and to the law because we have a situation of two men acting as judge and jury in relation to a man when they do not know the details that lay behind the sentence. And this would indeed be the result in my submission if this defence is allowed in law.
I ask this question rhetorically, are the jury to retry Blake? Are the jury to work out the appropriate sentence for George Blake? Are the jury to say, 'Well, we think he should only have received 5 years', or an effective five year sentence.
Alliott: I am going to stop you, Mr Bevan because what Mr Randle

was saying was that he was founding the possibility of necessity being a defence on the reasonable belief on the part of himself and Mr Pottle that 42 years was too long etcetera and I do not think it is necessary, for the purpose of his argument – I do not pretend to endorse it – but for the purpose of his argument I do not think it is necessary for him to have a total comprehension of the facts of Blake's case.

Bevan: I only relate to the point for your Lordship to understand the Crown's position that it is nonsensical in my submission for an individual to be allowed to say that the sentence passed by a court upon a man was inhuman and unjust and therefore I am entitled to allow that man to escape, especially in a case where the individual does not, in fact, know the facts that lie behind the case. I am only, if I might say so, making the point in order to strengthen the submission that I make, that where a person has been lawfully convicted and sentenced by a court that cannot provide the foundation for an individual charged with helping that individual escape, in relation to the defence of necessity. That is the point I am seeking to make. My Lord, may I go to the basic principles of the case of Martin.

Alliott: Yes, can we look at the that. I make no criticism of Mr Randle who is essentially a man of words, but it wasn't cited in the way a lawyer would, so can we look at it more fully.

Bevan: It may assist if I read the headnote, then we can all understand. 'The appellant drove his car while disqualified and was charged with contravening Section 99 of the Road Traffic Act and before arraignment he sought a ruling from the trial judge whether the defence of necessity was open to him in that he drove when he did because his wife, who was suicidal, threatened to kill herself if he had not driven at the time in question. The judge held that defence was not available because once it was established that the appellant was driving and was disqualified the offence was established, i.e. it was an absolute offence. The appellant thereupon pleaded guilty and relied in mitigation on the above circumstances which he would have raised as a defence of necessity and he appealed under a section of the Criminal Appeal Act on the grounds that the judge had erred in law in the things he did.'

My Lord, perhaps it is important to read not simply the headnote under 'Held' but to read part of the judgment.

Alliott: Yes.

Bevan: My Lord, the facts of the case are rehearsed at the beginning of the judgment and I indicate a passage in the middle, the appellant's case on the facts.

'The appellant's case on the facts was that he genuinely, and he would suggest reasonably, believed his wife would carry out that threat unless he did as she demanded. Despite his disqualification he therefore drove the boy. He was, in fact, apprehended by the police within a quarter of a mile of the house.' Then read to the words ... 'Duress of circumstances.'

Pausing there for a moment. As I understand it, the defendants are not making their submission under the heading of duress. I look to see whether or not I am right in making that submission, but your Lordship will see there is a distinction between duress and necessity which one comes to under two and three.

Randle: On that point, necessity is sometimes thought to be duress of circumstances.

Alliott: I have a note of your submission in those very terms, necessity is duress of circumstance.

Bevan: Some authorities, or two of them, the two of them go hand in hand, but if I might say this as a lawyer, this is not a case of duress in that either Mr Randle or Mr Pottle was under pressure from an outside source so that their will was overborne and therefore they had no choice.

Alliott: No, that has never been put. That is not how this submission has been made. Therefore, if I might put duress to one side.

Bevan: My Lord, I go to what the learned judge said.

'Certainly the defence is available only if, from an objective standpoint, the accused can be said to be acting reasonably and proportionately in order to avoid a threat of death or serious injury.'

My Lord, I am relying on the words 'from an objective standpoint.' The defence is available only if from an objective standpoint the accused can be said to be acting reasonable and proportionately in order to avoid a threat of the death or serious injury.

My Lord, insofar as the threat of death or serious injury in the circumstances of this case is concerned, there is not a shred of evidence that George Blake, at the time of his escape, was under the threat of death in the sense that death was imminent. Nor indeed is there a shred of evidence that he was, at that time on 22nd October, 1966, under threat of serious injury. He was then and there a fit man, before he broke his wrist having climbed over the wall.

Alliott: Yes, but you have heard how Mr Randle puts it. He says that anyone the subject of a 42 year sentence must be at risk from serious psychological injury.

Bevan: I understand the point that is being made but simply ask your Lordship to consider in the context of the defence submission, namely

the defence of necessity, whether the threat of serious injury although in a sense alive because the man had been sentenced to 42 years imprisonment, the serious injury is not going to occur until many, many years later.

In my submission, the authorities, such as they are, under necessity, appear to indicate that the threat of death or injury is not remote, it is in the foreseeable future if not imminent and it cannot be said on the facts of this case, that death or serious injury was imminent or indeed in the foreseeable future, if I might put it that way. It simply does not apply although Mr Randle may say that twenty years hence he may be a mental and physical wreck.

In my submission, when one considers the defence of necessity, that is far too remote, the threat of death or serious injury, if one is speaking in terms of years hence, and that is the point I make on that passage.

Going back to the judgment. 'Thirdly, assuming the defence to be open to the accused on his account of the facts, the issue should be left to the jury who should be directed to determine these two questions. First, was the accused, or may he have been, impelled to act as he did because as a result of what he reasonably believed to be the situation he had good cause to fear that otherwise death or serious injury would result.'

Alliott: You omitted the word 'physical'.

Bevan: I do apologise. 'Felt compelled to act as he did because as a result of what he reasonably believed to be the situation he had good cause to fear that otherwise death or serious physical injury would result. Have I still left out a word?

Alliott: No.

Bevan: My Lord, again I make the same point, 'otherwise death or serious injury would result.' Then that, in my submission, in the context of necessity, ten, twenty years later. The second point, and I go back to the judgment.

Alliott: This is a sort of echo of the provocation point, is it not, this next proviso.

Bevan: 'Second, if so, may a sober person of reasonable firmness, sharing the characteristics of the accused, have responded to that situation by acting as the accused acted.' As your Lordship said a moment ago that is a direct echo, in my submission, from the provocation cases. It is the reasonable person on the Clapham omnibus, the reasonable person, but sharing the same characteristics of the individual, age, and your Lordship knows the point I am making in so far as that is concerned.

Alliott: Yes.
Bevan: If the answer, going back to the judgment, to both those questions was yes, then the jury would acquit. The defence of necessity would have been established. That the defence is available in cases of reckless driving is established by Conway and indeed by an earlier decision of the court in Willer. I think Mr Randle mentioned the case of Willer during his argument. That was the case concerning the individual who was fearful when he was apprehended by two plain clothes individuals and drove away in a tearing hurry in fear of being robbed, assaulted or threatened and the like, and that was his defence. I need not go into the merits of it, but that was his defence.
The Court of Appeal when they considered that case did not say, 'No, there is no defence of necessity in driving cases.' There can be, but in that particular case the court decided it was not applicable because the individual, Mr Willer said in his defence when he gave evidence that he drove properly and not recklessly throughout the whole of my time. As a result of that evidence the court said …
Alliott: He was running a defence too many.
Bevan: The defence of necessity did not apply. I am afraid he over-egged the pud in relation to too many defences. So that was, as I remember it, the case of Willer. [In fact I had not referred to Willer at all, a confusion that was in due course cleared up.]
My Lord, it also cites, in the judgment of Martin, Conway as an authority also for the proposition that the scope of the defence is no wider for reckless driving than for other serious offences as was pointed out in our judgment, reckless driving can kill. 'We see no material distinction between offences of reckless driving and driving whilst disqualified so far as the application and scope of this defence is concerned. Equally, we can see no distinction in principle between various threats of death. It matters not whether the risk of death is by murder or by suicide or indeed by accident. One can illustrate the matter by considering a disqualified driver driving his wife, she suffering a heart attack in the remote countryside and he needing instantly to get her to hospital.'
My Lord, pausing there, that plainly would give rise to a defence of necessity if such a situation ever arose. I, on behalf of the Crown would not suggest otherwise.
'It follows from this the judge quite clearly did come to a wrong decision on the question of law and the appellant should have been permitted to raise the defence for what it was worth before a jury. In our judgment it is a great pity that that course was not taken. It is

difficult to believe that any jury would have, in fact, swallowed the improbable story which this defendant desired to advance …' I do not think it is necessary for me to read further. They then deal with the merits of the case.

Alliott: Can we just go to the top of page 344, the remainder of the headnote you broke off from reading, to deal with the facts.

Bevan: I am so sorry, 344.

Alliott: Yes, 'Held.'

Bevan: What it says is this. 'Held, in extreme circumstances English law recognises the defence of necessity most commonly as duress. Equally it could arise from other objective dangers threatening the accused or others, i.e. duress of circumstances. Two, that defence was available only if, from an objective standpoint, the accused could be said to be acting reasonably and proportionately in order to avoid a threat of death or serious injury. Three, assuming the defence to be open to the accused on his account of the facts, the issue should be left to the jury who should be directed to determine two questions:

a) 'as the accused, or may he have been, impelled to as he did' – and your Lordship will notice the word impelled – 'impelled to act as he did because as a result of what he reasonably believed to be the situation he had good cause to fear that otherwise death or serious physical injury would result, or

b), if so, might a sober person of reasonable firmness sharing the characteristics of the accused have responded to that situation by acting as the accused had acted?' If the answer to those two questions was in the affirmative the jury could acquit because the defence of necessity would have been established.

Alliott: Yes, then he goes on to deal with the instant case and it is the not a matter of concern.

Bevan: My Lord, no. The foundation of this defence of necessity must rest, must it not, on any view on the fact that George Blake was lawfully sentenced by a court, if that be the evidence accepted by the jury, to 42 years imprisonment, and their starting point is that they considered, and they consider. that sentence to be an inhuman sentence, and they did what they did on humanitarian grounds, if I can use but one word.

Therefore, they say, do they not, 'Taking the view that we did, that 42 years was an inhuman sentence we can properly say we acted under necessity and put forward to this court now charged with these offences the defence of necessity.'

Your Lordship will have to decide whether or not this defence is

> open to a person where the central individual, namely George Blake, was lawfully convicted and sentenced by a court, because that is the starting point of the defence that is being put forward. In my submission your Lordship should rule that in those circumstances this defence of necessity simply cannot apply. As I have already submitted to your Lordship, if the submission made by Mr Randle and Mr Pottle is right, it would allow an individual to take the law into his own hands and act as judge and jury. That is the natural, if I might say so, consequence of such a decision and it is not difficult to understand the consequences of that.
>
> The second point I make, as I have already indicated to your Lordship, in such a case of defence of necessity the threat of death or serious injury and the like must be or reasonably imminent, not 15, 20 years hence.
>
> My Lord, that in short is my submission but your Lordship has been quoted many other cases which I must confess as you will appreciate, I was given literally a minute before we started this morning and they produced them to your Lordship and myself, so I have not read all the authorities.
>
> Alliott: Thank you. Now Mr Randle is there anything you would like to say in reply?

My response comprised essentially a restatement of some of the points I had made earlier. However, I did point out that Bevan's objection that we were claiming the right to act as judge and jury would apply to every case where a defendant relied on the necessity defence. 'Someone backing down a one-way street is making a choice. He is acting as judge and jury in a certain sense by saying: 'In these circumstances I am breaking the law, but I think I am right to do so.'

Bevan then had a further opportunity to put the gist of his case.

> Bevan: If it was not made plain, if one looks very carefully at Martin – and I know it is a case these two defendants rely upon – if your Lordship looks at 346. We went through the three point. 'Secondly, the defence is available only if, from an objective standpoint the accused can be said to be acting reasonably and proportionately in order to avoid a threat of death or serious injury.' I have made my point. Thirdly, assuming the defence to be open to the accused on his account of the facts …
>
> Alliott: That is the issue I have to decide.
>
> Bevan: The test really is under two. If your Lordship were to decide, having considered those words, 'Yes, it could apply in this case,' then the questions to be determined by the jury are set out. It would appear

on a close analysis that it is under the second line; 'the defence is only available if from an objective standpoint the accused can be said ...' etcetera, and those would appear to be the key words whether or not the defence is available in any particular case.

Alliott: You are entitled to the last word Mr Randle.

Bevan: Of course, and I didn't ...

Randle: My Lord, what I want to emphasise is that the state of the law in relation to necessity is an open issue to some extent. Even the Law Commissioners when they were looking at this have gone back and forward. I could go through the cases if I had a few minutes but at one point the Law Commissioners said, yes, there should be a defence of necessity. Then in the next report, that was rejected entirely and it was then said, no, this should be totally ruled out, totally excluded.

This judgement was heavily criticised in particular by Professor Cross who said that to allow the defence of duress of circumstances but to rule out totally the defence of necessity was – and the phrase used was his – 'the apotheosis of absurdity.' So there is some leeway there. I think it was in 1985 that the Law Commissioners made their proposals on the codification of the law. They acknowledged that this was an area on which the law was uncertain. They did not want to propose anything in the statutes to change this. They said this would be going beyond their brief. But they did say that in so far as this defence existed in common law, it should be for the courts to explore and develop it. I haven't got the exact words, but that's roughly the idea of it.

So I think Simon Brown, J, has given us some guidelines and we have suggested already that these are not sufficient of themselves. They don't finally close the issue or deal with the whole question of immediacy and so on. These are matters which logically ought to be further explored.

We have not relied entirely on that case. In citing the position of the Security Service I think we make a point that is a very powerful one. Those are ordinary people. In the eyes of the law they are no different from Mr Pottle and myself, and yet one of the highest judges in the land has said, 'We all know that under certain circumstances they do break the letter of the law.'

So we are not asking for some huge expansion, we are asking for the merits of each particular case to be looked at and we think the merits of our case are very strong, are certainly strong enough that it should be left for the jury to decide whether or not the defence can be expanded if you like in that way – that the common law can be developed as the courts have the power to do.

Alliott without further ado gave his ruling:

Alliott: Yesterday, in the course of discussion following a question posed by Mr Randle to the witness Mr Lindley, it emerged that the defendants intended to run the defence of necessity. I indicated, since it would be likely there would be other questions that would raise the same issue, it would be sensible to decide once and for all in the context of this trial, whether the defence of necessity was open to the defendants in this case.

Unusually, at the express request of Mr Pottle and Mr Randle, the jury have been present in court throughout the consideration of this point of law. I have come to the conclusion, without any hesitation, that it is not open, on the apparently admitted facts of this case, for defendants to raise the defence of necessity.

I do not propose, in the presence of the jury, at this stage of trial, to give my reasons for that decision but out of courtesy to the careful argument of Mr Randle, and indeed to give a hostage to fortune if they care to test it in the Court of Appeal Criminal Division, I shall, at some later date, give my reasoned judgment.

For the time being I merely turn to the jury, who in ordinary circumstances would be brought into court after I had given my reasons, and say this. As a matter of law I rule that the defence of necessity is not open to the defendants. I shall continue to rule upon the cross-examination to reflect that ruling and when I come to sum the matter up to you I shall direct you as to issues that you are to consider.

What I propose to do is to break off now until noon. That will give you [the jury] an opportunity to stretch your legs, and perhaps even take some refreshment. If you would like to leave the court now and be back at noon.

It was 11.50. The jury members filed out of the courtroom. When they had gone Alliott turned to us.

Alliott: My real reason for adjourning for this brief period and without making any order under the Contempt of Court Act – I do not want to have this reported – is to give you Mr Pottle and Mr Randle a greater opportunity to discuss the state of affairs that now presents itself to you with Mr Birnberg and Mr Wadham, which perhaps can be done more conveniently if you were to leave the dock rather than across the bar of the dock.

We then left the court as well and held a further brief discussion with the lawyers. As far as we were concerned, nothing had occurred to make us consider changing our plea. It was a considerable satisfaction that the jury had been able to hear our necessity defence. With the benefit of that, and of having read the whole of our book, our case would not go entirely by default. But, as Ben, John and Tom warned us, we could now expect the judge to be even stricter in enforcing his ruling on the kind of argument and line of cross-examination he was prepared to tolerate.

Chapter 18:

Exploiting the Leeway

It was 11.50am. We all – Pat, myself, Ben, John and Tom – crammed ourselves into a tiny ante-room and reviewed the situation. Despite the judge's ruling, the mood was buoyant. No-one had expected Alliot to find in our favour, but at least we had been able to make our point strongly and in front of the jury.

The idea of changing our plea was not even discussed; it was simply not a possibility as far as we were concerned. But the lawyers did give us advice on tactics. We must now expect Alliott to be very strict and crack down hard on us if we tried to put questions he considered irrelevant in our cross examination. We should keep our questions short and snappy – that way we might get a few across before the judge or prosecuting counsel realised what was happening. The more we dragged it out, the less likely we were to get away with it.

We had the order of prosecution witnesses and knew that the first to appear would be prison officers, or former prison officers, from whom we mainly hoped to elicit evidence about the effects of long-term imprisonment. Almost certainly the judge would stop this line of questioning at an early stage in accordance with his ruling.

The first witness was Simon Hills, the Clerk of the Central Criminal Court. Under examination by Calvert-Smith, he confirmed that the court records showed that Blake was sentenced on 3 May 1961 to a total of 42 years imprisonment. Hills was quite a young man, born in 1962, a year after George was convicted. Pat and I concentrated on bringing out the uniqueness of the sentence:

> **Alliott: Mr Randle.**
> **Randle: I see from your statement you were born in 1962?**
> **Mr Hills: Yes, sir.**
> **Q: So these events took place when you were about 4 years old?**
> **A: That's right.**
> **Q: It must seem very remote. In your experience as a clerk to these courts have you ever come across a case where first of all a convicted person received a 42 year sentence? Have you come across any other cases of that length of sentence?**
> **A: I've come across many life sentences but not many for that total.**

Q: Thank you. Have you ever come across a case where an accused who pleaded guilty received maximum consecutive sentences, or would you be aware of that?
A: No, I wouldn't be aware.
Q: All right. Is it normal practice, or again is this something you would be aware of, for a defendant who pleads guilty to receive a lighter punishment rather than a maximum sentence? Does that show up at all in your court records?
Alliott: Can I help on this … Whatever the position prevailing in May 1961, it is now a standard sentencing practice that there is a discount for a plea of guilty and if follows that anyone who pleads guilty would not ordinarily receive the maximum.
Randle: Yes, I just wanted to bring out the uniqueness of this particular case, thank you for confirming that, my Lord.

Pat, to drive home the enormity of the sentence, put it to Hills that someone today sentenced to the same period as Blake would not be due for release until 2033. Hills agreed that would be the case.

So far so good. We had got what we wanted from the witness and neither the judge nor prosecuting counsel had raised any objections to our questions.

At 12.30, another former prison officer, Peter Clark, took the stand. He was an older man, born in October 1936 who had retired from the prison service two years earlier. He wore a chequered jacket and spoke with a slight West country accent.

Calvert-Smith took him through his statement. He had joined in the prison service in 1960, and had retired just over two years ago. In November of that year was posted to C wing. He remembered Pat and myself on the wing. Pat, he recalled, was 'a well-made man, tall, black hair, black beard, a quiet person'. Randle he remembered as being 'a very intelligent, supercilious person, of average height.'

Calvert-Smith: …Were they both on C Wing as you recall?
Clark: They were on C Wing on two landing.
Q: Do you remember the man George Blake?
A: Yes.
Q: Was he on the same Wing or a different Wing?
A: He was on the same Wing, on the same landing.
Q: Was he in some sort of special category as a prisoner?
A: He was what we classified as a special watch inmate at the time.
Q: In normal circumstances would such a prisoner associate with prisoners who were not in that category?
A: No.

Clark was the witness that Bevan had said he would produce to show that Pat, George Blake and myself had all been on C-wing together. We knew we could disprove this, and early on I had contemplated rubbing Clark's nose in it, particularly after his remark in his statement – repeated in court – that I was a 'supercilious' person. ('Trouble is,' Pat had said, 'the more you do rub his nose in it the more you will appear to prove his point'. The lawyers too advised a gentle approach).

I was first to cross-examine:

Randle: We are talking about a very long time ago, aren't we?
A: Correct.
Q: The escape happened in 1966. We are going back even further than that, 30 years now and it is easy for the memory to make mistakes after that length of time. You say that Mr Pottle and myself were on C Wing at the same time as Mr Blake?
A: As far as I can recollect. I believe George Blake came into the Scrubs in '62.
Q: '61?
A: '61, okay. And I can't remember exactly when you and Mr Pottle came in.
Q: Well it is not a large point, and it is very understandable after this period of time there should be a slight mistake. As a matter of fact there is a mistake and I can show – I do not want to take up too much time of the court, but in fact we have the evidence of the Mountbatten Report, and I have the paragraph 32 of that report which says that 'from the beginning of July to the beginning of October 1961 the inclusion of Blake on the escape list' – that's the same as special watch – 'was reviewed by the governor at monthly intervals and on 3rd October, 1961, after consultation with the Prison Commissioners and with their approval, he was removed from the escape list.'
And finally on paragraph 51 of the Mountbatten Report.
When Blake was removed from the escape list in 1961, he was transferred from C Hall to D Hall and it was from D Hall that he eventually escaped.
Would you accept that you probably made a mistake?
A: Certainly I accept that.
Q: There is no big issue there, but I thought we ought to clear it up … Do you know anything about the practice of prisoners who are serving long sentences? Is it the practice to put them in the prison hospital for observation when they come in?
A: When they first come into prison, this was the normal practice.

Q: Right. Would this be to study what the psychological effects would be?
A: Basically, yes.
Q: And whether there was any danger they might try to commit suicide and that sort of thing?
A: Yes.
Q: Thank you. Do you know if Mr Blake was admitted to the hospital wing on his arrival at Wormwood Scrubs?
A: I can't state categorically, but I would imagine he would have been in hospital for two or three days.
Q: While he was on special watch were you able to form an opinion of him as a person?
A: As a person he was very quiet, a gentle, pleasant person.
Q: Thank you. And was he liked by fellow prisoners?
A: A. Well, I think he was a curiosity, mainly due to the term of the sentence.
Q: Because of the length of his sentence?
A: 42 years, yes.
Q: Apart from people doing life, which is an indeterminate sentence and often is much shorter, 10 or 11 years would be the longest …
A: 42 years was something totally different.
Q: Yes, it was a unique sentence?
A: Yes, it was.
Q: The other prison officers, did he adopt this gentle good mannered relationship towards the other prison officers?
A: Oh yes.
Q: Thank you. Did you ever among yourselves, among prison officers, ever wonder or discuss how he could possibly cope with a sentence of this length?
A: Well I have my own opinions but I prefer not to state them … He seemed to settle down very well and particularly in view of what he'd gone through, I believe, in the Korean war, being in Wormwood Scrubs would be easy for him and I would have imagined he didn't expect to do that length of time. It would have meant serving 28 years out of the 42.
Q: If he had served that 28 years or if he had lost remission and served the whole 42 years, that might eventually have had quite a depressing effect upon him?
A: Presumably, yes.
Randle: Thank you very much.

Pat took up the cross examination.

Pottle: I am Patrick Pottle?

Clark: Yes, sir, I appreciate that.

Q: Please do not think in any way I am attacking you or your statement. I just want to clear up a few things. The easy way of clearing up any misunderstanding as to where we were in 1962 or where George Blake was in 1962, is to refer to, in fact, pages 8 and 9 of the bundles marked 'material evidence' the larger bundle. This is, in fact, a statement made by Mr Lesley Newcome, whom you will remember was the governor in 1966. If you look at his statement which was made …

Alliott: You do not have this members of the jury. It is part of a large wodge of statements that the defence have and the Crown have of course.

Pottle: It was made on 7th November, which is just a couple weeks afterwards. In the second paragraph it reads, 'I know that Blake was taken off the escape list sometime in 1961. He was received in prison following conviction.' So there it is quite clear at that point … But if I now look at this statement here, was it normal practice – you were a prison officer and came into contact with a number of prisoners – was it normal practice in those days this the prisoner had a half an hour visit once a month?

A: Yes.

Q: That was in a way the only time, whatever length of time they were doing, whatever their sentence was, that was the only human contact which one in a way could call normal.

A: The convicted prisoners half hour per month.

Q: It is very hard for people who have not been to prison, and Michael and I have been, you have been but on the other side, but even you get a very clear picture of how that once a month visit builds up in a prisoner's mind. This is my possible half an hour every month of some kind of sanity. I can hold on to my sanity by looking forward to that visit?

A: Yes.

Q: I want to go back to this statement made by Mr Newcome the prison governor. 'At no time did Blake have any unsupervised visits. All his visits took place in a small room at the entrance to the old administration block. On three occasions up to 1966 he had visits from the War Office and from MI5 personnel. These were in sight of prison officers but not in their hearing.'

A: Yes.

Q: So in fact what the governor is saying there is that Mr Blake was the only prisoner within Wormwood Scrubs who wasn't allowed a visit that wasn't supervised. All other visits were open, you had them, you met your family, you touched your wife, you kissed your mother, you cuddled your kids. But George Blake's, all his visits were in fact supervised, they were monitored, they were recorded with a prison officer standing next to him?

A: In sight and out of hearing.

Q: No, in sight and in hearing. The only time it was in sight and out of the hearing was when he was talking to MI6 and MI5. That's when it was in sight and out of the hearing. Otherwise, on normal family visits he would in fact always be monitored?

Pat now quoted a statement by John Leonard Rham, Assistant Governor Class 2 at Wormwood Scrubs at the time of George's escape, who had told the police on 3 November 1966:

> 'When Blake left D Hall, on every occasion he would be escorted by a prison officer. All of his visits, including those of his solicitor, took place in a separate room from normal visits and were within both sight and hearing of a prison officer.'

So clearly, even within the prison system they saw George Blake as somebody out of the ordinary?

A: He was still a special prisoner.

Q: He was not in patches at that time?

A: No.

Q: I will just carry on a bit on this. I will just refer back, to the governor's statement. He says, further on in his statement:

> 'It was rumoured in August, 1966, that a two way radio was operating in the prison. There was no evidence of this but it was realised that there were persons who were sufficiently skilled and had access to material that could manufacture such a device, these were seen by Mr Ralph who warned people of the consequences. No such device was ever found. Special searches are carried out as the result of direct information.'

If we then turn back to the Governor's statement, this same matter is covered by the governor; he relates the same story. He says:

> 'About 3 months ago I heard a jocular remark from a member of staff to the effect that radio Wormwood Scrubs was operating again. I didn't consider that was meant seriously. But at the same time we were aware that I did have men who were capable of making the transmitter and of obtaining access to the necessary materials. I did not consider that they would manufacture a transmitter because there was too much to lose

from their point of view, if they were discovered. I did, however, see all the men concerned and I warned them.'

Do you remember that at all, Mr Clark?

A: No.

Q: … I am only mentioning this to you, Mr, Clark not in any way critically. I want to establish that when we today talk about prison and high security, we are talking about television cameras inside the jail and outside the jail, fax machines, communication. This is an example of what it was like in 1966 When Seán Bourke for instance, smuggled in a two-way radio, that was unheard of. Every copper on the beat's got one today but in 1966 you did not see that?

A: Correct.

Pottle: Thanks very much?

Alliott: Thank you Mr Clark.

The state of prison security in 1966 was in a sense neither here nor there, but the story of how casually the assistant governor had treated a report that a prisoner was operating a two-way radio was too good to miss. More important was the corroboration from Clark that Blake's sentence was unique, that the strict supervision of his monthly visits deprived him of all privacy in his relations with his family; it supported our contention that Blake had been subjected to 'cruel and unusual punishment' as we had argued in the submission on necessity. The judge might have ruled out that defence but it would not necessarily be discounted entirely by the jury. It was good too to provide evidence that Blake as a person was liked and respected within the prison.

Clark, though appearing for the prosecution, had been an ideal witness from our perspective. But he now did something which gave us one of the biggest lifts during the whole trial – and which must have appalled and infuriated the prosecution. As he walked past us in the dock, and in full view of the jury, he gave us the thumbs up sign and said 'Good luck, lads!' I doubt if the Old Bailey has ever witnessed such an incident before in its entire history.

At lunch time in the pub we met Clark and chatted about the Scrubs in 1962, about the state of his health and the work he had now taken up as a landscape gardener. It was clear too, by now, that he had intended no insult in describing me as supercilious, and I thought how right Pat and the lawyers had been in saying we should avoid antagonising him, or indeed any witness where this was avoidable.

Next Calvert-Smith read out a statement by David Williams, the current Security officer at Wormwood Scrubs, who confirmed that the prison records showed that Pat and I had been admitted to the prison in 1962. The judge again carefully explained to the jury that if the defence did not require a witness to attend, his statement could be read and become evidence.

A second prison officer from the Scrubs in 1966, William Southward Fletcher took the stand. He wore a blue blazer with shiny brass button and held himself like a ramrod in the witness box.

Calvert-Smith took him through his statement. He had been on duty in D wing with prison officer Townsend and others on 22 October 1966 – the night of Blake's escape. At about 5.15 Blake was walking down the wing and remarked to him that the wrestling on the television was a farce. There was a film showing in a compound outside the wing. At 7pm he had rung the bell to signal the end of the recreation period which meant that the prisoners in the wing and those coming back from the cinema had to return to their cells for the night. When he went round the cells to close the doors, he noticed Blake was missing but was not unduly concerned since he might have been in another part of the wing and not yet have made his way back to his cell. But on the second check, he found Blake was still missing and raised the alarm. Later that evening, or early next day, he had seen a piece of metal which was part of the window frame lying outside the south end of the wing with a piece of black tape wrapped around it.

I cross-examined him, again briefly. My hope was that he would confirm that Blake was well respected within the prison not only by other prisoners but even amongst the staff. But, unlike Clark, he proved unbending.

> **Randle: The jury saw a video yesterday about the escape of George Blake and one of the people who appeared in that film was a man called Phil Morris. Do you recall that name at all?**
> **Townsend: It does ring a bell, yes.**
> **Q: Yes. He was, at the time, a prisoner in Wormwood Scrubs. He stated in the programme that there was elation among the prisoners when the news spread that George Blake had escaped. Can you recall the atmosphere when that happened?**
> **A: As far as I'm aware, it's going back a long time now, I didn't recollect any elation at all.**
> **Q: We have here in the book which forms the basis of this case – on page 113, my Lord and members of the jury. I start at 112, the quote from Zeno, the pen name of another prisoner who was in Wormwood Scrubs at that time. Mr Lemarque, you remember him?**
> **A: Yes, I remember him, Lemarque, yes.**
> **Q: I go to the last paragraph on page 112 where he has just heard on the radio that George Blake has escaped. He says:**

'A growing murmur of sound breaks into my thoughts. The men with radios'. Some had radios in their cells?

A: That's right.

Q: 'Are shouting the news to those without them. The excitement in the voices I hear is unbelievable. There must have been nearer 150 escapes in the years I have spent here but I have never known a reaction like this. By concentrating I can distinguish words and snatches of conversation. 'Blake over the wall.' 'George had it away.' 'Good old George'. Yells of Yipee, only once or twice sheer savagery directed against authority … and then faintly from the south end of the prison, singing, "For he's a jolly good fellow." ' You do not recall that?

A: The problem I had I was too busy.

Q: He then goes on to what happened the following day.

'My door is unlocked, pushed quietly open and I look up. A screw is standing in the doorway looking at me. This is unusual for the majority of the screws simply unlock the door and push it an inch or two. I continue to look at him, a blanket half folded in my hands. He's a decent screw but I wonder what's coming. Suddenly he grins, raises his shoulders in a silent laugh and walks on to the next cell. A dozen men come to my cell before I go down to breakfast, all of them hoping that I haven't heard the news and that they will be the first to give it to me. Their happy grins make me warm to them as little else could. On the landings I see screws standing … sheepishly, but none with an expression of anger or displaying the venom of the defeated. Now my heart warms to screws as it has never done before. They are human. They cannot feel anger or regret that a man they know to be kind and considerate may not have to complete another 22 years in prison When he arrives at our table to check the roll he counts the nine of us and starts to move off. Paddy says, 'Only George to come'. The screw smiles and goes on. It's extraordinary. I could never have forecast such a universal reaction within the prison. I liked George from the moment I met him and over the years I have become more and more attached to him. I have always known his popularity but until now I had never appreciated the extent of it.'

Does that correspond also with your experience of the reaction?

A: With regard to Sunday, I couldn't comment because I wasn't in that wing Sunday.

Randle: All right. I have no further questions.

The judge decided that it was 'a convenient moment' for lunch. When the court reassembled just after 2pm, the prison officer Colin Townsend took the stand. Bevan took him through his statement in which he stated that he was on duty with Fletcher on the night of Blake's escape. It was he who had discovered the broken window at the south end of the wing.

Pat this time conducted the cross-examination:

> **Q: Hello, Mr Townsend. I've only one or two questions. The statement that Mr Bevan has just taken you through, of course, is a statement based on the statements you made in 1966?**
> **A: Yes.**
> **Q: I mean, it would be impossible for you to remember events that long ago without being prodded?**
> **A: No, I couldn't remember that long ago, obviously.**
> **Q: Now you made two statements in 1966 about the Blake escape, to prison officers. The first of your statements in 1966, and I refer your Lordship to pages 22 to 24 of the bundles marked 'material statements'.**
> **Alliott: Thank you.**
> **Pottle: You made your first statement on 24th October, just two days after the escape, and you made a further statement on 1st November.**
> **A: I can't remember, quite honestly.**
> **Q: Perhaps what I could do is pass you the statement that you made, and perhaps you could just take us through it. Perhaps you could just start it as you have written it, perhaps you can take it on from there?**
> **A: You want me to read it out?**
> **Q: Yes, could you just read the statement that you made?**
> **A: With further reference to the statement I made …**
> **Alliott: No, I think go back to the other statement to start with. You are looking at your statement dated 1st November.**
> **Townsend: Yes.**
> **Alliott: I think Mr Pottle wants you to go, first of all …**
> **Pottle: No, my Lord, the first one I want, not the second.**
> **Alliott: I beg your pardon. You are right. I am wrong.**
> **Townsend: I am sorry, my Lord, do you want me to read …**
> **Alliott: Yes. I was wrong, you were right. Read what you have in front of you.**
> **Townsend: 'I have been asked why I changed my duty to the evening of Saturday 22nd October from A hall to D hall. The reason for this is that I am a D hall officer and most officers attached to a hall prefer to do duty in their own hall if possible. Prison Officer Giddings had no objection to changing. This is the normal procedure. I have been asked if I was playing table tennis in D hall on the evening that Blake escaped. This is not true.'**

Pottle: Can I just stop you there?
A: Yes, certainly.
Q: You mentioned playing table tennis at that stage. I believe a number of prisoners, when interviewed in 1966, said, well, the prison officer at the time of the escape was in fact playing table tennis, and you then had to make a further statement, which is the one we are talking about now, actually to show that you were not playing table tennis at the time of the escape?
A: Yes, I do remember this now, yes.
Q: Sorry, There is nothing wrong with playing table tennis?
A: No, nothing wrong at all, but it was suggestions made by one or two prisoners that might have had an axe to grind.
Q: Yes, of course, I can see the reason.
A: Hence the indication that I was doing something improper.
Q: Yes. Could you carry on with the rest of the statement at that point?
A: Yes. 'I am considered a bit of a bastard because I am a disciplinarian and have booked several inmates in D hall. Steward, Benmore, Titmus and others. The inmates of D hall would like to be rid of me for this reason. I have also had words with a number of inmates in D hall. From time to time prisoners complain about prison officers they dislike in order to get them shifted. This statement has been read to me and it's true.'
Q: So it is quite reasonable for you to have been asked by the police to make the statement because of these accusations?
A: Of course.
Q: Twenty-five years is a long time. We've all mellowed. I am assuming that you are not still a bit of a bastard?
A: One assumes that.
Alliott: He is the prison officer who might have been called "Fletcher".
Pottle: Yes.
Alliott: A lead balloon. Obviously you do not follow the series.

Alliott was referring to the TV series 'Porridge' which featured Ronnie Barker as the convict Fletcher. Pat and I were both fans of the series but didn't immediately get the drift of Alliott's remark.

Pottle: We got there late. (To the witness): You were on duty the night of George Blake's escape?
A: Yes.
Q: And you describe in your statements the events that took place that night and the events that followed?
A: Yes.
Q: I should imagine that there must have been a certain amount of

panic and a certain amount of running too and from. Was there a certain amount of panic?

A: No, no.

Q: Everything very English and stiff upper lip?

A: It was all quite calm and quite reasonably civilised.

Q: Yes. Let me just read to you from a statement taken at that time. This statement, my Lord, is pages 46 and 47 of the bundle marked 'material statements'?

Alliott: Thank you.

Pottle: This is a statement made by a police officer who was on duty in Shepherd's Bush Police Station, the very night that George Blake broke out, and it is the first communication they received from Wormwood Scrubs that in fact a prisoner had escaped. It was made on 2nd November, 1966, by Stanley Franklin, Police Constable 436F/137388 who said,

'On Saturday 26th October, 1966, I was employed at Shepherd's Bush Police Station on communications duty at a time recorded of 7.43 I received a 'phone call from a man who said he was the Deputy governor of Wormwood Scrubs Prison. To the best of my recollection, the conversation went as follows; This is the deputy Governor of Wormwood Scrubs. I have just been informed by my chief that we've lost one of our chaps over the wall. We think it's Blake. I said Blake? He said yes, the one doing 42 years. I said, Can you give a description and he said, Not at the moment. He's probably in prison grounds. He went over the east wall. Look, I'm a bit tucked up at the moment. I'm in the middle of releasing a man. I'll ring you back when I've got more information.'

The possibility of you playing table tennis seems to me has nothing on what we have read from this statement so far. The statement continues:

'I am aware that a coded form of message, Patterson called it, is in use for escape messages from the prison. This had not been used. I therefore asked the reserve officer PC 622F Child to ring the prison to verify the information.

Now we are not really talking urgent here, are we? We are not really talking George Blake has got over the wall, now the most wanted man, the man serving the longest prison sentence ever issued in an English court of law?

A: I would disagree. If I could just interrupt you, I would disagree with you there. There was a sense of urgency but not panic.

Q: Not panic?

A: You asked me in the first instance, panic.

Q: Well, he hadn't even given the password. This is the assistant

governor. The police have got to ring him back to say, "Is your call genuine?" And he said, "I'm a bit tucked up." It sounds to me he was tucked up in bed. That is the impression I get. I am not in any way attacking you or the Assistant Governor. What I am trying to establish is that even in D hall, which was a hall for long term prisoners, there was not the kind of prison security that we know today?
A: Oh, certainly not.
Q: No. But even in those circumstances it was really quite a lax atmosphere in relation to what we know today?
A: Oh yes, yes. I mean the prison service now bears no resemblance to what it was 25 years ago, none whatsoever.
Q: I'm glad to see that even though you were the officer on duty that night no responsibility was put on to you because I see that you are still in the prison service and in fact you are the Chief Officer now in the hall?
A: Principal Officer.
Pottle: Thanks very much.

I had no questions, and neither Pat nor I had anything to ask the next witness, the prison officer who testified he had been on boundary patrol on 22nd October 1966 and had discovered the rope ladder used in the escape.

It was quite a different matter with the next witness, Detective Inspector Helen Crampton who had interviewed Pat and myself on 30th October when the Sunday Times first headlined our involvement in the escape. After the briefest of examination in chief by Calvert-Smith, in which she confirmed she and another officer had interviewed us and that we had both declined to answer questions, I began the cross-examination:

Randle: Detective Inspector, were you actually in charge of investigations at that time as a result of those newspaper articles?
Crampton: Yes.
Q: You were. And you and Sergeant Lynch I think, were involved?
A: That's right.
Q: You also interviewed Mr Barrie Penrose at about the same time?
A: Yes.
Q: Were you surprised at all at being asked to interview someone about events that had taken place 21 years earlier? Was that unusual?
A: In my experience it was unusual, yes.
Q: So presumably when you were investigating that case, you had to remind yourself of all the documents, the previous documents that had come up in relation to it?
A: Yes.

Q: So you would have gone through the Special Branch documents relating to the case?
A: Yes.
Q: Did you also have the opportunity to consult MI5 files on occasions?
A: No, I didn't, no.
Q: You have said that it was newspaper articles that prompted the renewal of this investigation. Was it also the book by Mr Montgomery Hyde *George Blake, Superspy* - was that part of it?
A: Yes, that was looked at as well.
Q: The articles appearing I think in the Sunday Times were by Mr Barrie Penrose?
A: Correct.
Q: I have a question here. Did you learn anything from Mr Penrose's articles that was not known to the police in 1970 from police files?
A: I really couldn't say, sir, for sure.
Q: You do not recall any documents from Special Branch files which indicated that in the early months of 1970 the special branch actually named Mr Pottle and myself?
A: No, sorry.
Q: Do you know whose decision it was to interview us in 1987?[1]
A: It was my own decision.
Q: Well, the thing that surprises me is that we do know and we have had disclosed to us, a Special Branch document naming us in 1987 and comparing us with a description in Seán Bourke's book and positively identifying Mr Pottle and myself as probable suspects. You do not recall that at all?
A: No.
Q: I have here a copy of that document and at the back of that document there is an appendix which compares two characters in Mr Bourke's book, somebody he calls Pat Porter and somebody he calls Michael Reynolds, and there are points of comparison made between Mr Porter and Mr Pottle and Mr Reynolds and Mr Randle. It goes through the descriptions and so forth and compares them with ours. On Pat Porter on page 246 of the book it says friend of Michael Reynolds, and then the real Pat Pottle, friend of Michael Randle, 'described as more robust than Michael Reynolds and about two years younger'. The police description, height 6 foot and well built, four and a half years younger than Randle, born 8th August, 1938. Then it

1 A slip of the tongue on my part: I should have said 1970. The point was cleared up by the judge shortly afterwards.

says Pat Porter was a single man, and Patrick Brian Pottle was a single man. His address was a flat in Hampstead. The address, 'although technically he lived with his widowed mother at the latter's council flat at Aldborough Road W2, enquiries at that period show that he was seldom there. His girl friend, Susan Abraham, later his wife, however, lived at 98 Adelaide Road, Hampstead and he may well have had a flat nearby.' Then the occupation of Pat Porter is described at page 246 of Seán Bourke's book.

So there is a very positive identification and this was done to give the reasons for the special branch believing that the Pat Porter in Bourke's book was, in fact, Patrick Pottle. You do not recall any of that?

A: I don't recall that as being …

Alliott: Can I just make sure I have my note right. I have recorded three answers back, 'I don't know if the Special branch named Pottle and Randle in 1970. It was my decision to interview in 1987,' and then you (Randle) used the date 1987 in your next question and I have it in this way, 'I don't know of a disclosed document comparing in 1987 Bourke's characters,' as I have summarised it, 'with you two.' Is that correct in 1987?

Randle: Sorry, that was …

Alliott: By a slip of the tongue you said 1987. 'So the suggestion, Miss Crampton, is that Special Branch had made a detailed comparison of the characters referred to in Bourke's book and these two way back in 1970.' Were you aware of that?

Crampton: I am quite sure that I found it in my research of the case, sir, yes. I don't recall it.

Alliott: Is this a document that is in my papers that you have been quoting from?

Randle: I don't think it is there, my Lord.

The reason it was not was that it had been disclosed to us during the High Court hearing and was a document the prosecution would want to keep out of the trial itself. After the rehearsals with our lawyers I had been fully expecting Bevan or Calvert-Smith to jump up as soon as I quoted from it. But to my surprise they remained seated.

Alliott: Have you a copy for the lady to look at.

Randle: Yes, certainly.

Now at last Bevan seemed to wake up to the significance of what was happening and stood up.

Bevan: May I explain? I have been in this case, as Mr Randle and Mr Pottle know, for a long time. This case has a history, as your Lordship may know, with regard to abuse of process proceedings.

Alliott: Yes.
Bevan: During those proceedings documents were disclosed and this is one of those that was ultimately disclosed. It is a 1970 police report, as I remember it, on which Mr Randle is … concentrating. May I ask for your Lordship to decide the relevance of this in view of that fact that at the abuse of process proceedings heard in the divisional court it was decided by the court that there was no abuse of process and that these proceedings should continue. I must question, through your Lordship, what the relevance of this matter is to this case. I say that only as a marker, because of course these two defendants, representing themselves, must be given as much latitude as possible.
Alliott: I have been very conscious that a good many of the questions asked have been, as it were, in breach of my rules; but as they have not been taking up too much time I felt it might be dealt with more expeditiously.
Randle: We will try not to take up too much time.
Alliott: No, you are not. That is why I am not being punctilious about keeping you to my ruling.

Once again we had reason to be thankful to our legal team for the advice they had given. They had been exactly right. By limiting our questions and convincing the judge that we had no interest of wasting the court's time, we had gained ourselves the leeway to smuggle in the occasional question on issues which could have been ruled irrelevant.

Randle: What we are trying to establish at this time are the facts of the case. Mr Bevan made a very fair opening in which he went through the history of the case, but there were some omissions and the jury could form the impression that in 1987 this was the very first moment that … any suspicion was upon us.
Alliott: Let me see if I can help you. Members of the jury, this case was originally going to be tried before another judge months earlier than now. However, the defendants said, 'Just a moment, this is all far too stale. Too much water has flowed under the bridge for you to prosecute us now', and they went off to the Divisional Court and said the same thing. The Divisional Court has held that it is not too stale and therefore this trial is proceeding and what Mr Bevan has just said is that this is a document that was disclosed in the course of that hearing, on a different issue from the one you have to decide, and it is apparently quite plain – I have not seen the document myself – that someone made the comparison between what Bourke had written, and these two gentlemen's identities, way back in 1970. That is the context

and Miss Crampton has agreed that she must have found out about that during the course of her researches.
Randle: Again, to avoid taking up too much time, I don't want to go through the comparisons between the Michael Reynolds of Mr Bourke's story and the Michael Randle whom you see in the dock before you, but there is a close similarity. They go through a list of points and show that in all probability it must have been us.
Alliott: The jury will have read the passage in your book when I cannot remember who actually was the narrator at the time but there was a sort of shock-horror reaction as to how closely you have been identified by a book.
Bevan: I included it, I think, when I opened the matter to the jury, about how he provided clues.
Alliott: Because it was Anne Reynolds, too, and children of the same age and so on. You have it well in mind, members of the jury, I am sure.
Randle: Yes, but of course what we have to speculate in the book was whether the police knew or not. Did they put two and two together? We thought that probably they did, but now we have proof positive in these documents. Of course they did. It would be amazingly remiss of them if they did not. I think a comment made at the time was 'a boy scout could have traced this to us'.
We will obviously make copies of these documents and I wanted to go to the last paragraph. This is a report signed by Chief Inspector Watts of Special Branch. 'It should be stressed that at this stage there is no actual evidence to substantiate any of these possible identifications. No enquiries have been made by the police of the persons concerned.'
Do you find that strange, after one of the most massive police hunts for many decades that when, three and a half years later, two people were positively identified there were not even any enquiries made of these two people? Do you find that unusual in your knowledge of police procedures?
A: I am sorry, I wasn't actually involved in the enquiry at that time.
Q: No, but would it have been unusual in your experience if there had been a case that had involved a massive police hunt and evidence of some kind came up three years later, or some very strong clues, and the police were actually able to identify the likely suspects that then there was no follow up whatever, the those people were not even interviewed? Would that be the usual practice in your experience?
A: Well, as I say, I wasn't on the enquiry at that time. I can only speculate as to what went on.

Q: I understand that. I am just asking, as a matter of general police practice, if there had been an enquiry and then some evidence came up somewhere later, would it be normal practice to make enquiries and to approach the people concerned? Would that be normal practice? Not in this case, we will forget this case, but in the normal course of events?
A: I would have thought that it would certainly have been looked into.
Q: Right. The statement continues. 'It must be said, however, that if Bourke's story is true, these persons with their ideological beliefs, their militant backgrounds and their wide circle of associates, fit very well into the pattern of the escape as we know it. Even the final details of the escape where Michael Reynolds and his wife allegedly drove to Dover with Blake hidden in the secondhand Dormobile they had purchased would have been quite feasible for Randle and his wife, both of whom had current passports and had travelled abroad extensively.' It is extraordinary, is it not, that we were not interviewed at that time, that no enquiries were made in the words of the report?
A: As I say, I was not involved in the enquiry at that time. I really cannot comment.
Q: We may have here in another document a clue as to why this unusual thing happened. The transcript of Seán Bourke's book, an advance copy, was obtained by MI5, and we have disclosed to us a letter dated some time in January – 30th January, 1970
Alliott: Again this was in the abuse hearing, was it?
Pottle: As a result of that.
Randle: Yes, we got it through the abuse hearing. It says,'For the attention of Chief Inspector Watts', and he is the man from whose report we have been quoting. 'You may wish to have a preview of Seán Bourke's book, The Springing of George Blake.' The second paragraph: 'I have been asked to stress that this typescript was received on a confidential basis and we would ask you not to take any action.' I will repeat that: 'We would ask you not to take any action on matters revealed in the typescript or make any enquiries which reveal that it is in our possession.'
That forms some kind of explanation as to why, three and a half years later, no enquiries, no interviews, were made?
A: I'm not sure when that document was published, or indeed when Bourke's book was published.
Q: I can remind you of that. Seán Bourke's book was published in June 1970. I think there is a copy in the court that we can refer to if necessary. This letter was dated the 30 January, 1970. We can make a copy of that and it is a document that was revealed to us from the MI5

> files in the course of the abuse of process.
> So the sequence of events is that MI5 gets hold, through whatever means they have, of an advanced typescript. They send it along to Special Branch and they say, 'We would like you to have a look at this and to draw up a report on it, but we do not want you …' I repeat, 'We would stress, we would ask you not to take any action on matters revealed in the typescript or make any enquiries which would reveal that it is in our possession.' Do you think that throws some light on why no enquiries were made at the time of the publication of that book?
> A: I can only repeat that I was not involved in the enquiry but it's only a couple of months until the book was published, so it would have been public knowledge. I can't see that there is a problem there.
> Alliott: I am bound to say the same thought had crossed my mind. On publication it is in the public domain.
> Pottle: Yes, my Lord. The point Mr Randle is trying to establish is that this copy of this transcript had been obtained by MI5. MI5 said to Special Branch, 'Could you write a report on this transcript we managed to obtain. We don't want the source of where it's come from revealed.'
> Alliott: What Miss Crampton has said is that two months later the book is published, it is all in the public domain. It was her answer to the suggestion that the covering letter to the typescript might, in some way, account for inactivity on the part of the police. Miss Crampton, reasonably in my view, it is a matter entirely for the jury, says that the book was published two months later and then they were under no inhibition. That is your point, is it not?
> Crampton: Yes.
> Randle: That is exactly the point we want to establish, that as between January and the time of publication they had that advice and they had the warning from MI5 – don't take any action. But I absolutely take your point that once the book is published we are into a different ball game.

Having got away with quoting from the Watts' report, I made a quick decision to introduce the famous Note for File with the reference to the Big Fish and Little Fish. Pat and I had earlier decided to wait until Detective Inspector Eggington was in the witness-box before raising it. But it seemed right to seize the opportunity before the prosecution and the judge had had time to catch on to the implications of what we were doing and intervened more vigorously to stop us.

Randle: But we now have here on 29th April, we are now getting very close to the time of publication, and this is another document disclosed to us from MI5. It is dated 29th April and it is a record of a conversation that Miss A from MI5 had with Chief Inspector Watts of Special Branch. She says, 'When I was speaking to Chief Inspector Watts of Special Branch yesterday, he mentioned their report' – that is the report on the Seán Bourke book – 'and asked me if we had any comment on it. Chief Inspector Watts added that the Special Branch decision at present was to take no steps to interview or attempt to prosecute the Randles, Pottle' – and then there is another name of someone who in fact has nothing to do with the case. 'It was considered that to do so might be persecution – a big fish had got away so they were taking it out on the little fish. It was considered, however, that it had been necessary to investigate their suspicions and to place them on record'. I do not think I need to read further.

So there we have an explanation, perhaps, as to why, coming up to the time of publication, and subsequent to publication, we still have this extraordinary situation – no enquiries are made and we are still not interviewed. Is that right?

A: I couldn't tell you, I am sorry.

Q: Right. Then I shall leave it. I think I have probably said all I need to say about that point. But the point I wanted to emphasise is that when all this information was in the hands of Special Branch and MI5, a conversation was recorded in which the Chief Inspector who had drawn up the report was reported, and we have the document here, by an MI5 officer saying that it was considered that either to interview or prosecute the Randles and Mr Pottle, might be persecution. A big fish had got away and it would be taking it out on the little fish. Do you think as the officer in charge of the investigation that you ought to have been shown that document at that time in 1987?

A: I believe it was probably on file and it was quite open to me to draw the file.

Q: This would be on MI5's files.

A: I didn't have access to MI5 files.

Q: Is it not extraordinary that you did not have access to those files, given that this information on it was absolutely central to the case?

A: Unless they were of evidential value I don't think they would be obliged to show it to me.

Q: No, but would it not be normal for you to be informed of what the police knew at various stages, the police and MI5?

A: I'm really not quite sure what you are asking me.

Q: Let me put it another way. If a decision was taken, as it appears to have been from this note in 1970, on the basis of considerations other than evidence – namely to do with persecution and the big fish having got away – if a decision was taken in 1970, despite the knowledge of our involvement, would it not be extraordinary that in 1987, 17 years later, the officer in charge was not even informed that that decision had been taken or was not told about the history of the case up to that point?

A: Well, it was up to myself to research the case and make myself familiar with the history of the case.

Q: Yes. But do I understand that you were not given access to the MI5 files?

A: You do understand that right.

Q: But should you have been, given that there was evidence there that would have a very important bearing on the case?

A: I can't really say.

Q: You can't really say. I will not press you further on that point. Thank you.

Cross-examined by Pat.

Pottle: I have only a couple of questions. In answer to Mr Randle's question you said you actually looked through the files in 1987, because a newspaper article appears which says that the two people who broke George Blake out of prison are Michael Randle and Pat Pottle. You read this article and think you'd better investigate this. Before you do so you now say that you looked through the files of Special Branch to see if there was anything that would help. Did you come across this document. I wonder if I could read it to you.

My Lord, it is document 171 of the non material statements. It is a statement made by Detective Inspector Nichols on 2nd November 1966. This is just 10 days after the break. This statement is of a police officer who goes along to the landlady of Seán Bourke's last known address, ten days after the break in 1966. I shall read you the statement. 'At 5 pm today I visited 26 Perryn Road, W3, where I saw separately Mrs Brown and a Mr and Mrs Lucy. To each of them I showed a photograph of four men together' I will not name the other three men. One of them was Patrick Pottle. 'Mrs Brown and Mr and Mrs Lucy were not able to identify any of the four men and were quite certain they had never seen them visiting Seán Bourke at 26 Perryn Road.'

So here we are, ten days after the break, and my photograph is being

shown around, as a possible suspect. Did you, in fact, find that document within the MI5 files.
Alliott: She did not see the MI5 files. She saw the Special Branch files.
Pottle: The Special Branch files?
A: I simply cannot recall. It is some years ago since I researched them.
Q: So in fact you cannot help me on anything prior to 1987. You can't remember anything of what you saw in those files?
A: There are a number of files that I researched. I mean, obviously my …
Q: But you can help me with the investigations that you yourself carried out?
A: I certainly can.
Q: Then let us move on to 1987, the newspaper articles that appeared by Mr Barrie Penrose in the Sunday Times which prompted you to interview us. In those articles, which appeared on 4th October, 1987, and 11th October, 1987, a number of other people were named as being people who, if not actually involved in the case, could in fact supply the police with information about us – Michael Randle and myself. Is that correct?
A: Without re-reading the articles and refreshing my memory, I believe there were some other names in there, yes.
Q: Of course you are the officer in charge of the case. You read the articles which name us and it would be reasonable to assume that you also read the articles in relation to all the other people who were also named. And people actually spelled out in the newspaper the names and the possible kind of information that they could supply you, the police, with. I shall name a few of those people for you just to jog your memory. Mr Randle has already mentioned the author Montgomery Hyde who said in his book that he had two informants who had given him information about these two people. One of them is a man called Kenneth de Courcy and the other is a man called Nicolas Walter. Did you interview either of those two?
A: No.
Q: You did not, even though the article in the Sunday Times said Nicolas Walter was somebody who has information that could be of great use to the police? He is the man who has given the information to Montgomery Hyde to put in his book and has also given information to Barrie Penrose to put in the newspaper articles. But you didn't interview him?
A: No.

Q: Those articles also named Terence Chandler, Vanessa Redgrave, Kevin O'Connor, John Papworth, Mr Gore-Grimes, Seán Bourke's solicitor. The article actually said that Seán Bourke had made a death-bed confession of some kind implicating all the other people involved in the case and it was just a simple case of getting in touch with Mr Gore-Grimes who had this information and he would then supply it. Did you get in touch with Mr Gore Grimes?
A: I made a number of enquiries seeking evidence in this case.
Q: But the people I have named, you had not at this stage been to see any of them?
A: No.
Q: Did you see a Mr Bernard Miles?
A: No.
Q: Did you see a Mr John Papworth?
A: No.
Q: Did you see a Dr Alex Comfort?
A: I don't think so.
Q: I want to get this absolutely clear. You are the officer in charge of the case. Accusations have been made in the newspaper that these two men are partly responsible for getting George Blake out of jail. Your job is to investigate those allegations. In those newspaper articles 14 other people are mentioned as possibly suspects, as possibly people who could have supplied you with information; in fact I just find it quite amazing that you never, ever, interviewed one of them. Why? I might be teaching you to suck eggs. I'm not a policeman, members of the jury are not policemen, but it does not stop us saying to ourselves, 'Well, I'm not a copper, but what I would have done is I would have gone and interviewed the very people being named by Mr Penrose.' Why did you not do that?
A: We were seeking not information solely. We have information on the files anyway. We were seeking evidence.
Q: I see. When were you taken off ... Are you still in charge of the case?
A: No, I am not.
Q: When did you cease to be in charge of the case?
A: Shortly after I interviewed you.
Q: I do not want to be crude, it seems to me to have been a cosmetic exercise at that time. A newspaper article appears naming two people who helped George Blake break out of jail. A number of people are asking questions in newspapers, in the Houses of Parliament and so on about what the hell is going on. You decide to interview. You open

up the Special Branch files and you see in those that the decision was taken in 1970 to do nothing, that no further investigations were to take place.

Bevan: May I just jog Mr Pottle's memory, my Lord, about the abuse proceedings when all these documents came to light. The documents did not come to light through Special Branch files. The one Mr Randle made mention of, the 'persecution note,' it came, as I remember it, from the MI5 files.

Alliott: As the witness has said more than once she did not see the MI5 files.

Bevan: No, so when Mr Pottle says the witness must have seen it, etcetera, he is saying effectively they were in the Special Branch files. Mr Pottle may remember that they were not.

Alliott: These 14 names, not all of which I have got but some of which I recognised, in which files were they, Special Branch or MI5?

Pottle: They weren't in any files, my Lord, they were all names in newspaper articles in 1987.

Alliott: They were all named in the Penrose articles?

Pottle: [The articles] that prompted Inspector Crampton to investigate them, my Lord. (To the witness): Just to go back to the point made by Mr Bevan I am sorry if I've given the wrong idea. I wasn't in any way referring to the MI5 document but it is clear from the documents with which we have been supplied by Special Branch, that in fact a decision was taken and is recorded in those documents, 'We will take no further action.' Here the matter would seem to rest. That is what's down in the documents. I put it to you, Inspector, that you saw these documents, the matter would interest you, you are under pressure, quite reasonably, people don't know what the hell's going on. Why aren't these people being investigated? And you carry out a simple little investigation that will not lead you anywhere but will enable you to say, if asked by the press of the world, 'Well, we have thoroughly investigated these allegations, and we intend taking no further action.' Is that not the case?

A: It would seem to me that there was no fresh evidence.

Q: I am not trying to be rude, honestly I am not, but here you had a whole host of names of people as having possible evidence. You are investigating the case. You can't say to this jury that you did not have any other evidence because you are doing what they did in 1970, you see, you are not looking for the evidence. I'll give you an example. Mr Bevan referred to it in his opening address. He said, I can't remember the actual date, but in January 1967, 3 months after the break, the first

hideout in Highlever Road is discovered. In that hideout the police find a number of sets of fingerprints. Some of those fingerprints are identified as those of George Blake. There are two sets of fingerprints completely unidentified, in the possession of the police. Did it occur to you, at any stage in 1987, to say, 'Well, this Randle and Pottle are mentioned. Why don't I compare their fingerprints which I have on file with those unidentified fingerprints taken from Highlever Road in January 1967 and see if they match, and if they match, I now need to go and interview all these other people because the evidence I'm looking for will now be in my possession.' Did you do that?
A: No, I didn't. I would have expected the officer investigating in 1967 to have compared known fingerprints against those unknown ones that he found at the scene.
Q: That is enough for you, is it, when you are investigating a case like this, you can actually say to yourself that it is quite obvious to you and straightforward? It may not be so obvious and straightforward. Those fingerprints were not compared in 1967. They were not compared in 1970. They were not compared when you were in charge of the case in 1987. They were compared in February last year. I find extraordinary your answer, 'I assumed they would have been'. Surely you don't assume; the least you could do was check. Did you check?
A: No, I didn't.
Q: You didn't?
A: No.
Q: You just assumed. In a way I can agree with your assumption because it is such an obvious thing, but obviously you would say to yourself that that must have been done, but you didn't actually check?
A: No.
Q: You were taken off the case in?
A: 1987.
Q: 1987. So you wrote a report, presumably, about the interviews. Did you submit that report to a superior?
A: I did.
Q: Did you hear any more of it?
A: No, no …
Q: So you know nothing since then. In a way, that was your only involvement with this whole investigation?
A: That's right.
Q: Thank you very much, Inspector.

Inspector Crampton had visibly withered in face of Pat's questioning. You could see it in her stance, in the way she clutched her hands in front of her, in the sideways tilt of her head. You could feel sorry for her, in a way, for she was a minor player in the drama, perhaps with little or no experience of giving evidence, and facing cross-examination, in court.

Calvert-Smith did his best to retrieve the situation in his brief re-examination.

> **Calvert-Smith: You were asked whether you had made any enquiries other than interviewing these two accused for about 5 minutes each. Did you?**
> **A: Yes, I did, sir.**
> **Q: About how long did you spend on the case before writing your report?**
> **A: Four months.**
> **Q: What was the conclusion that you came to, albeit it would not be your decision in the end, perhaps, but what was your conclusion?**
> **A: There was no fresh evidence which would be suitable to put before the court.**
> **Q: Just explain to the jury, who may be unclear, the distinction between information and evidence?**
> **A: Well, certainly information could be very useful in leading to the evidence, but information could be something that one had heard via somebody else and therefore is not direct evidence.**
> **Calvert-Smith: I have no other questions.**

Mr Calvert-Smith now read the statements by two people from Harrap, the publisher of our book – Susanne McDadd, the senior commissioning editor at Harrap with whom we had worked most closely during the writing of the book, and Jean-Luc Barbanneau, the Deputy Managing Director of the firm. These confirmed that we had been commissioned to write The Blake Escape for a fee of £15,000 each.

While this was going on, Pat and myself had an urgent consultation. It was vital, we decided, to get the Watts report and the MI5 Note for File into the hands of the jury. So as soon as the reading was finished, I stood up and asked the judge if there could be a short adjournment to allow us to raise a couple of points with him.

> **'I dare say a mid-afternoon break will not come amiss with you, members of the jury', he said.**

When the jury left I asked if the material referred to by Pat and myself could be added to the jury 'bundle'. Alliott suggested that in order to avoid interrupting the trial we consider the matter at the end of the day when the jury had gone home.

When the jury returned the next witness was the detective James Hill, one of the officers who had searched Anne and my house on 3 May 1989. He had testified in his statement to having found a copy of Minutes of the Social Defence Project (which referred to my involvement in the Blake escape), some photographs (taken in Goslar after we had dropped off George in East Germany), a negative (showing the inside of the van with the concealed compartment) and correspondence with Palach Press.

My cross-examination dealt mainly with this last item. The correspondence was with Jan Kavan, the Czech exile who had worked for twenty years in London assisting the Czechoslovak opposition before returning to Prague in 1989 and being elected in June of the following year as a Civic Forum MP in the Federal Parliament. I had worked on and off with Jan since December 1969, and he would be appearing for me as a character witness – so this was an opportunity of introducing his name to the jury.

But there was another reason I wanted to question Hill about the correspondence. It dated from the early months of 1989 and concerned plans to adapt a Transit van to take in further equipment to Czechoslovakia. Hill, in his written statement, identified it as exhibit JRH/2. But there was no such exhibit put in evidence. Nor was the correspondence among the items returned to our lawyers by the police as being of no relevance. My suspicion was that Special Branch had handed the letters over to MI5.

When I raised the issue, the judge intervened to explain that the reason it had not been produced as an exhibit in the case was because the Crown had concluded that it had no evidential value. I asked why, in that case it was not amongst the material returned to me. Bevan promised to look into the matter and to see I got it back. (For the record I never did.)

WPC Sharon Cole was the next witness – another officer who had taken part in the search of my house. Among other things, she had found the old passport of mine which we had used in the book to demonstrate how we adapted Pat's passport for use by Seán Bourke, an 'impression of an official stamp', a notebook with notes on the book including draft chapter headings, questions of paperback, foreign and film rights and so forth. Calvert-Smith carried out the examination in chief. When he referred to my passport (Exhibit 31), I stood up:

> **Randle: I am sorry to interrupt again, but wasn't it an 'ex-passport' rather than a passport?**

Calvert-Smith picked up at once on the Monty Python 'dead parrot' allusion.

Calvert-Smith: A late passport! The only point is to indicate that as it is set out in the book, in fact, this passport was issued because the previous passport had been lost, and that is set out at page 1077.
Pottle: I wonder if I could just interrupt you. I noticed in the opening of Mr Bevan he did actually say that Michael's passport which is a mistake. In fact it was my passport. So in case you are trying to establish that Michael's passport …
Bevan: It was pointed out to me that I opened the case from the book, the jury must appreciate, and I did make a mistake, no doubt one of many, but it was in fact Mr Pottle's passport that was used I think for Seán Bourke and not Mr Randle's, and I made a mistake. I said Mr Randle and it was Mr Pottle.
Alliott: Thank you.
Calvert-Smith: I was referring to the use by Mr Randle of the passport to go to East Germany.
Alliott: It has its corner snipped off, as we see from page 1075. That is indicating that Mr Randle is correct. It is an expired passport.

The final witness that day for the prosecution that day was Detective Sergeant William Lloyd who had transcribed the interviews conducted by Superintendent Eggington on 3 May 1989 with Pat, Anne and myself. He had also established from the register of electors that in October 1966 Pat Pottle had resided at flat 4C Willow Buildings in Hampstead. We had no questions for him.

When the prosecution called Superintendent Eggington to take the stand, Pat interrupted:

Pottle: My Lord, I wonder if I can address you on a matter a little earlier. I think it is quite important that while Superintendent Eggington is here we may well be referring once again to the documents we referred to earlier. In view of the lateness of the hour, as well, my Lord, I …
Alliott: I can see you are trying to win friends on the jury by suggesting an early rising on a Friday. Off you go, members of the jury. 10 o'clock Monday.

When the jury had filed out, Alliott turned to us:

'Now have you had any exchange with counsel for the Crown as to what you want to put in.'

Pat then requested that the documents we had referred to from those disclosed to us prior to the our first appearance at the Old Bailey and in the course of the High Court proceedings should be added to the jury bundle. Bevan did not object to the inclusion of statements obtained by the police during their investigations in 1966 – the statements by the prison governors Newcombe and Rham, by the prison officer Townsend, by the policeman Franklin on duty at Shepherd's Bush police station when the governor phoned through to say that 'one of our chaps has gone over the wall,' and by Detective Inspector Nichols who had showed a photograph of Pat and others to Seán's former landlady on 2 November 1966. But he did oppose the inclusion of the Watts report and the 'Fish document'.

> Bevan: … The point I raise with your Lordship with regard to these documents only arose, I submit on behalf of the Crown, as to the question of abuse. The core question in relation to the judicial review proceedings was not merely the elapse of time. The other core question the court had to consider was whether or not the decision has been made in 1970 not to prosecute these two defendants. That was a matter that was considered by the court and evidence was heard. These documents were produced and considered by that court during the abuse proceedings.
>
> My Lord, the only relevance of those documents in those proceedings, must, in my submission, go to the question of abuse, and that is not a matter which this jury could ever be asked to consider. An abuse of the proceedings is not a defence to the charge. It lies quite outside the charges themselves and there is no relevance, in my submission, so far as the issues before this jury are concerned to touch upon these documents. I anticipate Mr Randle and Mr Pottle would wish to submit to the jury, or certainly by way of invitation through the means of these documents, this: 'You look at these documents. They amounted to a policy decision made in 1970 not to prosecute us and it is now very unfair that we are being prosecuted.' No doubt they will put the argument far more forcefully and compellingly than I do. But that, as I understand it, will be the issue.

Alliott now acknowledged what had been immediately apparent to Pat and myself during the cross-examination of Inspector Crampton.

> Alliott: Yes. The thing is this, notwithstanding my strictures early in the case, I was not punctilious about enforcing cross-examination of Miss Crampton and some of these matters have been aired. I do not suggest for one moment that that entitles them to put in, and I look at the list, the Watts' report in its entirety or the abuse documents. But I think in order to make that which has emerged, albeit perhaps a more Draconian approach to the cross-examination would have prevented emerging, I would be minded to allow there to be a written form of that which has been put in; for instance, the passage in the Watts'

report setting out the comparison between the Bourke characters and the defendants, because that was raised in extension.
Bevan: And I think the conclusion of Mr Watts' report.
Alliott: Then there was the query whether it was persecution because a big fish had got away and this was taking it out on the little ones. I appreciate all that.
Bevan: As to the Watts' report, the comparisons, as I remember the cross-examination, the conclusions – I will be corrected if I am wrong, but that is how I remember it. Also, what I am going to call the fish letter the persecution letter.
Alliott: My present thoughts are that which has been raised by Mr Randle in the course of his cross-examination of Miss Crampton can be put before the jury in a more permanent form so that they do not have to carry it in their minds. I am certainly not going to allow the entire Watts report or all the abuse documents to go in. What I think I shall do is to leave the parties to mull over that view I have expressed to see whether it can be agreed what should be added to the jury bundle.

Bevan repeated his point that all the documents in question had been disclosed in relation to the abuse of process. Pat pointed out that some of them had been disclosed earlier in the hearings before Mr Justice Auld and Mr Justice Rougier in March.

Bevan: My Lord, I cannot enter into a conversation with Mr Pottle before your Lordship and I address your Lordship. Factually, what he says is entirely true with regard to Mr Justice Auld and Mr Justice Rougier, but I would submit that the purpose of seeing, or trying to see those documents – on some of which, I think the majority, public interest immunity was claimed – went to the abuse, not, if I might say so, to the issue that is before this jury. All those documents did go to abuse and I would submit that it is not right for this jury to have to consider the abuse proceedings and what lies behind them. That is not the issue they have to decide. That is the single point I make.
Alliott: To an extent, this is all beating the air, because I shall direct the jury on the narrow issue: have the Crown proved that these two defendants committed the acts set forth in the indictment. As I say, if you cannot reach agreement I shall consider the matter on Monday.
Bevan: As I understand the position, your Lordship has said that as a result of the cross-examination such parts of the documents as have already been read should be copied for the jury.
Alliott: Yes.
Bevan: At the moment, without having heard further from Mr Randle and Mr Pottle …

We signalled our agreement to the judge's proposal, scarcely able to believe our good fortune. It would have been better still had the whole of the Watts' report been handed to the jury but clearly the judge was not going to allow that. But the crucial passages from that report, and the still more crucial 'fish' document would now be in their hands.

Mr Calvert-Smith now firmly locked the stable door:

> **Calvert-Smith: I am simply concerned that the defence should be on notice that at least from now on reading from the document to a witness will not be allowed for that document to be photocopied and given to the jury.**

Alliot again acknowledged that the horse had already bolted:

> **Alliott: You see, we have made a rod for our own backs, we lawyers. Notwithstanding the warning shot I fired earlier on we have given these two leeway we would never have allowed had they been represented. You have not jumped up and objected, Mr Bevan, and I have not intervened. There we are.**

Pat and I left the court in a state of elation. Not so the two prosecuting counsel. They were conferring together looking distinctly crestfallen.

'It the oddest thing,' I said to Pat, 'Here are we facing certain imprisonment for several years, but it is they who are demoralised.'

Chapter 19:

Interrogating the Interrogators

After a relaxed weekend, which included a party on Saturday night at the home of one of our legal team, we returned to court on the Monday morning for what we knew would be the last day or two of the trial.

It began with my handing over to the judge, as he had requested, my notes on the necessity defence and the report on the Conway case, which I had cited – and which Bevan had confused with another case, that of Willer. The Conway case was the one in which a man drove off at high speed when approached by two plain-clothes detectives, and sped in the wrong direction down a one-way, afterwards claiming in court that he thought the two men who approached him were criminals intent on killing his passenger in the back seat. On appeal it was held that he ought to have been allowed to put forward a defence of necessity or 'duress of circumstances' to the charge of reckless driving. I returned to my argument about a hypothetical 'tug of love' case. If the driver of the car had been a mother who feared the abduction of a child – instead of an attack on a passenger – and had driven away at speed down one way streets etc. surely she ought in logic to be as entitled, as Conway was, to put forward the necessity defence, even though there was no immediate threat to the life and well being of the child. I invited Bevan to accept that point, and asked the judge to reconsider his ruling on our defence of necessity.

> **Alliott: Mr Randle, I am not going to call upon Mr Bevan again, nor will I change my ruling. It is fair to say that I have done some work on the reasons and I have very much in mind that the two extensions that you have contended for – one, there need not be an immediate risk and, two, it can be mental as opposed to physical injury. That is reflected in the draft I have made of my reasons, which I have not perfected because I wanted to have your notes before me before I did that.**
>
> **Bevan: May I just say that I was handed by Mr Randle the moment the jury came in the Conway case. On a very brief reading of that authority it does not alter the shape of the submissions I made to your Lordship.**

Detective Superintendent Eggington – the detective in charge of the prosecution took the stand. Examined by Julian Bevan she described how she had arrested and interviewed Pat and me on 3rd May 1989 at Gerald Road police station. We had declined to answer any questions. Later she had been in charge of a search of Pat Pottle's premises at 2 Dashwood Road. At the conclusion of the search she had driven Pat back to Gerald Road to be bailed, and subsequently offered him a lift home in a police car. On the journey back he had talked about the case and his and Randle's involvement in it.

This time Pat opened the cross examination and did the bulk of it. He concentrated on the fact that the police had known of – or at least strongly suspected – our involvement in 1970, on the various documents that had been disclosed to us during the High Court hearings or in the period leading up to our first appearance at the Old Bailey before Mr Justice Macpherson in April 1990. Eggington kept her nerve; she was more experienced than Inspector Crampton and it showed. She was careful to address all her answers to the judge and several times asked him to rule on the relevance of Pat's questions. But Pat achieved his main purpose. By the end of his lengthy cross-examination, the jury could not fail to have been thoroughly acquainted with the complexities of the case.

The sparring between Pat and Eggington, and between Pat and the judge began at once with his opening questions:

> **Pottle: Superintendent, in your experience, do people ever confess to crimes they never commited?**
> **Eggington: I'm not sure that this is relevant to this case, my Lord.**
> **Q: Well, it seems a straightforward question to me. Do people ever confess to crimes that they never commited?**
> **A: I've got no idea.**
> **Q: If somebody were to confess a crime to you, that they have never committed, how would you determine whether they were telling the truth?**
> **A: My Lord, this would be pure speculation on my part.**
> **Q: I'm sure. But I would certainly like to hear you speculate on what you would do.**
> **Alliott: What issue does this go to, Mr Pottle?**
> **Pottle: The issue it goes to, my Lord, is that Superintendent Eggington arrested us, as she said, on 3rd May. The evidence on which she arrested us was the Blake book we had written. It seems to me reasonable for Superintendent Eggington to read the book and say, 'My God, this is true, I'll arrest them.' What I am asking her is, was there any other evidence, other than that book? Why did she think that the book was true? It is a simple straightforward question.**
> **A: I can answer that question, my Lord. I arrested you on suspicion**

that you had committed the offences for which I did arrest you, and that suspicion was based upon the film which we have seen and which the jury have seen – the television programme – and also from the book which the two of you wrote.

Q: So you did not bear in mind the words used by Mr Bevan in his opening that, 'This is not a phantom dreamt up by two people seeking fame.' You did not take that into account?

A: I considered that when I was reading the book and when I saw the film. I saw the film, I might say, before I had any idea that I was going to be made the officer in the case. It was the following morning that I was given the case to investigate. I then read the book. Having read the book, I drew my own conclusion that it wasn't fanciful and that you meant what you said and that you believed what you said.

Q: And it would be reasonable to assume that having seen the film and then having read the book and said to yourself, – 'Well, this is not a fantasy, this obviously is true, but I must compare what they are saying in that book with the facts as known to us.' Would that be reasonable? For instance, if that book laid out a number of facts which completely contradicted the story as you knew it and the evidence that you already had, then it would mean that the book was untrue. So you must have compared the book with the known facts?

A: That is true, yes. With those known facts and the facts that could perhaps be discovered.

Q: Yes. So you read the book and it seems to me that you must have looked at the evidence you had, possibly within your own files, to see if they tied up?

A: I can say that there was no evidence in the files linking you …

Q: Not even …

Bevan: With respect, could the witness finish the question?

Pottle: Yes. I am sorry.

A: My Lord, in the files, in our records, there was no evidence linking you with the offence for which you were later charged.

Q: The only thing you did have, of course, was Mr Watts' report of 22nd, of the 23rd March, 1970, which clearly spelled out the suspicions you had at the Special Branch that Mr Randle and myself were in fact involved in the escape?

A: Of course I had sight of that report … But it was merely speculation. We had no evidence.

Q: Speculative as to the book on its own?

A: Yes, except in the case of the book you were saying you did it and also Mr Randle.

Q: And if you put those two documents together, the book and Mr Watts' report, it all fits. Mr Watts' report, on its own, you would claim is not good enough to substantiate a prosecution?
A: That's correct, my Lord.
Q: The book on its own could possibly fail in a prosecution in a prosecution were the two people who wrote it to deny that it was true?
A: That's correct, my Lord.
Q: But if you put them both together, that is the book and Mr Watt's report, the jigsaw is complete?
Alliott: I am afraid that is not so, because the Watts report is not evidence, had not been led as evidence and could not have been.
Pottle: I am sorry, my Lord.
Alliott: If the Watts report was evidence to go before this jury, Mr Bevan would have opened it. He scrupulously refrained from doing anything of the sort.
Pottle: That, I think my Lord is one interpretation you could put on it and I could accept that. I personally could put a completely different interpretation on it.
Alliott: I do not think you could have been listening to the opening, then.
Pottle: My Lord, no ... I realise certainly that Mr Bevan did not mention the Watts report in his opening. I would disagree with you on the reasons he did not mention it. (To Eggington). So you have now read the book, you have read the Watts report and you have arrested us. Am I right in thinking that it is your job as the officer in charge of the case, to compile the case against us, to gather all the evidence you possibly can and to submit that to the Crown Prosecution Service for them to consider?
A: That's correct, yes, but the case is based entirely upon your own confessions in the book and on the film and in subsequent interviews.
Q: That's fine. I am just trying to get technically what happened.
A: Therefore, my Lord, all we sought to do then was to corroborate the other facts, the fact that Blake was convicted, that he was sentenced, that he was imprisoned and that he escaped. Those sort of facts we had to prove.
Q: So you gathered the facts, raided our houses and established that we wrote the book and so on. You then compiled your case and you have now submitted that case to the Crown Prosecution Service for them to consider?
A: That's correct, my Lord.
Q: Did you, at that stage, give the Crown Prosecution Service any

indication whatsoever that your department had known about our involvement in the Blake case for the previous 17 years?
A: The answer to that question is, first of all, that our department did not know about your involvement for the past 17 years but the Crown Prosecution Service were certainly aware of all the information that we had on record about you.
Q: Did you, at that time, tell the Crown Prosecution Service that a report had been drawn up in 1970, giving chapter and verse as to why Michael and I were identified. Did you tell the Crown Prosecution at that stage that your department had taken the decision in 1970 not to prosecute?
A: Can I correct you there. There was never any decision not to prosecute.
Pottle: Well …
A: Can I answer the question?
Pottle: Of course, I am sorry. You want to say something else?
A: I am trying to answer your question. There was never any decision not to prosecute. The Crown Prosecution have always been in the light, as far as we are concerned, about all the facts all the information it has. I cannot recall exactly when they were told about the Watts report, but it would have been at a pretty early stage.
Q: I just want to get the atmosphere here. I think you would agree with me that the Crown Prosecution Service has a decision to make. This is quite a unique case in a way. It is a case that stretches back over 25 years. The Crown Prosecution Service have a number of considerations as to whether they should bring a prosecution. One would be the staleness, the fact that there has been a 25 year gap from the offence until the prosecution. I think you would also accept that in any case where there is direct involvement with the Security Service, that also becomes a consideration.
A: Is this a question?
Q: It is a question, yes.
A: Obviously the Crown Prosecution Service and the Director of Public Prosecutions have to take everything into consideration before coming to a decision, particularly in a case that is 25 years old.
Q: What I find amazing is that you did not tell the Crown Prosecution Service that in 1970 a decision was made by your department not to investigate the matter any further, not to look for evidence, not to try to obtain evidence against us. You did not tell them that. Bear in mind that it has to make this rather delicate decision whether it is in the public interest to prosecute after this length of time?

A: As I said before, my Lord, the Crown Prosecution Service, and I had a meeting with them myself and I cannot recall exactly what was discussed. But they were entirely in the light about what we had concerning you and any possible involvement in this case. There was never any decision not prosecute you but you are aware that there was a decision not to investigate further because it was considered that an investigation would be futile at that stage. I cannot comment on that decision. I was not there.
Q: At the moment, I want to try, if I can, to take it chronologically through. You were present in court when Mr Bevan made his opening address made up on the logical order of events. Perhaps I can do the same with you and we will eventually lead up to the things you just mentioned?
A: My Lord, can I seek your directions here. I am very happy to answer these sort of questions but I am aware that they are not direct evidence, they are just matters of which I have read and so on.
Alliott: Yes, well, notwithstanding my firm resolve at the start of the case I am inevitably allowing someone in person leeway and Mr Bevan has not intervened as yet. One has to be rather patient. The only issue is whether these two men did the acts complained of in the indictment, as I have said before the jury on a number of occasions.

Pat now raised directly the other issue to which his questioning had been directed – whether or not the court would be obliged to consider a renewed abuse of process application if facts emerged that had not previously been considered. We had prepared the ground for this on the opening day of the trial.

Pottle: Yes, my Lord, I am sure you are absolutely right. But were it the case in questioning Superintendent Eggington, or any other prosecution witness, evidence was to emerge that in fact a decision was taken in 1970 not to prosecute then I think it would be your duty … to take that into account and possibly even suggest that the case …
Alliott: Mr Pottle, as you know, this matter was a prominent issue in the abuse of process hearing which has been determined against by another court and which I am not reopening.
Pottle: Of course. And I am not at this stage suggesting that your Lordship …
Bevan: May I make something plain because I feel a duty on behalf of the Crown to make the position plain to your Lordship as Mr Pottle well knows because he was present during the whole of the abuse proceedings, and I on behalf of the Crown said to the Divisional Court, which is a High court, that adjudicated upon this matter and

indeed heard evidence, as Mr Pottle and Mr Randle will remember. Various witnesses took part in the investigation in 1970, including Mr Watts, but the position in so far as the Crown was concerned, was that if the court, on the evidence that they heard, said to themselves that a decision had been made in 1970 not to prosecute these two defendants, whatever their position was, the Crown would not seek to pursue this prosecution. I never resiled on behalf of the Crown from that position. The Divisional Court were aware of the Crown's position from start to finish. So if the Divisional Court, having heard all the evidence, was of the view that a decision had been made in 1970 not to prosecute these two defendants, whatever the circumstances, I on behalf of the Crown would not have submitted to the Divisional Court that these proceedings should be pursued. Mr Pottle and Mr Randle will remember well the words of the judgment. The Divisional Court decided that these proceedings were not an abuse of process, and that included the consideration with regard to the non-decision in 1970. I say no more otherwise I would be giving evidence and that I should not do.

Alliott: That which you have said was certainly in the public domain because, of course, the process was extensively reported. I was no more a member of the public, members of the jury, in reading it. I was not party to the Divisional Court, but obviously as a lawyer I am interested in legal affairs. I dare say some of you read the reports too.

Pat moved on to the Attorney General's Guidelines for Crown Prosecutors, and attempted to read out the section dealing with the issue of staleness. Bevan was on his feet at once:

Bevan: My Lord, I am sorry ... What Mr Pottle is effectively doing is reopening the abuse of process proceeding which has been adjudicated upon by the Divisional Court and it is not an issue that this jury have to consider. I have said it before, I say it again and I hope I shall not say it any more.

Pottle: I am afraid you are wrong. I am not trying to reopen the abuse of process. What I am trying to do is to try to put before the jury a number of things that have happened since 1966 up until this year. This is not a simple case of somebody writing a book in 1989 and that being the only possible evidence there was available to the police. It is simple, it is straight forward. All I am asking the superintendent who was in charge of the case at that stage is did she at the time of sending her report to the Crown Prosecution Service, bear in mind that there had, at that stage, been a lapse of 21 years between the offence being committed and the investigation. That seems to me to be a reasonable point.

> Alliott: With courtesy and charm you pay not a blind bit of notice to the ruling I have made, that is what it comes to. You just persist in the line notwithstanding what I say or Mr Bevan objects to.
>
> Pottle: Only, my Lord, because you are under a misunderstanding, but if you do not want me to, I shall not pursue it …

I stood up:

> Randle: I am puzzled as well. I mean, what we are trying to do is to find out the facts of the case. Mr Bevan did it in a very fair way but there were some gaps and those gaps ought to be filled in otherwise the jury might get the impression that in 1987 these Sunday Times articles came like a bolt from the blue and they [the authorities] had no clue whatever before and had not made any previous decisions not to investigate, which is a point that is conceded now. Surely the facts of the case ought to be put before the jury in a way that does not mislead them. If you start in 1987 they will be misled.
>
> Bevan: I only repeat the submission that I made. It goes to the abuse of process point that was fully ventilated. May I also say that as far as the opening is concerned, and I thank both Mr Randle and Mr Pottle for the praise they have given me, I could not, as your Lordship knows introduce to this jury the Watt's report because it is not evidence against either of these two gentlemen. It never has been and it not now.
>
> Pottle: What I am trying to establish, my Lord, is did Superintendent Eggington feel that this offence was so serious that even after the gap of 25 years she felt so strongly that she should submit her case to the DPP and possibly even recommend that a prosecution take place.
>
> Alliott: We all know that if you had not gone public and on television it is highly unlikely that you would have ever been prosecuted. But you did go public and you have been prosecuted and the Divisional Court has held that it is not an abuse of process to do so.
>
> Pottle: I accept that, my Lord. I am not in any way querying that. Let us say Miss Crampton was in the box … and if I asked her how she came to investigate in 1987. She could say that she came to see me in 1987 as a result of certain speculation and that would be correct and would create a certain impression within the jury's mind. But it is a half truth. I could say, yes, you came to see us in 1987 because of the those newspaper articles but they told you nothing that you had not known for 17 years. So unless one puts the whole question, a slight misrepresentation is put into the jury's mind. That is the point I am trying to make.

(To the witness): So, Superintendent Eggington, you felt that these charges were so serious that a prosecution should take place?
A: As I said, my Lord, my feelings had nothing to do with this. I was appointed officer in the case to investigate it following the film and the publication of the book and obviously it was done in consultation with the Crown Prosecution Service whose job it was to decide whether or not the prosecution should take place. Obviously, after such a long time this had to be carefully considered.
Q: It must be a consideration?
A: It wasn't my decision.
Q: Of course not, but it must be a consideration. I agree with you. Were the charges less serious, possibly the Crown Prosecution Service would say that after a gap of 25 years we will not go ahead with this but it is because the charges were so serious they agreed to go ahead with the prosecution?
Bevan: My Lord, I am sorry to interrupt. Again, I do not do it out of any sense of rudeness. The decision not to prosecute is not down to the Superintendent.
Alliott: She has just said so.
Bevan: I do not think that this officer should be asked the reasons for or against prosecution because she did not make the decision.
Pottle: No, it was just an observation I passed. It seems to me important what information you give to the CPS. If you do not supply them with any indication that the decision had been taken 17 years earlier to do nothing, then you are only supplying them with half of the case. That case then goes to somebody like Mr Bevan. They then say, this is the evidence against these two men, could you draw up an opinion? There is enough evidence there to prosecute. You then put Mr Bevan in the position that even he doesn't know of the existence of the Watts' report. Even he does not know when he has given his opinion that the decision was taken in 1987. Mr Bevan admitted before Rougier, J, that he had never seen the Watts' report, never heard of it, and in any case that as it touches on national security it is quite reasonable that even the prosecution do not see those documents.
Bevan: There must be a record of what I said or did not say. I am in the difficult position of saying things; I am not trying to give evidence but I have …
Alliott: Mr Bevan, what I have Miss Eggington saying is this, that the CPS was aware of all the facts and information that we have. 'I cannot recall when they were told of the Watts Report but it was at an early stage.' Have I got that right?

Eggington: That's correct, my Lord, yes.
Alliott: As far as this lady is concerned, certainly counsel could not take it further and I do not think that Mr Pottle should.
Eggington: My Lord, perhaps I can add to help there were rumours in the press that the book was going to be published and there were discussions at that early stage with the CPS as to what should happen should this event take place. I am almost certain that they were aware of everything that we had at that date.
Pottle: You are not talking about 1988. The year before you were in fact in charge of the case?
A: You are asking for my …
Q: You mentioned the rumours in the paper about us writing a book in 1988?
A: Yes, if you say so, yes.
Q: And are you seriously now telling this court that in 1988 the CPS were aware of the Watts report?
A: What I am saying, my Lord, is that following this speculation in the press and the fact that there was probably going to be a book written by two people confessing to the crime, then there were discussions. I cannot say whether they saw the Watts' report, but certainly they would be advised of the history and they would have been in discussion.
Q: They would have been told that your department …
A: They would not have been shown the police report because, quite frankly, it is not normal to let police reports on information and speculation go out of the police service.
Q: So you would not present them with the report but you made them aware of the fact that your department had taken the decision not to investigate?
A: I can't tell you what they were being told. They would have been about our suspicions.
Q: So, the position that we are now in 1989 is that the Foreign Office, the Home Office, MI6, MI5, CID and Special Branch are all aware that in 1970 a report is drawn up by Mr Watts clearly implicating Mike and myself in the escape of George Blake. Do you accept that?
A: I don't accept that. I was given a whole list of organisations …
Q: I refer you to the Special Branch letter that shows that copies went off...
A: The copies went to the Security Service, to the Home Office, and to a branch of the Foreign and Commonwealth Office.
Alliott: This is the distribution of the Watts report, is it?

Pottle: Yes, my Lord
Eggington: And to the CID officer who had been the investigation officer.
Pottle: This is a letter, my Lord, written on 18th March, 1970. It is an internal Special Branch memo written by Mr Rollo Watts, Chief Inspector, the chap in charge of the case at that time. He is writing an internal memo to his Acting Commander who I believe at that time was Mr Roger.
Alliott: This a document disclosed to you in the course the abuse of process hearing?
Pottle: Yes. It says, 'Sir, I understand …' And then we have a blanked out name for security reasons. 'I have understood from Box 500 that copies of Seán Bourke's manuscript have been sent to both Home Office and the Foreign Office. In this connection, Mr Fries of the Home Office telephoned me and asked me if a copy of the Special Branch assessment of the manuscript could be forwarded to Sir Philip Allen when completed.' Sir Philip Allen was then, I think, the Permanent Undersecretary at the Home Office. There is then another blanked out name. 'So and so also stated that Mr W … of the information research department at the Foreign Office.' My Lord, the information research office at the Foreign Office is in fact a euphemism for MI6.
A: Can I correct that, my Lord. That is not correct.
Q: This is not correct?
A: No.
Q: 'And asked Box 500 to pass on Special Branch comments about the manuscript in order to assist them to prepare for publication when the book appears.' So the position is that in 1970 the Home Office know, the Foreign Office know, MI6 know?
A: I've no idea if MI6 know.
Q: But MI5 know because, the CID know and of course Special Branch know. So all these different government departments now know that Michael and I are both suspects and that a report has been drawn up clearly implicating …
Alliott: Mr Pottle, just pause a moment. This is in theory cross-examination; that is to say, you asking the lady questions.
Pottle: Well, she indicated …
Alliott: Just a moment, I am trying to make sure that I have her answer. (To the witness): Are you accepting that the Home Office, the Foreign Office, MI5, the CID and the Special Branch all had a copy of the Watts report in 1970?

Eggington: Yes, my Lord.
Alliott: Thank you.
Pottle: So all these departments know of the Watts report and the only government department that does not know is the very department which has to make the decision whether or not to prosecute us?
A: My Lord, can I – because I am not sure how long you are going to go on for – say that it was speculation at that stage. There was absolutely no evidence, and for reasons that I cannot say because I was not there and it is not fully recorded, no further enquiries were made. Therefore, there would have been no reason for the CPS to have had a copy of that report.
Q: Or even Mr Bevan when he's drawing up the case against us?
A: Well he's slipped that one in.
Q: Well, is it a fact?
Alliott: We are dealing at the moment with 1970 and what the witness is saying is that there is no earthly reason for the CPS, if it existed then which it did not, but for the DPP to be informed because there was no question of a prosecution, there being no evidence. If you move on to a later time, please make it plain.
Pottle: Yes. I now want to start taking you through the chronological order of things. You have actually seen the report?
A: Yes, of course.
Q: So if anyone can answer them you actually can?
A: I have tried to remember, my Lord. I have read them but it does not mean I remember.
Pottle: Of course.
Bevan: I am sorry to interrupt but if Mr Pottle is going to embark on the evidence surrounding the abuse of process proceedings …
Pottle: Certainly not. I have no intention of doing so.
Bevan: … I formally object to him doing so because as I have said it is not an issue that this jury have to consider, it having been dealt with fully by another court. I say that I formally make objection to it.
Pottle: I have no intention to doing so, my Lord. Mine is going to be as simple as Mr Bevan was in his opening. (To the witness): I think we are all agreed, Superintendent, that George Blake did in fact escape?

Eggington smiled:

A: There is evidence to that effect, yes.
Q: There is also evidence, is there not, that on 2nd November, ten days after that escape, MI5 ring Special Branch suggesting that they make enquiries into Michael Randle and myself. I will stress again that there is evidence to that effect?

A: You are asking me that question?
Q: Yes?
A: There is a document, a telephone message to show that the names were put up as possible suspects, but you were eliminated almost immediately after a very simple enquiry.
Q: I put it no higher than that on 3rd November, the following day, my photograph is shown around to the last known landlady at the address where Seán Bourke lives?
A: Yes, my Lord, that is true.
Q: And if I can just summarise, the events in 1966, we are both suspects, but we are only two suspects …
A: Yes, hardly in the category of suspects, my Lord. There was an extensive enquiry and anybody who had any possible connection was being considered, so in fact it was more in that light.
Q: We are two possible suspects but among many suspects and in fact police enquiries go off in another direction and any enquiries into Mike and I are then not followed up. But that was, must have happened to a number of other people as well?
A: Yes, there was a very big set of files on this investigation, hundreds of people were interviewed and eliminated.
Q: We were, of course, never interviewed?
A: My Lord, if I can answer this because you keep getting the point in here. You were not interviewed because you didn't emerge into that category, where it was considered necessary.
Q: I accept your point. But in 1966 Michael and I were just very remote suspects because we had actually been in prison with George Blake. I suppose in a way that would make us slight suspects. You receive a telephone call from MI5, suggesting that they show my photograph. That is another point, but it is still not the answer. The only thing …
A: My Lord, can I say that was as a result of some article in the Telegraph … giving your first name, and it was MI5 trying to be helpful, really, saying – 'how about looking at these two?'
Q: Of course, we were possible suspects but we were never interviewed and enquiries went in another direction and we were never actually pursued in that way?
A: That's correct, my Lord.
Q: Now we move to January 1967 and we are just three months and two weeks after the escape and the first hideout is found in Highlever Road. In that hideout three sets of fingerprints are found, one set identified as belonging to George Blake and the others unidentified?

A: That's correct, my Lord.
Q: Nothing else developed in 1967 except that towards the end of that year it becomes clear that George Blake and Seán Bourke are in fact in Moscow. Seán Bourke returns to Ireland in 1968 and he wins his extradition case and in a way the Irish police there, the matter would seem correct.
A: Are you asking me?
Q: I am trying to put to you that that was the position.
A: Yes. My Lord, there were strenuous efforts to extradite Seán Bourke from the Republic of Ireland.
Q: Yes, there were strenuous efforts, as you say …
A: Yes, had Seán Bourke been extradited and brought here, possibly there would have been a case against you two as well.
Q: Whatever for?
A: We would have had the prime witness as well as the suspects.
Q: That's possible, of course, were we suspects. And it would only occur if Seán Bourke came back in 1968 and spilled the beans.
A: My Lord, at this stage Seán Bourke had written the book.
Pottle: He didn't write the book until 1970. We are talking about the extradition in 1968?
A: Oh well, okay, I stand corrected.
Q: Nothing then happened until 1970 and then MI5 obtained a transcript in advance of Seán Bourke's book which was due to be published 5 months later. Is that correct?
A: That's correct, my Lord, although I am not sure exactly of the timescale.
Q: Yes, we don't know exactly when they got it. What we do know is that they wrote to Special Branch, asking your department to read the book and give an assessment of it. On 30th January, 1970 – I think the jury now have these transcripts. On 30th January, MI5 …
Bevan: The jury do not. The documents your Lordship considered ought to be handed to the jury, namely those passages that have been read out during the cross-examination on Friday have been prepared but the jury do not have them. If they could be handed to them now. Does your Lordship have a copy?
Alliott: I have five documents.
Bevan: There are five documents. It would be easier if these documents, as a result of your Lordship's ruling, could be given to the jury and then they will understand the position.

These were then handed to the jury.

Alliott: Members of the jury, can I explain the position. You will remember that on Friday various passages were read to you. It is extremely difficult to follow what issues which you are concerned with those passages relate to. But as they have been read you could not be expected to carry them in your head. I thought it was sensible to rule that they could be added to the documentation you have. It looks as if the first page is the concluding paragraph of the Watts report. You see that is the name of the Chief Inspector.
Pottle: I could refer you to page 4. Have you got a set there?
A: No, I have not, my Lord. (She was handed a copy).
Q: If you could turn to page 4 of those, the original letter from MI5 dated 30th January.
A: Yes, I have it.
Q: It is a letter from an organisation called the 'Box 500' – which is in fact MI5. It is to the Deputy Assistant Commissioner, Special Branch, for the attention of Mr Watts, because it was already established at that stage that Mr Watts had in fact been involved in the original investigations and he would be the liaison officer really between MI5 and Special Branch?
A: My Lord, can I say that Mr Watts would have been one of the many officers involved and he was of a junior level at that stage.
Q: Of course. It says:

'You may wish to have a preview of Seán Bourke's book, The Springing of George Blake. I have been asked to stress that this typescript was received on a confidential basis and we would ask you not to take any action on matters revealed in the typescript or make any enquiry which would reveal that it is in our possession.'

So here MI5 are saying, could you please draw up an assessment but do not make any enquiries which can jeopardise our source?
A: It seems that is what the letter is saying, my Lord.
Q: They do not want the source to be revealed. But as His Lordship I think pointed out on Friday, that does not become a consideration once the book is published?
A: That's correct, my Lord.
Q: On February 25th, 1970 Chief Inspector Watts meets an MI5 officer and brings her up to date with his enquiries. He tells her that he has made tentative identification of Seán Bourke's book and he gives her his handwritten notes in which he identifies Michael and myself. That is this document here. I apologise that we only have a few of them, but this …

Alliott's patience was running out.

> Alliott: Mr Pottle, you have heard me umpteen times state to the jury the issue they will have to decide. What issue does this go to?
> Pottle: The only issue it goes to, my Lord, is just laying out chronologically, because it is a case that is complicated, it is a case that has been going for 25 years. It is not a simple case of did they write a book in 1989 and that is the end of it. For the jury to get the whole case they must know what has happened from 1966 to the present day.
> Alliott: Why?
> Pottle: Because otherwise they are under a complete misapprehension as to what has gone on. You can tell this story in a number of different ways. For instance, I could ask the simple question now and get her answer. Just one simple question and you can object to it afterwards. Superintendent …
> Alliott: (between gritted teeth): What I strongly suspect I shall do is tell you to shut up and sit down. That is what I would if you were counsel. Do you not appreciate that the issue here is not abuse of process which has been adjudicated upon by another court? That was the appropriate court at which to go into the long history of the matter. The crown is saying in this court, read the book, view the television documentary; upon that evidence we invite you the jury to say that these two defendants in your charge committed the acts reflected in the three counts on the indictment. For the last time, that really is the only issue to which you should direct your questions.
> Pottle: My Lord, Mr Bevan gave the chronological history of events from 1966 to 1990 in his opening address. I believe there were a number of omissions from that. I am not putting any interpretation on any of the documents. I am not in any way suggesting abuse. All I am saying is that there were a number of omissions, the jury should know what they are and if they want to put an interpretation on them either way, I am afraid that is out of my control. But they must be allowed to know. If Mr Watts can give a chronological order, surely I can.
> Bevan: I repeat the point I have already made. I have listened to Mr Pottle cross-examining this officer and it must be clear to every individual in this court that what Mr Pottle is aiming at really is this; you the jury should not find us not guilty because this all took place 25 years ago and these proceedings amount to an abuse of process, so find us not guilty. That, in ordinary language, is what Mr Pottle is doing. That is not the issue before this jury. I have said it more than once. The abuse of process proceedings have been adjudicated upon and Mr Pottle's aim in the questions he has asked and indeed the comments he

has made all point to this – Find us not guilty, it was all too long ago. I make my objection to that.
Pottle: It may well be, my Lord, that in my final submission to the jury I may well say that this happened so long ago, forget all about it. That is not what I am talking about now. What I am trying to do is to put before the jury, quite simply, a chronological order of exactly what happened from 1966.
Bevan: My Lord, the chronological order I gave to the jury emanates from the book, and the way I opened the case emanated from that book. The jury have read it and they can judge for themselves.
Pottle: Well, Mr Bevan, you did refer to a number of events in 1970. You did in your evidence, a number of times, refer to Seán Bourke. It seems to me if you can refer to Seán Bourke's book and the possible interpretation of it then surely I can.
Bevan: My Lord, I have made my point.
Alliott: It is extremely difficult, Mr Pottle. You have dispensed with the services of legal counsel deliberately in order to pray in aid the leeway that the courts traditionally give, and you crow in the book about exploiting in your original trial before Mr Justice Havers. I do not want to shut you up lest there be any suggestion of unfairness but the issue is a simple one; are you and Mr Randle telling the truth in the book, are you and Mr Randle telling the truth when you faced the television cameras. If the jury come to the conclusion they are then it may well be that they will not have too much difficulty in deciding their verdict.

I decided to intervene at this point to raise explicitly the abuse of process issue.

Randle: I am sure that is quite possible. Can I just ask a question. If evidence were to come forward relating to the abuse case, surely it would then be incumbent upon you as the judge of this court to reconsider the verdict notwithstanding that it had been heard previously?
Alliott: Mr Randle, this is a trial by jury on specific issues. If there were any reason to reopen the case of abuse, speaking without looking into the matter, I would have thought that should be renewed to another court.
Randle: I think formally the position is that you are entitled to reconsider it … I am not raising it at this point but I think that you are entitled, and therefore if some new evidence were to come out that had not been put before the other court it would be within your power to …

Alliott: I reserve my position on that, as to what I should do were that to happen. At the moment it has not and this is trial by jury on those very simple issues.
Bevan: My Lord, may I say that I have looked up the authority recently and I have a feeling that the question of abuse of process can, in fact, technically be raised at any stage during the course of trial. If that is what these defendants wish to do, an application has to be made to your Lordship to reopen that matter and for such new evidence that appears to exist from what they say, although I am not aware of any, to make that application in the absence of the jury and for your Lordship to hear the abuse of process application itself. That application has not yet been made.
Alliott: It has only been raised this morning for the first time.
Bevan: My Lord, can I say this, perhaps to assist the defendants. They made the application with regard to the abuse of process at the outset of these proceedings, put down their marker.
Alliott: I recall that but I did not realise that it was suggested that there was 'fresh evidence.' Fresh evidence has only been referred to this morning.
Randle: If it emerged.
Bevan: They made the application … they put down their marker. But if they are going to renew the abuse of process application on the basis that there is fresh evidence that is not a matter that concerns this jury. It would concern your Lordship, of course, and the matter would be dealt with.
Pottle: At some stage during this hearing we may well put an application to his Lordship on abuse of process. At the moment we are not doing that.
Bevan: My Lord, I can say no more.

Pat continued to probe the contents of the disclosed documents, emphasising again that no investigation was carried out after Watts had made his report and this had been circulated to various police and government departments. Eggington played her part skilfully, on the one hand repeatedly querying the relevance of Pat's questions, on the other hand trying to limit the influence they might have on the jury. Thus she described Inspector Watts as 'a junior officer' in MI5 in 1970, one of several officers who would have been looking into the Blake escape. (In fact Watts was not as junior as all that and had been specifically assigned the task of reading and evaluating Seán Bourke's book and writing a report which would be highly praised and sent to MI5, the Home Office and elsewhere.) Miss A was 'a junior officer' in MI5, and her Note for File was 'purely a note' of a 'conversation that had taken place between two individuals off the record if you like.' (But Miss A, however junior, was the MI5 officer assigned the task of liaising with Watts and reporting back to her superiors.) When Pat got on to the letter dated 7th May 1970 which a senior MI5 officer had written to the acting head of Special Branch, Commander Cunningham, Eggington overplayed her hand.

> **Pottle: We now go on to May 7th. MI5 are now writing in response to having received the Watts report. They received it on March 23rd and we are now on May 7th. They are responding to that report. We should bear in mind that in that period Mr Watts has already seen the MI5 officer of which she recorded the note for the file. So MI5 are fully aware of paragraph 2 in the notes?**
> **A: My Lord, if I can explain. This was a note by an individual junior MI5 officer and I cannot say that the writer of that letter was aware of this note.**
> **Q: Oh, now that's interesting. The writer of this letter which is now going to the head of Special Branch in response to the Watts report, may never have seen the note for file?**
> **A: Possibly not because I don't think it is relevant, quite frankly.**
> **Q: You were in court with all of us in the High Court on the abuse hearing, Superintendent. Do you remember Mr Arthur Cunningham the head of Special Branch?**
> **A: Yes, my Lord, I know Mr Cunningham.**
> **Q: Mr Cunningham, in his evidence, said that he was rung up by Miss A's section boss, we'll call him Mr B …**
> **A: Yes.**
> **Q: … Who said – Look, I just read Miss A's note and I'm a bit worried about it – that it means what it says. And Mr Cunningham said – 'My God, no, it's a load of old codswallop. Mr Watts didn't say that at all and if he did say that he shouldn't have said it, it's all a big mistake.' So clearly the section commander who is writing this response from MI5 had seen the note because according to Mr Cunningham he rang Mr Cunningham up about it and said – 'What's going on?'**
> **Alliott: Now just where are we getting to? This is your commentary – it may well be accurate I know not – of what transpired in another hearing relating to a document that the jury and I have not seen.**
> **Pottle: Sure.**
> **Alliott: We are going into a very difficult situation.**
> **Pottle: My Lord, Superintendent Eggington inferred that the person who wrote this letter was unaware of the note for file, or might have been.**

Eggington: My Lord, I accept what Mr Pottle has said about what happened at the proceedings, but I think the point I would like to make is that this had no real relevance. This was merely a note by an individual, junior officer of MI5, a note of accommodation, as was her habit to make.
Pottle: And it's the only note within the file that says anything like that. It gives the position, as told by Mr Watts, in 1970?
A: My Lord, it gives the position of a private conversation – which is this writer's interpretation of that conversation. There is nothing in Special Branch records to reflect this information, or in police records.
Pottle: I think you will recall that Miss A says in her evidence that it was routine to make these notes on file of meetings that took place. She has already made another one which I referred to earlier, on 25th February, so that she was the liaison officer between MI5 and Special Branch and when she had a meeting, or a telephone call from Special Branch, she would report and say this is what I said, this is what he said. That is what files are for. The files are so if I come along and know nothing about the case, I could read it and know about it. Would you accept that?
A: That is the object of a file, to give some indication of the subject matter, yes.
Q: So I do not think there is any dispute. We now get on to 7th May. We finally get the long awaited response from MI5. You will remember that Special Branch had made a decision not to do anything until they get this response. In fact, this letter is no more than a thank you letter for sending the report attached to the letter of 23rd March. 'We find the whole report extremely interesting and were very impressed by the highly likely speculative identification.' Paragraph 5, 'Unfortunately, for this very reason, we too have been unable to find any collateral to back up the suggested identification. So MI5 would have to say, 'Look, we like your identifications, we think they are very good, but we as an organisation cannot supply you with any evidence that may back up your suspicions?'
A: That seems to be the case. Yes.
Q: And they thank you again for the most excellent report. We agree that it provides the most acceptable explanation of events after the escape. Nowhere within that letter do they comment on the Note for File. Nowhere do they say we agree with your note and with Mr Watts.
A: Is this what you have just read out?
Q: They don't say, 'We disagree'; they say nothing. May, 1970, an internal memo sent around to various departments. Mr Rollo Watts

has now read the response from MI5 and he recalls in a memo which he sent round to all department heads, 'Box 500 appear to agree with the identifications in theory but are unable to add anything further. Apart from the warrants for Bourke's arrest which remain outstanding, the matter would seem to rest here. Do you accept that?

A: I accept that, my Lord.

Q: And of course there the matter did rest?

A: Yes; until 1987.

Q: And the kinds of consideration as to whether the matter should be left there aren't just simple ones. There are a number of political considerations too. As pointed out, think, and the jury saw, Mr Richard Helms on the TV documentary …

A: My Lord, can I interrupt here. There were no political considerations.

Q: You mean you have found things like that in the past?

A: There was certainly no indication in any of the files of any political considerations. It was purely a criminal matter, but obviously of interest to the Security Service.

Q: I mean you can say that with a certain authority?

A: I can say that with all the authority of having read all the files.

Q: You can't answer a lot of the other questions I have put to you, of course, with that same authority, because you tell me you don't know, but this one you can?

Bevan: With respect to Mr Pottle, I think that is an unfair question he has certainly put to the officer now. If Mr Pottle remembers when he was asking why things were not done in 1970, I got up and objected on the basis of how could the witness speculate as to what was in the … mind of the officer in 1970. To say now that she can answer this question and she cannot answer the others, with respect to Mr Pottle, seems a bit unfair.

Pottle: I apologise and I withdraw that remark. But I will refer you to what Mr Helms said on the television programme. I will start with the commentary and then go to Mr Helms. 'The rift between the intelligence of Britain and America brought about by the Blake escape took months longer to repair.'

'The reaction was how in the world did the British Authority …'

Alliott: There is a limit to the leeway, you know. This cannot be the subject of a question to this witness.

Pottle: My Lord, I was only trying to establish that when one has to make a decision of this kind in 1970 and your Lordship has to bear in mind, it seems to me, that MI5 are involved and when MI5 are

involved on any case it does take on political connotations … And one of the considerations surely must have been the relationship between MI5, MI6 and the CIA which we know, certainly according to Mr Helms in that film – relationships had suffered. That is a consideration when you are determining whether … Perhaps I can put it better, my Lord. I think the public conception at that time, 1966, was that this escape was remarkably organised by the KGB, if not by the KGB, then they were somewhere, they were behind the scenes. If I could ask Superintendent Eggington this, I believe that a Mr Marchant drew up a report, I think it was on the third of the fourth, 1967, which was referred to by Mr Bird in his later statement in 1989, that in fact, the public view and the police view at that time was that this escape had been organised very likely by Seán Bourke but with the help of a country hostile to the interests of the United Kingdom. I think that was the general view at the time?
A: Mr Marchant was the Detective Superintendent in C Department, as it was then known, of Scotland Yard. He was a crime investigator who wasn't a member of Special Branch, he was the officer in the case in the Blake escape, and if you say that is what he concluded, it probably was.
Q: I think that would fit in with the general idea around the world...
A: The mystery, I think, was my reading.
A: Yes, I think in general one had thought it was something that had been organised by the KGB?
A: There are all sorts of rumours and speculation which could be still around, I think.
Q: But in general one could say that the feeling was that somewhere behind the scenes you have this big organisation, very powerful, money in their pockets and they are up against another powerful organisation, one's the KGB, one's MI6. Possibly in MI6 minds, the KGB did it. Okay, this time we've lost one. Some you lose, some you win, next time it will be our turn, but that was the general view at the time, that it was a KGB operation?
Alliott: Miss Eggington has agreed that the escape was organised by Bourke with help from a hostile power.
Pottle: I think so.
Alliott: I think you have that answer from the lady already.
Pottle: If you could narrow the field, of course, that in fact the escape wasn't organised by the KGB but was organised by the Lavender Hill mob, the kind of relationship that Mr Helms was talking about on that TV programme would once again come into play, 'My God, they've

done it again.' You see we are talking about the sixties. We are talking about a whole period of Burgess, Maclean, Philby, Blunt, the Portland Spy Ring, the Christine Keeler affair, the Blake escape, Gordon Lonsdale, there's even talk of the top people in MI5 being Russian spies. Then this follows on. Relationships with the CIA have already reached rock bottom. Now, in 1970, to say to the Americans, look, this in fact was organised by two ban the bombers and an Irishman, not the KGB, that might be a consideration, and there's a kind of political situation I mentioned to you earlier. Do you think that would have been a consideration not to investigate?
A: Can I say, my Lord, that had your points been relevant then I imagine that no steps would have been taken by the police to try to extradite Seán Bourke. But there were strenuous efforts to extradite him and clearly one assumes he would certainly have been prosecuted had he been brought here and probably found guilty.
Q: Whatever the situation was in 1970, a decision was made not to investigate and that is the end of the affair?
A: The decision was made not to investigate any more at that stage.
Q: And of course it is not in a way just at that stage, unless, of course, you are saying to yourself we'll prosecute in 20 years time. You would not have had that in your mind in 1970. Once you made the decision that you are not going to do something in 1970, that in reality is the end of the affair.
A: My Lord, it certainly is not the end of the affair. It means what it says, at that stage, at present I think were the words used. It could be reopened at any time, which it was in 1987 and then again in 1989.
Q: We'll move on from that now. The whole affair now remains dormant for the next 17 years. No evidence comes to light for 17 years to help a prosecution, is that it?
A: I can't quite recall – no evidence, certainly, no.
Q: No. We all heard Inspector Crampton's evidence on Friday, including yourself, and she interviewed us in 1987 but admitted that she had made no attempt to interview other people named in those newspaper articles who could possibly have evidence to help the police. Do you remember her saying that?
A: I think she said that, my Lord, but without the record I wouldn't like to put words in her mouth.

Eggington in response to further questions stated that she had taken charge of the investigation in late April 1989, the day after the Thames Television documentary in which we featured. She had then read our book, and continued her investigations over the May bank holiday weekend. It was at this stage that she first saw the Watts' report.

Pottle: And of course you realised over that weekend that the Watts report had been drawn up at the request of MI5?
A: Yes, my Lord.
Q: Did you ask …
A: Only because, my Lord, they had the manuscript. They sent us the manuscript to ask for our views, for no other sinister reason.
Q: So after you realised in fact that MI5 has asked Special Branch in 1970 to draw up this assessment, did you then go to see MI5 and consult with them? I am talking about over that weekend or just after it, in 1989?
A: Specifically about the Watts Report?
Q: Not specifically about the Watts report but you realised, in fact, that the whole thing had been started off by MI5 because you had read the Watts report. So surely you must say to yourself, my God, MI5 are involved in this case, I better go and have a word with them.
A: My Lord, I was in contact with MI5. I can't remember, it would have been early the following morning after the bank holiday. I wanted to know, I asked the case officer, whether there was anything in the MI5 records that would assist me in my investigation and I wanted to know in effect whether there was anything politically sensitive that I should be aware of because my concern was that I would embark on a criminal investigation and then subsequent evidence or information would come to light which would embarrass the Crown and me and so on, so I took it upon myself to establish that there was nothing, no cover up if you want to put it in simple terms.
Q: So when you did speak to them and ask if there were any documents that could become embarrassing, any political considerations that you had not thought of, did they show you the files?
A: No, my Lord. Apparently that particular note was filed under some other, unrelated documents, and that is why it came to light later during the abuse process proceedings. It came as a surprise to myself and to everybody because it wasn't in the file MI5 had on their files of the case.
Q: You had, at that stage, no idea that that note on the file existed. It wasn't in fact in the file?
A: No, my Lord. Well, it wasn't readily available, it seems.
Q: Were there to have been in the file, were you to have read that paragraph 2, would that in any way have influenced your decision to recommend a prosecution?

A: I think what I can say is that if I had seen that I would certainly have made enquiries to see if that had any basis of truth, but I might say that at those early stages I took upon myself to speak to as many people as possible: officers who had been on the case, junior officers, senior officers, everybody I could get hold of really, to get their opinion as to what was the fact, and why no detailed enquiries had been made, and I was assured that there was absolutely no cover up at all.
Q: But you were not told about the note in the file. None of the people you spoke to could recollect ever seeing it in the file?
A: No. As I say, I had made enquiries from MI5 it was in their files, and they assured me there was nothing. As I said before, my Lord, this was merely a note. It is a note of a remembered conversation, an impression, and ex-Chief Inspector Watts himself has given evidence in the Divisional Court that he doesn't recall saying this. I spoke to Mr Watts early, obviously, having read his report. He was one of the first people I contacted to get his recollection of the case; no suggestion at all that this was his view or the Special Branch view.
Q: But of course he does not ever remember having the conversation at all, is that not true?
A: That's right, my Lord, but …
Q: As to what he said or didn't say …
Bevan: Could the witness finish the answer, if it is allowed.
Pottle: Yes, of course.
A: In the evidence he gave he said he could not remember this conversation, it was indeed a long time ago, but I would have assumed …

Once again Mr Justice Alliott, intervened in exasperation:

Alliott: I am sorry interrupting you, Miss Eggington, but this really is very unsatisfactory. You are not honouring the ruling I made. You are going into the abuse process by the back door.
Pottle: Okay, my Lord, I am sorry. I apologise for that. I thought we were getting on quite nicely.
Alliott: As long as we let you have your head you ramble on all over the place. It is only when we try and keep you to the issues that …
Bevan: The only disagreement that I have is with the back door; I would have said the front door.
Pottle: I've nearly finished. I've only a couple of questions to go. It seemed to me Superintendent Eggington had been shown the MI5 files, not necessarily been shown the files, been assured that there is nothing in them?

A: My Lord, I have not seen the files. I have been shown what they say they have in them.
Q: Sure. And in what they showed you there is nothing that can help you, or for you to determine whether there's a cover-up going on, whether a decision has been taken, whether it is politically – you don't know. They're giving you the information that …
Bevan: I am sorry, my Lord, I am sure that Mr Pottle appreciates that Mr Havers, acting as amicus, actually went through the MI5 file. I did not, but Mr Havers did. So it is not a question of a cover-up in the sense of MI5 saying you can't see it. Mr Havers, during the Divisional Court hearing I think said, I will be corrected if I am wrong …
Pottle: Yes, he said that he …
Bevan: Said that he himself had gone through the files to make sure, as counsel, that that was the position. It was not a question of MI5 saying that they would not give access. I personally did not see the files.
Alliott: Can I just explain to the jury. The Crown sometimes wears more than one hat and Mr Bevan is wearing the Crown's hat as prosecutor. On this occasion another barrister, from my chambers as a matter of fact, called Havers was appointed to act as *amicus curiae*, friend of the court, to deal with this particular issue, and he it was, apparently, who went through the files and gave the assurance that there was nothing else there. It is done this way so that Mr Bevan would not be embarrassed by wearing two hats on behalf of the Crown. A separate barrister is appointed to look into it.
Pottle: Thank you, my Lord. Certainly Mr Havers, I remember quite clearly, gave an absolute assurance that there was nothing within the MI5 files that in any way affect our case. But it is, of course, after he gave that assurance that the Note for File was produced which I believe came from another file.
Bevan: My Lord, we have heard evidence that came, Mr Pottle may remember, I shall certainly never forget, 4.13 one afternoon when that document was handed to me and I indicated to the court in the presence of both Mr Randle and Mr Pottle that this document had come into my possession. The Court immediately must look at it and indeed the Court did. That document surfaced during the Divisional Court proceedings and as Miss Eggington has said, came out not of the file one would have expected it to come out of but a different file.
Alliott: Not the file Mr Havers was speaking of but some other file?
Bevan: That is right.
Randle: There is just one point of fact there. I was not in court at that stage, I was in hospital.

Pottle: The position is, anyway, that the note, at some later stage, is produced from another file. You had no knowledge, at that time that the note ever existed, prior to the hearing at the high court?
A: No, my Lord. And I might say the fact it was on an unrelated file shows how little importance was attached to it.
Q: Well, now, you see once you start speculating about how important that document is, who drew it up, what was the rank of the officer who drew it up, then I must be allowed to get in, but because his Lordship has ruled, I am not going to pursue that.
Alliott: That is very gracious of you.
Pottle: I just have a couple of questions left. Has the fact that it was George Blake who we broke out of prison played any part in your decision to investigate and submit the case to the CPS?
A: I don't … the fact is it was George Blake and the fact is that you wrote a book and said you did it and you appeared on the file. That was the reason I was appointed to investigate. I can't speculate on whether it was a small time criminal escaping 25 years ago.
Q: So if, for instance, it was Joe Bloggs we had broken out 25 years ago and written a book about it, would you have felt that the case was so serious that it merited prosecution 25 years after it was committed?
A: My Lord, this is purely speculation, and the fact is that it wasn't.
Alliott: The answer I have written down, anticipating it, if it was a small time criminal you sprang you might not have been prosecuted. Is that fair?
Eggington: Possibly, my Lord, yes.
Pottle: Thank you very much, Superintendent. I'll sit down.

Pat had brought out and emphasised the essential points, so my cross examination was much briefer. I chiefly wanted to do some further preparatory work for our planned application for the abuse of process issue to be re-heard.

Randle: You will be pleased to hear that I have very few questions. It emerged in the cross-examination by Mr Pottle that the note of the file from MI5 on 29th April, 1970, did not come into your possession until long after we had been charged?
A: Yes, my Lord. It was as Mr Bevan said. I saw it the same time as him at 4.13 in the afternoon.
Q: So at the time that you made your report to CPS the CPS would not have had the benefit of that document in coming to their decision?
A: No, my Lord. Had they had it I am confident that it would have made no difference at all because it has no relevance.
Q: That is a judgment which perhaps a court of law will determine or this ought to be the subject of some consideration not simply of an

individual opinion, namely, the significance of that document and how it would have affected the case. There is certainly room for speculation there, is there not. I mean it is not a cut and dried issue. If the CPS considering a case that was more than 20 years old had seen a note from MI5 saying that the big fish had got away and there was clear evidence of the escape at that time it is really taking a very big step to say that this would not have affected their decision?
A: My Lord, the CPS was aware of the information we had on record so that a decision had been taken in 1970 not to proceed further. This note is merely a record of a conversation and somebody's private view. If Mr Watts had expressed that view that would have been his private view and it was not a policy decision or the view of Special Branch as such.
Q: It is some evidence that there might have been a policy decision. Did Miss A say that it was the normal practice when she appeared at the abuse process and judicial review, did she or did she not say that it was normal practice to make such notes of the developments in a case?
A: I am aware that she said that it was normal practice. It is whether it was for her or – I think probably for her, on my understanding.
Q: As I understand it, and we can refer if necessary to the transcript of that court, she was saying quite clearly – and I have a very distinct recollection of it – that it was normal practice, not that it was a private obsession of hers to make a private note, but that when something happened within the Service to have a note of that conversation. After all, that would seem the logical thing to do, otherwise important pieces of information might get lost, is that not so?
A: My Lord, I can't say. I think she probably did say that, but I can't remember. Certainly if I made a practice of making a note of a conversation –I just wouldn't do it myself.
Q: No. But perhaps this was sufficiently important that she did make that note?
A: That is her recollection of a conversation.
Q: And it was a contemporaneous note, done that evening or the following day. Is that correct?
A: From the date she is talking about, the 29th, she said it was yesterday, so.
Q: If we look again at the Code for Crown prosecutors, they have to take a number of things into consideration and what must be decided at different times. They would certainly have to take that note into account however important or otherwise they thought it to be.
A: My Lord, MI5 are not investigators. They have nothing to do with

the criminal process. They have nothing … to do with the criminal process and what they have recorded on this branch note or note for the file would have absolutely no bearing on the Crown Prosecution's decision.

Q: Nevertheless, Miss A did say in her evidence that it was inconceivable at that time that a prosecution would have gone ahead without consultation with MI5. Again we can, you know, if necessary, we can adjourn and produce the …

Bevan: I am sorry.

Randle: I am saying we do have the transcript of Miss A's evidence and if necessary we can refer to it, but maybe it is common ground between us that she did say this.

Bevan: My Lord, I am standing here now and can't remember what Miss A said in the course of those proceedings.

Alliott: No. It is quite apparent that that relates to the abuse process. We keep returning to it.

Bevan: My Lord, I've said it before, we seem to have entered the house, I would submit through the front door as opposed to the back door. Now we are inside the house. I repeat what I have already said. The court heard evidence surrounding the letter; I call it the fish letter, the document Mr Randle is referring to. The court heard Miss A give evidence. There is no doubt a transcript of her evidence. The Crown position was that if the Divisional Court were of the view on the evidence that a decision had been made in 1970 not to prosecute these two individuals for whatever reason, then the abuse of process application would be upheld. The Divisional Court, having heard all the evidence from Mr Cunningham, Miss A the writer of that letter, came to a different view and that was the adjudication that no decision had in fact been made in 1970, having heard all the evidence. Therefore the application regarding the abuse of process proceeding was dismissed. That is the position. My Lord, I can only repeat what I said earlier. This is not an issue for this jury to consider.

Randle: You said earlier, Mr Bevan, that you will not forget that [note]. In fact it is so clearly imprinted on your head that you can even give us to the minute the time it came forward. So you attached considerable importance to that conversation, did you not?

Bevan: As far as the Crown are concerned it must be obvious to the jury and everybody in this court that I attach enormous significance to that document because if a policy decision had been made in 1970 I, on behalf of the Crown, would have said it is unfair to go ahead now. I said that in court and I have never resiled from that position and it is contained in the judgment.

Randle: Well …
Bevan: Can I just finish? The court decided, having heard all the evidence, that no policy decision had been made in 1970 not to prosecute these two defendants, for whatever reason. The document lay at the heart of that matter, and indeed at the heart of Mr Randle's and Mr Pottle's application, not surprisingly.
Randle: In view of that reassurance that you gave then and which you have now repeated and in view of this Note for File, I invite you now to drop this case.
Bevan: This is an abuse of process application which has been heard by a court and the court has decided that this is not an abuse of process, namely this prosecution. They have heard all the evidence surrounding it and this case has to go on.
Randle: I return to the point of consultations with MI5. We can, as I say, refer to the …
Alliott: I remind of what you were putting. You were suggesting to this witness that Miss A in the Divisional Court hearing had said it was inconceivable the prosecution would go ahead without consultation with MI5.
Randle: Yes, that's right.
Alliott: Have you a recollection of something like that being said.
Eggington: I have a vague recollection, my Lord, I think that's quite probably that in 1970 there would have been consultation, but certainly MI5 wouldn't have dictated whether or not a prosecution should go ahead.
Randle: They would not have dictated it but they would have been consulted and indeed you yourself consulted MI5 very early on, you told us that?
A: Certainly, my Lord, because it was … George Blake was spying and therefore I knew that they would have some records on that at least.
Q: I now want to refer to a statement by Lord Denning, the former Master of the Rolls. This is the 1960 report on the Profumo affair. He said, 'The Security …'
Alliott: Put it in the form of a question.
Randle: Are you aware of the statement by Lord Denning, the former Master of the Rolls in the 1963 Profumo affair, and I quote, 'The Security Service in this country is not established by statute, nor is it recognised by common law. Even the Official Secrets Acts do not acknowledge its existence. The members of the Security Service are, in the eyes of the law, ordinary citizens with no powers greater than anyone else. They have no special powers of arrest such as the

police have. They cannot enter premises without the consent of the householder, even though they may suspect a spy is there.' Are you aware of that document?
A: I remember reading those words, my Lord. I can't recall it in that document.
Q: I am actually quoting from Lord Denning, Master of the Rolls in the 1963 report of the Profumo affair. So that was the position at that point, that MI5 had no position within the law or the constitution?
A: That is correct, my Lord.
Q: So as far as the constitution or the law was concerned these were a bunch of individuals?
A: I suppose you might deduce that, yes, my Lord.
Q: And yet senior officers like yourself are not allowed to go directly to see the files of these individuals. You have to take their word?
A: My Lord, I don't think that I can really answer questions on this. The fact is, no, I've never seen MI5 files. That's the answer.
Q: Even though these are files of individuals who, as Lord Denning says, have no special position within the law or the constitution?
A: I have never seen MI5 files as such.
Q: Just picking up on one or two points that came up earlier. You know, there is general agreement that the decision was taken in 1970 not to interview us; that comes from the Watts report and the other reports at that time. There was a decision at that time not to interview us?
A: Yes, my Lord.
Q: And we have heard evidence that the reason for that – either the reason or excuse given for that – was that we probably would not answer questions and it would turn into a fruitless task?
A: That's what other people have said, my Lord, yes.
Q: Are you aware that George Blake – that there was no evidence against George Blake, enough to bring him to court, until he was …
A: I don't know the details of the George Blake investigation, my Lord.
Q: But it was a confession on his part, was it not, that led to the trial in this court some 30 years ago?
A: I am aware that he pleaded guilty, my Lord.
Q: In fact, it was only when he was being interviewed that he broke down. I don't know that he broke down, but at a certain point he confessed that he had been involved in passing information to the KGB. I think that is a matter of record?
A: If you say so, yes.
Q: I just want to return, once again, to the facts and I will ask you

once again, am I right in saying that CPS did not have the benefit of seeing Miss A's note for file in which she talked the big fish and the little fish? They did not have the benefit of that when they made the decision to bring this prosecution?

Bevan: My Lord, I can make an admission as to that. The decision when this prosecution was launched and the committal proceedings took place and the defendants appeared before the Court, I on behalf of the Crown did not know of the existence of that note and it surfaced during the abuse proceedings.

Alliott interrupted to say that a chronology of the dates of the hearings in connection with the case would be useful, and Bevan undertook to provide this, including the date on which the 4.13 note appeared. My final few questions concerned the Montgomery Hyde book which had led us to being publicly named, but which Eggington said she had not read. Finally I asked her about the bail we had been granted from the period immediately following our arrest.

Randle: When we were arrested you did not raise objection to bail, did you?

A: No, my Lord

Q: And it was completely unconditional bail?

A: Yes, my Lord

Q: And you did not ask for our passports to be confiscated or any restrictions to be put on our movements?

A: No, my Lord, I don't think I did.

Q: Did you at any stage become aware that we were travelling abroad while on bail?

A: I believe you went to Southern Ireland, if I remember rightly, and also you went to Russia.

Q: That's right, yes. You weren't worried that we were going to go to Russia and not come back?

A: No, my opinion was, my Lord, that you were very keen to stand trial and tell the world what you had done.

Q: I don't know where you got the impression we were very keen from. I wish I could disabuse you of that feeling at the time because maybe you could have said, these two men have suffered enough, let's drop it. (Pat had used those very words to her at the end of our second interview in June 1989). No, I mean, we weren't keen to be prosecuted. We were keen for the truth to be out in the open and we would much prefer it if once it was out in the open that nothing more was done. I can assure you we are trying to make the best of the situation now that we are here but it was not our wish that we should be standing in the dock.

A: Perhaps I should say that I was pretty sure that you wouldn't run away.
Q: Right, fine, okay. So in a certain strange way you trusted us and trusted what was said and what you already knew about us?
A: I believed what you said, yes and I didn't think you would do a bunk.
Randle: Thank you, no more questions.

Inspector Bird took the stand. He confirmed in a brief examination-in-chief conducted by Calvert-Smith that he was one of the officers that had gone to my house on 3rd and 4th May and was also concerned to produce exhibits from various other sources.

Pat again opened the cross-examination, establishing that Bird had drawn up a report on the history of the case from the time of Blake's escape in 1966, and had subsequently, on the instructions of Mr Justice Rougier, produced a supplement listing the documents he had consulted in doing so. He established also that Bird had been charge of the investigation from the time it was re-opened in January 1989 until Eggington took over in late April, and questioned him about people he had or had not interviewed.

Q: Did you at that time look at the queries that had been raised by Inspector Crampton 18 months earlier?
A: I probably did.
Q: And do you think you read the report which prompted her to make raise these questions in the first place?
A: I believe I did.
Q: Did you come across, while reading those newspaper articles a list of 12 or 14 people all of whom according to the articles had information to give to the police?
A: I probably did. I can't recall definitely.
Q: And did you think, 'My God, why didn't Inspector Crampton go and visit these people? God knows she's made a mess up there. I'll go and do it now.' Did you do that?
A: I can't recall. I made my enquiries that I needed to make.
Q: You refer in your report to a newspaper article which came out in November in the Observer where, for the first time, according to your report, Michael and I admitted that we broke George Blake out of jail and that we were going to write a book about it. Do you remember that article?
A: I remember the article, yes.
Q: Did you interview the reporter who wrote the article?
A: No.
Q: You are now in charge, and the DPP has reopened the case. Days

after he reopens the case, Mr Barrie Penrose, in the *Sunday Times*, writes the article about the Blake escape in which he names a Dr Comfort. Do you recall that article?

A: Yes, I do.

Q: In that article he says, if anybody has been contacted by the police interested in Dr Comfort because he can actually prove that Michael Randle approached him for money prior to the break and so if the police are looking for evidence, this is the most important witness they can get. Did you go to see that doctor?

A: Yes.

Q: Did you interview him?

A: Yes.

Q: What did he say?

A: That he denied the report in the press.

Q: He denied ever writing the report for the Telegraph?

A: He denied saying the words that he said that were reported to him in the Times.

Q: Did you, at that stage, go to see Mr John Papworth?

A: Yes.

Q: And his response was …

A: On instructions given to him he refused to answer all questions, or allow an interview to be conducted …

Pottle: So we are now at this stage. You say that as far as 16 people, excluding Michael and myself, have now been named by the police as people helping with enquiries and as far as you are able to remember you have only interviewed two. Why not interview the others?

A: At that stage the enquiries that I was conducting required the questions to be asked of the people that I had asked.

Q: I go along with that. I am not knocking it. But it just seems to me that you have 14 names of people here. Why did you not interview them?

A: Because I didn't think it was necessary.

Q: The most important one mentioned in the newspaper report was the man who gave Montgomery Hyde the information for his book. His name is Nicholas Walter. He was named twice in 1987. He was named in 1988. He was named in 1989. Did you get in touch with him?

A: Yes.

It was a confident answer. But Pat had information that would rattle Bird.

Q: Can you tell the court when you interviewed him?

Clearly embarrassed, Bird said he would need to consult his pocket note book. Pat persisted:

Q: Wasn't it two weeks ago?[1]

A: Yes, about two weeks.

Q: So for the last three and a half years this man had been portrayed as somebody who had information that could probably be of help to your enquiries and you ring him two weeks ago and you speak to him on the telephone?

A: Yes.

Q: You haven't interviewed him, you haven't questioned him. Why not?

A: Because I didn't think he would be able to give me evidence. In fact, he couldn't.

Q: If you don't know what he has, how can you say that you are not going to see him?

A: I didn't think he had any and he didn't give me any information.

Q: It seems to me that you are taking the same line that people took in 1970, we are not going to try and gather evidence because there might not be any there. Isn't that, in reality, what you are saying now?

A: I don't know what people did in 1970. I tell you what I did.

Q: And what you did was to say, 'I'm not going to interview these people because I don't think they have any evidence,' without even knowing what they might have. Is that not the case?

A: Not entirely, no. I think you are misconstruing the situation.

Q: I am just about to finish. Can I refer you to the last paragraph of your report in November 1988. Articles appeared in the Sunday Times and the Observer, newspapers in which it was recorded that Randle and Pottle confessed. They are the articles we have just been talking about.

A: Quite.

Q: And that they had assisted Blake to escape and were proud of what they had done. Consequently, a number of MPs signed a motion urging that they should not be permitted to gain from their alleged crime by publishing a book about the escape. Now here you are being asked to draw up a summary of a police investigation. 110 MPs have signed a motion calling for our – I mean, you saw that as important?

A: No, I saw that as part of the reiterating for the benefit of the court the history of the case. I didn't view that as important.

Q: So you thought it was relevant?

1 The official transcript omits Pat's question `Can you tell the court when you interviewed him?' but it was in fact this question that prompted Bird to say he wanted to consult his pocket book.

A: Just reiterating what had happened over the course of the case, no more than that.

Q: I see. Thanks very much, Inspector.

I took up where Pat had left off:

Randle: I just want to follow up from that last point You thought that the fact that these MPs – I believe they were all Conservatives – had put down this motion calling for us to be prosecuted. You thought that was a relevant consideration which should go into your report?

Bird: I thought it relevant to give the history of the case.

Q: And you saw that as a relevant part, otherwise it was irrelevant?

A: If it was irrelevant it would not be there. It was part of the history of the case.

Q: Can you say it is a relevant part?

A: A part of the history of the case.

Q: If it was not relevant it would not be there?

A: It was put in purely and simply to assist the court to understand the history of the case.

Q: I am sure we have all got the point that you thought it was relevant and part of the history of the case.

A: It was part of the history of the case.

Q: One other small point. You said that you were on the case after the DPP reopened it in January 1989, and you carried out a number of interviews at that time, am I correct?

A: Yes.

Q: Can I remind you that you saw Professor O'Connell between then and when the book was published?

A: Yes.

Q: Yes. So on the basis of newspaper reports and on the basis perhaps of what has been said in the House of Commons. The case was reopened even though the book had not been published. You had to carry on investigating?

A: Maybe for some preliminary enquiries, yes.

Q: You said that you were a person on the case but I think you said that you were not in charge of the case?

A: No.

Q: Who was in charge of the case at that point?

A: At that point?

Q: Yes?

A: I believe I was in charge at that particular point, but …

Q: Your Lordship, I have nothing further. Thank you.

The court adjourned for lunch, and the afternoon began with the prosecution putting in evidence a number of items found in Pat's house or mine. The Items included Exhibit 15, a letter from Clive Edwards of Thames Television dated 14 November 1988, Exhibit 17, part of a print-out of Chapter 1 of The Blake Escape and other sundry papers, and exhibit 29, a copy of the Contract between Harrap and ourselves for the publication of the book. Two statements by a fingerprint expert, Irving, were also read out indicating that one print taken from 28 Highlever Road in January 1967 was that of George Blake, and that two other sets of prints had not been identified. We did not contest the validity of any of these items and Calvert-Smith was content for them simply to be put in evidence at that point, though adding that 'a detailed look at some of the documents may be necessary, depending on what defences may emerge.' The judge carefully explained the procedure to the jury:

> **Alliott: You follow the point, members of the jury. We have the provenance of these documents and Mr Calvert-Smith is saying that we shall wait to see whether we have to look at them in any detail. They have gone in evidence in that very swift way because the defendants have agreed that it can be done that way.**

Alliott then ascertained that Pat and myself did not want to have any other prosecution witness statements read and Bevan rose to say that this concluded the case for the Crown.

Chapter 20:

Self-incrimination I: Pat testifies

Our defence opened with Pat telling the judge that we would have completed our defence by lunchtime next day. He then took the stand and affirmed that he would tell the truth rather than swearing by Almighty God on the Bible.

> Pottle: I would just like to say to the court that I believe that anyone who was involved in the escape of George Blake bears no guilt and has no shame because the sentence …
> Alliott: Just a moment, I have to take a note.
> Pottle: Oh, you're writing it down?
> Alliott: Yes.
> Pottle: … would have no guilt or shame for what they did. I consider breaking George Blake out of prison to be a decent humanitarian act. That's all I have to say in relation to the statement. Thank you.
> Alliott: Then Mr Randle, it is for you to cross-examine first.
> Randle: Good afternoon, Mr Pottle. Were you born in 1938?
> Pottle: Yes, that's correct.
> Q: Had your family a long history of involvement with radical politics?
> A: Yes. My great-great-grandfather, for instance, was one of the leaders of the Chartist movement. He in fact was responsible for having Karl Marx thrown out of the labour movement. My great-grandfather owned a plot of land down in Brighton which included a stretch of beach which he refused to pay taxes on and was prosecuted. He maintained that the beaches belonged to the people and so refused to pay taxes. He was imprisoned and as a result of that dedicated the rest of his life to prison reform. I do believe up until about the 1930's beds in prisons were called after him, they were called Pottle Beds. Also my father was imprisoned in the 1920's for trade union activity.
> Q: Can you describe the circumstances under which your father and mother met?
> A: Yes, I can, certainly. My father and mother met on the Jarrow marches, the hunger marches in the 1930's and as a result of that they got married.
> Q: These were marches to protect against the intolerable conditions that the people of that time suffered under?
> A: Yes. There was a big depression on at that time.

Q: At what age did you leave school?
A: I left school at 14.
Q: What did you do after you left school?
A: I left school and then took on an apprenticeship to be a compositor in printing, which lasted 6 years.
Q: At that time there was still conscription in this country, is that correct?
A: There was and at the age of 20 I was called up and I did my National Service in the Royal Air Force.
Q: Your involvement in the Royal Air Force, did that prevent you from expressing your political views at all?
A: Certainly not. In those days national Service was two years and I formed a nuclear disarmament group on the RAF camp and after 18 months I was asked to leave the RAF even though I was doing two years National Service. I also remember taking part in the very first committee of 100 demonstration sit downs when I was in the RAF.
Q: That would be in 1961?
A: Yes.

We then covered briefly the history of the Committee, its stance against nuclear weapons of whatever country, the role Pat had played in it, including his arrest and imprisonment under the Official Secrets Act in 1962. The fact that it was in no sense a pro-Soviet campaign was concretely demonstrated by the fact that Pat himself had been arrested inside the Russian Embassy when he and others members of a delegation staged a sit-in protest there opposing the resumption of Soviet atmospheric tests. He described meeting George Blake in Wormwood Scrubs and the sympathy he felt for him despite disagreeing with him politically and with his espionage activities, and the first tentative escape plan communicated by Blake on the inside of a chocolate wrapper.

Randle: When you decided to help him, was this because you agreed with him and with what he had done in passing information to the Russians?
A: Absolutely not. At no stage had you and I ever supported any policies on espionage either by the Soviet Union or by our own country or by America or anyone; we were opposed to all of them. So in no way have we ever tried to whitewash or try to justify what George Blake did. We absolutely, completely, condemn it but on the other hand here was a human being who had been sentenced basically to death, and I was not prepared to stand by and see that happen. I am very sorry but I wasn't prepared to do that.
Q: Did you, on various occasions, talk to him about your disagreement with him?

A: Oh, we disagreed politically all the time, certainly while we were in prison. He did assure me in prison that the kind of rumours that had been spread about in national newspapers about what he had done and may not have done were completely untrue …

Pat then described his work as secretary to Bertrand Russell following his release from prison. He told of how he had been beaten up by Greek police when he took part in the anti-nuclear Marathon March soon after coming out of prison, of Russell's work on behalf of Soviet political prisoners, and of his own experiences as a kind of roving ambassador on Russell's behalf.

Q: I believe you were also involved in negotiations on behalf of Bertrand Russell in certain border disputes between India and China?
A: Yes, war had broken out between China and India and Lord Russell was asked to send a representative out to carry out negotiations between the Indians and the Chinese. I was sent in round about August, 1963, had several meetings with Pandit Nehru, the Prime Minister of India, and then went on to meet Mrs Bandaranaike the Prime Minister of Sri Lanka and eventually ended up, having discussions with the Chinese.
Q: You actually spent some time in China?
A: Yes, about four to five weeks.
Q: Were you actually arrested while you were in China?
A: Yes, I was arrested. Although one wasn't aware that one was being arrested at that time, as the same people who had been taking us round that day turned up and said that we were going off to a meeting. We went into a room, in a way very much like this but not quite so formal. Suddenly all the other people in the room stood up and started accusing me of various crimes against the state. It was an accusation meeting and the main complaint was that I had, in their view, tried to incite the Chinese people to overthrow the state. I can remember the kind of language they used. I was called a running dog, lick-spittle of the American imperialists and I was told that for what I had done I could get ten years in prison but because they held me in such high regard I was put on the first plane out and deported that night.
Q: Are you a running dog, lick-spittle of the American imperialists?

Breakthrough! For the first time several members of the jury laughed aloud.

A: Not of the American imperialists or any other imperialists.

We then went over again how we had both become involved in planning the escape of George Blake, the difficulty we had in raising money for it, and the near disasters after the escape which led to Pat putting up George and Seán in his flat in Hampstead. I asked him about the stress this had put him under:

Q: Can you please just describe a little about the atmosphere there, what it actually meant in human terms to have him there?
A: Although you actually prepare for something and actually plan it, … it still doesn't take away the effect. You know, I can remember sitting down some nights and watching the television and he [George Blake] was the first item on the news and there he was sitting next to me in the chair, and I would be terrified and suffering to a large degree from paranoia. I would never read about the case in public. It is easy now, in retrospect to say I wasn't worried, but of course there were incredible periods of worry. I thought every night when I came home from work – had the police found the place, and was I going to walk into a trap? Yes, no matter how I try to gloss over it now, it was a very, very worrying time.
Q: Was there one occasion, or perhaps there were two consecutive occasions, when people came to the door for one reason and were admitted into the flat at that time?
A: Yes, there was. Once the builders were carrying out work and a representative from the landlord came and actually came into the flat. The agreement was, we had fixed up a simple little pass knock, I can't remember what it was now, two long one short, or one long – whatever it was. There was a knock on the door and George actually went and opened the door and let this builder in. His face was in every paper and appearing on television and he showed the man around the flat and the man was describing what improvements they were going to make and George was saying that it would be nice. When he told me that night what he had done I was absolutely devastated. I thought it was incredible, I thought it was stupid. I was so annoyed, I couldn't even speak to him, I went off and sulked in the kitchen. I was fuming. He could have jeopardised everything by opening the door. So there were occasions when one was terrified, of course.
Q: Was there another occasion on which you came back to the flat in the evening and found – because at this point Seán was also staying there – was there an occasion when you found both of them with their hats and coats on ready to leave?
A: Yes. I should perhaps explain that Seán and I did not get on very well. We got on very well on a personal level, until I suggested doing anything about security, or telling Seán not to do this or that. I was the one who was to some degree always attacking Seán for his lack of consideration of security. So when he moved in with me he was very resentful. He was the one that actually threw the rope ladder over the wall and nobody could ever take that away from him. It was an

incredibly brave thing to do and something I could never have done. But once that was done and George was physically now over the wall Seán found his role in a way that of a minor figure as against the major figure, and I think he resented the fact that you and I to some degree had now taken over the organisation. So he used to talk to George when I was at work. He would go on about how worried he was. You had two young children and so on. So I think he convinced George that perhaps – in fact I can remember George saying that they were actually going to leave. They were going to go down to the docks and try to swim to get on a Polish boat or some European boat. The excuse in a way was that they were risking you and your family. I tried to explain that Michael, Anne and myself, all of us, had gone through the whole thing and the idea that it would fail just because we couldn't stick it out another week … In the end I talked them out of it.

Q: So it was a very anxious time in many ways?

A: Very anxious, yes.

Pat then described how he had doctored his passport so that Seán could use it to get out of the country, how we had emptied the flat at Highlever Road despite a telephone warning from Seán from Paris that on no account should we attempt this. We then covered Seán's return to Ireland in 1968, the failure of the British authorities to have him extradited, and the publication of his book in 1970 which convinced us that the police must know about our involvement. Finally we covered more recent events: the publication of Montgomery Hyde's book in 1987, the articles by Barrie Penrose in the *Sunday Times* naming us, and our eventual decision to write The Blake Escape saying what we had done and why. He was also able to bring out the fact that he had not made a fortune out of writing the book and indeed on the contrary it left him worse off than he would otherwise have been:

Randle: As a result of our discussions with Harrup, they finally drew up a contract offering a total of £30,000?

Pottle: Yes, that was to be fifteen thousand for yourself and myself. It was to be split into three payments, the first of five thousand each would be on signing the contract, another five on actually giving them the final draft and another five thousand each when the book was actually published.

Q: Was there a considerable amount of work involved in actually writing the book?

A: Yes.

Q: Can you give an estimate of how long it took from the time we started working on a draft chapter or two to the final finished version. How much, in terms of time, did that take?

A: It actually worked out for both of us to be a solid year. I am not saying that I spent every minute of every day on that book, because I had an antique business which I ran with my wife. But certainly as a result of that book my antique business suffered …
Q: As a result of the possibility of prosecution, did you decide to take certain steps to get rid of liabilities as it were?
A: Yes. We had an antique business. We had a four bedroomed house in Crouch End which we had a very large mortgage on. My wife, who has supported me all the way through on this, and I had to say to ourselves if we do go public I shall have to go to prison. How was she going to pay the mortgage?
The children at that stage although 17, that kind of age, were still at school, so we had to agree yes, we would sell the house, buy another house much smaller. We would have a smaller mortgage so that if I did go to prison my wife could then possibly cope with that mortgage. So yes, of course, we were conscious of the fact and we tried to make arrangements to alleviate it.
Q: So the money you received from the book did not make you such a fortune that you could afford to ignore these realities?
A: You know, if I say to anyone fifteen thousand pounds it seems an enormous amount of money and if you put that amount of money in relation to how much work you had put into what you are doing, plus the – fact that you are going to end up going to the nick, I don't think fifteen thousand pounds comes over as much in relation to what you are giving up.
Q: How have you been earning a living over the past year of eighteen months since we were first arrested?
A: Of course this case has dragged on for rather a long time. My wife and I decided to sell the house and buy a smaller one, as I said, so she could possibly keep the mortgage going, and this case was due for trial in this court last April. So we, as individuals have to say to ourselves – 'Well, it's physically going to happen in April …'
Q: This is April of last year?
A: April of last year. So the antique business had relied very much on the two of us doing it. We would buy something I would spend a lot of time repairing it and doing it up and then we would put it in the shop to sell at an exorbitant price. It meant me doing an awful lot of work. So we thought that if I went to prison we would not be able to run the antiques business and my wife would not be able to earn enough money off the antiques to keep the house and mortgage going. So we thought, here we are coming up to April and the start of the trial, we

will close the antiques business and my wife will try to get a full-time job. Of course, then the trial was put off for another year, so for the last year I haven't been doing any work at all. I was on income support round about Christmas time and just after that I managed to ring round a number of old friends. I have been trying to get work but it is very hard to get work when you get over fifty. It is also very hard to get work when you are having to explain to somebody that you might be coming up for trial. So it was a very uncertain time, but I did manage to get a temporary job through old friends which I have been working at for the last three months. I stopped working on that the week before this trial was due to start.

I then asked him if we had had any contact with Blake since the escape:

A: We had no contact with him whatsoever from the day he left my flat until last year. Last year you and I, our wives and two solicitors, went out to see him in Moscow and that is the first contact since the day he left my flat.

Q: Can you tell us just a little in your own words about that meeting?

A: Over the years we have obviously talked about it. When the Olympics were in Moscow I said to my wife – 'Why don't we go out there for the Olympics, and incorporate that with arranging a meeting with George.' But we couldn't just walk in and ask to see him so practically it became an awkward thing to do. So actually meeting him after all those years was an incredible experience. It was something I never really dreamt would ever come off. We met him. He has remarried. A lovely wife. He has a son of about, must be 20 now, who attends Moscow University. I don't care what the verdict of this court is now. I don't care what anybody says, but to actually see George Blake living a life – he's carved out some kind of normal life … He's remarried, he's got a family and I refuse to believe that he would have been better off rotting in some English jail than living a semi-ordinary life back in Moscow. I refuse to believe that we should have left him there to rot. And now having seen him and his family I think everything we did in 1966 was absolutely justified.

I had one final question to put to Pat about which we had had long and anxious debate. This concerned the fact that Bevan had offered to do a deal whereby if we pleaded guilty to the charge of harbouring the prosecution would be willing to drop the other conspiracy charge and the most serious charge of assisting in the escape of Blake. Ben and John had warned us that it was never done to reveal to a jury any deals or discussions about deals of this kind, and that if we went ahead with the idea the prosecuting counsel, and probably the judge too, would be furious. We could forget about the relatively relaxed atmosphere that had prevailed up to then; the gloves would be off. But I remember John pointing out that if we gained some benefit from this relaxed atmosphere, so did the prosecution. It was up to Pat and me to decide.

> **Q: One final question. Did our solicitors inform you that Mr Bevan had told us that he would recommend that the main charge against us would be dropped if we pleaded guilty to one of the lesser charges of harbouring and preventing rearrest?**
> **A: Yes, we've been offered that deal four times in the course of this trial. The first time was over a year ago. The last time, in fact last Monday in this very court, we were offered if we were to plead guilty to the lesser charge then the main charge of conspiring to break him out would be dropped.**

Bevan had a habit of pulling exaggerated wry faces when anything untoward happened, or anything to which he took strong exception. He now pulled a succession of grimaces, and turned to consult his junior, Calvert-Smith.

> **Q: We nevertheless refused to accept that offer?**
> **A: Yes. We don't like the idea of deals being done behind anyone's back. We felt it important the jury should know that we had had that offer. We feel it is important that the court should know we had that offer. We maintain that what we did was right. We maintain that there were certain times when any one of us is justified in breaking the law and we can all envisage some occasions, if say our children are threatened, that we are right in breaking the law. I'm not asking anyone to turn round and say, look at him, he broke the law now he wants us to forget it. If this court and if this jury want to find me guilty then find me guilty. And if it means going to prison then I don't want to but that's out of my control. But I will say that we believe what we did was right … and I refuse to believe that there is anyone who can honestly say to me, that you or I or the jury or the court or the country would have been better off by George Blake rotting in an English jail rather than living a normal life in Russia. I refuse to believe that there's anyone who would say that to me.**
> **Randle: I agree very much with that. Thank you very much. I have no further questions.**

Bevan conducted the cross-examination:

> **Q: Mr Pottle, I have very few questions of you, which may not come as a surprise to you. Were you aware that Mr Scrivener, who was the Queen's Counsel who represented one of you – was it you or Mr Randle?**
> **A: It was Mr Randle, yes.**

Q: Were you aware that when he represented you in this court in April of last year, he was the first to make an approach as to the possibility of the Crown proceeding on a plea of guilty not on all the counts but on one or two of those counts. Are you aware of that?
A: I am aware that at some stage counsel has gone to counsel and I accept that entirely, of course.
Q: As to 1988 …
Alliott: Just a minute. I think what was put to you was that Mr Scrivener, acting in fact on behalf of Mr Randle, first approached the Crown. Your answer was that you were aware that counsel went to [prosecuting] counsel.
Pottle: Yes.
Alliott: Were you aware that it was in fact it was on the initiative of defence counsel.
Pottle: Absolutely, yes.

Bevan was clearly surprised at Pat's complete openness on this point.

Bevan: That is very candid of you, Mr Pottle. In so far as 1988 is concerned, is it right that you and Mr Randle decided to write the book?
A: Yes.
Q: That is in fact what happened, you and Mr Randle jointly wrote the book?
A: Yes, we did.
Q: The jury have read the book. Is it true?
A: Absolutely true. We do make, I think on the very first page, a point that after a period of 25 years it is very hard to remember exact conversations; but, that apart, every word of that book is true.
Q: Also this; am I to understand on behalf of the Crown that you do not deny committing the acts alleged in this indictment?
A: Absolutely. Don't deny it whatsoever. In fact, I officially now in front of you confirm it. What we say in the book was absolutely true. We broke George Blake out of jail in 1966.
Q: Although Seán Bourke himself executed the escape, you prior to that had taken part in the planning?
A: Oh yes.
Q: No doubt gave Bourke some support and encouragement?
A: Of course.
Q: And also provided ideas?
A: Oh yes, most definitely.
Q: In so far as the second count on the indictment; if you want a copy in front of you, please have one?

A: No, unless it is getting terribly technical.
Q: That is a conspiracy count, namely that you and Mr Randle, as between 1st May and 31st December 1966, conspired together with Seán Bourke, knowingly to harbour George Blake?
A: Yes.
Q: And you did that?
A: Absolutely.
Q: And indeed at one stage, as you have candidly admitted, George Blake stayed at your home at Willow Buildings in Hampstead?
A: I think he stayed there overall for two months.
Q: Just to finish the indictment, it is right, is it not, that you, together with Mr Randle, and no doubt with Mr Bourke, gave assistance to George Blake in so far as spiriting him out of the country was concerned?
A: Absolutely true.
Q: And when the van, having been bought, was being constructed with the secret compartment, you no doubt took part in the planning and so forth so that the escape could be successful?
A: There is no doubt that the three charges against us we did whatever we are accused of in those charges; of that there is no doubt.
Q: Finally, Mr Pottle …
A: I am just trying to save you time.
Q: You do not have the book in front of you, so maybe it could be put in front of Mr Pottle. Would the jury turn to page 284, please. The second paragraph of that page. 'Although we are convinced we were justified in breaking the law by helping Blake to escape we do not claim any special rights or privileges and are prepared if necessary to face trial and go to prison for what we did'. Do you stand by that?
A: Absolutely, every word of it. Yes.
Alliott: You have the right, as it were, to re-examine yourself. If there is anything that you want to add arising out of cross-examination of either Mr Randle or Mr Bevan this is your opportunity to do so. It is of course evidence. You will have an opportunity to address the jury at a later stage.
Pottle: I fully understand. I have nothing further to say.
Alliott: Thank you very much. Then if you would like to make your way back.

Pat now returned to the dock and the judge turned to the jury.

> Members of the jury, Miss Coughlin, who takes down every word that is said in court has asked for a break. I have every sympathy with her

because when Mr Randle was asking Mr Pottle questions they went along at a cracking rate. We will have five minutes.

After a short break the hearing resumed.

Alliott: Yes, Mr Pottle, have you got a witness to call.

Pottle: I have my Lord. I would like to call, in fact, Mr George Blake to give evidence. Mr Blake unfortunately cannot be a witness but he has in fact made a statement, a Section 9 statement …

Alliott: Have you spoken to Mr Bevan about this.

Pottle: I haven't, my Lord.

Alliott: It is a pity. I think you should have a word now. What do you say about this, Mr Bevan.

Bevan: My Lord, I would like time obviously to read it, because as Mr Pottle has just indicated, I have not seen it. I am not criticising anybody but I have had no opportunity to see the statement and would like time to read it and to consider its admissibility.

Alliott: Yes.

Pottle: Would your Lordship like to see a copy of it.

Alliott: Yes, I would.

It was a crucial moment in the trial. Would the judge allow Blake's video taped statement made in Moscow, in the presence of Ben Birnberg and John Wadham to be played in court? Would Bevan object, and if so, how insistently. George Blake was not adding anything new to our evidence, simply confirming some points including, crucially, that we had at no time had any contact with Soviet Intelligence or received any financial incentive or reward. These points were by now not seriously contested by the prosecution yet having them confirmed by Blake himself would add something. More importantly, Blake's appearance – albeit on screen – in the same court where almost exactly 30 years earlier he had been sentenced to a record term of imprisonment could not fail to capture the attention of the press and the media. The outcome of the trial was unlikely to be affected by Blake's evidence, but its impact certainly would be.

Pat had his arguments well prepared.

Pottle: I think it fulfils, my Lord, all the requirements of Section 23.

Alliott: This is something that I shall deal with in the absence of the jury. I also want to give my reasons for my earlier ruling [the ruling on the defence of necessity]. What I shall do, members of the jury, is break off now as far as you are concerned and I shall carry on with these other matters. Would you be back and ready to resume the hearing at 10 o'clock tomorrow morning. If you would like to leave now?

The jury then withdrew, and Alliott turned first to his reasons for rejecting our defence of necessity.

> **Alliott: I think it is convenient if I gave my reasons for my ruling first and get that out of the way. It is not going to take very long. I do not make any contempt of court Act Order because I think it is a sledge hammer to crack a nut but I think it would desirable that these reasons, if they are of the slightest interest to anyone, were not published until after the jury's verdict.**
> **Randle: We are a bit puzzled. I mean earlier when the argument about this matter was discussed the jury were present. If there are reasons our arguments are rejected we would be very much happier if the jury were also present to hear them.**
> **Alliott: At the time I indicated my state of mind. I indicated that I would not give my reasons in the presence of the jury.**
> **Randle: I didn't understand that, my Lord.**
> **Alliott: I think I spelt it out quite clearly.**
> **Randle: Perhaps you can … I mean if they [the jury] were able to hear the argument, shouldn't they be able to hear the conclusion, or the reasons. Well, they have heard the conclusion but not the reasons for that conclusion.**
> **Alliott: I think not because in due course I shall sum the matter up to them and I think it is better if they have the summing-up and only the summing-up.**
> **Randle: Well, obviously it's your court …**
> **Alliott: Yes.**
> **Randle: … but I think it would be more satisfactory if they could mull it over before the final summing-up so that when we are talking they can bear that in mind the weight of those arguments, whichever way they are.**
> **Alliott: No, no, because they loyally have to adhere to my ruling. That is the way we work.**

Alliot then read his statement:

> During the afternoon of Thursday 20th June Mr Randle sought to justify the relevance of a question he was asking Mr Lindley by indicating his intention, and therefore Mr Pottle's, to raise the defence of necessity. I there and then doubted it would be open to the defendants to raise that defence but adjourned until Friday 21st June when I heard full argument on the topic at the express request of the defendants in the presence of the jury.
>
> At the conclusion of the argument I ruled that on the admitted facts of

this case the defence of necessity could not be run. I now give my reasons for that ruling.

Mr Randle attempts to bring his conduct and that of Mr Pottle within the extremely limited boundaries of the defence of necessity by the following argument. Three consecutive maximum sentences of 14 years, totalling 42 years, upon George Blake was, he contends, a cruel and unusual punishment which would inevitably destroy Blake whether by suicide in the short term or by serious mental deterioration in the long term, and the defendants were therefore entitled to take advantage of a limited window of opportunity to free Blake and thus, while breaking the law achieve the greater good by saving his life or sanity.

Mr Randle recognises he must bring the facts of the instant case within the most recent definition of necessity given by Simon Brown, J, in R v. Colin Martin, 1989, Vol. Cr. App. R. p.343, and further recognises that that definition to support his case must be extended to accommodate the lack of immediacy of the threat and the threat being one of mental as opposed to physical injury.

Mr Randle has cited a number of authorities to me in the course of his submissions but he will forgive me, I hope, if I concentrate upon the case of Martin because upon the defendants' account of what they did, their conduct cannot be brought within the judgment of the Court of Appeal, Criminal Division. In the judgment of that court, delivered by Simon Brown, J, the principles of the defences of necessity were summarised thus:

'First, the English law does, in extreme circumstances, recognise the defence of necessity. Most commonly this defence arises as duress, that is pressure upon the accused's will from the wrongful threats or violence of another. Equally, however, it can arise from other objective dangers threatening the accused or others. Arising thus it is conveniently called duress of circumstances. Secondly, a defence is available only if, from an objective standpoint, the accused can be said to be acting reasonably and proportionately in order to avoid a threat of serious injury.'

Whilst I am prepared to include mental or psychiatric injury in 'serious injury,' I have no doubt that the threat of death or serious injury must be reasonably imminent which is not so in the present case. In any event, the defendants' conduct cannot be said, from an objective standpoint, to have been acting reasonably and proportionately in assisting the escape of a prisoner lawfully convicted on his own confession and lawfully sentenced. Therefore harbouring that prisoner and subsequently, in Mr Bevan's words, spiriting him away, there is no room for the defence of necessity in this case.

Mr Randle, I am indebted to you for the notes and Miss Coughlin the shorthand writer has asked if she too may borrow them. With your consent I will hand them to her, although, if I may put it this way, you did not slavishly follow your notes, you ad-libbed on the basis of what was prepared.

Randle: Exactly, your honour.

Alliott: But if she can derive any benefit, I hand them to her. She will, of course, return them to you when she has made use of them.

Randle: Yes. Can I ask one point for clarification.

Alliott: Yes.

Randle: I think before I got into the main argument about necessity, I put forward reasons why the substantive issue should be left to the jury, it shouldn't be decided on just by the judge. Has your Lordship any comments on that. It was the question of proportionality.

Alliott: If it were open to you on the facts, I should leave it to the jury.

Randle: You have said that it is not reasonable and that proportionality does not apply in this case, but surely it should be for the jury, having heard those facts, to decide whether this was a reasonable act and whether it was proportionate to the damage that would be done by the action that we took.

Alliott: In my view, no. Only if admitted facts permit of the defence of necessity to arise, would I leave it to the jury. In some of those motoring cases that you cited, Martin for one, it was held that on the facts it was open to the jury to consider the defence of necessity and that is why the appeal was allowed in the case of Martin. In my view, on the facts of this case, necessity does not arise.

Randle: But we can, of course, appeal that to another court.

Alliott: Yes. Any decision of mine in law is appealable to the Court of Appeal.

Randle: The other thing you don't consider at all in your reasoning is the argument from Lord Donaldson and Lord Denning about the position of the Security Service and the argument – to use your own phrase – what's sauce for the goose is sauce for the gander. The argument that these [MI5] are ordinary citizens and Lord Denning or Lord Donaldson, I forget now which, are saying, the law applies to them as to everybody else and yet at the same time he is saying, you know, it's stupid for us to sit here and pretend that they are completely bound by the law. So the argument was if there are particular circumstances which make it right for a member of the Security Service to break the letter of the law that should also be applied to ordinary members of the public.

> Alliott: I have applied my mind as to whether, on the admitted facts of this case, there is room for the defence of necessity. For reasons I have just given I decided there was not.
> Randle: But you have and you have chosen not to deal with that particular argument?
> Alliott: No.
> Randle: Thank you.

Alliott returned to the issue of Blake's evidence and addressed prosecuting counsel.

> Alliott: Now, have you had an opportunity of looking at this, Mr Bevan, I scarcely have?
> Bevan: I have read the statement. Has your Lordship read it?
> Alliott: No, will you pause while I do.

There was a few minutes silence while Alliott read the statement. Then he continued.

> Alliott: As I understand it, Mr Bevan, the intention is to play a video tape that will consist of Mr Blake making this statement orally is that right.
> Pottle: Yes, my Lord. The film was actually shot in the presence of Mr Birnberg and Mr Wadham. It just starts off exactly as you see it in the section marked there. It's word for word.
> Alliott: What is your attitude Mr Bevan?
> Bevan: My Lord, my only query with regard to the statement of Mr Blake – I can understand why he cannot come to court to give evidence – is I query the relevance and the issues that the jury have to decide.
> Alliott: Yes. I entirely agree but considering that which is irrelevant that has already gone in I think we would be straining at a gnat to draw the line here.

Pat then came out with one of the classic lines of the trial:

> Pottle: I thought your ruling, my Lord, was whether the evidence was relevant and goes towards guilt or innocence. I would have thought quite clearly on reading Mr Blake's statement that it certainly goes towards guilt.
> Alliott: I do not think this begins to be relevant in the strict sense of the word but I am not going to exclude it.
> Bevan: I have made that point but on reading there is nothing that is objectionable. I have not seen the video. It must take but a minute. Would your Lordship allow me to see it.
> Alliott: Shall we have a dummy run? I think here again this ought not to be reported upon. You can report upon the decision if it is of

any interest as to what will happen, but not the fact we are having a preview.
Bevan: As I understand we are going to see a copy.
Alliott: If anything turns upon it Mr Birnberg is in a position to prove it.

The video was now played. As we watched it, we were more than ever convinced that if it was shown in open court the impact would be spectacular.

Alliott: I should be grateful if this one (video screen) could be made to work tomorrow. Does anyone want the actual witnessing to be shown to the jury?
Randle: Oh no.
Bevan: My Lord, I would like an opportunity to discuss with Mr Calvert-Smith the Crown's position with regard to the statement because I cannot accept the truth of the statement, but I do appreciate that it is an impossible task for George Blake to come and give evidence here. I accept the reality of the situation. Would your Lordship give me a moment to discuss the matter with Mr Calvert-Smith?
Alliott: Yes.
Bevan: I would like to do it outside court. I appreciate it is five to four.

Pat was straining at the leash to present the legal argument in favour of the video being shown:

Pottle: My Lord, a statement under Section 23 of the Criminal Justice Act … would be permissible if … 'a person who make the statement is outside the United Kingdom and it is not reasonably practical for him to secure an attendance.' So I think the actual statement fulfils those requirements. Then if we go and look at the Criminal Evidence Act 1968, Section 10 actually spells out what a document is, because things have changed, and a document includes in addition to a document in writing, 'any map, plan, graph or drawing, any photograph, any disk, tape sound track or other device … in which sound or visual images are involved.' The new definition of a document includes film or video so I think it fulfils all of the requirements of a Section 9 statement.
Alliott: At the moment I have indicated it should be given in evidence so you can keep your powder dry at the moment.
Bevan: My Lord, I am looking at Section 23. I have it in the supplement at page 35.
Pottle: It is at page 673 to 674 of the Supplement to Archbold.
Alliott: Thank you.

Bevan: The point I am making, my Lord, is this. It would be wholly misleading for the jury to consider that this statement in its entirety is accepted as entirely accurate by the Crown. That is the only point that I seek to make.

Alliott: Are you content to make that position plain, recognising the impracticability of Mr Blake coming to this country.

Bevan: I am bound to, yes.

Alliott: But subject to that …

Bevan: All I am saying is that it would not be right for this jury to say to themselves – 'and the Crown accept the contents of this statement in its entirety' – when we do not. That is all.

Alliott: Are you content, gentlemen, that Mr Bevan, whilst not persisting in an objection can make plain his attitude that he does not accept the total accuracy of the statement and of course he is totally inhibited from cross-examining.

Randle: Of course, my Lord.

Alliott: I think that is a sensible basis. If you have any thoughts overnight we will discuss them before the jury come in.

He then adjourned the case until 10.30 the next morning.

Chapter 21:

'Call Mr Blake'

So it was that on Tuesday morning, 25th June 1991, just over 30 years after being sentenced to 42 years imprisonment by Lord Justice Parker, Blake was back at No 1 court at the Old Bailey. The first time it had been in the flesh as the accused. The second time it was as an image on screen giving evidence on our behalf. The press were eager, the two prosecuting counsel plainly discomfited.

Before the jury came in, Bevan reiterated that the Crown did not accept in its entirety the truth of Blake's statement and said this should be made clear to the jury. In particular the Crown challenged the accuracy of a passage in Blake's statement in which he claimed that it had never been alleged at his trial that he was responsible for the death of agents.

> **Alliott: You made this quite plain yesterday and Mr Pottle and Mr Randle accepted that it would be shown on the basis of that.**
> **Bevan: Provided that is made plain, I …**
> **Alliott: It certainly was to me last night and I am sure it was to Mr Pottle and Mr Randle.**
> **Bevan: My Lord, yes. As Mr Calvert-Smith says to me, the jury were not here yesterday, so would your Lordship make it plain to the jury?**
> **Alliott: I thought you were going to. That was my understanding of what was agreed last night.**
> **Bevan: Then I will do that my Lord.**
> **Randle: Is the position then that that particular statement is neither confirmed nor denied – that is, you are saying it is not relevant as far as evidence is concerned? Because if there is going to be a challenge about the accuracy of one particular statement, then the proper thing would be … for a transcript of that trial to be made available. But if it is simply a matter of saying – 'Well, we don't accept this is relevant and we reserve our position' – that is an another matter.**
> **Alliott: The position is this, Mr Randle. Mr Bevan is indicating, I do not say as a precondition, but in return for the jury seeing this video, that he should be entitled to make plain that he does not accept the accuracy of the whole of this statement, a good deal of which is irrelevant to the issue the jury have to decide. You remember my reaction yesterday when relevance was raised was to say in the light of**

what had gone in it would be straining at a gnat to exclude it?
Randle: Yes.
Alliott: Are we all set? Let us have the jury in.

It was just after 10am when the jury filed in.

Alliott: Members of the jury, as part of the evidence led by the defendant Mr Pottle, you are going now going to see a video of a statement by George Blake who for very obvious reasons cannot come to this country to give his evidence in person. When that is concluded Mr Bevan will indicate the Crown's attitude to the video you will have seen, because for equally obvious reasons he is not in a position to cross-examine a video recording.

The showing commenced. As a film it would win no Oscars. Blake sat centre picture throughout, dressed in a blazer and muffler, reading his statement. Occasionally he would look up from the text, but mostly his head was bent forward. He was flanked on his right by Ben, on his left by John. The latter stood statuesque without moving a muscle for almost the entire time, one hand clasping the other. The sound quality was poor too and the statement was interspersed every few seconds with a noise akin to a glottal impediment – rather like you get with some of the early sound boxes provided to people who had had their larynx removed. At one point Bevan went to the set and turned up the sound – but succeeded only in making it less intelligible. Yet a Hitchcock thriller could not have been more riveting for everyone in the courtroom.

> I am George Blake, born on 11th November, 1932, of 23 Profsoyunaya Street, Moscow, USSR.[1] This statement consists of three pages each signed by me. It is true to the best of my knowledge and belief and I make it knowing that if it is given in evidence I shall be liable to prosecution if I wilfully state in it anything which I know to be false or do not believe to be true. Dated the 13th day of February, 1990.
>
> I am making this statement at the express request of Patrick Pottle and Michael Randle. I was a member of the British Secret Intelligence Service from August 1944 until the date of my trial, 3rd May, 1961. I was engaged in secret subversive operations directed against the Soviet Union, the Socialist Countries and world communism. It was my task to attempt the recruitment of Soviet citizens and in particular members of the Soviet Intelligence Services and those of other socialist countries. I have been advised by the solicitors acting for Patrick Pottle and Michael Randle that because of the operation of the British Official Secrets Acts, I can say no

1 23 Profsoyunaya Street was the address of the World Institute of Economics and International Affairs (IMEMO) where Blake worked.

more than this.

It is said that my actions led to the death of British and other agents. I can confirm that at my trial it was never alleged that in working for both the British Secret Intelligence Service and the Soviet Intelligence Service I was ever responsible for the death of agents. However, I will not deny that I disclosed the identity of a number of agents to the Soviet authorities.

After my conviction I was sent to Her Majesty's prison in Wormwood Scrubs where in 1962 I first met Patrick Pottle and Michael Randle.

I can confirm that neither Patrick Pottle nor Michael Randle were at any time in contact with the Soviet authorities or acting on their behalf helping me to escape in 1966 from Wormwood Scrubs prison. Nor did they receive any kind of financial assistance or reward at any stage for their assistance. Indeed I had to explain to the Soviet authorities once I arrived in Moscow who these two men were and why they chose to assist me.

There never was any doubt in my mind that Patrick Pottle and Michael Randle acted as they did out of purely humanitarian concern and specifically because of the length of my sentence. I say this as they repeatedly commented on the harshness of the sentence.

Furthermore both men asked me to intervene on behalf of two well known Soviet dissidents imprisoned at the time, Mr Daniel and Mr Sinyavsky. Moreover they frequently stated how much they would like to be able to bring a prisoner in Soviet hands back to the west on their return journey.

I should like to conclude this statement by saying that I am deeply grateful to Patrick Pottle and Michael Randle for having enabled me to lead a normal life over the last twenty four years.[2]

As agreed Bevan now told the jury the Crown's position on Blake's statement.

Alliott: I am sure the jury will readily understand that. Mr Pottle, is that the only evidence that you call or have you anyone else?

Pottle: No, I think that finishes my defence. I would just perhaps point out, if I could, that I found that the sound quality on that video pretty bad and possibly the jury have not actually understood all of it.

Alliott: I thought it was particularly good and was booming until Mr Bevan adjusted it. Did you hear it all right, members of the jury?

Bevan pulled one of his wry faces.

---

2 See Appendix 6 for a photocopy of Blake's witness statement in his own handwriting, signed by him and countersigned by Benedict Birnberg.

Bevan: That was not deliberate on my part, my Lord.

Alliott: It was better when you turned it down. You heard it all right, did you not, members of the jury?

Pottle: Would it serve better perhaps if it was possible for me now to duplicate off a number of copies of that so that the jury have a copy of that statement in their evidence? Or do you think it is enough that they heard it?

Alliott: I think it is enough that they heard it. It was not of any depth or length. What do you feel, members of the jury?

The jury seemed satisfied as things stood.

Alliott: (To Pat). I think you are all right. Mr Randle.

As I went to the witness-box to affirm, the press benches emptied.

'It seems, Mr Randle,' the judge remarked, 'that the press are more interested in Blake's statement than in what you have to say.'

This was true, but nothing we hadn't expected. The trial had been well covered in the media up to that point, particularly in the broadsheets, and had received mentions in radio and television bulletins. But the Blake video catapulted it into prominence in all the media – on radio and television, in the tabloids as well as the broadsheets. Some papers carried pictures of Blake, some part of his hand-written statement. All were struck by the fact that after 30 years he was again appearing, in sound and vision at least, at the same court where he had been sentenced all those years ago.

Chapter 22:

Self-incrimination II: I testify

Like Pat I testified instead of taking the oath. I too began with a short statement:

> **Randle: I just want to make a short opening statement to say that we have done everything of which we have been accused in this case. We did help, albeit not in a major capacity, in the escape from Wormwood Scrubs Prison, we helped finance and we helped with the planning of that operation.**
> **Alliott: Bear in mind I am taking a note.**
> **Randle: I will slow up.**
> **Alliott: 'We have done everything of which we have been accused in this case. We did help, albeit in a minor capacity.' Were those your words?**
> **Randle: Maybe – okay. Albeit in a minor capacity in the escape of George Blake from Wormwood Scrubs Prison. We helped with finances and plans. We did harbour him, and we did spirit him out of the country. However, we feel what we did was right in principle and in law. We have been faced with the stick of a possible longer sentence if we are found guilty and we have been offered the carrot of a deal whereby the main charge would be dropped if we plead guilty to one of the less serious charges. But we believe we have a defence, that this should be put to the jury, and that it should be the jury that decides on our guilt or innocence.**

Pat then cross-examined me. He took me through a tour of my involvement in political and protest movements, including two lengthy spells in prison, much as I had done with him. ('You'll get used to this double act,' Alliot told the jury at one point.) Answering his questions I told the court how my involvement had begun when I registered as a conscientious objector to military service and joined a direct action group initially called Operation Gandhi (subsequently the Non Violent Resistance Group) in 1953 through to joining the Direct Action Committee Against Nuclear War and the Aldermaston March Committee in 1957 and the Committee of 100 from its formation in 1962, and my association with various groups and movements throughout the period since then, in some cases working closely with Pat.

I was at pains to emphasise that I had actively opposed Soviet foreign and military policies. In 1956 I had undertaken a one person march from Vienna to the Hungarian border in an attempt to cross into Hungary and give out leaflets expressing pacifist support for passive resistance to the Soviet invasion and calling on Soviet troops to refuse orders to fire on unarmed demonstrators. In 1968 I had been closely involved in organising on behalf of War Resisters International simultaneous protests in Moscow, Warsaw, Budapest and Sofia against the Soviet-led invasion of Czechoslovakia, and subsequently from 1970 onwards had assisted the Czech dissident exile Jan Kavan in smuggling literature and equipment to dissident democratic organisations in Czechoslovakia. This work had continued right up to the time of my arrest on the Blake escape charge in April 1989. I also mentioned the year I had spent in Ghana in 1959-60 as a Direct Action Committee worker helping to organise an international protest team against the French atomic bomb tests in the Sahara. I hoped, while doing so, that the black member of the jury, a man of about my age, and the young Asian woman on the jury might be impressed by the fact that one of the leading members of the protest team was the American civil rights leader, Bayard Rustin, a close associate of Martin Luther King and the coordinator of the 1963 March on Washington at which King made his famous 'I have a dream' speech.

The narrative naturally included also my year-long imprisonment in Wormwood Scrubs where I had got to know both George Blake and the man chiefly responsible for organising and carrying out his escape, Seán Bourke. We then went through some of the highlights of the escape itself and the role Anne and I had played in smuggling Blake out of Britain to East Germany hidden in a secret compartment of a camper van. Inevitably at times there was an overlap with Pat's testimony, a fact which led to one caustic comment from the judge when Pat was asking me about the Greek Embassy demonstration in 1967 which had led to my receiving a year's prison sentence:

> **Randle: I don't think we really made it clear what demonstration.**
> **Alliott: We did actually have the mirror image of this, if you remember, when the double act took the form of you cross-examining – I use the word loosely, in inverted commas – Mr Pottle.**
> **Randle: Yes, all right. So perhaps the jury are already aware that we occupied the Greek Embassy and were arrested as a result of that. Pat managed to kick open the door of the police van and escape, but I wasn't so lucky.**

Pat, in his cross-examination, returned again to the question of making money from the book:

Q: You pointed out to me yesterday that writing a book is not easy. Did you find it time consuming?
A: It was extremely time consuming. I had other work at that time, and I was – I think that the phrase used is moonlighting. I was trying to do two jobs at once. I did have some holiday time so I was able to spend that on the book.
Q: I think as a result of that you developed a duodenal ulcer?
A: Well I was ill in – it would be 1988. And again last year I had to have an emergency operation. Of course, one can't say precisely what causes these things but certainly stress and overwork contributes to that condition.
Q: How much were you paid for writing the book?
A: I was paid £15,000.
Q: Some people would say that is a lot of money. That must have been a consideration, must have been an incentive to write the book?
A: I think it was an incentive in the sense that it provided some kind of security, because I knew that once I wrote the book I would have to resign from my post at the university. In fact this was agreed before the book was ever published. Many months before I agreed with the professor of Peace Studies that if I went ahead with the book I would resign my post. So I knew that security was gone. I also knew that if we went ahead with the publication of the book there was a strong possibility of arrest and imprisonment, and of course I wanted to provide some kind of security to my family if I was put away for several years.
Q: So, far from gaining from the book, in fact it was made clear to you that if you went ahead with it you would have to resign your position at the university?
A: Yes. We knew we would be paid for the book. We knew that what we gained on the roundabouts we would lose on the swings, and very much more than that. In financial terms, we would be worse off if we did go ahead – or that that would be the likely outcome.
Q: Are you working now?
A: No. I have been working free-lance. I have had occasional work, but since last December I have had no regular work and I have been relying upon the income of my wife who works as a staff nurse at a local hospital.

This was also an opportunity to impress on the jury that Pat and I faced the confiscation of our houses if we were found guilty. I also wanted to bring out the way the Crown had calculated the extent of my own gains.

Pottle: If I now move on to 1990. In 1990 I think it was the day before Easter, the prosecution went to the High Court to try to take our houses away from us, have charging orders put on our houses. That was an *ex parte* application. We never knew about it until it was made?
Randle: That is absolutely correct. I had never heard of charging orders, but the effect of it, as I am understand it, is that if we are found guilty our houses will be confiscated and sold and then the amount, whether it is a fine or in this case the amount that we earned from the book … could be taken. Then we would have to use the balance to try and find another house, I suppose.
Q: So what they are in fact saying is that the money you were paid as an author is in fact the proceeds of crime?
A: Yes. That is an argument which, if necessary, we will pursue in another court. But certainly the advice we had from our lawyers is that this is a quite wrong application of the Act.
Q: Not only are they claiming the £15,000 you received, they also say that in 1966 you received £1,000 to buy a camper-van?
A: Yes, in my case. I think in your case it is £15,000, the proceeds from the book. No account is taken of the fact that these are gross proceeds because the law in question was never intended to be used in this way. It doesn't say the gross earnings can be confiscated because in all normal cases if it is the proceeds of crime people don't declare it to the income tax. This is one of the absurdities of the situation. So your case it was £15,000, in my case, they took into account the £1,000 that I received to buy the van. As we say [in the book], we used that to buy the van and to convert it, to pay fares and expenses for Seán and so on. At the end of the day the van was sold and the money was returned to the person who gave it to us in the first place. Also … they say I was paid another one hundred pounds. This relates to a passage in the book where I say that I received an initial two hundred pounds. I also say that on such and such a date Seán Bourke records [i.e. in his book] that I paid him an initial one hundred pounds. Now the Crown assumes that I must have pocketed the other hundred pounds and they have added that on to the bill. So in my case it is £16,100.

Bevan was pulling wry faces as this was going on, no doubt aware of how such petty-mindedness was likely to strike the jury.

At the conclusion of the cross-examination I was able to re-iterate the basic philosophy underpinning our decision to defy the law on this and previous occasions:

Q: I want to move on, if I could, because it would seem to me that any ordinary person, certainly any member of the jury, must say to

themselves, well, look, you are prepared to take the law into your own hands. You're prepared to break the law when it suits you.
A: I think that any citizen has to consider that in the normal way one should obey the law, provided one is living in a country where the laws are determined democratically and where the laws are themselves just. The norm should always be to obey the law, if only out of consideration for the effects of breaking the law upon other people. There are, however, exceptional circumstances in which I believe it is right to break the law. Even in a democratic society unjust laws can be passed, laws which discriminate against people on the basis of their colour or their nationality or religion. In those circumstances I think the individual citizen has to ask himself or herself – 'would it be right to obey that law or would it be right to disobey that law?' There are other circumstances in which the law itself may be neutral. For instance, a law against obstructing traffic is a perfectly reasonable law, but it would seem to me to be perfectly legitimate to block traffic that was taking innocent people into a concentration camp. So the law itself is not unreasonable but the way in which it is being applied is unreasonable. I would say that again there are still other circumstances in which the law itself might be quite reasonable. It is not an unreasonable law that says it is an offence to help someone get out of prison or to harbour somebody who has escaped from prison. But in circumstances where the prisoner in question has been unjustly sentenced or where the harshness of the sentence means that it is totally inhuman for that person to stay in prison, it would be right to break the law.
We have actually had this debate with the jury present about the question of necessity, and it is conceded that there are circumstances in which a plea of necessity is perfectly proper and there have been successful cases. In those circumstances too the individual concerned has to decide, has to be judge and jury in his own cause, in a certain sense, but the final arbiter, in our view, ought to be the jury. Of course, one can exaggerate one's one interests, one can make a mistake, but in the final analysis it should be the jury who decide whether or not the decision was right in those particular circumstances, and that is the position that we are adopting here in this court.
Alliott: I am afraid not, because I have ruled that the defence of necessity does not arise in your case. I think I have made that plain on a number of occasions.
Randle: I'm talking about our approach. I mean you have made certain rulings, but I'm talking about our approach to the matter which is, of

course, at variance with the judgment you have made.
Alliott: I am afraid so far as this court is concerned everyone has to honour my ruling on the law. As I have explained, that can be challenged elsewhere if I have got it wrong.
Randle: Of course the jury are the final arbiters as to guilt or innocence.
Alliott: On the issue as I shall put it to them.
Pottle: Did you approve of George Blake passing secrets to the Russians?
A: No, I didn't agree with that, and I didn't agree with what he was doing when he was working for the British Security Service, when he was trying to get people from the other side to betray the trust that their countries had put in them. And I made that very clear in the debates that I had with him, both inside prison and after he got out of prison. We had numerous discussions on that and on wider political issues.
Q: Do you have any regrets in helping him escape from prison?
A: No. My feeling is exactly the same as yours on that. I went and saw George in Washington living – I beg your pardon, in Moscow, living a normal life, doing something useful with a family. And I mean the alternative – to think that he could have spent all those years in prison! To me there is just no choice involved. It was the right thing to do and I cannot regret it, seeing how things had worked out, and seeing that the security of this country was not in any way jeopardised by his escape. Then it seems to me that a bit of common sense and decency ought to come in even in a court of law which is bound by strict rules of law and evidence … I think the main function of the jury is to bring in that breath of fresh air and common sense.
Q: Now here we are Michael, 25 years after all these events took place. I think in 1966 you were aware, when carrying out these actions, of the risk of going to prison. Certainly in 1970 we had those same considerations in mind when Seán wrote his book. But here we are 25 years later standing in a dock for something we did a quarter of a century ago. Do you have any regrets at all?
A: No, I have said before that I don't have any regrets. I think it was the right thing to do and I now am quite prepared to face whatever consequences arise from that. I could not have lived with myself if we had turned down that man and I would now be thinking, well if we had only had the courage to take some action he might have been able to live a reasonable life.
Pottle: I have no further questions. Thank you.

Calvert-Smith conducted the cross-examination.

Q: Mr Randle, you are aware of the Crown stance obviously, as the case developed, of our contention that you, by your admissions, stated yourself out of court so far as a verdict is concerned, but I'm going, if I may to ask you a few questions about your state of mind at the time you did these acts. Did you at the time you agreed to help Seán Bourke and at the time you helped to shelter Blake after he escaped and take him to Berlin later, then believe that you had any more than a moral justification for what you did?

A: I believed that we had the moral justification and I didn't know the technicalities of the law but I thought that in all such cases it should be the jury who decides.

Q: Could you perhaps have a look at the book, a copy of which will be handed to you, at page 83.

A: Yes, I have the page.

Q: This is you talking and I think if we go back to 81 we can see 'Narrated by Michael Randle'?

A: Yes.

Q: You are talking about the time when you are deciding whether or not to get involved?

A: Which paragraph are we looking at?

Alliott: 'We also discussed.'

Randle: Oh, yes.

Calvert-Smith: Perhaps I can start at the previous paragraph:

'We went through our reasons for being involved and how we could put them across in the events of arrest and trial. We decided that if it came to it we would not deny our involvement or shelter behind a legalistic defence, but would concentrate on the moral and political issues involved.'

A: That is correct.

Q: We can all understand that the autobiographical evidence, as you described it this morning that you have given, goes to show that in your opinion you have a moral justification?

A: Yes, we did.

Q: I understand that. But when was the first time that it occurred to you that you might have a legalistic defence. It was not at the time you committed the offences, was it?

A: No, it wasn't – and I am not prepared to call it a legalistic defence. When we talked to our lawyers about it they said – well, you know you are wanting to raise the moral issues but there is something which at least partially recognises this in law, which is the defence of necessity. I

am quite frank that I did not know of this law at the time, and in fact I don't think it had been developed to the extent it has at the moment. I'm not prepared to call it legalistic because I think that there ought to be that kind of defence for actions that are taken on moral grounds.
Q: At the time of these acts – and I am turning to another area of the matter that you put before the jury, subject to his Lordship's ruling – did you believe or not that George Blake had been, or may have been, responsible for the death or serious injury of British agents.Pottle: My Lord, I'm very sorry to interrupt at this stage, but it seems to me that if Mr Calvert-Smith wants to raise those particular issues, which I have no objection to at all, then the only honest and true way he can raise them is by revealing the transcript of George Blake's trial, by revealing the transcripts of the evidence presented against him … All you can say is what was he was charged with and that it seems to me is it. To infer that, in fact, he was responsible for people's deaths when he was never ever charged with that, seems to me to be wrong.
Calvert-Smith: With the greatest respect, I was not inferring any such thing, I was asking what the defendant's state of mind was because the defendants have put forward their state of mind at the time as affording justification. And there is a passage in the book which we all read to which I wish to refer in the event of a particular answer. In my submission it is the defendants' belief which has any relevance at all, if any, in law, rather than the actual situation. Because the defendants are saying, 'Our belief was X, therefore we had the duty or justification for doing what we did,' and in my submission, since that is a something to which Mr Randle and Mr Pottle devoted considerable time, I ought to be entitled to explore what they said about it on another occasion.
Alliott: I suppose it could be said that in light of my ruling, which you must honour even if the defendants are disinclined to, the question is going to something that is irrelevant. But in the light of the stance taken by each of them I think I will allow you the inch.
Calvert-Smith: I am very grateful to your Lordship. (To the defendant Randle:) What was your belief at the time?
A: I knew that the Security Service of both East and West did horrendous things, and I can give some examples of that. Since you raise that issue I think I ought to be allowed to mention …
Q: I would be grateful if you will answer the question. Did you or did you not believe?A: I am going to answer the question but I'm saying you have now opened a much wider area. I did not know whether George Blake was or was not responsible, indirectly at any rate, for the death of agents, but I did know that people on both sides, agents on

both sides, were responsible for imprisonment, for deaths, for coups to overthrow democratic governments and so on. And I knew that some people …

Alliott: Just pause, please. This is a paraphrase; tell me if you agree. 'I didn't know whether or not George Blake had been responsible for the death of any agents, but I knew then – my words – 'hideous things were done on both sides.' Is that fair?

A: Yes, that's fair.

Q: If I could just ask this. The Antigone Chapter – is that yours or a joint effort?

A: It's a joint effort.

Q: And page 258 where you have a paragraph headed "Blood on his Hands"?

A: Yes.

Q: I appreciate that this is written long after the events and therefore your opinion or feeling may have changed between 1966 and 1989?

A: Not very much I think, but …

Q: So that your opinion in 1966 would have been, would it, 'Granted that the 42 year sentence on Blake corresponded to the number of British agents he betrayed is a myth, is it nevertheless likely that Blake does have blood on his hands. The answer has to be yes"?

A: I'm sorry. I haven't got the actual passage.

Q: I did refer you to, 'Blood on his hands,' question mark?

A: I think indirectly, yes, but we had no direct knowledge of what he had done. He always denied that he had been responsible for the death of agents. And of course we then go on to the passage underneath.

Q: To develop the hideous things on either side?

A: Not in those general terms but in specific terms, talking about attempts to murder the president of Egypt at that time.

Calvert-Smith: Yes, thank you very much, Mr Randle.

Pottle: My Lord, could I just ask Mr Randle one question?

Alliott: No. Mr Randle can.

Pottle: It was only on the very last question that Mr Calvert-Smith brought up about, 'Blood on his Hands'. My Lord, all I want to say is, whatever is done on either side …

Alliott: Just a minute. Is it something arising out of Mr Calvert-Smith's cross-examination?

Pottle: Yes.

Alliott: I think it would better, I am sure it could come equally from him, if Mr Randle did his own, as it were, re-examination. He is entitled to re-examine himself. I do not think you really are entitled to another crack. You had a pretty good one, if I may say so. (Addressing me). Is there anything you want to say either in relation to anything Mr Pottle has asked you or Mr Calvert-Smith?

Bevan: I think Mr Pottle wants to pass on information. I think that is what has been happening in this case.

Actually Calvert-Smith's line of questioning had given me the ideal opportunity to raise, or dwell upon, issues that the judge had earlier ruled inadmissible, including notably the facts surrounding the conviction and fining of the former head of the CIA, Richard Helms.

Randle: Well, I think I can rely upon my own resources in re-examining myself. We have made it clear time and time again throughout the book that we did not approve of what George Blake was doing. We did not know whether he was responsible for deaths. That was a rumour that was put about at the time and the circumstances in which it was put about were in fact quite disgraceful. On the very day that his appeal was being heard *in camera* and against the protests of Jeremy Hutchinson QC, who is now Lord Hutchinson, in spite of those protests that justice should be seen to be done in open court, on that very day a government inspired rumour was circulated that he had been responsible for the imprisonment, and the suggestion initially was possibly also for the death of some agents. That rumour, as you see from the book, has grown throughout the years so that now every time George Blake is mentioned it is said that he was responsible for 42 deaths. I do not know at this point or at any point whether he was responsible for deaths, and I doubt if he himself knows. What we have said in the book is that no evidence or even the rumours have suggested that he did the kind of things that we know have been done on both sides where people were actually assassinated, and we give the example here of attempts by MI5 or MI6, the plots to try and assassinate the president of Egypt. Other examples were Mr Richard Helms, if I had been able to pursue that line. Mr Richard Helms was actually convicted and sentenced to a suspended prison sentence because he told, under oath, a Senate committee that the CIA had not being involved in attempting to overthrow the democratic Government of Chile, that it had not been involved in passing money to opposition candidates to try and affect the outcome of democratic elections. As a result of that, because he gave that evidence and because it was decided that this was false information that he gave he was eventually taken before a court, convicted and he was sentenced to a $2,000 fine and to imprisonment. We do know that CIA and MI6, which is commented on in some detail in the book, were involved in a plot which was going to overthrow the Mossadeq government in Iran at that time. We know that Sir George Young who was involved on the MI6 side in that plot also helped to train the notorious SAVAK secret police and that when the Shah was returned to power those secret police tortured and killed people in Iranian prisons. We do know, therefore, the names even of people who were responsible for the death of others. Were those people prosecuted? No ladies and gentlemen, they were not. In fact, George Young, for his services on that occasion, was given a knighthood. That is the hypocrisy of the sentence that I referred to and wanted to bring out in this court.

Alliott: Thank you very much.

Randle: That's it.

Alliott: Yes. I got that impression. Have you any witnesses you wish to call, Mr Randle?

Randle: Yes. I have a character witness to call. He is Mr Jan Kavan.

Bevan: I see no objection from the Crown.

Alliott: Thank you. Come forward, would you please?

Chapter 23:

The Czech Connection

I was first introduced to Jan Kavan when he was an emigre student activist in London struggling to establish a regular means of communication with dissidents inside Czechoslovakia and keeping the outside world informed of what was going on in his country. I worked with him from time to time over the next 19 years. In 1989 he returned to Czechoslovakia and in June 1990 was elected MP to the Federal Parliament. The story of our collaboration is best related through his own testimony in the witness box at the Old Bailey.

Jan had agreed to appear on my behalf prior to the original date set for the trial in April 1990. Meanwhile, however, he had become embroiled in controversy within Czechoslovakia which might have led anyone less loyal and less courageous to have withdrawn his offer. In March 1991 he was among ten deputies in the Federal Parliament named in a special parliamentary committee as having collaborated with the StB, the secret police of the former communist regime. In Jan's case the accusation was that he was 'a confidential contact' from 1969-70 when he represented the Czechoslovak Students Union in London.[1]

The claim was manifestly absurd, given Jan's record of opposition to the regime, and was based on the flimsiest of evidence – if indeed it deserved that title at all. The circumstances were that during the period in question he had had dealings with a Mr Zajicek, Education Officer at the Czechoslovak Embassy, on behalf of fellow students facing visa problems following the Soviet invasion. When the StB files were uncovered after the fall of the communist regime, it emerged that Zajicek had been working at the time for that organisation and had named Jan as one of his contacts. Jan had no knowledge of Zajicek's double role, as the latter himself was to testify in court, but his political opponents made the most of the allegation to try to discredit him. He subsequently lost his seat in the elections of 1992 and it was not until January 1996 that his good name was finally vindicated in a judgement by the Czech appeals court.

When the accusations against Jan first surfaced I contacted him in Prague, and, with his encouragement, drafted a letter for the press and phoned

---

1 See the report by Susan Greenberg and Michael Simmons in the *Guardian*, 23 March 19.

round various of his friends and contacts in this country asking them to be co-signatories.[2] The *Guardian* and *Independent* carried the letter on 2nd April, the first signed mainly by people in and around the peace movement, the second by some weightier names, mostly well-known journalists. The Guardian also published an interview I conducted by phone with Jirina Šiklova, another prominent Czech dissident during the communist period, who was unstinting in her praise for Jan and the role he had played.[3]

I would have perfectly well understood if Jan, in the light of the accusations he was facing, had changed his mind about giving evidence on behalf of someone who, unbeknownst to him until it became public knowledge, had helped in the escape of a Soviet spy. But he never wavered, and flew specially from Prague to be present at the trial. I met him at Stamford Hill underground station the evening before he was due to give his evidence and went with him to a flat nearby which he still rented. It was crammed with office equipment and piles of the latest edition of East European Reporter which he had edited until shortly before then, and which, since its foundation in 1985, had reported events and debates within the opposition movements in the Soviet-bloc countries in Europe. We then went through the kind of questions I should ask him.

---

2 The Guardian letter was co-signed by Jeanette Buirski of European Dialogue, April Carter, Howard Clark of War Resisters International, Peter van den Dungen, Lecturer in the Department of Peace Studies, Bradford University, Judith Hempsling and Joanne Landy of the Campaign for Peace and Democracy, US, John Keane, Peter Rossman of Across Frontiers, and Dorothy and Edward Thompson. The Independent letter was co-signed by Neal Ascherson, Mark Frankland, John Keane, Arthur Lipow, Edward Mortimer, William Shawcross, Tony Smith, Ben Webb and again Dorothy and Edward Thompson.

3 `A Tragedy Comes to Light'. Of Jan Kavan, Jirina Siklova stated: `On the naming of Jan Kavan last week i would like to say this. The contribution to the opposition from the outside during the 1970s and 1980s by Jan Kavan from Palach Press and others was extremely important. It was Jan who first established a channel of communication with friends in the West starting in January 1971 when the first van was driven to Brno. From then on we received regular help from Palach Press, from Amnesty International and others. Jan's work was vital. For 10 years he and his friends brought in material by van until in 1981 the secret hiding place was discovered by the border guards. After that other ways had to be found.'

'Aren't your enemies in Czechoslovakia going to use your appearance at the trial to throw mud at you?' I asked him at one point.

'It's already happening! Some of the papers have got onto the fact that I'm coming here, but …'

He shrugged his shoulders and smiled wryly. He is a man well used to controversy.

Jan took the stand at the Old Bailey at 11.45 on the Tuesday morning, 25th June. He is rather thick set with a prominent balding dome of a head. In his dark suit and large horn-rimmed spectacles he has a distinctive presence. He answered my questions slowly and deliberately, and with impressive assurance. From time to time his eyes twinkled as we recalled some of the adventures and successes of the past. He was there to be a character witness for me, but I was anxious first of all to impress the jury with his own background and credentials.

Randle: You are Jan Kavan?

Kavan: Yes, I am.

Q: Are you an Independent Civic Forum MP in the Czechoslovak Federal Parliament?

A: Yes, I am.

Q: Have you flown over especially to be in this court?

A: Yes, I did.

Q: You were born in London, I believe, in 1946.

A: That is correct.

Q: Your father was, at that time, Czechoslovakia press attache in Czechoslovak Embassy in London?

A: That is correct.

I then went in some detail into his family and personal background. His father had fought with the Free Czechoslovak Forces during the war and was part of the unit that had liberated Belsen. His mother, Rosemary, was English, born in Leicester, but went to live in Prague with her husband in 1950. At around that time the notorious show trials of top communist leaders and others began, including that of the General Secretary, Rudolf Slansky who was among those executed. Jan's father had been arrested in 1951 and forced to give evidence on the prosecution side in the Slansky trial, before being tried himself and sentenced to 25 years imprisonment on trumped-up charges. The alleged offence was that he had acted as the main link between the Czechoslovak Communist Party and 'British Imperialist Agents,' supposedly led by the Labour MP, Konni Zilliacus. Ironically the latter was himself expelled from the Labour Party because of his left-wing views. Jan's father was released on Christmas Day 1955, but his health had seriously deteriorated during his years in prison and he died of a heart attack in May 1960.

Jan himself continued to live with his mother in Prague, and became involved as a student in the 1960s in a group known as the Prague Radicals, a small group of student leaders who campaigned for democracy within the Communist Party. Two of his closest friends had been expelled from university and drafted into the army to put a halt to their activities and to avoid a similar fate he came to Britain in 1969 to finish his studies and had remained there until shortly before the fall of the communist regime in November 1989. At the time of the Soviet invasion in August 1968 he was representing the Czechoslovak Students Union at the US Student Congress in Kansas but hastened back to help organise opposition. He and other radical students organised occupations and sit-in strikes in November 1968 which were supported by the industrial and agricultural workers and by practically all the trade unions in the country. He was also one of three or four main student leaders who signed political treaties with the industrial unions listing a minimum programme which they pledged to defend by all non-violent means, including the threat of a general strike.

At this point, Alliott interrupted.

> **Alliott: Mr Randle, I mean no disrespect to Mr Kavan but you are calling him as a character witness to say what a good chap you are, not to give us a lecture on the recent political history of Czechoslovakia. You follow the point?**
>
> **Randle: Yes I do. My point was to establish where Mr Kavan was coming from, as it were, and that would lead up to my own involvement with him.**
>
> **Alliott: You see strictly the only question a character witness can be asked is something along the lines 'what is the general standing of Mr Randle amongst his peers?' Now of course, it is stretched so that character witnesses can speak of the background as a rule of the defendant and the good things he has done in the past. But I really think this is going much wider to establish Mr Kavan's basis for getting to know you. You have touched upon it in our own evidence. (To Jan): There came a stage, did there sir, when you wanted printed materials and books and, as we understand it, Mr Randle was most helpful in getting material into the country?**
>
> **A: That is correct.**
>
> **Bevan: None of this evidence would be challenged by the Crown. Mr Kavan is a highly respected and honest individual and I would have no questions of this witness so Mr Randle could take it as shortly as he wished ...**

However, I did not want to take it that short. It was important for the jury, especially perhaps the younger members of it, to grasp the political and human significance of the events that Jan had been involved with.

> **Randle: There was a very dramatic event that took place in Czechoslovakia at that time. I am referring to Jan Palach. Can you just describe what happened and how you visited him with a friend in the hospital?**
>
> **A: Jan Palach was a 21 year old student who got so exasperated at the concessions made to the occupying forces by the government of the time in autumn and winter 1968/69, that he decided that the only way to stop this growing demoralisation and growing apathy of the population and acceptance of these concessions was to do something which would shock the nation out of its apathy and bring them back to the reality of what was happening. So he decided to offer the greatest price any human being can offer and sacrifice his life and set himself alight. He was taken to hospital, badly burned, where for three days he still fought for his life.**
>
> **During those three days, when it become clear to him he was going to die, he asked for one of the main student leaders to come to the hospital. I went with him to the hospital but did not enter the room where Palach was dying. Palach dictated a message to those other young people who, according to his note, were prepared to follow his example and die if his demands had not been met. I was very emotionally affected by this experience and realised that if he was prepared to die I should be prepared to at least do everything possible, short of offering my life which I was not prepared to do, being slightly too selfish for that. But I was prepared to do anything else I thought necessary to stop that political process.**
>
> **Q: So did you eventually decide to stay in Britain and work from Britain to help the democratic opposition in Czechoslovakia?**
>
> **A: Yes. My permission to stay in England, Czechoslovakian permission, expired on the 1st September, 1970. I then had to make a decision whether to stay here and become an emigre with a question whether I would be able to return to Czechoslovakia or should return and risk imprisonment. I couldn't make up my mind so I went back to Czechoslovakia illegally in August, 1970, to consult with my friends about what to do. The majority told me if I could manage to get back to England that it would be very useful if I could stay in the UK and meet their needs as they would define them and that is exactly what I did …**

Q: And I think it was round about that time, September or October, round about that time in 1970, we first met?
A: Yes. When I accepted the challenge to go to England to meet the needs of the opposition as they would define them I was told the first thing they would want was a very efficient electric duplicator ... As a young student in Britain I had absolutely no idea how you start raising money to buy duplicators and how you smuggle a duplicator across the border. I began therefore to make, as I hoped, discreet enquiries of most people I knew in this country at the time, people associated with the peace moment. And one of my friends in the peace moment introduced me to you, as you probably remember, as someone who might be able to help me with this particular task. And I am still, all these years later, extremely grateful for the efficient help you gave us, because I still can't think how else we would have solved the problem of not only purchasing a van big enough to carry a duplicator but building a secret compartment large enough for the duplicator – and cleverly disguising it so that various Czech customs officials, who at that time were very thorough indeed looking not just for Gestetner duplicators but for small pieces of paper, would not be able to find it. In fact, we used that system for many years, and many other vans with exactly the same compartment, built on your suggestions and with your help ... and were never caught or not caught until ... April 1981. This is due to your help for which we are grateful.
Q: Thank you very much. In January, 1970, did I make the journey – let us go before that. I think it was November 1970; did I make the journey to Prague as a courier on your behalf to make contact with some of the opposition?
A: Yes. In the last months of 1970 I was establishing a regular network, a regular channel of communication to Prague. I couldn't use a telephone and I couldn't use any open communication as they were all monitored by the secret service. As proof of that I received even recently a transcript of some of the letters I sent in at the time and transcripts of some of the telephone conversations I had. I was aware that the only way I could communicate with my friends without the knowledge of the Czech secret service was to use couriers and you were one of the first couriers I sent to Czechoslovakia.
Q: And in January 1971 I did in fact drive the first of the adapted vans to Czechoslovakia, is that right?
A: Yes. That is correct. At that time we had no experience in smuggling things across the border and did not know how the search would be conducted. Not wishing, with all due respect to you, to lose the

> Gestetner duplicator, we decided to send you on a dummy run – not quite a dummy run because that would be a waste of money we didn't have – but with a van full of books, Czech and western literature requested by the opposition. You drove it as the first person to risk being arrested or detained if the compartment was found. I agreed, of course, at that time it was more important for us to preserve the Gestetner, and you were prepared to take that risk and therefore you drove in the first load of books, the first of what eventually were one of a hundred similar van runs. Your successful dummy run allowed us to send, with the next van, the duplicator.

Jan's evidence at this point was neatly corroborated by a prosecution exhibit – Exhibit 31, the 'ex-passport' of mine which we had used to demonstrate in our book how we altered Pat's passport to get Seán Bourke out of the country.

> Q: I refer the court now to exhibit 31. This shows various pages of my passport at that time, and it is 1080 in the jury bundle. It's just to draw attention, if you could see it's marked page 11 of the visa page of my passport, or my ex-passport. You will see there is a Czechoslovak visa dated 3rd of the 1st 1971 … This would be the visa for that particular journey?
>
> A: Yes.
>
> Q: Now, the person I met there on that occasion was Jaroslav Sabata. Can you say something about him?
>
> A: He was one of the main organisers of the first underground opposition in Czechoslovakia. He eventually spent eight and a half years in prison for these activities in the seventies and early eighties. He was one of the main organisers of the border meetings between Czechoslovakia opposition and the Polish opposition. Today he is a minister in the Czech government.
>
> Q: There was a problem at a certain point when you were driving these vans into Czechoslovakia – the risk that because it was the same van all the time, it would be recognised by border guards and they would become suspicious?
>
> A: Yes, we learned on the job to become more or less professional smugglers of literature. I never had any training in this so I had to guess what would be the best way to protect the regular loads of literature. I realised that we could not afford to buy each time a new van. That would have been totally out of the question as we were not supported by any government secret services or any anything like that. What we did was that from time to time we changed the colour of the van and we changed the registration number, the two main facts which the custom officers would have to put into their computers,

and we hoped that therefore the computer would then treat these vans as separate vans and they would not be identified as being always the same van, which would obviously draw attention to us and rouse their suspicions. The problem, of course, was how to change the registration number each time, simply because, as you know, registration numbers are recorded in important documents which you have to present at foreign borders. You don't have to present the log book but you do have to present a Green Card which is proof of your insurance. That was a major headache because you couldn't obviously walk to a British insurance company and say, 'Please give us a different set of green cards for different registration numbers for each journey.' We therefore came to the conclusion that, unfortunately, the only thing we could do was to drive the van on the legal regular British registration number so close to Czechoslovakia borders and then change the numbers there, and arrive at the Czechoslovak border with the false number plates and the false Green Card. Once again we turned to you and asked you to help us to obtain false Green Card forms which I then filled in with a different registration number for each journey.

Q: Was that successful? Did the Czechoslovak border guards ever realise that this wasn't a genuine Green Card?

A: No. I still don't know how you did it, but the Green Cards which were used were perfect forgeries. We never of course tried them on the British insurance companies themselves or on the British custom officers, but on the Czechoslovakia border … They were always with no exceptions accepted as genuine.

Q: I was actually breaking the law by producing those green cards?

A: Yes, you were.

Q: Do you think I should be prosecuted for having done that?

Alliott: That cannot begin to be a proper question, but never mind.

Randle: Then I will not put it.

Alliott: I am not sure it was an offence to present the form, what I think was to suggest that a reputable insurance company had filled it in and issued it.

Kavan: In that case I probably violated the law more than you did.

Alliott: That is what I strongly suspect.

Kavan: I filled it in and presented it to the customs officer. Therefore I should probably be prosecuted. I, on the whole still today feel that this was justified. To give an example, recently in January this year I as a member of parliament in Czechoslovakia supported the Bill of Rights, the first Bill of Rights which we had for many, many years, and there was a long discussion about a clause which we eventually included, which specifically gives citizens the right to violate the law on those occasions when major principles of democracy are in question. It basically justified a kind of civil disobedience. The lawyers who put it in who consulted with a number of international lawyers before they did so, and obviously had in mind the Warsaw Pact invasion of Czechoslovakia. A number of people resisted passively … and therefore this kind of a clause [was included] which would allow people in extreme circumstances, when major humanitarian principles or democracy are in jeopardy, to violate the law … To me what the [communist] Czechoslovakia government did in prohibiting literature published in this country was wrong. It was literature which was not in any way seditious or pornographic, which would not in any way be contrary to either UK or international law – ordinary academic books about the political situation in Czechoslovakia. The fact that they prevented such literature coming into the country to me was illegitimate behaviour. Therefore I believe that I can challenge illegitimate behaviour by, in this particular instance, violating the law and in the same spirit I saw your helping in providing that support in exactly the same spirit. So I don't think you should be prosecuted for it.

Randle: Thank you. The feeling is mutual. I hope you won't be arrested on your way out of this court. Just to go through various things, not only did you do this kind of activity of smuggling material into Czechoslovakia but you also established a number of organisations to provide information about what was happening over there, to have a two-way communication and to put this on a regular basis. Tell us just briefly what those various organisations were?

A: Thanks to the van journeys, which were the most important thing in my opinion which we were doing, and thanks to their success, we began to receive via the same vans an enormous amount of current literature and periodical information [from inside Czechoslovakia] with the request to publicise them in the West. By 1974 the flow of such information was so huge that we decided to institutionalise the way of handling the information and set up a limited company, a press agency, called Palach Press named after Jan Palach and in memory of his sacrifice. It was the main unofficial voice of the opposition and eventually of Charter 77 in English-speaking countries and supplied information about what was happening in Czechoslovakia to British newspapers, internationally and so on. A few years later when the volume of work we were doing in Czechoslovakia – supporting underground university seminars, supporting translations of English academic books into Czech which were published underground in Czechoslovakia, sending technical help: first duplicators and other things, and eventually in the early eighties, video cameras, computers, printers, etcetera – we set up a charity called the Jan Palach Information and Research Trust registered as a UK charity to raise money here for the support of educational and cultural activities in Czechoslovakia.

Eventually I was involved also in similar work, not just with Czechoslovakia but vis-a-vis the entire central and eastern Europe and I cooperated with other similar organisations based primarily in the UK, but also in France and elsewhere, who were doing similar things vis-a-vis Poland, Hungary and eventually other countries. For that reason, in Spring 1985 we set up another charity which basically very briefly did two things. It produced a quarterly journal which tried to inform not just the British public and the Western public as to what was happening in those countries but also to inform some editors in those countries who could read English what was happening in neighbouring countries for them to understand that people in Poland knew far less of what was happening in Czechoslovakia than people in London or New York.

Alliott: Mr Randle, I am sure all this is an immense contribution to the much happier state of affairs that prevails in Czechoslovakia today. I remind you again, you called this gentleman as a character witness for you.

Randle: Well, perhaps we can move on then. At that time in that period, I was also quite active in the peace movement and writing about the relationship between the peace movement in this country and the opposition movements in Eastern Europe. Did you read some of those studies and articles that I wrote at that time?

A: Yes. I don't know if I read all of them but I read quite a number of them, primarily because at the time I was involved in mediating and facilitating a dialogue between some Western peace groups and human rights activists in Czechoslovakia. It was a very uneasy dialogue, full of distrust and prejudices on both sides because they were both influenced by propaganda in their own countries.

Randle: Thank you. Just a couple more questions, one which I meant to clarify earlier. When I first met you and was adapting this van, you had no idea of my involvement in the escape of George Blake?

A: None whatsoever.

Q: And you first found out about it when it become public knowledge?

A: I found out about it when the book was published.

Q: Do you remember writing to me in the early months of 1989 asking for further help with adapting a Ford transit van to get more equipment into Czechoslovakia?'
A: Yes, I do. As I mentioned earlier, in April 1981 one of our vans using the same system which you helped to build in 1970/71 was apprehended by the Czechoslovakian authorities and from then on we couldn't of course use the same system. We had great problems in continuing the smuggling of literature into Czechoslovakia. However, we continued to do so on a smaller scale. By 1988/89, the opposition was so well organised and there were so many more new groups, that the smaller scale smuggling operation … couldn't meet that demand. I therefore decided that we had to restart van journeys on the same basis, carrying the same quantity of material … As you so efficiently helped us in 1970 I wrote to you and asked whether you would be able to come up with a different system with the same purpose and enabling the same quantities to be hidden in the van. So I wrote to you a letter asking whether you could help us to adapt the Ford transit which I then had at my disposal.
Q: Do you remember telling me telling you at a certain point that when the police searched my house they seized that correspondence?
A: I remember in fact that you told me that a few days after they searched your house that various papers were taken and then you phoned me and apologised that among the papers taken was also my letter to you.
Q: You returned to Czechoslovakia some time in late 1989?
A: I returned on 25th November, 1989.
Q: So the stirring events were still going on at that time I believe?
A: Yes. I attended in the first few days of what is now known as the velvet revolution – thirty-four hours after the Presidium of the Communist Party resigned, but quite a long time before the government fell and the first non-communist government was appointed on 10th December, 1989.
Q: Did you have any problems getting into the country?
A: I was arrested, detained rather, as soon as I landed at Prague Airport. I was interrogated for 12 hours and eventually – on the Monday morning of 26th November – allowed to go. Twenty-four hours later, at 7 seven o'clock in the morning, I was picked up in my hotel and taken for yet another interrogation. After that I was again allowed to continue my activities which were to join Civic Forum where I eventually worked in the address department. As days went

by the powers of the secret service diminished fairly rapidly and the interrogations did not have any long term effect on me.
Q: In June 1990 did you stand as a candidate for the Federal Parliament?
A: Yes, I did. I was selected by Civic Forum and in June 1990 I was elected to the Parliament.
Q: So 20 years after your exile you returned and were elected to the Federal Parliament?
A: Yes, that is correct.
Randle: Thanks very much.
Alliott: Any questions, Mr Pottle?
Pottle: No.
Bevan: No questions, thank you.
Alliott: Thank you very much. Like all other witnesses you are free to leave if you wish to do so.

Jan's testimony was crucially important not only in the context of the trial itself but in a wider political sense. Much more powerfully even than Blake's own video statement, it showed that we had no sympathy with repressive Soviet-style regimes and were prepared actively, and at personal risk, to contribute to the efforts of movements inside them for democratic reform. Blake had noted in his statement that we had several times expressed the wish that we could have used the van in which he made his escape to smuggle someone out of East Germany who wanted to leave it and was unable to do so. Obviously that was completely impractical. But what did prove practical, and was infinitely more effective than any one-off gesture, was using the skills and experience gained in his escape to provide long-term assistance to a dissident democratic movement in another East-Central European country.

Jan's testimony also lent powerful support to our argument about necessity. For who could doubt that Jan's own technical breaches of the law – in particular in presenting forged Green Cards to the Czechoslovak border guards – was morally and politically justified? Another impressive point in a legal sense was the fact, as Jan had pointed out, that the new Czechoslovak Constitution contained a clause recognizing the right of the citizen to engage in acts of civil disobedience in exceptional circumstances where the authorities were acting in breach of the constitution or of human rights.

We were now moving into the final act of the drama, but had one further surprise in store for the bemused prosecuting counsel.

Chapter 24:

Abuse Again

As soon as Jan had finished giving his testimony, Alliott asked Bevan how long he thought his final address to the jury would take.

> **Bevan: Extremely short, but what I wish to say to your Lordship now is essentially this. In view of the fact that these defendants have admitted the allegations contained in the three counts of this indictment, and that your Lordship has ruled that the defence of necessity is not available in any case, it strikes myself, on behalf of the Crown, that no useful purpose would be served addressing the jury. And I also very much take into account that neither of these two defendants are represented.**
>
> **Also although technically I could perhaps make a speech to the jury on behalf of the Crown, in view of the fact that some evidence through the television interview of George Blake has been shown to the jury, it is but a technicality that they have called evidence as to fact. In these circumstances, and for those reasons, I do not propose to address the jury.**

Well certainly you couldn't get any shorter than that! Bevan's reference to the fact that only in a very technical sense had we called evidence as to the facts with Blake's statement was an acknowledgement of the legal procedure which debars the prosecution from making a closing address to the jury where no witnesses to the facts have been called. Alliott had allowed us to present Blake's testimony though doubting if it really had any evidential value.

Pat told the judge that he expected his final address to last somewhere between half an hour to an hour – and I said I expected mine to be of around the same length.

> **Randle: … I am a little bit unsure of how to proceed because it's been a long morning.**
>
> **Alliott: I am not going to ask either of you to start now. I dare say, although you are probably prepared you could do with a little more preparation time.**
>
> **Randle: I could really do with overnight.**

What I was angling for here was for Pat's and my closing speeches and the judge's summing up to occur at the same sitting. Our lawyers had advised us that it would work to our disadvantage if our speeches were followed by an overnight break and the jury went into the juryroom with only the judge's summing up fresh in their minds. But Alliott resisted my suggestion.

> **Alliott: I do not think I can accommodate you that far. The sensible thing will be if Mr Pottle begins at two o'clock and then we have a short break after he has concluded his speech, then we will have you Mr Randle and then we will call it a day. Then I will sum the matter up to you and you will be out mid-morning, members of the jury, something like that. Let us work on that timetable and give ourselves a little extra this lunchtime.**

Over lunch we reviewed the situation. The time had come, we decided to resurrect the issue of abuse. We had earlier decided that I would present the argument, relying on cases researched by the lawyers, especially by Tom MacKinnon. We thought there was little or no chance that Alliott would find for us, or that it would delay proceedings by more than fifteen or twenty minutes, but it would provide us with an appeal point after we had been convicted.

As soon as the judge came back to court after lunch I stood up:

> **Randle: Before we start, I would like to make a submission on the question of abuse, particularly in the light of evidence that has come out in cross-examination.**
>
> **Alliott: This is a matter that Mr Bevan indicated was for me alone. Is that your understanding of the position, Mr Bevan?**
>
> **Bevan: Your Lordship, this application takes me by surprise. I had no warning of it. I need perhaps a moment to make sure I am right, but a defendant is allowed to raise the question of abuse during the course of the proceedings and it is for the learned trial judge to decide the matter.**
>
> **Alliot: Yes. It is certainly no part of the trial by jury, is it?**
>
> **Bevan: It is not. It is not even a matter relating to trial on indictment. I use those words because the only jurisdiction that the Divisional Court had is very limited. The Divisional Court in the abuse proceedings decided that an abuse of process application is not a matter relating to trial on indictment, which just goes to emphasise this is not the matter that concerns this jury one iota.**
>
> **Alliott: No. The history that we have heard is that Macpherson, J, made a ruling upon it which was challenged by judicial review to the Divisional Court. And now Mr Randle, having raised it initially before the jury was sworn, raises it again now. How long do you think it will take you?**
>
> **Randle: I do not think it will be very long. With the decision … maybe ten minutes, quarter of an hour.**

> **Alliott: All right. I will say quarter of an hour, members of the jury, if you like to leave court and I shall deal with this because this is a matter for me, as you will appreciate.**

It was just a minute or two after 2 o'clock when I began my submission. We hadn't got much to go on but it was worth trying. I began by repeating the point we had raised on the first day before the jury were sworn and again during the cross-examination of Chief Inspector Eggington, namely that the fact that the Divisional Court had ruled against us was not a bar to the Crown court reconsidering the matter if fresh evidence came to light: in legal jargon, there was no issue estoppel. Thanks to the lawyers researches I was able to cite case law to this effect, relying on the judgement of Judge Denison in *R. v Grobb and Hart* (1990) – which indeed I had cited at the very outset of the trial at their suggestion, and 'put down our marker' on the abuse issue.

There were two substantive points, I said, which the Divisional Court had been unaware of but which had emerged during the course of the present trial. First there was the plea-bargain offer by the Crown – their offer to drop the most serious charge of aiding Blake escape if we pleaded guilty to one of the lesser charges (or to both of them according to Bevan's recollection). The seriousness of the charges against us, I argued, had weighed strongly with the judges in the Divisional Court, as was clear from their judgement. Second there was the fact, as Chief Inspector Eggington had testified, that the Crown Prosecution Service had not been aware when they initiated the prosecution of the MI5 Note for File which strongly indicated that a policy decision had been taken in 1970 not to proceed against us because of the embarrassment this would cause when 'the big fish' had got away.

Another question of an entirely different character had arisen in relation to the decision of the Divisional Court. Anthony Scrivener had argued that the Divisional Court should not have taken upon itself to reconsider the substantive issue of abuse, and to hear live witnesses. If the judges decided that Mr Macpherson had acted wrongly in refusing to hear the witnesses we wished to call – which they did – they should have sent the issue back to the Crown Court for a new hearing of the question.

Bevan responded by recalling the history of events – the application for disclosure of documents before Mr Justice Auld, the Old Bailey hearing in April 1990 before Macpherson, the hearings in the Divisional Court, and finally Lord Justice Watkins' rejection of an application to certify that an issue of public importance was raised by the case. He pointed out, in relation to this last matter, that originally Geoffrey Robertson had stated two grounds for applying for the certificate: the gap of 25 years between the offence and the prosecution, and the action of the Divisional Court in hearing witnesses and making its own ruling on abuse rather than ordering the Crown Court to reconsider the matter. The implication was that he had concluded there was no substance in that complaint.

After the discussion had been going on for a while, Alliott intervened to say he was concerned about the position of the jury 'the only people who are here without any reason other than they are called to do a public service.' It was most unfortunate he concluded, 'but I think what I had better do is send the jury away for the day.' However, he did not do this straight away.

> **Alliott: Mr Pottle looks somewhat anguished at the thought of that delay. Perhaps you'd better have a word to see if you really do intend to proceed with this. I am not shutting you out but I indicate that the odds of me disagreeing with the Divisional Court who heard all those witnesses, as present advised, is remote.**
> **Bevan: My Lord, may I say, and this may help, I know not. In so far as the Divisional Court is concerned, they very much concentrated on and considered Miss A's evidence, she being the author of the 4.13 document.**
> **Alliott: I have already indicated that the CPS acknowledged this point. I think the inference was overwhelming, but there is another matter that he has raised.**
> **Bevan: Completely and utterly irrelevant, in my submission.**
> **Alliott: But Mr Randle has said that the offer made by the Crown, entertained by the Crown, whichever way it went …**
> **Bevan: Much has been said about this in this court to my consternation. As your Lordship knows Mr Scrivener approached the Crown with regard to their view as what course and what count might or might not be acceptable in this matter, but since these defendants, as I understand it, certainly from counsel were never going to plead to any kind of indictment, come what may … (addressing me directly) … that is true?**
> **Randle: Yes.**
> **Bevan: … it never proceeded. In so far as any discussion between the Crown and the defence is concerned, during the course of these proceedings your Lordship will remember the 45 minute adjournment when we first started this case. I seem to remember some conversation, either by myself and Mr Wadham or Mr Birnberg, of what had been said earlier that the Crown would certainly consider not pursuing every single count, the three counts in this indictment … and that justice might be able to be done by a plea, let us say, to counts 2 and 3 rather than 1. But this, as your Lordship knows, is a discussion**

that can go on and has gone on as between counsel for the Crown, generally the professional advisors of the defendant, normally other counsel, as to whether or not it is possible to shorten the case and justice being done by accepting a plea. But it never got to the stage of a deal ever because as Mr Randle and Mr Pottle will no doubt accept, it was never indicated that they would.
The Crown has never taken instructions as to whether they would or would not; it was nothing more than a debate. I, on behalf of the Crown, have never sought the instructions of the Director of Public Prosecutions and said, 'Can I do this because this is being actually offered?' It never reached that stage and I hope Mr Randle and Mr Pottle, who have no doubt come to know me over the years, will accept my word for that.
Alliott: I merely raise that point because although I think nothing at all of Mr Randle's second point that there is something new, that is to say that the knowledge of the CPS did not embrace the 4.13 document, there was nothing in that because obviously everything that happened in the Divisional Court made it perfectly plain they had no idea of its existence until later. But I have reminded you there was an another factor that he had earlier said was something I should take into account which was something the Divisional Court did not know about. (Turning to me)
Mr Randle, what I think I must do in order that the jury are not mucked about, is to say would you please have a word with Mr Pottle, a word with Mr Birnberg and Mr Wadham. Do you want formally to renew the abuse of process application? If you do, then I will send the jury away for the day. If you do not then they can come back and Mr Pottle can address them. Just have a word.
Bevan: May I just say one word to your Lordship so that their legal advisers may hear it.
Alliott: Yes.
Bevan: It would be my submission that if this application was pursued, and I would concentrate now on what they consider the plea bargain, which is totally misleading, what goes on between counsel on behalf of the Crown and the defendants and their legal advisors as to whether or not a plea might be acceptable or not, does not touch upon, with respect, the seriousness of this case. Of course the Crown in the abuse proceedings argued that helping Blake escape was in itself a serious offence. The fact that the Crown were approached by Mr Scrivener and the Crown said thereafter, 'We could consider accepting a plea; let's take counts 2 and 3, in the circumstances of this case,' does not

diminish one iota, in my submission, the seriousness of the matter that had to be considered by the Divisional Court. Maybe that is a point Mr Wadham and Mr Birnberg will take into account.

Alliott: I do not overlook the fact, of course, as well that had counsel continued to represent these two, the matter would never have come into the public domain in court. If it had done so through inexperience or malice on the part of counsel, no doubt disciplinary steps would have been taken.

Pottle: I would just like to point out just on the last point …

Alliott: No criticism of you. One of the advantages of being in person is that you can breach all the rules.

Pottle: It was really what Mr Bevan said.

Alliott: Please, you know I have got uppermost in my mind the jury.

Pottle: Just a simple point – what is Mr Bevan saying? I think what he is saying, he was basing his whole argument before the High Court on the seriousness of this charge, the 5 years, that is what he got over to the two Lords in the High Court. The reason this is active after 25 years, is the seriousness of the charge. When it was put to him, 'Look it's equivalent to a man going into a police station and saying, I have had something on my conscience for 25 years, 25 years ago I slapped somebody in the face which could be GBH.' What would the policeman have said? He would have said – 'On your bike!' He certainly wouldn't have said, 'Right that offence is so serious that it must be considered after 25 years.' And had those two judges been aware of the fact that the Crown was quite willing to accept the lesser pleas …

Alliott: Mr Pottle, please take this decision. If I am going to have to consider abuse of the process I must read what the Divisional Court said, but it is going to take time. I want to release the jury if you are minded to pursue that particular court. Please take your joint decision.

Ben and John came up to the dock and we had a brief discussion. We were all agreed that there was nothing to lose and something to be gained from pursuing the abuse issue.

Pottle: I think we have to proceed with the abuse of process and I apologise deeply about the time, but it is a point that we do need, in fact, to pursue.

Alliott: Are you content that I send a message to through the jury? I think, Miss Russell, I shall ask you to do it personally. Would you say that they are released for the day and the explanation is that which Mr Randle mentioned in their presence, the abuse of process, is going to be pursued and will take the rest of the afternoon.

After he had ascertained that there were copies of Macpherson's and the Divisional Court's judgements he could skim through, Alliott adjourned the hearing for 15 minutes.

Pat and I were walking on air. We had thought the abuse issue would be over and done with in ten or fifteen minutes. Now the jury would hear our final speeches and the judge's summing up at one sitting, and both would be fresh in their minds as they retired to consider their verdict.

As we walked out into the main lobby and turned to the left to the little box room where we held our adjournment discussions, I caught sight of Mr Calvert-Smith talking to some fellow barristers.

> 'Oh Randle's got a brilliant point …' he was saying, his voice rising to a sarcastic nasal whine on the word 'brilliant.'

I didn't stop to hear him explain what my brilliant point was but I was laughing aloud as I walked down the narrow corridor to our room to tell the others what I had overheard. Anne told me afterwards that she had left the courtroom next to Chief Inspector Eggington who had sighed aloud and said to her: 'Is he as stubborn as this at home too?'

When we had crowded into a tiny ante room, Tom Mackinnon wondered whether we shouldn't try to insist on a complete re-hearing of the abuse issue, including recalling Watts, Cunningham, Miss A, and Kevin O'Connor.

'Of course it would mean that if we lost the abuse case, the whole trial would have to start again in front of a different jury.'

Pat and I groaned aloud. Tom regarded us with his big, solemn eyes:

> **'I know it's a frightful thought,' he said. 'I understand how you must feel. But on the other hand I've been watching the jury's reactions and I don't think I've ever come across a worse jury.'**

But the thought of further delays was too awful to contemplate. Instead we went rapidly through the points I should stress when the hearing resumed.

At 3.15 we were back in court.

> **Alliott: May I say three preliminary things. First or all, I shall have to rise at ten to fifteen past four because I have a presiding judges' meeting in the Royal Courts of Justice. Secondly, I think that although the fact that the trial by jury has been interrupted for a further argument on abuse of process can of course be reported, I do not think the argument should be reported until after the conclusion of the trial. I am always loathe to make a Section 4 order which is a sledge hammer to crack a nut, but I hope that review will be honoured. Thirdly, skimming over that which is irrelevant, for instance going to jurisdiction, I have now read, albeit very quickly, and you must all refer me to specific passages, the judgments of Macpherson, J, and**

the Divisional Court in the instant case and the judgment of Judge Denison in the Grobb and Hart case. Yes Mr Randle.
Randle: Yes, thank you very much.
Alliott: Can I indicate the note I have. You were saying that it is open to you to renew the application to stay a case on the basis it is an abuse of the process of the court – there is no issue estoppel – and you have indicated to date two points which I will summarise as the plea bargaining unknown to the Divisional Court and the 4.13 document not known to the CPS.
Randle: Right. Well we have made our point on the fish document or the 4.13 document. I am not going to say any more on that. I'm going to try to be as brief as possible and to make this the last interruption of this kind.

I want to concentrate on the plea bargaining issue, and to say that there were four occasions on which this offer was made. The first was when Mr Scrivener spoke to Mr Bevan on 2nd March, 1990, and we do have a contemporaneous note of that. The offer that was made at that time was if we pleaded to count 2 the other two charges would be dropped, not only the first charge of assisting in the escape but also the other conspiracy charge.

There were three other occasions on which this was raised. One was during the judicial review proceedings, another was on Friday 24th May this year when we were applying for leave to appeal to the House of Lords and the final occasion …

Alliott: 23rd of May?
Randle: Friday 24th May of this year. And the final one was on Monday 17th June at the beginning of this present trial. That first occasion I meant to add on 2nd March, 1990, was on the occasion of a hearing in this building before Auld, J. Now that was the only occasion on which our counsel actually approached Mr Bevan. On all the other occasions it was Mr Bevan himself who approached our legal advisors and renewed that offer.
Our point is that if one looks at the judgment at the judicial review it is stated at several points, the seriousness of the offence has to be taken into account.

I developed this point, referring to passages from the Divisional Court judgement which bore it out, and to the judgement in the case of *Jago* that delay in itself, if sufficiently prolonged, could constitute abuse. The important thing was not whether Mr Bevan had taken instruction on a plea bargain but the fact that he was willing to canvass this kind of bargain on behalf of the Crown. Finally I referred briefly to the court decision that it would be an abuse of process to go ahead with the prosecution of three policemen charged with conspiracy to pervert the course of justice in relation to the Guildford Four.[1]

After a short statement from Pat, again underlying the significance of the plea-bargain offer, Bevan replied. As his Lordship was aware, it was Mr Scrivener who first raised the issue of what pleas might or might not be accepted. There had never been any concrete offer on the part of the Crown because he had never been in a position to go to the Director of Public Prosecutions.

> **'It takes two to tango,' the judge intervened to say. 'These two have never been minded to plead to anything.'**

Bevan went on to argue that even if the Divisional Court had heard there had been those offers – or rather offers of consideration – 'it would not ... have altered their view or judgement or attitude one iota.' The only conceivable ground for the Crown not pursuing every single count in the indictment would be humanitarian, bearing in mind that the offences charged had taken place 25 years ago. Furthermore neither Mr Robertson nor Mr Scrivener, who knew about the discussions about pleas, had ever sought to raise the question during the hearing before Mr Justice Macpherson or in the Divisional Court. The case of the three policemen in the Guildford Four affair was completely different. Their counsel had argued that after 17 or 18 years the men's recollection of events was such that they could not put forward a proper defence, and that other officers involved in the investigation either did not remember, or were reluctant to remember, the events of 1974. Our case could not be more different, for it was Pat and myself who had chosen to write our book and give the television interviews that formed the basis of the prosecution's evidence. They were not prejudiced by lack of recollection. 'Their recollection of the events of 1966 is better than that of any other human being in this court.'

Alliott intervened to say that he thought 'at first flush' he would be entitled to take into account also the fact that both of us under affirmation had said they did the acts set out in the indictment. Bevan eagerly agreed, and pointed to a passage in the Divisional Court judgement in which the judges had stated: 'There is a significant difference in our judgement between a case where guilt is squarely in issue and one in which it is suspected that it is not or may not be. The value to be attached to that in the judgement of the court depends entirely upon the circumstances.'

At the end of the submissions and exchanges, Alliott gave his ruling.

> **Alliott: Right at the outset of this case when the defendants were being arraigned, Mr Randle indicated that he wished to raise the question**

1 I mistakenly referred to a Divisional Court decision in relation to the three policemen: in fact it was the magistrate who decided at that point that the case ought not to proceed.

again of an application that this trial was an abuse of the process of the court. In a brief exchange between us he did mention the case of Grobb and Hart. I then indicated that I felt that the issue of abuse, if I may use that shorthand phrase hereafter, had been decided by the Divisional Court and it was not for me to take a contrary view. For the time being, Mr Randle was content to let that matter stand in that way.

At the conclusion of the evidence in the trial before this jury, however, Mr Randle renewed the application and he urges upon me, and this is not in any way dissented from by Mr Bevan for the Crown, that there is no issue estoppel and it is open to me to consider the position de novo.

Two matters are raised in particular and I deal with the second first of all because when I indicated a preliminary or tentative view Mr Randle really did not persist in it. It can be summarised in this way, that the Crown Prosecution Service, when they took the decision to initiate this prosecution, were not aware of the Note for File, variously described as the '4.13 document' or the 'fish document.'

It is quite manifest from everything I have heard, mainly from Mr Bevan, I must confess, being as it were a witness at the forensic process, that that document came as a surprise to him late in the day, was instantly shown to the Divisional Court and by the Divisional Court to these defendants, then of course applicants.

The inference that anyone in court and anyone hearing the events could only draw was that the document came to light then and there for the first time, and I have no doubt that the Divisional Court had well in mind that the decision to initiate the prosecution was taken in ignorance of that document.

The second matter relied upon by Mr Randle, and indeed Mr Pottle who supports this submission, is this: notwithstanding the fact that the Crown have made an allegation in three counts in an indictment, indicating three dimensions of criminality that total a maximum possible sentence upon conviction of 9 years, notwithstanding that it was emphasised to the Divisional Court that these were grave matters, when the matter came before Auld, J.on a preliminary point in this building, Mr Scrivener then acting on behalf of Mr Randle, spoke to Mr Bevan as to whether or not pleas to one or two of the second and third counts would be acceptable upon the basis that the plea to count 1 would then be dropped.

Mr Bevan did not reject that out of hand but certainly entertained the possibility. I now learn that there were three other occasions when the possibility of accepting pleas were aired; on 24th May, on 17th

June, and speaking extempore, as I do, I do not seem to have a note of the third occasion. Suffice it to say that they were spreading from 2nd March until the very start of this trial. And, say the defendants, that attitude, humanitarian as Mr Bevan describes it, invalidates the Crown's attitude that these are serious matters.

That, it is contended, is something that is so serious that the fact that the Divisional Court was not aware of it impeaches their decision and should be a matter that I should take into consideration in arriving at a different conclusion.

I disagree. Whatever transpires between counsel or behind the scenes cannot, in my view, as our system operates, invalidate that which occurs in open court, and in this particular case, as the defendants have been at pains to emphasise, they have never contemplated for one moment pleading to any count on the indictment. Another matter which I am fortified in my initial view that I am entitled to take into consideration in the hearing before me, is the fact that before this jury both defendants have, on affirmation, accepted they did the acts alleged in the three counts of the indictment. That is clearly an aspect of the matter that the Divisional Court, in anticipation of those events, as they set out at page 48 of the perfected judgment – I do not take up the time of the court by reading it; it has been cited to me by Mr Bevan very recently – that was clearly a matter that the Divisional Court took into consideration then as I say, in anticipation, and I am clearly entitled to take into account now that it has in fact transpired.

So as to reviewing the matter de novo I reject the application that the trial held before me amounts to an abuse of the process of the court.

Mr Pottle I return your copy of the judgment. Thank you. It enabled me to correlate the two editions.

I did indicate to the jury before lunch today that I would send them out tomorrow. I will consider that. It depends really how far we go. What I will do is have a break between your speeches and I will then see how much time I have to sum-up. I know not how long the jury will take, one can never tell, but it may be I will decide that first thing in the morning would be more appropriate than later in the day. I will reserve that if I may.

Anything else gentlemen?

There was nothing else, and we left the court happy enough at how events had gone that day, but well aware that by the following night we would almost certainly be behind bars.

Chapter 25:

'No Apologies, No Regrets'

The Blake video turned the trial into a major news story. It was a leading – in some cases the lead – story on radio and television on that Tuesday evening, and made the front pages of many of the papers on Wednesday. The tabloids which had paid little attention to the trial up to that point carried pictures and reports. For us this was an important success. Not only could we now be sure that the trial and its outcome would be widely known and discussed, but we could be confident that the humanitarian motives for our actions – which George stressed in his statement – would be well publicised. Jan's testimony was less widely reported though it did figure in both the *Guardian* and *Independent* reports.

That night – not for the first time during the trial – I stayed up into the early hours working on my computer in Richard's office on the top floor. On this occasion I was re-working my final speech. The lawyers – and John in particular – had strongly advised us against making a long speech. At one point they suggested that we should address the jury for no more than ten minutes, but after discussion we settled on twenty minutes to half-an-hour. Looking through my extensive notes, I decided I had nearer two-hours worth, and I would need to make extensive cuts and revisions. Anne came up several times to ask when I planned to come to bed. I needed, she said, to be fresh and alert next day; if I carried on much longer, I would be ill. At 2am I crept down the stairs to the bedroom.

In the dock the next morning, Pat was first to make his final speech to the jury. He stood tall and spoke with confidence, using plain down-to-earth language. No one could have suspected – certainly I did not suspect – that he was fighting hard to control his nerves. He told me afterwards, however, that his leg muscles were trembling all the time he was talking. 'I was thankful,' he said, 'that the front of the dock prevented the jury and the other people in the court from seeing the way my legs were shaking.'

> **Pottle: This is the only opportunity I have of speaking directly to you. Sitting in the jury box must be boring and frustrating. If it's any consolation to you, I can assure you it beats sitting in the dock. Let's open the windows, let the fresh air in, and blow away the cobwebs. Let common sense, for once, be champion over legal technicalities.**

The Judge and Mr Bevan have told you that the issue you have to decide is simple. I disagree. It is not a simple case. First, the events in question took place 25 years ago, before some of you were even born. Second, the only evidence in this case is the book that we wrote. Third, the police knew about us 21 years ago and made a decision to take no action.

This prosecution is taking place today not because of what we did 25 years ago, but because 110 MPs signed a motion calling for our prosecution and because of the threat of a private prosecution by the inaptly named Freedom Association.

It is necessary to consider all the elements in this case. It is not simply a matter of guilt or innocence. The judge and the prosecution say that the only question for you to consider is – did we do the things we are accused of? Of course we did. We have admitted it from the dock. They say all the other issues are irrelevant. My answer is rubbish! You are the jury. No matter what the judge or Mr Bevan may say to you the final decision is yours. No one can take away that power from you.

If we go back for a moment to last Monday week. Think how nervous we all were – you as well as us. None of us knew the procedure. We were awed by the surroundings, by all those people in fancy dress. The atmosphere was claustrophobic and overpowering.

We spent the first few days eyeing each other up, rarely making direct eye contact. The judge is nervous. It isn't every day he sits in a court where the accused face trial for things which happened 25 years ago and freely admit the facts of the case. Even Mr Bevan is nervous. He is thinking to himself: If I play my cards correctly and win this case, I'll get no credit. If I play them wrongly, I'll lose.

Members of the jury, let me say at this point that if you think I'm being in any way evasive at any point, please stop me. Just shout out – Stop! I'll do my best to explain.

Michael and I would like to return to the situation that existed prior to October 1987. At that time the only people to know of our involvement were MI5, Special Branch, the CIA and the CID. We were content to remain quiet – and so was the prosecution. Then in 1987 we were named in a newspaper. The speculation began about our motives and about who else might have been involved – MI6, MI5, the KGB. There were rumours we might have been working for a foreign power. Innocent people were named. What do you do in those circumstances if you put a value on the things you have done in the past? We felt the only honourable thing to do was to say – yes we did it, and this is why we did it.

Your task today would be a lot easier if this were a simple case of guilt or innocence, but it is not. It is a case of right and wrong. It is a case of politics, a case of how governments lie, cheat and manipulate, and then cover their tracks in a smokescreen of official secrecy.

This is not just a case of a man given an inhuman sentence and of us freeing him. This is a political trial. A political decision was taken in 1970 not to prosecute. When we were publicly named in 1987 it came as no surprise to the police: they had known about us for 17 years.

In 1970 it had been too embarrassing to prosecute us. By 1989 it had become embarrassing not to do so. The Prosecution say that the police did not have the evidence to prosecute. But that evidence could have been obtained in 1970. The decision not to prosecute was taken before even the most routine enquiries had been made. If the police had been seriously looking for evidence they would have checked our fingerprints against those found in the hide-out in Highlever Road. They never did that. We don't know, you and I, how to investigate a case. But even we could have done better than MI5, Special Branch and CID in 1970.

Why were there no routine enquiries? Because a decision had been taken not to conduct them. This is the only explanation that makes sense. The police knew it was us. They could easily obtain more evidence. Why not pursue us and charge us?

The police enquiries were conducted by Special Branch. This is the part of the police force that deals with political offences. If we were talking about France or Russia we would refer to them as political police. Any case with political overtones is dealt with by Special Branch. George's escape certainly did have political overtones.

We have to remember we are talking about a period when the Cold War was at its height. The Cold War was still dominating political thought. Paranoia about Russia and its intentions were still rife.

The 1950s and 1960s had been a terrible time for the British intelligence agencies. There had been the Burgess and Maclean scandal, Philby, Blunt, rumours of a 5th man and a 6th man, the Portland Spy ring, the George Blake escape. British Intelligence was becoming a laughing stock. The CIA regarded it as incompetent and dominated by the old school network. The US was threatening to stop co-operating with British Intelligence.

The accepted theory about George's escape at the time was that it was organised and carried out by the KGB. The British Intelligence services were obviously embarrassed by what had happened, but at least they could argue the escape was carried out by an equal organisation. Then they read Seán Bourke's book and realised that it was not organised by the KGB. What would the revelation that a petty criminal and two peace activists had carried it out do to our relations with our allies? It was better that the world continued to believe that the whole thing was organised by the KGB rather than the Lavender Hill Mob.

I believe this is the truth of the matter. What is my proof? – the MI5 Note for File of April 1970. Other than this I have nothing. We had no access to MI5 files. The prosecution say that the decision was taken in 1970 not to prosecute because of lack of evidence. But if the police adopted the attitude that they wouldn't ask questions if they thought people wouldn't answer them, no crime would ever be solved. George Blake was suspected of being a double-agent. It was only while he was being interviewed that he confessed. There was a cover-up in 1970 by MI5, MI6 and Special Branch. That is the only explanation for the farcical non-investigation in 1970 and again in 1987.

The judge has ruled that our reasons for freeing George are irrelevant. We disagree. He may tell you that the case is simple. The accused admit the facts and they do not have a defence in law. Their reasons may be honourable, but you have no choice in law but to find them guilty.

I disagree with the judge. The idea of a jury system is that you can look at whole case, not just the legal mumbo-jumbo. You are twelve independent people. Unlike most judges you exist in the ordinary world of everyday life. You are able to use your common sense and humanity and not have your hands and minds tied by legal technicalities. Common sense must tell you that our reasons for helping to free George from prison must be relevant. If you accept the narrow legal position that the judge may direct you to do, you diminish your own role as jurors.

The moral indignation that Lord Parker expressed at George's trial about his work for the Russians is something I completely agree with. But moral outrage is only genuine if it is applied to both sides. Have our values become so perverted that we only claim moral outrage at the other side's activities and not our own?

What George did for British intelligence and the KGB was wrong – we have never tried to justify it nor whitewash it. But espionage is a dirty business, where rumour becomes fact and fact becomes fiction. The individuals involved in it are exploiters and in turn exploited. Even when caught they can still be used as international pawns in a game, some to be swopped, some to be given immunity, and the unlucky ones left to rot in prison. No one who supports this kind of thing can hold their heads high.

George was no threat to you, to me or to our children. He had been caught spying for the Russians, just as they had caught people spying for the West. His usefulness as a spy was over, his spying activities at an end. What purpose was served by giving him such a vicious sentence? As Jeremy Hutchinson said at his appeal: 'This sentence is so inhuman that it is alien to all the principles by which a civilised country would treat its subjects.' Anyone with a spark of humanity would see that this was a vicious revenge. Would anyone really prefer to see him rotting in a British jail, rather than being in Moscow living a normal life? If we have to go to prison for helping him, so be it.

The sentence on George was influenced by the climate of the Cold War. Judges are human, like you and I. The formal position is that they don't let outside pressure interfere with their judgement. But this does happen. When Lord Parker sentenced George to 42 years imprisonment, he was affected by the climate of the times, the Cold War. He manipulated the law by imposing three consecutive maximum sentences on George. Lawyers can argue about the legal view of this. But it ain't justice.

The 42 year sentence was counterproductive. The Security Service want spies to confess, but who would do so if they stood to get a sentence of 42 years? What sentence would Lord Parker have imposed if George had not pleaded guilty? Would he have given him more than 42 years? When the government and its judges allow themselves to be dictated to by mob hysteria you end up with a society whose laws and penal institutions are based on revenge and nothing else.

What did George do that set him apart from other spies uncovered at that time? He was not really British, was he? Not of the old school, not one of us. Deep down he was a foreigner and half jewish to boot. He was never part of that privileged undergraduate set at Cambridge in the 1930s. Not like dear old Kim, who was offered immunity, or dear old Anthony who was not only given immunity but allowed to continue his work as Surveyor of the Queen's Pictures.

The law must act even-handedly. It is not for the Secret Services to decide who is and who is not subject to the law. The different treatment meted out to spies goes against the whole idea of equality before the law.

Mr Bevan has stated in this court that if we produce a piece of evidence to show that there was a policy decision in 1970 he would ask the CPS to drop the case. I make a personal appeal now to Mr Bevan to throw out the case at this stage.

Alliott: There is no place in a final address to the jury for an appeal of

> that kind.
> Pottle: The judge has thrown out our defence of necessity. Michael made a powerful case for allowing the necessity defence, but the judge turned it down. Never again will you hear such a powerful and convincing case put forward on this issue.
> When you retire to the jury room you should ask yourselves this question. Would this trial be taking place if the prisoner in question had not been George Blake? The maximum sentence for helping a prisoner to escape is 5 years. If you or I walked into a local police station tomorrow and confessed to doing something 25 years ago which carried a maximum sentence of 5 years – hit someone perhaps – they would not listen. It was who we broke out of prison that led to our prosecution, not what we did.
> You are being asked to convict us not because of what we did in 1966 but because we wrote a book. His Lordship himself said that if we had not written the book we would not be on trial today.
> You will shortly be retiring to the jury room. I suggest you put aside your bundle of papers. You don't need them. All you need is the book, and the MI5 Note for File.

Pat now walked solemnly to the back of the dock and rested his hand on the enclosed banister by the steps leading down to the cells.

> I am standing by the steps that lead to the cells. I would like to take every one of you over here to have a look. Every building has a sewer running underneath it. These steps lead to the sewer underneath this court. 42 years down in that sewer means death.
> You are twelve individuals with minds of your own. The decision is up to you. We think that what we did was right. If you think the same, then obviously you will find us Not Guilty.
> In the end it comes down to this: a fellow human being asked for help. That help meant breaking the law. I feel no shame in having done so, but I would have felt great shame had I turned down George's request for help.
> Yes I helped George Blake escape. I did it for purely humanitarian reasons. I think we were right to do so. I would it again. I have no apologies to make and no regrets.
> I will finish by quoting Bertrand Russell: 'Remember your humanity and forget the rest.'

It was a dramatic and fine performance. During a short interval which the judge allowed us before I made my closing speech, Pat received the congratulations not only of our own friends and legal advisors, but of other lawyers and barristers who had come to the court out of interest and curiosity on the final day of the trial.

'How do I follow that?' I asked Pat.

I had been surprised, however, at how much the judge had allowed Pat to get away with, especially given the very tough stand he had taken at the beginning of the trial. He was far more lenient in the event than Lord Havers had been during our trial in 1962 when Pat had been interrupted and warned several times even during his final speech. Seeing what Pat was been allowed to get away with, I was busy during the few minutes we had flagging passages from the longer version of my closing speech which I had decided to cut out.

One thing which boosted our morale was the fact that some of the lawyers not directly involved in the case were clearly on our side and wanted to help us. One of them approached John during the break and suggested I should emphasise the point about the jury being the final arbiter by asking them what was the point in them attending the trial at all over the last ten days if they were now simply to do as the judge directed them.

At 10.55 the court resumed. Below is my final speech as I reconstructed it from my notes just after the trial ended.

> **Randle: Members of the jury, I don't want to spin out this case any longer than necessary. Pat and I are as anxious to get back home as you are – perhaps slightly more so.**
>
> **This is in one sense the simplest of cases because the facts are not in dispute. Pat and I have made clear throughout the trial that we did carry out the acts of which we are accused.**
>
> **Yet it is in another sense the most complicated of cases because you have to decide whether what happened – almost a quarter of a century ago now – was a criminal act meriting our conviction and punishment or whether the exceptional circumstances of George Blake's case justify what we did and enable you in good conscience to bring in a Not Guilty verdict.**
>
> **Finally it is the most bizarre of cases because it relates to events of 25 years ago and because, as the documents you have before you clearly show, the police knew of our involvement and did nothing about it twenty years ago.**
>
> **There has been a suggestion during the course of the trial that we are seeking martyrdom and do not mind the prospect of being sent to prison. Nothing could be further from the truth. True we wrote the book that forms the main evidence of the prosecution case. But we did so after we had been publicly named and all sorts of rumours began to circulate about us and about others who had nothing whatever to do with the escape.**
>
> **I spent my honeymoon in 1962 on bail, and my first year of marriage**

in Wormwood Scrubs. My eldest son was born while I was there. The last thing I want is to go back to prison now. Nevertheless this is something Pat and I and our families are prepared to face if that is what it takes to put the record straight.

We helped George Blake escape because of the unprecedented sentence he received. As his Counsel, Jeremy Hutchinson, now Lord Hutchinson of Lullington, stated at his appeal: 'This sentence is so inhuman that it is alien to all the principles on which a civilised country would treat its subjects.'

The sentence contravened stated Home Office policy. To quote Lord Hutchinson again: 'The policy of the prison commissioners and the Home Office was not to keep a man in prison so long that his resulting mental and physical deterioration would prevent him returning to the life of the community.' Yet that could not but be the effect of the 42-year sentence passed on George. With maximum remission he would have been released in 1989 at the age of 67. If he had served his full sentence – which he might well have done after a failed escape bid – he would have been released in 2003, an old man of eighty. The much more likely outcome is that he would have died in prison.

This was a sentence which reflected the obsessions of the Cold War not considerations of justice. It contravened the 1688 Bill of Rights, one of the great Documents of Liberty in this country. The Bill of Rights prohibits 'cruel and unusual punishments.' George was sentenced to 42 years imprisonment and was not even allowed privacy during prison visits. If this is not a cruel and unusual punishment, what is?

It was to save him from a slow death in prison that we helped him to escape. We believe that that was the right decision, right in principle and right in law.

A basic principle of justice is equality before the law. That principle is routinely flouted in the way spies are dealt with. Some like Blunt and Philby are not prosecuted at all. Others are sentenced to long terms, but swopped within a few years. Gordon Lonsdale was sentenced to 25 years in prison in March 1961, just two months before George. He was swopped in 1964 for the British businessman, and self-confessed spy, Greville Wynne.

There are those who say that because George Blake was a spy he deserved what he got. But he was a spy for this country before he was a spy for the Soviet Union. His job was to persuade members of the Soviet and East European military and Security Service to betray the trust placed in them by their countries. How is this done? Anthony Cavendish, a former MI6 officer who retains an absolute loyalty to the

service, explains in his recent memoirs the kind of methods that are used:

'Blackmail can be used either to recruit a conscious source or to recruit an agent who will run an unconscious source. Blackmail can also be used in other ways, for example by threats to the family of valuable informants. An operative of SIS (MI6) cannot automatically rule out such methods of achieving the required result in an intelligence mission. Similarly, theft. deception, lies, mutilation and even murder are considered if and when necessary.'

I was waiting at every line of this quote for the judge to intervene but he had clearly decided to let us have our say. Perhaps he was satisfied to do so because very soon he would have the final word.

George Blake does bear a moral responsibility for the fate of the agents he named to the Soviet Union. But it is clear that his hands would not have been clean if he had continued working faithfully for the British Intelligence Service.

There is another sense in which double-standards are applied here. Double-agents who pass information to the Soviet side are reviled as the worst kind of criminals. But double-agents who pass on Soviet military and intelligence secrets to the West are regarded as heroes. George Blake's actions exactly parallel those of the Soviet KGB officer Gordievsky who turned double-agent and eventually defected to the West. Gordievsky passed on information to British Intelligence about KGB operations and agents, just as George had told the KGB about British operations and agents. Gordievsky was responsible for naming Geoffrey Prime, the young man from GCHQ who had naively presented himself at the Soviet Embassy offering his services and is now serving a long prison sentence under soul-destroying security conditions. Very possibly agents named by George to the Russians suffered similar – or worse – fates. Gordievsky was smuggled out of the Soviet Union by MI6 in 1985 hidden in a secret compartment of a Commer van.[1] George was smuggled out of Britain by us nineteen years earlier in a converted Commer van. If our action in smuggling George out was a crime – which we contest – then the MI6 action must be regarded as a copy-cat crime.

No, we do not condone George Blake's activities. But Lord Parker who sentenced him to 42 years did so. Not of course his efforts on behalf of the Soviet Union but his work for British Intelligence. As he said

1 I was relying here on the account by Nigel West in The Friends: Britain's Post-War Secret Intelligence Operations, Coronet Books (Hodder & Stoughton), 1990,

in passing sentence, George's activities had 'rendered much of this country's efforts (i.e. espionage efforts) completely useless.' Lord Parker supported those efforts. We do not.

Our defence in law is that of necessity; in this instance, we argued, the evil of obeying the letter of the law was socially greater than the evil of breaking it. The law had to be broken to achieve a greater good.

The judge has rejected that defence. He has indicated that he will direct you to ignore it. We believe he is wrong and intend to challenge his ruling in a higher court.

In your absence he has given his reasons for rejecting this defence, though I understand he proposes to explain them to you in his summing up. He has accepted that preventing serious psychological injury could provide grounds for a necessity defence – just as much as preventing death or serious injury. But he has ruled that the necessity defence applies only in an emergency where the threatened injury to life, or physical or mental well-being is imminent. We say that position makes no sense. If the injury is inevitable, though delayed, and the opportunity to remedy it must be taken at once, the necessity defence ought in logic and commonsense to apply.

The judge in his ruling also ignored our argument about the Security Service, MI5. Prior to the 1989 Security Service Act, members of MI5 were in the eyes of the law no different from any other citizens; yet Lord Donaldson stated in the Court of Appeal during the Spycatcher case that it was 'silly for us to sit here and say that the Security Service is obliged to follow the letter of the law.' We say what is sauce for the security goose is sauce for the citizen gander. If it is right, in exceptional circumstances, for members of the Security Service, to break the letter of the law, the same must apply to every other citizen. Since the passing of the 1989 Security Service Act, the status of members of the Security Service has changed. But the Act has only made matters worse, and in a way strengthens our argument. The act forbids members of MI5 from making any unauthorised disclosure no matter what the circumstances, and imposes a lifelong legal obligation of secrecy. Yet we now know that, certainly in the past, MI5 has been involved not simply in minor or technical breaches of the law but in major crimes which can never be excused. It would be the public duty of anyone in MI5 who knew such crimes were being committed to expose them. As the law now stands, however, they could be prosecuted for so doing. And if his lordship's ruling were accepted, they would have no defence. We say the defence of necessity ought to apply in such cases.

> There are circumstances in which it becomes a duty to disobey the law – the apartheid laws in South Africa, for example. In other cases the law itself may be reasonable but be used to protect practices that are indefensible.
>
> You have heard yesterday how Mr Kavan, the Civic Forum MP from Czechoslovakia, and I conspired to break the law by forging official documents in order to smuggle books and equipment into Czechoslovakia. It is unlikely in the extreme that he will now be extradited to this country to face charges. But if he were to be so, and if he and I were to be charged with forgery, do you think it right that we should have no defence in law to the charge?
>
> In 1967 I forged a passport for a Greek radical being sought by the neo-fascist Colonel's regime in Greece. Had he been captured he would have faced imprisonment and very possibly torture. Other Greek friends of Pat and myself had been arrested and tortured. If I had been arrested and charged for that, ought I not to have been allowed to put forward a defence of necessity?

Ben Birnberg told me he was smiling wryly to himself at this point. What would the judge have said, he wondered, if he realised that it was at the request of his wife Felitia that I had forged the Greek passport in 1967? The individual concerned safely escaped from Greece on the forged passport and came to in Britain.

> You also heard Mr Jan Kavan yesterday describe how in the new democratic Czechoslovakia a draft law is in preparation which would recognise the right of individuals to break the law in exceptional circumstances.[2] This is based on recent experience under the old communist regime of conscientious lawbreaking by members of the opposition, many of whom are now involved at various levels in the new democratic government. Clearly this country needs a similar law – or needs the existing law of necessity to be developed to cover a broader range of circumstances.
>
> His lordship has ruled that the defence of necessity is not applicable to the circumstances of our case. But only a few years ago he would very probably have ruled that the defence of necessity did not exist at all in English law, since at that time many legal experts took that view. Now the Courts have clarified the situation and established that the defence of necessity does exist.

---

2 I had got this slightly wrong. As the transcript of Jan's evidence shows, he testified that the new constitution incorporating the possibility of a necessity defence had not simply been drafted but adopted.

The Law Commission – the body responsible for making proposals to clarify the law – argued in a report in 1985: 'the courts should retain the power they now have to develop or clarify the defence (of necessity).' Clearly it does need clarifying in the direction of the broader law now being introduced in Czechoslovakia. But the judges alone will not make such a clarification unless pressed to do so by juries. You can exert that pressure by your verdict today.

The judge in rejecting our defence has stated that you must accept his ruling on a point of law. But in fact you have complete independence to act according to your conscience. If you come to the conclusion he is wrong, or that his ruling defies commonsense and humanity, you can ignore it. If you don't have that freedom of action, if you simply have to follow the judge's direction, what on earth have you been doing sitting here for the last ten days? Juries down the centuries have from time to time defied directions from judges and in doing so struck some of the most important blows for civil liberties, commonsense and humanity.

A former Lord Chief Justice, Lord Goddard, stated in 1955: 'No one has ever yet been able to find a way of depriving a British jury of its privilege of returning a perverse verdict.'[3]

But 'perverse' needs in many cases to be in inverted commas. The penalty of hanging for stealing sheep was abolished in this country because juries refused to convict people who were clearly guilty of that offence. As far as the judges and the lawyers were concerned, their verdicts were 'perverse.' Today we see that it was the punishment that was cruel and perverse.

We are not asking you to act against your conscience. Of course you must do what you believe is right. But whereas the concern of the lawyers is the law, your concern must be justice.

In 1670, two Quakers, William Penn & William Mead, were accused of causing an unlawful and tumultuous assembly after preaching on a Sunday afternoon in Gracechurch Street in the City of London. The judge directed the jury to find them guilty and when they refused to do so he locked them up overnight. They were, to quote an account of the time 'without meat, drink, fire or other accommodation: they had not so much as a chamber-pot, though desired.' When they persisted in their refusal to bring in a guilty verdict he fined each of them 40 marks and sent them to prison. Finally one of them obtained a writ of habeas corpus and the Court of King's Bench found in their favour.

Now I am not suggesting that if you bring in a Not Guilty verdict his

3 Cited by Patrick Devlin, Trial by Jury, Stevens 1966 edition, p.84.

lordship is going to lock you up.

At this remark – for the first time I think during the whole trial – all the members of the jury laughed. This was a breakthrough indeed.

I am saying that, like the jury in the Penn and Mead case, you have to reach your own independent decision, whatever the judge may say.

An outstanding English judge, Lord Devlin, made this comment on the jury system:

'The first object of any tyrant in Whitehall would be to make Parliament utterly subservient to his will: and the next to overthrow or diminish trial by jury, for no tyrant could afford to leave a subject's freedom in the hands of twelve of his countrymen. Trial by jury is more than an instrument of justice and more than one wheel of the constitution: it is the lamp that shows that freedom lives.'[4]

But that is only part of the truth. Institutions alone do not guarantee freedom; that depends crucially on the quality of the people involved in those institutions. The simple existence of the jury system will not ensure freedom unless juries maintain the tradition of independence which has made them the scourge of mandarins and bureaucrats down the centuries.

Six years ago, in 1985, a senior civil servant, Clive Ponting, was prosecuted under the Official Secrets Act for disclosing documents to the Labour MP, Mr Tam Dalyell. The documents proved that government Ministers had lied to Parliament and the public about the circumstances surrounding the sinking of the Argentinean cruiser Belgrano during the Falklands' war.

There are important parallels with the present case. First the essential facts were not in dispute; the documents concerned were confidential and Clive Ponting did pass them to Mr Dalyell. Second, the Prosecuting Counsel, Mr Roy Amlot, offered a deal to Mr Ponting before the case opened: if Ponting would resign his civil service post, the prosecution would be dropped. Ponting turned down the offer. He was convinced that what he had done was right, and his public duty. At his trial he pleaded Not Guilty, arguing that his actions had not been, to quote the words of the Official Secrets Act 'contrary to the safety and interests of the State.'

The judge, Judge McCowan, in his summing up to the jury virtually directed them to find Clive Ponting guilty. He told the jury that the interests of the State were synonymous with the policies of the State and these were determined by the government of the day. Ponting's motives, he said were irrelevant. The jury should forget about any

---

4 Devlin, p.164.

> concept of moral duty.
>
> But the jury did not forget the concept of moral duty or were unwilling to accept the judge's contention that the interests of the state were synonymous with the policies of the government. They brought in a verdict of Not Guilty.
>
> The lamp of freedom shone more brightly that day, and a dangerous shift towards arbitrary power was avoided. I appeal to you today to keep that lamp burnished and shining and to allow considerations of humanity and common sense to guide your judgement. I invite you to agree with us that what we did was right and to find us Not Guilty.

Once again there was a short adjournment. At 11.40am we returned to court to hear Alliott's summing up.

> Alliott: Members of the jury, it is now for me to sum the matter up to you. May I begin by reminding you of our quite separate roles. I have to preside and try and keep the case conducted in accordance with the law as I understand it. It has not been entirely easy in this case. At this stage I have to direct you upon the law. But you and you alone are the judges of the facts. You decide the facts of the issues that I propound to you, and you will decide them in accordance with your own consciences, of course.
>
> Let me direct you upon the law. The first thing is that the burden of proving the case that the Crown brings is upon the Crown, and that burden remains with them throughout. It does not shift because the defendant gives evidence, and the burden is a high one. They have to satisfy you so that you are sure that each of the three counts upon this indictment has been established.
>
> Would you take your copies of the indictment, please, because I next direct you upon the offences, and really the language is such that there is no arcane point of law at all. Count 1: Aiding a prisoner in escaping from prison. That is no more and no less than what is used in every day language. Harbouring – perhaps not a word we use every day – in count 2. That means providing a place for the escaped prisoner to remain. As you know, there were some three different hiding places, and he was harboured for some two months. Finally, count 3: That is also assisting an escaped prisoner. In fact, conspiracy is alleged, as it is in count 2. Conspiracy merely means an agreement, and there the phrase used by Mr Bevan in opening the matter to you is 'spiriting' Blake out of the country in that adapted van. You know that Mr Randle drove the van. Mr Pottle was not there. But, as has been emphasised on all sides, although the defendants have pleaded not guilty, and it is therefore for the Crown to prove the case, in fact the

defendants do not challenge the allegation made. They have admitted it in the book you have read; they have admitted it in the television documentary you have seen, and they have admitted it in their evidence.

You remember Mr Pottle made a brief opening statement. He said, 'I believe that anyone who was involved in the escape of George Blake would have no guilt or shame for what they did. I consider breaking George Blake out of prison to be a decent, humanitarian act.' And when he was cross-examined by Mr Bevan he said, 'The book is true; absolutely true.' He added the proviso that they could not report precisely conversations all that distance ago, and he said, 'I don't deny the acts alleged in the indictment. I confirm the truth of the book. We did what we are accused of in those charges.'

When Mr Randle came to give evidence, he said in his opening statement, 'We have done everything of which we have been accused in this case. We did help, albeit in a minor capacity, in the escape of George Blake from Wormwood Scrubs. We helped with finances and plans. We did harbour him and we did spirit him out of the country.'

In those circumstances, the review of the evidence led by the Crown can be brief.

You will remember that Mr Hills produced the Certificate of Conviction, which you have got in your bundles – do not trouble to turn it up – it is at page 1033.

George Blake pleaded guilty to five counts of unlawfully communicating information contrary to section 1 (1) (c) of the Official Secrets Act 1911 at this court on 3rd May, 1961, and was sentenced to three consecutive terms of 14 years' imprisonment, totalling 42 years.

Then you remember a number of former or present prison officers gave evidence: Messrs. Clark, Williams, Fletcher, Townsend and Buckley. They proved between them that these two defendants were in Wormwood Scrubs at the same time as George Blake, and how George Blake escaped on 22nd October, 1966.

Various items were seized from the defendants by police officers, and those items demonstrate that they were indeed the authors of the book. And, of course, we have also had the evidence of the two employees of Messrs. Harrap the publishers, Mrs McDadd and Mr Varley, who also gave evidence that they dealt with the two defendants.

Thus, on the sole issue you have to decide the evidence is all one way. Nevertheless, it is your decision. In respect of each count in the indictment you must ask yourselves: Are we satisfied so that we are sure that each defendant did the things the Crown say he did? If the

> inevitable answer is Yes, you will find the defendants guilty.
> As you are aware, the defendants contend they are not guilty because they consider their conduct to be morally justified and the prosecution politically motivated. They persist in that stance, notwithstanding my ruling on the law, in respect of the very, very limited defence of necessity. I have ruled that that defence is not open to them on the admitted facts of this case. It is presumably because they anticipated such a ruling that they dispensed with the services on Legal Aid of Queen's Counsel to act on their behalf, so that they could persist in the line they have, whereas counsel, of course, would be inhibited from so doing.
> You must loyally honour my ruling on the law, whatever view you have formed of the defendants. I do not know; you may sympathise with them, or you may abhor what they did. That matters not. I have given a ruling in law, and you must honour it.

At this point I called out: 'Remember the Ponting case!' I thought Alliott might threaten to order me to be taken below, or actually do so, but he ignored my interjection and continued.[5]

> If I am wrong, I can be put right by the Court of Appeal, Criminal Division, and that is a place apparently that Mr Randle is already determined to go should you convict him. I have given my reasons for my ruling in your absence. Mr Randle somehow got the impression I was going to repeat them to you. I am not going to repeat them to you. He has his hostage to fortune from me, if he wants to impeach my rulings in the Court of Appeal. I do not refer to them before you.
> Other issues have been raised: Whether to prosecute these defendants after all these years is an abuse of the process of the court. That, as you know, was raised before another judge in this building, was taken to the Divisional Court by way of judicial review, and was raised before me yesterday afternoon. Each one of those hearings resulted in an adverse view being taken of the application. That is not a matter for you as the jury. It is a matter either for the single judge or for the Divisional Court.
> You have heard that apparently charging orders have been made on the houses of these two defendants, with a view to recouping the money received for the book. That is an entirely collateral matter which you are not concerned with in any way. You are solely concerned to decide whether the Crown has proved the defendants, and each of them, did the deeds alleged against them.
> Necessarily, you have heard in this case that the defendants have been

5 My interjection, however, is not recorded in the court transcript.

> in prison before. Ordinarily, that is something the jury would not hear about. But whatever view you have formed of the defendants, you will not regard them as being of bad character in the usual sense, and their previous convictions are in no way probative of guilt.
> So far as character is concerned, you heard yesterday from Mr Jan Kavan who expressed his gratitude for what Mr Randle did for him and Czechoslovakia.
> The evidence was wide-ranging. Wide-ranging partly because of an indulgence shown by counsel for the Crown and myself to those appearing for themselves. I have reminded you of the only facts that are relevant to the issues you have to decide, and I do not propose to remind you of the evidence that you have heard comparatively recently on those wide-ranging matters. You do have a straight-forward case to decide, whatever may have been submitted to you by the defendants. What you have got to decide is this: Are you satisfied so that you are sure that the defendants, and each of them, aided Blake's escape, harboured him, conspired to hide him, and conspired to spirit him out of the country? If you are so satisfied on one or more of those counts you will convict. If you are not so satisfied you will acquit.
> If you will pause now while the jury bailiffs are sworn, I will ask you to retire to consider your verdicts.
> I have omitted one matter. I should have said this to you: You are probably aware that in certain circumstances I can accept from you a verdict which is a majority verdict. Those circumstances do not prevail when you first retire to consider your verdicts. Before I can accept a majority verdict I have to have you back in again to give you a further direction. The verdicts I seek from you, therefore, are unanimous verdicts; that is to say, verdicts in which all twelve of you concur. Now will you retire.

It was an entirely fair summing-up. In fact, five minutes into it, Pat scribbled a note to me which read: 'This isn't too bad!' But it really left the jury with no option but to convict. We left the courtroom and trundled upstairs to the canteen to drink coffee and await the verdict.

Chapter 26:

High Noon

The jury retired just before 12 o'clock to consider their verdict. High Noon. After the judge's summing up – fair though it had been – it was not a question of what the verdict would be but of how quickly the jury would reach it.

> **'Let's hope they spin it out till lunch time,' I said. 'I could do with a last drink.'**

We had been granted bail again 'within the precincts of the court' a term we interpreted in a broad sense – as the lawyers would say – to include the pub across the road. This time the situation was different.

> **'You'd better hang on here till one o'clock,' Ben said. 'You should be safe enough then to go out, because the jury aren't going to bring in a verdict during the lunch hour.'**

We adjourned to the canteen on the floor above, pushing several tables together to make room for us all. Pat's wife Sue was there and their two sons, Julian and Casper. Anne was there too with our sons Seán and Gavin, and Gavin's new partner Anna whom we had met for the first time during the trial. Then there were our two solicitors, Ben Birnberg and John Wadham, and the student barrister from Geoffrey Robertson's chambers, Caroline Bowman, who had been taking full notes for us of the proceedings, and finally the ever loyal Tom Mackinnon who had taken a fortnight's holiday so that he could be present during the trial.

We drank endless cups of coffee. Chatted. The atmosphere was brittle; we laughed too loudly at our own quips. I emptied my pockets and gave everything to Anne except for my glasses, some tissues, a book and a toothbrush. Pat too emptied his pockets – but, being a smoker, kept a pouch of tobacco. It saved time to be carrying very little when the screws were listing your possessions. Every so often the loudspeaker crackled, signalling the start of another announcement – 'Would all those connected with such and such a case return to court x.' The conversation would stop; the stomach muscles tighten.

We didn't discuss the verdict for we were in no doubt what that would be. But we did speculate about the sentence.

> **'When we first decided to write the book,' Pat said, 'I wrote down on a piece of paper what I thought the sentence would be and put it in a drawer. I reckoned three years. I still think that.' Whatever the**

> sentence, it was Sue and Anne who could face the most immediate problem if the judge ordered the confiscation of our houses as the charging order gave him power to do. The lawyers thought our best bet was not to try to argue the legal points with the judge but to tell him we were appealing against the order to the Court of Appeal.

We had been mulling over the issue for some time when Tom intervened:

> 'Why don't I appear on your behalf to argue the point? I would be happy to do so free of charge.'

We greeted the suggestion with enthusiasm.

> 'The only problem is,' he said 'that I haven't brought my wig and gown with me. Without those, the judge could refuse to hear me.' He reflected for a moment, looking anxious and uncertain, then added: 'Perhaps I could ask around and see if I can borrow one.'

He hurried off in search of this attire so essential for upholding the majesty of the law, and returned some ten minutes later pulling at the sleeves of a gown that was way too short for him.

> 'It's the best I could do, he said, looking sheepish.

When the laughter and teasing subsided, we had a serious discussion about what he would say. We were not in a strong position given the fact that the High Court in March had refused to reverse the charging order. But Tom thought he might be able to say enough to persuade the judge to defer a decision.

As one o'clock approach we became restless. (Look at that big hand move along.) We strained our ears at every announcement. That last drink and sandwich, that last draught of freedom had become crucially important. At five to one, Ben said: 'I think we're safe to go out now. They're not going to come to a decision within the next five minutes.'

We all piled out into the warm sunshine outside, and then into the welcoming, noisy hubbub of the pub. No rounds on Pat and myself that day: others could pay for the last square meal of the condemned. A journalist, Mark Whitehead, interviewed me for the Bradford *Telegraph & Argus*. He seemed reasonable. Perhaps for once the paper would publish something sympathetic.

Lunch over, the tense wait in the canteen resumed. We tired of drinking coffee. The jokes and conversation flagged. At a quarter to three, Pat said:

> 'Well, they've been out now for almost three hours. That's not bad. We must have given them something to think about.'

I looked down at my nails and suddenly it became immensely important to file and clean them. Strange the obsessions which possess you in moments of stress. I hunted out a nail file from my briefcase and disappeared with it into the lavatory, working away feverishly at each finger. I had just finished the manicure when the announcement came. Time for a final quick pee. As I re-zipped the announcement was repeated.

> **'Will all those concerned with the case of Pottle and Randle please report to court number one.'**

The others were just coming out of the canteen as I reached it. Anne and I held each other tightly. (Do not forsake me oh my darling.) She whispered in my ear:

> **'If you can cope, so can I.'**

We walked through to the spacious hall which gives access to Court No 1 and waited in a little knot for the door to be opened. Julian Bevan, Chief Inspector Eileen Eggington, Superintendent Bird were there too and several others on the prosecution side. Many others we did not recognize were milling around.

The jury have got a verdict,' Ben said quietly to us. I wondered how he could know? (I think there is in fact a minimum period of time before the jury can come back to say they have failed to reach a verdict.)

Inside the courtroom the atmosphere had subtly changed. People were alert, expectant – and there were many more of them. The well of the court was filling with the gowns and wigs and dark suits of barristers and solicitors. But the most striking difference as far as Pat and myself were concerned was that two uniformed prison officers were waiting up in the dock for us. Previously, apart from the first day when there was one custody officer present, we had been alone. As I went into the dock I glanced again at the steps leading down to the cells below, and at the walls to the side of them lined with cracked white tiles. As Pat had told the jury, it was like the entrance to a public lavatory.

Now the jury came back. We watched them carefully as they took up their places on the bench. I tried to catch the eye of the two women who had smiled briefly at us on the second day of the trial when they were still reading the book. But neither glanced in our direction. I did notice, however, that the juror called Michael who normally sat on the extreme left at the front during the trial now took up a different position on the front right. He was perhaps in his mid-thirties, dressed informally in an open-necked coloured shirt and a light anorak. I took it that he had been elected foreman, and this proved to be the case.

Three knocks on the door at the back of the judge's bench announced his lordship's arrival.

> **'Be upstanding in court!' the usher commanded. Mr Justice Alliott took his usual seat and laid his silk gloves nonchalantly on the bench in front of him.**

'Will the accused please stand,' said Mrs Russell, the clerk of the court.

As Pat and I stood up, the two prison officers moved up close behind us.

'Well, this is it!' I muttered to Pat. We had last stood together in the same dock almost thirty years earlier. On that occasion, as soon as the judge pronounced sentence the officers firmly gripped each of us in turn by the elbow and led us straight down the stairwell to the cells beneath. In minutes now the scene would be repeated.

'Mr Foreman,' the Clerk said, standing and turning to face him, 'will you please confine yourself to answering my first question, either yes or no. Members of the jury, have you reached a verdict upon which you are all agreed?

Foreman of the Jury: Yes.

In spite of myself, I felt a twinge of disappointment. After all our efforts, they were going to find us guilty with not a single dissenting voice.

Clerk of the Court: Members of the jury, in respect of count 1, aiding a prisoner in escaping from a prison, do you find the defendant Pottle guilty or not guilty?

Foreman of the Jury: Not Guilty.

He said it in a firm, clear voice. A shout like a football supporter's victory whoop came up from somewhere in the well of the court. It was just that. Pat's younger son Julian is a keen Spurs supporter. Others too in the well of the court, and in the crowded public gallery overlooking it, shouted and clapped. The official transcript states in parenthesis: 'Cheers from the public gallery.'

I was in a state of shock. I could hardly take in what was happening. But then I told myself – 'Hold on! The jury might decide to acquit us on the most serious charge, carrying a five-year maximum sentence, but convict us on one or both of the other counts. After all it was in harbouring George, and smuggling him out of the country that Pat and I (and of course Anne) had played a central role.

Down in the well of the court Anne was trying to comfort – and at the same time forewarn – our two sons, Seán and Gavin. Both as children had been unwitting accomplices in the flight of George Blake from the country. Seán, the eldest, burst into tears as soon as the foreman pronounced Pat 'Not Guilty.'

'It's not over yet,' she told them. 'They could still convict Dad – and there are the other two charges.'

Clerk of the Court: Do you find the defendant Randle guilty or not guilty?

Foreman of the Jury: Not Guilty.

Further uproar. Here the official transcript notes 'Demonstrations from the public gallery.'

> **Alliott: Silence. If there is any further disturbance I will order the court to be cleared.**
>
> **Clerk of the Court: In respect of count 2 conspiracy to harbour an escaped prisoner, do you find the defendant Pottle guilty or not guilty?**
>
> **Foreman of the Jury: Not guilty.**
>
> **Clerk of the Court: Do you find the defendant Randle guilty or not guilty?**
>
> **Foreman of the Jury: Not guilty.**

Was this real? Were the jury who had so depressed us by their apparent passiveness actually going to acquit us on all counts. I tried to suppress a mounting excitement. There was still count 3.

> **Clerk of the Court: In respect of count 3 conspiracy to assist an escaped prisoner, do you find the defendant Pottle guilty or not guilty?**
>
> **Foreman of the Jury: Not guilty.**

Now his voice was less firm. He too was beginning to be affected by the emotion of the occasion.

> **Clerk of the Court: Do you find the defendant Randle guilty or not guilty?**
>
> **Foreman of the Jury: Not guilty.**
>
> **Clerk of the Court: Members of the jury, you find the defendant Patrick Pottle and the defendant Michael Randle each not guilty on the three counts of this indictment and that is the verdict of you all.**
>
> **Foreman of the Jury: It is.**
>
> **Mr Justice Alliott: Let the defendants be discharged.**

Pat and I turned and spontaneously hugged each another in the dock.

Mr Justice Alliott was not amused. Instead of observing the usual courtesy of thanking the jury for their efforts, he said testily:

> **'Members of the jury, will you please vacate those benches. We have another case to hear.'**

I was unaware of this incident till friends told me about it afterwards. I was too dazed and bewildered to take it in.

A court official opened the door at the back of the dock and said to Pat and me: 'Please leave now!'

In the hall outside the courtroom we rejoined our relieved – yet tearful – families from whom we had parted not ten minutes before expecting a long, tough separation. Newspaper and media journalists crowded around looking for comments, or arranging interviews, while court officials pleaded vainly for us all to leave the area. Then to our surprise and delight the jury filed out, using, for the first time, the same door as us to leave the court. We hugged or shook hands with each in turn, thanking them for their decision. Our one regret about the day is that we did not, there and then, decide to hold a party and invite them to it. But we were in a daze at the turn of events and by the time the thought had occurred to us the moment was gone.

Chapter 27:

Postscript: The Member of the Jury

Our acquittal was headline news in all the media. It was the verdict no-one had anticipated, us least of all. There were on the spot radio and television interviews with us as we left the courtroom, and arrangements made for further interviews and appearances in the days that followed. Thames Television that night re-ran their drama-documentary film *The Blake Escape* which we half-watched during a euphoric celebratory party thrown by Pat and Sue. Ben Birnberg and John Wadham were at the party, so too was Tom Mackinnon and his wife Katya, Jan Kavan, Richard Norton-Taylor and several of the other journalists who had been reporting the case, the young barrister and her boyfriend whom we had first met during our trip to Moscow and Leningrad in 1990, and many friends and relatives. George Blake phoned from Moscow to congratulate us, clearly both delighted and relieved at the outcome. Ed Fitzgerald sent his apologies together with a Magnum of Champagne and a note congratulating the 'little fish' for their victory over the Leviathan.

Next morning Pat and I were interviewed on early morning television, and later that day, on the *World Service* of the BBC. As we came out of the BBC studio, a woman ran out into the corridor from another room to offer her congratulations. Walking back up the road, we were recognized by a young black man standing just inside a shop-front shop who grinned and said 'Well done!' In the underground on the way back to Pat's place someone else recognized us and added his congratulations. In the evening Pat, Sue, Anne and myself were chauffeur-driven to Birmingham courtesy of Central Television to appear on an hour-long discussion programme on whether, and under what circumstances it was right to break the law. Norris McWhirter, the man from the *Freedom Association* who had threatened to take out a private prosecution against us was there sharing the panel with us, and the audience included the barrister and Conservative MP, Ivan Laurence, who commented that while he regretted the fact we had been acquitted it was in a strange way a vindication of the jury system.

When Anne and I got back to Bradford there was a further hastily arranged surprise party, to welcome us home (by our good friends in Yorkshire) at the house, and a week or so later a full-scale benefit party at a venue in the town centre organised by our friend Mandy Farrar. She laid on a local band, Scarlet Heights, which specialises in traditional Irish music and rounded up friends from far and wide to attend. Max Madden, the MP for Bradford North was there, and there were messages of congratulations from, amongst others, Bob Cryer, our local MP from Bradford West, Tony Benn and the writer and columnist Paul Foot. (Foot in his message quoted the Penn and Mead case which I had referred to in my closing speech.) From collections and the sale of books, enough money was raised for Anne and myself to go off the following week for a holiday with friends and relatives in Ireland.

Naturally not everyone was pleased. Back in Bradford I even received one telephone death-threat, though somehow I couldn't take it seriously. One neighbour took deep offence and refused ever after to speak to us, but he was the exception. Mostly local people were curious but supportive. One elderly man who had a lock-up garage next to ours, a plain-spoken Yorkshireman said: 'Well done, lad! You beat the buggers – that's the main thing.'

There was quite a lot of flak too at the political level. The Bradford *Telegraph & Argus* quoted Graham Riddick, the Tory MP for Colne Valley who tabled a motion in the Commons in 1988 calling for our prosecution, as saying: 'It seems to me that the jury has collectively gone soft in the head. George Blake was one of the most notorious traitors I have ever known. I am appalled.' Sir Marcus Fox, MP for Shipley commented that he was 'absolutely astounded.' By contrast Max Madden said: 'I would like to congratulate the jury on their excellent verdict. It reflected commonsense and justice.'

The newspapers on the day after the acquittal were divided. All gave the event prominent coverage, many with photos of Pat, Sue, Anne and myself coming away from the Old Bailey with our arms around each other's shoulders, and broad smiles on our faces. But in general the comments and editorials in the more conservative papers expressed shock and outrage. The *Daily Telegraph* ran an editorial headed 'A Bad Day for British Justice' – though to their credit they included in their condemnation the grudging comments by the Appeal Court in quashing the convictions of the Maguire Seven, comments that fell far short of clearing their name after the appalling injustice they had suffered. (Bradford's *Telegraph & Argus*, also linked our case with that of the Maguires but for them the disgrace was that the Maguires' convictions had been quashed at all!) Janet Daley in *The Times* of 28th June devoted her column to attacking us and the jury's decision – and was replied to very effectively by Ben Birnberg in a letter published on 3rd July. The *Daily Mail* and *Daily Express* also ran editorials critical of the jury's decision. The *Mail* in its report quoted Tory MP Rupert Allason as saying 'These men were guilty of a despicable act which directly led to the death of British operatives' – a comment which they were forced to retract a few days later. The *Sun* waited a day and then, true to form, ran an editorial headed 'Stinkers of the Old Bailey.' We hope, they said, that 'Pottle and Randle now crawl back under the stone from which they should never have emerged.' But they reserved the real venom for the jurors: 'And the 12 jurors? They have given fresh hope to criminals all over Britain. Ladies and gentlemen of the jury, you stink.'

In the *Sunday Times*, Barbara Amiel devoted her column to a virulent attack on Pat and myself headed 'Shabby day at the Bailey with moral high horses in full gallop.' Her central – and valid – point is that due legal process is crucial. In support of this she quotes the celebrated jurist Frankfurter who stated that 'the history of liberty has largely been the history of procedural safeguards.' On these grounds, although she deplores what we did and the stance we took at the trial, she thinks the jury were right to acquit us because it was, in her view an abuse of the judicial process to have prosecuted us in 1991 when the police knew of our involvement in 1970. The government, she argues was 'criminally negligent' in not bringing us to trial 20 years earlier. 'I disagree vehemently,' she writes, 'with the High Court judges who permitted this case to come to trial now.' However, it is this very procedure that leftists, ourselves amongst them, forget. 'Randle himself', she states, 'in his summing up to the jury spoke contemptuously of these legal technicalities as "mumbo jumbo".'

But her piece, though commending due process, is based on a careless reading of hearsay evidence. It was not me but Pat who spoke of legal mumbo jumbo. Moreover he did so not to dismiss proper legal procedure as rubbish but to urge the jury to take into account the fact that the police had known of our involvement in 1970, i.e. the very point which Amiel herself argues they were right to do, and which in her view justified their decision to acquit us.

Amiel also decries the fact that Blake was able to give evidence on video rather than appearing in person when he could be cross-examined, and suggests that allowing children to give evidence on video was the thin end of a very thick wedge. This is to overlook the fact that the practice of accepting written witness statements in court with the agreement of both sides is of long standing. Had Blake's statement simply been read out by one of us, he still could not have been cross-examined on it. The prosecution made clear that they did not accept everything in Blake's statement – presumably a reference to his claim that there was no suggestion at his trial that he was responsible for the death of agents. As a witness of fact, he simply confirmed the facts as already agreed by prosecution and defence. As a witness of character, he said nothing about our own conduct that the prosecution contested for it was no part of their case that we had acted in collusion with Soviet Intelligence or accept money from them.

Amiel attacks us also for failing to distinguish between liberal democracy and red fascism and suggests that our actions against Soviet imperialism in Hungary and Czechoslovakia indicates that 'unlike some run-of-the-mill fools who are not consistent in their moral equivalency they were extraordinary fools consistent in their errors.' It is not clear whether she is arguing that our actions against 'Soviet imperialism' were in themselves wrong or simply an indication of an underlying false premise. In fact in *The Blake Escape* we draw a clear distinction between democratic systems and totalitarian systems of right or left while taking a stand against the crimes and excesses of each side. The fact that a leading Czech dissident and Civic Forum MP was prepared to fly specially from Prague to speak in my defence is vindication enough of our 'folly.'

Ben Birnberg, who had agreed to reply to press comments in the aftermath of the trial, had a short but effective letter in the *Sunday Times* of 7th July. It reads:

> Barbara Amiel was not in court during the Pottle and Randle trial. (News Review last week). As their solicitor, I was. There was nothing 'shabby' about the trial or its outcome. My clients did not defend George Blake or the crimes he committed. On the contrary, they made it clear that they assisted Blake to escape only because of the enormity of his 42-year sentence, which his counsel Lord Hutchinson described as 'so inhuman that it is alien to all principles by which a civilised country should treat its subjects.' However, Barbara Amiel hit the nail on the head when vindicating the jury for its 'necessary verdict' if lynch law is not to operate in this country. 'Legal technicalities' are indeed the 'stuff of law' and the prosecution came unstuck because the jury sensed the abuse of process, even though the judges, after days of argument in pre-trial proceedings, did not.

By contrast there was sympathetic coverage and features in the Guardian and *Independent*. The *Guardian* editorial was headed 'Escape into pantomime.' There was an element of Ealing Comedy, it said, about the escape itself and it was 'natural to cheer at the not guilty verdict on Randle and Pottle.' It 'stuck in the craw' that the Security Service had known of our involvement so long ago but had been too embarrassed to take action until after the publication of our book when it became even more embarrassing not to prosecute; the jury had seen through the humbug and asserted their independence. The *Guardian* also carried a highly sympathetic piece from Richard Norton-Taylor, and a shortened version of Pat's final address to the jury. The *Independent* too carried a feature by Nick Cohen headed 'Blake escape pair win hearts of the jury.' Some weeks later, on 10th July, Richard Norton-Taylor had a feature on the *Guardian's* law page headed: 'Campaigners who bucked the system.' It concluded as follows:

> The two also had the advantage of being ideal defendants-in-person: they were convinced that what they had done was right; they could easily master the evidence; they were articulate; and they were palpably, almost suicidally, honest.

But the division of opinion wasn't entirely on predictable lines. The eminent QC Louis Blom-Cooper wrote in the *Observer* that Sunday a piece entitled 'Juries that should be in the dock' condemning Pat's and my action in helping Blake as 'by any standards a wicked offence' and argued that 'perverse' jury verdicts should be subject to review by the courts. 'What ... is so sacrosanct about a jury's verdict of acquittal?' he asks. 'Other European legal systems do not countenance such a bizarre rule.'

However, as he knows, European legal systems do not in general have a jury system. And although he was not advocating its abolition in Britain his proposal, if put into effect, would radically, and perhaps fatally, undermine it. It would mean that in principle every jury acquittal would be subject to appeal and review – and it is not difficult to imagine the pressure that would then build up to replace lay jurors altogether with trained lawyers on the grounds that they would be less likely to bring in perverse verdicts in the first place.

The following week the three lead letters in the paper were from people taking issue with Blom-Cooper – one from a solicitor, Rosemary Gordon from Weston-super-Mare, one from the Labour MP for a Leeds constituency, Michael Meadowcroft, and one from a Peter Nettleton from Richmond in Surrey which put the counter argument succinctly:

> Louis Blom-Cooper is deservedly respected as a tireless legal and penal reformer. The song and dance he makes over the Pottle and Randle case is therefore surprising.
>
> Twelve of his fellow citizens selected at random, having listened to prosecuting counsel, the two defendants themselves and the judge, decided, unanimously, that punishment in this quite exceptional case was

not called for. That's all.

The Spectator attacked the jury system as present constituted in a leader headed 'The Jury is an Ass.' This called for the reinstatement of an educational *and property* qualification for jurors – 'the former for obvious reasons, the latter because property owners have an automatic stake in the preservation of law and order.' (I replied in the letter pages the following week). However, in the same edition of the journal Auberon Waugh had a splendid, swingeing attack on the 'punishment freaks' in the Conservative Party who were in danger of losing it the next election. The 110 MPs who had called for our prosecution, he said, had made fools of themselves, and moreover 'large parts of the Conservative Party – all the rows of clones of Kelvin Mackenzie, the editor of the Sun, who have been filling the back benches since 1979 – have miscalculated the mood of the nation.' He went on to quote in full the *Sun*'s vitriolic editorial, detecting in it evidence not so much of petulance as of panic.

> 'In fact I always doubted whether the British public was quite as sadistic or quite as moronic as it appeared from conversations with cab drivers, in public bars and opinion polls. It occurred to me that people produced these revolting reactions only because they thought it was expected of them to do so. Put the same people on a jury, or ask them to vote in a referendum which would actually restore hanging, and you might have a very different response.
>
> 'Or so I have often mused. Needless to say, no such thoughts seem to have occurred to the new Tories. It is noticeable how the bond which once united the Duke of Worsthorne with his gamekeeper, the London businessman with his cabby, has now been adopted by the mop-haired be-cardiganed cretins bobbing around in Mrs Thatcher's wake as a talisman. The new hybrid 'classless', overweight, androgynous young Tory-in-a-basket now sees penological sadism as his only way of ingratiating himself. As a result, after 11 years of Mrs Thatcher, we now have a higher proportion of our citizens in prison than any other country in the world; we have more life sentence prisoners than all the other countries of Western Europe put together ...'

The attacks on the jurors increased the regret Pat and I felt that we had not managed to get any of their addresses or had not invited them to the party at Pat's house at the end of the trial. The 14 pacifists from the British Withdrawal from Northern Ireland campaign, acquitted at the Old Bailey in the 1970s – some of them incidentally defended by Louis Blom-Cooper – had done so in court at the end of the trial, and several of the jurors had turned up.

We had, however, made a note of their names as they were sworn in at the beginning of the trial, and we knew roughly the catchment area from which

Old Bailey jurors are drawn; so we had at least some kind of lead.

The first step was to ascertain the precise legal position. We checked with Geoffrey Robertson, a specialist in this area, who told us that while the jurors are forbidden by law to speak about anything that goes on in the juryroom, they are free to talk about their own thoughts and feelings on a case, or indeed about conversations they have had with other jurors outside the juryroom itself.

Having got this clear, I began systematically to go through the relevant London phonebooks, making dozens of calls. There were some awkward and embarrassing moments when I was explaining to complete strangers who I was and why I was phoning. Eventually, however, I struck lucky and got through to one of the women jurors whom I shall call simply Maria to protect her identity. She agreed at once to see Anne and myself, and had a cake newly baked for us when we arrived.

I will not describe Maria beyond saying that she would have passed both the educational and property tests that the *Spectator* would like to see in place. She was intelligent and open, and freely explained her own thoughts and conclusions about our case.

I apologised to her early on for the fact that we had totally misjudged her and the other jurors. We had thought they were completely unsympathetic because they seemed so unresponsive to us and what we said.

> **'That was deliberate,' she said. 'Right at the beginning we all agreed that as we might end up having to find you guilty it would be quite unfair to raise false hopes by nodding and smiling.'**

I was moved by this evidence of responsible forethought on the part of the jurors, in such marked contrast to the stereotype proposed by the *Spectator* in its editorial, or in the *Sun*'s diatribe. Not only had they made that decision but they had had the discipline to carry in through to the end – so much so that Tom Mackinnon was led to conclude that they were the least sympathetic jury he had ever encountered.

In answer to a question from me, Maria said that she had been strongly persuaded by the necessity defence I had put forward, and could not understand why the judge had not wanted the jury to hear it. A point that weighed even more strongly with her was that the police had known of our involvement in 1970 and taken no action until we had published our book. But she was impressed too by some of our broader points – in particular the fact that some spies are given immunity, others swopped after a short time, and still others made to serve out their sentence.

She was struck by our sincerity; this was really important for her. She admired too the thoroughness with which we had prepared our case. Afterwards she had had to serve on several other juries, and sometimes the barristers were obviously ill-prepared and had not done their homework as we had done ours.

The threat of the long prison sentence hanging over us was another consideration. 'If I thought you would have got say nine months it would have been different.' One of the papers had got it right when they mentioned that point. She was also shocked – as she thought were the other jurors – that our houses were likely to be confiscated. 'That seemed totally unfair,' she said. There was a nice irony here. The confiscation order on the houses was a nasty little twist of the knife. It was quite unnecessary too, for the judge, had we been convicted, could have imposed a heavy fine in addition to imprisoning us.

There were other interesting details, particularly about the way the jurors were treated after they delivered their verdict. They were immediately dispersed to be sworn in on other cases and remained at the court for several weeks. They also had to hand in their copies of our book as soon as the case ended. Fortunately an enterprising bookshop nearby had copies on sale at a reduced price, and as soon as she got out of the building that afternoon she went round and bought one. (She went off at this point to fetch her copy and got Anne and myself to sign it.)

She and the others had been deeply shocked by some of the attacks on them in the press, particularly by the *Sun* editorial. They had tried their utmost to do the right thing – and had not the judge himself said to them that it was for them to decide?

Most moving was her description of how the atmosphere amongst the jurors had changed in the last day or two. At the beginning they were light-hearted, going off in twos and threes at lunch time to chat and get to know one another. But as the case drew to a close, people became solemn and thoughtful, realising how much depended on what they decided. On the Tuesday lunchtime everyone went his or her own separate way.

> **'There were people of several different religions among us', she said. 'But people went to their own place of worship and tried to think out what was the right thing to do.'**

It was a quite remarkable testimony, and put to shame the ignominious attacks to which the jury were subjected after the trial in some quarters. I can only repeat the comment I made as I stepped out of the Old Bailey a free man: 'Thank God for the jury system, and the independence of jurors.'

It is unlikely in the extreme that the members of the jury will ever have a plaque to them in the precincts of the Old Bailey as did the jurors in the

17th century trial of the two Quakers, Penn and Mead. Yet it is clear that theirs too was an act of conscience, arrived at after a deep consideration of the issues involved. It was a 'rebel' verdict not a 'perverse' one, part of a long and honourable tradition which has helped rid the judicial system of some of its worst excesses. For this they deserve to be remembered and thanked.

Appendices

On the folowing pages the appendices refered to in the text are copied. All, but number 8, are slightly modified originals. Number 8 is re-typed.

Appendix 1 - Copy of the Public Interest Immunity Certificate signed by the Home Secretary, David Waddington, on 24 April ~~1970~~ 1990

IN THE CENTRAL CRIMINAL COURT

R

-v-

POTTLE AND RANDLE

CERTIFICATE OF THE RT. HON. DAVID WADDINGTON QC, MP,
SECRETARY OF STATE FOR THE HOME DEPARTMENT

---

1. I understand that by letter dated 12 April 1990 to the Crown Prosecution Service, the Defendants' solicitors, Messrs B N Birnberg & Co have indicated that they will seek an Order for disclosure of three police reports. This Certificate relates to those reports.

The reports in question are as follows:

1. Report dated 26 October 1966 by Detective Inspector Murray of Special Branch reporting on information received and subsequent enquiries.

2. Report dated 4 March 1967 by Detective Superintendent Marchant to the Chief Superintendent reporting on the escape by Blake from HM Prison Wormwood Scrubs and reporting the result of enquiries into the matter.

3. Report dated 23 March 1970 of Detective Chief Inspector Watts commenting on and analysing the material contained in the manuscript for a book written by Sean Bourke.

2. I have carefully read what purport to be true copies of these reports and am of the opinion that it is necessary in the public interest that these reports should be withheld from production. They are internal police reports in pursuance of criminal investigations. As such they belong to a class of documents which should be protected from production for the reasons which follow.

3. It is necessary for the proper and efficient functioning of criminal investigations that officers involved at all levels in such investigations should be able to comment freely and with candour upon all matters arising out of their investigations. This includes freedom to comment upon the strengths and weaknesses of evidence and on the reliability or otherwise of witnesses including personal information about the witnesses. Reports may also include allegations in respect of suspects who are not subsequently charged and suggestions of lines of investigations which at the time of the writing of the report have not yet been pursued. In my opinion police officers would be inhibited in carrying out their functions if their own opinions, suggestions and assessments were exposed to public view, particularly where those opinions and assessments are recorded at a stage where investigation is incomplete.

4. It is further necessary to withhold police reports from production since, as a class, they may contain information which has been received in confidence. If it were to be thought that such documents might at some future date pass into the field of public scrutiny such information would not be forthcoming and the criminal investigation authorities would thereby be deprived of that information. Additionally, if such information were to be made public, informers might be placed in danger.

~~480~~ 481

5. If police reports were disclosed, there would also be a risk that persons who had featured in police enquiries and against whom allegations had been made or suspicions recorded, but who had never been charged, might be held up to public suspicion and contempt.

6. It is, further, in my view undesirable that the inner workings of the criminal investigation process should be revealed. Such information could prove to be of use to criminals by revealing police methods and the information available to the police about suspected crimes.

Dated this 24th day of April 1990.

[signature]

....

Secretary of State for the Home Department

Appendix 2 – Copy of the report of 23 March 1970 by Chief Superintendent Rollo Watts, Special Branch and Chief Superintendent M.D.Rogers

SECRET

S.B. No. 1 (Plain)

METROPOLITAN POLICE

SPECIAL BRANCH

Special Report

23rd day of March 19

SUBJECT Sean BOURKE

Reference to Papers 588/UNREG/51.W

1. With their letter dated 30 January 1970, reference PF.607,084, K3/NLM, MI5 enclosed a photostat copy of the manuscript for a book written by Sean BOURKE which, it is understood, will be published by Cassell & Co Ltd, 35 Red Lion Square, WC1 in May this year. They ask for comments regarding the material contained therein.

2. It will be recalled that BOURKE returned to the Republic of Ireland from Moscow on 22 October 1968, and was quite open about the part he had played in assisting George BLAKE to escape from HM Prison, Wormwood Scrubs, on 22 October 1966 and in subsequently arranging BLAKE's escape to the USSR. He later successfully appealed against an application to extradite him to this country.

3. The manuscript has been examined closely and it gives every indication of being BOURKE's own work rather than that of a 'ghost writer' employed by the publishers. BOURKE has always considered himself to have a flair as a writer and the style and phraseology is typical of the articles he wrote when editor of the prison magazine "New Horizon" and of the many long letters to his brother and others of which we have copies. In fact, many of the Moscow incidents recorded in the manuscript are virtually identical with the descriptions contained in the letters which he wrote to his brother, Kevin at that time.

4. It also appears that BOURKE has basically written the true story. From the very extensive enquiries which were made at the time, a great deal was learned of the plans for the escape and the escape itself, and BOURKE's subsequent activities in the USSR were known to us through his brother, Kevin, and from other more delicate sources. Almost without exception, the facts recorded in the manuscript agree with those known to us and, apart from disguising the identities of those who assisted him, BOURKE app[ears] to have written the story of the escape as it happened and in a [way] consistent with his delight at having beaten the authorities.

5. An appendix detailing those parts of the manuscript which a[re] of main interest to police, is attached to this report (Appendix The manuscript deals briefly with BOURKE's childhood and the [events] leading up to the incident for which he was sentenced to seven years imprisonment in December 1961. He writes of life in Wormw[ood] Scrubs, his meeting and association with George BLAKE and the latter's request to arrange an escape. The details of BOURKE's approach to Mrs BLAKE and her daughter, Adele, for money to fi[nance] the project, are included and the manner in which they decided t[o]

BOURKE goes on to describe the persons who did, in fact, assist him and the plans which he made with BLAKE regarding communication by two-way radio after he was released from prison. Mention is made of a prisoner who helped them by acting as a courier, of the car which BOURKE purchased and the various "rehearsals" which he undertook. The escape itself and the hide-out at Highlever Road, W12 are dealt with in detail and of particular interest is the information regarding BLAKE's subsequent movements before leaving the country.

6. BOURKE describes the important part played by his friends, Michael and Anne REYNOLDS, who not only obtained the financial backing for the escape, but arranged for a doctor to set BLAKE's arm, which he broke falling from the prison wall, and provided transport and assistance during the move to other accommodation. One such hide-out was the flat of Pat PORTER, a friend of REYNOLDS' and another was the home of a further friend - a writer. It was REYNOLDS and his wife who eventually bought an old Dormobile, adapted a hiding place in it for BLAKE, and drove him via Dover and the Continent to East Germany.

7. The story tells of BOURKE's decision to join BLAKE in Moscow, the way in which he achieved this and his reception by BLAKE and the Russian authorities. There follows a description of BOURKE's travels in the USSR, his gradual disillusionment with BLAKE and the communist way of life, and his attempt to seek sanctuary in the British Embassy in Moscow. From there, the story is brought to an end, telling of his brother's visit to Moscow, the arrangements the latter made to obtain a travel document for him, and the eventual journey from Moscow to Ireland.

8. In all, the manuscript is a story BOURKE tells with considerable bravado and with no attempt to hide his delight in outwitting the authorities whom he openly despises. It is also a bitter condemnation of BLAKE himself and shows clearly the way in which BOURKE was cleverly recruited, flattered and used by BLAKE from the outset.

9. Reference is made earlier in this report to a prisoner in Wormwood Scrubs, who was known to have assisted in the escape plans and to have acted as a courier between BLAKE and BOURKE whilst the latter was in the prison hostel. Although it was not possible to obtain any firm evidence, it was strongly suspected that this person was Philip MORRIS, CRO No 44041/43 who was an associate of both BLAKE and BOURKE and who, as a 'red band', frequently moved between the prison and the prison hostel. If this suspicion is correct it is of interest to note that in naming the prisoner 'Peter MARTIN', BOURKE has retained the correct initials. This may be considered a typical example of BOURKE's bravado.

10. Using the assumption that BOURKE has similarly retained

the correct initials of the other persons who assisted him, a search of records concerning persons who came into the scope of police enquiries into the escape, reveals some strong possible identifications. The most important of these are, of course, the persons named as Michael REYNOLDS and his wife, Anne, and BOURKE describes them in some detail.

11. A very probable identification thus comes to light in the form of Michael Joseph RANDLE, very well known to Special Branch for his militant activities with the Committee of 100 and similar organisations, and his wife, Celia Anne, nee PARR. For ease of comparison, the points of similarity are listed as Appendix 'B' to this report.

12. On 20 February 1962, RANDLE was sentenced to 18 months imprisonment for offences against The Official Secrets Act, 1911 (conspiring to enter and to incite others to enter a prohibited place), and it was whilst serving this sentence in Wormwood Scrubs, that he came to know BLAKE and BOURKE. He is known to have felt sympathy for BLAKE, considering the length of the latter's sentence to be inhuman, and after his discharge sent him occasional greetings cards. There is certainly a discrepancy in BOURKE's story in that he describes BLAKE's predicament to 'Michael' as though the latter had no knowledge of it. However, even BOURKE would be unlikely to identify him as a former prisoner possibly known to have been sympathetic to BLAKE.

13. Apart from the personal similarities between RANDLE and 'Michael REYNOLDS', this identification would explain many points which caused confusion during the enquiries following the escape. It was perfectly obvious that BOURKE must have received assistance from someone, and that that assistance must have been given for financial, political, ideological or personal gain. BOURKE's range of acquaintances was limited and were virtually confined to the people he knew in Crawley prior to his imprisonment, and to prisoners and staff whom he met in Wormwood Scrubs whilst serving his sentence. Very extensive enquiries were made of these persons without success and although RANDLE came under scrutiny at one stage, when it was found that he had known BLAKE in the prison, there was nothing whatsoever to associate him with BOURKE since his release.

14. Now, however, his complicity would make sense and answer many of the questions previously left unanswered. BLAKE was known to be very loath to involve criminals, realising that once freed and in their hands, he could be 'sold' to the highest bidder. RANDLE, on the contrary, was obviously an extremely sincere person, with a large number of contacts in his pacifist sphere. The reaction of 'Michael REYNOLDS' to BOURKE's approach is what might be expected from RANDLE who, through his beliefs, has been prepared to flout the law and accept the resultant sentences of imprisonment. A further point worth considering is that 'Michael REYNOLDS' was apparently able to raise the money needed to finance the escape and was also able to obtain the

services of a doctor to set BLAKE's broken arm. It is well known that amongst RANDLE's political/pacifist friends were numbered several quite wealthy persons and, more pointedly, several medical doctors.

15. In his manuscript BOURKE describes how 'Michael REYNOLDS' recruited the help of a friend 'Pat PORTER' who was prepared to assist in a practical way. Again, by using this person's initials, a possible identification can be made, because a close friend of RANDLE's throughout his Committee of 100 activities, was Patrick Brian POTTLE. A table of points of comparison between "PORTER" and POTTLE is attached as Appendix 'C', (the latter served a similar sentence of imprisonment with RANDLE in Wormwood Scrubs).

16. The story also tells of BLAKE and BOURKE being hidden at a house in Cromwell Road, not far from Gloucester Road Underground Station, the home of a person whom he does not name. A possible identification might be made here of Clive Lionel GOODWIN, of Flat 4, 79 Cromwell Road, SW7, a well known left-wing extremist with anarchist leanings. BOURKE describes the owner as aged about 40 years, tall and thin, hair almost shoulder length, flamboyantly dressed, who was a writer by profession and employed a secretary who worked at his home address. GOODWIN was, in fact, then only 34 years old but his description contained in a 1968 Special Branch report showed him to be 5'11" tall, slim build, long face, pale complexion, brown curly hair worn long, casual dress; a self-employed literary agent. There are, however, various discrepancies in this last identification as the story speaks of a 'house' as opposed to 'a flat', and mentions the owner's mother whilst no such person was shown on the electoral register at that time. BOURKE also describes meeting the owner's wife whereas GOODWIN in fact, is believed to be a single man.

17. It should be stressed that, at this stage, there is no actual evidence to substantiate any of these possible identifications and no enquiries have been made by police of the persons concerned. It must be said, however, that if BOURKE's story is true, these persons, with their ideological beliefs, their militant backgrounds, and their wide circle of associates, fit very well into the pattern of the escape as we know it. Even the final details of the escape, where 'Michael REYNOLDS' and his wife allegedly drove through Dover with BLAKE hidden in the secondhand Dormobile they had purchased, would have been quite feasible for RANDALL and his wife, both of whom had current passports and had travelled abroad extensively.

R.B. Watts
Chief Inspector

M.D. Rodgers
CHIEF SUPERINTENDENT

SECRET

APPENDIX 'A'

In the attached copy of Sean BOURKE's manuscript, the following are of particular interest to police:

1.	Author's Note	
2.	Pages 7 to 173	Agreement to arrange the escape. (Pages 154-161, and 163-168, are missing and are believed to have been cut out by the publishers as of no interest).
3.	Pages 180 to 192 and 196 to 210.	Plans for the escape and the system of communications.
4.	Pages 211 to 262	Further plans and meetings with accomplices.
5.	Pages 278 to 336	Final plans and the escape. The hideouts and BLAKE's departure from the country.
6.	Pages 338 to 345	BOURKE's departure for Moscow.

SECRET 487

SECRET

APPENDIX 'B'

Comparison as at May 1966 Michael REYNOLDS	 Michael Joseph RANDLE
Page 212 Aged about 30 years, slight build and pale-faced Son of an Irish mother and an English father - brought up as a Catholic.	Aged 32, (born 21.12.33), height 5'8 thin build, pale faced. Son of an Irish mother and an English father - brought up as a Catholic.
Page 211 Married to "Anne" aged about 25 years. Two children aged 4 years and 2½ years.	Married to Celia Anne PARR aged 25 (born 7.8.41). Two children aged 3 years 8 months (born 19.8.62) and 2 years 4 months (born 12.1.64).
Page 212 Had been to University and gained a BA degree. Was a clerk earning £14 per week.	In 1963 was a student of English at University College, London. Our report of August 1966 showed him to be on the Board of Directors of 'Peace News'.
Page 211 Lived in a modest house about 20 mins. walk from Camden Town Station.	Lived at 25 Torriano Cottages, NW5 about 15/20 mins. walk from Camden Town Station.
Page 211 He was a Socialist at heart but not a communist.	Political sympathies well-known.

SECRET 488

SECRET

APPENDIX 'C'

Comparison as at August 1966	
"Pat PORTER"	Patrick Brian POTTLE
Page 246 Friend of 'Michael REYNOLDS'. Described as 'more robust' than Michael REYNOLDS and about two years younger. A single man	Friend of Michael RANDLE Height 6' and well built. Four and a half years younger than RANDLE (born 8.8.38.) A single man
Address: A flat in Hampstead	Address: Although technically he lived with his widowed mother at the latter's council flat at Alfred Road, W2, enquiries at that period showed that he was seldom there. His girl friend Susan ABRAHAM, later his wife, however, lived at 98 Adelaide Road, Hampstead and he may well have had a flat nearby.
Occupation: Page 246 About a year ago, had started in business with two other men. All the profits were still going in HP repayments on equipment.	Occupation: On 3.2.65 "Stanhope Press" was formed as a printing company by POTTLE, his twin brother and Douglas BREWOOD. The business operated from 96A Stanhope Street, NW1.

SECRET

489

Appendix 3 - Copies of additional documents from Special Branch files released by the Crown as soon as it was ordered by the High Court to produce the Watts Report

18.

Press cuttings - action thereon —18A-E.

19.

DAC to see please on 24.3.70.

A/DAC to see please.

A/Commander 'Ops' to see, please

Paragraph 2 of Box 500 letter draws attention to the need to protect the source from which the manuscript was obtained prior to its publication. You may agree that at this stage we should merely,

1. Send copy 19D to Box 500 under covering letter as in draft.
2. Send copy 19D (less appendix of references) to Sir Philip Allen, Home Office, under covering letter as in draft. (By hand)
3. Commander Wilson to see, please.
4. Send copy 19D to D.I. Chapman C.1.
5. Await comments from Box 500

SB
25.3.70.

M D Rodgers
Chief Superintendent

20.

21

ACC ✓ MVB 31/3

You may wish to see 19D for information. The possible identifications are interesting, but there is no evidence to substantiate any charge.

SB
25.3.70.

A. Cunningham
A/DAC

496

SECRET & PERSONAL

Correspondence to this address must be under *double* cover.
The *outer* envelope should be addressed to:—
THE SECRETARY, BOX 500, PARLIAMENT STREET B.O., LONDON, S.W.1.
and *not* to any individual.

BOX No. 500,
PARLIAMENT STREET B.O.,
LONDON, S.W.1.

Telephone Nos. 01-734 6050 Ext. 662
01-930 6789 Ext.

Our Ref.: ————

Your Ref.:

The Deputy Assistant Commissioner,
Special Branch.

For the attention of Chief Insp. R. Watts.

You may wish to have a preview of Sean BOURKE's book "The Springing of George BLAKE".

2. I have been asked to stress that this typescript was received on a confidential basis and we would ask you not to take any action on matters revealed in the typescript or make any enquiries which would reveal that it is in our possession.

3. The book is expected to be published in May, but this will give you advance knowledge of its contents.

4. It is assumed that much of the material on the actual escape is inaccurate and misleading and that BOURKE has deliberately altered names and places. You will no doubt be able to draw some conclusions from this as a result of your investigation of BOURKE at the time.

5. We shall be interested to have your comments and to see whether there is any possibility of countering some of the statements in the book if and when it is published.

6. If you want us to institute any enquiries abroad resulting from BOURKE's account of the escape, no doubt you will let us know.

30 January, 1970.

SECRET 19C

MEMORANDUM

A/Commander 'Ops'

Sir,

I understand from ______________, Box 500, that copies of Sean BOURKE's manuscript have been sent to both Home Office and Foreign Office.

In this connection, Mr Fries, Home Office, telephoned me and asked if a copy of the Special Branch assessment of the manuscript could be forwarded to Sir Philip Alan when completed.

______________ also stated that Mr Welfer of the Information Research Department, Foreign Office, had asked Box 500 to pass on Special Branch's comments about the manuscript, in order to assist them to prepare a reply for publication when the book appears.

18.3.70

R W Watts
Chief Inspector.

SECRET

Our reference:
588/UNREG/51W

Your reference: —

Box 500
(for the attention of
————)

23 March 1970

Manuscript of a book by Sean BOURKE

1. In answer to your letter dated 30 January 1970, I enclose a copy report dealing with an assessment of BOURKE's manuscript and the possible identifications of persons mentioned therein.

2. We understand that the Information Research Department, Foreign Office have asked you to pass on our comments in respect of the assessment. Whilst there is no objection to this, as far as comments on the manuscript itself are concerned, you will appreciate that it would be undesirable, at this stage, to disclose the possible identifications which have been made.

3. Your comments on the attached report would be appreciated. A copy has been sent to Sir Philip Allen, Home Office, at his request.

A/DAC

SECRET

SECRET

588/UNRIG/51W

Sir Philip Allen KCB
Home Office
SW1

23 March 1970

Sir,

1. I am directed by the Commissioner to forward a copy Special Branch report giving an appreciation of the contents of a manuscript written by Sean BOURKE regarding the escape of George BLAKE which is to be published shortly.

2. You will see that some possible identifications of persons who assisted in the escape are included.

I am, Sir
Your obedient Servant

for Assistant Commissioner

SECRET

SECRET

Correspondence to this address must be under *double* cover.
The *outer* envelope should be addressed to :—
THE SECRETARY, BOX 500, PARLIAMENT STREET B.O., LONDON, S.W.1.
and *not* to any individual.

Telephone Nos. 01-734 6050 Ext. 640
01-930 6789 Ext. ....

BOX No. 500,
PARLIAMENT STREET B.O.,
LONDON, S.W.1.

Our Ref.: ——————

Your Ref.:

7 May, 1970.

Dear Arthur,

Manuscript of a book by Sean BOURKE

Thank you for sending us the report attached to your letter of 23 March.

2. In order not to disclose the possible identifications you have made, we forwarded only paragraphs 2, 3 and 4 of the report to the Information Research Department of the Foreign Office.

3. We found the whole report extremely interesting and were very impressed by the highly likely speculative identifications.

4. We have been through the report in detail and there is not a single point on which we would take issue and heartily endorse the conclusion that if BOURKE's story is true the three candidates fit the pattern of the escape. This would account for the fact that no information of value was forthcoming on the criminal or the security nets.

5. Unfortunately for this very reason we too have been unable to find any collateral to back up the suggested identifications.

6. We have been able to match some suggested identities with those of BOURKE's contacts in Russia, but here again we are unable to prove these.

7. Thank you again for this most excellent report. We agree that it provides the most acceptable explanation of events after the escape.

Yours

Commander A. Cunningham, Q.P.M.,
Special Branch.

SECRET

No. 477

Corres. No.

22.

Letter from Box 500 ....22A

D.A.C. to see. pse

A/Commander 'Ops' to see, please

Box 500 appear to agree with the identifications in theory but are unable to add anything further. Apart from the warrants for BOURKE's arrest, which remain outstanding, the matter would seem to rest here.

S.B.
9.5.70

A/Chief Superintendent.

Appendix 4 - Copies of the two MIS 'Notes for File', dated 25 February 1970 and 29 April 1970, produced in the High Court on 25 July 1990. p.499.

NOTE FOR FILE

I saw Chief Inspector Watts at S.B. today to discuss Sean BOURKE's book "The Springing of George BLAKE". [redacted]. Chief Insp. Watts gave it as his view that the book was probably BOURKE's own writing and not ghosted. He thought it was probably 99% true and said that much of what was described fitted in with their knowledge of minor events not directly connected with the escape.

2. We discussed his suggested identification of Sean BOURKE's accomplices in the BLAKE escape. He has a considerable amount of work to do before he will be able to say that the identifications are anything like confirmed, but at present he believes it is possible that "Michael REYNOLDS" (page 211) = Michael RANDLE [redacted] and that "Pat PORTER" (page 246) = Patrick POTTLE [redacted]. Two longer shots are the possibility that the unnamed writer with the house in the Cromwell Road (page 322) might be [redacted] and the doctor who attended BLAKE (page 306) might be [redacted]

3. Chief Insp. Watts asked if we were interested and I said we were very interested although of course any action was a matter for the Police. What particularly interested us was any evidence, or evidence to the contrary, of any Russian involvement in the escape.

4. Chief Insp. Watts said that Michael RANDLE had been in Wormwood Scrubs at the same time as BLAKE and knew him there. He thought it was possible that BLAKE himself might have assessed RANDLE as an idealist who would have sympathy with an attempt to help him escape from his 42-year incarceration and asked Sean BOURKE to approach him.

5. Chief Insp. Watts gave me his hand-written notes comparing the descriptions of REYNOLDS - RANDLE and PORTER - POTTLE and these are attached.

6. He said that even if the identities are confirmed it is very unlikely that any of those identified could be prosecuted unless they themselves admitted their involvement. However a course of action would be decided after his preliminary investigations were completed.

25 February, 1970.

7

NOTE FOR FILE

While I was speaking to Chief Inspector Watts of S.B. yesterday he mentioned their report [redacted] and asked if we had any comments to make on it.

2. Chief Inspector Watts added that the S.B. decision at present was to take no steps to interview or attempt to prosecute the RANDLEs, POTTLE or GOODWIN. It was considered that to do so might be persecution - a big fish had got away so they were taking it out on the little fish. It was considered, however, that it had been necessary to investigate their suspicions and place them on record.

3. First of all I said I already had it in mind that S.B. would want to know how much of their report had been passed on to I.R.D. and I said that in order not to prejudice their enquiries we had omitted all parts which disclosed the possible identifications they had made.

4. Secondly, I said that before commenting on their report we were awaiting the results of our own enquiries. I said I would see that S.B. would receive our comments as soon as possible.

29 April, 1970.

Appendix 5 - Copy of the contemporaneous note 'in shorthand and gobbledegook' made by Kevin O'Connor of his conversation with ex-Chief Superintendent Watts in 1984 at the offices of Saladin Security near Sloane Square.

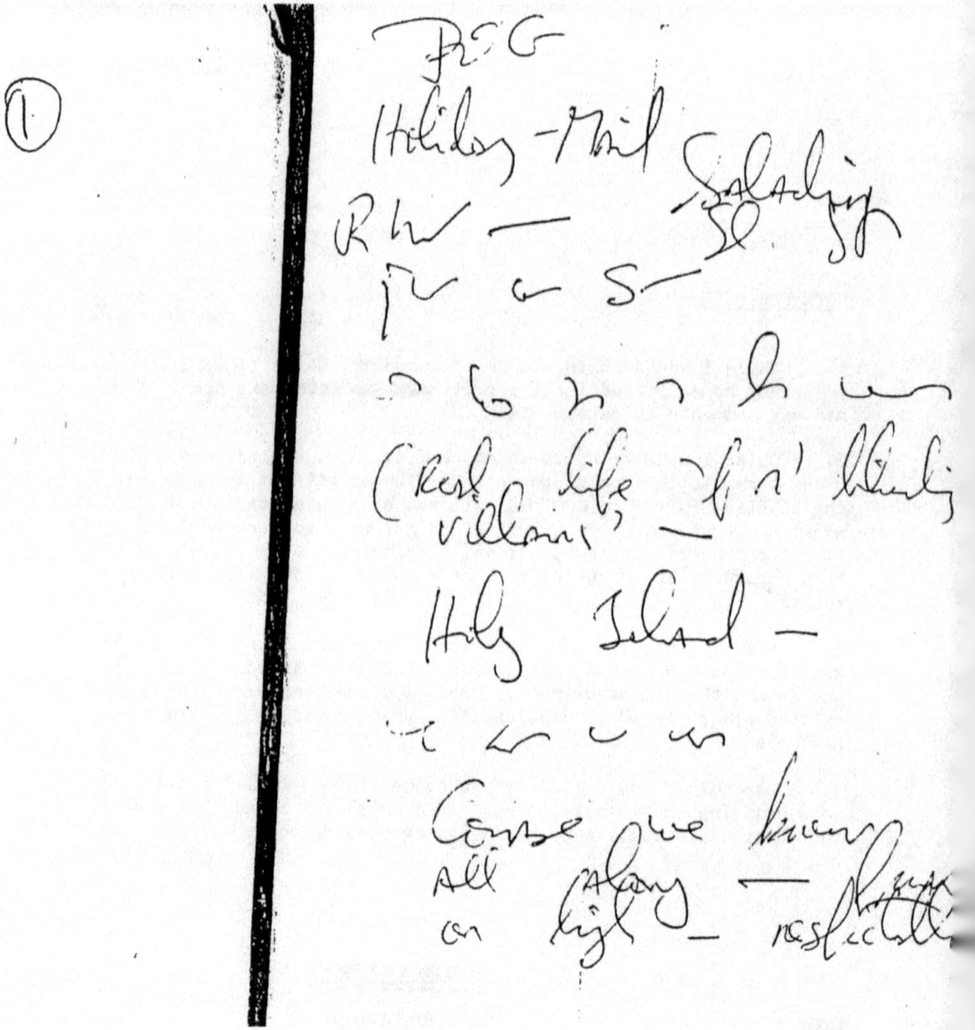

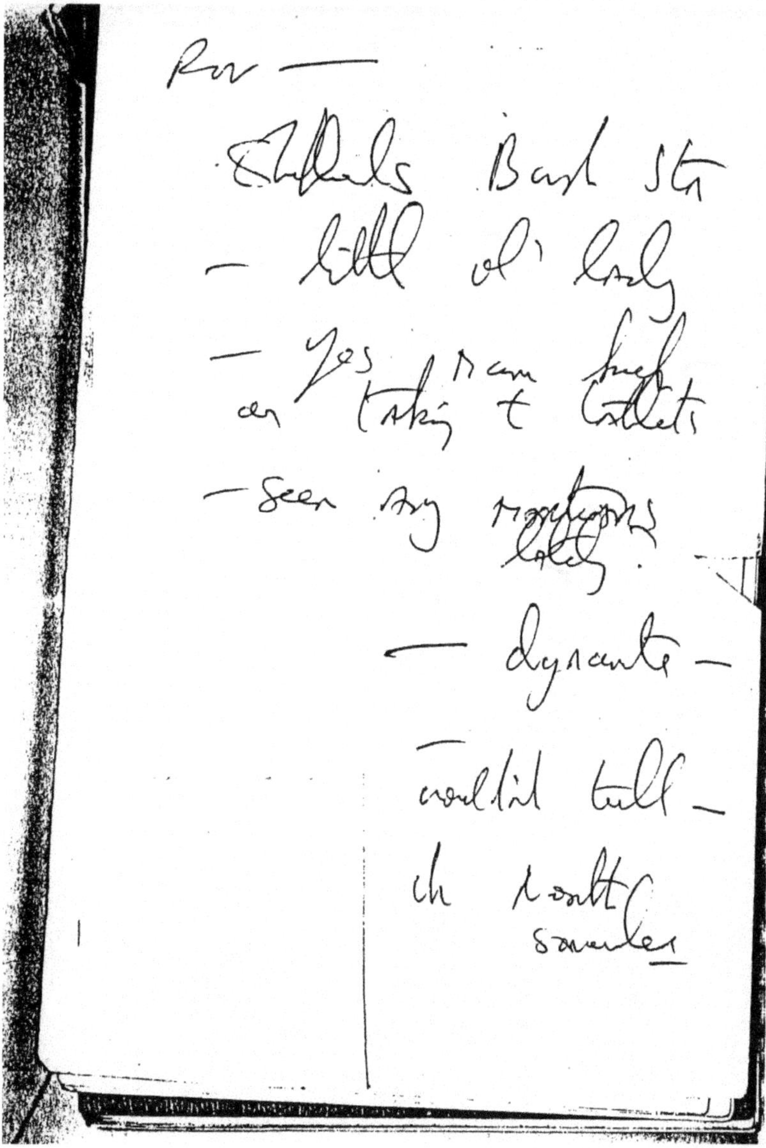

Rov —

[illegible] Bank Sta

— little ol' lady

— Yes ma'am kept
on taking the tablets

— seen any mushrooms
lately.

— dynamite —

— wouldn't tell —

ch [illegible]
somewhere

Kew

— Shaw SOD's

ASSO.. in W.S.

—

ppendix 6 – Witness Statement by Kevin O'Connor
1 March 1990

2-08-90 WED. 12:54 P.03

No. 991

Evidence Stmt 16

02 MAR 1990

STATEMENT OF WITNESS

(C.J. Act. 1967, S. 9; M.C. Act. 1980, S. 102; M.C. Rules, 1981, r.70)
S.23 Criminal Justice Act 1988

Statement of KEVIN O'CONNOR

Age of Witness (Date of Birth) OVER 21

Occupation of Witness JOURNALIST

Address and Telephone Number 52 EDENVALE ROAD
RANELAGH
DUBLIN 6

This statement, consisting of 3 pages each signed by me, is true to the best of my knowledge and belief and I make it knowing that, if it is tendered in evidence, I shall be liable to prosecution if I have wilfully stated in it anything which I know to be false or do not believe to be true.

Dated the 1st day of March, 19 90

Signed K D O'Connor

Signature witnessed by Joan Bergin

I AM A JOURNALIST AND RADIO PRODUCER WITH RTE THE STATE BROADCASTING SERVICE IN THE IRISH REPUBLIC. IN JANUARY 1984 I WROTE AND PRODUCED A DOCUMENTARY FOR RADIO ENTITLED ' A DEATH IN JANUARY' WHICH WAS ON THE LIFE OF SEAN BOURKE.

AFTER THE PROGRAMME WAS BROADCAST, I WAS CONTACTED BY A NUMBER OF PEOPLE WHO SAID THEY HAD FURTHER INFORMATION TO OFFER. ONE OF THESE MENTIONED THAT MICHAEL HOLIDAY THEN A REPORTER ON THE MAIL ON SUNDAY HAD SEEN SEAN BOURKE BEFORE HE DIED. I SUBSEQUENTLY MET HOLIDAY. HE INTRODUCED ME TO THE CRIME CORRESPONDENCE OF THE MAIL. HE ARRANGED FOR ME TO MEET ROLY WATTS.

SOMETIME IN 1984 I WENT TO THE OFFICES OF SALIDON SECURITY IN SLOANE STREET AND MET MR WATTS. WE HAD A MEETING FOR ABOUT 20 MINUTES IN WATTS OFFICE.

WATTS WORE A BUSINESS SUIT 3 PIECE PIN STRIPE. HE TOLD —

K D O'Connor Joan Bergin

S.23 CRIMINAL JUSTICE ACT 1988

Statement of Witness (C.J. Act, 1967, S.9; M.C. Act, 1980, S.102; M.C. Rules, 1981, r.70)

Kevin O'Connor

CONTINUATION OF STATEMENT OF ME THAT MONTHS AFTER SEAN BOURKE RETURNED TO IRELAND FROM MOSCOW, BOURKE WOULD TELEPHONE HIM FROM IRELAND AND THEY WOULD HAVE A CONVERSATION, ALONG THE LINES THAT BOURKES, OLD HUMBER WAS STILL IN THE METROPOLITAN POLICE POUND AND WHEN COULD HE ARRANGE TO CLAIM IT.

WATTS SAID THAT HE WAS AN EX SCOTLAND YARD OFFICER A SERGEANT, WHO WAS INVOLVED IN THE INVESTIGATION WHICH SURROUNDED THE ESCAPE OF GEORGE BLAKE. HE SAID THAT THE AUTHORITIES HAD KNOWN WITHIN A VERY SHORT TIME THAT THERE WERE TWO OTHER PEOPLE BESIDES SEAN BOURKE INVOLVED IN THE ESCAPE. THEY KNEW THAT TWO OF THE PEOPLE WERE PART OF THE ' INTELLECTUAL MAFFIA ' AT THE PRISON. WATTS SAID THAT THERE WERE CONVERSATIONS ~~BAOUT~~ ABOUT THE PROSECUTION OF THESE TWO PEOPLE AND HIS SUPERIORS HAD TOLD HIM THAT THEY SHOULD LEAVE WELL ENOUGH ALONE.

WATTS SAID THAT THE POLICE HAD QUICKLY ESTABLISHED BOURKE AS THE PRIME SUBJECT DAYS BEFORE THE DESCRIPTION OF BOURKE WAS RELEASED TO THE MEDIA.

I HAVE A NOTE OF THE CONVERSATION AND WATTS SAID " OF COURSE WE KNEW WHO THEY WERE IN A SHORT TIME BUT A DECISION WAS TAKEN NOT TO PROSECUTE THEM. THE REASON (WHICH CAME FROM ABOVE) WAS THEY WERE PERFECTLY LAW ABIDING CITIZENS IN EVERY OTHER RESPECT. ONE WAS A TEACHER MARRIED TO A TEACHER THEY HAD YOUNG CHILDREN WHY BREAK UP THE FAMILY AND PUT THEM AWAY AT THE COST OF THE TAX PAYER, WHEN THERE WERE LOTS OF OTHER REAL VILLAINS ABOUT THAT IT WAS OUR JOB TO CATCH?"

AT THAT STAGE FROM INFORMATION AVAILABLE FROM ELSEWHERE I KNEW THAT RANDLE LIVED IN BRADFORD. I TRIED TO GET WATTS TO SAY WHERE THE TWO MEN WERE NOW AND HE SAID

Signed K O'Connor Signature witnessed by Joan Bergin

No. 991B Page No.

2-08-'40 WED 12:55 P.05

Statement of Witness (C.J. Act, 1967, S.9; M.C. Act, 1980, S.102; M.C. Rules, 1981, r.70)

CONTINUATION OF STATEMENT OF KEVIN O'CONNOR

SOMETHING TO THE EFFECT OF 'UP THE MIDLANDS SOMEWHERE'.

IT WAS CLEAR TO ME HE KNEW MORE THAN HE WAS PREPARED TO SAY IF ONLY TO PROTECT THE FULL IDENTITY AND LOCATION OF RANDLE.

X Signed K D O'Connor Signature witnessed by Joan Borghi

No. 991B Page No.

M.P.86

Appendix 7 – Witness Statement by George Blake in his own handwriting witnessed by Benedict Birnberg, 13 February 1990

STATEMENT OF WITNESS

(C.J. Act, 1967, S. 9; M.C. Act, 1980, S. 102; M.C. Rules, 1981, r.70)
C.J. Act 1988, S.23

Statement of GEORGE BLAKE

Age of Witness (Date of Birth) 11 - 11 - 1922

Occupation of Witness RESEARCHER

Address and Telephone Number c/o INSTITUTE OF WORLD ECONOMY AND INTERNATIONAL RELATIONS 23 PROFSOYUNAYA STREET, MOSCOW USSR.

This statement,* consisting of 3 pages each signed by me, is true to the best of my knowledge and belief and I make it knowing that, if it is tendered in evidence, I shall be liable to prosecution if I have wilfully stated in it anything which I know to be false or do not believe to be true.

Dated the 13th day of February, 1990

Signed G. Blake

Signature witnessed by Benedict Birnberg

I am making this statement at the express request of PATRICK POTTLE and MICHAEL RANDLE.

I was a member of the British Secret Intelligence Service from August 1944 until the date of my trial 3 May 1961. I was engaged in secret subversive operations directed against the Soviet Union, the socialist countries and world Communism. It was my task to attempt the recruitment of Soviet citizens and in particular members of the Soviet intelligence services and those of other socialist countries. I have been advised by the solicitors acting for PATRICK POTTLE and MICHAEL RANDLE that because of the operation of the British Official Secrets Act I can say no more than this.

It was said that my actions led to the death of British and other agents. I can confirm

Signed G. Blake Signature witnessed by Benedict Birnberg

No. 991B

STATEMENT OF WITNESS

(C.J. Act, 1967, ss. 2, 9; M.C. Rules, 1968, r. 58)
C. J. Act 1988, s.23

Continuation of statement of GEORGE BLAKE

that at my trial it was never alleged that in working for both the British Secret Intelligence Service and the Soviet Intelligence Service, I was ever responsible for the death of agents. However, I do not deny that I disclosed the identity of a number of agents to the Soviet authorities.

After my conviction I was sent to H.M. Prison Wormwood Scrubs where in 1962 I first met PATRICK POTTLE and MICHAEL RANDLE.

I can confirm that neither PATRICK POTTLE nor MICHAEL RANDLE were at any time in contact with the Soviet authorities or acting on their behalf in helping me to escape in 1966 from Wormwood Scrubs prison. Nor did they receive any financial assistance or reward at any stage for their assistance. Indeed, I had to explain to the Soviet authorities once I arrived in Moscow who these two men were, and why they chose to assist me.

There never was any doubt in my mind that PATRICK POTTLE and MICHAEL RANDLE acted as they did out of purely humanitarian concern and specifically because of the length of my sentence. I say this as they repeatedly commented on the harshness of the sentence.

Furthermore both men asked me to intervene on behalf of two well-known Soviet dissidents imprisoned at the time Mr Daniel and

G.B.
[initials]

Signed G. Blake, Signature witnessed by [signature]

STATEMENT OF WITNESS

(C.J. Act, 1967, ss. 2, 9; M.C. Rules, 1968, r. 58)
C J Act 1988, s. 23

Continuation of statement of GEORGE BLAKE

Mr Sinyavski. Moreover they frequently stated how much they would like to be able to bring a prisoner in Soviet hands back to the west on their return journey.

GB. I should like to conclude this statement by saying that I am deeply grateful to PATRICK POTTLE and MICHAEL RANDLE for having enabled me to lead a normal life over the last twenty four years.

G. Blake.

[signature]

Michael Randle - Biographical Note

Michael Randle was one of the pioneers of nonviolent direct action in Britain, against nuclear war and in support of radical social change. In 1952 he registered as a conscientious objector to conscription and joined the recently formed activist group, *Operation Gandhi* (subsequently renamed *The Direct Action Committee Against Nuclear War*, or *DAC)*, centred round the weekly pacifist paper *Peace News* and its editors, J. Allen Skinner and Hugh Brock.

In December 1957, he took part in an attempt, sponsored by the DAC, to walk from Vienna to Budapest with leaflets in Hungarian, German and English, which expressed opposition to the Soviet military intervention in Hungary and in support of the ongoing civil resistance there to Soviet control.

He was a member of the Aldermaston March Committee, set up by the DAC to organise the first march from London to the Atomic Weapons Research Establishment at Aldermaston over the 1958 Easter period. The Committee adopted the now ubiquitous nuclear disarmament symbol, designed by the artist Gerald Holtom.

Michael was Chair of the Direct Action Committee against Nuclear War (1958-61), and Secretary of the Committee of 100 (1960-61), headed by Bertrand Russell.

For acting on his convictions, Michael was imprisoned several times. In 1962-63, he, along with five other Committee of 100 members—Helen Allegranza, Terry Chivers, Ian Dixon, Trevor Hatten and Pat Pottle—were sentenced to 18 months imprisonment for their part in organising a nonviolent occupation of Wethersfield USAF Airbase, in protest against the deployment of nuclear weapons there. Michael served a further eight months in 1967-8 for participating in an occupation of the Greek Embassy in London, following the Colonels' Coup in Greece.

In 1968, he co-ordinated simultaneous international demonstrations by the pacifist organisation, War Resisters International, in Moscow, Warsaw, Budapest and Sofia, opposing the Soviet-led invasion and continued domination of Czechoslovakia.

In 1966, Michael and Anne Randle, along with Pat Pottle and another ex-prisoner, Sean Bourke, sprung George Blake from Wormwood Scrubs prison. The details of this incredible story and the subsequent 1991 trial at the Old Bailey, are contained in the pages of this book.

Michael served on the Council of War Resisters International from 1960 to 1987, and as its Chair from 1966 to 1973. He co-ordinated the Bradford University-based based Alternative Defence Commission from 1980 to 1988 which published two major reports, *Defence Without the Bomb* (Taylor & Francis, 1983), as well as *The Politics of Alternative Defence* (Paladin, Grafton Books, 1987).

Michael's publications include:

The Blake Escape, with Pat Pottle (Harrap, 1989); *Alternatives in European Security*, co-editor with Paul Rogers (Dartmouth,1990); *Civil Resistance* (Fontana,1990); *People Power* (Hawthorn Press, 1990); *Civil Resistance* (Paladin, 1994); *How to Defend Yourself in Court* (Civil Liberties Trust, 1995); *Challenge to Nonviolence*, editor and contributor (Bradford University, 2002); *A Guide to Civil Resistance*, co-editor with April Carter and Howard Clark, (Green Print, Volume One 2013, Volume Two 2015).

More recently, Martin Levy published a biography of Michael called *Ban the Bomb* (Ibidem, 2021), based on interviews with him.

[illegible]

[illegible]

[illegible]

[illegible]

[illegible]

[illegible]